Class Structure in Australian History

Class Structure in Australian History

Documents, Narrative and Argument

R. W. Connell and T. H. Irving

Longman Cheshire

Longman Cheshire Pty Limited
346 St Kilda Road
Melbourne 3004 Australia

Offices in Sydney, Brisbane, Adelaide and Perth. Associated companies, branches and representatives throughout the world.

First published 1980

Set in 10/11 pt Baskerville Roman
Printed in Singapore
by Multiprint Services

National Library of Australia
Cataloguing-in-Publication data

Connell, R. W.
Class structure in Australian history.

Index
Bibliography
ISBN 0 582 71092 8
ISBN 0 582 71091 X Paperback

1. Social classes — Australia — History.
I. Irving, Terence H., joint author.
II. Title.

301.44'0994

Front endpaper shows 'A Camp of Jolly Miners' (1909), *State Library of Tasmania*
Back endpaper shows 'Wedding Breakfast, Queensland' (1909), *Oxley Memorial Library, Brisbane*

Contents

Acknowledgements

The documents in this book are reproduced by kind permission of: Angus & Robertson Publishers, Sydney, for extracts from R. G. Menzies, *The Forgotten People* (5.13), and H. Fallding, 'Inside the Australian Family', in A. P. Elkin (ed.), *Marriage and the Family in Australia* (5.14); the author and the Australian National University Press, Canberra, for extract from *Settlers of the Latrobe Valley* by J. Zubrzycki (5.10); Archives Authority of New South Wales (2.2, 2.5); Archives Office of Tasmania (2.10, 2.18, 4.3); the author and the Australasian Meat Industry Employees' Union (Victorian Branch), for extract from *The Meat Workers Unite* by A.E. Davies (4.9); Betty Collins, for extract from 'Work: The Coal Miner', in *Outlook* (5.9); the author and Constable & Company Limited, London, for extract from *Caddie: The Autobiography of a Sydney Barmaid* (4.16); Conzinc Riotinto of Australia Ltd (5.11); Current Book Distributors Pty Ltd, Sydney, for extract from *The Trade Unions* by L. Sharkey (5.7); Fryer Memorial Library, University of Queensland (2.17, 4.10, 4.13); Pauline Grenfell Price (5.2); Institute of Public Affairs, Victoria, Melbourne, for extract from *Looking Forward: A Post-War Policy for Australian Industry* (5.4); editor, *Journal of the Institution of Engineers, Australia*, for extract from 'To Raise the ... Status ... of the Profession of Engineering' (5.16); La Trobe Library, State Library of Victoria (2.7, 3.6); Mitchell Library, Public Library of New South Wales (2.13, 2.14, 2.15, 3.3, 3.7); Denis Murphy, Department of History, University of Queensland (4.14); the author and Thomas Nelson (Australia) Limited, Melbourne, for extract from J. Paterson, 'Outsiders: Those Who Have Not', in J. Rigg (ed.), *In Her Own Right* (5.15); Norton Smith & Co., Sydney (3.7); John Oxley Library, Brisbane (4.15); South Australian Archives (3.16); State Library of South Australia (3.4, 3.10, 3.11, 3.17, 3.19); State Library of Tasmania (3.20).

The illustrations are reproduced by kind permission of: John Arnold (pp. 125, 128); Battye Library, Perth (pp. 59, 124); Dixson Gallery, Sydney (p. 55); Herald & Weekly Times Ltd, Melbourne (p. 307); Mitchell Library, Public Library of New South Wales (pp. 52, 60, 133, 194); Public Library of New South Wales (pp. 192, 209); John Oxley Library, Brisbane (p. 215); South Australian Archives (p. 117); State Library of Tasmania (pp. 121, 199).

In addition, acknowledgement is made to the following for permission to reprint copyright material: the author and Victor Gollancz Ltd, London, for extract from *The Making of the English Working Class* by Edward P. Thompson; the author and Hutchinson Publishing Group Limited, London, for extract from *The Class Structure of the Advanced Societies* by A. Giddens; and the author and New Left Books, London, for extracts from *Classes in Contemporary Capitalism* by N. Poulantzas.

Permission to reproduce material was refused by: Repco Limited, for extracts from a history of the company published in the house magazine; and the Pastoralists & Graziers Association of Western Australia, for a secret circular of 1913, dealing with the need for organisation to meet the challenge of the shearers' union, which is in the Battye Library.

While every effort has been made to trace and acknowledge copyright material, in some cases the source has proved obscure. Should any infringement or incorrect acknowledgement have occurred, the authors and publisher tender their apologies.

Abbreviations

A.E.H.R.	*Australian Economic History Review*
A.F.R.	*Australian Financial Review*
A.G.P.S.	Australian Government Publishing Service
A.J.P.H.	*Australian Journal of Politics and History*
A.N.U.	Australian National University
A.N.U.P.	Australian National University Press
A.N.Z.J.S.	*Australian and New Zealand Journal of Sociology*
B.A.H.	*Business Archives and History*
C.U.P.	Cambridge University Press
H.R.A.	*Historical Records of Australia*
J.R.A.H.S.	*Journal and Proceedings of the Royal Australian Historical Society*
M.L.	The Mitchell Library, Sydney
M.U.P.	Melbourne University Press
N.S.W.S.A.	New South Wales State Archives
O.U.P.	Oxford University Press
P.T.H.R.A.	*Proceedings of the Tasmanian Historical Research Association*
S.M.H.	*Sydney Morning Herald*
S.U.P.	Sydney University Press
T.S.A.	Tasmanian State Archives
U.P.	University Press
U.Q.P.	University of Queensland Press

Foreword

We live at a moment in history when the opposition to capitalism faces fundamental problems. Widely believed to be dying half a generation ago, working-class and socialist movements in the West have come back with signs of rude health and continued vigour. But they have come back to a thorny nest of strategic and theoretical problems. Capitalism itself has done a fair job of flourishing; neither the official marxism of the mainstream Communist parties, nor the reformism of labour parties and union confederations, has given much of a grip on it in the post-war decades. While the leading intellectuals on the left have gone exploring increasingly esoteric variations on marxism, many radicals—especially youth—have ditched working-class socialism altogether as a basis for opposition. Their energies have gone into constructing enclaves of total negation in the nooks and crannies of the system, either in the wistful hope that a counter-culture can transform its environment by pure example, or in the belief that personal liberation is itself the main goal. Some radical groups, notably parts of the women's movement, have continued to face questions of changing social structure, but have focused on other structures as either theoretically prior to, or posing more immediate problems than, class relations. These partings are not final, of course, and some reunions have occurred, on the streets as well as in ideas. But it is clear that a fundamental rethinking of socialist ideas has to occur.

While this has to take account of new lines of thought, especially those raised by the sexual liberation movements, it is crucially important that it should also re-examine the traditional bases of socialist accounts of capitalist society—which means, above all, class analysis. Without a thorough understanding of classes, class dynamics and their place in the whole social structure, arguments about socialist strategy are simply hot air; and without a *rethinking* of ideas about class, they will simply be expressions of nostalgia. That rethinking has already begun; to be strictly accurate, it never ended, but it is certainly going on at a greater pace than before. In Australia, there has been in the last ten years a notable revival of socialist theoretical work, concrete research and strategic argument. This book is intended to bring some of the products together and shape them into a coherent account of the history of class in this country.

Our intention is political—to help people gain a clear understanding of the pattern of class relations they live in and have to act on here and now—and it may therefore seem curious to some readers that a history-book is the result. (There is not much political mileage left in the First Fleet.) But there is a very basic reason for doing this. To anticipate briefly the arguments of Chapter 1, one of the basic differences between socialist and bourgeois understandings of class is precisely that the former is historical and the latter is not; which makes excellent sense given that socialist thought is directed to understanding the conditions for a fundamental historical change in social relations. The concept of class itself, we will argue, is a historical one, referring to patterns of social polarisation and transformation that can only be understood as processes in time. And while some theories—notably though not exclusively marxist ones—do give a way of analysing these massive changes, no theory can substitute for a close study of the shape they have actually taken on the earth of these islands. Applying *a priori* notions of the way class relations *should* go has been one of the besetting sins of the Left; and is arguably an important reason for its decline a generation ago.

To put that more simply: people facing the task of changing a society need an accurate account of the way it came into being and the way it has worked up till now. This has to be the history of the society as a whole, not just bits and pieces of it; the problem is to write the history of a structure. The actual region studied is a bit arbitrary—for some purposes 'Australia' is too big a unit, for others too small, and our choice of these boundaries is merely a practical compromise: two lives are not enough. But whatever the area in question, the key point is that the topic is the structure of class relations, and the activity of people as they make and remake that structure.

Most history is conceived differently; and though we will be summarising the results of orthodox historical research extensively, it will be with a critical eye. 'Class' figures in orthodox historiography mainly as a set of boxes to stuff people into at a given point of time, or as a set of quotable reflections—images of magnates and servants, dangerous classes and fat oppressors—in the eye of the literate beholder. Most of the useful research on topics such as companies is done by people entirely innocent of questions of class. Labour historians have a much more developed sense of classes as historical forces, though there are obvious limitations on history conceived as the history of a single class. Those few people who have attempted to grasp the historical pattern of class relations as a whole—in Australia the most important, until recently almost the only, example was the work of Brian Fitzpatrick in the 1940s—have been the chief inspiration of this work.

The book begins with a theoretical chapter. This is abstract and reasonably difficult; many people may prefer to skip straight to the narrative, though we hope they will come back to it afterwards. It is intended to establish a case for the kind of analysis the rest of the book offers, to defend the conception of class structure that the rest of the book works out and to explain in a preliminary way the main concepts used in it. The critical reader will observe that no formal definition of 'class' is given in that chapter, and the attentive reader will see why. The whole book is a contribution to the definition of class.

The chapters that follow consist of three parts: a narrative and analytic text, a set of slightly discursive footnotes, and a set of documents with brief introductory comments. These are meant to be taken together, and all are important. The text offers our interpretation of the structure and dynamics of class relations in the period being discussed. The notes are not just a guide to the sources of the information, but a partial bibliography of the subject and the forum of our arguments with previous interpretations. The documents are meant to convey further detail on points that the other sections treat generally, and particularly to convey the lived reality that we hold to be crucial to an understanding of class formation. They are theoretically important, not mere illustrations.

There are four narrative chapters, and the periodisation is deliberate: it is based on our interpretation of the main stages in the development of class relations and the transformation of the ruling class. Somewhat more weight is given to the first century or so of settlement than might normally be thought apt in a general history, but again this is for a reason. The routine reproduction of patterns of social relations in the later period makes it necessary to go back to their first construction in Australia, and most of the essentials of capitalist social relations were in fact constructed (or reconstructed) by the first few generations of settlers. Hence there is a good deal of attention to such things as the initial construction of a capitalist labour market and a colonial capitalist state. They have more than antiquarian interest.

Intellectual work is necessarily a collective enterprise, and this project has drawn on the help of many people over the last nine years. Most particularly, we have drawn on the assistance, support and criticism of Pam Benton, Sue Scott and Jack Arnold (who worked on the project for a year, with energy and enthusiasm, as research assistant). We have relied at many points on librarians and archivists in every state; friends, relations and colleagues (including Ron Witton, John M. Ward, Brian Dickey and Tim Rowse, who made detailed comments on drafts); not to mention the hundreds of other researchers mentioned in the notes. The extensive and often intricate typing was done by Linda Benson, Rebecca Jackson, Heather Williams and Joy Cook. Funds were supplied initially by an advance from the publisher, a grant from the Australian Research Grants Committee, and subsequently by grants from Flinders University and the University of Sydney. Our thanks to all; for any deficiencies remaining, don't blame us — we are merely the bearers of a structure.

The book is dedicated to the socialist activists of the 1950s and 1960s, who kept up the struggle when the going got tough. It is, in a basic sense, a product of their work.

1 Class Analysis and History

Introduction

The subject of class analysis is social power: how it is organised, on the largest possible scale; how it is won and used, stabilised and overthrown; what its effects are in everyday life. It goes beyond 'power' as the business of giving and taking orders, for those who give orders are themselves powerfully constrained by the way the whole society is organised. Class analysis is concerned with the political nature of the entire social structure. And it is therefore itself political. Structures of power are not just objects of academic research, they define the fate of actual people—realities of oppression and exploitation, possibilities of liberation, questions of life and death. To understand or misunderstand them has profound consequences: in the final analysis, it is a question of whether history can be brought under human control.

Our approach is based on the tradition that explicitly aligns intellectual work with the struggle of working people to control the making of their history: the tradition of socialism. Modern socialism grew out of the working-class revolt against capitalist industrialisation in the nineteenth century. Out of that experience, it developed a theory and method of social analysis that saw antagonistic class relations as the fundamental structure of the society that was being produced.

Capitalist industrialisation was experienced by those who first went through it as a rupture, a violent invasion of existing ways of life, the creation of a new order of things. The social order it created was therefore known to be historical and contingent; it was produced by events that were held in memory, and it was capable of being overthrown in its turn. That knowledge was the ground of the historical approach to social structure that is basic in class analysis. In brief—and to foreshadow some later argument—social relations are grasped as a series of situations. Society is always seen as something being produced, coming into being and passing away. Even its stability is understood not as the stability of an object like a stone, but as a process of constant reproduction. The concepts of class analysis, to be adequate, must themselves be intrinsically historical concepts, dealing with processes and situations. This does not for a moment imply a belief that all is flux and change is easy, which would be absurd in the light of working-class experience itself. On the contrary, class analysis is very much concerned with the intractability of situations, and no realistic analysis of power could be otherwise.

The importance of this understanding of the historical nature of social structure is underlined by the struggle needed to sustain it. It has not been easy to hold to it, especially in periods and places where capitalism has achieved reasonable stability and begun to look like part of the order of nature. In social theory, as in mass politics, there have been constant attempts to bleed history out of the knowledge of social relations, to define existing structures ideologically as immutable forms. Ideology constantly presents one race as 'naturally' inferior to (or different from) another, women as 'naturally' subordinate to (or different from) men, and private wealth as the 'natural' reward of talent and hard work. To reject this, root and branch, is often difficult; but it is essential.

The ahistoricity that is characteristic of ideology should not be confused with the absence of *any* concept of change. Change was a commonplace of bourgeois thought in the nineteenth century, and slicker versions of the Victorian notions of Evolution, Improvement and Progress are still with us — urban development, economic growth, automation, and the well-known brand of aspirin that kills pain 2¼ times faster. It is not the awareness of change that is at issue, but the way it is understood: whether as some kind of natural law of society, operating eternally and outside the control of mere humans; as some kind of accident, or pile-up of accidents, within a framework of relationships that is basically taken for granted; or as itself the texture and substance of social life, the product of human passion, conflict and routine, capable of being understood and — in principle — directed. The third is the approach of class analysis.

To the generation of workers who lived through the disruption of handicrafts, the crowding of the workforce into factories, the tyranny of the machine, the incessant pressure on wages, and the breakdown of traditional rights, capitalist industrialisation was experienced not just as a rupture in historical time but also as an assault on the fabric of everyday existence. The business of producing commodities was separated from everything else, in the daily lives of the workers and in the larger social order. The new industrial magnates were rulers who seemed to have cut themselves adrift from all morality and all mutual obligation in their pursuit of profit. Much of the early protest against industrialism was an attempt to reassert the moral unity of society in the new conditions — Blake's poems are perhaps the supreme example. As ideas of the New Jerusalem retreated and socialist thought began to develop along its own lines, it carried with it a stress on the theoretical as well as the moral unity of society. It emphasised the social character of human existence; the interdependence of politics, economics and private life; and above all, the collective and co-operative basis of production, which remained fundamental however quickly the product was seized and converted into private wealth.

The 'point of view of totality', as Lukacs[1] called this principle, is in one sense merely a rule of method. It states that bits of social reality should not be analysed in isolation; that one should always look for the context, the connections, and work back from them. This approach will constantly drive the argument across boundaries that have come to be recognised conventionally as defining separate sciences — economics, psychology, sociology, and so forth — and whose main function in practice is to prevent controversy spreading. However, the principle of totality can be taken as much more than a negative rule. The aspiration of class analysis is to discover those structures of relationships that operate most generally and most powerfully. It has this aspiration precisely because this is a criterion for practical politics: socialist political movements need to identify those points from which fundamental change *can* proceed, from which the intractability of power structures can be overcome. Radical politics is always relational: seeing connections, being able to interpret personal experience as a political problem, is at the basis of radical responses as diverse as the sexual liberation movements and the working-class politics of housing. Socialist theory is concerned to make relational interpretations structural, in the most general sense of the term.

Again, this is a way of understanding the world that has to be sustained against opposition. On the one hand, there is bourgeois individualism, the hand-grenade approach which explodes society into a multitude of competing individuals, dominant in many branches of social theory and historical writing, as well as mass ideology. On the other, there are concepts of society as a pre-given unity, a kind of overgrown happy family — whether the corporate unity of Catholic and fascist social philosophy, the moral unity of Durkheim's sociology, or the functional unity that flourished in post-war American sociology and still lurks in dark corners of educational sociology and economics. Many reactionary political movements have traded profitably on nostalgia for wholeness in a deeply divided society, and still do. The concept of society in class analysis is neither of these. It is, rather, the concept of a structured whole, bound together by relationships that also divide it, and that define the directions in which it may be changed.

These comments have been rather abstract and abrupt, but we do not want to labour preliminary observations. The basic point can be put briefly. To change a society in any fundamental way in the direction of increasing human freedom and self-determination, it is necessary for people to understand its basic structures, the processes that have produced it and the forces that are capable of changing it. That is the kind of knowledge that we hope to produce, if inevitably in a partial and sketchy form; and our concepts and methods are those that seem most apt for the purpose. Of course, we cannot prove by algebra that this society *ought* to be transformed; but some reasons to think so might emerge from the story that follows.

Bases of the Concept of Class

To the worker on a production-line, there is not much doubt about the meaning of class — it is an immediate reality in the noise, pace and discipline of the line, in the size of the weekly pay-packet, and the contrast with the pay, conditions and authority of management. In discussions of the concept, the brute obviousness of class relations in industry should always be borne in mind, especially by those who do not work in such a setting. Class is not an invention of the intellectuals, to be conjured up or conjured away by tricks of definition.

Still, what is immediately obvious is rarely a guide to the whole situation. There are spheres of life where class relations are not obvious — the leisure world of the commercial mass media is deliberately so — and there are many people who do not use the language of class even for their work experience. If we try to define 'class' by what people at any given moment take it to be, as a number of historians and sociologists have done, then we dissolve the concept of a society into a kaleidescope of competing views-of-society, any one as good as any other. Through this we lose the concept of a social totality (except in the extraordinary case where everyone agrees in their perceptions), and lose the possibility of explaining, within a theory of class, why there are such things as production-lines and people obliged to work on them.[2] Though the consciousness of people in class relations is immensely important in understanding those relations and how they develop, we cannot take the concept of class directly from their consciousness. Some further basis of theory is needed. In this section, therefore, we shall examine conceptions of class that are current in theoretical discussion, trying to develop an approach that is consistent with the principles already stated and that is adequate to the task of analysing a very complex historical process.

The most elementary meaning of 'class' is simply a category; a social class can be trivially defined as a set of people who share any identifiable characteristic — wealth, red hair, deplorable morals, a taste for new beer. These are all 'classes' as logicians use the term, and as nineteenth-century speech often used it, in discussions of 'the criminal class', 'the educated class', 'the useful classes', and so forth. In itself, this concept has no particular relevance to the kinds of issues we are concerned with, but it can be made into a theoretical model in two ways.

In the first case, the argument is confined to such characteristics as wealth, power or prestige, which imply some sort of hierarchy and allow two or more categories to be discovered on top of each other. Being very simple, this idea has naturally appealed to professional sociologists, who have called it 'social stratification' and made it the basis of a flourishing branch of academic research. In its more sophisticated versions, it grows into a concept of dimensions on which people can be arrayed, and much learned debate has arisen over what dimensions should be recognised, how they can be measured, how many classes — or 'strata' as they are more often called — should be distinguished on each dimension, and so forth. Most survey research that touches on class adopts this model; and though it tends strongly to have conservative ideological implications, it can on occasion point up unrecognised forms of exploitation. An interesting recent example of this is the concept of 'housing classes' that has become current in British sociology as a way of analysing social differentiation and conflict in cities.[3]

In the second case, a characteristic or relationship defines two sets of people, who are simultaneously defined as being in conflict with each other. A careless or highly simplified interpretation of Marx on capitalism (both of which are common) will interpret his class theory as being of this kind, with the two classes, defined by the magic formula of 'relation to the means of production', glowering at each other across the profit margin. The radical-feminist concept of 'sex class' advanced by Firestone and others is a very clear-cut example, with two sharply defined sets of people and a fundamental opposition — man, as Johnston put it, 'the natural enemy of woman'.[4] The populist vision which pits 'the people' against 'the monopolists'; theories of the 'new class' in Eastern Europe; and concepts of the 'managerial revolution' in the West, all typically involve models of this form.

The first of these models can be useful as a way of representing some of the effects of class dynamics, the second as a rough approximation to an antagonistic social structure. But in neither case does the concept of 'class', as a set of people marked out by a defining characteristic, begin to be adequate for sustained historical analysis. The approach is in itself ahistorical.

Stratification theory is logically incapable of modelling historical transformations, providing at best a grid through which people and time may flow; the notion of opposition and conflict in itself is no more historical than the notion of stratification, as Johnston's remark illustrates. To use this kind of class concept in a historical analysis requires a resort to metaphor, where the 'class' becomes a collective person with emotions, wishes and purposes of its own;[5] thus losing the notion of a situation, the response of people to a situation, and the intractability of situations. Even if some notion of place in a social relation is introduced (say, relation to the means of production) as the defining characteristic, the concept of a class as a set of people will still rapidly yield paradoxes. A familiar example is the objection to marxist accounts of contemporary capitalism, that many workers are (small) owners of shares and many businessmen are salaried employees of their companies. When classes are taken to be simply bounded sets of people, the difficulties of defining boundaries unambiguously will constantly appear to be a decisive objection to a class analysis.

This problem is handled with almost ridiculous ease by the approach to class inspired by Althusser's influential reformulation of marxist philosophy. This approach insists on the priority of theory over the empirical observation of groups. This is firmly stated by Dos Santos and Poulantzas:

> In the last analysis, determination of the basic social classes of society is not a task of empirical observation but one for theoretical investigation of the mode of production that makes the society.[6]

> Social classes are not empirical groups of individuals, social groups, that are 'composed' by simple addition; the relations of these agents among themselves are thus not inter-personal relations. The class membership of the various agents depends on the *class places* that they occupy ...[7]

This view follows from the sharp distinction drawn by Althusser between empiricism and the kind of science represented by marxism. It rests on a view of science which we can hardly pursue here, but which has strong implications for the order in which the analysis of society must proceed. The starting-point is the theoretical analysis of the most general forms of social organisation, which in the usual marxist view are the different 'modes of production'. In some modes of production, the central fact is a division between labourer and non-labourer, an antagonistic relation because the one lives off the other; classes can be defined in a preliminary way by this antagonism. It is the *relation* that is the object of theory and the basis of the concept of class, not a set of people, however defined.

A mode of production, however, is not an actual society; it is rather a structure of relations, defined abstractly, which can be discovered, mixed up with others, in the analysis of real societies. The classes of our experience, and of actual political struggle, are reached by an argument from this abstraction to the concreteness of the real world. Opinions differ somewhat about the stages of this 'process of progressive concretion', as Dos Santos elegantly terms it. The commonest view treats actual societies as 'social formations', which can be summarily defined as compounds of particular modes of production that have been created by a particular sequence of historical events. Analysis of the modes of production involved in a given social formation, and of their interaction, allows the theorist to define:

> certain objective places occupied by the social agents [i.e. *people*] in the social division of labour... It may thus be said that a social class is defined by its place in the ensemble of social practices, i.e. by its place in the social division of labour as a whole.[8]

This idea of a class 'place', or in Poulantzas' synonymous phrase, 'the structural determination of class', is the nub of this whole approach. Classes considered as sets of people are simply the occupants, for the time being, of these places. There is no ambiguity of boundaries in the definition of class places. The structure of social relations very clearly has theoretical priority over the people.

The concept of structural determination is a useful way of grasping the intractability of historical situations, the difficulty mere humans find in changing the conditions of their lives. It offers an approach to the things that stratification research takes as basic—differences of wealth, prestige, etc.—as the products or effects of class determination. In its more sophisticated versions, it goes well beyond the idea of class as a simple economic category, which all too many people have taken as properly marxist. When Poulantzas defined a class by its place in 'the social division of labour *as a whole*', he meant explicitly this, that class determination involves political and ideological relations as well as economic ones. In the Althusserian concept of the mode of production, several types of social relations are distinguished, usually the three just mentioned. A class place as a structural concept is defined by a particular patterning at all of these levels, and a patterning of relationships between them. Poulantzas, for instance, distinguishes the proletariat from the 'new petty bourgeoisie' largely in terms of ideological relations.

These virtues are, however, bought at a stiff price. The whole analysis hangs on the comprehensiveness and precision of the original model of the mode of production. Any weakness here will be magnified as one works down to the level of the concrete. And—even without questioning the truth of the basic Marxian model—it appears that very great ambiguities arise in this interpretation of it. Wright has shown, for instance, that Poulantzas' interpretation of the categories yields a definition of the working class that embraces less than 20 per cent of the workforce in the United States. By interpreting the role of political and ideological relations differently, Wright gets the figure up towards 50 per cent.[9] The priority of theoretical concepts does not seem to yield very clear-cut conclusions when we work down to particular cases.

Further difficulties arise in putting the structural concepts to work in history, in the analysis of events. To avoid treating a class as merely the shadow of a structural category, Poulantzas is repeatedly obliged to draw a distinction between what might be called two fields of analysis. The first is the field of the structural relations that constitute classes, in which the class *places* are defined. The second is the field of the 'conjuncture', or as we might put it, the actual historical situation; and in this field, classes (supposedly still defined in the same way) have *positions*. In this second field, as Poulantzas develops his analyses, we see classes adopt positions that may not at all correspond to the interests defined by their places: they manoeuvre for control of the state, making and unmaking alliances with dazzling promiscuity; and in general they behave rather wilfully, and oddly like the flesh-and-blood human beings whom Althusser had so carefully read out of scientific marxism at the start.[10] Not to labour the point, it appears that this theory can get a grip on historical events, and simultaneously maintain the epistemological purity of its structural categories, only by introducing a covert distinction between the concepts of class used in each of the two fields, by defining a separate system of class relations in each. The treatment of class in the second field is, perhaps, historical; the treatment of class in the first is certainly not; and the relationship between them is more a matter of metaphor than anything else.

We may take this point further. The priority of structural determination in this approach, its hostility to any notion of personal agency in history, means that it separates the basic concept of class from the process of class formation. Classes, in a fundamental way, are taken as given in the structural categories. But the structural categories themselves do not have a necessary historical sequence which might model class processes. They can be, and are, applied wherever and whenever they are thought to be relevant, and in almost any combinations. It is this that gives the analysis of 'determination' in marxist structuralism its uncomfortable feeling of rabbits being produced from a hat. A sceptic could interpret its methodology as basically a translation device, enabling one to talk about any situation at all without ever having to change one's vocabulary. It does not seem possible, along these lines, to develop an approach to class that does justice to its complexity, its intractability and its historical character at the same time.

In the final analysis, the conception of class as a place in a structure of theoretically-defined relations fails because it yields only an abstract, top-down approach to the politics of class. Classes *are* real groups of flesh-and-blood people, formed under particular stars at particular times and places, who work out their fate together — and whose fate is what politics is all about. We cannot get away from this without falling into a doctrine in which real history is derivative from many possible histories; in which real people become puppets in a cosmic ballet; and in which politics itself becomes *a priori*, the answers known before the problems arise.

On the other hand, the notion of classes as sets of people leads to no politics at all. The fact that people can be classified into a category means no more than that potatoes can be put in a sack. The experiences and actions of a group of people are not given simply by their existence — they refer to the situation in which they occur. And the meaning of actions is not just a matter of what is intended. A given situation has ways in which it can and cannot be transformed. Some choices, some actions, come to nothing, or result in changes that were quite unintended. Other choices may work — and sometimes this is the extraordinary choice for a new social order, made in a revolutionary situation, which works because it has become the common interest of a revolutionary class. To understand a class fully is to be concerned with people in situations, and that means to be concerned with the structure of situations: their limitations, their intractability; and their potential for fundamental change. This is to say that the understanding must be historical. The antinomy in class theory between set and structure can only be resolved by a historical analysis, which shows how both are produced at one and the same time.

A first step towards this is taken when the categories which, in stratificationist arguments, define classes, are seen rather as the matrices in which classes form. In this conception, a system of social differences defines sets of people—'quasi-groups' as they are sometimes called—who may become aware of their common position in the social structure, enter into conflict with other such groups, and develop common ideas and organisations to promote their common interests. Classes are understood as the organised groupings produced when these processes occur. As a representative definition puts it:

> Classes are formed when an aggregate of persons defines their interests as similar to those of the other persons in their aggregate, and as different from and opposed to the interests of another aggregate of persons.... The big difference between social stratification and social class is communalisation. (Krauss)[11]

Though it has no recognised name or attendant school, this conception of class is quite widespread. Some warrant for it can be found in passages of Weber and even Marx, whose famous distinction of a class 'in itself' from a class 'for itself' is constantly quoted. It is sometimes adopted by stratificationists when the limits of their approach become too stifling; it is implicit in the writings of those marxists who solder a conception of class consciousness on to the concept of relation to the means of production; it has been formally developed by theorists such as Dahrendorf; and it has been used in some substantial historical researches, such as those of Neale and Laslett. Its importance is precisely in its stress on 'communalisation', or more broadly class formation, as a process central to the concept of class itself.

Class formation is genuinely a historical concept, referring to actual events and real transformations. But a fundamental division still exists within the theory between structure and history. The historical process of class formation is superimposed on a structural division, whose roots are outside that history, which is not produced by historical processes recognised in the theory. This can be seen in the historical studies that have used this conception of class. Neale's research on nineteenth-century England hardly refers to the structures, concentrating rather on the ideologies and practical politics of the people defined by them. Laslett, though a fine descriptive historian, is so far from the concept of the historical production of a structure that he is able to argue seventeenth-century England was a 'one-class society' because only one grouping in it showed a high degree of mobilisation and self-consciousness. His notion of social structure is the static stratificationist idea of a status hierarchy.[12]

In Dahrendorf's theoretical treatment, it becomes even clearer that the root of the problem lies in the treatment of structure. The structural basis of the quasi-groups underlying classes is the relation of authority (as defined by Weber) in 'imperatively co-ordinated associations', and class conflict is regarded as inherent in the relationship between those roles which do and those which do not have authority. Having generalised away from the concepts of surplus-value and capital accumulation through which Marx attempted to link structural conflict and historical change in capitalism, Dahrendorf is left with an ahistorical opposition, an abstract polarity, as the basis of his concept of classes. He is left with a notional class struggle that can have no effect except temporarily shifting the balance of forces, or shifting particular people between pigeon-holes, within a structure whose basic form is always renewed. The best that struggle can achieve in the long run, in this conception, is a circulation of anti-elites — someone else goes to the bottom of the heap.[13]

The stress on class formation is valuable, but the approach is not yet fully historical — there is no theoretical conception of the historical transformation of structures. The view of class proposed by Thompson moves a long way towards this, by placing the process of class formation firmly in centre-stage. As this argument is central to our own approach, we beg indulgence for quoting his formulation at some length:

> By class I understand a historical phenomenon, unifying a number of disparate and seemingly unconnected events, both in the raw material of experience and in consciousness. I emphasise that it is a *historical* phenomenon. I do not see class as a 'structure', nor even as a 'category', but as something which in fact happens (and can be shown to have happened) in human relationships.
>
> More than this, the notion of class entails the notion of historical relationship. Like any other relationship, it is a fluency which evades analysis if we attempt to stop it dead at any given moment and anatomise its structure. The finest-meshed sociological net cannot give us a pure specimen of class, any more than it can give us one of deference or of love. The relationship must always be embodied in real people and in a real context. Moreover, we cannot have two distinct classes, each with an independent being, and then bring them *into* relationship with each other. We cannot have love without lovers, nor deference without squires or labourers. And class happens when some men, as a result of common experiences (inherited or shared), feel and articulate the identity of their interests as between themselves, and as against other men whose interests are different from (and usually opposed to) theirs. The class experience is largely determined by the productive relations into which men are born — or enter involuntarily. Class-consciousness is the way in which these experiences are handled in cultural terms: embodied in traditions, value-systems, ideas, and institutional forms.[14]
>
> The making of the working class is a fact of political and cultural, as much as of economic, history. It was not the spontaneous generation of the factory system. Nor should we think of an external force — the 'industrial revolution' — working upon some nondescript undifferentiated raw material of humanity, and turning it out the other end as a 'fresh race of beings'. The changing productive relations and working conditions of the Industrial Revolution were imposed, not upon raw material, but upon the free-born Englishman — and the free-born Englishman as Paine had left him or as the Methodists had moulded him. The factory hand or stockinger was also the inheritor of Bunyan, of remembered village rights, of notions of equality before the law, of craft traditions. He was the object of massive religious indoctrination and the creator of political traditions. The working class made itself as much as it was made.[15]

As these passages indicate, Thompson's conception revolves around a notion of agency. Though some phrases sound a bit like Krauss or Dahrendorf, this is not a matter of a historical process of mobilisation superimposed on an ahistorical structure of roles, quasi-groups or strata. As Thompson himself remarked in reply to Dahrendorf, 'the question, of course, is how the individual got to be in this "social role", and how the particular social organisation (with its property-rights and structure of authority) got to be there. And these are historical questions.'[16] The things which in that approach were taken to define categories, are here taken as the historically produced material of experience, which is acted on — along with the other historically produced material of cultural tradition — in a process of construction out of which a class as a category of people emerges.

Even that is a slightly too mechanical way of putting it; fundamentally, in Thompson's work, 'class' *is* the process of construction. As against marxist structuralism, which of course shares his emphasis on struggle though not on agency, Thompson locates the production of categories in real historical time, in the action of real people. Class is a historical relationship in a full and integral sense that does not admit of a distinction between a field of structural determination and a field of conjunctural interaction.

The main thrust of Thompson's research is concerned with the making of one class, but he is clear that one class cannot be conceived of by itself. Nor can two or more, by themselves. As Poulantzas remarked, 'social classes do not firstly exist as such, and only then enter into a class struggle. Social classes coincide with class practices, i.e. the class struggle, and are only defined in their mutual opposition.'[17] This requires an extension of the notion of agency and its effects. What is created cannot be a class, it must be a-class-in-relationship-with-another-class. The labour of class formation always gives birth to twins. Indeed, what is produced is not so much two classes as one class structure, an ordering of society around a class relation (or several class relations, if the situation is a complex one). Giddens has proposed a term for this, 'class structuration', which can be understood as the effect, at the level of the whole society, of the processes construed as class formation in an analysis such as Thompson's.

As Giddens observes:

> It should be evident that structuration is never an all-or-nothing matter. The problem of the existence of distinct class 'boundaries', therefore, is not one which can be settled *in abstracto*: one of the specific aims of class analysis in relation to empirical societies must necessarily be that of determining how strongly, in any given case, the 'class principle' has become established as a mode of structuration.[18]

Structure itself, in other words, is something historically produced, and its production cannot be logically separated from the actual events that make up the process of class interaction: it is all in the one field of analysis.

These views lead to an unexpected difficulty. If the historical approach is pushed to an extreme, it seems to make class well-nigh undefinable. 'A fluency which evades analysis' except as fluency, does not seem a very firm foundation for world history. A class that makes itself, whose consciousness of itself as a class is a crucial part of its constitution as a class, is all very well; but this seems to make popular consciousness very much the arbiter of theory, which is a position we rejected at the start. What happens if the people involved (or any part of them) *lose* this consciousness? Thompson's own formulae seem to work a good deal better for the heroic age of a nascent working class in the last century than they do for the tortuous history of workers and the Left in our own. More generally, if class is not *a priori* defined but is a category (or relation) constructed in history, at what point in the process of class formation or class structuration can one say that classes are finally here? At what point does the infant come of age? There seem no grounds of principle for choosing a particular cut-off point in this process, any more than there are for defining strata on a dimension in stratification theory. One can define a process of class formation with considerable rigour; but never, it would seem, 'class' itself.

This unhappy result, however, is not peculiar to Thompson's analysis, nor indeed to the writings of professional researchers. To take just one example, consider the following statement from the 1970 theses of the 'Il Manifesto' group, an Italian left-communist movement of unimpeachable militancy:

> The proletariat, representing the majority of those exploited in modern society, is the central motor and directing force of the revolutionary historic bloc built around a communist perspective. In an advanced capitalist society, however, the proletariat is not a reality that is sociologically definable with precision. It cannot be identified with the traditional factory workers: for the boundaries of the force of wage labour have been considerably enlarged. It cannot any longer be defined as those who produce surplus value: for the limits between productive and nonproductive labour appear less rigid. Thus the concept of proletariat runs the risk of being watered down until it signifies everything and nothing. In an advanced capitalist society, just as Marx had seen, the proletariat constitutes itself as a class especially through its struggle, its relationship to the reversal of the system. It is that part of the force of wage labour that, by its social aspect, its level of struggle, its degree of organisation, stands up to capitalist relations of production. This is why the fundamental means for the construction of a socialist alternative in the West does not consist in alliances between the proletariat and other social strata, but in the unification and constitution of the proletariat as a class through the politicisation of its economic struggle and the socialisation of its political struggle.[19]

A reality not sociologically definable—a class defined by its stance against capitalism—a class constituting itself as a class by the unification of economic and political struggle—it is uncannily like Thompson on the early nineteenth century, and raises the same conceptual difficulties, compounded by the fact that this is not so much a historical definition as a teleological one, more hope than science.

This difficulty is not easily overcome in theory, arguably cannot be overcome at all except in an actual analysis. But we can indicate at least the way in which the argument would have to proceed. The key weakness of other approaches that we have identified is their tendency to separate concepts of structure from concepts of situation or the real existence of groups of people. A consistently historical approach will escape total 'fluency' and regain the structuralists' sense of the intractability of class relations, to the extent that it succeeds in re-integrating these levels of analysis. Structure is an ordering in relationships; the existence of a given set of relationships is a situation. 'Structures' can of course be found in almost anything; but we are interested only in those which have some generality and have some relation to the determination of historical change, which express the constraints and potentials discoverable in a situation. What is often referred to as 'structure' in the theoretical literature that separates it from situation and process is basically the persisting order in relationships that links a series of situations. The analysis of such structures is not mysterious; it is a matter of accounting for the reproduction of this order in relationships through real historical time. And that is a familiar issue in socialist class analysis; as the master himself remarked, in a well-known passage of *Capital*:

> Capitalist production, therefore, under its aspect of a continuous connected process, of a process of reproduction, produces not only commodities, not only surplus-value, but it also produces and reproduces the capitalist relations; on the one side the capitalist, on the other the wage-labourer.[20]

Recently, Carchedi[21] has shown in detail, if in a rather structuralist vein, how the reproduction of class relations in production can be analysed. Of course, one must go beyond the economic process itself—if twentieth-century marxism has taught us anything, it is that the reproduction of social relations has a political and cultural dimension of the first importance. The point is that the persistence of constraints and potentials can be analysed in the same framework as the character of, and the events occurring in, situations—there is fundamentally no difference.

The History of a Class Structure

Taking a working-class perspective in history was originally a matter of writing the history of the labour movement itself. This was certainly justified, if only to claim a fair share in the past for the people normally treated as cannon-fodder by the historians of empires. It had a political point, making clear to working-class activists the depth and vigour of the tradition they carried; and naturally, it concentrated on the most visible and dramatic expressions of that tradition—'the subject matter usually considered the proper sphere of labour history', as Gutman has put it: 'trade-union development and behaviour, strikes and lockouts, and radical movements'.[22] In the work of a number of English historians, most notably Thompson and Hobsbawm, this approach has broadened into what is sometimes called 'the new labour history', but is in effect an attempt to write the history of the working class. This is a vastly more complex and comprehensive exploration of the experiences of working people, the social and economic changes that overtook them, their often contradictory responses, and their presence and power in the societies being created by the earthquake of industrial capitalism. The reasons for this shift in historiography are themselves complex: in part it is a simple development in technique; in part a response to changed emphases in socialist theory; and in part a directly political change, the decline of triumphalist labour history reflecting growing doubts about the effectiveness of traditional working-class organisations, at least in the English-speaking countries, and a search for new resources for socialism outside official socialist politics.

With the publication of Gutman's book of essays, *Work, Culture and Society in Industrialising America*, American labour history has signalled that it recognises the shortcomings of the institutional approach. Acknowledging a debt to Thompson, Gutman admits to shifting his theoretical focus away from 'the community' to 'the working class', with a consequent stress on the active role of that class, both in terms of its own making and its effect on the wider society. However, it is also clear from the title-essay that Gutman manages to assimilate this approach to behaviouralism. His main conceptual frame is industrialisation, not capitalism; it is cultural modernisation rather than class struggle that he sees as the motor of change in his period. This assimilation of the notion of class-as-event to behaviouralism is connected with a weakening of the category of structure. The stress on the making of *one* class, despite Gutman's disclaimers, makes it appear as if the process of class formation can be understood in its own terms, independently of situation; or with situations presented merely as episodes through which one can observe the process of a class making itself. A class analysis with definable terms becomes difficult to see in operation.

Gutman's work shows why non-marxists can welcome Thompson's work, stressing his marvellous feel for cultural fact; and more than that, how cultural analysis can be lifted to the level of a new explanatory principle, a self-acting dynamic. It illustrates very clearly why labour history, even in its broadened form, must be seen as theoretically limited. As Thompson observed in a passage already quoted, 'we cannot have two distinct classes, each with an independent being, and then bring them *into* relationship with each other.' If the argument in the previous section is even roughly correct, the concept of class structure is prior to the concept of class, and the project of analysing a class makes theoretical sense only as part of the project of analysing the whole structure. This applies of course to the analysis of other classes; it is precisely what gives point to research on the ruling class, such as Zeitlin's study of American corporate ownership and Miliband's study of the state, and distinguishes their work from the 'sociology of elites'.[23] Detailed studies are absolutely essential for an analysis of the whole structure that is to be anything more than doctrinaire; but they must be put together; in fact, they must be done with a constant awareness of the context of the whole. Some notion of how they fit together is already implicit in many of the authors cited, who plainly have views on the structure of the entire social order and the nature of the process of historical change. To make them explicit, however, is to step to another level of historical analysis: the history of the structure itself, which is, in the final analysis, the proper object of socialist historical study.

The practical analysis of a social totality, so far as it has been done at all, has usually been done in local and regional histories, and is usually quite innocent of theoretical intent. Regional historians typically do investigate a range of social groups and at least the more spectacular episodes of interaction between them; good regional histories also try to investigate the routine interactions between them. Where the society happens to be class-structured, this will often lead to a local history of classes and an empirical analysis of class formation; there are a number of good examples of this in Australian historiography, such as Kiddle on the Western District, Bolton on North Queensland and Waterson on the Darling Downs.[24]

Where this kind of study is combined with a theoretical appreciation of class processes, it can produce analyses of remarkable force and interest. Perhaps the best recent example of this is Foster's *Class Struggle and the Industrial Revolution*,[25] principally concerned with the textile manufacturing town of Oldham in England. This study is based on a remarkably detailed analysis of the town's working class and its radical leadership, the origins and structure of its bourgeoisie, the labour process and capital accumulation. It analyses the course of local politics in terms of the construction of a system of class relations and the specific way this town fitted into—and in some important ways differed from—the general patterns of socio-economic relations in industrialising England. Foster's accounts of the nature of the 'labour community', the nature of the resistance it made to the imposition of capitalist social relations, and the price the bourgeoisie paid for their eventual success, are models of theoretically informed historical analysis.

Local events, however, are local; as Foster makes clear, the working class in Oldham could not in the long run maintain its extraordinary control of local politics because of overwhelming bourgeois power at the level of national politics. For the history of social structure at that level, the models are much less satisfactory. Orthodox 'general history' usually weaves its comments on social conditions around a narrative of politics and rarely achieves much grasp of social process. To balance it, there is a well-developed genre of 'social history', which has typically meant the history of customs and tales of everyday life—child-rearing and church-going, crinolines and corsets. This does, like traditional labour history, provide important materials, though in most cases they remain very raw. Searching beyond those genres, however, it is possible to find some notable examples of structural analysis on a large scale. Perhaps the most splendid is Bloch's *Feudal Society*, which treats feudalism precisely as a distinctive form of the structuring of human relations, and investigates in great detail the material and historical circumstances in which that structuring arose and the transformations through which it passed. A more recent example, and closer to our theme, is Perkin's *Origins of Modern English Society*, which attempts to analyse 'the rise of a viable class society' out of the Industrial Revolution, as a revolution in the entire social structure. Indeed, a number of historians have recently made methodological statements arguing for the analysis of a total social structure—'the history of society' instead of 'social history', as Hobsbawm has put it—though usually without specifying in any detail the way in which the totality is to be understood.[26]

Perkin asks about the emergence of a 'class society', which is a notion not exactly covered by the discussion so far; it has to be related to the concept of class structure. In some versions of marxism the problem does not arise, since the two are defined in the same gesture, via the idea of a mode of production based on antagonistic relations of production: class society and class structure always appear together, by definition.[27] Without taking that step, most class analysis since Marx has taken it for granted that class relations form the basic or fundamental structure of any society in which they appear. But this is not a position that can be held if a fully historical approach to class is taken. For any society at a given time, one can raise the question of how far the 'class principle', as Giddens put it, dominates other forms of division and relation. Precisely this question is often raised in political debate about the contemporary situation. Many authors on the right, and some on the left, have argued that though class dynamics were dominant in the past, they are no longer in the Western social order; and radical feminists have made a more general claim for the priority of relations between the sexes over relations between classes.[28]

Since most writers have taken an *a priori* position on this, little attention has been given to the question of how the issue can be decided. It is not simple. If we ask how far class relations fill up, so to speak, the space of a given society, we nudge the circularity that plagues arguments in this field—for how do we mark out that space? A society is not a self-defining unit; its boundaries blur in time and space and analytic depth. If we push out to find the 'intelligible field of historical study', as Toynbee[29] (one of the few to address the problem) put it, we cannot define a limit without some criterion for what is inside it; and that criterion must have something to do with our notions of what the effective dynamics of a society are, that is, what are its defining relations. It would seem then that we cannot assess the dominance of a given set of social relations without also taking those relations as a means of defining the space that is dominated: which is, on the face of it, circular.

This circularity can be overcome. It depends on taking the notion of a society as given, and taking the concept of class society as the extent of class structuration in a 'given' setting—thus again separating structure and situation. Rather, it is necessary to see the way class relations come to dominate other patterns of relationship as an aspect of the process of carving out a distinct region for the operation of class relationships, the process of *creating* a social 'space' of a certain kind. The process of colonial expansion in the nineteenth century that created 'Australian society' shows this very clearly, as interlocking class processes in metropole and colony constructed a new kind of social unit. The problem of 'class society' comes down to the extent to which class relations themselves redefine historical regions (or cease to).

The unity of a region in class terms, then, cannot be assumed *a priori*; it is a constructed unity, and is only to be demonstrated by following out the process of construction and showing that its main dynamics follow class patterns. What is involved in such an argument is particularly well illustrated by Bowles' and Gintis'[30] argument about educational reform in the United States, where the school system has been a very important vehicle of political integration. Each of the major waves of reform, they suggest—the creation of the common schools, the progressive movement, and the expansion of higher education—has been a response to developments in economic relationships between classes, specifically a means of resolving contradictions between the processes of accumulation and reproduction that have given rise to heightened class struggle. Similar arguments can be developed about politics, urban structure, and many other matters. But the claim of a class dynamic is more than a list of arguments from economic conflict to other spheres. Education, the physical pattern of settlement, the course of political events, all feed back into the economic structure and play a part in constituting the classes that appear on the economic stage. The notion of a class dynamic in history is not one of economic determinism, but one of a complex pattern of historical causality in which class is an emergent—in which the structures constraining the principal transformations can be specified in class theory. And a 'class society' is, from the methodological point of view, a unit for which this pattern of historical analysis can, on the evidence, be sustained.

Social history has long been beset by a type of evolutionism in which the emergence of a class society appears as a kind of natural process. Metaphors such as 'the *rise* of a viable class society' are seductive; and we have already referred to the triumphalism of traditional labour history, which sees the emergence of working-class consciousness and labour organisations in much the same light. Althusser's critique of simplified conceptions of historical time is useful here: the kinds of processes—political, economic and cultural—that class theory speaks of, do not go on in orderly, logical unison. They can, on the contrary, get badly out of phase (at least, out of the correspondences that a simple evolutionism might suggest).[31] The processes of mobilisation that are crucial in class formation do not by divine ordinance always go one way—demobilisation can also occur. Though this point has not often occurred to class theorists, it is common sense to working-class activists, who are often faced with the possibility of a weakening of class consciousness, the defeat and on occasion the destruction of working-class organisations, and at best a routine daily struggle to maintain a given level of mobilisation. The important thing to remember is that class struggle is genuinely struggle; and though it is possible to pick out long-term trends in it, no one direction of historical change is guaranteed by natural law.

In writing the history of a structure, then, we will be badly in error if the interpretation is organised around any unilinear or uniform conception of historical change. In fact, one of the main tasks will be to identify structural disjunctions, those transitions where the ordering of relationships and the possibilities of action are reconstructed in major ways. The creation of the first working class is one such change, which has now been analysed in considerable detail by English historians; and its demobilisation, 'liberalisation', or whatever one wishes to call it—that is, the creation of a bourgeois hegemony in the mid-Victorian period—would seem to be another. In Australia, we will be concerned to analyse the ways in which a society polarised around capitalist production relations was created, and the major transitions that then occurred within it—the linked changes of the dominant groups within the ruling class, of capital formation and the production process, and of the scale and depth of working-class resistance. It is not a history of triumph, nor (as some historians suggest by discarding everything after 1921) one of ignominious defeat. It is the history of a social structure, as the history of the people who variously made and endured it; and it is certainly not yet over.

Concepts for Class Analysis

In the course of this enterprise we will be using a number of technical terms, and it may be useful to give a brief explanation of them here. These definitions, it should be made clear, are not attempts to specify what will be found in the historical materials; this is not intended to be the outline of an *a priori* theory. Fundamentally these are summarising concepts, their validity depending wholly on the patterns that can be found in the events.

It is a striking fact that neither of the two greatest theoreticians of class, Marx and Gramsci, offered a clear basic definition of the term. Apart from accidents (such as Marx's dying in the middle of a chapter on the subject) the basic reason is that class is not an elementary logical category of class analysis—it is a concept that emerges in conducting it. Ollman[32] is right in suggesting that the definition of class in Marx inheres in his whole analysis of capitalist society, and is bound up with his substantive claims about the way it works. Still, the analysis has to start somewhere, and the following concepts, if not complete, may at least provide guidance.

Power, Property and Commodity Production

As we suggested at the start, the main subject of class analysis is power, its institutionalisation, use, and effects. Power is a concept notoriously difficult to define, and we are not going to try solving the main problem of political science here. We can, however, usefully distinguish two forms of it and explain the way we are *not* going to use it.

The commonest conception of power is a matter of someone issuing orders — and having them obeyed. Weber formulated it neatly by defining power as 'the possibility of imposing one's will upon the behaviour of other persons', adding, in some versions, despite resistance and regardless of the basis on which the possibility rests. This is a definition that will do for the power of a Prime Minister, for the power of a foreman, for the power of a husband (as in Millett's definition of politics as 'arrangements whereby one group of persons is controlled by another'); and is obviously of great importance for our analysis. Power in this sense may sometimes have to be traced through to people in the background, such as the businessman–politician Sir Arthur Warner in Bolte's Victorian cabinet in the 1950s; this is often difficult to do in practice, but creates no theoretical problems in itself. Theoretical difficulties arise when this is taken as the *basis* for an analysis of the social structure and its workings, as in stratificationist analyses that make 'power' in this sense (or 'authority', that is, legitimate power) a fundamental stratifying variable. It is possible in principle (though fiendishly difficult in practice) to give everyone in a given society a score for power in this sense, and hence to stratify them; but the trouble is that this gives no theoretical grip on what they *do* with it, and hence yields no conclusions about historical process. The best that can be done is to postulate some inherent conflict between those who are high and those who are low in power, making social structure and politics basically a contest of Who's Who versus Who Isn't — and with that we are back to the eternal cycles of bourgeois elite theory.[33]

We need a more impersonal concept of power, which refers to the constraints on holders of personal power, and is not necessarily defined in terms of the formulated will or intention of any person or group. The classic case of such constraint is the competitive market, where the interaction of many individual wills produces a result that no one individually intended. The constraints in such a situation can be very strong indeed; there is, it would seem, power of some sort here, though not coming from a particular person. So also at the receiving end. To achieve many intentions, it is not necessary to issue commands — one can simply issue money and buy the result desired. This also seems to be power, but not over a particular person; rather over a situation, through the abstract agency of the medium of exchange. Where these two forms of constraint come together, we may have a very strongly constrained system of social relations, but one that can only be analysed by an impersonal conception of power. The classic case is the capitalist labour market based on the institution of private property.

'Property' or private ownership is the enforceable claim to exclusive use or disposal of something by a person or an association of people, involving an extension of that claim to the products of its use. It plainly depends on consent by, or intimidation of, other possible users; and thus may be regarded as a specific form of power, one that is formalised and impersonalised to an extreme degree. (Capitalism, strictly, should not be spoken of as a system of power based on property but as a system of power organised in the form of property.) The institution of property was established, together with an apparatus of enforcement, with the first white settlement in Australia. It has undergone some change towards greater scale and impersonality of form, along lines familiar in the history of capitalism (notably the nineteenth-century shift to the corporate organisation of productive property), but the basics have changed little.

Private property occupies a central place in the socialist analysis of power, not because of obsession with Mine and Thine, even less because of some belief that people are governed by their baser instincts, but because of its remarkable practical effects in the sphere of production. Not all property—perhaps not even most—is employed in production. Hobhouse once made a happy distinction between 'property for use', such as household utensils, and usually the house, and 'property for power'.[34] Though the juridical forms are often indistinguishable, the practical differences are immense. Property for power, deployed in the sphere of commodity production, is capital. Capital as a form of organised power depends on the mass of workers' being excluded from control and disposal of their tools, materials and products. In fact it is partly defined by this situation, the concept 'capital' thus fundamentally *meaning* a particular organisation of social relations in production.

Power in the form of property, property in the form of capital, is crucial in modern history because of what may be called its generative capacity. The rapidity with which capital can be accumulated in a production system increasingly organised for it, and employing machine production in at least some key processes, yielded an extraordinary economic dynamism, and a capacity for the social relations of production to dominate other kinds of social relationships, which has marked the last two centuries off from all other periods of history. In some forms of socialist theory, it is assumed that relations of production are central to the analysis of all social structures whatever; we doubt this as a grand historical generalisation, but in any case it suffices that it is true for capitalism. In capitalism, of course, class relations are not *confined* to production. Class struggle and exploitation occur in other spheres, for instance the allocation of housing and the functioning of cities, though connections with production relations can normally be traced.[35]

Capitalist production relations may, and usually do, coexist with other forms of economic organisation. Ownership by the direct producer, in the form of family farms or the small businesses of craftsmen and craftswomen, may persist alongside capitalist agriculture and factories; in some circumstances it may flourish and expand, as in the Australian wheat-belts in their prosperous periods. But these forms of production are liable to be integrated into the capitalist order, either as specialist suppliers of goods or services most easily handled on a small scale (as in many professions), or by the co-ordination of their activities by other institutions (such as the role of banks in financing and organising rural production in Australia, gradually replaced by the state), which mediate their relationship to the capital and commodity markets.

The dominance of capitalist commodity production in the whole social order is marked by a separation of economic life from domestic life, driving a division between paid work in the economy and unpaid work in the home.[36] One should not conclude from this that those who perform domestic labour — typically married women — are in any sense outside of class relations, or related to 'class' only through their attachment to wage-labourers. The making of a class is in one of its most important aspects the construction of certain types of communities that link households in private and domestic life as well as public and economic. When we say that 'class' involves a structuring of society *around* the labour market, we mean explicitly that it is *more than* the labour market itself. Actual classes embrace more than direct employers and employees: they include the very young and the very old, as well as the economically adult; the unpaid housewife as well as the paid hand and the paid domestic; the unemployed and partly employed as well as the 'full-time' employed. A full class analysis must be concerned with what is specific to the position of these different groups of people, most importantly the complex effects capitalism has on the relations between the sexes; and above all, must be concerned with the way these positions are produced by the historical changes with which the theory of class is concerned.

Labour Market, Class Boundaries and the Structure of a Class

The social relationship which is capital is mediated by a market, in which the labour power of the workers is sold — as Marx put it, labour power becomes a commodity itself. This market is the central structure of the capitalist system, the pivot on which the dynamic of the system turns. By 'labour market' we mean more than simply the employment bureaux, the pick-up at the gates of the dock, and the direct bargaining over the terms of the sale, the wages and conditions to be gained. We mean the whole complex of institutions and arrangements that make labour power a commodity, and keep it a commodity — the fact of private ownership of tools, machines and materials, the fact of the ownership of the product by the capitalist, the dependence of the workers on wage income, and the possibility of the accumulation of capital out of the labour process.

This structuring of production relations did not fall from the sky; it was produced historically by a long and often violent process, which is, in fact, still going on at the margins of the capitalist world. Marx spent a good deal of the first volume of *Capital* in analysing its course in England, the dispossession of the direct producers which he regarded as 'the secret of primitive accumulation'. Even in such a high-technology industry as steel production in the nineteenth century nothing like a pure capitalist labour market existed; the skilled steel-workers were in effect contractors to the capitalists who owned the plant, controlling the labour process, typically engaging their own labourers, and in effect sharing profits with the steel masters by a sliding scale of payments. As Stone[37] has shown in a detailed examination of the American steel industry, it was only after a conflict in the early 1890s in which a dozen workers were killed and the plant manager shot and nearly killed in return, that direct wage–labour relations and capitalist control of the production process were established. As this and Foster's analysis of the parallel process in the British cotton industry show, the establishment of a capitalist labour market is itself in part the *product* of class struggle; it would be in error to think of class conflict as necessarily *flowing from* capitalist production relations. The labour market is always the focus of that struggle, but the nature of the struggle changes according to the degree to which capitalist relations have been established in it. In fact, it is wise to think of those relations as always being imperfectly established, and class conflict as never being entirely within the labour market or exclusively over the terms of the exchange of labour power for wages. Working-class responses, even after such frightful defeats as the Homestead massacre of 1892, always have in them some element of resistance to the nature of the system as a whole and foreshadow alternatives; conversely, the ruling class always must expend some energy in preventing those alternatives arising.

The general labour market that structures the basic relations of a capitalist social order is just that: a general structure. The actual situations faced by workers and their employers are varied. The labour process in different industries calls for different proportions and types of skill, and the workers affected have different skills and different positions of strength and weakness according to their organisation and social situation. In many circumstances, there is a strong tendency for a series of separate 'labour markets' (in the restricted sense) to form, with resulting conflicts between different groups of workers. The creation of an ethnic 'under-class' (as it is sometimes called) in Europe, the United States and Australia in the post-war period is now well recognised, and similar processes can be found much earlier. Much more generally, a segregated labour market exists for women, concentrated in particular types of jobs and almost universally with worse conditions of pay and security than are available to men. Changes in the labour process itself may be introduced where it is in the interest of capital to differentiate jobs and introduce lower-paid groups of workers.[38]

Even at the economic level, then, the working class can never be regarded as homogeneous, and one of the major tasks of its history is to analyse its changing internal structure and the connection of those changes with the evolution of the system as a whole. The same goes for the owners of capital. Their forms of organisation change, as we have already noted in the case of the transition to corporate capitalism. Events such as the concentration of power in a small number of giant companies, shifts of profitability and political power between different industries, and changes in the distribution of power within companies, pepper the history of the ruling class. Both major classes in capitalism are internally diverse—though both, in a crisis, may mobilise in a way that overrides these diversities.

One of the most important features of the internal differentiation of classes is the emergence of leadership groups. The 'labour community' analysed by Foster was politically effective largely because it developed a radical and experienced leadership; and the modern corporate management, over which so much ink has been spilt in the 'managerial revolution' debate, is quite analogous—an operating leadership group within a class. This conception of leadership, which relates to the historical process of class formation (a constantly continuing process), must be clearly distinguished from the notion of an elite in stratification theory. It has to do essentially with the role of small groups in processes of mobilisation—mobilisation of political resources, mobilisation of economic resources (such as the mobilisation of capital that occurs in company formation), and so on. This may, in periods of stability, amount to the occupation of top positions in formal organisations, but need not do so.

As the positions of the major classes differ fundamentally, so do their typical patterns of leadership. Among capitalists in the pre-corporate period, leadership often amounted to the local prestige and informal authority that defined a 'notable' among landowners, magistrates, and so on. In the period of corporate capitalism, economic and political leadership to a considerable extent become differentiated; the one based on the mobilisation of capital directly and depending on mastery of organisational power in companies, the other based on the mobilisation of resources in political class struggle and — where a party system emerges — depending on mastery of organisational power in conservative parties. Working-class economic organisation, mainly through unions, is profoundly different, though here too organisational power becomes significant when unions are institutionalised and a bureaucratic organisation can emerge. The leadership of such unions is liable to be in tension with the 'rank-and-file' activism that emerges in the workplace, and also may be in tension with the political leadership that emerges when working-class parties are organised to carry on political class struggle in the arena of the state. This too may become institutionalised, and a very similar tension often arises between bureaucratic leadership in parties and activism at the level of the mass membership or political activity that rejects the major party organisations.

We have discussed the question of the internal differentiation of classes before the vexed question of the 'boundaries' between classes, because from this perspective the latter is not a fundamental problem. Many people still think that class analysis is basically a matter of drawing lines through a society; and if clear-cut lines cannot be drawn, that class theory is thereby refuted. The growth of a mass of white-collar workers, for instance, is often supposed to have 'blurred' class boundaries and thereby refuted socialist analyses of capitalism. The stratificationist assumptions of this line of argument should be evident, and we have already given the answer in principle. 'Class' is not a layer in a layer-cake; it is an emergent structure in a historical process. Class boundaries, where they become clear as divisions in an entire social structure, are constructed historically by processes of mobilisation and struggle. They are *normally* 'blurred', uneven, incoherent; they should be expected to be; and they may become more blurred, uneven and incoherent depending on changes in the organisation of production, the fortunes of politics, the processes of cultural change. They may also become more sharply defined; and when they do become sharply defined, then some kind of crisis is normally at hand.

The State, Hegemony and Crisis

The political class struggle just referred to is, in one of its most important aspects, a struggle for control of the state. Its importance is sufficiently defined by a remark of Neumann's: 'ultimately the fight to smash the power of property will have to be waged in the citadel of the rule of private property, the state'.[39] In the meantime, the struggle to define the limits of 'the power of property' is constantly carried on through the state. Throughout

Australian history, capitalists have attempted to use the state to control the price of land, control immigration, etc., to ensure a supply of wage labourers; and conversely, workers have petitioned, pressured, and eventually attempted to capture state power in order to 'civilise capitalism'—or abolish it.

The state is as difficult to define as power; the difficulties are closely related, and a similar polarity can be traced between concepts of the state that rely on notions of direct personal power, exercised through the state organisations, and more structural definitions that define the state by its functions and effects. In socialist writing, there have been two main perspectives on state power. The anarchist tradition has seen the state as directly the instrument of oppression, though communist anarchists such as Berkman have argued its close integration with production relations, its function as the basis of economic exploitation in capitalist production. The marxist tradition has seen the state essentially as the product of class antagonisms, the instrument of ruling classes in containing conflicts that would otherwise shatter the social order.[40] To capitalism, we would suggest, both conceptions apply. It is useful to distinguish the *state organisations*—parliaments, courts, government departments, military and police forces, over which and in which class conflict will occur as already noted—from the *sphere of the state* as a system of social relations. The state in this broader sense may be defined as the sphere of regularly enforceable direct power relationships. Our discussion of class so far has stressed indirect relationships, notably in markets. Markets, both general commodity markets and the special case of the labour market, depend on the system of property, which requires the enforcibility of claims to ownership. The state as a system of control thus underlies the market itself; it has a *constitutive* role in the generation of a class structure, at a deep level. Nevertheless, the enforcibility of claims requires enforcers—laws, courts, police—and thus the state organisations are involved at this level too. The creation of a capitalist labour market involved a struggle for control of the state and the creation of a form of the state integrated with capitalist production relations; and the struggle to change those relations is also a struggle against that form of the state.

Enforceable claims to property require either coercion or consent. Consent is in large measure a cultural and psychological problem, and even coercion raises these issues, for one has to account for the consent of the enforcers, which is not always reliably given. This is an issue that has received a good deal of theoretical attention since the defeats of the European Left in the 1920s, receiving its most general formulation in Gramsci's theory of hegemony. Gramsci used the term in two main senses, to refer to the role of political leadership held by one class in an alliance of classes, and to a situation of cultural dominance held by one class in the society as a whole; it is the second meaning that will mainly concern us. It refers to a situation where, parallel to the control exercised by a ruling class over the coercive machinery of the state, there is an effective control over the relations and organisations of private life or 'civil society'—churches, schools, families, and so forth. More generally, hegemony can be seen as a situation where the subordinate class lives its daily life in forms created by, or consistent with the interests of, the dominant class, and through this daily life acquires beliefs, motives and ways of thinking that serve to perpetuate the class structure.[41]

The concept is fundamentally a situational, that is, historical, one. The concept of hegemony-as-a-situation must be clearly distinguished from the concept of the mechanisms of control (such as intimidation, persuasion through education or the mass media, bribery) that may be operating, in different combinations, to create any given hegemonic situation. Too great a concentration on mechanisms leads theorists all too readily into postulating total control—implicit in theorists as diverse as Marcuse and Althusser—and underplaying struggle.[42] Gramsci avoids this trap, perhaps partly by ambiguity, but also by paying close attention to the formation of hegemony, the historical sequences by which a hegemonic situation is created. (In this, the divisions within the working class that we have already noted in discussing the labour market can be of the first importance.) A hegemonic situation may be regarded as one where the dominant class is highly mobilised, in some respects at least, and the subordinate one very little. The formation and maintenance of hegemony may thus be regarded as a process whereby the holders of power—whether by conscious policy or standing institutional arrangements—*resist the process of class formation* on the part of the labour force, and especially resist the development of a heightened class consciousness. Anything that serves to disorganise the working class, to disrupt class solidarity, or to contain or deflect the action of working-class groups, will then be a mechanism of hegemony. The differentiation of the labour force, which sets group against group in economic competition; the psychological pressures analysed by Sennett and Cobb,[43] which turn working people's discontents against each other and their aspirations towards the individual advancement of their children; and the political forms which direct working-class mobilisations into struggles which, whatever their outcome, cannot damage the basic system of exploitation; all will serve. Here we meet one of the most fundamental features of the capitalist state, for in a great measure, it is the state that is active in the these matters; in the routine management of affairs, the state is capable of substituting for the mobilisation of the ruling class.

The resistance to class formation is never entirely successful; there is always tension in and around the labour market. To handle it, there must be a degree of organisation and expenditure of energy by the owners of property, some element of class mobilisation; and this is typically the role of conservative parties. On the other side, the subordinate groups will often respond to power in a hegemonic situation by mobilising as a class within the confines of the ruling political and legal system. The strategy of reformism adopted by many unions and labour parties, which allows labour leaders to raise a limited set of class demands in parliament, or to conduct industrial battles via the legal manoeuvres of the arbitration system, is just such a working-class response to hegemony. Reformist mobilisation, though limited, is still a form of class mobilisation, and any form of class mobilisation carries at least the shadow of a threat to the system. This is a fact that goes some way towards explaining the intense emotional support attracted, for a time, by quite moderate leaders such as Lang in the Depression; and the intense hostility generated in some ruling-class quarters to the rather benign Whitlam government.[44]

Hegemony can also be directly opposed; and there is a long history of groups and movements that have deliberately set themselves to follow a counter-hegemonic strategy. To think only of Australia in this century, such movements range from the I.W.W. in the 1910s to the counter-culture of the present. As we suggested much earlier, the meaning of an action is dependent on the structure of the situation in which it occurs; and a counter-hegemonic strategy is not an effective choice unless it is made in a situation that has developed crisis tendencies. The analysis of capitalist crisis is one of the most obscure and difficult areas of class theory, and we will only make two observations here beyond pointing to the issue. The most developed form of socialist theory, i.e. marxism, has traditionally sought the roots of crisis in basic contraditions of the capitalist system, most generally in the contradiction between an inherently social and co-operative form of production and an anti-social private appropriation of the products. The angatonism in the relations of production that expresses this contradiction was expected to be the basis of a revolutionary response to a system that, by its own logic, would be driven into a series of economic crises.

That economic crises have duly occurred is beyond doubt. That the revolutionary response has normally not, at least in the ways anticipated, is also fairly clear. A number of socialist theorists have taken up the problem, and their analyses, often of very different specific issues, have in common the idea of the displacement of crisis. The analysis of imperialism developed in the years before the Russian Revolution suggested an economic and political displacement, a postponement of the reckoning in the leading capitalist powers by means of the export of capital and the exploitation of the rest of the world, and a conversion of tensions between classes into rivalry between countries. The theory of hegemony developed after the Russian Revolution suggested the possibility of the displacement of crisis between spheres in the social structure of the metropolitan powers, an absorption of tensions generated in the relations of production by the psychological and cultural resources of the system. Whether, as Habermas[45] suggests, there are limits to this displacement, and crisis tendencies within the realm of culture, is a moot point, though the fact that the main mobilisations against the capitalist order in this century have corresponded to wars rather than economic depressions gives some point to the idea. Given its dependence on the international capitalist order, one would hardly expect to find major crises originating in Australia. But as a vulnerable capitalist economy — because of that dependence — with a relatively highly organised working class, there is a good chance that we would find the dynamics of cultural crisis particularly clear to view. Australia in this sense is a laboratory of hegemony, and perhaps a test-case of its demise.

Objections

The line of argument and the concepts sketched above are meant to be vulnerable to counter-argument, counter-example and disproof. Propositions about class should not be made true by definition, nor 'produced' by production processes that occur exclusively in the theorist's head. Swallowing a good rich dose of awkward facts is the best medicine for theoretical mistakes. But this is not a simple matter of confronting fact and theoretical claim, as suggested by empiricist epistemology — the kind of argument illustrated by critics who reject a class analysis of Australian society because there is not a high level of social polarisation or sharply defined class boundaries in it at present. (Some people, it seems, expect to find what would practically amount to a revolutionary situation before they will admit the existence of a class structure at all.) The relation of fact to theory is much more complex, because the relevant facts (or at least their relevances) are partly constituted by the theory, as well as the theory being partly suggested by late-night meditation on the known facts. And class theory is particularly difficult to sort out because it is historical and concerned with processes; our very language makes it difficult to think consistently in these ways.

Nevertheless, the application of class theory can be refuted in various ways. It can be argued that the structures modelled in the theory do not share the form of the structures of the actual society. Some such claim is implied in the claims of theorists of the managerial revolution or welfare capitalism, that property has now gone through an internal evolution that has removed or reduced its capacity to structure social relations, or has replaced it with a different structure of power. It can be argued that the processes specified in class theory, though they occur, are not the most basic or determinant ones—we have already considered this line of thought. Or it can be argued that the patterns partly picked up in this theoretical outline may be better understood by a different organisation of ideas, which produced a more comprehensive theory.

What is 'better understood' is not simply a cognitive matter. Logic might construct many models of the world for us, all with intellectual appeal. The claim of class theory is to a very large extent pragmatic: that its concepts and postulates enable one to make sense of the historical evidence and lead to effective political action. Plainly, a test of such a claim is extremely difficult. Historical evidence is complex and ambiguous; people will differ over whether explanations and tactics do work; political practice is, in a well-known phrase, a slow boring through hard boards. Yet it is in this direction that the test of a theory that claims to speak of large-scale social dynamics, and the structure of historical situations, must lie. And the test is not independent of the political process that might confirm it. As we argued at the start, social analysis is inherently political, and conducting a class analysis in a particular way is a political act that has a bearing, however slight, on the future of class relations.

People answering polls sometimes refuse questions about class, complaining that they 'don't want to be in any class'. We sympathise, as have others. A Sydney *Herald* editorial argued in 1844:

> To instil into the minds of what are called the working men a feeling of class separation, or of class independency, or of class antagonism and rivalry, towards the classes from which alone they can obtain employment, and with whose welfare their own is necessarily interwoven, is... a cruel wrong to society at all times.[46]

And especially with Chartism shaking the gates in England, not to mention a depression and a nicely brewing struggle for state power in the colony! But that is the authentic conservative response to class analysis—to reject it because it is socially disruptive—just as the authentic radical response is the reverse, for the same reason. To argue *for* class conflict involves, of course, an ethical risk. Class struggle involves social disruption; has often meant bloodshed on a considerable scale when pushed to the point of major confrontations. Ruling classes are often prepared to fight. But the alternative does not prevent either risk or bloodshed. Intellectuals may prefer a soft life, hoping that the trouble will be contained and the killing will keep well out on the edges of the system, in unimportant places like Vietnam. Most people do not have that option. The system depends on pressure to maintain economic exploitation—nearly 500 000 were unemployed in Australia at the last count, countless others under-employed or vanished from the carefully manipulated statistics. And the violence is in the heart of the system as well as on its fringes. An activist in a housing campaign was murdered not long ago in Sydney in the course of a confrontation with capitalist developers; and on the night this page was written, police attacked a demonstration in Melbourne against the export of uranium arranged by a reactionary government in the interests of multinational mining companies and (by a complicated system of international blackmail) Australian rural capitalists.

The most devastating objection to the theory, in the final analysis, is what it may itself lead to. Class analysis is intimately connected with the critique of the existing social order and the project of constructing socialism. It is a *possible* outcome of class analysis that socialism cannot be achieved by any foreseeable transformation of the existing order. Most 'proofs' of this so far are products of wishful thinking by conservatives or fatigue on the part of radicals, which on examination boil down to the usual circularities of elite theory. But there have been some serious historical arguments along this line, such as those of Marcuse, which must be respected. If that is really the conclusion, if the historical signs really do read 'No Exit', then the point of the analysis is removed. One may continue to struggle for ethical reasons, or from force of habit, but the place of struggle is irrelevant and analysis is a waste of time. In some groups within the Left, there does seem to be an impatience with theory, which comes from a pessimism born of repeated defeats, a sense that the battle is always going to be lost. But until theory says that—unambiguously—theory has a place. We don't yet know the answers; and a necessarily slow and patient process of research and analysis is a part of the total practice that may find them. It is not simply a matter of harping on fundamentals, insisting that basics have got to change, as socialist writing has all too often done. Many of the outworks of the class system have not been recognised as such by the labour movement in Australia. Until they are identified, analysed and dealt with, socialism will remain a dream.

Notes

1. G. Lukacs, *History and Class Consciousness*, Merlin, London, 1971, p. 27 (first publ. 1923).

2. For an example of this among historians, see R. Gollan, *Radical and Working Class Politics: A Study of Eastern Australia, 1850–1910*, M.U.P., Melbourne, 1960; and among social scientists, R. R. Centers, *The Psychology of Social Classes*, Princeton U.P., Princeton, 1949; and P. Hiller, 'Social Reality and Social Stratification', *Sociological Review*, vol. 21, 1973, pp. 77–99. For an example of the way production-lines *can* be explained, see H. Braverman, *Labor and Monopoly Capital*, Monthly Review Press, New York, 1974.

3. For an analysis of the character and limits of stratification theory, see

R. W. Connell, 'Logic and Politics in Theories of Class', *A.N.Z. J. S.*, vol. 13, 1977, pp. 203–11; and for a particularly clear exposition of its empirical techniques and their problems, E. F. Jackson and R. F. Curtis, 'Conceptualisation and Measurement in the Study of Social Stratification', in H. M. Blalock and A. B. Blalock (eds), *Methodology in Social Research*, McGraw-Hill, New York, 1968, pp. 112–49. A recent review of the latter problem is C. Bell, 'On Housing Classes', *A.N.Z. J.S.*, vol. 13, 1977, pp. 36–40.

4. S. Firestone, *The Dialectic of Sex*, Paladin, London, 1972, esp. ch. 1; and J. Johnston, *Lesbian Nation*, Simon & Schuster, New York, 1973, p. 276.

5. As was noted, in comments on a schematised Marxism, by E. P. Thompson, 'The Peculiarities of the English', *Socialist Register*, 1965, p. 342.

6. T. Dos Santos, 'The Concept of Social Classes', *Science and Society*, vol. 34, 1970, p. 172.

7. N. Poulantzas, *Classes in Contemporary Capitalism*, New Left Books, London, 1975, p. 17; emphasis added.

8. Ibid., p. 14.

9. E. O. Wright, 'Class Boundaries in Advanced Capitalist Societies', *New Left Review*, no. 98, 1976, pp. 3–41. The uncertainty about the meaning of 'determination by the economic' that this exchange reveals has been noted by other critics of Marxist structuralism; see, for instance, A. Callinicos, *Althusser's Marxism*, Pluto Press, London, 1976.

10. These remarks apply particularly to the analysis in Poulantzas' *Political Power and Social Classes*, New Left Books and Sheed & Ward, London, 1973; the position in *Classes in Contemporary Capitalism* on this issue is cruder — the field distinction appears on occasion, but there is a greater tendency to treat classes in action simply as the personifications of the economic categories.

11. I. Krauss, 'Some Perspectives on Social Stratification and Social Class', *Sociological Review*, vol. 15, 1967, pp. 134–5.

12. R. S. Neale, *Class and Ideology in the Nineteenth Century*, Routledge & Kegan Paul, London, 1972; and P. Laslett, *The World We Have Lost*, Methuen, London, 2nd edn, 1971.

13. R. Dahrendorf, *Class and Class Conflict in Industrial Society*, Stanford U.P., Stanford, rev. edn, 1959, esp. ch. 5. B. Jones, 'Max Weber and the Concept of Social Class', *Sociological Review*, vol. 32, 1975, pp. 729–59, raises another objection to this approach, that at least in the case of Weber, the notions of structure (here market structure) and of class formation (or social class) are logically incompatible because they are defined in different frameworks, which make it 'impossible to produce a concept of social class in the sense of a *unity* of economically determined individuals'. That seems consistent with the argument on historicity here, provided one does not attempt to solve the difficulty by retreating to the level of class determination alone.

14. E. P. Thompson, *The Making of the English Working Class*, Penguin, Harmondsworth, rev. edn, 1968, pp. 9–10.

15. Ibid., pp. 212–13.

16. Ibid., p. 11.

17. Poulantzas, *Classes in Contemporary Capitalism*, p. 14.

18. A. Giddens, *The Class Structure of the Advanced Societies*, Hutchinson, London, 1973, p. 110.

19. *Il Manifesto* Group, 'For Communism', *Politics and Society*, vol. 1, 1971, p. 436; cf. Thompson, *Making of the English Working Class*, p. 546 and *passim*.

20. K. Marx, *Capital*, vol. 1, 1867, ch. 23.

21. G. Carchedi, 'Reproduction of Social Classes at the Level of Production Relations', *Economy and Society*, vol. 4, 1975, pp. 361–417.

22. H. G. Gutman, *Work, Culture and Society in Industrialising America*, Knopf, New York, 1976, pp. 11–12. There are, of course, notable exceptions to this pattern: such as G. D. H. Cole in England, Brian Fitzpatrick in Australia, and others in America listed by Gutman, who besides writing labour history of this kind also attempted to write the history of the class.

23. M. Zeitlin, 'Corporate Ownership and Control: The Large Corporation and the Capitalist Class', *American Journal of Sociology*, vol. 79, 1974, pp. 1073–1119; and R. Miliband, *The State in Capitalist Society*, Weidenfeld & Nicolson, London, 1969; these are, of course, only meant as illustrative examples of socialist ruling-class analyses, though they are particularly clear and useful ones.

24. M. Kiddle, *Men of Yesterday*, M.U.P., Melbourne, 1961: G. C. Bolton, *A Thousand Miles Away*, Jacaranda, Brisbane, 1963; and D. B. Waterson, *Squatter, Selector and Storekeeper*, S.U.P., Sydney, 1968.

25. J. Foster, *Class Struggle and the Industrial Revolution*, Weidenfeld & Nicolson, London, 1974.

26. M. Bloch, *Feudal Society*, Routledge & Kegan Paul, London, 2nd edn, 1962 (first publ. 1940); H. Perkin, *The Origins of Modern English Society, 1780–1880*, Routledge & Kegan Paul, London, 1969; and E. J. Hobsbawm, 'From Social History to the History of Society', *Daedalus*, vol. 100, 1971, pp. 20–45.

27. B. Hindess and P. Q. Hirst take the cake for managing also to define the state and politics in the same fruitful move: see *Pre-capitalist Modes of Production*, Routledge & Kegan Paul, London, 1975, p. 13 and *passim*.

28. For example, M. Bookchin, *Post-scarcity Anarchism*, Wildwood House, London, 1974; and C. A. R. Crosland, *The Future of Socialism*, Cape, London, 1956; and among feminists, Firestone, *Dialectic of Sex*; and R. Dunbar, 'Female Liberation as the Basis for Social Revolution', in R. Morgan (ed.), *Sisterhood is Powerful*, Vintage, New York, 1970, pp. 477–92.

29. A. J. Toynbee, *A Study of History*, abr. D. C. Somervell, O.U.P., London, 1946, pp. 1–11.

30. S. Bowles and H. Gintis, *Schooling in Capitalist America*, Routledge & Kegan Paul, London, 1976.

31. L. Althusser, 'The Errors of Classical Economics: An Outline for a Con-

cept of Historical Time', in L. Althusser and E. Balibar, *Reading Capital*, New Left Books, London, 1970, pp. 91–118. If taken to an extreme, this produces a total disengagement from historical sequence of the kind we have already criticised in marxist structuralism; but within limits, it is an important and practical argument.

32. B. Ollman, 'Marx's Use of "Class"', *American Journal of Sociology*, vol. 73, 1968, pp. 573–80.

33. Weber's definition is quoted in R. Bendix, *Max Weber*, Anchor, New York, 1962, p. 290; cf. the expanded definition in *Wirtschaft und Gesellschaft*, I, 1, §16; Millett's definition is in *Sexual Politics*, Sphere, London, 1972, p. 33. For an archetypical stratificationist position, see W. G. Runciman, 'Class, Status and Power?', in J. A. Jackson (ed.), *Social Stratification*, C.U.P., London, 1968, pp. 25–61. Dahrendorf's *Class and Class Conflict* is an example of the tendency to postulate inherent conflict, as noted earlier; and it can also be seen in radical writings such as C. W. Mills, *The Power Elite*, O.U.P., New York, 1956, esp. ch. 13.

34. Quoted in A. Weinberg and F. Lyons, 'Class Theory and Practice', *British Journal of Sociology*, vol. 23, 1972, pp. 62–3.

35. See, for instance, the attempt to analyse urban process in terms of the circulation of surplus-value in D. Harvey, *Social Justice and the City*, Edward Arnold, London, 1973.

36. This question is now coming in for concentrated attention; see, for instance, D. L. Barker and S. Allen, *Dependence and Exploitation in Work and Marriage*, Longman, London, 1976, and the sources cited there. On effects on the household, see the stimulating hypotheses of E. Zaretsky, *Capitalism, the Family and Personal Life*, Canadian Dimension, n.d. (1974)?, (repr. Harper & Row, New York, 1976), which has interesting parallels with the work of Sennett and Cobb cited below.

37. K. Stone, 'The Origins of Job Structures in the Steel Industry', *Review of Radical Political Economics*, vol. 6, no. 2, 1974, pp. 113–73.

38. On labour market segmentation, see the very important study by S. Castles and G. Kosack, *Immigrant Workers and Class Structure in Western Europe*, O.U.P., London, 1973; for a review of the American debate on the issue from the point of view of class theory, D. M. Gordon, *Theories of Poverty and Underemployment*, Heath, Lexington, 1972; on Australia, J. Collins, 'A Divided Working Class', *Intervention*, no. 8, 1977, pp. 64–78; and M. Power, 'The Wages of Sex', *Australian Quarterly*, vol. 46, no. 1, 1974, pp. 2–14. Braverman, *Labor and Monopoly Capital*, discusses the differentiation of the labour process itself.

39. F. Neumann, *European Trade Unionism and Politics*, League for Industrial Democracy, New York, 1936, p. 11.

40. On the first point, see the celebrated exchange between Miliband and Poulantzas in *New Left Review*, nos. 58, 59, 82, 1970–73. For the Communist anarchist view expounded by A. Berkman (who, by the way, was the man who shot the steel-plant manager referred to earlier), see his *A.B.C. of Anarchism*, Freedom Press, London, 1968 (first publ. 1929); for the basic mar-

xist perspective, see the discussion of classic texts in Poulantzas, *Political Power and Social Classes*.

41. This account is based on A. Gramsci, *Selections from the Prison Notebooks*, Lawrence & Wishart, London, 1971; and the essay on 'The Southern Question', translated in *The Modern Prince and Other Writings*, International Publishers, New York, 1957, pp. 28–51. There are a number of short expositions of his conception in English, of which the best is perhaps still the earliest, G. A. Williams, 'The Concept of "Egemonia" in the Thought of Antonio Gramsci', *Journal of the History of Ideas*, vol. 21, 1960, pp. 586–99.

42. Cf. H. Marcuse, *One Dimensional Man*, Routledge & Kegan Paul, London, 1964; and L. Althusser, 'Ideology and Ideological State Apparatuses', in *Lenin and Philosophy*, New Left Books, London, 1971, pp. 121–73.

43. R. Sennett and J. Cobb, *The Hidden Injuries of Class*, Vintage, New York, 1973.

44. Here we differ from H. McQueen, *A New Britannia*, Penguin, Ringwood, Vic., 1970, p. 236, who describes the Labor Party as 'the highest expression of a peculiarly Australian petit-bourgeoisie'. We regard it as a much more ordinary thing, a product of class mobilisation under hegemony; if a formula must be found, it fits Gramsci's category of formation 'which assert the autonomy of the subaltern groups [i.e. classes], but within the old framework'; see 'History of the Subaltern Classes: Methodological Criteria', *Prison Notebooks*, p. 52. On Lang, see R. Cooksey, *Lang and Socialism*, A.N.U.P., Canberra, 1971; on responses to Whitlam, R.W. Connell, *Ruling Class, Ruling Culture: Studies of Conflict, Power and Hegemony in Australian Life*, C.U.P., London, 1977, ch. 6.

45. J. Habermas, *Legitimation Crisis*, Heinemann, London, 1976.

46. Quoted in M. Roe, *Quest for Authority in Eastern Australia, 1835–1851*, M.U.P., Melbourne, 1965, p. 30.

2 Convict Settlement and the Origins of Colonial Capitalism, 1788–1840

The search for origins is deceptive. White society in Australia is so easily dated to Sydney Cove in January 1788 that the question of origins can appear simply a matter of the Tories' motives for planting a penal settlement there and then. Indeed, the precise balance between the delicate motives of evacuating human refuse from the gaols and hulks of Britain, bolstering profits in the whale and tea trades, and providing a naval base for imperialism in south Asia, continues to fascinate historians.[1] But though we can learn a little from that debate — notably the multiple roles of the state from the settlement's first conception — it misses the main point. The creation of a white society in Australia was not accomplished in 1788; nor were its major directions in the long run set by that beginning. As a purely convict colony, the settlement was experimental. For half a century, succeeding cabinets and parliaments in London remained uncertain whether or not it was a failure. By the time they decided that it was, their judgement had become irrelevant: a colonial capitalism and an expanding white settler society had already come into being. In this process lie the origins of the modern social structure in Australia. It was not a product of official policy, but it was also not a matter of chance; it was the outcome of hard-fought struggles and grinding labour, from which the power structures of mercantile and pastoral capitalism successively emerged.

We start the analysis with the first important actor, the state, enquiring how state organisations and property relations were constructed and reproduced in the new settlements. We then consider the character of the labour market (in the general sense already defined) and its complexities in the penal context. As the crucial feature of the early settlements was the penal system, we then turn to the situation of the convicts, their experiences and responses. We then consider the more orthodox processes of class formation among other groups, notably landowners in the countryside and merchants and working people in the towns, the principal groups whose struggles created the situation in which the penal system met its inglorious end and the British state relaxed direct control. Finally, we return to the state and the question of the cohesion of this growing mass of tensions and contradictions, considering the first attempts to create a hegemonic situation in the Australian colonies, the reasons for their failure, and the beginnings of a new cultural order.

Construction of the State

It has often been observed that the state has played an unusually important role in Australian history, from the comprehensive management of the convict colonies to the extensive economic activity of colonial governments in the later nineteenth century, and arbitration and welfare activity in the twentieth. But the state that planted the first settlements and the state of the post-gold-rush boom was not the same thing. For all its influence and the undoubted continuities, the British state was not simply transplanted into Australia. The state as a set of social relations simply cannot be lifted from one spot and set down in another — it has to be constructed, or reconstructed, in the new conditions. In Australia this construction was undertaken deliberately, using the resources of the British state, and modelled on many of its features, but departing from the model in a number of ways.

The first departure was in the provision for repression. The British state was no stranger to force; but the settlement in Australia involved two generations of violence of an intimacy, continuity and scale very different from the home model. From the moment of the first occupation, force was applied on two fronts, against convicts and blacks — controlling the white workforce by the lash and the gallows, and creating the space within which the settlement could grow. Though official policy towards blacks had an element of sympathy and conciliation, which at times predominated in the governors' counsels, in normal practice the government provided military support to white settlers at the frontier, and often enough, troops and police took the lead in skirmishes and massacres. Whatever the motives, force was the basis of the pastoral explosion of the 1830s and 1840s which swept across the south-east of the continent, wrecking Aboriginal society and causing perhaps a hundred thousand deaths by murder, starvation, disruption and disease, out of a population that was probably no greater than 300 000 at the start.[2]

Coercion was carefully provided for in the First Fleet. Governor Phillip may have been short of everything else, but he did have a marine garrison with a tough and experienced commander. In 1791, this force was replaced by an army unit specially raised to be a colonial garrison. Like the marines, the New South Wales Corps fought a number of skirmishes with blacks, and hunted down escaped convicts; it also faced, and beat, an organised convict rising in 1804. In 1810, after its mutiny against Bligh, the Corps was replaced by regular army regiments, in rotation. These too fought on the frontiers with blacks, and several times fought small guerrilla campaigns against bushranging convicts, particularly in Van Diemen's Land. The actual fighting was done as infantry with muskets, or as mounted police troops; in reserve were artillery and naval forces. Their control of the colonies was never in danger, and only in 1804 seriously challenged. This permanent imbalance of military power was the most decisive fact about the early settlements: it was the frame within which everything else happened.[3]

The military were not directly involved in the management of the convicts. Major Robert Ross, the marine commander, refused this task in 1788, and the refusal stuck. Though the military did in time provide guards for chain gangs and penal settlements, and military officers became police magistrates, the colonial authorities had to build a separate system of control for the mass of working convicts. Phillip improvised an administration using any men he could lay hands on: his personal servant and a purser off a wrecked ship became key officials. He also improvised a police force, including convicts under the supervision of civil officials acting as magistrates. The colony had been provided by the English authorities with a system of courts, principally a criminal court, a civil court, and magistrates to hear minor charges. This system of control, needing an executive arm, rapidly acquired floggers and hangmen, and in due course gaols and gaolers, paid out of a local police fund. A network of penal outposts was set up to deal with convicts who bucked against discipline, committed crimes in the colony or were suspected of sedition, beginning in the early 1800s with Newcastle. After the general tightening of convict discipline in the 1820s, it produced Port Arthur, Moreton Bay and the second settlement at Norfolk Island, the hell-holes that have gone down in legend as signifying the convict system. They were, more exactly, part of the apparatus of terror by which the regular convict system was enforced.[4]

Apart from the military, the state organisations were constructed in the colonies, beginning with the dozen officials who sailed with the First Fleet. Phillip soon added convict overseers, and a rough structure of three tiers began to emerge. At the top were officers, typically appointed by Royal warrant, and paid salaries from England that were sharply graded from around a hundred pounds per annum for assistant surgeons and the like, to ten or twenty times that amount for the governor. Most had a background as military officers, and all considered themselves gentlemen. In the second rank, on the other side of a sharp social divide and at distinctly lower salaries, were supervisors, such as the tradesmen who did the government's carpentry, and minor paid officials with clerical jobs. These were a mixture of free immigrants, ex-soldiers and ex-sailors, and time-expired or pardoned convicts. Some were sent out from England, but most were scraped together locally by the governors. At the bottom were the overseers of convict gangs, usually convicts themselves, still serving their sentences but rewarded by extra food, clothing and privileges. Order in the whole structure was maintained by the threat of dismissal, tacit bribery and the lash.

An administrative structure of this kind was able to run the colonies for thirty years without great strain. With the large increase in convict numbers that followed the rising level of class conflict in England after the Napoleonic Wars (arrivals climbed from a few hundred a year to two or three thousand a year), with the review and toughening of transportation policy that followed in the 1820s, and not least with the reform and regularisation of colonial administration in England, there was a considerable shift towards bureaucratic rigour in the colonies. Respectable convicts and ex-convicts, who on the whole had been rising in influence and dignity up to about 1820, were squeezed out of positions of authority. Immigrant professionals such as lawyers and surveyors became more prominent in the administration; the courts were reformed and convict administration was bureaucratised, most effectively in Van Diemen's Land.[5]

At the same time, there was a development in quite another direction: towards amateurism in the shape of unpaid magistrates. When the role of Justices of the Peace became a point of sharp political conflict in the 1830s, it was no accident. The magistrates in fact played a critical part in the evolving system, and their story provides the key to the changing role of the state in early Australian history.

In contemporary England, magistrates were a basic part of the system of government. In the countryside especially, they carried the administration as well as forming the courts. Almost all being landowners, they united economic and legal power with social prestige, forming local oligarchies that were in effect the major counterweights to the central government in London. In the Australian settlements there were originally no landowners, so military officers and civil officials were made magistrates to get the courts going. They soon took on administrative tasks—for example, supervising the police and fixing the price of bread—which expanded into a general supervision of the non-convict population along English lines. As the civilian population grew, non-official magistrates, such as the merchant Robert Campbell, were appointed. As is well known, Governor Macquarie appointed a few rich ex-convicts as magistrates, to the scandal of local gentlemen and the displeasure of his superiors in England. His successors appointed increasing numbers of rich free immigrants.

Though it had been a point of conflict before, this practice took on major significance only with the expansion of convict numbers and the growth of pastoral capitalism in the 1820s. Convicts were taken off the hands of the government by being 'assigned' to private settlers, that is, supplied to them as labour on condition of being fed, clothed and housed. As this scheme expanded, the pastoralists became an arm of the state, a vast outdoor department of penal supervision. Conversely, the state became a partner of the pastoralists, supplying labour and guaranteeing its discipline. The magistracy articulated the scheme into a system. For it was the magistrates in the countryside who were responsible for the supervision and discipline of the convicts. And those who were appointed as magistrates were, of course, the respectable local landowners, that is, the leading pastoralists. Thus in the Australian countryside, on a penal basis, the English combination of economic and legal power was re-created and a local gentry began to form.

Though this reacted against the authority of the governors, they could not prevent it: only gentlemen could be made magistrates, and in much of the countryside the only gentlemen available were pastoralists. An attempt was made in 1825 to balance them with stipendiary magistrates, employing among others seconded army officers; but their numbers (26 in 1840, when the population of New South Wales was nearly 130 000) never made stipendiaries an effective alternative, even if they had been disposed to challenge the social position of the pastoralists.[6] Conflicts arose over which particular men were to be appointed magistrates, and reforming governors such as Bligh and Bourke roused remarkable hostility by failing to reappoint as magistrates men with whom they had fallen out politically; but not even Bourke thought to challenge the social assumptions on which the state and pastoralism were linked, or the general character of the magistracy.

The close relationship of private business with the state in pastoralism was not in principle unusual. The earliest merchants in Sydney and Hobart were the settlements' civil and military officers, buying imports with the salaries, regimental funds and government bills that represented practically the only 'foreign exchange' at the time. The enterprising gentlemen who could wring a profit out of a gaol at the end of the world did not stop with importing. They were granted land, they got free labour in the form of assigned convicts to work it, and then sold the produce to the government commissariat. As the botanist Caley drily observed in 1803, 'they had hit upon a genteel plan of getting money out of the British Treasury'.[7] For half a century, imprisonment was the colonies' main industry, and it was an industry from which many ingenious profits were wrung. The state long continued to be the largest customer in the colony; it pioneered many industries and even opened up the tracks for pastoralism, as is dramatically shown by the squatting rush into Victoria within months of Major Mitchell's exploration of the Murray Valley in 1836. Some historians of early Australia have pictured the state and capitalism in opposition, as if they represented rival social systems. Nothing could be more misleading. The state organisations provided both a base and a field of operations for private entrepreneurs. State power and private control of production were articulated in many ways, from the magistracy to the organisation of immigration. The form of the state certainly changed, moving closer to the English pattern, but it was never substantially opposed to private production. Above all, the state became involved in constructing and guaranteeing the relations of private ownership on which the labour market and capitalist production would rest.

The first fleeters brought with them the usual English assumptions about private ownership of personal goods, though for the moment they regarded the general resources of the colony as belonging to the government. The coercive apparatus of the state immediately began enforcing property rights. Of the first forty-odd prisoners brought before the Bench of Magistrates in Sydney in 1788, two-thirds were brought on charges of theft. A private retail system spread through the settlement, relying heavily, in the absence of currency, on credit transactions. As early as 1798, the courts were convulsed by the resulting debt cases and the attempt to enforce property rights; Governor Hunter actually had to promulgate an order to prevent convicts being prosecuted for debt, to stop interference with their labour. By the 1810s, the civil courts were handling highly complex cases, and the full system of English commercial law was in force.[8]

This eventual result was not in doubt; but there was more scope for doubt about private property in land, especially in a penal settlement. The British government claimed ownership of all land for the Crown (ignoring any Aboriginal claim absolutely); but provided in the first governor's instructions for small grants of farming land to ex-convicts, then to ex-servicemen. This provision was brought into operation in 1791 with the famous grant to James Ruse at Parramatta. The officers, discovering that they were not entitled to grants, complained of this as a hardship, and after a few years' delay in London, permission was given. The authority arrived in the colony in 1793 and was immediately used to set up substantial farms, John McArthur racing in the lead. Some feeble attempts were made to impose conditions on grants, but in practice farm land became a commodity, freely able to be sold or leased. (In one bizarre episode, some prime wheat land at the Hawkesbury was actually leased back to the government.) Land was granted to new settlers, in rough proportion to their wealth. By the 1820s, practically all the usable land in the Sydney region had passed into private hands.

An initial attempt was made by the governors to keep control of the town centres, yielding colonists only temporary rights to build houses. But that great leveller Macquarie, impressed by the 'opulence' of the colonial merchants, got approval to grant away this land too; and the great urban property market was launched. In new townships, land was granted (in Perth) or sold (in Adelaide and Melbourne) from the start. Thus, by one track or another, every type of land in the settled districts came to be a simple commodity.[9]

Pastoral land was a different story. The earliest stock-owners got large grants and quietly occupied the 'waste lands' nearby. Small men, when they got stock, just took usable land until forced off it—hence the earliest complaints about 'squatters'. When the British government realised it could make money out of colonial lands, it began to sell them; after a complex policy dispute, free granting was finally abandoned in 1831 for sale by auction. Much ink was spilt over the question of the minimum price that would be low enough to encourage pastoral capitalists, but high enough to raise a good revenue and deter working men from becoming pastoralists. With land being sold, there was of course a greater incentive to squat. The colonial government attempted to control this by introducing annual licences for people wishing to occupy Crown land in the settled areas. With the big rush beyond the Limits of Location when the pastoral export business boomed, this system was extended to the new districts in 1836, tacitly legalising the great land grab that had occurred. Occupation by pastoral licence was so cheap that it was practically a loan of the land to the squatter, hardly even a lease. But it conveyed no rights of sale, inheritance, or renewal. In the 1840s land was being held by at least five different titles—grant, purchase, lease, licence, and brute force—and the most economically important forms were the most unstable. Thus the stage was set for the land struggles of the mid-century in New South Wales and Victoria, with the squatters fighting for secure tenure of their land, the imperial government resisting the loss of control or at least hoping to make them pay for it, farmers and urban radicals claiming the land for other purposes, and the emerging colonial parliaments as the battleground.[10]

The struggle over land in large measure took the form of a struggle for control of the state organisations, and in this the fundamental connection of business, the state, and the system of property was made very plain. Access to state power was desired because it reacted directly on private fortunes. The factional politics of the early settlements (that is, the politics of the respectable) largely revolved around the issue of access. The McArthur–Bligh dispute was fuelled by Bligh's exclusion of his opponents from the magistracy and from informal decision-making. Some of the most bitter arguments of Macquarie's time were about access of ex-convicts to government office and to practice in the courts; and the emancipist–exclusive controversy of the 1830s also involved access by ex-convicts to minor authority, notably in juries, as well as the disputes over the magistracy already mentioned. Until the 1840s, when the first elected legislative and municipal councils were set up, the government remained formally a bureaucracy—but a bureaucracy rent with faction, surrounded with intrigue and gradually changing in form as its slow reactions helped or hampered different groups among the emerging colonial capitalists.

Formation of a Labour Market

The changes in the forms of the state just sketched are obviously closely linked with the growth of a system of private production. At the very start of settlement, though there was private property in personal goods, there was no labour market in the sense defined earlier. Property was wealth, but not capital. The state directly controlled labour: it grew or imported its own food, set up its own smithy and shipyard, provided its own services. Throughout the convict period, in a variety of ways, the government continued to play an active role in production. This need not be romanticised as public enterprise; it was forced labour for penal purposes, and the buildings and bridges still standing as memorials to Macquarie and Arthur must be seen in this light. With the growth of capitalist production, nevertheless, the government's economic activity became more ambiguous, controversial, and eventually contradictory. On the one hand, under pressure from London to cut costs and make transportation really penal, the government was a direct producer of its own necessities. This brought it into conflict with local capitalists, who thought they were being denied their divine right to cheap labour (especially skilled labour) and saw themselves cut out of a lucrative local market. On the other hand, the government did provide the infrastructure for capitalist development (such as roads and port facilities), and provided itself with the means for the efficient importation and distribution of an expanding workforce (such as Macquarie's convict barracks). With many hesitations and reversals, reflecting changes in British penal policy as well as local fluctuations in the labour supply, the second role came to predominate over the first, and a recognisable capitalist state began to emerge from the workings of a prison administration.

Though the consummation was long in coming, the direction was set very early, for the government ceased to exert direct control over the labour process within a very few years of the initial settlements. The first faint sign of what was to come was the farming done by some of the First Fleet officers — or, more precisely, by convicts lent them by the governor. When the officers, and later other respectable immigrants, were granted land, there was a much greater potential for employment. Most of the convicts shipped to the colonies were soon absorbed as household servants and agricultural and pastoral labourers. Around this 'assignment' relation, which persisted as a major form of employment into the 1840s, a complex structure of regulation and custom grew up. The distribution of convicts among employers was a constant point of conflict, and the supervision of assignment, once made, varied from the fairly tight control maintained by Arthur in Van Diemen's Land to total laxity at other times and places. The legal basis of assignment was decidedly marxist, the convicts' labour-power being regarded as a kind of commodity that was granted to the settler by the government, which maintained (in theory) control over the convicts' persons. The convicts were thus supposed to be performing unpaid prison labour. However, their masters typically found that pure coercion was bad business. The custom grew of supplementing the lash with incentives, notably in the form of drink, and sometimes also low money wages. A certain amount of competition for convict craftsmen developed among masters, given the rarity of skills in the colony and the importance of such men as carpenters and blacksmiths in pioneering conditions. Thus a muted but definite labour market developed in private agriculture and grazing, even within the penal framework of assignment.

As the assignment system evolved, another structure of employment was growing alongside it. When convicts became free, by pardon or expiry of sentence, or came 'off the stores' with a ticket-of-leave, they had to fend for themselves. Some, though it seems never more than a quarter, took up grants of land. Others worked for themselves in the towns; others became wage labourers. The government soon developed a system of 'tickets-of-leave' whereby convicts still under sentence went off, under loose police supervision, to fend for themselves. Thus, as early as the 1790s, the convict system began to generate a pool of men and women in search of work. Their numbers were swelled in time by free immigrants, and the children of convicts and free people born in the colony. Within twenty years of the foundation, these groups considerably outnumbered the convicts serving sentences in New South Wales. Some of the enterprises built on their labour were substantial: in a document of 1810, for instance, the merchant Robert Campbell claimed to be the employer of 126 'free men'. The ratio swung back towards convicts under sentence with the big shipments after the end of the Napoleonic wars; but the free-labour pool remained an essential part of the colony's social structure. There were normally some free employees even on pastoral properties at the height of the convict system. By the end of the 1820s its permanence and importance had to be acknowledged, and duly were by a repressive Masters and Servants Act passed by the New South Wales Legislative Council in 1828.

In the pastoral boom, with a rising demand for labour and increasing uncertainty about convict transportation, the government went much further. It swung from a policy of encouraging rich immigrants whose capital would absorb convict labour, to a policy of encouraging, indeed subsidising, working-class immigrants, thus stimulating the growth of a colonial labour market. A scheme of large-scale assisted migration got under way in 1832; by 1851, when the population of the eastern colonies was approaching 450 000, more than 100 000 immigrants had been subsidised. Most of the men who came, up to the time of the gold-rushes, were labourers, and most of the women were domestic servants. A minority had trades and hence had a chance of setting up on their own, but most were unskilled (many being from Irish agricultural districts) and dependent on finding employment when they arrived in the colony.[11]

A propertyless labour force is only one side of the capitalist labour market: there must also be capitalists possessed of the needful. Where did the power to employ come from? The first private capital in the colony, as we have noted, came from officers' salaries and official funds—hence, indirectly, from the social surplus extracted by taxation in Britain. But a process of accumulation in the officers' hands began immediately private trade and agricultural production was organised, that is, in the early 1790s. Some ex-convicts whom the officers had used as retail agents also began to accumulate profits in the 1790s. The details are obscure, and probably always will be, because very few commercial records have survived from these years. It is clear that some of the profits were extracted from convict labour by sales of produce to the government, on the system already described. It is also clear that some profits were extracted from small landowners, by credit sales of imported goods at monopoly prices, often leading to foreclosure on the land. No doubt there were other devices too; the pioneers of free enterprise in Australia were a tough and grasping group. In the 1800s there were a number of men—officers such as McArthur, ex-convicts such as Simeon Lord—worth some thousands of pounds and able to be employers on a fair scale, on the basis of capital accumulated in the colony. The generative powers of private property acted promptly.

Local capital was rapidly supplemented by imported capital, which became significant in trade as early as 1800. It developed first as a credit network linking local traders with established merchant houses in Calcutta and

London, who would consign goods to Australia either speculatively or as agents. Campbell's business, for instance, was built this way. The importance of such credit was shown soon after Macquarie took over: the British commercial crisis of 1810–11 forced a commercial depression in the colony that practically wiped out the first generation of traders.[12]

Imported capital was even more important in beef and wool. The cost of setting up as a pastoralist was high. In the early period, the British government insisted on emigrants having a certain air of affluence: £500 was the atmosphere required, around 1810. Land was granted and convicts assigned in proportion to the sum brought. Later, wealth was automatically demanded by the fact that Crown land was being sold. In the back country, this cost could be evaded by squatting, but the costs of transport, wages, equipment, and of course stock, remained. The most detailed of contemporary calculations, in the 1840s, reckoned the cost of establishing a substantial station, running 20 000 sheep, at about £8000. Other estimates put the minimum for setting up as a pastoralist at £500 to £1000. The smallest of these sums was far more than most working people in the colony, whose money wages might amount to £20 or £30 a year, could ever hope to own.

There were, then, high barriers to entry into pastoralism. Only those who already had money could get in. Some, such as McArthur and Campbell, went into pastoralism with the profits of agriculture and trade. Some squatters in the boom raised loans from merchants and bankers in Sydney. But the typical route into pastoralism was an import of personal or family capital from England. The pastoralists, that is to say, were usually men of some wealth, who came out to the colonies hoping to turn a modest fortune into a big one. Some of the most familiar figures of the convict and pastoral age, including the Blaxlands of New South Wales and the Hentys of Victoria, began their colonial careers this way.[13]

Commercial agencies and family enterprises could organise an import of money or credit that could become capital, but they could not seize really big opportunities for business and profit. For this, the available English model was the joint-stock company: a committee of wealthy men trading as a partnership or under a charter given by the state. Company formation in early Australia followed much the same course as family capitalism, though with a lag of about twenty years. The first step, the formation of the Bank of New South Wales in 1817, was a mixture of official and private enterprise. It was set up to handle general currency problems, and provided by Macquarie with a (probably illegal) charter. Leading officials were prominent among its owners and directors, and the bank was even listed as a government department in the young Wentworth's book about the colony. But it was in fact privately owned, and its healthy profits flowed into the pockets of the officials, merchants and pastoralists who held shares. Not long after, colonial entrepreneurs began linking up with British ones to promote companies in Britain, and this was followed by local companies formed independently of the government (though still closely linked to the state in their operations).

Most of these companies provided specialised services in finance and transport: they were banks, insurance and steamship firms. Manufacturing was still only a small part of the economy, though the Australian Gas Light Company (1837), with a capital of £45 000, reached a respectable size. Initially, the local companies had a simple structure. The banks, for instance, depended on share capital rather than deposits for their funds, and were basically devices for broking loans between the shareholders and borrowers. A fairly small, but very active, group of merchants, officials and some pastoralists was involved in the formation of a range of different companies. The merchant Alexander Brodie Spark, for instance, at his bankruptcy in the crisis of the early 1840s, held shares in ten companies, several of which he had promoted or directed, and which gracefully subsided alongside him. The numbers of people from whom these entrepreneurs raised their capital was also small; the Australian Gas Light Company in the 1840s, for instance, had only about 150 shareholders. The expectation that only the wealthy would be subscribers was shown in the size of shares, which were commonly in £25 or £50 denominations. Within that group, however, there was a good deal of capital to be raised. In the boom conditions of 1838–40 there was a wave of company formation both in Sydney and in Hobart, and despite the massively larger capital market in London, it seems likely that local investment in Australian companies outstripped British investment in the period up to the gold-rushes.[14]

Several of the native-born companies attempted to raise capital on the British market, through shares or deposits, but this was at the time (before the telegraph) difficult and risky. It was more readily done by companies formed in Britain. The first of any importance seems to have been a Scottish company, formed in 1822 to engage in shipping to Australia rather than to invest in the colony itself. A series of substantial companies intended to invest soon followed: the Australian Agricultural Company (1824) and the Van Diemen's Land Company (1825), which got huge grants of pastoral land; the Bank of Australasia (1835) and the Union Bank (1837), which revolutionised local techniques with branch banking and deposit finance; the South Australian Company (1836), formed to take up a convenient shortfall in the sales of land for the new colony, later engaging in everything from whaling to banking; the Australian Sugar Company (1839), which set up the biggest factory in the colony, collapsed, and after much turbulence became in 1855 the Colonial Sugar Refining Company, still one of the largest firms in the country. Though not all British–Australian companies were big, there was certainly a concentration of British capital in the biggest companies. The problem of long-distance control bedevilled them, but even with that they could turn a profit. Despite early blunders, the Australian Agricultural Company seems to have returned its proprietors about 200 per cent profit on their investment over its first thirty years.[15]

This development, of course, meant a radical shift towards impersonality in the relationship of owner to enterprise. The supply of funds increasingly came from the general London capital market rather than from people with a personal connection with the colonial project (the shareholders of the Bank of Australasia did not even see a balance sheet until eight years after the bank began trading); and profits flowed back into unknown pockets. Even when formed in the colony, companies took on an existence independent of the particular businessmen who formed them. It is important to realise how early this happened in Australian history. By the 1840s there was a corporate structure as well as a wide network of partnerships, commercial credit and family property. Colonial working people were confronting an increasingly organised colonial capitalism, closely linked to the state, when they raised their first demands for reform.

The first industry to create a solid demand for 'free' labour was not pastoralism but sealing, which was conducted on quite a large scale by colonial merchants and shipowners in the 1800s. Advertisements for seamen and gangs of sealers are common in the *Sydney Gazette* in this decade. And advertisements can represent only a fraction of the actual labour market, especially for labourers, who were often illiterate or unlikely to see the newspaper, and who must usually have been found by word of mouth. There was some element of wage labour in this, but typically the sealers were paid by 'lays' or percentages of the catch, which spread the risks of the enterprise to them and reduced demands on the sealing masters' liquidity. The sealers might end a year of heavy and dangerous work at Bass Strait or Macquarie Island with only a few pounds profit, or even owing money to their employers. In the field, they were more or less at the masters' mercy and were vigorously exploited, cheated in the quality and amount of their food, and sometimes abandoned for months on the islands.[16]

The seamen normally were paid on a wage basis, as were the shipyard workers. In the towns, a number of manufacturing enterprises developed, such as milling, brewing and salt-making. Typically, these establishments were very small, little more than a craftsman at work with a few assistants. But scale grew with rising population and the organisation of companies, and some mills, breweries and foundries had plant on a considerable scale, if not very highly specialised. One sign of early mechanisation is the fact that in June 1840 a dozen steam engines were being built by local engineers in Sydney; another is the existence of a metal-working industry in South Australia which was able to produce a significant advance in agricultural technology — Ridley's reaping machine — only a few years later. Some manufacturing moved outside the towns; the Australian Sugar Company, for instance, developed Canterbury, south-west of Sydney, on the English pattern of a large factory in a semi-rural setting, with workingmen's houses clustered around. By the mid-century, at the copper mines in South Australia and on the coalfields at Newcastle, similar miners' villages sat in a pastoral or agricultural countryside. Little is known about the nature of the employment relation in these settings, but it would be unwise to assume simple wage labour even where companies existed. On the contrary, their technical sophistication points to the presence of craftsmen — it is certain that skilled workers were imported for the sugar works and the mines — and that probably meant a form of contracting for production rather than wage labour.[17]

By the rigid custom of the time, women did not come on to the general labour market. Of about 190 jobs advertised in the *Sydney Gazette* in 1810, only seven were for women. But they did dominate one category of work. All but one of these seven advertisements were for household servants. It was automatic that people with money would have servants to look after their children, their houses and clothes, and their cooking. (The detail that conveyed the terrible hardships of the squatter's life most vividly to English audiences was that he had to do his own cooking.) Convict women were typically assigned as servants, but the supply did not reliably meet the demand. Some wealthy colonists anyway preferred hired labour to forced labour in their immediate households: convicts were supposed to be a corrupting influence on children. Thus a sex-segregated labour market was established. It was on this that the government-sponsored female immigration scheme of the 1830s relied, and Mrs Chisholm depended in her charitable labours in the early 1840s. Her female immigrants were almost all placed in employment as housekeepers and maids.[18]

In working for wages as servants, women were of course doing exactly the kind of work they would do, unpaid, as wives. Fragmentary official records suggest that about half the female convicts sent out got married in the colonies. Many others lived as *de facto* wives of male convicts, soldiers, settlers and (in the first generation) a good many officers. Some married women, though it is not clear how many, came out at government expense to set up house with their convict husbands. To some extent, marriage would have accelerated turnover in the female labour market; on the other hand, it began the process by which the domestic labour of women came to subsidise wages. Wives in wealthy families generally had the management of their household and the supervision of domestic servants; neither they nor their daughters would ever be employed. However, when their husbands were away, such women might take on the management of a pastoral business, as did Elizabeth McArthur for years during John's absences in England; Esther Johnston, a convict *de facto* wife, during George Johnston's absence for his court-martial after the 1808 coup against Bligh; and Harriet King while her naval husband was at sea.[19]

From the 1820s, the most vigorous demand for labour came from the pastoral industry, and this demand was almost entirely for males. Convicts on assignment were of course an important part of the labour found. But it appears that they formed the bulk of the pastoral workforce only in a limited area for a limited time: in east-central New South Wales for perhaps twenty years, and for a somewhat longer period in central and eastern Van Diemen's Land. Apart from that, 'free' labour was the order of the day. Workmen might be hired in the towns when a squatter first set out, or came down later with his clip; or they might be hired while tramping around the back country. This was wage labour, and the nearest thing to a simple labour market in the early colonies, though the wages were not exclusively in money and the period of hire was much longer (often a year) than was typical in towns.

Opinions differ about the relative bargaining positions of pastoral workers and pastoral capitalists. Employers at the time bitterly lamented shortages of labour, high wages and the independent attitude of workmen. Most historians have accepted this view; but it has been argued that the main constraint on pastoralism in the wool boom was shortage of capital rather than shortage of labour. Wages fluctuated a good deal with the state of the industry and the local supply of workmen, so it is difficult to fix a characteristic rate: perhaps £20 a year, plus rations, can be regarded as a typical rate for shepherds, though it could go as low as £10 or as high as £40. (The highest figures are quoted by employers.) This was of the same order as typical rates for labourers in the towns, and the earnings of sealers, so far as these can be calculated. Taking the comparison further afield, the money wages of shepherds in Australia were not very different from those of agricultural labourers in England at the beginning of the century. One must add provision for keep; but subtract provision for truck: as Mr Commissioner Bigge remarked, 'it is necessary...to observe, that all labourers in New South Wales are paid for their work, as well in articles of subsistence as in money, and goods.' The employers supplied only a bare minimum of rations free, and charged anything else the employee wanted against his wages at inflated prices. Some contemporary estimates suggest that the nominal wage should be reduced by a quarter or a third to allow for this. We may therefore read the pastoralists' claims about very high wages with considerable scepticism.

Tradesmen certainly did better. There was, rather generally, a ratio of about 2 : 1 between tradesmen's and labourers' rates in England; the ratio of actual earnings typically a little lower. This differential was reproduced in Australia. Artisans got about double the labourers' rates in the Sydney shipyards, and this seems to have been fairly general in urban trades, though fluctuations in the labour supply, and the quasi-contractual situation in which skilled work was often done, could produce sharp variations—earnings of £1 per day for masons were quoted in the Adelaide building boom of the late 1830s. In the pastoral industry, overseers and tradesmen commanded between 50 per cent and 100 per cent above the base rate. Overseers on the sealing-grounds got up to four times the cut of the men in the gangs, but experienced or skilled men got 50 per cent to 100 per cent above. Though one cannot compare earnings without having information about regularity of employment, it appears that the differentials in rates survived general rises and falls in wage levels.

It is difficult to see how this apparently stable relationship would have been produced spontaneously by the changing market forces in early Australia. It would appear that the colonial wage structure was governed more by custom, and less by supply-and-demand, than is often supposed; as, indeed, it seems to have been in industrialising England. The dominance of market forces in wage-fixing was only gradually established. The strength of custom, of imported attitudes and social expectations, is evident in other institutions such as kinship, and is dramatically shown in the creation of ethnic networks such as the Irish-Catholic settlements that spread south-west of Sydney. The colonial craft unions that appeared after these wage differentials had been established can be seen in part as a means of defending them, and in this respect as a form of resistance to the rising influence of the labour market, an attempt to regulate its impact.[20]

The dependence implied by wage labour, or at least the discipline that accompanied it, could also be avoided by anyone who could survive by working for him or herself. This was clearly a significant option, though it is impossible to state the exact numbers who took it. If she could get hold of a stock of materials, and had the relevant skill and push, a woman might set up as an independent trader: plying a trade such as millinery or dressmaking, setting up a restaurant or hotel. It is clear from advertisements and court reports that numbers of women supported themselves in this way, especially in the towns. A few even appear in textbook history, such as Rosetta Terry, an innkeeper when she married Samuel Terry in 1810 and rapidly accumulated one of the biggest fortunes in the colony; or Mary Reibey, who conducted a prosperous mixed business by the 1820s. It was even possible for unmarried women to be pastoralists, such as Anne Drysdale and Caroline Newcomb near Geelong in the 1840s. But this was rare; most independent business by women was certainly on a small scale and more reliant on a craft than on capital.

For men, the commonest form of small business was small farming. This was established by the grants in the 1790s, and on the Hawkesbury at least was quite prosperous in the early 1800s; studies of the census records suggest that considerable numbers stayed on their farms for at least two decades, so they must have been making a living. Small-farmer settlement continued on agricultural reserves after the land sale policy was adopted. A private farm, however, did not necessarily mean independence. Most smallholders, lacking capital, were early engulfed in debt to merchants, mortgaging their land. Dependence through debt also seems to have been characteristic of the relationship of retailers to the larger merchants who could finance imports.[21]

To sum up: there was a push towards the formation of a labour market and the organisation of production on capitalist lines, but throughout this period it was severely restricted. The first generation of pastoralists had a largely convict labour force; sealing and (probably) mining involved a crude profit-sharing arrangement; many urban craftsmen and labourers took contracts for work, and this merged imperceptibly into independent small business. There was a whole spectrum of relationships between those with wealth and those without, from mortgage financing through informal credit arrangements, contracting and profit-sharing to truck payments and pure wage labour. What was common was hierarchy and dependence; but this was imposed on a population with very irregular work habits and more than a little inclination to resistance and evasion. It was only very gradually, in Australia as elsewhere, that the wage system and its characteristic labour discipline became predominant; and as the following chapter will show, the resistance to this process, and the search for independence by working people, was a major theme of the politics of the next generations.

The Convict Experience

The main reason why the social structure of the colony differed from English and Irish patterns was of course the convict system. 'That colony', wrote an emancipist of New South Wales, 'is certainly the fruit of the convicts' labour.' This was true in a literal sense: whatever gentlemen got the credit and the profit, it was convicts and ex-convicts for the most part who cleared and hoed the ground, made the roads, built and kept the houses, raised the children, lumped casks off the ships, and walked after the first generations of sheep. This is familiar. The crucial thing is the social relationships in which they did this work, and their experience of them.[22]

The convict men who did the developmental work of road-making and town-building were mostly working under government control. Some labouring jobs were done by chain gangs, whose members had been sentenced for colonial crimes; but in the early period especially, most government work was done by convicts of 'normal' status under no particular restraint. They were usually organised in gangs of about twenty, larger or smaller according to the work, each under an overseer who represented the bottom level of the administrative apparatus already sketched. Around the towns, convicts would commonly be distributed according to trades; at outstations, such as the agricultural settlement at Castle Hill in the 1800s or the penal station at Norfolk Island from 1825, there would be a larger concentration of convicts doing heavy labouring.

The convicts who formed the bulk of the agricultural and pastoral workforce, during the period already delimited, were in assignment to private settlers. The complexities of the administrative history of assignment have already been noted. Some features remained constant, such as the legal basis of the arrangement as a tacit contract between the government and the settler. But the actual context of assignment varied so much, and the situations into which convicts were thrust were so different, that from their point of view it was completely unpredictable. They seem to have regarded assignment with great anxiety; for in practice, the settlers had wide control over their lives. Convicts who got a conciliatory master would be in a position hardly distinguishable from that of a labourer or household servant in England. But those who got a grasping or hostile master, or one infected by a sense of righteousness and a mission to punish the transgressor, might be in for years of brutality and oppression. In cases of dispute, the government would almost certainly step in on the settlers' side.

It was this that gave labour relations in early Australia the horrific cast that distinguished the colonies even from the black country of industrialising England. As the records of punishments show, penal authority in Australia had, via assignment, become the tool of labour discipline for capitalist enterprise. Such offences as 'insolence and neglect', 'neglect of duty', 'disobedience of orders and absenting', 'feigning sick', 'threatening his overseer' and 'general bad conduct', were typical charges against assigned servants, all liable to be punished by public flogging. Statistical research has shown that the average male convict faced such charges several times in the course of his career, and about 30 to 40 per cent were actually flogged — and that reckoning leaves out the unofficial beatings, deprivation and abuse that are commonly mentioned in convict narratives but were not reported to the magistrates. Should the convicts rebel against the control of settlers and the local magistrates, the whole state system of force stood in reserve. In the final analysis, the sanction of death stood behind labour discipline and the maintenance of social order. The governors repeatedly staged public executions to drive the lesson home.[23]

The convicts' situation, then, had a more complex structure than appears on the surface. The fact of repression, backed by overwhelming force, was constant (though there was much minor corruption at the lower levels). But the types of work into which convicts were sent varied: clerks and tradesmen might get to work at their usual jobs, though they might also be set to labouring; labourers might be set to quarrying stone for a church, doing general work on a farm, or following a flock of five hundred sheep around in the bush. Women would not be sent to heavy outdoor labour, but might indiscriminately find themselves doing housework in central Sydney or deep in the bush. The personal relations in which this work was done varied unpredictably from permissiveness to brutality in both public and private sectors. It is important to grasp this variety, and to realise that it was not simply different groups of convicts who had these different experiences. A single convict's career, starting with arrest and imprisonment in Britain, might lead through all these types of situations in a few years. The convict narratives that have survived make this very clear. Joseph Platt, for instance, a convict sent out in the 1830s, was first assigned to a pastrycook in Sydney; after a couple of years and various beatings, he attempted to escape by ship, was betrayed and sent to Norfolk Island; after three years there he was assigned to a settler near Campbelltown; escaped into the bush, lived with Aborigines, was recaptured and put in a chain gang; then worked in various

places and jobs on a ticket-of-leave before losing it and being sent to the quarry and road gangs, and finally serving out his sentence. The story as told in his pamphlet *The Horrors of Transportation* is no doubt highly coloured, but the basic feature of unpredictable movements between quite different situations is common to most of these memoirs.[24]

A situation with this structure made resistance through open organisation extremely unlikely. But there was another order of resistance, just below the level that would attract major penal sanctions, that was very widespread. The convicts replied to coercion with the classic response of forced labour, the slow-down. Colonial officials and gentry themselves, unconsciously, give abundant proof of the convicts' tactics. Early dispatches show governors almost foaming at the mouth over the difficulty of getting the convicts to raise crops, even when the settlement was starving. Slow-down is the meaning of the 'neglect of duty' charges that crop up so often in the punishment books. It is the situation behind respectable settlers' endless complaints about the laziness of the convicts, and behind the endless calculations, in the debates over transportation, of how many convicts gave equivalent work-value to one free labourer.

In circumstances where the master was anxious to get work done, this was a very effective weapon, and the enterprises of men who were driving for quick profit were just such. The convicts were in fact able to force substantial concessions. They early won a restriction on the hours of work; then the right to work for pay for part of the day. In many places they won a tacit payment for assigned work, often in the shape of rum. And it was not only the labour demands of the pastoral boom that produced this. Tacit bargaining and accommodation to the convicts was going on long before, as early as the 1790s. Some concessions were actually lost at a later stage. The reforming governors who came out to correct the 'abuses' of the convict system, men like Bligh, Darling and Arthur, were to a very large extent attacking the concessions that had informally been won by the convicts.

There were other forms of resistance in the workplace and in private life, other ways of clogging up the system or wringing something out of it. The convict clerks in the government stores in King's period had an organised scheme of fraud based on forgery of the governor's initials. Resistance could be expressed in non-cooperation with minor officials, especially the 'bloody traps', the police. It could be expressed in speech and private habit; this is the explanation of the constant complaints of convicts' insolence, foul language and viciousness made by colonial gentlefolk (including 'gentlemen convicts'), who were particularly scandalised by the convict women. A mocking hostility to the pretensions of authority comes through in the folklore of the convicts, such as their few surviving songs, and in many incidents recorded in the newspapers and courts.

All of these forms of action, it should be observed, have a strong collective character. The slow-down, like most other forms of labour action, is ineffective unless done on a mass scale; cheating on authority will be discovered

Left: Discipline for the penal workforce. A contemporary drawing of a convict being flogged at Moreton Bay. The three figures on the left are also convicts, one just flogged; it was usual to assemble the rest to watch, to increase the deterrent effect.
Source: Frontispiece to W. Ross, *The Fell Tyrant, or the Suffering Convict*, Ward, London, 1836. The original is tinted.

unless others support and conceal it; maintaining a 'criminal' subculture in opposition to official morality is by definition a collective act. We thus have very strong grounds for inferring a widespread solidarity among the convicts—at least among large sections of them—independent of the contradictory statements of officials and visitors on this point.[25]

On the basis of this partial solidarity, more violent forms of resistance arose: bushranging and insurrection. Bushranging was mainly the product of assignment, a simple consequence of a coercive labour system and a thinly occupied countryside. The term covered several forms of action. The commonest was that of assigned convicts who simply escaped into the bush and tried to support themselves by robbery on the fringes of settlement or by passing for free men. Sometimes bushranging meant organised gangs of robbers, who had connections in the towns and made a business of sticking up travellers and isolated homesteads, much as the post-goldrush bushrangers like Gardiner and Hall were to do. Sometimes it meant rural terrorism such as burning the ricks of unpopular masters, on a familiar British model. On a few occasions—in Van Diemen's Land in 1813 and during 1824–26, and in the Bathurst district in 1829—it took on the character of a guerrilla resistance, with gangs upwards of twenty men able to fight off military search parties and contemplate raids on towns. Matthew Brady's career in Van Diemen's Land in 1824–26 shows dramatically how convicts with skill and resolution could maintain themselves for long periods as outlaws in the back country. But it also shows the ultimate limits on this form of action. The military force available to the government was always adequate to defend the main centres, and eventually to erode and destroy the outlaw force.

The final step that the convicts could take was open mass revolt. Several insurrections occurred within the convict system, the most serious being at Castle Hill in 1804 and on Norfolk Island in 1834. A number of other risings seem to have been planned, but were discovered and broken up by the authorities. While bushranging was a product of assignment and dispersal, the insurrections occurred at government out-stations, where there was a concentration of convicts in a common situation. The overriding motives of the Norfolk Island revolts seem to have been revenge and escape. A close study of the Castle Hill rising shows that its central aim too was escape; 'Their cry was death or liberty, and a ship to take them Home.' The convicts under the stonemason Philip Cunningham directed their first attack towards the harbour, and only retreated towards the Hawkesbury agricultural districts when their attempt to capture Parramatta was frustrated. They were caught and shot down by a military detachment before they got the chance of calling up a rural rising.[26]

The immediate reason why the convicts were not more constantly in revolt was, plainly, effective repression. All the risings were defeated, all the bushranging gangs were dispersed and their leaders hanged or shot. The sustained official terror against convicts also produced breakdowns of solidarity and betrayals, as in other situations such as prisons and concentration camps. But there were also more deep-seated reasons why the convicts did not mobilise as a class.

Given the character of English radical politics at the time, one might have expected leadership to come from the literate and the skilled workers. In the colony, however, these men were mostly divided from the mass of labouring convicts. There is much evidence of disdain for the rough, uneducated, vice-ridden mass, even on the part of political radicals or physical-force men among the educated convicts such as George Loveless and Joseph Holt. Loveless, one of the Tolpuddle martyrs, regarded himself and his friends, but not transportees in general, as victims of injustice; the bulk, he wrote, were 'such monsters as I never expected to see'. This savage remark is quite typical. The authorities themselves reinforced the division, sometimes physically segregating the educated convicts (who were regarded as especially threatening) and giving privileges to the skilled. Only in the penal outposts was the bulldozing effect of the convict system able to override the status divisions imported from England, and only in the insurrections that occurred are there many signs of political leadership by the skilled and educated.[27]

Two other forces inhibited organisation. The first was religion. Most of the convicts were certainly not conventionally religious; but to those who were, religion carried a strong message of social quiescence and persuaded them of the need to cut their connections with the 'corrupted' mass. The parallel with official Wesleyanism in England is close. Religion—at least evangelical religion—interpreted the situation of being a convicted criminal as a consequence of personal sin rather than social oppression. In the letters of James Grove, a Van Diemen's Land convict of the early days, it is impossible to distinguish the sense of religious from the sense of legal guilt; he actually ended up being glad he was punished.

Grove also had material grounds to be pleased with his God—'his temporal mercies to us are singular'—and the fact that *some* convicts did very well out of the system is the second point to be borne in mind. Simeon Lord and Samuel Terry may have been exceptions, but they did exist and were known; and there was a wider spread of smaller convict capitalists, landowners and publicans who had kept out of trouble and got to be comfortably off. The effects of religion and material success reinforced the divisive effects of class origin among the convicts: they cut off, inhibited or realigned a potential radical leadership.

When a political movement did emerge from the ranks of educated convicts in Sydney around 1820, it was mainly among well-to-do ex-convicts. Its focus was the legal rights of emancipists; its leaders, men like Eagar, Lord, and Terry, were aligned with respectability, and their demands were progressively merged with those of colonial liberals such as W. C. Wentworth and Sir John Jamison in the democratic movement. This alignment meant that emancipist politics separated, rather than linked, the activists and the mass of working convicts. A movement of ex-convicts that was both popular and distinct from the liberal and radical politics of free immigrants emerged only in Tasmania in the years around 1850. This was at the end of the period of transportation to the eastern colonies and hence was of no significance in the mobilisation of the convict workforce.[28]

This is not to suggest that popular revolts and radical politics are created by leaders. It is to suggest that the mass of convicts in Australia were in a considerably tougher situation than working people in Britain. Not only did they face the penal system of repression. To develop a movement against it they would have to do something quite new: create a movement with very little participation from the literate and the skilled. The consequence of this double barrier was that convict movements, though several times reaching a fair scale, were short-lived and did not accumulate experience of organisation. There was little of the continuity that underlay radical politics in contemporary England. There was some absorption of members of older bushranging gangs into new ones, but it was severely limited by the mobility of the convict population and the authorities' habit of killing rebels at the time of capture or soon after.

In the final analysis, the convicts did not mobilise as a class in Australia for reasons that all led back to the fact that they were not a group generated by the operation of the property system in Australia. They were a category of labourers generated by the state's enforcement of the property system in Britain. They could cause local upheavals in the system, but the potential of their solidarity and resistance, even of their aggression, was limited to that. They could not, by any *possible* process of mobilisation, force a transformation of the social system. At the psychological level, 'the convict' was made by a convict career that began with arrest and charge in Britain. Within this career, the acts that led to his or her being oppressed in the colony occurred in the home country. The rationale of the situation, so far as it had any sense or reason at all, lay in relationships there. This is why transported radicals have disappointed local historians by failing to become the core of a colonial radicalism.[29] They continued to focus on the English ruling class as the source of their oppression, and saw their colonial masters, if they criticised them at all, merely as agents. The convict rebels also had their eyes on their homes. They may have had a temporary lust for revenge, but so far as they had any long-term aim, it was escape and return home. Throughout the convict period, there was a steady stream of escape attempts by ship or boat, some leading to epic voyages and most to quick disasters. Not many did get back.

The convict experience, then, seems on the face of it to be a sterile tragedy. One hundred and sixty thousand men, women and youths were transported, and all they seem to have left as cultural inheritance were some elements of folklore to a rural counter-culture, and some claims of legal rights to urban liberalism. But to stop with this judgement would be to treat history as purely linear, to ignore the fact that colonial capitalism grew in an interacting social structure. The convicts did have their influence on what followed, by affecting the conditions in which classes began to form. Their resistance in the workplace strengthened the position of immigrant and native-born workmen in the free labour market, which was much better than it would have been in competition with a totally dominated slave labour force. Their resistance in the countryside was one of the issues that fuelled the democratic movement in the towns in the 1830s, which did launch the tradition of Australian radicalism. Their labour created the wealth, and their resistance shaped the attitudes, of the pastoralists who bid for power in the mid-century.

Processes of Class Formation

Though the convict system was central, it can hardly be said to have been entirely determinant, given the early appearance of a private labour market and the influence of kinship and other traditional relations. Many events that occurred in the colonies are recognisable examples of the processes of mobilisation that were then producing a new class structure in England. Within the theoretical framework already stated, we may speak of processes of class formation without implying that a full-blown class society was present in the colonies. It would be possible simply to list these processes and leave them with the implication that in each case the generation of a class was incomplete. So in a sense it was; but that would be to fall into the trap of treating classes as independent entities. It is the structure of a set of relations as a whole that is crucial. The complexities and conflicts of the early Australian settlements become more intelligible if we postulate that there were two structures being produced at the same time, which were not entirely compatible. One was the sharply polarised structure centred on the assignment relation in the pastoral industry; the other, the much less polarised structure centred on mercantile capital and small production in the towns and gradually extending as wage–labour relations in the primary industries. Both were based on private property and the state, though the former was much more closely integrated with the state organisations, in ways already described. Both were fundamentally capitalist, though the former differed from the classic pattern in having a directly coerced labour force, that is, it followed the pattern of a plantation economy; and the latter had simply not reached the point where large-scale production units and direct wage labour were characteristic. In course of time, their incompatibility became more plainly a contradiction, the development of one being blocked by the other. The political struggles of the 1830s and the 1840s, at one level a contest for state power between two groups of capitalists, were at a deeper level a clash between two orderings of colonial society.

The structure centring on assignment defined two major groups, the working convicts and the pastoral gentry. The latter, of all groups in the colonies, became the most highly organised and self-conscious. Their consciousness can be traced from well before the pastoral boom. The officers of the original settlements imported a prickly sense of their own status as gentlemen, which was maintained by a ceremonious code of interaction (it was taken as an insult to leave the word 'Esquire' off the address of a letter), and a constant display of deference from social inferiors (it was taken as an insult not to raise one's hat to a gentleman in passing). Civilian immigrants who possessed both respectability and money were admitted to equal status. 'The officers civil and military and the principal inhabitants' formed a well-recognised group both in private life and in public ceremony, though they did not necessarily have a common economic interest.[30]

The accumulation of wealth turned a considerable part of this social elite into an economic force which moved from trade towards pastoralism, seeking not only profit but also the traditional prestige of large land ownership. In the 1810s and 1820s, this 'ancient nobility' was joined by the increasing numbers of moneyed newcomers who went directly into the pastoral industry. By the 1830s, something approaching a regional ruling class had formed in the countryside of Van Diemen's Land and central New South Wales, with a common economic base, a common experience in the management of a mostly convict workforce, a firm consciousness of status, and political power in the countryside through the magistracy.

Their numbers were small. In 1821, about eighty men held 60 per cent of all alienated land in New South Wales, working it with assigned convicts. In the 1830s, it has been estimated, there were about 400 gentry estates in New

South Wales and 250 in Van Diemen's Land. However their wealth, contacts in London, and capacity for common action rendered them powerful beyond their own demesnes. Their cohesion in the colonies was maintained by informal networks rather than formal political organisation. (A Pastoral Association in New South Wales was formed only in 1844, and then represented squatting interests as well as the gentry.) Marriage was typically at the same social level—a few of the pioneers married convict women, but this was rare in the pastoral age—and some of the gentry families thus became interlinked as kinship networks. The women rarely emerged into political activity, but played an active role in maintaining class consciousness through their policing of gentility, and in maintaining contacts through correspondence, visits and entertainments. Other networks were kept up among the men through exclusive clubs, and of course in business and on the Bench. The teaching of their children was mainly done by tutors, but in the pastoral boom, a number of elite private schools were formed, notably The King's School founded in 1832 by the Anglican hierarchy in New South Wales.

Pastoralism under the gentry created a polarised, patriarchal society in the countryside, a deep gulf of status, property and power separating the workforce from the rulers. The gentry attempted to entrench themselves politically in the institutions of the state and physically on the land. Here they created a notable monument to themselves in the only distinct ruling-class domestic architecture in Australian history. Solid Classical and Georgian homesteads proclaimed their style and confidence, and with surrounding clusters of barns, barracks and cottages, embodied the social relationships of the time. Some homesteads in Tasmania still have the ring-walls that were built for defence against blacks and bushrangers, material reminders of the violence on which the gentry's power was founded.[31]

The fact that their power was dependent on the state did not inhibit the gentry from bitter opposition to the government on occasion. In the mid-1830s, confronted with a liberal governor in Bourke and policies that appeared to threaten their status, there was a conservative mobilisation; in the mid-1840s, confronted with land policies that appeared to threaten their economic interests, the gentry of New South Wales coalesced with squatters and urban workers to deliver a sharp defeat to Gipps. However, it would be a mistake to over-estimate either the power or the political unity they achieved. Their representatives in the Legislative Councils set up in the 1820s never dictated policy, and the central administration remained firmly under the control of Whitehall until the 1850s. And the conservative gentry of the 1820s and 1830s were opposed by men such as Wentworth and Jamison who were equally landowners and pastoralists. In the squatting boom alignments became even more complicated. The squatters who rushed the outback, though moneyed men, were disruptive in terms of the structure based on assignment and land ownership, relying on a form of wage labour and a form of land piracy. But they were the main market for the gentry's production of surplus flocks (the sale of sheep rather than the sale of wool is

Left: The colonial gentry. Panshanger, 'the seat of Joseph Archer Esq.', a rich and respectable landowner near Longford in Van Diemen's Land; rendered (inaccurately) in the style of an English landscape. The building dates from the early 1830s. Other pictures show more plainly a high defensive wall around the farm buildings.
Source: Mitchell Library, Sydney, PXC 284f. 19.

reckoned to be the key to the early pastoralists' profits), and many of the gentry themselves became involved in squatting. After a sharp struggle, leading members of the gentry came to accept the end of transportation in New South Wales and the end of assignment in Van Diemen's Land. This was far from being the end of pastoral capitalism, nor even of attempts to create a hierarchical rural society, which developed later in the nineteenth century in the Western District of Victoria and the Darling Downs of Queensland. But these were on a wage–labour basis and had to concede financial and political pre-eminence to the cities. The possibility of a distinctive pastoral ruling class in colonial society as a whole appeared only once, and was aborted even as it appeared.[32]

The structure of relations which eventually predominated first developed in the towns. Though there is a danger of exaggerating the clarity of social divisions, we may usefully trace its history through two opposed groups, the owners of mercantile capital and urban wage workers. Merchants were central to the colonial economy from the start: Sydney especially was a trading and shipping town, and it was traders and shipmasters who launched the first important export industry, sealing. But as everyone who was a substantial merchant in the first generation was also necessarily a landowner and pastoralist, there was then no basis for a separate social group. Close links between pastoralists and merchants continued throughout the period. Merchants provided a good deal of the finance for the wool trade, and pastoralists appear in numbers second only to merchants on the share lists of the early companies; Thomas Icely, for instance, one of the leading pastoralists, was also one of the most prominent company promoters. Capital could be, and was, transferred between land, stock and trade. The merchants in no sense formed a separate class; the view sometimes taken, on the basis of occupational figures in census returns, that the social order was characterised by a very small 'middle class' is highly misleading, a good example of the stratificationist fallacy of counting heads and ignoring relationships.

They were, however, increasingly identifiable as a distinct interest among property owners. Trade became a more specialised activity around 1820, when importing began to settle down from the hair-raising high-profit adventures of the earliest period into a routine business living off a regular turnover. Men trained in British merchant-houses, such as Alexander Spark, Richard Jones and William Walker, moved in and took up the running from officers and emancipists. Merchants were still commonly landowners, but landowners were no longer usually merchants. Sydney traders produced a modest expression of a sense of identity, a Chamber of Commerce, in 1826, which organised the employers in the country's first strike wave (over currency changes) in 1829. It folded in 1833, but it was revived; as was the attempt to set up an Exchange in Sydney, chartered under an Act of 1837, though not built until twenty years later. The more effective means of articulation was through companies, whose boards and committees provided an institutional base for a group of very active businessmen. The process of capital-raising itself created a situation where promoters and directors (who still did most of the day-to-day management) stood in a definite leadership relation to the owners whose capital they mobilised. In this regard, they were in a stronger position in the long run than the prominent pastoralists, whose leadership of the gentry depended on prestige and personal influ-

The near-gentry: wealth without prestige. Jane Tompson, wife of a prosperous emancipist landowner at Clydesdale, near Windsor, and mother of the poet Charles Tompson.
Source: Portrait in watercolour by R. Read in Dixson Gallery, Sydney; done in 1836 or 1837.

ence, given the fragmented family ownership of most pastoral property at this time.[33]

The importance of company promotion, however, should not be exaggerated; most trade was still carried on by individuals or by private partnerships. There were also other institutional structures developing, notably the system of courts, which from the late 1810s (in Sydney) began to have a regular workforce of lawyers. There was also an increasing number of newspapers, after the monopolies of the two *Gazettes* were broken in 1824 and 1825, and schools beyond the elementary level. These developments provided the base for a growing group of professionals, an embryo intelligentsia which immediately became important in politics.

In the towns, there was nothing like the social cleavage of the pastoral countryside. From craftsman as employee to craftsman as employer, from shopkeeper to merchant, from journalist to lawyer to lawyer–landowner, were no great leaps. The democratic movements that grew out of this matrix in the 1830s were not the product of a sense of middle-class distinctiveness. Indeed, it is a mistake to see them as essentially middle-class at all. They were, like the factions that formed around men like Bligh and McArthur in the early settlement, alliances across social levels. This they explicitly set out to be: the Political Association in Hobart, for instance, laid down that it 'admits as equal members, all Free Persons whatever';[34] the Patriotic Association in Sydney included some of the colony's largest pastoral landowners (Wentworth, Jamison) and leading professionals (Bland, Carmichael) as well as merchants and a popular following. They were more unified by common enemies than common interests; a vigorous populist rhetoric was a thin glue for what proved shortly to be divergent aims.

Yet these movements were important in the development of urban bourgeois politics, in two ways. Firstly, their agitation brought leading businessmen and professionals together at the head of a larger alliance, thus prefiguring the general structure of politics after the mid-century and developing the political skills that made the transition possible. Secondly, before they broke up in the 1840s, these movements had had some influence in shaping the framework of the emerging state. Though some in them flirted with republicanism, the movements generally defined colonial liberties in terms of the rights of Englishmen and traditional parliamentary government. Constitution-making took another twenty years, but its terms were essentially set by the limits of the democratic alliances of the 1830s. The state power given up by the British government would necessarily be handed over to one or both of the two groups who could dominate a parliamentary system: the representatives of pastoral or mercantile capital.

Outside the pale of respectability and wealth was the mass of the free population: domestics, housewives, labourers, shepherds, craftsmen, shopkeepers, and so on. As the property system produced a labour market, and labour produced profits, some consciousness of the process and some attempts to control it appeared. These appear to have been confined to men: there is no record of organisation among working women in this period, nor any signs of concern about women from the labour organisations set up by men, until the Early Closing movement. This was partly due to the conventions of femininity, but also to the fact that most working women were domestic servants, isolated from each other and under the close surveillance of their employers. There certainly was bargaining over terms of employment, and at times a skilled domestic could command good wages, but there are no signs of organisation.

Among men, signs of resistance and organisation appeared almost as soon as the labour market itself. The first recorded 'combination' to raise wages was in 1795, among reapers at the wheat harvest. Through the following decades, agricultural labourers repeatedly demanded, and got, higher rates than they were officially supposed to. In the maritime trades, there was also organisation and resistance. Seamen sometimes struck by refusing to take their ships to sea, or struck harder by mutiny: in 1806 four seamen were flogged around Sydney Cove for a planned 'mutiny' on the colonial vessel the *Governor Hunter*, and some ships were lost to rebellious sailors at sea. Sealers sometimes abandoned their work when they were dissatisfied, and some hit back at their employers on return to port by taking them to court, occasionally winning judgments. Wharf-labourers in the early 1820s staged protests over pay, and in 1824 there was a strike by coopers that drew in several other groups of workers. In 1829, when a currency reform was introduced, there was a two-week strike in several industries in Sydney, demanding payment at the better rate of exchange. Through the 1830s, a number of short strikes were fought by the new trade societies in the towns, with mixed success; the Hobart journeymen tailors, for instance, lost a strike for higher wages in 1834.[35]

Employers of course resisted these actions, with the general support of the government. Official concern with the issue is in fact one of the strongest evidences of worker resistance. Governor Hunter launched the state on the endless task of wage control in response to the farmers' complaints. A series of regulations followed over the next two decades, fixing piece-rates and wages in the interest of farmers; Bligh actually invoked an Elizabethan statute to check 'the evil tendency of the workmen now demanding, and the settlers paying much larger sums for labour than they can afford'. The regulations were obviously ineffective. General labour codes followed: a proclamation by Macquarie in 1818 giving magistrates power to hear disputes and punish servants, and the New South Wales Act 'for the better regulation of Servants, Labourers, and Work People' in 1828—the year before shipwrights formed the first trade society in Sydney. By 1840, when a more drastic Masters and Servants bill was introduced into the Legislative Council, a labour movement was in being and able to campaign successfully to amend it.[36]

There are, then, strong if inferential grounds for thinking that there was a considerable amount of organising among working men from a very early stage. It is notable that these signs appear among labourers more than craftsmen, and in industries where there was, relatively speaking, some scale in employment early on. The origin of labour organisation in Australia, we may infer, was an autonomous local development from the human situation created by the structure of property. It was not imported, and it was not produced by craft exclusiveness. This informal, and often illegal, organising and resistance lay behind the craft societies when they emerged in the 1830s, and without any doubt continued alongside them.

Like the gentry, working men and women created family and friendship networks, which could provide information, relief and support. In some parts of the towns, such as The Rocks at Sydney, a considerable social solidarity could develop against colonial respectability. Crowds often gathered for illicit sports like cockfighting and boxing, sometimes tolerated and sometimes raided by the authorities. The magistrates periodically attempted to control liquor and put down 'disorderly houses', obviously with little success. On occasion there were riots and minor disturbances, usually fired by drink. To the sanctimonious, such things were evidence of 'the Immorality and Vice so prevalent among the Lower Classes of this Colony'; to historians, they have usually represented light relief and colour. We should see them, rather, as signs — distorted by the nature of the historical record — of the attempt by working men and women to carve out their space for living from a highly repressive environment.

This is not to imply, however, that stable 'working-class' settlements were typical. The Rocks was a portside district with a large floating population; the factory and mining villages noted earlier held only a small fraction of the workforce. Labouring men in general seem to have been fairly mobile, travelling from place to place in search of work, trying their hand at a variety of jobs and entering various kinds of relationships with employers. Benjamin Boyce in Adelaide, for instance, started as a seaman, jumped ship to follow his girlfriend, and within a couple of years worked as a dairy-hand, cut hay to sell on his own account, worked as a logger and house-builder, and worked for the owner of a grog-shop. This kind of mobility is characteristic of the irregular work habits of a pre-industrial population. It was itself a weapon: except in times of serious unemployment, a workman could bargain simply by moving on, and the effectiveness of this is suggested by the stress in the Masters and Servants Acts on forcing employees to stay and serve out their contracts. But it also hampered organisation, just as the variety of relationships in which the work was done, from servant to contractor to small entrepreneur, prevented the crystallisation of class consciousness around wage labour.[37]

This variety of relationships also shaped the trade societies that emerged in the towns in the 1830s. By the mid-century, about twenty of these had been established in Sydney, though they were unstable and some soon collapsed; perhaps half that number was formed in Hobart and a few in Melbourne and South Australia. Small, with memberships ranging from twenty to sixty, they were usually formed by skilled men who wished to regulate their particular trade. This regulation might involve a wide range of activities: setting up a 'House of Call' or labour exchange (usually at a named hotel); controlling entry to the trade, by resisting the employment of convicts and apprentices, resisting the importation of labour, and guaranteeing the quality of workmanship; setting up funds to pay funeral expenses and benefits in sickness or unemployment, fixing wage rates and conditions by collective bargaining and, on occasion, by striking. They represented the craftsman-as-entrepreneur as well as the craftsman-as-employee, though naturally there was a trend towards the representation of employee interests. In the course of time, benefit societies with a basically insurance function became more distinct from trade unions.

The trade societies covered only a fraction of the workforce. At an absolute maximum, they cannot have had a total membership of more than 1000 at

Right: Housing for the rural workforce. This photograph dates from 1851; the slab hut at right is obviously older, and is typical of accommodation for poor settlers, selectors and rural labourers throughout the century.
Source: View of Allen's farm, Fremantle. Battye Library, Perth, 66B.

any time before 1850, and the actual total was probably much less (in a total colonial population of around 200 000 in 1840). They were mostly confined to limited categories of workers. But however small and exclusive, they did co-operate with each other in strikes and petitions, and provided a permanent presence that could generate a sense of working men as a distinct 'interest' in society, with some claim to representation even in a Whig view of politics. At times when this interest was threatened by competition from convict or immigrant labour, the trade societies could draw larger numbers of workers into a political campaign. There was an agitation on the unemployment issue in Hobart in 1834, and against the probation system and transportation generally in the 1840s. In Sydney, campaigns against competition and unemployment led to early attempts to form organisations of a general kind, the Society of Emigrant Mechanics (1833) and the Mutual Protection Association (1843), contemporaneous with the Grand National Consolidated Trades Union and the Chartist movement in England. An effective agitation against the Masters and Servants Act amendments was mounted in 1840. But apart from the last episode, these were not cases of political organisation of working men against their employers. For the most part, politically minded working men connected with the trade and benefit societies in the 1830s formed a wing of the urban democratic movement, accepting the leadership of liberal capitalists and professionals, and directing their fire against the gentry and the government.[38]

The trade societies, or craft unions as they became, were one of a number of pressure groups that took their place in the political order being formed in the pastoral period. As that order crystallised towards the mid-century on the pattern of a democratic parliamentary regime, it is worth noting who were excluded from it. Women, who by custom were kept out of public affairs, were denied the vote when elective councils were established, and still more, the possibility of being elected. Many groups of men, through distance, poverty or lack of organisation, were only loosely connected to the political centres, whether or not they had the vote—notably urban labourers and practically the entire rural workforce. Aborigines were totally excluded. Children had no means of public expression, though a great deal of politicking went on over their education. 'The people' that Australian democracy apostrophised were thus a minority in the population from the start, even before one starts to reckon the concentration of power in the hands of particular groups within the political society of the later nineteenth century.

The Struggle for Hegemony

The officials of the first settlements had a clear view of their place in the world. They were responsible men engaged in the public service—'service' implying obedience to orders, vigour in carrying them out, economy in the use of public resources. This conception was closely tied to a hierarchical and static view of social relations, for guardianship of the public interest entitled the higher orders to deference and obedience from below. It was a

Left: Urban industry. View of a pottery at Camperdown near Sydney, probably in the 1840s, which employed about twenty-five men.
Source: Copy in Mitchell Library, Sydney, Small Picture File.

cause of astonishment and resentment if anyone tried to rise above his or her assigned station in life, not only an error of taste but an offence against morality and religion. The proper task of the lower ranks of society, convict or otherwise, was to work hard and keep quiet.

Some attempt was made to impose corresponding beliefs on the lower ranks: but that was likely to be difficult, given a workforce that, by the mere fact of being convicted as criminal, seemed to have declared its independence from conventional morality. Many of the officers were entirely sceptical of any success and made no effort; most had better things to do. But an attempt was made, principally through the Church. Official chaplains were appointed to evangelise the convicts, distributing tracts and preaching sermons on such topics as 'Duty and Submission to Government'. A doctrine of political quietism, social stability, obedience, repentance and moral reform was the social gospel according to the Church of England in Australia. It was reinforced by the official newspapers, by the homilies and judgments of the magistrates, and by the proclamations and ceremonial acts of the central government.[39] By and large, the sceptics were right. Conventional religion and morality did not penetrate deeply among the mass of convicts, though it had a very strong influence on a few. A belief in God, Hell and a Judgement was widespread; but there is much evidence of indifference to official theology and hostility to the clergy, including one episode where a church was burned down. Convict congregations were small when voluntary, and inattentive when coerced. The state's first ideological effort paid few dividends apart from the immobilisation of some potential leaders of revolt; force remained the basic technique of control.

The ideology of service and stability in the earliest settlement had a fatal flaw: it was a non-capitalist, in some ways a pre-capitalist, framework. It did not embrace, explain or defend the activities of the local entrepreneurs, and something had to be done about that. The second generation of immigrant churchmen who, led by Bishop Broughton, attempted to apply a Tory theory of hierarchy and stability in the 1830s and 1840s, had already been left behind by local developments.[40] Ideology in the colony moved in two directions, broadly corresponding to the two major structures of class relations described in the previous sections.

The first was the creation of the pastoral gentry, or at least those of their number whose gentility was tender enough to be threatened by the rise of ex-convict entrepreneurs, whose money offended the traditional equation of wealth with respectability. The social recognition of emancipists by Macquarie posed an acute status problem, out of which grew a theory of a 'moral ascendancy' in the colony. The term was probably borrowed from the Anglican 'Ascendancy' in Ireland; it conveyed the idea of a group of families who had come to the colony without a convict taint, who were both wealthy and virtuous, and who were the chief bulwark of social order against a sea of crime and immorality. The economic welfare of the colony lay in their hands, in the development of pastoralism, and the government had to ensure a supply of labour for them, whether convict or free. Convicts were moral degenerates, to be held in check, and just possibly reformed, by strict daily work under the supervision of the elect.

There was hardly a breath of this doctrine in the colonies until the last years of Macquarie's rule. Then its essentials were expounded to Commissioner Bigge; and it was fully developed by the mid-1830s, when it was widely held by the gentry, expressed in Mr Justice Burton's famous 'charge to the jury' in 1835 and the exclusives' constitutional petitions of 1836, and expounded at length in books circulated by James Mudie and James Macarthur. It was, clearly, a struggle ideology, generated by conflict and used as a weapon. But it was not principally struggle with the workforce that sparked it, so much as struggle with another group of entrepreneurs. There was always a section of landowners who denied it, and after their factional conflicts had been resolved, the ideology rapidly faded away. Notions of moral ascendency over a depraved workforce remained hardly more than an echo (except in Tasmania, where anxiety over the 'convict stain' continued to colour social attitudes in the later nineteenth century), until the age of Malcolm Fraser.[41]

It is understandable that there was little attempt to persuade the convict workforce of all this: the unwashed remained unevangelised. To the very limited extent that a hegemonic structure emerged in the gentry's countryside, it was in an entirely different way, in the course of struggle with the Aborigines. For all the hostility and the depth of the social gulf between pastoral owners and pastoral workers, they shared a clear interest in smashing the Aboriginal tribes, and there is much evidence that they set about this together. The racist doctrines that were almost universal in the countryside (and in most of the city press) had the effect of cementing this alliance. What remained for the most part tacit became very clear in the *cause célèbre* of 1838, the Myall Creek trials, where a group of pastoral workers were hanged for being caught out after a particularly brutal lynching party. The gentry of a pastoral heartland formed a committee to defend the men, called with remarkably bad taste the Hunter River Black Association; their mouthpiece the *Sydney Herald* campaigned violently for an acquittal; and pastoralists in the Council later effectively resisted legislation to protect blacks.[42] This alliance persisted as long as the blacks' resistance did, outliving the penal structure in which it first appeared.

Ultimately more powerful than the doctrine of ascendancy, and broader than racism, was an ideology of economic development. Like all social thought at the time, this presupposed the system of private property; but it saw property, in combination with enterprise, as a dynamic force capable of transforming society. W. C. Wentworth brilliantly formulated the issues in a youthful book, first published in 1819, called *A Statistical, Historical, and Political Description of the Colony of New South Wales*. No title could be more modest. What the book contained was a critique of British policy and a view of colonial development informed by a reading of contemporary political economy. Wentworth saw a contradiction between Australia's enormous productive capacity and its limited capacity for consumption. He mapped out a future in which Australia, through the immigration of men of property and enterprise, would become a supplier of raw materials to the manufacturing economy of England, the key product being wool. A local representative government based on landed proprietors would liberate this economic development from the artificial restraint placed on it by despotic government.

What was first systematically stated here, to be developed in countless ways later on, was a doctrine of progress as capitalist expansion. Wentworth put his finger on pastoralism as the immediate growth industry, and was right, but the argument was more general: it achieved an identification of the public good with the state of private profits in the leading industry. This equation transformed a doctrine of economic progress into a doctrine of social prosperity. It was a lasting legacy, becoming a central part of the parliamentary ethos as the new political order crystallised. Henceforth governments took credit for prosperity, blame for contraction, and attempted to prop themselves electorally by guaranteeing the profitability of the leading industries. 'Your flocks, Sir? What have I to do with your flocks?', Governor Bligh is supposed to have shouted at John McArthur. None of the later colonial governments would have dreamed of asking such a question.

A doctrine of progress was a much more effective theme for hegemonic cultural relations than the exclusives' excuses for their own power, and its effectiveness was demonstrated in the democratic movement's campaign against the 'factious oligarchy' of exclusives itself. Though one could hardly say that a bourgeois hegemony had already been established, the ideological initiative had passed out of the hands of the pastoralists and their intellectuals as early as the 1830s. Alternatives were already emerging in the towns. The Protestant churches were lively and argumentative, in some cases expressing a vigorous artisan radicalism. In the new settlement of South Australia there was practically a dissenters' colony, where religion was ingeniously interwoven with the hope of profit in the South Australian Company. An equally dissident press flourished in the port towns. New movements arose that expressed a desire for respectability without a doctrine of hierarchy, notably the temperance movement and some new developments in education, where the confusion of voices was loudest.

From the start, the education of the people had a cultural rather than a technical rationale: it was believed that the improvement of 'Learning and Morals' went together. Schooling was part of the effort at moral reform and social control, exactly parallel to the evangelisation of the convicts; and it was supported by the colonial governments, and supervised by the Church, for precisely this reason. It was because control over education meant control over culture, that when the different sects emerged in the 1820s and 1830s they fought so viciously over popular education. Deadlock resulted, luckily for the children; but the basis for the secular compromise that was reached later in the century was laid in the 1830s, in the form of a new cultural rationale for education. Emigrant teachers such as Henry Carmichael brought out a concept of moral improvement through the spread of knowledge. This was distinctively expressed in the School of Arts movement, a scheme for adult education aimed at working men and apprentices, launched in Sydney in 1833. Few workers in fact turned up, so the hegemonic impact at the time was slight; but those who did, would have got a very particular type of culture. On the ship out from Britain, Carmichael already had thirty mechanics studying *The Wealth of Nations*. In the 1830s, the doctrines of bourgeois political economy began to be propagated widely in pulpit and press, and were well represented in colonial libraries.[43]

In the 1830s, all this was ferment; it had yet to crystallise in a social and political practice. But at a very basic level of social structure, the level at which class relations articulate with sexual relations, some of the foundations of a stable bourgeois order were being constructed. It will be appropriate to end this survey of the period of penal settlement with some notes — they can hardly be more, for the problems have been very little studied — on developments at this level.

The social code of the elites of the early settlements attached honour to a gentleman's person more than to his actions. Thus it was possible for colonial officials to contract sexual relations quite freely with convict women, and to acknowledge, and sometimes legitimise, the children. A governor-to-be (King), two lieutenant-governors (Collins and Sorell), and a commander of the garrison (Johnston), all lived in *de facto* relationships. It was a male privilege: women of the same rank could not contract *de facto* relationships with convict men; though they had a certain freedom of action in other matters that flowed from their unchallengeable status. Moralists such as Bligh, Macquarie and Marsden criticised the lax morality displayed, but did little about it.

In the 1820s a tightening began. The movement in England by evangelicals against the sexual laxity of the aristocracy soon acquired colonial agents. The Protestant clergy were prominent, with the bitterly intolerant Lang in the lead, who seems to have driven at least one person to suicide; while Governor Arthur was the toughest and most successful moralist among the officials. In 1824, Sorell was removed from office in Van Diemen's Land, despite his acknowledged ability and success, for living with someone else's wife. At least Sorell was an acknowledged adulterer; in 1846, a successor, Eardley-Wilmot, was dismissed on the basis of unchecked rumours, and the shock seems to have killed him. Particular venom was directed against the homosexual relationships formed by many convicts and pastoral workers, though unmarried convict women got a fair pasting as sluts and whores. The 1812 parliamentary inquiry into transportation had hardly raised a question about sex; the 1837 inquiry and report positively smouldered with innuendo, scandal and moralising.[44]

The imposition of a much more repressive sexual morality led to a complex change in the position of women. Working women, especially convicts, had been vulnerable to sexual exploitation by their social superiors. The insistence on marriage as the condition for sex improved their bargaining position at the expense of their libido. Sexual restraint and marriage were equated with the dignity of womanhood. The connection of women with cultural conservatism and instinctual repression, characteristic of bourgeois culture, was established.[45]

But as women were tied in more closely to the institution of marriage, their opportunities outside it were sharply reduced. After this period we do not hear of women entrepreneurs comparable to Mary Reibey or Rosetta Terry. We hardly even hear of women playing a leading role in the management of family properties like Elizabeth McArthur, or taking a major initiative in cultural affairs like Anna King with her orphan school in Sydney or Lady Franklin with her artistic circle in Hobart. Caroline Chisholm, from this perspective, appears as the end of an era in the history of Australian women rather than the beginning of one. They disappeared into domesticity in the age of the bourgeois ascendancy.

And in a fundamental way, domesticity itself was devalued. In the older social ethic, a person was what she (or he) was, prior to what she did or what she achieved. An age of 'progress' had an ethic of performance, not being, and especially economic performance. The increasing rationalisation of a capitalist economy tended to separate the household from the process of production. Thus the means of successful performance were progressively removed from the sphere in which women were progressively confined. The increasing dignity of womanhood inexorably deepened the subjection of women.

Retrospect

The convict settlements and the mercantile and pastoral economy that grew in intimate connection with them established the basis of capitalism in these parts, and are worth close study if only for that reason: private property, family relations, the state, have all been reproduced continuously and autonomously in Australia since then. Compared with this fundamental point, the question of whether the structure of social relations at the time was strictly 'capitalist' or not is a trifle academic:[46] no one can doubt that capitalism was in process of being constructed, nor that its construction took a distinctive form because of the peculiar combination of penal settlement and pastoral expansion. The decisive factor in the early colonies was state power, and their political economy has some resemblances to mercantilism, if that is taken to be a system where a developed state organisation is both the base and field of action for profit-making entrepreneurs. Class formation followed a circuitous route here partly because of the singular role of the state. The nearest thing to a sharp class polarisation was in the established pastoral districts where assignment predominated, and this happened to be precarious because assignment could be ended by a change in state policy; the situation of convict labourers was not autonomously reproduced. The ironic result was that the increasing predominance of orthodox capitalist relations led to a decline in apparent class polarisation — though only for one generation, and that was also helped by the immediate effects of gold. Overall, attention tends to focus on the countryside because that is what was most distinctive and dramatic; but political power remained centred in the towns, and that was where the economic and sexual order characteristic of the period of bourgeois hegemony began to be formed. The colony may have been the fruit of the convicts' labour, but other hands came to the harvest.

Notes

1. For the latest round in this epic contest, see A. Frost, 'The East India Company and the Choice of Botany Bay', *Historical Studies*, vol. 16, no. 65, 1975, pp. 606–11; and 'The Choice of Botany Bay', *A.E.H.R.*, vol. 15, 1975, pp. 1–20; A. Atkinson, 'Whigs and Tories and Botany Bay', *J.R.A.H.S.*, vol. 61, 1976, pp. 289–310; G. Martin, 'Economic Motives behind the Founding of Botany Bay', *A.E.H.R.*, vol. 16, 1976, pp. 128–43; and A. Frost, 'Botany Bay: A Further Comment', and A. Atkinson, 'Botany Bay: A Counter-riposte', ibid., vol. 17, 1977, pp. 64–82. On this point, we think the instinct of an older generation of historians, notably E. O'Brien, *The Foundation of Australia (1786–1800)*, Angus & Robertson, Sydney, 2nd edn, 1950; and C. M. H. Clark, *A History of Australia*, vol. 1, M.U.P., Melbourne, 1962, is sounder. Exactly why the colony was landed there is trivial; what happened once it was, is the question.

2. C. D. Rowley, *The Destruction of Aboriginal Society*, A.N.U.P., Canberra, 1970, comprehensively proves the connection of pastoral expansion with violence against blacks. R. H. W. Reece, *Aborigines and Colonists*, S.U.P., Sydney, 1974, shows this in detail for one district, and explores the ambiguities of official policy; his account of 'Major Nunn's campaign' on the Gwydir in 1838 shows the initiative of the State in some of the largest-scale killings. It is impossible now to discover the exact numbers killed. But various estimates suggest the Aboriginal population was reduced by something like 200 000 during the nineteenth century (F. L. Jones, *The Structure and Growth of Australia's Aboriginal Population*, A.N.U.P., Canberra, 1970), and it seems reasonable in the light of the history of contact to attribute at least half of that to deaths caused in the impact of pastoralism.

3. M. H. Ellis, 'British Military Regiments in Australia', *J.R.A.H.S.*, vol. 37, 1951, pp. 313–43, establishes the background experience of the regular troops used from 1810. There has been a futile dispute among historians over the 'quality' (i.e. respectability) of the troops of the N.S.W. Corps; the main point is that they could and did fight effectively. H. King, 'Some Aspects of Police Administration in New South Wales, 1825–1851', ibid., vol. 42, 1956, pp. 205–30; and 'Problems of Police Administration in New South Wales, 1825–1851', ibid., vol. 44, 1958, pp. 49–70, is the most important study of the repressive apparatus of the State, describing the use of soldiers in the well-hated Mounted Police, and the inefficiency and corruption of the constabulary apart from this force.

4. The convict industry and convict administration is comprehensively discussed in A. G. L. Shaw, *Convicts and the Colonies*, Faber, London, 1964. W. D. Forsyth, *Governor Arthur's Convict System*, Longman, London, 1935 (repr. 1970), though much older, is methodologically better, since it relates convict administration to the structure of social relations in the countryside. D. Denholm, 'Port Arthur: The Men and the Myth', *Historical Studies*, vol. 14, 1970, pp. 406–23, is a useful survey of the penal outpost system and a corrective against literary distortions.

5. The classic study of state organisations in early Australia is A. C. V. Melbourne, *Early Constitutional Development in Australia*, O.U.P., Oxford, 1934 (repr. 1963). This is useful only at the level of law and high policy; its social analysis is faulty and its political analysis misleading, representing colonial politics essentially as inadequate responses to imperial policies—in which it has been followed by a school of imperial historians. Our view of administrative structure is based on the material on convict administration cited in Note 4 above; and on A. McMartin, 'The Payment of Officials in Early Australia, 1786–1826', *Public Administration*, vol. 17, 1958, pp. 45–80; 'The Treasury in New South Wales, 1786–1836', ibid., pp. 213–28; and 'Aspects of Patronage in Australia, 1786–1836', ibid., vol. 18, 1959, pp. 326–40; R. W. Connell, 'The Civil Administration of N.S.W., 1788–1810', B.A. history thesis, University of Melbourne, 1965; and R. L. Wettenhall, 'The Introduction of Public Administration into Van Diemen's Land', *P.T.H.R.A.*, vol. 7, 1959, pp. 44–57, 66–75. A striking picture of a colonial official is given by R. Crossland, 'The Boyes Diaries', ibid., vol. 3, 1954, pp. 46–51. For the change in English practices, see J. C. Beaglehole, 'The Colonial Office, 1782–1854', in M. Beever and F. B. Smith (eds), *Historical*

Studies: Selected Articles, 2nd series, M.U.P., Melbourne, 1967, pp. 1–29. For the professionalisation of the courts, see C. H. Currey, *The Brothers Bent*, S.U.P., Sydney, 1968.

6. In 1836, there were over one hundred unpaid magistrates in New South Wales and its dependencies, and only a third that number of stipendiary magistrates; in 1840, at the height of the pastoral boom, about ninety new unpaid magistrates were appointed and about a dozen stipendiary magistrates. See J. Macarthur (attrib.), *New South Wales: Its Present State and Future Prospects . . .*, Walther, London, 1837, p. 132; and *New South Wales Government Gazette*, 1840, *passim*. For the social history of the magistracy in England, see E. Moir, *The Justice of the Peace*, Penguin, Harmondsworth, 1969. No Australian historian seems to have tackled this subject with the care it deserves, though there are discussions of the magistracy in the context of general accounts of the gentry (see below, Note 31), and the stipendiary magistrates are discussed in King, 'Problems of Police Administration'. J. K. McLaughlin, 'The Magistracy and the Supreme Court of New South Wales, 1824–1850', *J.R.A.H.S.*, vol. 62, 1976, pp. 91–113, has useful points on the legal framework, but little of consequence on the issues raised here. For some abuses of power by unpaid magistrates, collected by Wentworth, see C. H. Currey, *Sir Francis Forbes*, Angus & Robertson, Sydney, 1968, p. 183.

7. Caley's comment is in an essay sent to Sir Joseph Banks; see G. Caley, *Reflections on the Colony of New South Wales* (ed. J. E. B. Currey), Lansdowne, Melbourne, 1966, p. 88. J. M. Powell, 'The Squatting Occupation of Victoria, 1834–60', *Australian Geographical Studies*, vol. 7, 1969, pp. 9–27, notes that it was Mitchell's news of good land more than his actual blazing of a trail that was important, and stresses the private exploring efforts of companies and individual pastoralists. The economic role of officials such as John McArthur and D'Arcy Wentworth in the early days is familiar. Its continuation is illustrated by the career of J. E. Manning, court registrar and public trustee in the 1830s, who used his control of trust funds to become a leading company promoter and investor. The classic local formulation that pits State against capitalism is E. Shann, *An Economic History of Australia*, C.U.P., Cambridge, 1930 (repr. 1948). The continuing importance of the State for colonial capitalism was argued by K. Dallas, 'Transportation and Colonial Income', *Historical Studies*, vol. 3, 1949, pp. 297–312; and decisively proved by S. J. Butlin, *Foundations of the Australian Monetary System, 1788–1851*, M.U.P., Melbourne, 1953.

8. Details of the initial cases are in Sydney Bench of Magistrates, 'Minutes of Proceedings, February 1788–January 1792' (N.S.W.S.A., C.O.D. 17). For the debt cases of 1798, see Hunters' dispatch of 21 February 1799, *H.R.A.*, Series I, vol. i, pp. 243–78. The fullest account of the development of trade, making use of court records, is D. R. Hainsworth, *The Sydney Traders*, Cassell, Melbourne, 1971.

9. That the Aborigines' occupation of the land was legally ignored is acknowledged even by B. Bridges, who curiously argues that their failure to hold and farm land on the whites' terms was somehow their own fault: 'The Aborigines and the Land Question', *J.R.A.H.S.*, vol. 56, 1970, pp. 92–110. For the original power to grant lands, and the six years of negotiations to extend it, see *H.R.A.*, Series I, vol. i. *passim*. Actual alienation of land is

traced by T. M. Perry, *Australia's First Frontier*, M.U.P., Melbourne, 1963; and K. W. Robinson, 'Land', in G. J. Abbott and N. B. Nairn (eds), *Economic Growth of Australia, 1788–1821*, M.U.P., Melbourne, 1969, pp. 74–104. For the lease-back episode, see B. H. Fletcher, *Landed Enterprise and Penal Society*, S.U.P., Sydney, 1976, pp. 30–1. Town land in Sydney was first granted by the military government in 1808, but Macquarie launched the policy formally; see *H.R.A.*, Series I, vol. vii, pp. 4, 13–14, 269, 366. For the granting and building of country towns, see D. N. Jeans, *An Historical Geography of New South Wales to 1901*, Reed Education, Sydney, 1972. A racy story of the first land sales at Melbourne is in *Garryowen's Melbourne* (ed. M. Weidenhofer), Nelson, Melbourne, 1967, pp. 22–4.

10. Land tenure is discussed, with varying degrees of clarity, in all works concerned with pastoralism. K. Buckley, 'Gipps and the Graziers of New South Wales, 1841–6', *Historical Studies*, vol. 6, 1955, pp. 396–412, stresses the variety of titles and the different grievances against the government that all came together in 1844. A detailed account of official policy is now available in P. Burroughs, *Britain and Australia, 1831–1855*, O.U.P., Oxford, 1967; and G. J. Abbott, *The Pastoral Age*, Macmillan and Dalgety, Melbourne, 1971, ch. 6.

11. On the development of an ex-convict and free labour force, see R. Ward, *The Australian Legend*, O.U.P., Melbourne, 1958 (2nd edn, 1966); and A. G. L. Shaw, 'Labour', in Abbott and Nairn, *Economic Growth*, pp. 105–18. Campbell's return of his possessions, listing a 'family' (i.e. household) of 21 and 126 'Free Men Employed', is enclosed in Darling's dispatch no. 93, 20 October 1831 (M.L. A1267–12), pp. 1058–9. There is an excellent formulation of the (interrupted) trend back towards English social patterns in M. Roe, 'Colonial Society in Embryo', *Historical Studies*, vol. 7, 1956, pp. 149–59. For the schemes to assist migrants, see R. B. Madgwick, *Immigration into Eastern Australia, 1788–1851*, Longman, London, 1937 (repr. 1969); and A. J. Hammerton, '"Without Natural Protectors": Female Immigration to Australia, 1832–36', *Historical Studies*, vol. 16, 1975, pp. 539–66; for their occupations, see ibid., and R. J. Schultz, 'Immigration into Eastern Australia, 1788–1851', *Historical Studies*, vol. 14, 1970, pp. 273–82.

12. Hainsworth, *Sydney Traders*; M. J. E. Steven, 'The Changing Pattern of Commerce in New South Wales, 1810–1821', *B.A.H.*, vol. 3, 1963, pp. 139–55. The process in the 1790s is particularly obscure, but from a slightly later period, G. M. Dow, *Samuel Terry: The Botany Bay Rothschild*, S.U.P., Sydney, 1974, is able to identify the varied sources of one emancipist's growing wealth: a shop, a spirit licence, grazing, general trade, rents and mortgages, land ownership, milling, brewing, shipping—and later, company shares. It is remarkable how little attention economic historians have given to the crucial question of the process of capital formation in the colony, apart from the somewhat mistitled sketch by K. Buckley, 'Primary Accumulation: The Genesis of Australian Capitalism', in E. L. Wheelwright and K. Buckley (eds), *Essays in the Political Economy of Australian Capitalism*, A.N.Z. Book Co., Sydney, 1975, pp. 12–32. There is a chapter on 'enterprise', but not on accumulation, in Abbott and Nairn's *Economic Growth*. B. Fitzpatrick, *British Imperialism and Australia, 1788–1833*, Allen & Unwin, London, 1939 (repr. 1971), tried to handle the problem through the concept of a

local monopoly. This certainly did exist in the 1790s, but was dead at the end of that decade; it probably speeded up the initial stages of accumulation, but is far from being an explanation of the whole process. As ties with merchants overseas were established, small local entrepreneurs could expand their capital through mercantile credit. For the troubles of the early 1810s in three separate cases, see Hainsworth, *Sydney Traders* (Lord); M. Steven, *Merchant Campbell, 1769–1846*, O.U.P., Melbourne, 1965; J. Ker, 'Merchants and Merinos', *J.R.A.H.S.*, vol. 46, 1960, pp. 206–23 (Riley). We have laboured this point a little because of its importance in understanding the generative effects of the property structure.

13. The estimates of costs are discussed in Burroughs, *Britain and Australia*, pp. 120–32; and Abbott, *Pastoral Age*, pp. 121–2. The import of one family's capital is traced in immense detail in M. Bassett, *The Hentys*, O.U.P., London, 1954.

14. This last claim is speculative, but is suggested by H. Kolsen, 'Company Formation in N.S.W.: 1828–1851', *B.A.H.*, vol. 1, no. 6, pp. 11–21; Spark's holdings are given in G. Abbott and G. Little, *The Respectable Sydney Merchant: A. B. Spark of Tempe*, S.U.P., Sydney, 1976, p. 167. For company formation in Hobart, see R. M. Hartwell, *The Economic Development of Van Diemen's Land, 1820–1850*, M.U.P., Melbourne, 1954, pp. 170–80, 214–16. For studies of particular local companies, see R. F. Holder, *Bank of New South Wales*, vol. 1, Angus & Robertson, Sydney, 1970; S. J. Butlin, 'Charles Swanston and the Derwent Bank, 1827–50', *Historical Studies*, vol. 2, 1943, pp. 161–85; J. Ginswick, 'Foundations of the Australian Gas Light Company', *J.R.A.H.S.*, vol. 45, 1960, pp. 226–65; and 'Early Australian Capital Formation, 1836–1850: A Case Study. The Australian Gas Light Company', *B.A.H.*, vol. 1, no. 6, pp. 22–49, no. 7, pp. 43–9. B. Dyster, 'Prosperity, Prostration, Prudence: Business and Investment in Sydney, 1838–1851', in A. Birch and D. S. Macmillan (eds), *Wealth and Progress*, Angus & Robertson, Sydney, 1967, pp. 51–76, cautions against over-estimating the role of companies in regularising the capital market, which was still turbulent and largely composed of private lenders.

15. J. Robinson, 'The Australian Agricultural Company and the Port Stephens Fiasco', *J.R.A.H.S.*, vol. 50, 1964, pp. 216–29, calculates that an investor of 1824 would have subscribed £30, but got back £16.8.6 in dividends, with £50 bonus and paid-up shares worth £35 in the reorganisation of 1852–53. On the other companies mentioned, see D. S. Macmillan, 'The Beginning of Scottish Enterprise in Australia', *B.A.H.*, vol. 2, 1962, pp. 95–105; S. J. Butlin, *Australia and New Zealand Bank*, Longman, London, 1961; 'British Banking in Australia', *J.R.A.H.S.*, vol. 49, 1963, pp. 81–99; and *Foundations of the Australian Monetary System*; D. Pike, *Paradise of Dissent*, Longman, London, 1957 (2nd edn, 1967); A. Birch, 'The Origins of the Colonial Sugar Refining Company, 1841–55', *B.A.H.*, vol. 5, 1965, pp. 21–31; and A. Birch and J. F. Blaxland, 'The Historical Background', in Colonial Sugar Refining Company Ltd, *South Pacific Enterprise*, Angus & Robertson, Sydney, 1956, pp. 11–52. The first involvement of big British capital with Australia actually goes back before this time, but did not involve a special corporate structure; see the material on whaling in M. Roe, 'Australia's Place in "the Swing to the East", 1788–1810', *Historical Studies*, vol. 8, 1958, pp. 202–13.

16. Hainsworth, *Sydney Traders*; and 'Iron Men in Wooden Ships: The Sydney Sealers, 1800–1820', *Labour History*, no. 13, 1967, pp. 19–26; and B. Little, 'The Sealing and Whaling Industry in Australia before 1850', *A.E.H.R.*, vol. 9, 1969, pp. 109–27.

17. G. P. Walsh, 'The Geography of Manufacturing in Sydney, 1788–1851', *B.A.H.*, vol. 3, 1963, pp. 20–52; and 'Factories and Factory Workers in New South Wales, 1788–1900', *Labour History*, no. 21, 1971, pp. 1–16; E. S. Richards, 'The Genesis of Secondary Industry in the South Australian Economy to 1876', *A.E.H.R.*, vol. 15, 1975, pp. 107–35; M. T. Daly, 'The Development of the Urban Pattern of Newcastle', ibid., vol. 10, 1970, pp. 190–203 (see also Turner's critique, ibid., vol. 11, pp. 179–90); and I. Auhl *et al.*, *Burra—A Glimpse of the Past*, Burra Record Print, Burra, n.d. (1971?).

18. Hammerton, 'Without Natural Protectors'; M. Kiddle, *Caroline Chisholm*, M.U.P., Melbourne, 1950 (abr. edn, 1969). It is very rare to find evidence of the experience of convict women servants; the happier side is given in the letters of Margaret Catchpole, in Margaret Catchpole Papers, ML A1508.

19. The marriages and other experiences of women convicts are discussed in L. L. Robson, *The Convict Settlers of Australia*, M.U.P., Melbourne, 1965, who is too prone to accept official slanders as truth; and in H. S. Payne, 'A Statistical Study of Female Convicts in Tasmania, 1843–53', *P.T.H.R.A.*, vol. 9, no. 2, 1961, pp. 56–69. Harriet King's letters are printed in D. Walsh (ed.), *The Admiral's Wife* (a splendidly sexist title!), Hawthorn Press, Melbourne, 1967; and Elizabeth McArthur's in S. Macarthur Onslow, *Some Early Records of the Macarthurs of Camden*, Angus & Robertson, Sydney, 1914.

20. For the debate on labour supply in the pastoral industry, see W. A. Sinclair, 'Was Labour Scarce in the 1830s?', *A.E.H.R.*, vol. 11, 1971, pp. 115–32; and the reply by Abbott, ibid., vol. 12, 1971, pp. 179–84. Scattered details on wages and the truck system are available in many secondary works, such as Hainsworth, *Sydney Traders*; Abbott, *Pastoral Age*; and Hartwell, *Economic Development*. Bigge's remark (apropos building workers) is in J. Ritchie, *The Evidence to the Bigge Reports*, Heinemann, Melbourne, 1971, vol. 2, p. 174. The fullest published compilation is still T. A. Coghlan, *Labour and Industry in Australia*, Macmillan, Melbourne, 1969, vol. 1 (first publ. 1918). For the point about custom and a discussion of English wage-rates, see E. Hobsbawm, *Labouring Men*, Weidenfeld & Nicolson, London, 1964. For the Irish settlements, see J. Waldersee, *Catholic Society in New South Wales, 1788–1860*, S.U.P., Sydney, 1974, which has important information on the role of property in establishing these groups in an unsympathetic environment, and the role of kinship and custom in organising them.

21. These relationships are mostly seen in the records from the point of view of employers and creditors; a valuable attempt to reconstruct the situation of one of the dependent groups is B. H. Fletcher, 'Development of Small-scale Farming in New South Wales under Governor Hunter', *J.R.A.H.S.*, vol. 50, 1964, pp. 1–31; and 'The Hawkesbury Settlers and the Rum Rebellion', ibid., vol. 54, 1968, pp. 217–37. For later developments, see D. N. Jeans, 'Crown Land Sales and the Accommodation of the Small Settler in N.S.W., 1825–1842', *Historical Studies*, vol. 12, 1966, pp. 205–12.

22. E. Eagar, *Letters to the Rt. Hon. Robert Peel, M.P.... on the Advantages of New South Wales and Van Diemen's Land...*, London, 1824, p. 21. There are three major studies of the convict workforce: Shaw, *Convicts and the Colonies*; Robson, *Convict Settlers*; and C. M. H. Clark, 'The Origins of the Convicts Transported to Eastern Australia, 1787–1852', *Historical Studies*, vol. 7, 1956, pp. 121–35, 314–27, together with the account given in the first three volumes of *A History of Australia*.

23. The charges quoted are taken from the appendices to the *Report* of the House of Commons Select Committee on Transportation of 1837, (*British Parliamentary Papers*, 1837, vol. 19, p. 1). Robson, *Convict Settlers*, pp. 101, 104–5, 136, gives a more exotic (and hence possibly misleading) selection. Denholm, 'Port Arthur', confirms that the more serious penal sanctions also were mainly imposed for offences against labour discipline, in the assignment period. Robson has established the crucial details of how many of the convicts were officially charged and punished. For a sample ceremonial execution with a forced audience of convicts, see *Sydney Gazette*, 26 March 1803. One of the condemned escapees was reprieved on the scaffold; this was quite often done, as it was supposed to have a good moral effect.

24. J. Platt, *The Horrors of Transportation...*, London, 1862. Platt is closer to the average working convict than are the authors of better-known (and republished) narratives such as Vaux or Mortlock. An interesting reconstruction of a convict career quite like Platt's is S. M. Ingham, 'A Footnote to Transportation to N.S.W.: James Ingham, 1824–1848', *Historical Studies*, vol. 12, 1967, pp. 522–40. Convict reminiscences are discussed in an excellent article by A. Conlon, '"Mine is a Sad Yet True Story": Convict Narratives, 1818–1850', *J.R.A.H.S.*, vol. 55, 1969, pp. 43–82.

25. The comment about 'bloody traps' comes from an incident leading up to the murder of the chief constable at Port Dalrymple; see *Hobart Town Gazette*, 26 July 1817. Ward, *Australian Legend*, has assembled folklore and literary evidence of the convicts' resistance and solidarity. H. McQueen, 'Convicts and Rebels', *Labour History*, no. 15, 1968, pp. 3–30, rightly points out that the literary evidence is contradictory. But in stressing the convicts' *petit-bourgeois* outlook and denying them a role in the origin of Australian radicalism, he overlooks both the political character of their 'depravity' (as seen by respectability) and the effect of their resistance in the workplace on the conditions in which non-convict labour began to organise. L. Thomas, *Development of the Labour Movement... 1788–1848*, Australian Society for the Study of Labour History, Canberra, 1962 (written in 1919), picked up the latter point, but oddly attributed it to the convict tradesmen, who if anything were more integrated into the system.

26. On bushranging and convict risings, see Ward, *Australian Legend*; McQueen, 'Convicts and Rebels'; R. W. Connell, 'The Convict Rebellion of 1804', *Melbourne Historical Journal*, vol. 5, 1965, pp. 27–37; and M. Hoare, *Norfolk Island*, U.Q.P., St Lucia, 1969. The connection that the authorities saw between bushranging and the convict workforce is clearly shown by their responding to outbreaks by threatening reprisals against convicts in assignment and on ticket-of-leave; see, for instance, the proclamations regarding the Carcoar district, *New South Wales Government Gazette*, 1840, pp. 538, 751.

27. G. Loveless, *The Victims of Whiggery*, Wilson & Hetherington, London, 1837, p. 11; and *Memoirs of Joseph Holt, General of the Irish Rebels* . . . , Colburn, London, 1838. Holt resents, when sent to Norfolk Island on suspicion, 'labouring like a slave, and being compelled to herd with the vilest wretches in the creation' (vol. 2, pp. 238–9) — so much for revolutionary leadership! Other precautions taken against educated convicts are noted in Robson, *Convict Settlers*, p. 99.

28. J. Earnshaw, 'Select Letters of James Grove, Convict . . .', *P.T.H.R.A.*, vol. 8, 1959, pp. 30–41. Loveless, *Victims of Whiggery*, p. 23, tells the story of a convict who actually had his master in his gunsights, but was restrained by the fear of hell; this kind of information must be set against the evidence of hostility to churchmen collected by Ward, *Australian Legend*, pp. 89–94. On emancipist politics, see P. E. LeRoy, 'The Emancipists, Edward Eagar and the Struggle for Civil Liberties', *J.R.A.H.S.*, vol. 48, 1962, pp. 270–301; and N. McLachlan, 'Edward Eagar (1787–1866): A Colonial Spokesman in Sydney and London', *Historical Studies*, vol. 10, 1963, pp. 431–56, which also notes the connection with evangelical religion. Both of these authors see the emancipist movement as progressive, ignoring the fact that it was moving *away* from the convicts and labourers. In many respects, it was a defensive move by one section of colonial wealth, attempting to guarantee their share of power. For the movement in Tasmania and its conflict with working-class organisations, see P. Bolger, *Hobart Town*, A.N.U.P., Canberra, 1973, pp. 49 ff.

29. McQueen, 'Convicts and Rebels'; G. Parsons, 'The Cato Street Conspirators in New South Wales', *Labour History*, no. 8, 1965, pp. 3–5; E. J. Hobsbawm and G. Rudé, *Captain Swing*, Lawrence & Wishart, London, 1969, ch. 14; and G. Rudé, 'Early Irish Rebels in Australia', *Historical Studies*, vol. 16, 1974, pp. 17–35.

30. M. H. Ellis, *John Macarthur*, Angus & Robertson, Sydney, 1955, has probably the best illustration of this status consciousness; H. V. Evatt, *Rum Rebellion*, Angus & Robertson, Sydney, 1938, is still interesting for an analysis of its political consequences, though his account of class dynamics is hopelessly wrong. The tale of the hat is told in M. C. Kemp and T. B. Kemp, 'Captain Anthony Fenn Kemp', *J.R.A.H.S.*, vol. 51, 1965, pp. 10–22.

31. For origins and parallels, see J. J. Auchmuty, 'The Background to the Early Australian Governors', *Historical Studies*, vol. 6, 1954, pp. 301–14; and G. C. Bolton, 'The Idea of a Colonial Gentry', ibid., vol. 13, 1968, pp. 307–28. Bolton takes the superficial view that the attempt to form a gentry is a sign of colonial 'immaturity', when in fact it expresses changes in the relations of production, and between groups of power-holders, in the colony. By far the best account of the gentry is M. Roe, *Quest for Authority in Eastern Australia, 1835–1851*, M.U.P., Melbourne, 1965, ch. 2. The only serious difference we have with his account is that he puts too much stress on the attempt to recreate feudal social forms such as traditional village life. This was always marginal in Australia, where the reality was, and remained, pastoral capitalism — wealth based on dispersed flocks minded by a landless workforce. The estimates of numbers are from Roe, for the 1830s, and from T. G. Parsons, 'Does the Bigge Report Follow from the Evidence?', *Historical*

Studies, vol. 15, 1972, pp. 268–75. The social life of the gentry is richly illustrated in M. Barnard Eldershaw, *The Life and Times of Captain John Piper*, Australian Limited Editions Society, Sydney, 1939. Two central Tasmanian homesteads that still have the surrounding wall are Somercotes and Bona Vista. These are both shown in the superb volumes by E. G. Robertson and E. N. Craig, *Early Houses of Northern Tasmania*, Georgian House, Melbourne, 1964; which, with E. G. Robertson, *Early Buildings of Southern Tasmania*, Georgian House, Melbourne, 1970; and R. Roxburgh, *Early Colonial Houses of New South Wales*, Ure Smith, Sydney, 1974, comprehensively illustrate the gentry's architectural self-expression.

32. For the struggle in the 1830s, see H. King, *Richard Bourke*, O.U.P., Melbourne, 1971; and for the 1840s, Buckley, 'Gipps and the Graziers'. An interpretation of the squatters as disruptive members of the propertied class seems to be required by the course of political events, as well as the economic facts. They were not a separate class, as is shown by the fact that many of the gentry also indulged in squatting; but they did have opposed interests on some issues and rapidly became the larger sector of the wool industry.

33. On the business leadership and its relationships with pastoralism, see especially Kolsen, 'Company Formation'; and Butlin, 'Charles Swanston' (Note 14). There were of course pastoral companies from the 1820s on, but they were not nearly as important in the industry as they were to become in the later nineteenth century. For the view that there was 'a very small middle class', see the passages quoted in R. A. Wild, *Bradstow*, Angus & Robertson, Sydney, 1974, pp. 6, 8. For the development of merchants' organisations, see W. J. Lyons, 'Notes on the History of the Royal Exchange of Sydney', *B.A.H.*, vol. 1, no. 2, pp. 1–7. For the emergence of an entrepreneurial group in the other main port, see Bolger, *Hobart Town*, pp. 11 ff. By far the richest picture of a merchant's activities and outlook is given in the Spark diaries, reprinted in Abbott and Little, *The Respectable Sydney Merchant*.

34. *Rules and Regulations of the Political Association, of Van Diemen's Land*, Bent, Hobart, 1835, p. 6.

35. D. Collins, *An Account of the English Colony in New South Wales*, Cadell & Davies, London, 1798, p. 438, mentions the reapers' action; T. A. Coghlan, *Labour and Industry*, p. 212, was thirty years out in identifying the earliest combination. For the 'mutiny' of 1806—it is not clear what the seamen's purpose was—see *Sydney Gazette*, 13 and 20 July 1806. For sealers' work conditions and court proceedings, see documents in D. R. Hainsworth (ed.), *Builders and Adventurers*, Cassell, Melbourne, 1968, pp. 100–3. For the stoppage of 1829, see J. McDonald, 'Australia's First Trade Union Secretary', *Labour History*, no. 3, 1962, pp. 44–51; and for that of 1834, Hartwell, *Economic Development*, p. 75.

36. For Hunter's response, see Fletcher, *Landed Enterprise*, p. 99. Bligh's effort is published in *Sydney Gazette*, 7 December 1806. The Act of 1828 is reprinted in C. M. H. Clark (ed.), *Select Documents in Australian History, 1788–1850*, Angus & Robertson, Sydney, 1950, pp. 416–18. A useful survey of labour and early attempts to regulate it is F. K. Crowley, 'The Foundation Years,

1788–1821', in G. Greenwood (ed.), *Australia*, Angus & Robertson, Sydney, 1955, pp. 29–38.

37. The quotation on immorality comes from Macquarie's proclamation against *de facto* marriage and disorderly houses, *Sydney Gazette*, 24 February 1810. The best account of the life of working people is in C. M. H. Clark, *A History of Australia*, vol. 2, M.U.P., Melbourne, 1968, ch. 7. E. Richards, 'A Voice from Below: Benjamin Boyce in South Australia, 1839–1846', *Labour History*, no. 27, 1974, pp. 65–75, is a fascinating case-study. The point about the mobility of labour is confirmed, of course, by contemporary observers; see Ward, *Australian Legend*, pp. 88–9; and A. J. Hopton, 'Rural Port Phillip, 1834 to 1851', *J.R.A.H.S.*, vol. 36, 1950, p. 283.

38. The formation of trade societies and agitation by working men is traced by Thomas, *Labour Movement*; Hartwell, *Economic Development*, pp. 85–93; Pike, *Paradise of Dissent*, pp. 335–7, 347–50; and the important study by L. J. Hume, 'Working Class Movements in Sydney and Melbourne before the Gold Rushes', *Historical Studies*, vol. 9, 1960, pp. 263–78. Hume, concentrating on formal associations, overlooks the evidence of organisation before 1830 already discussed. The weakness of the interpretation he and Thomas give of the societies is that they take 'working class' as a fixed category, and do not understand their work as a study of class formation. This problem is formulated—but discussed without much reference to the trade societies—by Ward, *Australian Legend*; and H. McQueen, *A New Britannia*, Penguin, Ringwood, Vic., 1970.

39. The attitudes and programmes of the chaplains are best conveyed in Clark, *History of Australia*, vol. 1. The sermon quoted was preached by the Reverend Robert Knopwood to a chain-gang; see his diary, reprinted in *Early Van Diemen's Land*, Royal Society of Tasmania, Hobart, 1954, p. 78.

40. In the most systematic account of ideology in the period, Roe, *Quest for Authority*, ch. 1, sees these churchmen as representing a colonial 'conservative ideology'. This cannot be right: they were in fact trying to impose a traditionalist social and religious theory on a society that was already capitalist. Roe has to exaggerate the feudal elements in the gentry's life (see Note 31) to make them fit. They were not even 'reactionary', since there never had been a society in New South Wales corresponding to a squire-and-parson concept of established religion. B. Dyster, 'The Fate of Colonial Conservatism on the Eve of Gold-rush', *J.R.A.H.S.*, vol. 54, 1968, pp. 329–55, points out from a different perspective that leading gentry did not share this concept, and that their brand of 'conservatism' was not defeated. Strictly, there was no colonial *conservatism* in the pastoral age—merely different justifications of a new situation.

41. For its early formulations, see the description of the Bigge Enquiry of 1819–21 in J. Ritchie, *Punishment and Profit*, Heinemann, Melbourne, 1970. For its developed versions, see J. Mudie, *The Felonry of New South Wales*, London, 1837 (repr. 1964); and Macarthur, *New South Wales: Its Present State and Future Prospects* .... The backgrounds to these two books are discussed in B. T. Dowd and A. Fink, 'Harlequin of the Hunter: "Major" James Mudie of Castle Forbes', *J.R.A.H.S.*, vol. 54, 1968, pp. 368–86, vol. 55, pp. 83–110;

and J. Metcalfe, 'Edward Edwards: His Association with "New South Wales: Its Present State and Future Prospects"', ibid, vol. 38, 1952, pp. 152–80. The latter book was ghost-written by a young English intellectual from material supplied by Macarthur and other exclusives, to support their petitions to the British government. It was more genteel than Mudie's ranting, but equally a weapon. The lingering of moral ascendancy notions in Tasmania is traced by Bolger, *Hobart Town*; and H. Reynolds, '"That Hated Stain": The Aftermath of Transportation in Tasmania', *Historical Studies*, vol. 14, no. 53, 1969, pp. 19–31.

42. See especially Reece, *Aborigines and Colonists*.

43. V. W. E. Goodin, 'Public Education in New South Wales before 1848', *J.R.A.H.S.*, vol. 36, 1950, pp. 1–14, 65–108, 129–210, has useful material on the intentions of the authorities, and on literacy. The notion that moral education was central was shared even by liberals who dissented from the view that religion had to be its basis; see W. Foster, 'Education in New South Wales under Governor Sir Richard Bourke', ibid., vol. 47, 1961, pp. 255–80. Historians of education have typically taken a blandly meliorist view of education itself, and hence have seen in these battles only obstacles placed by prejudice in the way of progress. Its cultural and political significance was well understood at the time; see the fascinating material in J. M. Goldstrom, *The Social Content of Education, 1808–1870*, Irish U.P., Shannon, 1972, which refers to English and Irish textbooks that were no doubt used in the colonies. For Carmichael, see C. Turney (ed.), *Pioneers of Australian Education*, S.U.P., Sydney, 1969, pp. 68–72; on economic doctrine, C. D. Goodwin, 'Political Economy in Australia', *B.A.H.*, vol. 6, 1966, pp. 1–33. Roe, *Quest for Authority*, places temperance and adult education in the context of a general movement for moral enlightenment, and points to their significance in the formation of bourgeois hegemony.

44. For the Lang and Sorell episodes, see *Australian Dictionary of Biography, 1788–1850*, vol. 2, M.U.P., Melbourne, 1967. K. Fitzpatrick, 'Mr Gladstone and the Governor: The Recall of Sir John Eardley-Wilmot from Van Diemen's Land, 1846', *Historical Studies*, vol. 1, 1940, pp. 31–45, argues that Eardley-Wilmot was scapegoated for the failure of the probation policy. The *Report* of the House of Commons Select Committee on Transportation of 1812 (*British Parliamentary Papers*, 1812, vol. 2, p. 573) comes to the issue of morality only after traversing economics and administration, and then coolly observes (p. 12) that the 'prostitution' complained of is probably due to the imbalance of the sexes and could be rectified by sending out more women! The contrast with the attitude of the 1837 Committee could hardly be greater. Clark, *History of Australia*, vol. 2, pp. 334–45 comments on the irony of the hyper-moral approach taken by the free-thinker Molesworth.

45. These concerns are summed up in the ideas and work of Caroline Chisholm, who, notably, was a Catholic—it is tempting to think of all this as the work of the evangelicals. See Kiddle, *Caroline Chisholm*, especially on the Family Colonisation Loan Society.

46. However, since this has been a point at issue in recent writing about this period from the viewpoint of class theory, we should indicate our view. Broadly, we agree with K. Rowley, 'Pastoral Capitalism: Australia's Pre-

industrial Development', *Intervention*, no. 1, 1972, pp. 9–26; and D. Clark, 'Australia: Victim or Partner of British Imperialism?', in Wheelwright and Buckley (eds), *Essays in the Political Economy of Australian Capitalism*, pp. 47–71, that production in the colonies was essentially capitalist; against the view of M. Dunn, 'Early Australia: Wage Labour or Slave Society?', in ibid., pp. 33–46, that there was a 'slave mode of production', which was dominant up to about 1840. The transferability of capital between enterprises in the different structures, the fact that pastoral production under assignment involved a typical dynamic of capitalist accumulation, the labour market phenomena within it that we have outlined, all make it impossible to construe as being outside the capitalist mode of production; and if 'state power is the necessity for the dominant class of the dominant mode' (Dunn, p. 34), the gentry never had it in its unity. To suggest that the slave-owning class controlled the Legislative Council, which was set up to allow its interests better expression (pp. 37–8), is just wrong. (For details of its origin and functioning, see S. G. Foster, 'A Piece of Sharp Practice? Governor Bourke and the Office of Colonial Secretary in New South Wales', *Historical Studies*, vol. 16, 1975, pp. 402–24.) Nevertheless, Dunn is correct in seeing an important difference between the structure of production centering on assignment and that centering on wage labour, and a consequential transition within pastoralism, which Rowley and Clark blur. All three authors underplay small-scale production and the variety of relations of dependence in production, especially in the towns. Thus Rowley (p. 14) assumes an automatic transition from assignment to wage labour, and incongruously accepts the view that labourers could easily become landowners (p. 15), both of which are wrong and must lead to a miscalculation of the social situation and political struggles of the mid-century, allowing him to exaggerate the similarity of the pre- and post-gold-rush situations.

Documents

The State

2.1 Coercion: The control of minor offences
2.2 Establishing the property system
2.3 Assignment: The legal basis

The Labour Market

2.4 Convict labour on an early property: The owner's perspective
2.5 Labour troubles on the same property
2.6 Accumulation: The Macarthur fortune
2.7 Accumulation: Company formation
2.8 Labour market in the pastoral countryside
2.9 Labour discipline, Port Phillip

Convict Experience

2.10 Assignment: A convict letter
2.11 Chain gang
2.12 Floggings
2.13 Convict resistance: Bushranging
2.14 Convict resistance: The Castle Hill rising

Class Formation

2.15 Status consciousness and sexual code
2.16 Club gentility
2.17 Household structure in pastoral expansion
2.18 A craftsman's social outlook

Ideology

2.19 Social hierarchy
2.20 Moral ascendancy
2.21 A vision of progress
2.22 Democratic movement: Representation of the people

2.1 Coercion: The control of minor offences

A sample of proceedings before the magistrates at Hobart. Note the differences in the treatment of free men, convict men, and convict women.

Source: *Hobart Town Gazette*, 27 September 1817.

BENCH OF MAGISTRATES.—On Wednesday *Ann Bass*, a crown servant, was brought before a Bench of Magistrates, charged with behaving in a riotous and disorderly manner to her mistress, and attempting to quit her place without leave, contrary to the Colonial Regulations. The charge being most clearly proved, she was sentenced to be put in the stocks 8 hours, at two different periods, with an iron collar placed upon her neck, and to be imprisoned in the county gaol for 3 months. The complaint was peculiar aggravating, this woman having only been released from prison a few days back on a similar case.

John Gwynn, a free man, was fined five pounds, for attempting to inveigle the above woman from her place.

We trust this example will be a warning to all young women who are assigned as servants in this Island; and cause them to remain peaceable and contented in the situation allotted them by Government, and not to be seduced by those who in a short time may leave them friendless and distressed.

This day *William Mason*, a crown servant and cooper of His Majesty's Store in this town, was charged with stealing 7 lbs of sugar from the said store; for which offence he was sentenced to receive 100 lashes, and to work 12 months in the gaol gang.

David M'Coy, a settler and stock-owner, was fined 20 *l.* for killing a sheep without a licence, contrary to Government and General Orders. *William Smith*, a prisoner, was also sentenced to work 2 months in the gaol gang, for assisting in the same offence.

2.2 Establishing the property system

The first legal case in the white settlement—a dispute over ownership. This is the kind of situation that led to the convict women being regarded by the respectable as 'whores'.

Source: Sydney Bench of Magistrates, 'Minutes of Proceedings, February 1788—January 1792', N.S.W. State Archives, C.O.D. 17, pp. 1–3.

Head Quarters—Port Jackson

At a Meeting of two of His Majesty's Justices of the Peace for the Territory of New South Wales—19th Feb^{r}. 1788.—

Present—

David Collins, Esq .—Augustus Alt Esqr.—

Mary Jackson, a Convict, was brought before them, charged with detaining a Shirt, a Pair of Trowsers, and a new Frock and a Pair of Stockings—the Property of Edward Dease, a Seaman, belonging to the Lady Penrhyn, Transport.

Edward Dease, a Seaman, being duly sworn, deposes that, he gave the Articles mentioned in the Charge to the Prisoner, Mary Jackson, for the Purpose of getting them washed, on or about last Tuesday night—giving her at the same Time ½ a Pound of Tea to satisfy her for her Trouble—and some Soap to wash them—On Saturday night last, he procured a Pass from the Master of the Transport, to go on shore, and get his Things from the Prisoner, who told him at first, that they were lost out of the Tent but that if the Corporal (who was sent with the Evidence) would go with her, she would endeavour to find them—that, when she came to the Tent, she said she would not restore them, giving at the same Time much abuse—that the Evidence, not being able to get his things from her, went away—returning again on the next Morning, applying to Major Ross—who sent a Private Man to the Prisoner, with Directions to her, to deliver the things or he would send a File of Men for her—that the Prisoner, would not comply with these Orders, & a File of Men was sent for her—that then she gave up the Things, first cutting or tearing the Frock, & throwing the other Things out of the Tent & that he then returned to the Major, and informed him of his having got his Things, producing to him the Frock where it had been cut.

[Two marines give evidence of having gone under orders to seize the clothes, which Mary Jackson eventually gives up, under protest.]

Mary Jackson, being asked what she had to say, says, that Dease gave her the Shirt—and told her, the Frock she might have for a Shift, if she would bleach it, and the Trousers, she might have to mend her Stays—that she told him she would mend whatever he had that wanted mending, that in Return for the Trowsers he gave her, he asked her for a Canvas Petticoat she had, which would make him a good Pair of Trowsers—that the Stockings he gave her, for a Pair of worn Ones, he had worn often in the Cold Weather—that he asked her often to go on Board with him one Night bringing a Hat and great Coat, to take her off in Disguise—and that she refused to go with him, & that in consequence of such Refusal, he came to demand his Things of her—that she told him she would speak to some of the Officers & tell them her story, & if they thought she should, she then would give them up.

The Prisoner was reprimanded for not giving up the Things when she was sent to by the Major—and it appearing, that the Prosecutor had cohabited with her during the Passage, had given her the Articles for her own Use, & required them again, on her refusing to go on Board ship with him, she was discharged.

2.3 Assignment: The legal basis

Evidence of Sir Francis Forbes, the first Chief Justice of New South Wales, to the House of Commons Select Committee on Transportation of 1837. Note his comments on the powers of magistrates.

Source: *Report . . .*, Minutes of Evidence, 14 April 1837, pp. 7–11 (*British Parliamentary Papers*, vol. 19, 1837).

93. *Chairman.*] Will you explain to the Committee what is the nature of the law or authority which determines the state of the convict in the colony

on account of a crime committed in England?—Suppose a convict commit a particular offence, liable to be punished by transportation, the law merely affixes transportation to the crime, as the punishment of seven years, 14 years, or for life, according to the degree of the offence, and goes no further. The Transportation Act, 5 Geo. 4, c. 84, provides, that as often as a convict shall be sentenced to transportation, it shall be in the power of the Secretary of State to appoint a place within His Majesty's dominions to which the convict shall be transported. It further directs, that on his arrival in the country he shall be delivered over to the governor, who shall have a property in the services of such convict, and who may assign such convict over to any resident within the colony, who shall have a like property in the services of the convict for the term of his transportation, with a power of assigning to any other person, with the assent of the governor, each assignee having a property in the services of the offender. It is from this right of property that the whole authority over the convict is derived, and without it I apprehend the convict, on being banished, would become free.

94. In short the convict is, properly speaking, a slave?—I cannot say that, because by the word "property," I mean such as the master has in his apprentice; I can only read the term property, in the Act of Parliament, as it is understood by the law. I know of no property in slaves now, since the abolition of slavery, but it is something analogous to the property a master has in his apprentice.

95. Sir *George Grey*.] He has an interest in the services of the convict?—A property in the services.

96. *Chairman*.] State what are the obligations of the master towards the person in whose services he has a property?—He is bound to maintain and protect him, I apprehend, and may exercise a domestic control and authority over him according to the common law of England; this, however, is only matter of opinion.

97. What are the convict's means of redress if his master ill-treats him and over-works him?—The local government, however, have entirely removed from the master any power of corporal punishment over his servant; the master is bound, as I have before stated, to supply his convict servant with stipulated food and clothing, failing which, the servant may apply to a magistrate, who will see that the government regulations are enforced, or will take away the servant from the master and return him to the government.

98. Is the master liable to no other punishment than losing the services of the convict?—Not by law.

99. Would he, for instance, for blows, positive cruelty of any kind, would he not be liable to punishment?—To prosecution by the government, to public prosecution for assault and battery, according to circumstances.

100. Then the convict's means of redress is through a magistrate?—Entirely, through a magistrate.

101. Will you state what are the magistracy of New South Wales, and by whom appointed?—The magistracy of New South Wales are appointed by the governor, under his instructions from His Majesty; they are composed of gentlemen settled in towns and in distant parts of the colony, and have very large powers, comprehending all powers of magistrates in and out of sessions in England, and the peculiar powers in the colony over all offences below the degree of capital, committed within the colony by transported convicts....

117. Will you state when and by what means the condition of the convict

is changed; how he obtains, for instance, a ticket of leave, and what is a ticket of leave?—By local regulation, from the beginning of the settlement in Australia, the governors of the colony were in the habit of granting what are called tickets of leave, as the reward of good conduct, and also formerly as remuneration for extra work and labour, skill or ingenuity. During the government of Sir Thomas Brisbane, however, a regular scale of time was established, by which a convict transported for seven years, and who conducted himself well for four; or a convict transported for 14 years, who conducted himself well for six; or for life, and good conduct for eight, were respectively entitled to a ticket of leave. This instrument is resumable at the discretion of the government, and is forfeited upon proof of any misconduct or conviction, and the holder, during the time that he holds a ticket, is in all respects liable to the summary jurisdiction of the magistrate, and to the same extent of punishment as while he continued a convict, or rather before he received his ticket.

118. What is the advantage of the ticket of leave; what is the right of the convict when he has a ticket of leave?—The right of a holder of a ticket of leave is to work for his own benefit.

119. Mr. *Hawes*.] To obtain work wheresoever he can in the colony?—To obtain work where he can within the limit of his district; tickets of leave being limited in terms to a particular district appointed by the government in such tickets...

149. *Chairman*.] Now with regard to the state of freedom, how does the convict become free?—By two modes; by the expiration of the term of his transportation as originally adjudged, and by the remission of the governor in pursuance of the Act of Parliament, 30 Geo. 3, c. 47, and 9 Geo. 4, c. 83.

150. Sir *George Grey*.] You do not exclude the prerogative of the Crown, which may grant a pardon generally?—There is in the Transportation Act an express saving of His Majesty's prerogative of mercy.

151. *Chairman*.] In what cases are the pardons of the governor given?—The governor grants pardon in consequence of good conduct in the colony for a length of time, but without any regulation as to that time that I am aware of, excepting that it cannot be given within the period limited by the Act to which I have before alluded.

152. What is that period?—At four, six and eight years; it says, "ticket of leave or pardon."

2.4 Convict labour on an early property: The owner's perspective

Evidence of George Johnston to the House of Commons Select Committee on Transportation of 1812. Johnston was military commander both in the suppression of the 1804 convict rising (see Document 2.14) and the 1808 coup against Bligh. The 'slops' referred to are rough clothes.

Source: *Report* ..., Minutes of Evidence, 13 April 1812, pp. 73–4 (*British Parliamentary Papers*, vol. 2, 1812).

...if any American ship, or any other arrived, the officers, or any others who had money, were allowed to purchase as much spirits as they liked; some of us had grants of land at that time, and we used to barter the spirits to pay the labourers for clearing our grounds.

What was the largest quantity of spirits you ever recollect being given to one officer by the Governor?—I think the most that ever I was allowed to purchase was a couple of casks of spirits in Governor Hunter's time, out of the Ganges, or the Britannia. I was enclosing a very large piece of ground, and building houses upon it in the country, and I asked that as a particular favour.

Do you recollect at what price these casks of spirits were allowed to you?—I do not exactly know whether it was five shillings, or nine shillings, it was one or the other, but I have paid as high as £.3 a gallon for spirits, and I have the Bill to show.

At what price were those spirits bartered to your neighbours?—At the same price they were sold at in the shops; they have paid at from twenty to thirty shillings a gallon, and when our ground was cleared, the labourers used to have slops and flour from us, and some spirits.

What quantity of land had you in your hands?—I do not think it is 3000 acres. Governor King gave me 2,000 acres for quelling an insurrection that happened in the country from the Irish convicts.

What number of convicts were allowed you to cultivate this land?—In the first instance, Governor Grose allowed me ten men, but they were not turned over to me till I had a comfortable house to shelter them in.

Did you maintain those men yourself at your own expense?—Not in Governor Grose's time. There was an order came that all the people that were allowed by Government, were to be victualled, except the people who were in civil situations; and, as a magistrate, I was allowed four by Government, and three as commanding officer; latterly I had only two, and did not apply for a third; when I came away I victualled and clothed twenty-three off the stores, besides my own family....

Were not the convicts allowed to work on their own account after certain hours?—Yes, after their task was done.

In what manner could they obtain employment without a pass?—The overseers of the different farms about, used to inquire of them if they had any spare time, and wanted employment; and if their master did not hire them they were at liberty to go to other people.

In what manner could they obtain employment, if the master refused to give them a pass to leave his premises?—If the master refused to give them a pass, they had a right to complain to the bench of magistrates; in the first instance they were obliged to offer their services to their master; and if they were not contented with the wages offered them by the master, they had a right to hire themselves to another person.

Was the price of labour ever fixed by the Governor?—Yes, it was.

Was that price acquiesced in?—I have heard it was not; up at the Hawkesbury the people would not work at the price that was fixed for their labour.

Was the price of labour in the neighbourhood of Sydney regulated by the Governor?—There were prices put upon the different articles, such as splitting paling, splitting shingles, felling timber, and in short all field labour; but you were in general obliged to give more than the Governor had ordered, for the people would not work for it.

2.5 Labour troubles on the same property

The court record of charges against four of the convict labourers assigned to Johnston.

Source: Sydney Bench of Magistrates, 'Minutes 1798–1800', 8 December 1798, N.S.W. State Archives, 1/298.

Cummings, *Calvin*, *McCabe* and *Dunn* charged by Capt. Johnstone's overseer with neglect of Duty and Disobedience of orders.

The three former were brought up and being called upon for their Defence declared that the Accusation against them was false, illfounded and proceeded wholly from the malignity of mind of Thos. Biggars (the overseer) whose cruel Treatment of & general ill-Behaviour to the unfortunate men under him they stated to be universally known to all Descriptions of people in the Colony—that said Biggars is in the constant Habit of knocking the men down without Cause or provocation and otherwise abusing and ill-treating them—that their allowance of Food is so extremely scanty as to be insufficient to support them in Labor, yet the said Biggars allots them more work than twice the number of men could perform in the time—that altho' they had 50 Rods to reap, each man daily, they contrived with great Labor & application from the dawn of Day until night to accomplish their Task work with a view to have friday to themselves and when Friday came & their week's Task Work was finished they thought themselves at liberty to leave the Farm for their own Earnings—wholly deny any Disobedience of orders.

Remanded to the Custody of the Gaoler until Capt. Johnstone could be written to on the Bus^{s}. that he may have an opportunity if he pleases, of attending himself or directing Thos. Biggars so to do in order to establish the Charge. . . .

On Monday morning *Galvin*, *Cummins* & *McCabe*, the three men complained of by Captn Johnstone's overseer, were in Consequence of the Charges being substantiated against them,

Sentenced to receive 50 Lashes each & to be discharged, to their former Labor.

[Note in margin:] Sentence inflicted.

2.6 Accumulation: The Macarthur fortune

James Macarthur's account of the family wealth, in evidence to the Select Committee on Transportation of 1837. Note the reliance on the state at almost all points.

Source: *Report* . . . , Minutes of Evidence, 23 May 1837, pp. 186–8.

James Macarthur, Esq., called in; and further Examined.

2858. *Chairman.*] Have you any explanations or additions to make to your last examination?—If the Committee will permit me, I am now prepared to state the quantity of land which my family possesses in the colony of New South Wales, and the nature of its tenure. The number of acres possessed by my two brothers and myself is, in round numbers, about 50,000 acres. As that seems a very large extent, I should wish, if the Committee will permit me, to explain the manner in which we have become possessed of it.

My father went out as an officer in the 102d regiment, in the second fleet, in the year 1791. Some years after his arrival in the colony, a grant of land was made by the governor to the officers of the regiment, as well, I believe, as of the marine corps to the extent of 100 acres each, with an understanding that whoever brought his 100 acres first into cultivation should have an equal quantity in addition. My father obtained the additional grant, making 200 acres, which was all that he obtained by grant at that period. He afterwards purchased land to the extent, as nearly as I can state, of between 3,000 and 4,000 acres. In the year 1797 he became possessed of three rams and five ewes of the Merino breed. He had been induced to turn his attention particularly to the production of fine wool from observing the great improvement which took place in the fleeces of Cape and Bengal sheep, which had been previously the only sheep-stock of the colony, by crossing them with some sheep bearing wool, which, I believe, came from England or Ireland.... In the year 1801, my father, then a captain in the New South Wales corps, arrived in England, and he made representations to the Privy Council and to the Government, a copy of which I beg to put in....

In consequence of the proceedings before the Privy Council, a communication was made to Lord Camden, then principal Secretary of State for the Colonies, recommending that my father should receive a grant of 5,000 acres of land in the colony, which was carried into effect, with an understanding, that upon realizing what he had undertaken to perform, that is, upon the successful introduction of the fine-woolled breed of sheep, he should receive 5,000 acres more. On the arrival of Mr. Bigge, the Commissioner of Inquiry, in New South Wales, in 1818, this was one of the subjects on which he was directed to report, and in consequence of his report an additional 5,000 acres was granted to my father. During his absence from the colony about 700 acres of land had been granted to my mother, Mrs. Macarthur, by Governor Macquarie, in consequence of the great improvements she had made on the property during my father's absence, and the various improvements in agriculture that were introduced by her, such, for instance, as taking the stumps out of the ground, and the making of hay for sale, both of which were quite new in the colony; as well as for the general regularity and excellent management maintained under her direction of a large establishment of convict servants. In 1815 my father, being again in Europe, visited the wine districts of France, and made a valuable collection of vines and fruit trees. On his preceding voyage he had introduced the olive into the colony, and he procured other varieties of the best kinds of olive on this occasion. Myself and my younger brother travelled with my father, for the express purpose of acquiring useful knowledge in the cultivation of the vine, the olive, and of these products generally which are grown in warmer climates and not in this country....

[2865.] In consequence of our attention to these pursuits, my brother and myself received a grant of 5,000 acres, by order of Earl Bathurst, having previously received 2,300 acres from Governor Macquarie; so that in round numbers the total quantity of acres held by my brothers and myself at this moment, and derived by grant from the Crown, is 18,000. There have been acquired at various times by my late father, by my brothers and myself land to the extent of 32,000 acres by purchase, which completes the 50,000 acres I stated in the outset. . . .

2867. [Sir *G. Grey*.] Were all the 32,000 acres purchased nearly at the same time, or at different periods?—At different periods. A part, to the extent of 4,368 acres, was acquired in exchange for sheep sold to the Government of Van Diemen's Land in the years 1819–20, which was the first introduction of fine-wooled sheep into that colony.

2868. What was the price of that land?—The price, I think, was 7*s*. 6*d*. an acre, and the sheep were valued at 5*l*. or five guineas.

2869. When was that?—That was in the end of 1819 or the beginning of 1820.

2870. Have you made any extensive purchases since the year 1831?—We have.

2871. To what extent?—I am scarcely prepared to state now, with accuracy.

2872. To a considerable extent?—I think to the extent of from 5,000 to 7,000 acres.

2873. Has that been bought at public auction?—It has.

2874. Do you know what has been the average price per acre of the land you have purchased?—Generally speaking, it has been purchased without competition at the minimum price; but for some lots we have given a very high price.

2875. What is the highest price that you have given?—I think 18*s*. per acre.

2876. Was that for agricultural purposes, or in a township for building?—It was purchased rather with a view to prevent encroachment on our lands by others. It would have been exceedingly inconvenient if other parties had obtained possession of it.

2.7 Accumulation: Company formation

An example of the small companies formed in the colonies. One of two auction companies formed by rival groups of capitalists to profit from the Port Phillip District wool boom in 1840.

Source: Australia Felix Auction Co., 'Minute Book', 8 April 1840, La Trobe Collection, State Library of Victoria.

The Gentlemen who Signed the requisition for a meeting to be held on Thursday the 16th Current to take into Consideration the necessity of forming a Joint Stock Auction Company in Melbourne, assembled together this day Wednesday the 8th April 1840 by *Mutual Consent*, at the office of William Meek Esqre and deeming delay injurious to the prospects of the Company, formed themselves into a Joint Stock Company, appointing Directors with power to add to their number, and Officers and issuing a prospectus of the Company of which the following is a Copy. . . .

From the unexampled prosperity of the Town of Melbourne the Capital of Australia Felix, especially in a Commercial point of view, from the rapidity with which it has become in the short space of Three Years, the Second town in the territory of New South Wales & from the Constant & daily increase of its Trade, both in Stock and merchandise of every description almost the whole of which is disposed of thro' the medium of Public Auction.

It is proposed in order to meet the wishes of the World Generally, as Well as those of the resident Stockholders & Graziers of this magnificent district and also to further the interests of Gentlemen introducing Stock for Sale from the elder Colony, to form a Joint Stock Auction Company in the Town of Melbourne to be denominated

"The Australia Felix Auction Company"

with a Capital of £50.000. to be raised in shares of Ten pounds each. The Said Company to be managed by Twenty Resident Directors and one Managing Director. That the plan & principle upon which the Sydney Auction is conducted & which have been found to work so admirably be adopted as the System of conducting the affairs of this Company.

While the projectors of this Company admit that the profitable results of such an institution must mainly depend upon its judicious management they at the same time feel confident that the period has arrived for the formation of such a Company and that no public Institution as yet formed in Melbourne offers so many advantages to the Proprietors with so little risk and so small an outlay of Capital. . . .

Fifty Shares to qualify for Directorship.

2.8 Labour market in the pastoral countryside

As described by an educated convict who worked in the mounted police and as a clerk in New South Wales in the 1840s.

Source: C. Cozens, *Adventures of a Guardsman*, Bentley, London, 1848, pp. 230–3.

The general rate of wages to farm-servants throughout the Colony, though considerably diminished from what it formerly was on my first arrival, may still be considered high, and, as near as I can recollect, averages as follows per annum, rations, as per scale, included: — Stockmen, from fifteen to twenty pounds; shepherds, fifteen pounds; watchmen, twelve pounds; bullock-drivers, fifteen pounds; and field labourers from twelve to fourteen pounds. The usual scale of rations allowed with the above consists weekly of beef or mutton, the former generally salt, ten pounds; flour twelve pounds, or a peck of wheat; tea a quarter of a pound, sugar a pound and a half to two pounds: all other necessaries the men must find themselves, such as tobacco, soap, clothing, &c., or any extra supplies of the above. This, when compared with the present rate of wages in the mother country, might be considered good, and, in itself, so it certainly is; but then there are many great drawbacks, which must likewise be considered. In the first place, where the principal diet throughout the interior, with a few exceptions, is bread, beef, and tea three times a day, the allowance is insufficient, especially that of tea and bread. The number of claimants almost daily upon the hospitality of the settlers, no matter how remote or secluded their situation, is very surprising.

As the general characteristic of the country is hospitality, it rarely if ever happens, particularly in distant localities, that a traveller is not entertained on the best the house affords, even in a shepherd's hut; for such entertainers know not, from the peculiar customs of the colony and the uncertain tenure of their position, how soon they may be placed in the same predicament, and require a return of such civility.

The most wealthy settlers themselves are often, when travelling in the bush, indebted to a shepherd for a night's entertainment. This tends much to reduce the shepherds' limited allowance still more; and often, long before the week has expired, they repair to the head station, distant perhaps fifteen or twenty miles, to draw an additional supply, which is, of course, booked against their wages. Clothing, tobacco, too, and soap, they require in great abundance; and for such articles the employer thus finds a market, charging in some instances two hundred per cent. on every article he issues (never less than cent. per cent.) to indemnify him, as he says, for the expense of carriage from Sydney or elsewhere. The poor creatures cannot do without such supplies, and have them they must at any price, as there is no other store perchance within a hundred miles of them; and, if there were, they could not avail themselves of it, as their employers will make no advance to expend at another's profit.

Such is the general system, and a most pernicious one it proves to be, for it seldom happens that the poor operatives have more than a few shillings due to them at the end of the year; and, in many instances, they are considerably in arrear. Thus it is that settlers can afford to lend such good wages, for in reality the wages must be viewed in this light.

In-door servants, married and single, sometimes do very well, particularly married ones without incumbrances; the husband being often retained as cook and butler, and the wife as housemaid and laundress, at joint wages of from twenty-five to thirty pounds, exclusive of rations. The single ones in such capacities, or as grooms, gardeners, or coachmen, may be respectively averaged at from twelve to fifteen pounds, and, in special and peculiar cases, twenty pounds. Tradesmen's and mechanics' wages rate generally very high; and they must be very inferior workmen indeed, if they do not make from thirty shillings to two pounds a week. The best trades in New South Wales, more especially in the interior, are carpenters, blacksmiths, wheelwrights, shoemakers, and tailors: these generally secure a good run, and, when once a connexion is established, success is certain. Masons, bricklayers, plasterers, cabinet-makers, turners, and white-smiths are almost useless in the bush, and do best in Sydney, Port Philip, or some large and flourishing township, where their particular branches of trade are in greater request.

2.9 Labour discipline, Port Phillip

An example of the prosecution of employees under the Masters and Servants Acts, from a newspaper report in the 'Local Intelligence' column.

Source: *Port Phillip Patriot*, 13 May 1841.

HIRED SERVANTS.—On Friday last Captain Smythe of Heidelberg, appeared at the Police Office, to prefer a charge against two of his hired servants named James and Agnes Brown, the former for shamefully maltreating a valuable horse belonging to the complainant, gross neglect of duty in losing off the dray the box referred to in another paragraph, and also for absconding. The female was also charged with leaving her hired service without permission. Brown pleaded guilty to the charges, and begged that Captain Smythe would take him into his service again, where he would work until his master's loss was repaired. This the complainant refused, alleging that Brown was considerably in his debt, and he was determined to have him punished; he was sentenced three months imprisonment. The woman, as it was suspected she had acted under the influence of her husband, was discharged.

2.10 Assignment: A convict letter

From an illiterate convict labourer in Van Diemen's Land. Note the postscript from the person who wrote it down.

Source: Richard Dillingham to his parents, 29 September 1836, Dillingham Letters, Archives Office of Tasmania, NS 157/1.

Vandemans Land Septer 29 1836

Dear Father And Mother I have After A long Absence from you Imbraced the opportunity of of writing to you hopeing those few lines may find you And All my Brothers And Sisters In Good Health As I Am happy to Inform you that this leaves me quite well at this time thank God for it I have likewise to Inform you that I Am Arived Safe In vandemans Land but I Am Sorry to Inform you that we had but A verry unpleasant Voiage for After we left Woolwich the Cholera raged on Board our Ship whitch Obliged us to Return Back to Chatham And lay there 21 days and we had 22 Persons died but I had but A Slight toutch of it my Self you must Excuse me for Not writeing Before As I have till Now been A Long way up the Country And have Not been Able till Now to get A Letter to the Post with any Safety but I Am happy to Inform you that I Am Now verry Comfortabley Situated within A mile of Hobart Town the head Town In the Collony I Am Situated In A Large Market Garden belonging to A Gentleman by the Name of Mr David Lamb Esqr And My Imploy Is to Drive A Horse And Cart Into Hobart Town with the Produce of the Garden for Sale As to my Liveing I find it Better than Ever I Expected thank God I want for Nothing In that Respect As for tea And Sugar I almost Could swim in it I am Alowed 2 Pound of Sugar and ¼ Pound of tea Per week And Plenty of tobaco And Good white Bread And some times Beef Some times mutton sometimes Pork this I have Every day Plenty of fruit Pudings In the Season of all sorts And I have two Suits of Cloths A year And three Pair of shoes In A year And I want for Nothing but my Liberty but though I Am thus Situated It Is Not the Case with all that Come As Prisonners It Is all Owen to A Persons Good Conduct that they Get Good Situations for some through their misconduct Get Into Road Partys and some Into Chain Gangs and Live A misaberable Life my kind Love to my Brother James and I hope that my misfortune will be A worning to him and to all I send my kind Love to my Child An I hope that he Is well and besure Send me word how he Is And how Providence have Provided for him Since my departure from him As to the State of this Country Is As follows A Tradesman of Any kind will get from 6 to 7s Per day And A farming man will get A dollar Per day whitch Is 4s 4d. And Bread Is 4d the 2 Pd loaf Cheese Is 1s 6d Per Pound Butter fresh Is 2s 6d Per Pound Beef 8d to 10d Per Pound Mutton 6d to 7d Per Pound Sugar And tea Is verry Cheap I have known good Sugar at 2d Per Pound And tea at 1s Per Pound But It Is Rather dearer at this time Sugar 4 and tea 1s 6d Per Pound As to the Produse of the Collony It Produces all Sorts of Grain and fruit of Every discription And wool and Oil Is the Cheif thing that Is sent from the Collony In the Shipping As for the Climate In this Country it Is A fine Climate we have but verry little winter And there Is not A tree but what may be Propperly Called An Ever Green As they are Green all the year long And what Is Termed the Bush Ground that Is not Cultivated Is Adorned with Beautiful flowering Shrubs of all Sorts and Ground flowers of all sorts as for the Timber In this Country it [grows] verry large and high some trees Called the Gum tree Grows 200 feet high [There] Is others Called Stringebark [ ] Peppermint tree but the Gum tree Is the Best for Use the Howses In this Country Are Cheifly Built of Stone And the Roofs are Covered with wood Called Shingals they Split Allmost In the form of tiles About 14 Inches long and 5 or 6 Inches Broad and Each one fastened with A Nail When you write to [me] you must be [sure And Pay] the Postage of the [le]tter to London or I sha[ll] not have it And you must direct As follows for Richard Dillingham at [Mr] D Lambs Esq[r] Sanday Bay Hobart Town Vandemans Land And besure and Pay the Postage of the Letter to London or I shall not have it And I hope you wil not delay w[riting] to me As Soon As Possable So I Conclud(e) with my kind love to you all and Still Remain your Unfortunate Son

Richard Dillingham

there Is one thing that I the writer this Letter have to State to I daresay your Great Sattisfaction that Is your Son Richard I can say Is Verry [illegible] Steady for though Liquor Is verry Cheap And he have the means and the opportunity of Geting it he Never gets more than do him Good Rum Is 2s the Pint and that Is the Cheif that Is drank Wine Is verry Cheap It Is 9d the Pint and the Cape Wine Is 7d the Pint the distance from England to Vandemans Land Is 18000 Miles and It Is day here when it Is Night in England

2.11 Chain gang

An example of the convict narratives that stress the horrors of life in the colonies — to be read together with Document 2.10, to get a sense of the variety of experiences undergone by convicts. After this episode, the writer tried to escape.

Source: C. A. King, *A Warning Voice from a Penitent Convict*, London, 1840.

An order having been issued that all the convicts must leave the town of Sydney, he was transferred into a road party, and where they were working there was also chained to a gang; and there, for the first time, he saw the miseries of transportation. Long before the stars had left the skies they were roused to work, and after partaking of a miserable breakfast of homily, they went to work under a guard of soldiers. The clanking of their chains was most dismal.—Every gang had a pair of triangles; and, for the most trivial offence, or act of disobedience. they were brought before a military man, the case was stated to him, and the convict was immediately tied up and flogged, and then sent to work again under the heat of a burning sun, and this might be repeated two or three times a-day for the least offence. At night they all lay together in one apartment, with only a little bark as a bed, and should a word be spoken, or the least noise heard, the offender was ordered up by the sentinel on duty. and he was either handcuffed or his hands tied behind him. and compelled to stand in the place till morning, and sent as usual to his work afterwards. It was here his life became a burden to him. One night, after working all day, he looked around him, and saw 300 men, all breakers of their country's laws, and for the first time in his life he felt the degraded and debased situation in which he was placed, and thought of obtaining his liberty.

2.12 Floggings

Details of the effects of flogging, collected by the colonial government in response to complaints by some pastoralists that punishments were too lenient. The names following those of the convicts are the ships in which they were transported.

Source: House of Commons, Select Committee on Transportation of 1837, *Report . . .*, Appendix no. 2, pp. 87–90.

James Clayton, Phoenix, absent without leave and neglecting his duty, 50 lashes. The skin was lacerated at the fifth lash, and there was a slight effusion of blood: the prisoner subdued his sense of pain by biting his lips. The skin of this man was thick to an uncommon degree, and both his body and mind have been hardened by former punishments, and he is also known to be what is termed "flash," or "game;" nevertheless, I am of opinion, that if all his former (or perhaps only his first) punishments had been as vigorously administered as this last, his indomitable spirit would have been subdued.

Thomas Holdsworth, Parmelia, pilfering from his master, 50 lashes. At the first lash the prisoner uttered piercing screams, and continued screaming at each succeeding lash, and appeared to suffer greatly; the fifth lash brought blood, and the flesh was considerably lacerated at the conclusion of the punishment. This man says he was never flogged before, nor did there appear on his back any marks of former punishment. I am of opinion that he was sufficiently punished at the 25th lash, for his bodily strength was nearly exhausted, as was manifested by his staggering gait when cast loose.

Joseph Kenworthy, Camden, accessary to pilfering from his master, 50 lashes. The first lash elicited loud cries from this prisoner; at the 18th lash the blood appeared; at the 25th lash the blood was trickling, and at the 32d flowing down his back; the bleeding continued until the end of the punishment. This man was very severely punished. I am of opinion that he would have been sufficiently punished at the 25th lash. He says he was never flogged before; his back exhibited no signs of former punishment; he was very fat, with a thin skin. The sufferings of this prisoner were evinced by his unnerved state of body when cast loose; he could scarcely stand.

2.13 Convict resistance: Bushranging

A letter from a farmer in Van Diemen's Land describing an action by the group of bushrangers led by John Whitehead and Michael Howe. Humphrey was an extremely unpopular magistrate; the author was district constable; the burning of their stacks was thus a political act.

Source: B. Reardon to J. Piper, 8 April 1815, Piper Papers, vol. 3, Mitchell Library, A256, pp. 787–9.

. . . thare as been nothing else hear for this Twelve Months Past but Roberies Committed, and driving Hurds of Cattle and focks of Sheepe in to thay woods, it is Dun Principalley by Banditeys of men that are Rainging of thay wods I Expect you have heard of thay loss i Met with on thay ninth of March last in thay Ded of thay night sum malissis Scoundrells set fire to Two of my Corn Stacks which set fire to Five more and to my barn which was Consumed to hasshes without saving a single Busshell of weate out of aney of thay Stacks or aney Part of thay Corn, thay fire was one of thay most Dredfull Sites i Ever saw no person Could git within fifty yards of it, it was with a grate Difficulty that i Saved my Hows which was one Hundred yards from thay fire, ad it not been discovered before it was Long on fire my wife and two Poure littell girls most likely would have been Burned in thare Beds which would have been thay worst Loss of all, I did not luse less then two thowsend Bushells of grane Likewise a barn which was thay best one that Ever was bilt in this Countaurey that Caust me Five Hundred Pounds Stirling, Mr Humphreys Stacks were set fire to about fifteen minuts after mine according to thay best of my Jugment from thay apperince of thay fire wen i saw it about ½ a mile distent from mine—hee Lost about Eight Hundred Bushells of weat, It is Expected by thay Gentalman hear that Colnell Macquarie will in sum measure Remunirate us for our Loss and if he Shuld bee so inclined i trust that you will Stande my friende in aney thinge you Can say to Him on thay bisness.

2.14 Convict resistance: The Castle Hill rising

Narrative of the rising and its suppression, in a private letter from the commander of the troops. Governor King's handwriting was notoriously difficult to read. 'Death or Liberty' had been a slogan of the rebels in Ireland a few years before, who were sometimes referred to as 'croppies'. Cunningham was hanged, wounded, the next day.

Source: G. Johnston to J. Piper, 12 April 1804, Piper Papers, vol. 3, Mitchell Library, A256, pp. 325–30.

Annandale,
Ap.[l] 12.th 1804

Dear Piper

I receiv'd yours of the 20th. of February, on on Sunday 4th: Ult[mo]: & that very night at twelve oClock I was awoke out of my sleep, & inform'd that a Trooper wanted to speak to me, when I got up he inform'd me the Governor was just behind & wanted to see me, I immediatly walk'd to the Parramatta road & soon after he came up, he acquainted me the Cropy's were in Arms to the number of 5 or 600 & that before he left Sydney he had given directions for a Detachment of 2 Serj[ts]: & 52 rank & file under the command of Lieu[t]. Davies & Quarter Master Laycock to proceed to my House, when I was to take them under my orders & proceed directly to Parramatta, about ½ past one in the Morn[g]. of the 5th: the Detachment arriv'd & having ascertain'd that they were all loaded & good flints in their Pieces, I form'd an advanced guard, & march'd the rest in four sub devisions or rather sections (which just fill'd the road) to Parramatta, where we arriv'd at the dawn of day . . . the Governor gave me his Orders in *Writing* how to proceed, & seeing I could not make it out, he said he supposed I cou'd not read it, I told him no, he might as well have given me Greek he then read it himself, which was, that with half the Detach[t]. I was to go in quest of the Rebels who had lately been at the Park Gate to the number of 5 or 600 & if I did not meet them there, to proceed to Toongabbé, & then wheel in to the right & go to Castle Hill, where I was to wait for further orders, but in one part of them he desir'd me to fire upon any person that attempted to run away when call'd to, which I told him was all I wanted; I directly divided the Detachment giving L[t]. Davies the Command of the left Division (& who had different instructions) & taking Mr. Laycock & the other half with me I march'd as quick as possible to Toongabbé, on our arrival I was inform'd there were four hundred of the Rebels laying on the top of Sugar loaf hill, all well arm'd, I instantly detachd the Corp[l]. with the advanced Guard (5 in all) with about 6 or 8 Inhabitants (arm'd with Musquets) by the Hawkesbury road to take them in flank, whilst Laycock & myself with the rest of the soldiers & about 12 arm'd Inhabitants ascended the face of the Hill behind Doctor Masons, & when we gain'd the sumit we found they had push'd on for the Hawkesbury & by every account we could learn there were at least 400 of them, I immediatly advanced as rapidly as possible (the day being intensely hot) & having heard before we arriv'd at the Governm[t] Stock fence that they were not above a mile before us I desir'd Handlesack (the only Trooper I had with me) to take my Handkerchief & wave to them as a flag of truce & acquaint them them the Governor was coming, as I thought that might delay them whilst we were gaining ground upon them—He went to them & spoke to them but they wou'd hear no terms, they however took the flints out of his Pistols & & allowed him to return, I then sent Dixon the Priest to them, (still with a view of detaining them) but they wou'd not listen to him; shortly after having taken one prisoner arm'd with a fusee that had separated from them, & understanding from him they were not above half a mile before us I ask'd the Trooper if he was affraid to ride up along with me to speak to them, he replied he wou'd go to hell with me (I desired Laycock to push on with the soldiers,) & we immediately gallop'd after them; when we came up with them I call'd to them to stop that I wanted to speak to them, they desir'd me to come into the middle of them as their Captains were there, I told them their Captains must have very little spirit if they wou'd not come & speak to me as I was within Pistol shot of them (& I do assure you expected to be compleatly riddled every minute) at length two men of the names of Johnston & Cuningham came from amongst them, when I reason'd with them upon the impropriety of their conduct they wou'd not hear it, I told them I only wish'd to stop the effusion of blood & that I wou'd even bring their Priest up to convince them they were wrong & desir'd them to Persuade the People to surrender, whilst I return'd to bring up the Priest I soon join'd the Detachment, & desiring Laycock to push forward with the soldiers (10 file our only front) I rode again within Pistol shot of the Rebels, & call'd to speak with the two People I had before seen, with some reluctance they again came to me, (whilst their Main Body form'd line on the second Hill on this side the last half way Pond) the Priest as well as myself spoke to them, wishing them to surrender to prevent Bloodshed, which they wou'd not listen to, at last I ask'd Cuningham what he wanted? his reply was Death or Liberty, I instantly cock'd a Pistol I had stuck in my sash, & clapping it to his head order'd him instantly to join the Detachment, (that just then appear'd in sight) else I wou'd blow his soul to Hell the Trooper did the same by the other, & in this Manner we drove them forcibly into the Detachment, which I order'd to advance & fire & instantly charge, the firing immediatly commenced & both sides & the Rebels soon fled in all directions, when we join'd (after the pursuit at the last Pond we found 9 Kill'd) & since that there has been six more found 6 or 7 wounded, & when we arriv'd at the Hawkesbury we had 26 Prisoners, 27 stand of arms that we took from the Rebels, besides, Pistols, Cutlasses, Bayonets Pikes & Pitchforks. — I never in my life saw men behave better than those under my command, & the only fault I had to find with them was their being too fond of Blood, for I do assure you I sav'd the lives of 6 miserable wretches, that the soldiers wou'd have butcher'd, if I had not presented my Pistol at their heads & swore I wou'd shoot them if they attempted to kill them in cold blood. —

2.15 Status consciousness and sexual code

Extract from a letter by one officer of the New South Wales Corps to another, about the scandalous behaviour of a third, in Sydney.

Source: E. Abbott to J. Piper, 30 October 1805, Piper Papers, vol. 1, Mitchell Library, A254, pp. 61–4.

It gives me extreme uneasiness to relate to you any unpleasant news concerning any person belonging to this Corps, and especially about Mr. Laycock senior whose conduct has been so extremely improper since his wife has left the Colony as to be noticed by almost every person and if possible every succeeding day has been marked in him with some some fresh act of folly, indecency or un-officer-like behaviour, After having been admonished by the Major without making any amendment, and his setting all authority at defiance, in using threats and language in the public Streets of the most mutinous tendency he was at last put into arrest at large. Here, one would naturally have imagined (who knew Laycock at all) he would have been brought to his senses but instead of which his behaviour continued as I am informed worse if possible on which account he has since been confin'd to a close arrest, and it is in agitation to send him a prisoner to England for want of officers to try him here; as there is only one officer at Head Quarters who could sit on his trial, and also but one could be had from the out posts, nor could his Son sit for obvious reasons. It is with regret that I add the father's bad example has been follow'd by the Son—You will perhaps scarcely credit that Lt Laycock escorted his fathers convict whore through the streets arm and arm on duty in full Regimentals & had the indecency to walk with her on the public parade last Sunday whilst the Band of the Regiment was playing—I have given you but a concise account of the business, as I wish to fill my letter if possible with something more agreeable to you.

2.16 Club gentility

Selections from the Rules of the South Australian Club, established in the early days of the settlement. It later collapsed, and in due course its place was filled by the celebrated Adelaide Club.

Source: *Established Rules and Regulations for the Government of the South Australian Club*, Adelaide, 1838.

Rules and Regulations

of

THE SOUTH AUSTRALIAN CLUB

I.

Establishment of the Club.

The SOUTH AUSTRALIAN CLUB shall consist of Gentlemen, resident in the Province.

II.

Admission of Strangers.

That the signatures of any three members of the club shall authorise the admission of any *Stranger* to the benefits of the club, for the space of *one* month *only*, such members being answerable for his gentlemanly conduct....

V.

Members and Candidates.

That the following gentlemen shall constitute the original members of the club:—

[A list of sixty-one names follows.]

All future members to be ballotted for by the general body, one black ball in ten to exclude, such ballot to take place the first Monday in every month.

VI.

That from the 10th of August, any gentleman wishing to become a member of the club, must be proposed by a member, and seconded by a member, at least fourteen days previous to his being ballotted for, the name of the candidate, proposer, and seconder, to be inserted in the book of candidates. No ballot shall be valid unless twenty members actually ballot....

VIII.

Entrance and subscription.

The entrance fee shall be ten guineas, and the annual subscription shall be two guineas payable in advance; the year to commence 1st January, 1839; except the original members, whose entrance fees already paid, cover all subscriptions to 1st January, 1840....

XXVIII.

Any member wilfully infringing the rules and regulations of the club, or the ordinances of the committee, or whose conduct in and out of the club after his election shall, in the opinion of the committee, be derogatory to his station in society, shall be subject to expulsion, under the award of a general meeting, which it shall be the duty of the committee expressly to convene, for the purpose of investigating the charges brought against such member; the opinion of such general meeting to be obtained by ballot; when, if two thirds of the members present at such general meeting decide that the offending member has merited expulsion, he shall thereon cease to be a member of the club; his subscription for the present year being returned to him.

2.17 Household structure in pastoral expansion

Domestic organisation from the point of view of a squatter's wife, in the northern district of South Australia.

Source: M. Cudmore to her brother and sister, 3 December 1837, Cudmore Family Papers, Hayes Collection, Fryer Memorial Library, University of Queensland.

Wilachra Creek Dec 3—1837

My dear Brother & Sister

I should have written to you long since but I expected to move farther north & Dan talked of going to Port Lincoln to purchase some sheep but his men mutinied which prevented his going. I was very much obliged to them as I felt very uneasy at his going as the Blacks have killed several people there, I fear the daily Employment in the bush wont interest you much. I lived all last year with the children at the old run we get up at six in summer the children are put in a cold bath by the Irish servant girl every morning all the year, then breakfast, then I teach them Spelling reading writing figures untill one when we dine, then needlework at four when the children go for the Cows, at five we have tea and put the calves up feed the fowls, and Dimmy reads the Bible and we go to bed this is the way we spend the summer, we make our own bread and yeast with hops I have 3 Cows & we scald the milk when it is twelve hours old and scim it when it is 48 hours old which makes the cream very easy to churn in cold weather increases the quantity of butter and keeps the milk quite sweet in the very hot weather for the children to drink, when the rain comenced Dan sent down a flock of sheep with the rams which the children were obliged to mind, then our troubles began nothing will please a shepherd, and we had the yard to shift every day with the servant girl 62 hurdles & sometimes raining all the time, as Dan stayed at the new run and our doing so saved 18/ a week for a hut-keeper, the first of September Dan and all the sheep shearers drays horses Bullocks & & came packed us all up and sent us off to his lambing station as he wanted to shear in the house as it was built for that purpose, in a month the shearing was over and we were ordered to pack up and be ready to start to the new run we sent all the things on the bullock dray and we followed in the horse dray driven by the girl, and Dan rode after with the cows, as, James started a week before with two flocks of sheep, and Uncle Robert who came while we were sharing with his son he left his daughter with mother in Adelaide— . . . [story of journey and a lost child] . . . we rested for a forthnight at one of the winter stations and Dan went in search of the Bullock dray. he found it broken down he had to ride 60 miles to borrow one. he came back in a week and took us over flinders range where a white woman or child never went before, you may judge of the terrible journey we had when it took two days to go 10 miles walking nearly all the way and draging the luggage up every hill we crossed as the horse could not take it up, we stoped 2 months at another winter station where the water lasts untill Ja[nuary] while Dan went to town and got up building materi[al] and built the kitchen wing of a house on the Willachra creek.

2.18 A craftsman's social outlook

Discussion of politics and conditions in the furniture trade in Van Diemen's Land, in a letter home to England. 'Mr Cole' is the author's brother-in-law, a carpenter.

Source: G. Best to W. Christmas, 17 May 1837, Archives Office of Tasmania, NS 252 A.

My Dear Brother

Time when fully employed flies quick and day after day passes almost imperceptibly but as Coulton says "Wisdom walks before it, opportunity with it, and repentance behind" had we the gift of prescience we are apt to think we could live to better purpose doing this and omitting the other so had I come out here 5 years ago in all probality I might now be rich but had I stayed at Richmond I might now have been in your much loved society but were you all here I would then give the preference to this place, as it is I may not be rich but having health & Gods blessing on my labor, shall live with rather less care & anxiety than in England and my children may reap the fruits if they are industrious, the want of which is often seen in the victims of the Emigration Society a parcel of useless drones who eat up the food without increasing the resources of the colony coming here with high expectations which when they find not realized they take to drinking & both men & women for the most part are living nuisances—indeed we have quite mechanics enough of the lower order, the poor are sent from England to pauperize this Colony and relieve your parishes at the expense of this, we have of late had large importations of them, and furniture, but which furniture does not appear to affect us at present as on Account of the cheapness of cedar we are able to make up furniture at less expence and nearly as good looking being all solid it stands well while the english being veneered it is constantly coming to pieces, but to obtain a profit & get sale for his furniture a man must labor himself or he will gain but little, a good workman will not work for another under 7/ or 8/– a day, while many indifferent hands work on their own account and do not average so much—I expect you have heard we have a new Governor Sir John Franklin, he was received with every testimony of respect, much is expected from him, and I fear more than is possible to be realized as of course he will act from orders, which however detrimental to the Colony must be adhered to, as for instance it is much desired to see the present system of land regulations abolished, we see occasionally a wealthy propritor making a large purchase or squaring up his property by buying a mile or two of rocky tier to save him fences—but the country beyond is but little explored—under the present system a man may spend some weeks or months in Seeking for land & when put up to sale it is snatched from him by the wealthy, or indolent, or the land jobbing Jew, the thing most desirable appears to be the sale of land at fixed prices, varying from 3/– to 5/– per acre with *personal occupancy and improvements* as the *indispensable conditions* at present there are many estates of from 1 to 5000 acres and some even 12000 acres and do not cultivate corn enough for the consumption of their own Laborers, but the whole in a state of nature for sheep runs allowing one acre for one sheep and for the most part boundary fences of rock or rivulet at once defeating the designs of the legislature & making us tributary for corn &c but in many places the land if obliged to be fenced in is not worth having at a gift and therefore requires to be searched for if required for small farms, there has been great speculations in Land, and in many cases losses have ensued, the land has been thought to be invaluable through a sort of mania, but which bubble has now burst as better land is found at Port Phillip & other places and then as to Town Allotments the holders have kept them back so long that now these are falling instead of rising except in *very good* situations those who came out about 10 years ago have enriched themselves by obtaing free grants of land and Town allotments and selling them without any improvements except fencing which has produced them thousands, many of whom have returned to England leaving others to fight about titles and quit rents to their ruin, a linen draper of the name of Cameron who lately returned to England has sent out 74 packages of chairs, and another of the name of Welch sent out Cabinet furniture bought of Siddons to the ammout of £950 some of which is selling off by auction, another Linen draper of the name of Robertson left about 2 months ago intending to send out goods of all kinds. his brother managing the business in his absence as they are partners—there have been many failures here and not to be wondered at as many transact their business in a careless mad headed way and then escape by benefit as they call it of the insolvent act, two Carpenters fail'd to the Amt of £7000 they kept from 20 to 30 men and *kept no books* of course their contracts were lower than others and they took care to draw money in advance & left some of them unfinished—

...I go on much as usual in business but there is but little doing just now owing to a stagnation in the money market. I think I keep one man and an assigned servant who is very useful as he polishes & we are very comfortable having all the necessaries & some of the luxuries of life for which I wish to be thankful to the Great Giver of all good we have a nice little garden out of which we had some melons a short time ago, apples we have bought at 5/- a bushel potatoes from 5/- to 6/- the Cwt—we all live on very good terms having each others welfare at heart the business is carried on in my name and David has what he can do. James works for him now as a journeyman and has one apprentice, I have the trouble of looking after the orders & the money for which he allows me 5 per cent—Mr Cole has plenty of work in the building line. he generally attends Mr Price (Independent) D.B. the Scotch church & I Mr D [ ] the two first are rather of the modern stamp but Mr Dowling has a very [ ] congregation chiefly his own family (about 20 in all) but he Recieves a Stipend [ ] as well from Goverment as Catechist or teacher to the convicts of as I have heard £150 per annum he is going to build a chapel, Mr Price is building one as large as that in the vineyard without gallery so we shall have plenty of chapels—

...Since writing the above the Governor has very properly stopped Emigration of the poor for the present, that Marshall ought to be hanged for the misery he has entailed on hundreds of poor sent out here and most of the female emigrants are on the Town—it is the rich settlers we want no one ought to come without some little money if it is only to keep them till they get into employ. I will send you a paper in which you will see a letter written by our Cole on emigration which is worth reading—people imajine there is employ as soon as they arrive & high wages forgetting it is only by strict economy & denial of many things which they may have accustomed themselves to, that money is saved, for London porter is 1/- per pot and gin 7d a glass butter 2/- per lb cheese 1/6 lb all of which may be dispensed with, there are so many of the convicts here equal to the free labor that they, get employed first, being cheaper & on the whole as little trouble, as the greater number of the free in general are both idle & saucy as well as intemperate, habits they contract on board of ship in coming out.

2.19 Social hierarchy

A discussion of social morality and a critique of social mobility from the point of view of the educated. Note the image of society as a pyramid depending on the health of all its parts, a common eighteenth-century view.

Source: *Sydney Gazette*, 7 August 1803.

To the Printer of the Sydney Gazette,

SIR,

By an attentive perusal of a Moral Contemplation contained in your Publication of last Week, I feel it my duty to assist the exertions of AMICUS, however feeble my capacity.

A consciousness of the blessings we enjoy may truly be considered as indispensible to human happiness; though we oftentimes regard with thankless indifference those comforts, to have hoped for which might in all probability at a former period have been considered a presumption; whence it may be generally inferred that ambition is subservient more to our immediate circumstance than to the dominion of reason, and that we sometimes sacrifice the blessings of composure and tranquillity to indulging in the anticipations of unbridled fancy.

From the word ambition may be understood a desire to be, or perhaps only to be considered as moving in a sphere, or being possessed of qualities to which we may not reasonably pretend. These qualities may be briefly distinguished into natural and accidental; the first existing in the mind, the latter derived from the possession of riches, both of which are capable of improvement, and of being applied to the general advantage of society, few are stimulated to obtain a rank with the former; but many supposing the latter within their reach perpetually devote themselves to hope, doubt, and fear alternately, and in pursuit of a shadow, lose the substance altogether....

Society may be compared with a magnificent structure, which step by step ascends to its most elevated and exalted pinnacle, the symmetry of which is equally dependent upon all its parts; in either of these if an imperfection be discovered, it must, for the benefit of the whole, be rooted out. To the human mind the allusion may also be applied, as a single blemish must disfigure, and if not eradicated in time, destroy the fabric. Most of our evils orginate in discontent of our circumstances and situations, to alter or AMEND which, recourse is too frequently had to a precipitancy by which we are enveloped in surrounding storms.

It may fastidiously be argued that contentment is not indiscriminately attainable to every rank in life; but to so shallow a presumption it may be answered, that the blessing exists only in the mind, in which it assumes an angel shape, that can minister consolation in the most humble retreat.

The labouring orders in this Colony are amply furnished with the materials requisite to contentment in the exercise of industry, and the consequent reward to all that are deserving. The fields and forests alike present resources, and their comforts are lessened or increased by their frugality, oeconomy, and perseverance. These are essential qualities, easy of attainment, and principally constitute the duties of the poor.

PHILO

2.20 Moral ascendancy

Extracts from the first section of the exclusives' petition of 1836 on legal and constitutional reform, conveying the intense status anxiety of the gentry faced with ex-convict wealth.

Source: J. Macarthur (attrib.), *New South Wales; Its Present State and Future Prospects*..., Walther, London, 1837, Appendix 2.

TO
THE HONORABLE, THE COMMONS OF
GREAT BRITAIN, IN PARLIAMENT
ASSEMBLED;

THE humble PETITION of the undersigned
Members of Council, Magistrates,
Clergy, Landholders, Merchants, and
other Free Inhabitants of New South
Wales,

RESPECTFULLY SHEWETH;

THAT although the Colony of New South Wales, as regards its Agriculture, Commerce, and Revenue, presents an aspect of extraordinary and unexampled prosperity, yet, apprehending the best interests of this community to be threatened with serious danger, which a timely enquiry may avert, your Petitioners feel it to be their duty, on the occasion of the expiration of the existing Act of Parliament, and the enactment of a new Law for the Government of the Colony, humbly to submit, for the consideration of your Honourable House, a statement of the principal evils they are at present exposed to, and the grounds of their apprehensions for the future.

Your Petitioners would, in the first place, entreat the attention of your Honorable House to the fearful increase of crime that has of late years taken place in this Colony....

Your Petitioners would, in the next place, beg to advert to the existing Colonial Law for the regulation of Juries in the Supreme Court, and in the Courts of Quarter Sessions; by the provisions of which law, individuals who have undergone sentence of transportation, and other ignominious punishments, as well as persons of bad repute and low standing in society, have been placed upon a footing with Magistrates and Colonists of the highest respectability....

That if persons who have undergone punishment for their crimes, and of bad repute, be entitled to sit as Jurors, the same reasoning, carried a step farther, would render them eligible as Judges—a proposition revolting to every right feeling, and too monstrous to be for a moment entertained....

That the law, in its present shape, was passed through the Legislative Council, in opposition to the votes and conscientious opinions of the most experienced and independent members; and, as your Petitioners are informed, was intended merely as an experiment, the failure of which, they have reason to believe, is now fully admitted by the supporters of the measure.

That one of the obvious and natural effects of this law is to encourage crime, by the facility it affords to the guilty to devise plans for ensuring acquittal; whilst its operation, on the other hand, as regards innocent persons, might be such as your Petitioners tremble even to think of, were its pernicious tendency not restrained by the right which is still left in criminal cases, to the party upon trial, to demand a Jury of military officers. And your Petitioners would humbly submit, that if the law be continued upon the same principle as at present, and extended to all cases, both criminal and civil, it will necessarily have the effect of deterring men of character from investing capital, or becoming settlers, in the Colony, and prove a manifest injustice to the emigrant, and the native-born inhabitants, and to all persons of respectability, of whatever class; who will thus be virtually deprived of the right of trial by their peers, in cases involving property, reputation, liberty, and life; and that too, in a community in which perjury is of every-day occurrence.

Your Petitioners would entreat your Honourable House to bear in mind, that from the facility of acquiring wealth in New South Wales, by dishonest and disreputable practices, the possession of property affords but slight proof of good character; a state of things which your Petitioners are of opinion must necessarily prevail, so long as transportation is continued, unless an entire change in the management and discipline of the convicts can be effected, which, under the present circumstances of the Colony, they conceive to be hopeless, and almost impracticable.

Your Petitioners would therefore humbly submit, that if it be proposed to confer free institutions upon this Community, property ought not to form the sole standard for the regulations of the elective and representative franchises. . . .

[signed by:]

6	Members of the Legislative Council.
57	Justices of the Peace.
4	Clergymen, including the principal Chaplain of the Colony.
5	Solicitors of the Supreme Court.
355	Landholders, Merchants, and other Colonists.
427	Total.

2.21 A vision of progress

A fantasy of the future of Australia, supposing that the inland rivers recently discovered by John Oxley flowed across the continent to the north-west coast.

Source: W. C. Wentworth, *A Statistical, Historical, and Political Description of the Colony of New South Wales* . . ., Whittaker, London, 1819, pp. 77–89.

If the sanguine hopes to which the discovery of this river has given birth, should be realized, and it should be found to empty itself into the ocean, on the north-west coast, which is the only part of this vast island that has not been accurately surveyed, in what mighty conceptions of the future greatness and power of this colony, may we not reasonably indulge? The nearest distance from the point at which Mr. Oxley left off, to any part of the western coast, is very little short of two thousand miles. If this river, therefore, be already of the size of the Hawkesbury at Windsor, which is not less than two hundred and fifty yards in breadth, and of sufficient depth to float a seventy-four gun-ship, it is not difficult to imagine what must be its magnitude at its confluence with the ocean; before it can arrive at which it has to traverse a country nearly two thousand miles in extent. If it possess the usual sinuosities of rivers, its course to the sea cannot be less than from five to six thousand miles, and the endless accession of tributary streams which it must receive in its passage through so great an extent of country, will without doubt enable it to vie in point of magnitude with any river in the world. In this event its influence in promoting the progress of population in this fifth continent, will be prodigious, and in all probability before the expiration of many years, give an entirely new impulse to the tide of population: and here it may not be altogether irrelevant, to enter into a short disquisition on the natural superiority possessed by those countries which are most abundantly intersected with navigable rivers. [He does so, at length.]

The probable course of this newly discovered river, being thus in every respect so decidedly favourable for the foundation of a rich and powerful community, there can be little doubt that the government of this country will immediately avail itself of the advantages which it presents, and establish a settlement at its mouth. What a sublime spectacle will it then be for the philosopher to mark the gradual progress of population from the two extremities of this river; to behold the two tides of colonization flowing in opposite directions, and constantly hastening to that junction, of which the combined waters shall overspread the whole of this fifth continent!

What a cheering prospect for the philanthropist to behold what is now one vast and mournful wilderness, becoming the smiling seat of industry and the social arts; to see its hills and dales covered with bleating flocks, lowing herds, and waving corn; to hear the joyful notes of the shepherd, and the enlivening cries of the husbandman, instead of the appalling yell of the savage, and the plaintive howl of the wolf; and to witness a country which nature seems to have designed as her master-piece, at length fulfilling the gracious intentions of its all-bounteous Author, by administering to the wants and contributing to the happiness of millions.

What a proud sight for the Briton to view his country pouring forth her teeming millions to people new hives, to see her forming in the most remote parts of the earth new establishments which may hereafter rival her old; and to behold thousands who would perish from want within her immediate limits, procuring an easy and comfortable subsistence in those which are more remote; and instead of weakening her power and diminishing her resources, effectually contributing to the augmentation of both, and forming monuments which may descend to the latest posterity, indestructible records of her greatness and glory.

2.22 Democratic movement: Representation of the people

The ideas of the Political Association of Van Diemen's Land, formed in the same year as the Patriotic Association in Sydney, though not nearly as successful an organisation.

Source: *Rules and Regulations of the Political Association*, *of Van Diemen's Land*, Bent, Hobart, 1835.

The following are the objects of the POLITICAL ASSOCIATION, *established in Van Diemen's Land—passed by a General Meeting of Members of the Association*, *October* 19, 1835.

I.—To obtain by every just and loyal means, a REAL AND EFFECTUAL REPRESENTATION OF THE PEOPLE OF VAN DIEMEN'S LAND.

II.—To enquire, consult, consider, and determine, respecting the rights and liberties of the People of Van Diemen's Land, and respecting the legal means of preserving those we are in possession of, and obtaining those we have a right to, but which we do not possess.

III.—To prepare Petitions, Addresses, and Remonstrances, to the Crown and Legislative Bodies, respecting the *preservation and restoration of our rights as*

British subjects, also, respecting the repeal of *bad laws*, and the enactment of *good laws*.

IV.—To prevent and redress, as far as practicable, *all local public wrongs and oppressions, and all local encroachments* upon the rights, interests, and privileges of the community.

V.—To promote peace, union, and concord, among all classes of His Majesty's subjects in this Colony, and to guide and direct the public mind into peaceful, uniform, and legitimate operations....

The following are the Rules and Regulations of the POLITICAL ASSOCIATION *of Van Diemen's Land*:—

I.—The Constitution of this Society is essentially popular. It admits as equal Members, all Free Persons whatever, whose names shall be registered on the Roll of Association, so long as they shall conform to the Rules and Regulations thereof.

II.—The general management of the affairs of the ASSOCIATION is committed to a COUNCIL, chosen annually at a GENERAL MEETING of the MEMBERS of the ASSOCIATION, and subject only to the controul of each annual or other yearly Meeting.

III.—All Persons becoming Members of the Association, are expected to contribute such donations, and weekly or quarterly subscriptions, as they can conveniently afford, the subscriptions not being more than one shilling per week....

The following are the Duties of the Members of the POLITICAL ASSOCIATION OF VAN DIEMEN'S LAND:—

I.—To be good, faithful, and loyal subjects of the King of Great Britain.

II.—To obey the Laws of the Land; and where *they* cease to protect the Rights, Liberties, and Interests of the Community, to endeavour to get them changed by just, legal, and peaceful means, ONLY.

III.—To present themselves to all General Meetings of the Political Association, as far as they conveniently can; to conduct themselves legally and peacefully at such Meetings, and to depart to their respective homes, as soon as the Chairman shall leave the Chair.

IV.—To choose only just, upright, and able men, as Members of the POLITICAL COUNCIL, and to dismiss them, and elect others in their stead, whenever they shall cease to watch over, and defend the RIGHTS, LIBERTIES, and INTERESTS of the PEOPLE.

V.—To obey strictly all the just and legal directions of the POLITICAL COUNCIL, so soon as they shall be made public, and so far as they can legally and conveniently be obeyed.

VI.—To bear in mind that the strength of our Association consists in the PEACE, ORDER, *unity*, and LEGALITY of our proceedings; and to consider all persons as enemies, who shall, in any way, invite or promote violence, discord, or division, or any illegal or doubtful measures.

VII.—Never to forget that by the exercise of the above qualities, we shall produce the peaceful display of an immense organised moral power, which cannot be despised or disregarded; but that if we do not keep clear of the *immediate and intricate laws* which surround us, the *Lawyer* and the *Soldier* will, probably, break in upon us, and render all our exertions vain.

3 Hegemony of the Mercantile Bourgeoisie, 1840–1890

Capitalist Institutions

When the *Empire* in 1853 asked, 'Is Capital property or not?', in the early stages of the struggle between pastoral 'property' and urban 'capital', changes in the institutional framework of colonial capitalism were just beginning. By the end of this period, there would be a reduction in the sphere of the state, an expansion of property relationships and, inevitably, a decline in the opportunities for self-employment. The triumph of urban capital, which established a 'fully fledged market system', increasingly transformed work into wage labour.[1]

The major contraction in the sphere of the state occurred when convict transportation to eastern Australia ended in the early 1850s. In the labour market, the retreat of state intervention had begun much earlier. The bargaining relationship that grew up between assigned convicts and their private employers reduced the state's role in the discipline of convict labour. Then in 1839 the supply of convict labour to private employers was abolished. By this time, state-assisted immigration had vastly expanded the free labour market, but the abolition of assignment came just as the depression of the early 1840s put enormous pressure on the squatters to reduce their labour costs. They asked for the revival of transportation. The reversal of state policy on transportation was impossible in such a short period, but the British government did produce a sanitised version of convictism to assist the squatters. Known as 'exile-ism', this scheme allowed convicts, supposedly partially reformed before transportation, to enter the free labour market in eastern Australia. Of course, the 'exiles' were not really free labour because their movement was restricted and they depended on the state for their ultimate release from bondage. Only about three thousand exiles arrived before the early 1850s, but their effects — the reduction of wage rates and the stigmatisation of free labour — were well understood by colonial workers, who began to mobilise against transportation in 1846. The movement grew, became a major issue in the crystallisation of colonial urban bourgeois politics, and achieved its ends after the gold-rushes convinced the British government that bourgeois dominance was feasible in the colonies. Although the state continued to be involved in the supply of free labour to all colonies through assisted immigration, and although in Queensland it regulated the private supply of identured coloured labour, this was the end of the insertion of state supplied and controlled labour into the labour market.[2]

The role of the judicial arm of the state in the discipline of labour also diminished in this period as pastoral employment declined relative to urban employment and mining. As a free labour market developed in the pastoral industry, the colonies passed Masters and Servants Acts to make the labour contract enforceable (on both sides, but as the preamble to the 1828 Act in New South Wales said, it was mainly 'for the better regulation of servants, labourers and workpeople') and to protect the property of the master against spoilage or loss by workers. These provisions accurately reflected the type of resistance engaged in by workers in the early pastoral industry; they were less effective when workers in the expanding urban labour market embarked on collective resistance, or when absconding from pastoral employment became a mass phenomenon during the gold-rushes. The exact details of how the Masters and Servants Acts fell into disuse are not clear. We may suppose that the labour shortage of the 1850s was crucial and that the gold-seeking immigrants who had expected to achieve independence were not disposed to sign long-term contracts at fixed wages, especially given the rate of inflation. When jobs became scarcer from the 1860s onwards, some urban workers were obliged to sign contracts that they later regretted. There were cases in the courts of immigrant tradesmen charged with absconding, or sometimes with breaking their agreement through striking. But increasingly, employers of urban labour relied on the constraints of the market, especially unemployment, and on the laws to protect property and prevent conspiracy, despite continuing complaints about the unreliability of the labour-force.[3]

The state also withdrew in a significant way from the organisation of private property in this period. Before 1863 in Victoria and 1874 in New South Wales, companies were incorporated by acts of the colonial parliaments, passed only after select committees had examined their viability. Between 1837 and 1874, seventy-one companies in New South Wales received this privilege, allowing their owners, a small group of finance capitalists, to avoid unlimited liability. The passage of general limited liability laws, extending this privilege as a general right of shareholders, coincided with mining booms, which involved rapid expansion of capital markets: 470 mining companies were formed in New South Wales between 1870 and 1874. The forerunner of the Sydney Stock Exchange appeared in 1872, in 'Greville's Rooms', where a number of brokers operated. In Victoria, the greater scale of mining activity produced an informal stock market and a company boom in the late 1850s and a stock exchange in 1865. So began the period of minimum state control of companies.[4]

The rush of acquisitive individuals to the goldfields in the early 1850s constituted a new area for private property. None the less, in common law, minerals belonged to the Crown, and there were at least some members of the ruling class who proposed that all mining should be carried on by the state. However, the governments of Victoria and New South Wales issued licences that, although recognising private ownership of the proceeds of mining, did not immediately overcome one major constraint on the development of market forces on the diggings. That constraint was political: the alluvial miners' attachment to the principle of economic independence created a problem of social control on the goldfields. In the course of establishing and then defending their economic independence, the alluvial miners formed associations that practised direct democracy, at first as organs of self-government (settling disputes about water rights, for example) and then, when state officials arrived on the fields, as political movements. The regime of the state officials on the fields was oppressive, basically because it was linked to policies that discriminated against the small alluvial miners in favour of large mining companies. Both Victoria and New South Wales in the early 1850s offered special leases of large tracts of land to capitalists at the same time as they stepped up the enforcement of the licence system, which was so onerous to the would-be independent diggers. Most of the agitations that developed on the diggings were potentially rebellious and eventually, at Ballarat's Eureka Stockade in December 1854, a clash of arms occurred. The diggers were crushed, but in the face of protests from a colony-wide democratic movement the Victorian government gave up its repressive strategy. It conceded to the diggers citizenship, the liberal-bourgeois solution to political resistance that challenged the power of capital in the era of working-class formation. As well as the parliamentary franchise, the diggers were given the right to elect their own regulatory bodies, the miners' courts. Of course, as the miners were expectant capitalists and as the franchise for these courts was tied to a property right (ownership of the proceeds of mining), the decisions of the courts reflected the logic of capital accumulation: larger and larger mining claims were allowed. In this way, mining companies replaced the independent and unruly diggers, and the authority of the state was confirmed. The victory of big capital in mining was recognised when mining companies became the first to receive limited liability by Acts in 1855 in Victoria and 1861 in New South Wales.[5]

As most of the land occupied by the pastoral industry up to the 1850s was Crown land, the squatters represented a major impediment to the consolidation of property relationships in eastern Australia, not because there was no right of purchase but because the privileges of Crown land occupancy 'locked up' a valuable resource. In fact, the urban capitalist opponents of the squatters were not hostile to the pastoral industry any more than they were sympathetic to the land hunger of the working men and women of the towns. Even before the series of land reforms in the three eastern mainland colonies, the pastoral industry had entered into a period of capital-intensive expansion. The most important parts of the Land Acts, as well as the way the state administered them, preserved the squatters' occupancy and discriminated against the small farmers. 'Free selection', when it figured in the Land Acts, facilitated the penetration of urban capital into the pastoral industry by encouraging the squatters to become landowners. For this they needed to borrow, and by 1890 almost half the pastoralists of New South Wales were mortgaged clients of bankers or brokers. Meanwhile, new capital formation in the industry required more labour, migratory men and women who refused to be treated as 'servants'. The great pastoral arc was throwing off the constraints of a plantation system and, by concentrating labour and capital, setting the stage for the bitter class conflicts of the 1890s.[6]

The extension of property relationships in the mining and pastoral industries inevitably extended the scope of the labour market, at first slowly and always unevenly. In the pastoral industry, while some squatters fruitlessly campaigned for the resumption of transportation, others set about importing Indian and Chinese 'coolies'. Later, sugar-planters in Queensland used indentured 'kanakas', Pacific Islanders recruited by blackbirders. In the mining industry, the first response of the independent diggers to the rigours of competition was to form co-partnerships, but there were always diggers without any capital working for wages paid by the co-partners. In agriculture, 'free selection before survey' (but without capital assistance) was a mainly symbolic compensation to ex-diggers for the decline of economic independence on the goldfields. There were a few thousand bona fide selectors, but those that survived into the 1880s frequently did so by part-time wage labour, as fencers, shearers or stockmen. The remainder of the 'independent' men who were squeezed out of the mining industry returned to wage labour in the cities and towns, but even here there were attempts by governments and private employers to promote a subcontracting system, especially in building and construction. Yet despite these imperfections in the labour market, the mainland colonies gradually developed a fairly unified labour market and the institutional framework for bourgeois and working-class politics came into existence.[7]

State Power

The history of the Australian capitalist state in this period was partly constituted by two related but ultimately divergent trends in the ruling class. First, there was the movement of urban businessmen into representative parliamentary institutions as part of the political struggle for dominance between factions of the colonial bourgeoisie, and secondly, there was the growing autonomy of the state, as the bureaucracy and a separate public sector of the economy developed in response to the victory of the urban faction. However, both these changes were in turn related to the redistribution of state power in the middle of the nineteenth century within the imperial system. Self-government for the Australian colonies and the form taken by the state in Australia were interrelated processes.

All the Australian colonies except Western Australia received self-government in the 1850s. Independence had been won by thirteen North American colonies at the end of the eighteenth century, but the 'second British empire' managed to contain the challenges to imperial power that arose in the remaining North American colonies, in the West Indies and to a lesser extent in New South Wales in the 1830s and 1840s. The imperial economy by that time rested on free trade instead of exclusive mercantilist arrangements between mother country and colony, which characterised the 'first' empire. Free trade was guaranteed by the supremacy not only of the British Navy on the trade routes but also of British industry in world markets. This made possible a contraction in the sphere of the imperial state in relation to colonies of British settlement; there was room now for the exercise of local autonomy by regional sections of the imperial ruling class in these colonies, provided that colonial interests were always subordinated to those of the mother country. The policy of free trade, of course, would have to be followed by the colonies. Further, the presssures of class conflict in Britain were rising. Colonies of British settlement were also safety-valves, where working-class immigrants could practise the constitutional liberties of free-born Englishmen that were proving so troublesome for the ruling class at home. Hence a new imperialism held together by the bonds of free trade and British 'civilisation' was bound to reproduce in the regional centres of state power the bourgeois-democratic form of government that developed in the imperial centre during the 1830s and 1840s.[8]

In the Australian colonies, the connection between the transfer of state power and the change in the form of the state was clearest in New South Wales, for it was there that class forces were most developed. The first move came when the squatters, who dominated the partly elected Legislative Council in the 1840s, sought to extend its legislative powers (so that they could secure the tenure of their pastoral runs) and to ensure that their representatives would occupy the positions of executive government. But their demand for responsible government came before the new imperial design was sufficiently clear to British statesmen. More significantly, when squatters asked for these changes, it made the British government wonder whether the time had come to concede them. The problem was not whether a colonial economic interest would interfere with an imperial economic interest, for specialisation in primary production by the colonies was to be one of the features of the imperialism of free trade. Rather, the problem was how to achieve the right balance between democratic representation and class rule in a parliamentary system. Too much democracy (and most ruling-class intellectuals thought that colonies of settlement were prone to democratic excess) would mean inefficient, *petit-bourgeois* government, which might also interfere with property; too much 'class legislation' (as it was called) from the representatives of the ruling class in the colonial legislature would lead to internal dissension and a strengthening of the democratic working-men's movement. In the Whig-liberal political rhetoric of the time, British statesmen argued that finding the balance depended on the growth of a 'middle-class' politics, that is, of an alignment of class forces resting on the appropriation by capital of skilled craft production in an urban setting, as well as of a more diversified primary production for export, and on the political leadership of urban businessmen. But in the meantime, the squatters threatened stability by their open resistance to democracy.

Thus it was not surprising that, while the North American colonies gained responsible government in the 1840s, New South Wales did not. Meanwhile, the British woollen manufacturers and shippers were lobbying on behalf of the squatters. So the Colonial Secretary, Earl Grey, attempted an act of high statesmanship: the economic interests of the squatters (and of the Empire) were to be met by the concession of leases of up to fourteen years and by the resumption of transportation, while the political fluidity of the colonies would be contained by an elaborate new constitutional system, involving a federation of the colonies and three tiers of representation, of which only the lowest, and least powerful, would be democratically elected. The protests of the colonists and British reformers killed the constitutional scheme, but in 1850 the colonies did receive a wider sphere of legislative authority and the right to alter their constitutions by providing for two houses of parliament. However, there was still no concession of responsible government.[9]

Six years later, responsible governments were inaugurated in four colonies. What happened so quickly in those years was twofold and interrelated: firstly, a further clarification among British ministers and their advisers that imperial economic and cultural ties would continue to bind to the mother country the colonies of settlement after they were self-governing and had ministers chosen by and responsible to the majority party in the popularly elected lower house. British thinking was affected by developments in various colonies of settlement: New Zealand, Jamaica, Cape Colony and Newfoundland, as well as Australia, where the gold-rushes were decisive. Running through official British assessments of Australia in the gold era were three themes: the stability of society in the face of social dislocation, because gold-mining brought wealth and wider property ownership; the fortunate coexistence of a thriving primary industry, whose products suited the imperial economy, and a growing market for British manufacturers; and a healthy British culture in a growing society of immigrant settlers. Hence, in 1852, the British government at last conceded control of land, a major productive force still, and the right to draw up new constitutions. Secondly, there was the failure, also attributable to the gold-rushes, of the democratic movements in the colonies to threaten the accumulation of capital. After raising the need for responsible self-government, and after linking it with a democratic electoral system and the composition of the upper house, the radicals lost momentum during the gold-rushes. When they returned to the battle in 1853 and 1854, they were much more moderate, defending the rights of property and dissociating themselves from 'democratic' as a party label. Not only British statesmen picked up the change; in New South Wales, conservatives revived their support for responsible government, albeit they hoped without the clamour and tension of party politics. The conservatives dominated constitution-making and although the British government removed some of the clauses of the colonial constitutions that would have favoured pastoralism, the upper houses remained conservative bastions. In the lower houses, there was to be a fair field for all starters, and so the liberal bourgeoisie prepared for party government. The British government, as well as the colonial liberals, understood that the structural preconditions for liberal democracy now existed: a weak gentry and working class and a strengthening bourgeoisie. The introduction of responsible government, therefore, occurred not only in the context of a reorganisation of imperial relationships but also of a change in the balance of class forces within the colonies.[10]

Responsible government also involved changes in the administrative arm of the state. Before 1856, boards of commissioners were often used to run such services as education, railways and aspects of public health, but one by one, as state activity grew in these areas, the boards were absorbed into ministerial departments. From time to time, political struggle developed around this change, with the liberal politicians of the urban bourgeoisie supporting the move to departmental administration, and the conservatives supporting the boards. When the conservative chairman of the National Education Board in New South Wales was sacked in 1858 for publicly rejecting the concept of cabinet responsibility, James Macarthur, the squatters and the previous officials mounted an unsuccessful campaign to have him restored. But it was in the railways, where state activity was most important, that the move to departmental arrangements occurred with the greatest speed, in the 1850s. Education departments followed in the 1870s and 1880s, but by this time the principle of political control of the administration was under attack from a new quarter—the public servants themselves and their ministers.[11]

The patronage that the departmental system afforded ministers was a crucial cement in the system of parliamentary factions that provided governments with majorities before modern parties emerged in the late 1880s. Expectation of gaining a state post created a chain of favouritism running from the cabinet into the electorate. Politicians could be rewarded in various ways, although paid positions in the emerging bureaucracy were regarded as incompatible with being a member of parliament. But there were unpaid positions on prestigious committees, contracts for public works and of course members could resign to take up a state post. Some transferred from parliament to a judgeship. In New South Wales between 1856 and 1890, about 10 per cent of the Legislative Assembly members accepted offices of profit after leaving parliament. As for overall recruitment to the public service, Victoria may serve as an example: between 1862 and 1882, only a tenth of the persons entering the public service took the examination; the rest, almost 16 000, owed their appointment to patronage.[12]

The administrative effects of patronage were not disastrous, yet in the mid-1880s a period of administrative reform began, ending two decades later in the modern public service: independently controlled, and bureaucratically integrated and regulated. One reason for reform was cost: inefficiency and bloated size made the civil service a target for financial cuts as governments struggled to balance budgets at the end of the 'long boom'. Political control, which had created this situation in the service, also had other effects. In 1885, almost half of the New South Wales Legislative Assembly were businessmen in commerce, mining or manufacturing. The problems caused by business influence in the legislatures were illustrated in Victoria in the 1880s, when small investors could not be protected from fraudulent urban land companies because 'the same persons were directing the affairs both of the government and of a number of the companies'. When the rate of company failure rose in 1891, these businessmen–politicians passed the Voluntary Liquidation Act, which severely hindered creditors and the courts in liquidation proceedings. Businessmen were also important at the top levels of the public service, and for some of them, too, it was difficult to tell where private took over from public activity. Geoffrey Eagar rose to a high position in the Bank of New South Wales before he became Treasurer of the colony and used that bank to float the largest loan up to then in New South Wales. He next spent almost twenty years as the top public servant in the Treasury department. In the location of public works, especially railways, political 'log-rolling' produced patronage of whole constituencies (the construction of branch lines increased local property values and provided local work), but the problem was the same. The overlapping personnel of the business leadership and the state elite was bringing the state into disrepute just when the expansion of state activities was necessitating greater legislative concern with the state's administration. Whether the solution was the bureaucratisation of the public service, or, as in the case of the railways, a statutory corporation, the need was to strengthen the state's legitimacy by developing its autonomy. Thus political neutrality for the administrative arm developed as a principle in the state elite. For the faction leaders in parliament it was not too harsh a blow, because of the appearance at this time of political movements in the electorate. Ultimately, however, the sectional and class conflicts of the 1890s sealed the fate of the faction system.[13]

In the economy, the autonomy of the state emerged in the 1850s and grew rapidly in the 1870s in the form of a massive programme of public capital formation. It was this separate public sector of the economy that demonstrated the state's economic autonomy by showing its ability to reorganise the capitalist class. For example, the assumption by the state of railway ownership flowed not just from the economic weakness of Australian capital but from the disorganised condition of the bourgeoisie. The mercantile faction understood the importance of railways for the expansion of the domestic market, but the squatters at the beginning of this period were distinctly indifferent to this goal. Moreover, there was always the possibility that privately owned railways, protected from competition as natural monopolies, might retard the advance of the market into the countryside by charging exorbitant rates and providing inadequate services. As merchant Robert Campbell wrote to Henry Parkes in 1854, the railways were too important to become the plaything of adventurers and stock-jobbers. By this time, liberal bourgeois journalists and politicians had found the right ideological point: railway communication, wrote the *Empire*, was 'a universal law of civilization'. The liberals in New South Wales therefore advised the government to take over the existing railway companies. The necessary infrastructural works of the public sector—railways and telegraphs, the water and sewerage works, the public buildings and assisted immigration schemes—were not simply protected from private misuse, they were necessary to the process by which the capitalist class was reorganised on a higher level. The plantation ideal of the pastoralists was weakened as the public sector legitimated the ideology of development and pastoral capital was absorbed into mercantile capital as the economy expanded on the bases of government activity. The mercantile capitalists emerged as the leading fraction of the reconstituted bourgeoisie. Thus the term 'public' in public sector really meant 'system-maintaining'; economically and ideologically, the constitutive role of the state was prominent in this period.[14]

The growing autonomy of the state did not prevent it offering direct and indirect services to particular groups of businessmen. The Land Acts served to protect the tenure of the squatters in Victoria and New South Wales, when radicals in the towns and goldfields were demanding that the lands be unlocked. Bankers were assisted in Victoria by legislation in 1864 to lend money on pastoral land. For the manufacturers, there were protective tariffs in Victoria, although they were not as effective as the radical working-men and liberal businessmen liked to believe, and in both Victoria and New South Wales, there were contracts for railway equipment. Moreover, the public sector of the economy also enriched particular businessmen, for example contractors on public works. And because public capital formation was actually a case of the state organising *private* capital, there were private profits (mostly to overseas investors) as well as 'public' benefits. Government borrowing in the London capital market also provided a shield behind which private borrowers could operate, such as the colonial land speculators who borrowed in London at 4 to 5 per cent and re-loaned in Australia at 10 per cent.[15]

The legacies of the convict system, the first stirrings of political mass action by working-men, the gold-rushes and the rural conflicts that nurtured bushranging in the 1860s and 1870s created problems of social control in this period. There was a Society for the Protection of Life and Property formed in Sydney as early as 1850. Yet there was no general mobilisation of a subordinate class and hence no need for extensive state activity to integrate the class structure. A rebellion of would-be entrepreneurs was easily crushed at Eureka in 1854 and riots were stopped or forestalled on many other goldfields by the threat of force. In the cities, collective violence was frequent in the 1840s and 1850s, but quite containable. None the less, ruling-class fears of widespread disorder continued, leading in part to two important changes in the organisation of the repressive arm of the state. The permanent military forces were joined by volunteer corps of city and rural gentlemen, who were used to back up the troops during social disorders. Thus in 1861 the Sydney Volunteers performed guard-duty while the permanent garrison went west to keep order during the anti-Chinese riots at Lambing Flat, and the Volunteers in Hobart patrolled during the religious riots of 1879. The other major organisational change was the removal of police control from local magistrates in each of the colonies, except Tasmania, during the 1850s and 1860s. As the local magistrates were leading pastoralists, this was another sign of the passing of the 'plantation' option for development. The context of this change, the urban and goldfields disturbances, indicated that the traditional police priority of maintaining public order (over crime prevention) was to continue, but the form of the reorganisation pointed forward to a new role for the police, as agents of the central government when cultural intervention became necessary in the period of working-class mobilisation.[16]

In other expressions of an integrative function, state power was also used in a limited way to make concessions in the labour market. By 1871, colonial governments were the most important employers and the focus of collective bargaining with the unions. Soon they became the pace-setters in the labour market, conceding wage rises and the eight-hour day for state employees, and employment agencies and public works for the unemployed. On the other hand, colonial governments passed virtually no protective legislation for wage-earners before the 1890s. For the most part, the leading manufacturers and merchants provided reasonable working conditions for the employees, and the working class was too weak to mount a campaign against either the great bulk of small, substandard, urban employers, or the large pastoralists. The state, in fact, could limit its activity in these areas because of the nature of the urban bourgeois mobilisation, which rested on the strategy of politically co-opting the urban workers. In the education and welfare areas, the same was true. For example, in education, before the centralised and compulsory state educational systems developed in the 1870s and 1880s, the state relied on the part-time and voluntary effort of local businessmen and clergy to administer the schools and the Mechanics' Institutes. And although the state became increasingly involved in financing and organising social welfare, it was still in essence a private system based on voluntarist and charitable principles.[17]

Conflict in the Ruling Class

The changes within the imperial ruling class that made possible the transfer of state power to colonies of settlement necessarily coincided with changes in the colonial ruling class. In eastern Australia, the unity of the ruling class dissolved in the 1840s and a struggle for control of the state developed. On the political stage, the conflict was projected in terms of rival social orders: plantation capitalism versus *laissez-faire* capitalism. Politics in this period became the main dimension for the development of class society, a process noted by one observer who remarked of the colonists, 'All are politicians and love the name of independence.'[18]

The first sign of disturbance within the ruling class occurred in the depression of the 1840s over imperial land policy. The more established landowning gentry supported the imperial policy of selling land at a high price to finance settlement by immigration (of course they had mostly obtained their land at a very low price or as a gift from the government), while the squatters favoured either a low price or, more usually, cheap long-term leases. After the first elections to the Legislative Council in 1843, the squatters were able to use their new political power to put themselves at the head of an anti-imperial coalition when the Governor issued new squatting regulations in 1844. His objects were to raise revenue, to control the expansion of squatting on Crown lands and to encourage free immigration. The squatters and their allies among the urban businessmen put together an alternative programme: security of tenure through long pastoral leases, the resumption of convict transportation and responsible self-government. The ideological justification for these demands was partly physiocratic: grazing was the only productive interest, and partly mercantilist: the wool trade defined the imperial tie, through the exchange of colonial raw materials for British manufactured goods. Meetings across the countryside, an active press and pamphlet war, the despatch of an agent to lobby British politicians and businessmen, and the formation of the New South Wales Pastoral Association signalled an organised challenge to the gentry's leadership of the ruling class.[19]

Representation in the legislature provided the possibility of access to state power for urban interests — the mercantile bourgeoisie and the working-men. The gentry, with their access assured through the magistracy, never really adjusted to electoral politics, although some of them organised their tenants and labourers to vote for them in the 1840s. By the elections of 1848, the city bourgeoisie was turning its attention to winning the country towns and hamlets, and in the period up to the 1870s, some country towns, especially those near the goldfields, became important outposts of city liberalism. For the gentry, this meant being squeezed politically on both sides. Some of them, like T. A. Murray, Charles Cowper or Charles Windeyer, sided with the city businessmen as a recognisable liberal politics emerged in the late 1840s. Others, who were also lease-holders, defected to the squatters. After the reorganisation of capital, and the constitutional changes to the form of the state in the 1850s, the remnants of the gentry leadership ultimately became members of the conservative upper houses.

In the late 1840s, after vigorous winnowing by depression in 1843, there were only about sixteen large capitalists and less than a dozen companies in Sydney. One man, A. B. Spark, probably invested in half of the companies formed between 1828 and 1851. Some specialisation and managerial expertise developed in the 1840s, but the absence of a share market for the mobilisation of capital indicated how weak urban property still was as the basis for an alternative leadership of the ruling class. It was only in the process of campaigning on the political ground already staked out by the squatters, the conflict between imperial and 'colonial' (i.e. squatting) interests, that liberal philosophy became linked with urban capital. In the issue known as 'the corn question', in the opposition to the resumption of transportation and in the discussions of constitutional change, the squatters were increasingly challenged by liberal businessmen for political leadership of the bourgeoisie.[20]

The corn question of the mid-1840s was the earliest and most transitional. The two demands of the campaign — tariff protection for wheat-growers and the maintenance of the British tariff's preference for Australian wheat and flour — were never likely to be achieved as the British government became more firmly attached to free trade, but the arguments and the coalition of campaigners pointed to a new political alignment. The liberal rhetoric of the British anti-Corn Law movement was used to justify a campaign on behalf of the farmers. Although its supporters argued that they were only trying to defend the farmers as they had earlier defended the squatters against imperial discrimination, the campaign implicitly challenged the pastoral ideology by asserting that agriculture, too, could be a productive interest. As for the composition of the movement, there were not many farmers, but there were liberal landowners, radical newspaper editors and urban businessmen.

If there were two productive interests, there could easily be a third. Indeed, during the anti-transportation movement of the late 1840s and early 1850s, the urban capitalists consciously clarified their programme by contrasting it with that of the squatters. Thus free immigration was preferred to cheap convict labour, and economic diversification to pastoral dominance. Underlying these differences of interest was the conflict between the plantation style of social order favoured by the squatters—an attempt to revive the set of relationships surrounding the assignment system, which had established the leadership of the gentry in the earlier period—and an urban bourgeois social order. This was clearly understood. Just as the squatters had justified their programme in terms of the good of the colony, so now the urban merchants and manufacturers associated a 'free' labour market with a free society, and profits with prosperity for all. A liberal individualism was easily inserted into these arguments. There was even a tinge of nationalism; a single, strong domestic market, whose entrepreneurs would be strategically placed to exploit the Asian and Pacific markets as well, formed part of grandiose dreams of national greatness. But the Australasian League for the Abolition of Transportation provided some material basis for these dreams. Its mobilisation of thousands of supporters through petitions, fund-raising and mass rallies, was intercolonial, and trading vessels did begin to fly the League flag. Of course there was also a widespread newspaper-inspired abhorrence of convictism as a moral evil, but from the point of view of bourgeois class formation, what was more significant was the way 'moral enlightenment' was linked explicitly with the ideology of economic development.[21]

Democracy was a more problematical issue for the liberal bourgeoisie. After their experience of mobilising the anti-convict movement and of transferring its mass support into electoral politics, they understood the advantages of a 'democratic' constitution, that is, of extended suffrage, a redistribution of electoral districts to favour the urban areas and an easing of the property restrictions on membership of parliament. On the other hand, they feared that it might be difficult to prevent a mobilised democracy from interfering with capital accumulation: gold-mining, land settlement and state-assisted immigration were looming as issues to divide the mercantile bourgeoisie not only from the squatters but also from the small and would-be capitalists. Moreover, the *petit-bourgeois* programme for economic independence was becoming increasingly associated with a radical movement that challenged state authority on the goldfields and demanded a more democratic constitution. This situation in the colonies of eastern Australia gave rise to a compromise between liberals and conservatives on constitutional reform in the 1850s.[22]

With their access to the state assured by the new constitutions, the liberal bourgeoisie were well placed to take over the political leadership of the ruling class, and they had mastered the necessary skills. They had mobilised political resources and were learning how to use the organisational power residing in legislative factions, electoral networks and *ad hoc* movements around particular issues or principles.[23] They proceeded to use their superior organisation to commit the executive and legislative arms of the state to a programme of economic development that further articulated the difference between their model of the social order and that of the squatters. Even the resistance of the upper houses, that produced fierce constitutional conflicts in Victoria, New South Wales and South Australia, could not alter the changed disposition of political forces in the ruling class; the conservatives could only exercise a veto power, and mostly they were too demoralised to do even that. But political leadership was only part of the picture. There remained to complete the emergence of a hegemonic situation the parallel growth of commercial business leadership and the alliance with the *petit-bourgeoisie*.

The organising base for the mercantile bourgeoisie in business was the company. In New South Wales one study has shown nearly 1100 companies formed between 1865 and 1890, and over 250 prominent directors. Nearly all of these men were entrepreneurs, not salaried managers, and this meant that their leadership in business, like that of the bourgeoisie in politics, was organisational: they mobilised capital and organised it into companies. The leadership of the commercial bourgeoisie, whether in business or politics, needed the same kind of skill, and it was this common skill, as much as the need to control the state, that accounted for the extraordinary overlapping of business and political leadership in this period. About 40 per cent of the Sydney directors were also politicians. The mobilisation of capital began with banks and insurance companies, which tapped the savings of skilled workers and small capitalists. Moreover, insurance and banking were hegemonic mechanisms. The press spoke of them in terms of 'progress' and 'thrift', the government in New South Wales allowed Clerks of Petty Sessions in country areas to collect the premiums for the Australian Mutual Provident Society (formed in 1848), and the National Bank of Australia hired a radical agitator to drum up shares among the Victorian diggers. When general limited liability laws extended the company form of capital organisation into other areas, the main banking and trading families remained pre-eminent in business. They undertook the transformation of the pastoral industry, sometimes through the banks, but mainly through pastoral-finance companies, using London funds. But the mining booms, which the new share markets facilitated in Melbourne and Sydney, produced a further mobilisation of capital and a new group of entrepreneurs. A third layer was added to the business leadership during the urban land booms of the 1880s, when local capital was again mobilised, often in a new form of investment company, the building society.[24]

As the economy diversified and competition increased, separate business interests emerged and were organised in business associations. After some false starts in the 1820s and 1830s, Chambers of Commerce were active in Sydney, Melbourne, Adelaide, Launceston and Hobart in the 1850s. They then appeared in Brisbane in 1868 and Fremantle in 1873. The merchants

Right: Palace of finance. The Bank of South Australia in King William Street, Adelaide, about 1883.
Source: South Australian Archives, Adelaide, B2534: 109.

were concerned to achieve self-regulation of certain aspects of trade and to influence government regulation of others, particularly the customs tariff. The bankers in Melbourne, then the strongest financial centre in the colonies, began to regulate interest and exchange rates in 1857 through the 'Associated Banks'. In coal-mining, a 'vend' appeared in New South Wales in 1873, to moderate the effects of competition among the owners. Industry associations were slower to start in manufacturing and urban construction, and when they did appear, mainly in the 1880s, they represented the response of employers to problems of industrial relations. But the protectionist possibilities of the tariff also produced a separate political intervention by the manufacturers, who organised Chambers of Manufactures in Melbourne in 1865, Adelaide in 1869 and Sydney in 1885.[25]

The leading capitalists who emerged in this way, and who were also prominent in politics, were mainly based in the capital cities. However, there was another level of bourgeois mobilisation in the country towns. As closer settlement of the agricultural districts proceeded, particularly in the 1870s and 1880s, country-town merchants engaged in political campaigns against the squatters. They were joined by local manufacturers in brewing, wool, sugar and flour-milling, brickmaking and in agricultural machinery. From Victoria to Queensland, a vigorous rural politics emerged, supported by town-based farmers' associations and a gutsy country press. The first of a steady stream of country-town businessmen entered the colonial parliaments. Yet there was no complete, economic as well as political, regional mobilisation of capital on class lines in the eastern colonies, while in South Australia, Adelaide capital was dominant on both fronts. As the railways spread out from Melbourne and Sydney, urban capital encroached on country markets, displacing many of the rural traders and, with the advantages of superior technology, setting up branch factories or flooding the local market with cheap city-made goods. Only temporary regional share markets developed outside the metropolitan centres and branch-banking ensured that provincial banks could not compete with those based in the cities. Rural capital produced some wealthy family companies and the political leadership for an aggrieved rural electorate, but it never challenged the many-sided power of urban capital.[26]

The struggle in the political arena against the conservatism of pastoral capital was the strongest dynamic in the emergence of the commercial bourgeoisie as the leading section of capital. Secondly, there was the need to relate to state action. This applied particularly to the merchants because of the economic dominance of the trading link with Britain and the political importance of free trade in the regional redistribution of state power as the colonies became self-governing. During the 1840s, British ministers responsible for the colonies had prohibited differential customs duties, that is, those that varied according to the country of origin of the imported goods. Britain's interest was to prevent the colonies exchanging tariff preferences with foreign competitors of Britain, but this policy, which was written into the Australian Colonies Government Act of 1850, also retarded Australian industrial development by preventing intercolonial tariff preferences. It was not until 1873 that the self-governing colonies of Australia were allowed to impose differential duties on intercolonial trade, and 1895 that this power was widened to cover trade with foreign countries. Meanwhile, the merchants engaged in trade between the Australian colonies could at least hope that it would flow freely. To this end, and using what fiscal power the 1850

Act had bestowed, the merchants set about achieving uniformity in the various colonial tariffs. The Chambers of Commerce in 1851–52 lobbied the governments, exchanged letters and emissaries, and mobilised members and supporters in the legislatures of New South Wales, Victoria and Van Diemen's Land. Their success in these three colonies, and in South Australia soon after, was 'one of the best things done by us', as Cowper wrote to Parkes. The movement among the merchants had strengthened mercantile links with liberal politics: certain merchants, such as William Westgarth in Victoria and John Lamb in New South Wales, were confirmed as political and business leaders, and free trade was separated from sectional connotations to become, at least for the 1850s, a principle of class identification.[27]

A third structural force pushing businessmen towards class awareness was the emerging organisation among the subordinate class. In the second half of the 1850s, groups of employers met to discuss their response to the Eight Hour Day campaign. The rate of formation of employers' organisations picked up in the 1870s, when trade unionism began to spread. It appears from Victorian figures that the increasing militancy of the workers and the co-operation between the unions in the mid-1880s was a turning-point for many employers. The paternalism of employers towards their workers, especially in the manufacturing industry, was checked by defeats in four major strikes and the formation of a Trades Hall Council. An Employers' Union was formed in 1885 (1887 in South Australia and 1888 in New South Wales) to co-ordinate industrial action against the trade unions. The language of class war was used publicly by such prominent businessmen as Bruce Smith for the first time.[28]

Populism and Hegemony

Before the 1880s the extent of class organisation and action among the workers was limited, although, as we shall see, the movement for shorter hours, which began in the 1850s, did anticipate the appearance of working-class politics. However, between the 1840s and the 1860s, the workers were part of a third political force: populist radicalism. The main features of the populist situation that produced this challenge to both liberalism and conservatism reflected the complex pattern of formation of the class structure in this period.[29] First, there was the relative weakness of class organisation among the workers, which occurred in the context of declining opportunities for self-employment and small-scale production. The wage-earning workers who expected to become independent, the artisans who were, and the small employers in manufactories, shops and alluvial mines, all felt threatened by the development of wage labour and the accumulation of capital. Radicalism was based on an agglomeration of people inside and outside the labour market, and those inside it were further divided by being on opposite sides of the labour/capital relationship. Thus radicalism could not be constituted as a single movement by the operation of relationships within the basic capitalist institutions. Although its goal was to protect the *petit-bourgeois* ideal of economic independence, radicalism was more than a *petit-bourgeois* movement; it was a populist movement, constituted by the need to relate to state action. These heterogeneous class elements formed a single political movement in response to the commercial bourgeoisie's access to parliamentary power, and their radical strategy combined a populist *émeute* with drastic legislative action.

Secondly, there was the conflict in the ruling class, which added another stress line to the class structure, and which was associated with the transfer of state power and the construction of the parliamentary form of the state. The preoccupation of the ruling class with its internal relationships made an opening for the radical ideology of 'the middle way' between pastoral 'barbarism' and urban 'civilisation'. At the same time, the commercial bourgeoisie needed political allies outside the ruling class, not only to ensure its political leadership of the ruling class but to demonstrate political consensus and thus the fitness of the colonies for self-government. Accordingly, the commercial bourgeoisie had to co-operate with the mobilisation of the working-men and small producers, a mobilisation that existed because of the connection between ruling-class conflict and the change in the form of the state. This co-operation strengthened the reliance on both mass action and legislative reform in radical strategy, as well as the ideological notion of 'the people' versus 'the monopolists' or squatters.

Thirdly, there was the problem of social disorder, which existed because bourgeois hegemony was weak. 'Independence' in workers meant not only *petit-bourgeois* aspirations but also resistance to the work discipline required of wage labour. The Deputy Adjutant-General of the Military Forces in Australia clearly saw in 1852 the connection between work and disorder: 'The day labourers of Sydney are notoriously idle, drunken and dissolute. They work . . . four days, then drink and riot.' Inevitably, when working-men organised, their political activities were unruly and spontaneous around the edges, and again the effect of work patterns was obvious. 'Monday, jocularly called by the labouring classes Saint Monday, because they often take a half-holiday on that day', was favoured for public meetings. From the beginning of electoral politics in the 1840s, partisan feelings ran high, and in subsequent years religious, racial and industrial conflict produced disorder and violence, not only in Sydney and Melbourne but in the smaller towns and goldfields. State repression was one response. Party processions were banned by New South Wales legislation in 1846, while obstructing the streets around Parliament House, Government House and the Police Office could bring a month in goal after 1853. By this time, the troops had been alerted or called out on several occasions during the anti-transportation campaigns and goldfields agitations. At Eureka in 1854, a rebellion against lawful authority occurred within the context of a developing policy of state coercion of working-men. At the same time, members of the ruling class in Sydney risked personal harassment from a 'cabbage-tree-hat mob' if they appeared in public wearing a 'black hat'. They organised meetings to call for the defence of 'life and property' in 1844 and 1850. They did more than exert pressure on the State—in the early 1850s, the men of property extended their political mobilisation into the extra-parliamentary organisations of the working-men.[30]

Between 1843, when the Mutual Protection Association was formed in Sydney by small capitalists and leaders of the trades societies, and the 1860s, hundreds of radical organisations appeared. They continued into the 1870s and 1880s, but by this time the political intervention by workers was being organised by the trade unions, and radical movements increasingly became satellites of the Trades and Labour Councils. But in 1872, the radical impulse was still dominant in the organisation that became the Australian 'section' of the First International, the Democratic Association of Victoria. Few radical organisations lasted longer than a year, the most notable exception being the Land Convention (1857–60) in Victoria. Their membership was small, perhaps a hundred or so in the cities or larger towns, but they mobilised many thousands through their posters, handbills and newspapers. At these 'monster meetings', symbolic politics came into its own. Effigies were burnt, slogans chanted and respectable members of the bourgeoisie became, temporarily, the saviours of the people. In 1848, the future Chancellor of the Exchequer of Great Britain was embarrassed to find himself greeted by crowds in Sydney who cried 'Lowe and Liberty!'.[31]

Rural poverty. Tasmania in the nineteenth century.
Source: State Library of Tasmania, Hobart, NS 126/38.

Populist in composition and style of organisation, radicalism was also populist in ideology, particularly in its view of class and politics. Although radicals were aware of the formation of the working class in Britain, they refused to discuss colonial politics in class terms. Using the British Whig concept of interest, they discriminated between 'the people', whose interests were reconcilable by good government, and 'the classes', who selfishly oppressed the people through their control of the state ('class legislation' arose in this way). If the colonies were becoming divided by class, the radicals attributed this to a deliberate political strategy by the squatting monopolists. It followed that politics would provide the means for liberation, through popular participation at meetings and elections, to cut the usurping link between government and vested interest, and through legislative panaceas, like land reform or protection, which once introduced would eliminate monopoly and restore harmony in social relationships.[32]

The radical 'middle way' declined in support as the class structure developed a dichotomous shape. In this period, the significant changes occurred in the space that the commercial bourgeoisie was carving for the dominant class. It included the state, where parliamentary democracy provided inhospitable country for radical working-men and small capitalists. Within the radical movement, while 'doctrinaires' studied the experiences of republicans and socialists in the European revolutions, the 'realists' advocated citizenship as the path to reform. The mass mobilisation and the legislative panacea were emerging as separate strategies. The doctrinaire wing took a step towards an alternative political theory when it proposed the need for 'associational' rather than 'individualistic' principles to guide the people's mobilisation.[33] But the realists scoffed at 'old world' delusions, and pointed instead to the benefits of alliance with the liberal bourgeoisie. After the gold-rushes, they linked the ownership of property with political rights, ignoring the extension of the labour market and the accumulation of capital. The realists argued that as working-men now had 'a stake in the country', their votes would count, thus ignoring the distinction between small and large property. The liberals applauded, for the acceptance of the 'stake in the country' argument by working-men guaranteed the success of the liberal programme of extending parliamentary democracy, and of their assumption of leadership of an anti-squatter alliance. If ownership of property made democrats, it also made those with the most property the best democrats.

The assumption of leadership in mass politics by the commercial bourgeoisie was effected in three ways. First, the bourgeoisie set the tasks for the alliance against pastoral capital. In the age of 'progress', when British enterprise dominated world markets and British colonists displaced indigenous peoples, the tasks of economic development and the maintenance of the superiority of the British race in Australia were heavy with liberal bourgeois values. Moreover, in the practice of these tasks, working-men were cast as followers. If the squatters could be accused of hindering development, it was because of their indifference to the dynamic union of 'capital and science', which the bourgeoisie understood and promised to promote for the benefit of all. Bourgeois support for exploration (commercial rivalry helped to finance the Burke and Wills expedition), for exhibitions of colonial goods and for scientific societies was hegemonic in that it presupposed working-men who would believe that their labour in developing the country depended on the efforts of capitalist entrepreneurs. Similarly, the practice of race relations, in the campaigns against the Chinese and Melanesians, saw workers endorsing the bourgeois model of the social order, in which equality of opportunity stemmed from the freedom of wage labour, and rejecting the stratified 'plantation' model resting on 'unfree', indentured coloured labour. For both tasks, the fact that massive injections of capital were contemplated underlined the superior resources of the urban bourgeoisie in this alliance.[34]

Secondly, bourgeois political leadership was effected by capturing the leadership of the radical mass movements of the working-men. The working-men developed the ward-by-ward political mobilisation (in Sydney, during the 1848 elections and the subsequent anti-transportation movement), set up radical 'reading-rooms' to educate their followers, published frantically and greatly increased the number of public meetings, especially on 'Saint Monday'. Sites for informal, spontaneous meetings developed—the Eastern Markets in Melbourne, the Queen's statue in Sydney—and from them, marches would set off to parliament or town hall. The resource of organised numbers was created in this way, but money, educated leaders and influence within the state organisations were not as easily generated by working-men. These were the resources that liberal property-owners brought to the popular movements. By the late 1850s, when the merchant William Westgarth acclaimed the public meeting as 'the great vehicle of progress', liberal politicians had become prominent speakers at them. Soon land-reform leagues, electoral-reform leagues, protectionist and liberal political associations were characterised by a rank-and-file of working-men but a leadership of prominent bourgeois politicians. This process was facilitated by ambitious men within the radical movement—like Henry Parkes—who welcomed the chance to join forces with the bourgeoisie, and by the liberals' need to win the votes of the working-men. The influx of politicians into the radical movements was always greatest when elections were approaching. Conservatives rightly recognised that popular movements were being transformed into electoral campaigns.[35]

Thirdly, popular issues were transformed from demands based on real grievances to rhetoric and symbolic legislation. Consider land reform. Initially, in the 1840s, radicals were demanding small allotment land schemes, financed by government. By the late 1850s, land reform, now a liberal issue, meant equality of opportunity through free selection. The 'reform' clauses of the various Land Acts in Victoria and New South Wales between the 1850s and 1870s provided a symbolic possibility of land ownership, which only a few, those with considerable savings, could take advantage of. Similarly, the electoral reforms in those two colonies in the late 1850s allowed liberal politicians to pose as democrats and talk of the achievement of political equality, but the reality was altogether different. Electoral districts were far from equal in size (the largest in terms of number of voters were in the workers' suburbs) and the franchise was far from universal (women could not vote and nor could migratory workers). And as members of parliament were not paid, workers could be represented by men of their own class only by a prodigious organising effort to raise funds to pay their representatives.[36]

The political leadership by the bourgeoisie of the anti-squatter alliance was important not only because the victory of liberal democracy in political theory and practice dished the squatter-Whigs and co-opted the dangerous working-men, but also because it gave the question of order a social dimension, by making order a goal of 'democracy'. Henceforth, democratic citizenship was used to legitimate the actions of the main agencies of cultural control—the family, the churches and the Mechanics' Institutes. The State was, therefore, intimately involved in cultural processes, not only through particular policies but also indirectly, through the predominance in bourgeois strategy of the struggle to control a state resting on political consensus. In this period, *direct* state intervention in cultural processes was limited.

The family was not yet a spectacular success as an agency of cultural control. Marriage in the colonies was not as prevalent as it was in England and Wales, due to quirks in the sex and age structures of the colonial population, and perhaps, ironically, to the heavy ideological stress placed on the family, causing working-men and women, as well as the bourgeoisie, to defer mar-

Rural affluence. A picnic party near Armadale, Western Australia, about 1890.
Source: Battye Library, Perth, 2432B.

riage until 'the proper time'. Ideally, the family fostered a domestic morality and entrenched the wider morality of bourgeois society. It would be structured as an independent household, with male breadwinner, housewife and children, and would practise, privately, consumption in the name of progress, sexual repression in the name of respectability, and domestic order in the name of training for citizenship. No doubt there were families, especially among the bourgeoisie, that worked in this way. The sprawl of suburban villas, the increase in personal savings invested in building societies and savings-banks, and the market for domestic gadgets reflected the stress on economic progress at the family level. The increasing voluntary work of bourgeois women in private welfare organisations and the temperance movement indicated a strong commitment to the 'God's police' stereotype. As for the family's connection with political order, it was said of the Mayor of Sydney in 1880 that 'he began life as a practical citizen by getting married'. Yet the extent to which the ideal of the bourgeois family was realised in the working class is open to question.[37]

Firstly, not all women were destined to become bourgeois housewives, because some bourgeois women expected to manage the domestic labour of other women, as female servants. Therefore, through immigration schemes and even legislation, a pool of unmarried women had to be created.

A respectable couple. The man has a patch on his left trouser leg.
Source: Collected by John Arnold in Benalla, 1972.

Moreover, the flight from domestic service did not always end in the haven of familial domesticity. Certainly, working-class women in the colonies avoided domestic service if they could by marriage, but there was a high probability that, after marriage, they would end up in part-time domestic employment—washing, ironing, cleaning, sewing—for those same bourgeois women.

So, secondly, the working-class mother could not always exercise the prescribed role of moral guardian of her family. It was necessary for her to supplement her husband's uncertain income; of course, if widowed or deserted (as many wives of migratory workers were), she became the sole breadwinner. In many cases, this took working-class wives completely out of the home, and into either the factories or the houses of the bourgeoisie. The children often worked too—in brickyards and leather, clothing and tobacco factories—because women's wages were so low. By the 1860s the lack of parental guidance and education among working-class children was recognised as a major problem of social control. Moreover, if a good wife improved the husband's productivity, as the secretary of the South Australian Chamber of Manufacturers said in 1875, something would have to be done to make women stay at home and to improve their housewifely skills. But it was not until the next period that working-class women were subjected to organised state and voluntary pressures to conform to bourgeois ideals.[38]

Thirdly, a suitable standard of domestic privacy was not easily obtained for working-class families. It is easy to be misled in this area by the aggregate figures, and international comparisons based on them, of the economic historians. They show a low population density, even in the most crowded suburbs of the cities, the absence of European-type slums, a rise in housing standards, the disappearance of the housing shortage by 1871 and a housing boom in the 1880s. What these figures ignore is the differential impact of economic and social forces on classes, and on strata within classes. Research here is thin, but it is noteworthy that inadequate accommodation for working-class families is a preoccupation of liberals from the 1860s to the 1890s. One witness told a New South Wales parliamentary inquiry in 1860 that working-class accommodation in Sydney was worse than in London, and another revealed that only 3 of 31 married men in his woollen mill were home-owners. If the aggregate figures for 1891 show that 60 to 70 per cent of housing in Melbourne and Sydney was tenanted, not owner-occupied, it is highly likely that throughout this period the families of labourers, and of deserted wives and widows, lived in rented accommodation which by contemporary colonial bourgeois standards was overcrowded and unhealthy. For a country without slums, it is surely strange that 35 per cent of houses inspected in Sydney in 1901, after the bubonic plague had swept through the inner-city area, were 'in such a dilapidated and unsanitary state that it was impossible to make them fit for habitation'.[39]

The churches played a diminishing role in the cultural sphere. Their near monopoly of education was broken when state education systems at the primary level were established between the 1860s and the 1880s. Moreover, their moral leadership faltered. The passing of convictism reduced the need for moral coercion as an object of state policy and there were few churchmen who could devise an alternative liberal justification for the Church's role in the community. Indeed, it was a secular ideology that accompanied the rise of the mercantile bourgeoisie; the belief in progress largely bypassed the churches at this time. One of the policy achievements of the bourgeoisie in eastern Australia, the removal of state aid from the churches in the 1860s and 1870s, was a triumph for liberalism, but only in the state organisations. The churches had neither moved away from the convict period's dogmatic theology, which united the conservative stress on hierarchy and the idea of moral ascendancy, nor captured the 'free' worker communicant. Church attendance was quite low among working-men and women. Anglican clergymen in particular were regarded, correctly, by the workers as supporters of a privileged upper class. To the extent that religion excited interest among working-class intellectuals, it was often in forms depised by the churches, such as spiritualism and deism. Secularism, too, attracted many educated immigrant workers during the 1880s with a programme that linked atheism with republicanism, land nationalisation and other counter-hegemonic demands. Not surprisingly, then, the face that the churches turned towards the workers was still remote and admonitory. Although the Salvation Army realised the need for a closer involvement with working-class life (but unsuccessfully, its members coming from other denominations), evangelical religion at this time approached the working class from the outside, in a series of wowserish campaigns against drink, desecration of the Sabbath and prostitution.[40]

Clergymen and businessmen were prominent in the voluntary organisations that sought to guide the working-men when they left the relative safety of home, workplace or church. Organised horse-racing had appeared as early as the 1820s, but from the 1850s spectator sport expanded rapidly. Huge crowds went to regattas, athletic meetings and cricket and football matches, and whether sponsored by businessmen for profit or by clubs of businessmen for more altruistic ends, their effect was hegemonic in its stress on colonial or national identification. Working-men played little part in the growing regulation of sport that occurred in this period, but there were other leisure-time activities that involved them more. Of prime importance were the various adult education societies—Schools of Arts, Mechanics' Institutes, working-men's institutes and debating clubs—which were often supported financially and in other ways by the State. The classes, on subjects literary and 'moral', failed to attract more than a bare minority of the workers, who preferred practical courses to keep them abreast of new technology. In 1855, there were 1000 members of the Sydney Mechanics' Institute, of whom 100 were skilled workers and the rest mostly clerks and shop assistants. But for these workers, and others in benefit societies, unions and co-operatives, the lessons were really about self-government and order. There was a great stress on rules, and on penalties for breaching them, and on rituals and other formalities of meeting procedure, which inculcated orderliness and regularity. Even some bourgeois parents had to be taught the importance of order, because it was a common lament of teachers in the expensive private schools that parents continually undermined school discipline. Of course, the state schools, apart from teaching basic literacy for citizenship and the ideology of progress, also provided a form of social control for workers' children.[41]

Expensive schools, city clubs, the temples of commerce erected as offices by the leading banks and trading companies, the museums and art galleries endowed by wealthy philanthropists: these were symbols of bourgeois cultural dominance. But beneath their appearance of solidity and restraint was

Horrors of childhood — I. A girl and other objects in a Sandhurst (Bendigo) photographer's studio, nineteenth century.
Source: Collected by John Arnold, Bendigo, 1972.

a very different quality. This was a hegemony in the making, and it was not very entrenched. There could have been more disorder; the working-men and women could have held out longer for a small-allotment land scheme and greater political equality. The squatters could have imported more cheap indentured labour to strengthen the plantation economy and British investors could have been less enthusiastic about the Australian colonies. There was nothing natural nor automatic about bourgeois ascendancy. Indeed, in view of the absence of mobilisation among a subordinate class, it may even be doubted whether hegemony accurately describes the main principle of control in the class structure, at least at the beginning of this period. Certainly, the struggle for *political* domination by the commercial bourgeoisie bulked very large, and it was in relation to it that a resistance from below developed in the form of populist radicalism. And it was the advance of capitalist corporate enterprise that disorganised small producers and checked the upward mobility of wage-earners. Yet there was a hegemonic situation. Cultural processes were operating, especially through the mechanisms that were so important for the commercial bourgeoisie's economic and political domination: the savings-bank, the joint-stock company, the mutual insurance fund, the building society and, in the political arena, the forms of representative, parliamentary democracy. On the other hand, the pattern of sex-roles and family life was still shallow among groups of workers, and the organisations of civil society had difficulty in reaching a broad range of workers. When the subordinate class mobilised at the end of the century, the balance between these mechanisms would shift towards the family and civil society and a new hegemonic situation would develop.[42]

The Organisation of Workers in the Labour Market

Although this period opened with a surge of self-employment during the gold-rushes and, on a smaller scale, during the land reforms of the 1860s, the relationships of wage labour continued to spread. We have seen how company mining brought more and more independent diggers within the scope of the labour market and how small rural proprietors alternated between working their own selections and working for the squatters. Moreover, the scope of the labour market was also extended geographically, as better transport and communications developed. This process of geographical unification of the labour market was occurring in other capitalist countries, and between them. Indeed, the era of mass migration that began in the middle of the nineteenth century made the reach of capitalist labour relationships almost global. Throughout this period, the Australian labour market was vulnerable to pressures on labour supply generated in other parts of the empire, pressures that the imperial and colonial governments tried to regulate through immigration policy. When the State could not successfully meet the needs of capital for cheap, tractable labour, employers had to organise their own supply. It was not only the squatters and planters who sent their agents to Europe, Asia, the Pacific Islands and to other colonies. Henry Parkes, whose Sydney printery seems to have had more than its share of industrial conflict in the 1850s, recruited compositors in Melbourne and in India. On the other side of the wages system, the workers responded to the increasing scope of the labour market by organising across geographical and ethnic boundaries. During the struggle in the Victorian building trades in 1859, the masons sent money and instructions to the English Society of Operative Stonemasons, to prevent the agents of colonial employers recruiting workers at less than the prevailing colonial wage rates and for a longer working day. When German masons were recruited, the Victorian union had to wait until they arrived, but then it had some success in persuading the Germans to demand new contracts with conditions in line with union standards, particularly the eight hour day.[43]

The labour market was also showing signs of becoming increasingly differentiated. In Queensland, employers introduced about 60 000 Melanesians for the sugar plantations, so that field labour became a separate segment of the labour market, where inferior working and living conditions persisted because of the racist disdain of white workers for 'nigger work'. In the boot, tobacco and clothing trades of Victoria and New South Wales, women and children became the major component of the workforce in the 1870s, displacing several hundred male workers at a time when near full employment and sluggish immigration was forcing wages up. Further, the capitalist mode of management appeared in certain trades, as a tobacco factory manager explained in 1876: his workers were 'not allowed to learn more than one thing, excepting, of course, the managers'. The average wage of these women in the 1880s was less than half that of male factory workers and barely placed them above the level of subsistence. Twice as many women were in domestic service, but if their earnings (wages, board and lodgings) were slightly better than those of the factory girl, their work was already stereotyped by the processes of labour market segmentation as being fit only for 'slaveys'—unskilled female labourers. Reinforcing the trend to complexity was the continuous policy of assisted immigration—which employers admitted was to cheapen the cost of labour. Many of these immigrants were skilled men who posed as unskilled in order to receive the subsidised passage to Australia. When they arrived, their skills were not in demand and they experienced transitional unemployment, which was a particular problem in the 1880s. Earlier, in the 1860s, there had been structural unemployment, especially in Victoria, while the ex-alluvial miners waited for the price of their labour to decline sufficiently for import-replacement manufacturing to become profitable. There was also some cyclical unemployment, which affected skilled as well as unskilled workers, every five years or so after 1854. In the cities, a zone of blighted living conditions existed for the worst-paid workers, the aged and sick, and the non-European workers who drifted in from the bush.[44]

Yet although the labour market was beginning to follow the classic path of increased exploitation of labour through differentiation, it did not produce overnight discontinuities and sufferings on the scale of industrialising European capitalism. On the last page of the first volume of *Capital*, Marx proclaimed the existence of a 'relative surplus population' even in Australia—that is, of a body of unemployed or partly employed workers that functioned as a labour reserve to depress wages and provide workers stigmatised by sex or race (or some other characteristic) for more intensive exploitation. But Marx spoke too soon. The chronic unemployment of the 1860s passed, and for the rest of the period unemployment was low—perhaps about 3 per cent—except during periodic brief recessions. By early in the next century, the Chinese had been excluded, most of the Melanesians repatriated, and the labour movement and liberal reformists had made so obvious their opposition, on racist grounds, to cheap contract labour that it was very difficult for employers to indenture even Southern Europeans without being accused of damaging White Australia. Nor was it clear that the status distinction between skilled and unskilled workers was becoming more rigid in the colonies. The 2 : 1 wage differential was broken down when the shortage of unskilled labour caused by the gold-rushes and the later railway and urban building booms created a range of wages for unskilled men. Fluctuations in demand sometimes pushed wages of an experienced navvy or a builder's labourer to about 80 per cent of tradesmen's rates. The trades unions increasingly recognised that to insist on the demarcation between craftsmen and labourers was not a wise policy in colonial conditions: the unions recruited men who had not served proper apprenticeships, organised unions for labourers, established inter-union councils in the building and iron trades, and by adopting the objective of a standard minimum rate, indicated their concern to secure wage justice for the least skilled worker. Lastly, the mobility of labour, particularly the rural–urban interchange, tended to unify the labour market.[45]

How, then, was the development of an industrial reserve army and labour market segmentation retarded in this period? Firstly, the economy was still pre-industrial in its main sector, primary production for export, and the factory system that emerged in the 1870s to serve a small domestic market did not look to expansion via labour-saving machinery. There was no 'mechanical revolution' producing a depressed stratum of displaced artisans. Where there was technological innovation — in pastoralism and mining — special circumstances mitigated its impact on the workers. In the pastoral industry, where many labourers were also part-time small producers, a migratory work pattern protected the 'independence' of those who were not. Besides, the pastoral industry was profitable and paid high wages. In mining, the workers underground preserved some autonomy by exercising a degree of control over production, through the system of task-work, that is, payment for completion of a set amount of work. In a new country the conquest of the physical environment, through primary production and transport and communication networks, created in the ideology of development a stress on work *per se*, which not only blurred differences between classes but also those within the emerging working class. When a full working-class mobilisation occurred at the end of this period, it was the heroic pre-industrial labourer who confronted 'Mr Fat' in the cartoons of the labour press.[46]

Secondly, the overwhelming proportion of assisted immigration was from Britain, and although many of the unskilled were Irish, they were not sufficiently different from other British immigrants to be easily separated as a permanent minority group. The demand for unskilled labour, on public works and in the rural industry, ultimately evened out the brief periods of excess labour and there was always a gold-rush or 'the outside track' to absorb the least tractable workers. This was the third reason: fairly full employment. Fourthly, there was the effect of organisation by the workers. When there was unemployment, these workers did not hesitate to create public disorder. By the 1870s, their mass protests were an integral part of a campaign, which continued until the end of the 1880s, to stop assisted immigration. The trade unions lobbied and the workers used their votes against employer–politicians who supported mass migration. In an early version of welfare capitalism, which alleviated the worst effects of labour market stratification, governments responded to working-class pressure by providing free transport out of the cities, board and lodgings, employment on public works, and labour exchanges for the unemployed between the 1840s and the 1890s.[47]

Alongside the extension and increasing complexity of the labour market went the organising of production into larger units. By 1885, less than a quarter of the mines on the New South Wales northern coalfields employed more than 60 per cent of the workers. The average workforce in these large mines was 360, while the largest employed 850. Mort's Dock in 1886 had 1000 employees. Railway-yards and large urban construction sites also had large workforces. Thus the institutional setting of working-class politics existed, as did the opportunity for organisation presented by concentrations of workers, either on the job or in factory suburbs, waterfront areas, and towns like Bourke and Wagga where shearers gathered to pick up work. But how would this organisation occur? To what extent would it develop along highly stratified, instrumental lines, reflecting capital's tendency to create a differentiated labour market, and to what extent would it represent a class-based mobilisation? Because bourgeois hegemony in the formal political arena was particularly firm, this tension within the politics of an emerging working class was largely resolved in labour market struggles in this period. There were two main determinants of labour market organising by wage-earners: the balance of power between labour and capital in the labour process, and the challenge of bourgeois ideology.[48]

The struggle for control of the labour process created a range of organising situations for workers. Those with craft traditions, such as the compositors, retained some collective autonomy in production. Work that could not be minutely supervised led to a similar position for engine-drivers and underground miners. In this situation of partial control of the labour process, workers needed arrangements among themselves to regulate the job, distribute the work and/or bargain with the employer over the rate for the job. Although some workers were quick to form unions to protect their position, amongst other workers in the same industry the arrangements were often informal, which was how they would have stayed without the pressures created by capital. Recessions and the competition for markets led employers to intensify the exploitation of labour. Disputes arose about the ratio of skilled to unskilled men, the use of apprentices, the rate for the task or piece, and the organisation of production. In fact, it was the struggle around control of the job that characterised the efforts of workers to organise in this situation. Existing unions were activated and new ones replaced the older informal arrangements. While it may be said that these workers were content to share production with capital, the relationship was not placid and one-way. From the workers' point of view, their organisation was both defensive and offensive, a strengthening of their position, but also a step forward, a working-class reply to the bourgeois principle of self-help. These were the earliest workers in Australia to support the principles of co-operative ownership; they set up co-operative mines, printeries and factories on several occasions. But most significantly, their reply came in the form of collective action. Whether this job-control unionism was conservative or radical depended on the extent to which its activity fed into a class-based mobilisation. In this period, the printers adopted a fairly conservative stance. But when the tailoresses, who worked on their own sewing-machines, struck in Melbourne in 1882–83, so powerful was the class response among the workers that even the subcontractors supported the strike and the newly formed union. One should not dismiss the workers in this situation, by speaking of their partnership with capital, without examining how the relationship was experienced and what the workers made of it.[49]

A different organising situation occurred where the employers were in undisputed control of production. Here the tightening of labour discipline and the increase of labour exploitation could not be offset by the bargaining strength derived from partial control of the labour process. There were various responses. The skilled engineers attempted to enforce a minimum wage rate by controlling the supply of local labour. But the geographical expan-

Masters and men. The P. N. Russell and Co. engineering works, about the 1870s.
Source: Mitchell Library, Sydney, Small Picture File.

sion of the labour market and recurring unemployment in the metal trades weakened this strategy. Inevitably, the Amalgamated Society of Engineers moved towards union co-operation on an industry basis. A similar path was taken by unskilled workers when they attempted to control the labour market through the 'closed shop'. But mass unionism among these workers was also a response to the practices of labour control — the methods of payment and of hiring, and the penalties for bad work, damage to property, lateness, insubordination — and to the attempts to reduce wages. It was not only pastoral workers who resented a draconian work regime; in New South Wales, the general union of railway and tramway employees arose to check the 'petty tyranny' of management, and in Melbourne, the coal-lumpers organised in 1885 when the employers reduced wages and eliminated the Eight Hour Day holiday. And as factories grew in size, union leaders drew the attention of the machine operatives to the increase of inspectors and foremen. Thus the natural style of this unionism was instrumental, focusing on control of hiring and the conditions of work. Moreover, as the need for industry-wide collective bargaining was greater in this situation, union leadership had to be more powerful. This is not to suggest that the workers in this situation were submissive; on the contrary, they were capable of sustained militancy, including physical violence against strike-breakers, in defence of 'their' union. But by the same token, the union dominated their social horizon, and they were ready, later, to support compulsory arbitration, with its promise of union recognition by the state.[50]

The second determinant of labour market organising by the workers was their response to the challenge of bourgeois ideology, in particular to democracy and equality. Democracy, which gave them the status of citizens, also legitimated unionism, or rather it was legitimated by *liberal* democracy, as an expression of the right of each economic interest to organise. This process contributed to the integration of the labour movement into bourgeois society. Egalitarianism encouraged *petit-bourgeois* aspirations among workers, some of whom undoubtedly regarded the union as an avenue of social advancement. Together, these processes created a union leadership committed to a reformist strategy of legislative action and collaboration with employers. But was it necessary for union leaders to adopt this strategy? In fact, workers were far from being *petit-bourgeois*, liberal democrats in the workplace. Because it seems difficult to convince Australian historians of this, here are some examples. In 1866, unemployed navvies seized a train to take them to Brisbane to demonstrate against unemployment caused by government finance cuts to public works. When the South Australian boilermakers and ship-builders made the transition from informal to formal organisation in 1880, they stated that their new union would aim 'to cultivate a better class of workmen, as they were going wild at the time'. During the strikes of the 1880s, there were many cases of 'wild' workers using physical violence against strike breakers. More significantly, they often resisted the moderating influence of their union leaders. Indeed, one of those leaders, W. E. Murphy, in his history of unionism, written in the mid-1880s, makes the tension between leadership and workers a principle of interpretation: 'The "going wild at the time" theory was probably the cause of the establishment of the Trades and Labour Council of South Australia. The unions . . . were more or less in need of a controlling executive.'[51]

Murphy's account is a justification for a particular kind of union leadership and its strategy. The reformism and conservatism of these union leaders should not be taken to characterise a class-in-formation, whose very disturbance of existing class patterns made the role of these leaders necessary to the bourgeoisie. If these union leaders embraced liberal-democratic ideology, there were other workers who did not. Interest-group status for labour and the individual advancement of the worker were not things-in-themselves, whose meaning was unaffected by the specific context of labour–capital relationships. Group interest could easily become class interest, given a shift in the balance of class forces. And while there is no doubt that a *petit-bourgeois* orientation persisted among the workers, if they could not own the soil, they might as well control their working conditions. Once again, if class relations altered, the transformation of 'independence' into a collectivist ideal was possible.[52]

It was the Eight Hour Day movement that began this transformation, anticipating the full class mobilisation of the 1890s and later. The movement, especially in the building and metal industries, was fuelled by the employers' attempts to reduce wage costs, as they competed for new markets or resisted the regular downturns in business. In 1861, for example, the workers at P. N. Russell's engineering works in Sydney were on strike for six months; they began by refusing a 10 per cent wage cut, but soon added to this a demand for the eight hour day. Also, any reduction in the hours of work was seen as a way to spread job security; not surprisingly, the demand for shorter hours grew louder after periods of unemployment. Sometimes shorter hours were conceded, and accepted, at the expense of hourly wage rates, but by the 1870s it was common for unions to link the demand for shorter hours with demands for overtime pay and increased hourly rates. There was, thus, a conflict of class interests in the shorter hours question, and while a 'democratic spirit' in Victoria may have accounted for the movement's earlier success in that colony, the significance of the eight hour day struggle for the workers lay in its contribution to their class mobilisation. Two preconditions for a class mobilisation were strengthened during the eight hour day campaigns — the extension of organisation among the workers and their consciousness of having a separate collective identity — but it was the way the campaigns highlighted the relationship between labour and capital that directed the workers' movement beyond the liberalism of interest-group politics. Firstly, for those workers without a share of control of production, the conflict over hours of labour broke the custom of passively accepting the work-rules imposed by the employer. Secondly, the emergence of the movement placed a strain on the radical political alliance. Although initially land reformers and protectionists were drawn into the shorter hours question, before long its tendency to check the power of property placed the workers' movement in a separate political category. Thirdly, the fear of unemployment that motivated many workers in this struggle forced attention on to the unequal relationship between labour and capital in the wages contract. A labourist political economy took deeper root in the colonies as a result.[53]

Notes

1. *Empire*, 30 August 1853, editorial; and W. A. Sinclair, *The Process of Economic Development in Australia*, Cheshire, Melbourne, 1976, p. 100.

2. 'Exile-ism' is dealt with extensively in T. H. Irving, 'The Development of Liberal Politics in New South Wales, 1843–1855', Ph.D. thesis, University of Sydney, 1967, ch. 5.

3. The Masters and Servants Acts await proper study, using archival sources, such as magistrates' bench-books. Meanwhile, a picture of the function of the Acts in the labour market can be gained from the many references in T. A. Coghlan, *Labour and Industry in Australia*, 4 vols, Macmillan, Melbourne, 1969 (first publ. 1918). See also B. Fitzpatrick, *The British Empire in Australia: An Economic History, 1834–1939*, Macmillan, Melbourne, 1969, appendix 8 (first publ. 1941). Resistance in the labour market by workers is discussed later.

4. R. A. Ferguson, 'New South Wales Company Formation, 1860–1890', B.Ec. (Hons) thesis, University of Sydney, 1968; and A. R. Hall, *The Stock Exchange of Melbourne and the Victorian Economy, 1852–1900*, A.N.U.P., Canberra, 1968.

5. G. Serle, *The Golden Age: A History of the Colony of Victoria, 1851–1861*, M.U.P., Melbourne, 1963, chs 1–6; and G. Blainey, *The Rush that Never Ended: A History of Australian Mining*, M.U.P., Melbourne, 2nd edn, 1974, pp. 21–2, 52–8. Jan Nicholson, 'Procedures and Perceptions of Authority: The Gold Rush Camps of Australia, Canada and the United States', *Public Administration* (Sydney), vol. 32, 1973, pp. 392–403, has insufficient evidence to support her claim that Australian miners' associations did not function as organs of self-government. The contrary view is taken by Irving, 'Development of Liberal Politics', pp. 466, 507. Nicholson also neglects the conflict of interests between small and large capital on the fields.

6. This account of changes in the pastoral industry is based on D. W. A. Baker, 'The Origins of Robertson's Land Acts', *Historical Studies*, vol. 8, no. 30, 1958, pp. 166 ff.; and N. G. Butlin and A. Barnard, 'Pastoral Finance and Capital Requirements, 1860–1960', in A. Barnard (ed.), *The Simple Fleece: Studies in the Australian Wool Industry*, M.U.P., Melbourne, 1962. The political implications are discussed in T. H. Irving, '1850–1870', in F. Crowley (ed.), *A New History of Australia*, Heinemann, Melbourne, 1974, pp. 153–9.

7. There are few adequate studies of nineteenth-century labour market relationships. F. Strahan, 'The Growth and Extent of Company Mining on the Victorian Goldfields in the 1850's', B.A. thesis, University of Melbourne, 1955, deals with wage labour and co-partnerships. Indentured labour in the sugar industry is sketched by Kay Saunders, in R. Evans, K. Saunders and K. Cronin, *Exclusion, Exploitation and Extermination*, A.N.Z. Book Co., Sydney, 1975, pp. 167–208. From the 1840s into the early twentieth century, the principle of subcontracting divided the working class, but there is as yet no systematic account of it. See, for example, Coghlan, *Labour and Industry*, vol. 2, p. 1030, for a New South Wales government scheme in 1870, and the resistance of the unemployed to it. See also, Irving, 'Development of Liberal Politics', chs 5 and 6 for the 1840s.

8. Amongst historians of empire, there has been a long debate about how imperialist the industrial bourgeoisie were, and how important their

economic self-interest was in the making of imperial policy. See J. M. Ward, *Colonial Self-government: The British Experience, 1759–1856*, Macmillan, London, 1976, ch. 7, for a discussion of this debate and of the new imperialist vision. Throughout his book, Ward stresses the influence of British constitutional, and to a lesser extent economic, developments. Our approach, which sees imperialism as an aspect of the development of the capitalist state, necessarily accepts that there was an 'imperialism of free trade', but considers that questions about economic versus other 'factors', interests versus ideals and colonists versus imperial administrators are limited in their usefulness to a general analysis of imperialism.

9. T. H. Irving, 'The Idea of Responsible Government in New South Wales before 1856', *Historical Studies*, vol. 11, 1964, pp. 190 ff.; M. Barratt Brown, *After Imperialism*, Heinemann, London, 1963, ch. 2, who sketches the economic basis of the imperialism of free trade; and Ward, *Colonial Self-government*, pp. 291–6, for the British government's approach to constitutional reform in Australia.

10. Ward, *Colonial Self-government*, ch. 9; Irving, 'Development of Liberal Politics', ch. 9; and W. G. McMinn, 'Government and the Land Problem in New South Wales', and S. G. Foster, 'The Concession of Responsible Government to New South Wales', both in *New South Wales—Autocracy to Parliament, 1824–1856*, Parliament of New South Wales, Legislative Council, Sydney, 1976, pp. 3–26 and 27–56.

11. *Sydney Morning Herald*, 13 November 1857, editorial (Document 3.1); J. N. Molony, *An Architect of Freedom: John Hubert Plunkett*, A.N.U.P., Canberra, 1973, pp. 251–60; and R. Wettenhall, 'Administrative Boards in Nineteenth Century Australia', *Public Administration* (Sydney), vol. 22, 1963, pp. 255–67.

12. P. Loveday, 'Patronage and Politics in New South Wales, 1856–1870', *Public Administration* (Sydney), vol. 18, 1959, pp. 341–58; G. N. Hawker, *The Parliament of New South Wales, 1856–1965*, Government Printer, Sydney, 1971, p. 79; R. S. Parker, *Public Service Recruitment in Australia*, M.U.P., Melbourne, 1942, p. 21; and K. W. Knight, 'The Development of the Public Service in New South Wales from Responsible Government (1856) to the Establishment of the Public Service Board (1895)', M.Ec. thesis, University of Sydney, 1956, pp. 71–4.

13. K. W. Knight, 'Patronage and the New South Wales Public Service: The 1894 Royal Commission', *A.J.P.H.*, vol. 7, 1961, pp. 166–85; Hawker, *Parliament of New South Wales*, pp. 16 and 19, where he shows that between 1858–59 and 1883, 'internal administration' bills in the New South Wales Assembly rose from 12 per cent to 30 per cent, while 'conservation and development' bills dropped from 34 per cent to 20 per cent. E. A. Boehm, *Prosperity and Depression in Australia, 1887–1897*, Clarendon Press, Oxford, 1971, pp. 265–7, for the Victorian businessmen–politicians; P. N. Lamb, 'Geoffrey Eagar and the Colonial Treasury of New South Wales', *Australian Economic Papers*, vol. 1, 1962, pp. 24–41; R. L. Wettenhall, 'Early Railway Management Legislation in New South Wales', *Tasmanian University Law Review*, vol. 1, 1960, pp. 446–74; and *Railway Management and Politics in Victoria, 1856–1906*, Royal Institute of Public Administration, A.C.T. Group, Canberra, 1961; and P. Loveday, A. W. Martin and R. S. Parker (eds), *The*

Emergence of the Australian Party System, Hale & Iremonger, Sydney, 1977, pp. 41–3, 453–87, who stress the development of organisational practices to account for the emergence.

14. N. G. Butlin, 'Colonial Socialism in Australia, 1860–1900', in H. G. J. Aitken (ed.), *The State and Economic Growth*, Social Science Research Council, New York, 1959, pp. 35 ff., for a discussion of the separate sectors of the economy. Butlin also notes that the public sector retarded private capital formation, but does not see this as the price paid for reorganisation of the class as a whole. On railways, see Irving, 'Development of Liberal Politics', pp. 480–2; Campbell to Parkes, 3 May 1854, Parkes Papers, M. L. (A878); and *Empire*, 24 April 1853, editorial.

15. A fuller discussion of the purposes of the Land Acts is in Irving, '1850–1870', pp. 153–9. The 1864 legislation is in Boehm, *Prosperity and Depression*, pp. 220–1; G. D. Patterson, *The Tariff in the Australian Colonies, 1856–1900*, Cheshire, Melbourne, 1968, pp. 164–7; and A. R. Hall, *The London Capital Market and Australia, 1870–1914*, Social Science Monograph 21, A.N.U., Canberra, 1963, ch. 5 on the Australian demand for capital and the role of government, and p. 167 for the land speculators. Also N. G. Butlin, *Investment in Australian Economic Development, 1861–1900*, A.N.U.P., Canberra, 1972 (first publ. 1964), p. 335.

16. Social disorder is discussed in a later section of this chapter. For the response to it, see D. M. MacCallum, 'The Early Volunteer Corps: The Origins of the Modern Australian Army', *Arts*, vol. 1, 1959, pp. 142–66; and K. L. Milte and T. A. Weber, *Police in Australia: Development, Functions and Procedures*, Butterworths, Sydney, 1977, pp. 1–31.

17. Butlin, 'Colonial Socialism', pp. 63–4; Hawker, *Parliament of New South Wales*, p. 19; J. Hagan, 'Employers, Trade Unions and the First Factory Acts', *Labour History*, vol. 7, 1964, pp. 3–10; M. J. Ely, 'The Management of Schools in New South Wales, 1848–1880: Local Initiative Suppressed?', in R. N. Spann and G. R. Curnow (eds), *Public Policy and Administration in Australia: A Reader*, Wiley, Sydney, 1975, p. 248; A. Wesson, 'Mechanics' Institutes in Victoria', *Australian Journal of Adult Education*, vol. 12, 1972, pp. 3–10; and B. Dickey, 'Charity in New South Wales, 1850–1914: Outdoor Relief to the Aged and Destitute', *J.R.A.H.S.*, vol. 52, 1966, pp. 9–32.

18. C. P. Hodgson, *Reminiscences of Australia*, Simpkin & Marshall, London, 1846, p. 139.

19. Irving, 'Development of Liberal Politics', chs 2–4; B. Dyster, 'Support for the Squatters, 1844', *J.R.A.H.S.*, vol. 51, 1965, pp. 41–59; K. Buckley, 'Gipps and the Graziers of New South Wales, 1841–6', *Historical Studies*, vol. 6, 1955, pp. 396–412 (Part I); and ibid., vol. 7, 1956, pp. 178–93 (Part II); and Roe, *Quest for Authority*, ch. 2.

20. Kolsen, 'Company Formation', p. 20; G. Abbott and G. Little (eds), *The Respectable Sydney Merchant: A. B. Spark of Tempe*, S.U.P., Sydney, 1976; and B. Dyster, 'Prosperity, Prostration, Prudence: Business and Investment in Sydney, 1838–1851', in A. Birch and D. Macmillan (eds), *Wealth and Progress*, Angus & Robertson, Sydney, 1967, pp. 51–76.

21. Irving, 'Development of Liberal Politics', pp. 82–99, on the corn question, and ch. 8, on the bourgeois nature of the anti-transportation movement. The existence of the League flag, containing a representation of the Southern Cross, points to the origin of nationalism among substantial liberal capitalists, several years before *petit-bourgeois* radicals raised their flag at Eureka. Roe, *Quest for Authority*, pt 3, for all its excellence as a study of the emerging bourgeois ideology, ignores the material basis, in the power of property, for the authority of 'moral enlightenment', and thereby excludes political economy from bourgeois ideology.

22. A full study of constitution-making in the context of class forces has yet to be made. Irving, '1850–1870', pp. 128–33, stresses evidence for class forces at the ideological level; as does R. A. Gollan, *Radical and Working Class Politics: A Study of Eastern Australia, 1850–1910*, M.U.P., Melbourne, 1960, p. 6. The historiographical debate concentrates on the political level and on the role of ideas, in this case political philosophies; see, for example, J. M. Main, 'Making Constitutions in New South Wales and Victoria', *Historical Studies*, vol. 7, 1957, pp. 377–8.

23. Alan Powell, *Patrician Democrat: The Political Life of Charles Cowper, 1843–1870*, M.U.P., Melbourne, 1977, for details of liberal political leadership in New South Wales.

24. The data on businessmen and company formation is from Ferguson, 'New South Wales Company Formation', appendices. These lists of companies include some formed before 1865 and omit others that were formed in the period. The biographies of entrepreneurs (misleadingly referred to as 'professional' directors) must also be used with caution. For the A.M.P. Society, see Dyster, 'Prosperity, Prostration, Prudence', p. 68. James McEachern was the radical agitator; see G. Blainey, *Gold and Paper: A History of the National Bank of Australasia Ltd*, Georgian House, Melbourne, 1968, pp. 12–13. On the pastoral companies, see N. G. Butlin, 'Company Ownership of N.S.W. Pastoral Stations, 1865–1900', *Historical Studies*, vol. 4, 1950, pp. 89–111; and Butlin and Barnard, 'Pastoral Finance'. The urban land booms are discussed in Ferguson, 'New South Wales Company Formation', chs 3 and 7; and in M. Cannon, *Land, Boom and Bust*, Heritage, Melbourne, 1972.

25. Trevor Matthews, 'Business Associations and Politics: Chambers of Manufacturers and Employers Federations in New South Wales, Victorian and Australian National Politics to 1939', Ph.D. thesis, University of Sydney, 1971, sect. 1, 'Origins'; and T. G. Parsons, 'An outline of Employer Organization in the Victorian Manufacturing Industries, 1870–1890', *Journal of Industrial Relations*, vol. 14, 1972, pp. 23–8. The information on banking is from Hall, *Stock Exchange of Melbourne and the Victorian Economy*, p. 41. On the vend, see E. Ross, *A History of the Miners' Federation of Australia*, the union, Sydney, 1970, p. 33.

26. The regional expansion and contraction of manufacturing is treated by G. J. R. Linge, 'The Forging of an Industrial Nation: Manufacturing in Australia 1788–1913', in J. M. Powell and M. Williams (eds), *Australian Space, Australian Time: Geographical Perspectives*, O.U.P., Melbourne, 1975,

pp. 153–80. The decline of country-town business can be traced in T. G. Parsons, 'Technclogical Change in the Melbourne Flour-milling and Brewing Industries, 1870–90', *A.E.H.R.*, vol. 11, 1971, pp. 133–46; and W. S. Logan, 'The Decline of Victoria's Southwestern Outports, 1890–1900', ibid., vol. 16, 1977, pp. 25–46. For South Australia, see J. B. Hirst, *Adelaide and the Country, 1870–1917: Their Social and Political Relationship*, M.U.P., Melbourne, 1973, which deals in passing with economic power. On rural politics in this period, see A. W. Martin, 'Pastoralists in the Legislative Assembly of New South Wales, 1870–1890', in Barnard (ed.), *Simple Fleece*, pp. 577–91; D. B. Waterson, *Squatter, Selector, and Storekeeper: A History of the Darling Downs, 1859–93*, S.U.P., Sydney, 1968; and R. B. Walker, *The Newspaper Press in New South Wales, 1803–1920*, S.U.P., Sydney, 1976, ch. 15. Regional sharemarkets, attracting metropolitan and local capital, were found in mining centres such as Bendigo and Charters Towers; see Hall, *Stock Exchange of Melbourne*, pp. 81–3; and G C. Bolton, *A Thousand Miles Away: A History of North Queensland to 1920*, Jacaranda, Brisbane, 1963, pp. 126–7, 290.

27. J. M. Ward, *Empire in the Antipodes: The British in Australasia, 1840–1860*, Arnold, London, 1966, pp. 29–30; and J. A. La Nauze, 'Merchants in Action: The Australian Tariffs of 1852', *Economic Record*, vol. 31, 1955, pp. 77–89.

28. Parsons, 'An Outline of Employer Organization', pp. 23–8; and Matthews, 'Business Associations', pp. 25–7.

29. T. Irving and B. Berzins, 'History and the New Left: Beyond Radicalism', in R. Gordon (ed.), *The Australian New Left: Critical Essays and Strategy*, Heinemann, Melbourne, 1970, pp. 78–81, on the populist situation at the beginning of this period. The explanation therein fails to distinguish structural principles from their effects. See also M. Roe, *Kenealy and the Tichborne Cause: A Study in Mid-Victorian Populism*, M.U.P., Melbourne, 1974, on Australian populism in the 1880s, who suggests that populism is linked to class structuration (p. 192) and that its demise is linked to the success of parliamentary democracy (p. 195).

30. The problem of social control in this period continues to be neglected. K. S. Inglis, *The Australian Colonists: An Exploration of Social History, 1788–1870*, M.U.P., Melbourne, 1974, pp. 184–90, sees disorder as inchoate anti-imperialism. *Eureka, Rebellion Beneath the Southern Cross*, ed. Geoffrey Gold, Rigby, Adelaide, and Widescope International, Melbourne, 1977, is also concerned with the anti-imperial aspect, although H. D. McQueen's chapter points to how work methods (in deep shafts) contributed to digger organisation and grievances. T. H. Irving, 'Some Aspects of the Study of Radical Politics in New South Wales before 1856', *Labour History*, November 1963, no. 5, pp. 18–25, raised the issue of widespread disorder. P. N. Grabosky, *Sydney in Ferment, Crime and Official Reaction, 1788–1973*, A.N.U.P., Canberra, 1977, is a superficial piece of behavioural history. G. C. Mundy was the Deputy Adjutant-General; see his *Our Antipodes, or Residence and Rambles in the Australian Colonies with a Glimpse of the Gold Fields*, Richard Bentley, London, 1852, vol. 1, p. 50. 'Saint Monday' is referred to in *S.M.H.*, 18 August 1853 (letter) and *Sydney Journal and Daily Advertiser*, 10 August 1847 (editorial). The English origins of 'Saint Monday' in small-scale, domestic and out-work industries is discussed in E. P. Thompson, 'Time, Work-Discipline

and Industrial Capitalism', in M. W. Flinn and T. C. Smout (eds), *Essays in Social History*, Clarendon Press, Oxford, 1974, pp. 50–3. Details of bourgeois and state responses to disorder are in Irving, 'Development of Liberal Politics', chs 6–10. See also A. W. Martin, 'Drink and Deviance in Sydney: Investigating Intemperance, 1854–5', *Historical Studies*, vol. 17, 1977, pp. 358–60.

31. Irving, 'Development of Liberal Politics', chs 6 and 10. Bede Nairn, *Civilising Capitalism: The Labor Movement in New South Wales, 1870–1900*, A.N.U.P., Canberra, 1973, for the Trades and Labour Council of New South Wales; H. Mayer, *Marx, Engels and Australia*, Cheshire, Melbourne, 1964, pt 1, for the First International in Australia; Serle, *Golden Age*, chs 9–10, on the Land Convention; Roe, *Kenealy*, and B. Mansfield, *Australian Democrat: The Career of Edward William O'Sullivan, 1846–1910*, S.U.P., Sydney, 1965, on radicalism in the 1840s; and Ruth Knight, *Illiberal Liberal: Robert Lowe in New South Wales, 1842–1850*, M.U.P., Melbourne, 1966, ch. 6.

32. On radical ideology, see Irving, 'Development of Liberal Politics', ch. 10; and Gollan, *Radical and Working Class Politics*, chs 1–2.

33. A radical critique of individualism as a barrier to popular mobilisation was developed in the *People's Advocate* (Sydney) during 1850 and 1851; see issues of 2 September and 16 November 1850, and 1 March and 19 July 1851.

34. 'Development' is discussed in Irving, 'Development of Liberal Politics', ch. 11; on racism and liberal ideology, see Ann Curthoys, 'Race and Ethnicity: New South Wales, 1856–1881', Ph.D. thesis, Macquarie University, 1973, Conclusion.

35. The capture of the leadership of radical organisations by the bourgeoisie is discussed by Irving in 'Development of Liberal Politics', ch. 8; and 'Electoral Reform and the Liberal Movement', B.A. (Hons) thesis, University of Sydney, 1959.

36. Irving, 'Electoral Reform'; and G. R. Quaife, 'The Diggers: Democratic Sentiment and Political Apathy', *A.J.P.H.*, vol. 13, 1967, pp. 221–46.

37. Peter F. McDonald, *Marriage in Australia*, A.N.U.P., Canberra, 1974, ch. 5, is a detailed demographic study that contradicts contemporary opinion that social conditions contributed to a higher marriage rate among workers in the colonies than in England. Michael Cannon, *Australia in the Victorian Age, Volume 3: Life in the Cities*, Nelson, Melbourne, 1975, provides lively and contrasting sketches of bourgeois and working-class domestic life. The role of women in the family is treated by Anne Summers, *Damned Whores and God's Police: The Colonization of Women in Australia*, Penguin, Ringwood, Vic., 1975, ch. 9. For the Mayor of Sydney's entry into citizenship, see *Bulletin* (Sydney), 21 August 1880, p. 2.

38. See McDonald, *Marriage in Australia*, p. 51, for the New South Wales Act of 1852 requiring all single women receiving assisted passages to be indentured for two years. The female immigration schemes are discussed by Summers, *Damned Whores*. Kay Daniels, 'Introduction', in Kay Daniels, Mary Murnane and Anne Picot (eds), *Women in Australia: An Annotated Guide to Records*, A.G.P.S., Canberra, 1977, vol. 1, pp. v–xix, shows the role played

by bourgeois charity in reproducing poverty and hence the need of some women for domestic employment. This excellent introduction to a valuable guide to sources also stresses the part-time wage labour of working-class wives, and, *contra* Summers, the occasions on which state policy actively discouraged family immigration in order to secure sufficient domestic servants for the bourgeoisie. The view of the housewife as reproducing labour power comes from J. F. Conigrave, *A Paper Read at a Meeting of the Chamber of Manufacturers on Monday, November 8, 1875*, Adelaide, 1875, p. 18.

39. R. V. Jackson, *Australian Economic Development in the Nineteenth Century*, A.N.U.P., Canberra, 1977, pp. 103–4 and 121–6, for these comforting conclusions; and p. 128, for the tenancy rate in 1891. Max Kelly's *A Certain Sydney*, Doak Press, Sydney, 1977, describes working-class housing and the parliamentary and newspaper investigations of this housing between 1851 and 1900. See also Cannon, *Life in the Cities*, pp. 264–7, for slums in Sydney and Melbourne. For the 1860 inquiry, see G. P. Walsh, 'Factories and Factory Workers in New South Wales, 1788–1900', *Labour History*, no. 21, 1971, p. 12. The quotation is from Kelly (n.p.).

40. The place of religion in the colonial social structure has not attracted much attention from religious historians. However, Ronald Lawson, *Brisbane in the 1890's: A Study of an Australian Urban Society*, Q.U.P., St Lucia, 1973, ch. 8, deals with religion, although within a stratificationist framework. A similar approach, but equally as valuable in its detail, is Renate Howe, 'Social Composition of the Wesleyan Church in Victoria during the Nineteenth Century', *Journal of Religious History*, vol. 4, 1967, pp. 206–17. Geoffrey Serle also makes clear the distance between the churches and the workers in *The Rush to be Rich: A History of the Colony of Victoria, 1883–1889*, M.U.P., Melbourne, 1974, chs 4–5. See also F. B. Smith, 'Joseph Symes and the Australasian Secularists Association', *Labour History*, no. 5, 1963, pp. 26–47. Most histories of the churches deal with the limited success of liberalism in the churches; see P. J. O'Farrell, *The Catholic Church in Australia: A Short History, 1788–1967*, Chapman, London, 1969, pp. 58–88.

41. Inglis, *Australian Colonists*, pp. 125–36, on the growth of spectator sport. For the class basis of adult education, see A. Wesson, 'Mechanics Institutes in Victoria', *Australian Journal of Adult Education*, vol. 12, 1972, pp. 3–10; and D. I. McDonald, 'The Diffusion of Scientific and Other Useful Knowledge', *J.R.A.H.S.*, vol. 54, 1968, pp. 176–93. Our Documents 3.17 to 3.20 illustrate cultural control through voluntary organisations. Education is dealt with in the next chapter, but see R. E. N. Twopenny, *Town Life in Australia*, London, 1883, pp. 131–3, on disciplinary problems in schools for bourgeois children.

42. Most of the general histories of Australia give a sketch of the outward form of bourgeois culture in this period. Michael Cannon's three-volume *Australia in the Victorian Age* adds not only more detail but a sense of class differences in culture. Brian Dickey's '"Colonial Bourgeois"—Marx in Australia? Aspects of a Social History of New South Wales, 1856–1900', *A.E.H.R.*, vol. 14, 1974, pp. 20–36, mistakes class analysis for a description of economic categories; Dickey seeks the dynamic of society in 'dominant ideas', with the result that the formation of bourgeois culture is taken for granted in his analysis.

43. There is no systematic analysis of the structure and scope of the colonial labour market in the work of the economic historians. Coghlan, *Labour and Industry in Australia*, remains the best general description of immigration, wages and employment. Sinclair, *Process of Economic Development in Australia*, is more sensitive to fluctuations in employment and wage rates than is Butlin, *Investment in Australian Economic Development*. A valuable corrective to over-generalisation about the job security of skilled workers is K. Buckley, 'A New Index of Engineering Unemployment, 1852–94', *Economic Record*, vol. 43, 1967, pp. 108–18. See E. J. Hobsbawm, *The Age of Capital, 1848–1875*, Weidenfeld & Nicolson, London, chs 3 and 11, for the global patterns of labour supply. On Parkes, see [J. Norton (ed.)], *The History of Capital and Labour . . .*, Oceanic Publishing Co., Sydney, 1888, p. 49; and Coghlan, *Labour and Industry*, vol. 2, p. 774. Our Document 3.13 deals with a walk-out by compositors working in Parkes' printery. On the Victorian masons, see Coghlan, vol. 2, pp. 737–8.

44. Basic data about the ethnic composition of the workforce is in F. K. Crowley, 'The British Contribution to the Australian Population, 1860–1919', *University Studies in History and Economics*, vol. 2, 1954, pp. 55–88. Assisted immigration is discussed as a political issue, but not in class terms, by A. A. Hayden, 'New South Wales Immigration Policy, 1856–1900', *Transactions of the American Philosophical Society*, new series, vol. 61, 1971, pt 6, pp. 5–60. Labour market segmentation is suggested in E. C. Fry, 'Outwork in the Eighties: An Examination of Outwork in the Infant Industries of the Eastern Australian Colonies, 1880–90', *University Studies in History and Economics*, vol. 2, 1956, pp. 77–93; Evans *et al.*, *Exclusion, Exploitation and Extermination*, pp. 19, 216, 221–2; and D. McDonald, 'Child and Female Labour in Sydney, 1876–1898', *A.N.U. Historical Journal*, vols 10–11, 1973–74, pp. 40–9, who quotes the tobacco factory manager. Although B. Barrett's *The Inner Suburbs: The Evolution of an Industrial Area*, M.U.P., Melbourne, 1971, mistakes 'community values' for the full range of class forces, which were expressed through land use and settlement patterns and which produced the living areas for the lowest stratum of workers, it is a most valuable history of certain working-class suburbs. For data on female wage rates, see Coghlan, *Labour and Industry*, vol. 3, pp. 1587–9.

45. The first edition of *Capital*, vol. 1, appeared in 1867. See Evans *et al.*, *Exclusion, Exploitation and Extermination*, pp. 5–6, for attitudes in Queensland to Italian workers. Data for the calculations on the ratio of skilled to unskilled wages comes from Coghlan, *Labour and Industry*, vol. 2 (pt 5, ch. 5) and vol. 3 (pt 6, ch. 6). J. Child, *Unionism and the Labor Movement*, Macmillan, Melbourne, 1971, pp. 34–40, refers to the difficulties of the skilled unions in relation to unskilled workers. Geographical mobility of labour in Victoria is mentioned by D. U. Cloher, 'A Perspective on Australian Urbanization', in Powell and Williams (eds), *Australian Space, Australian Time*, pp. 126–7.

46. For the absence of technological innovation in this period in the metal trades, see K. Buckley, *The Amalgamated Engineers in Australia, 1852–1920*, A.N.U.P., Canberra, 1970, p. 21. In the boot and clothing industry, full mechanisation did not occur until the end of the period, as Fry shows, 'Out-work in the Eighties', pp. 82–3.

47. There were Irish landowners to the south-west of Sydney and Irish

businessmen involved in Melbourne banking. M. de Lepervanche, 'Australian Immigrants, 1788–1940: Desired and Unwanted', in E. L. Wheelwright and K. Buckley (eds), *Essays in the Political Economy of Australian Capitalism*, A.N.Z. Book Co., Sydney, 1975, vol. 1, assumes that immigrants formed a low status group in the working class (which she takes as given). However, she contradicts herself to conclude that British immigrants 'did not form a permanent, physically differentiated minority group' (p. 91). A sample of demonstrations by the unemployed is referred to in Coghlan, *Labour and Industry*, vol. 2, pp. 700–3 (N.S.W., 1859–60), pp. 1056–9 (Qld, 1866), p. 1073 (S.A., 1870). On government response to them, see Hayden, 'N.S.W. Immigration', pp. 52–3.

48. Norton, *History of Capital and Labour*, p. 99, has figures for size of coal-mines; Buckley, *Amalgamated Engineers*, p. 15, for Mort's Dock. There is a general survey in Walsh, 'Factories and Factory Workers in New South Wales', pp. 1–16.

49. Information about workers' collective autonomy in production can be found in J. Hagan and C. Fisher, 'Piecework and Some of its Consequences in the Printing and Coal Mining Industries in Australia, 1850–1930', *Labour History*, no. 25, 1973, pp. 19–39; J. C. Docherty, 'The Rise of Railway Unionism: A Study of New South Wales and Victoria, *c.* 1880–1905', M.A. (History) thesis, School of General Studies, Australian National University, 1973, pp. 3–14; and Child, *Unionism and the Labor Movement*, pp. 73–5 (coal-miners) and p. 60 (gold-miners). Co-operatives, usually formed by workers during strikes and lock-outs, must be distinguished from the proposals for co-partnership made by liberals and their supporters in the unions. For the liberal position, see G. K. Holden, *An Enquiry into the New Relations between Labour and Capital*, William Maddock, Sydney, 1867; and William Roylance's speech to the First Intercolonial Trade Union Congress, Sydney, 1879, reprinted in R. N. Ebbels, *The Australian Labor Movement, 1850–1907*, Australasian Book Society, Sydney, 1960, pp. 93–5. For workers' co-operatives, see Ebbels, *Australian Labor Movement*, p. 86; Buckley, *Amalgamated Engineers*, p. 22; J. Hagan, *Printers and Politics*, A.N.U.P., Canberra, 1966, p. 28; and Ross, *History of the Miners' Federation*, pp. 23–4. On the tailoresses' strike, see Fry, 'Out-work in the Eighties', p. 81.

50. On the A.S.E., see Buckley, *Amalgamated Engineers*, p. 41. W. G. Spence, *History of the A.W.U.*, Australian Worker, Sydney, 1911 (repr. 1961), ch. 1, on oppressive clauses in the labour contracts of shearers. Norton, *History of Capital and Labour*, pp. 108–10, on N.S.W. railway and tramway employees, pp. 180–1, on Melbourne coal-lumpers, p. 153, on factory foremen, and p. 185, on violence against strike-breakers.

51. Norton, *History of Capital and Labour*, p. 232, on boilermakers, pp. 181–5, on militant workers, and p. 235, for the quotation on the South Australian Trades and Labour Council. Coghlan, *Labour and Industry*, vol. 2, p. 1056, for railway labourers.

52. Because labour historians have ignored the processes of class formation, they have written one-sided accounts of the labour movement in this period. Thus N. B. Nairn, in various studies, has documented the growth of labour as a legitimate political interest, and H. McQueen has focused on the *petit-*

bourgeois outlook of unions and unionists. Neither seems aware of the existence of the illegitimate and disruptive activities of workers, which made necessary the processes they write about. See N. B. Nairn, 'Some Aspects of the Social Role of the Labour Movement in New South Wales in the 1870's', *Bulletin of the Australian Society for the Study of Labour History*, no. 1, 1962, pp. 6–15; and 'The Role of the Trades and Labor Council in New South Wales, 1871–1891', *Historical Studies*, vol. 7, 1957, pp. 421–40; and H. McQueen, *A New Britannia*, Penguin, Ringwood, Vic., 1970, pp. 204–8. R. Markey, 'Civilizing Capitalism', *Arena*, no. 36, 1974, pp. 61–4, reviewing Nairn's book of the same title, points out that McQueen and Nairn agree about the integration of the labour movement, but while 'Nairn rejoices in the product, McQueen does not'.

53. A one-sided stress on the importance of increased leisure time to the workers in the eight-hours movement is found in Inglis, *Australian Colonists*, pp. 117–25 ('the sacred gift of time'). A more balanced account is in Buckley, *Amalgamated Engineers*, ch. 4, who shows how some workers also linked job security and wages with the shorter hours question. Helen Hughes, 'The Eight Hour Day and the Development of the Labour Movement in Victoria in the Eighteen Fifties', *Historical Studies*, vol. 9, 1961, pp. 396–412, is valuable for its detail. She points to the broad outlook of the craft unions, who aided organisation of the unskilled, and the increasing separateness of the workmen's movement from the radicals. J. Niland, 'In Search of Shorter Hours: The 1861 and 1874 Iron Trades Disputes', *Labour History*, no. 12, 1967, pp. 3–15; and 'The Birth of the Movement for an Eight Hour Working Day in New South Wales', *A.J.P.H.*, vol. 14, 1968, pp. 75–87, contain evidence for an interpretation of the movement as moving from a concern with self-improvement to the collective improvement of a subordinate class. He also stresses the way the movement challenged notions about work-rule establishment and change. Child, *Unionism and the Labor Movement*, p. 51, refers to Victoria's 'democratic spirit'. On labour political economy, see the suggestion in C. D. W. Goodwin, *Economic Enquiry in Australia*, Duke U.P., Durham, N.C., 1966, p. 352; and W. E. Murphy, *History of the Eight Hours' Movement*, Spectator Publishing Co., Melbourne, 1896, p. 66, for speech by C. J. Don.

Documents

The State

3.1 Political control of public servants
3.2 Government and business: The Overland Telegraph
3.3 Parliamentary politics: The end of the one-party system

Business

3.4 Income from capital
3.5 The growth of a family shipping firm
3.6 The organisation of businessmen
3.7 Speculative capital in the 1880s

Economic Independence: Ideology and Reality

3.8 The lower depths
3.9 The skilled worker's budget
3.10 A worker makes it — with the help of his wife
3.11 Prodigal tradesmen

The Labour Market

3.12 Employer equals master
3.13 Strikers guilty of conspiracy
3.14 Railway strike: Police versus labourers
3.15 Violence on the picket-line
3.16 Management

Cultural Control

3.17 The formation of a Mechanics' Institute
3.18 A children's temperance organisation
3.19 The formation of a church school
3.20 Securing order in a voluntary organisation

Bourgeois Ideology

3.21 Development
3.22 Education for citizenship
3.23 Co-operation between labour and capital
3.24 Qualifications for public office

3.1 Political control of public servants

Conservatives reacted bitterly when responsible government led to political control of public servants, especially when, as in New South Wales in 1857, the squatters' lands were at stake. Not only were public officials in the departments connected with the land system sympathetic to the squatters, but the development works that contractors carried out as part of the liberal programme weakened squatter control of the pastoral districts. Conservatives therefore favoured the retention of Boards of Commissioners, appointed before responsible government, to run sensitive government activities.

Source: *Sydney Morning Herald*, 13 November 1857, editorial.

The Cowper Ministry has expressed an opinion against the use of Boards in Government.

... The cry for "popular Government" in this colony is a deceptive cry. It is pernicious as a diversion of the public mind from the real danger. It is impossible for anything to prevent the Government being made dependent on the votes of those electors who choose to vote. When the so-called reformers pretend there is some despotic power — some class domineering over the rest, in virtue of rank or wealth — they are merely gulling the populace. No such power does exist, and until some ages have passed, none such will be found in the colonies. ...

It is not in that direction that we have to fear any obstruction to popular Government. But an evil is at our doors, of a far more serious nature than any supposed by political theories. This is the sale of Government patronage; the bribery of public officers, and generally the use of popular institutions to get a vote, and to make it a matter of barter and sale.

The peculiar circumstances of this colony offer every facility to this bribery. We have a vast estate, and by the proposed law its distribution will be in the hands of Ministers. ...

Beside the land management, there is the patronage of an ever extending web of offices, multiplying daily, and comprehending appointments of great value. It is fearful to reflect that judicial offices as well as others of great trust are at the disposal of parliamentary majorities, such as the present House gives; still more alarming when we look at the ever downward tendency in the popular choice.

But we have another grand field of jobbery and corruption, full of intricacies and obscurities — the *Contract* department.

That there might be every guarantee of fairness, the late Governments established Boards to deal with tenders. We are told that Boards are screens. They may be so; but it is far more likely that a bargain struck by a head of a department would be corrupt if acting alone — and it is equally likely, under the same circumstances, a bargain would be struck by a corrupt Minister. It is the impossibility of trusting several parties with a secret that makes it not only safer, but indispensable that no transaction involving money be left to one or two men. It is not at all impossible that a Minister will receive direct bribes; history does not lack examples. But it is positively certain that they will tacitly assent to a system of bribes, if necessary to the duration of their power.

... The object of a Board is to have a chance that a bona fide opinion of what is best for the public may be obtained; that discussion may take place;

that reasons may be given and recorded; and, finally, that a Minister, who goes in the teeth of a competent authority, may be under some practical responsibility.

The general responsibility of Ministers, we repeat, as a protection against bargains, is a delusion. What does it amount to?

They may be turned out of office by the Assembly, but who is to make the Assembly turn them out. The late Ministers were threatened with the loss of supporters, purely on selfish grounds,—that is, for not giving what was equivalent to public money. The responsibility of Ministers is a great cheat—the reverse of the popular idea; a responsibility to men who may, if they choose, sell their votes for whatever the Minister can bestow. Boards are a check on one large department of bribery,—for wherever money is to be expended, a honest Minister will desire a check; and a roguish Minister ought not to escape one.

3.2 Government and business: The Overland Telegraph

Development works assisted local businessmen (as contractors) and the system of business. However, in bourgeois ideology, 'development' was 'a great triumph of science and civilisation'.

Robert Dalrymple Ross retired from a successful career in the Army Commissariat to become a businessman and politician in South Australia. He was chairman of the Adelaide Steamship Company and Speaker of the Assembly.

Source: *Illustrated London News*, 22 February 1873.

THE AUSTRALIAN TELEGRAPH

The completion and opening, at the end of October last, of the great Overland Australian Telegraph, from the north coast, across the whole width of that vast continent, to the town of Adelaide, South Australia, brought all the Australian colonies into electric communication with Europe, Asia, and America.... In 1869 Captain Sherard Osborn announced to the various Australian Governments that it was contemplated to lay a cable to North Australia, either by way of Madras and Java or direct from Ceylon. He invited them to arrange among themselves for the completion of their land lines from the farthest point they had then reached in Queensland to Port Darwin, Arnhem's Land, on the north-west coast.... There were rival projects launched in the same year—one for connecting Java with Burketown at the head of the Gulf of Carpentaria, without entering South Australia at all; and another for laying a cable from Ceylon to Swan River, on the west coast, with a continuation from King George's Sound to Adelaide, on the south coast. These last were hampered with stipulations for subsidies or guarantees which the colonies were not disposed to concede. Captain Sherard Osborn, as agent of the Telegraph Construction and Maintenance Company, then undertook to lay a cable on the sole condition of finding a land line to which it could be attached.

Mr. Charles Todd, Postmaster-General and Superintendent of Telegraphs in South Australia, had already proposed to lay an overland line from

Adelaide directly north to Port Darwin, along the track of Stuart, the explorer, who in 1861 crossed the Australian continent in that direction. This plan was again taken up by Mr. R. D. Ross, a gentleman long resident in the colony, who was then in England. He gained for it some influential supporters here, and recommended it to Sir James Fergusson, then newly appointed the Governor of South Australia. It was urged that efforts should be made in the colony to secure the route, which would place Adelaide and Melbourne in the most favourable relation to the through traffic.

In the early part of 1870, when this scheme was hatched, South Australia had a population of about 170,000 souls. It had incurred heavy liabilities for railways and public works within its settled districts.... Mr. Ross advised the South Australian Government to Americanise its policy, and "run" a telegraph through these 1700 miles of inhospitable bush. Sir James Fergusson, and his Premier, the Hon. H. B. T. Strangways, heartily entered into the scheme; and Mr. Ross's suggestion was answered, by return mail, with a proposal to Captain Sherard Osborn that they would lay a trans-continental line in time to meet his cable at Port Darwin. Commander Noel Osborn soon after arrived in Adelaide as agent for the British Australian Telegraph Company, and a contract was speedily concluded. Its terms were that the land line—1700 miles—should be completed by the end of 1871, and that it should be maintained in working order at the sole expense of the South Australian Government. In the event of communication being interrupted for a certain number of days in the year, the company was to be at liberty to erect an alternative line into Queensland.

The execution of the work has been superintended by Mr. Charles Todd. He began it, two years and a half ago, with a Parliamentary credit of £120,000 for expenses. The two end sections were let to local contractors, one taking 500 miles from Port Augusta northward, and the other 250 miles from Port Darwin southward. Nearly a thousand miles, embracing the least known and most inaccessible part of Central Australia, had to be constructed by the Government. ... Mr. Todd returned to Adelaide on Oct. 30, and was received with a public demonstration of welcome. The whole line of telegraph had been opened a week before, messages of congratulation being received from London on the 22nd, which had been transmitted in less than seven hours. It will be remembered that this great triumph of science and civilisation was celebrated in London, on Nov. 15, by a banquet at the Cannon-street Hotel, with the Earl of Kimberley, Secretary of State for the Colonies, in the chair.

3.3 Parliamentary politics: The end of the one-party system

The faction system depended on the political supremacy of the urban bourgeoisie and on agreement among 'able and true' men. When Parkes wrote to Bernhard Ringrose Wise, formerly a minister in his government, the faction leader's power was already being undermined by the rise of the party system and the political mobilisation of business interests and the working class.

Source: H. Parkes to B. R. Wise, Wise Correspondence, vol. 2, Mitchell Library, 1327/2.

Balmain
December 15th, 1889

My dear Wise,

I see so little of you of late and I have so little time for calling to mind those who are out of my place of work, that when I think of you it seems strange that I should be so ignorant of what you are doing. I hear of you saying this, that and the other thing to people at Clubs which seems to make me still more ignorant of you. And yet we ought to look to you as a power in the land, as one, and not the least one, to whose hands we dying men may safely leave the country. In a very few years, perhaps 2, 3, 4 or 5 and all the old men will be gone. There will be none left who stood by the cradle of Australian freedom.

At this time, in New South Wales, there is a danger—not fully seen as yet—of men of crude and narrow minds, of brutal instincts, and absolutely ignorant of the principles and rules which govern those entrusted with the management of the affairs of a nation; a positive danger of such men getting possession of the country. The next Election will turn the tide. How much, then, depends upon the next Election.

There is no use in disguising the fact. I am too old for much physical exertion. But those who have the strength should use it to the utmost. Really there is much more than free trade or protection at stake.

Our first work is to find men, and we must look to the native-born to supply our ranks. "Able and true" should be our motto. You must have thought of this and you can bring large help.

Sincerely,
Henry Parkes

3.4 Income from capital

When barrister John Hindmarsh, jun., the son of the first Governor of South Australia, calculated his household budget (not without mistakes) in the late 1850s, he expected to pay less than 2 per cent of his income (from rents and interest) in taxes. It appears that he listed his current expenses in a 'Red Book', subtracting for this budget his permanent from 'annual' expenses over two months. 'F and W' were probably bankers; Frederick Henry Botting was an Adelaide builder.

Source: Notebook of John Hindmarsh, Jr, 1850's and 1860's, State Library of South Australia, D4735 (L).

Estimate of Expenses—

Red Book			*Permanent not Annual*				£	s	d
						1 Year's expenses as per Red Book	162	13	6
11	17	10	11	12	0	Servant	23	8	0
4	19	8		4		Garden	6	0	0
5	10	8	2	8		Wine	10	0	0
				10					
2	19	4				Total House	202	1	6

				2	15		10 per cent in			
8	16	3		2	6	8	addition	20	4	1
3	4	2			1	6				
								222	5	7
8	7	8		2	6	0	Rent	45	0	0
5	4	6				6	Taxes	5	0	0
					2	6	Total Expenses	272	5	7
1	1	2			1					
					1	6				
52	1	3			1					
24	19	0			1					
27	2	3	for 2 months	2	14	8				
					7	6				
		x 6			5	3				
162	13	6	for 1 Year	1	0	0				
					3	6				
					3	6				
				6	12					
				1	2					
				24	19	0				

Income

Cash	£	s	d
Cash now in F & W's hands	1187	15	9
To be received from W Taylor	228	0	0
	1415	15	9
Six months expenses	150	0	0
	1265	15	9

Say £1300 to Invest at
10 per Cent = £130.

Mortgages	£	s	d
Botting Interest at 12½ per Cent on £575	71	17	6
F & W Interest at 10 per Cent on £300	30	0	0
	101	17	6

Rents	£	s	d
Barn	50	0	0
Stone House	30	0	0
Section 2913 Macclesfield	19	4	0
Section 19 Encounter Bay	40	0	0
	139	4	0
Section 116 Rent of or produce of	25	0	0
Rents	164	4	0

Recapitulation	£	s	d
Money	130		
Mortgages	101	17	6
Rents	164	4	0
	396	1	6
	272	5	7
Ought to save	124		

3.5 The growth of a family shipping firm

In the era of mercantile capitalism, shipping was a profitable activity and capital was accumulated easily by successful trading. This document omits the role of the shipowners in the defence of this capital (they were prominent in the anti-union organising of the 1880s), although it does suggest the ideological advantage of placing shares on the market and claiming to be a 'public' company when working-class militancy rose again in the 1910s.

Source: *1876–1926*: *Huddart Parker Ltd*, Huddart Parker, Sydney, 1926, pp. 3–5, 10, 15–16.

Geelong may fairly claim to be the birthplace of Huddart Parker Ltd.

It was in 1853 when His Excellency Charles Joseph La Trobe was Lieutenant Governor of Victoria that Mr. Thomas James Parker, representing the London firm of J. & D. Parker & Co., arrived at Geelong and established himself in business there as an importer and merchant. Realising that he was going to a new country which was absolutely "in the raw," he took the precaution to bring with him in the ship, along with an assortment of saleable merchandise, an iron store in which to display it. . . . .

Another citizen of Geelong at that early period, whose name was destined to live on indissolubly linked with that of Mr. T. J. Parker was Captain Peter Huddart. Captain Huddart, who came from the North of England, had been the master of the ship *Aberfoyle*. He commanded the *Aberfoyle* on a voyage to Melbourne, and he landed there in 1852. . . . Captain Peter Huddart appears in a Geelong Directory of the "fifties" as "Shipbroker and corn agent, Yarra Street, North."

Next to food the commodity in most general demand was coal. No coal was available in Victoria at that time. It had to be imported from New South Wales and a busy trade quickly sprang up with Newcastle. The fleet of colliers that carried on the trade between Melbourne or Geelong and Newcastle was composed of sailing craft—small barques, brigs and schooners. Captain Peter Huddart was one of the first to engage in that trade.

Mr. T. J. Parker was never associated in business directly with Captain Peter Huddart, and it was not until many years had passed in the independent development of the two businesses—Mr. Parker's and Captain Huddart's—that an amalgamation took place, and Mr. James Huddart, nephew of Captain Huddart, joined Mr. Parker and those associated with him. Before that occurred the tide of events set Mr. T. J. Parker definitely towards the career of a shipowner.

The screw steamer *Express* was put on by her owners to run in the trade between Geelong and Melbourne, and Captain Thomas Webb, who was afterwards associated with Mr. T. J. Parker and Mr. John Traill, joined her as chief officer. Mr. T. J. Parker took up the agency of the steamer in Geelong, and early in 1855 Mr. John Traill joined him as manager of the Express Steamer Agency. The *Express* carried passengers and cargo daily between Melbourne and Geelong, and gave excellent service to the public. ...

Mr. T. J. Parker's career as a shipowner began definitely when he acquired Captain William Howard Smith's half share of the little *Express*. When that event occurred, Mr. Parker left Geelong and took up his residence in Melbourne, assuming charge of the Express Agency there, while Mr. Traill remained in sole control at Geelong. ...

While Mr. Parker and his two associates were thus engaged, Captain Peter Huddart, the former master of the *Aberfoyle*, had not been idle. He controlled a fleet of small sailing craft engaged in bringing coal from Newcastle to Geelong, and he had built up a prosperous business there in association with his nephew, Mr. James Huddart, who joined him in the early sixties, and who established a business also in Ballarat. ...

It was in 1876 that Mr. James Huddart joined Mr. Parker, Mr. Traill and Captain Webb, forming the firm of Huddart Parker & Co., coal importers and merchants, at Geelong. Each partner had an equal interest, and Mr. Huddart was appointed manager. This was the foundation of Huddart Parker Ltd. The date upon which the combination was effected was August 1st, 1876.

The date of the foundation of Huddart Parker Ltd. is significant. The last quarter of the nineteenth century began in 1876. Historians relate that the last quarter of the nineteenth century comprised the period of the British Empire's greatest expansion. It was a period in which new territories in Asia, in Africa, and in Polynesia were continually coming under the British flag, and in which the Dominions, including Australia and New Zealand, were developing fast. The last and greatest forward move was being made by the British race, and Kipling was the poet who sprang forward as the authentic voice of the age. In that period of intense political, commercial and industrial activity, when the need for sea transport in the outlying parts of the Empire was being keenly experienced as essential to the development of all the local resources, Huddart Parker & Co. came into existence naturally, and, it would almost seem, inevitably. Ships, ships, and yet again more ships, that was the demand of the time and of the place.

The busy shipping activities of the "nineties" offer a startling contrast to the position that was developed later. It is true that there were strikes even in those days. The great maritime strike of 1890 is not forgotten. Its appearance coincided with the early days of the Labour party in Victoria, and it was a remarkable manifestation of the influence wielded by those first labour leaders. But when the strike was over the shipping industry settled down to a long period of peaceful progress.

The noxious growth of "job control" had not yet appeared, and the trade and commerce of the Australian colonies could be carried on without interruption and for the benefit of all. Shipowners could plan with confidence for the future.

On 1st January, 1912, the business was formed into a public company under its present name, Huddart Parker Limited, with a capital of £1,000,000, divided equally into preference and ordinary shares. Of these shares 125,000 preference and the same number of ordinary shares were made available for public subscription, applications being received at the different ports to which the company traded in the various States of the Commonwealth and New Zealand. The flotation was an unqualified success, 2,448,996 shares being applied for. This is believed to be a record for the Stock Exchange of Melbourne. In March, 1923, the capital of the Company was increased to £1,250,000 by the issue of an additional 250,000 ordinary shares. Strengthened financially, and broadly based on the wide support accorded to it by the public, Huddart Parker Ltd. was well prepared for any troubles that might be impending.

By the beginning of the fateful year 1914, it was clear that the period when the directors of a shipping company were left free to manage their own business had to be counted with "the good old days." The Labour Administration which was in office in the Federal sphere had shown that its policy favoured Government interference with the management of business by private enterprise, and the unions were not slow to take the hint. In addition to a serious strike in New Zealand lasting for eight weeks, there were strikes of wharf labourers at Hobart, of coal yard men in Melbourne, and of wharf labourers in Sydney. All these stoppages reacted most unfavourably upon the Company's receipts. Moreover, the lack of facilities at Newcastle caused delay to ships, reducing the earnings of the company's colliers by about 30 per cent. The running of the steamers and loading and discharging of cargoes again showed increased cost. The Navigation Act increased the cost of the manning of steamers, and claims for time off, annual holidays, and overtime payments meant an increased expenditure of thousands of pounds. Worst of all, according to the directors' report, the new conditions defined by the Navigation Act "induced a growing indisposition to work which makes labour distasteful and unfits officers for responsibilities ever present in the navigation of ships."

Before the next annual report was presented to the shareholders of the company, the Great War broke out, and the interests of every shipping enterprise became subservient to the supreme interests of the nation and the Empire.

3.6 The organisation of businessmen

Businessmen mobilised in this period mainly to regulate the market and to put pressure on the state. These functions were often expressed in separate organisations. The purpose of the second organisation considered here was to extend state action to assist property owners; the first was formed to regulate subcontracting on government construction works.

Sources: *Rules of the Builders' and Contractors' Association of Victoria*, Melbourne, 1869, La Trobe Collection, State Library of Victoria.
Rules, Regulations, and By-Laws of the South Australian Lands Titles Association, State Library of South Australia, Adelaide, 1873.

RULES
of the
BUILDERS' AND CONTRACTORS' ASSOCIATION
OF VICTORIA

I. —That this Association, formed for the purpose of protecting its Members in the fair and proper execution of such works as they may from time to time contract to execute, shall be styled "THE BUILDERS' AND CONTRACTORS' ASSOCIATION of VICTORIA."

II. —That this Association shall consist of builders and contractors of good moral character, and who shall be duly elected. That any party desirous of joining this Association shall give notice of such intention at one of the regular meetings; and the votes of at least two-thirds of the Members present at the subsequent meeting of the Association shall be required for the admission of such candidate. In the case of firms, each individual member will be required to join this Association.

VII. —That all Tenders shall be opened by the parties inviting tenders, in the presence of the parties tendering, and at a time of which due notice shall be given by being inserted in the specification of works tendered for. That, in all future contracts, the Members of this Association tender only in the gross amount, and when it is intimated that the tender of any particular Member is accepted, then only shall such Member furnish a schedule of his prices, on being required so to do, but in no case shall he give up his bill of quantities.

XIV. —That we do not recognise the right of the Board of Land and Works, or any Corporate bodies, Engineers, Architects, Proprietors, or Clerks of Works to interfere with the workmen engaged on works under contract—the foreman excepted.

XV. —That if any Member of this Association, in carrying out or having completed any contract, shall consider himself unjustly dealt with by the Board of Land and Works, Engineer, Architect, or Proprietor of the building or other works, and shall require advice or assistance from this Association, he shall state his grievance in writing to the Secretary, who shall lay the same before the Committee; and, if they consider his grievance to be a just one, they shall appoint a deputation of its Members to examine the works in dispute, and adjust the difference, if possible. If the deputation fail to arrange the dispute they shall report the same to the Committee, who shall obtain a legal opinion before any further proceedings are taken in the matter. That if the legal opinion be in favour of proceedings being taken, the Secretary shall call a General meeting, and have the case fully explained to them. If put to the vote and carried, that it be tried in a manner determined upon, half the costs, if any, shall be defrayed out of the funds of the Association, and the other half by the Member so aggrieved.

Rules and Regulations

of the

South Australian Land Titles Association

NAME

1. The SOUTH AUSTRALIAN LANDS TITLES ASSOCIATION.

OBJECTS

2. To maintain the fundamental principles of the South Australian Real Property Act, commonly known as Torrens' Act, which are—

To give security and simplicity to all titles and interests in land....

3. To promote the development of the system in accordance with the foregoing principles;

To guard against every measure or practice calculated to encroach on them;

To advocate laws and machinery as safe, simple, and cheap as the Real Property Act, relative to property left by deceased persons, to the rights of orphans, and to any similar subject;

And generally to extend the benefits of the system—

By watching carefully the action of Parliament, the Government, and the Courts, and obtaining the co-operation of the country.

SECRETARY

9. The Secretary shall be appointed by the Committee, and remain in office at their discretion, and the first Secretary shall be Ulrich Hubbe, LL.D.; and his duty shall be to see that the rules of the Association be conformed to. ... He shall also, under the direction of the Committee, conduct all correspondence, prepare all business for the Committee meetings, collect and circulate information he may be able to procure, and generally transact any business requiring his attention.

10. Until the annual subscriptions shall exceed the sum of £75, the Secretary shall be paid the amount of the subscriptions, ...

PRIVILEGES

13. Every member, clear on the books, shall be entitled to vote personally on all questions; by proxy only in the election of Officers or financial arrangements of the Association. Provided that when the annual contribution is paid in the name of a firm, only one vote shall be allowed to the firm; but every partner may attend the meetings, make propositions, and enjoy all other privileges of membership, except the voting as individuals. ...

3.7 Speculative capital in the 1880s

Although Samuel William Gray (1823–1889) was not a member of Sydney's central capitalist network, his business interests and political connections were typical of the speculative capitalist. Originally a pastoralist, he was elected to parliament for rural electorates on five occasions between 1859 and 1882, and was a supporter of the Cowper and Robertson factions. According to R. A. Ferguson ('New South Wales Company Formation, 1860–1890',

B.Ec. thesis, University of Sydney, 1968), he directed fifteen companies in the 1880s, including one in insurance and ten in mining. When he died, he had a bank overdraft of nearly £53,000.

Source: Papers of S. W. Gray (Norton Smith & Co. Papers — Clients' Documents), Mitchell Library, A5355, Item 49.

Inventory, with Full Particulars and Value of the Estate and Effects of S.W. Gray deceased [excluding 32 Queensland properties]

	Particulars	Value £.	s.	d.
Real Estate	*New South Wales Properties*			
	Lots 10, 11, 12, 13 North Annandale Estate . . . Johnston St	900 —		
	850 acres Jerdwangla	750 —		
	820 acres Broughton Villiage	250 —		
	1/2 share in Billambi Est. 91 acres Parish Woonona, Camden	300 —		
	4735 acres Conditional Purchase, Murruwillumbah, Tweed River	15540 —		
	1/2 share 874 ac. 2r. 16p. ditto ditto	1029 —		
	1174 ac. 2r. Freehold ditto ditto	2989 —		
	82 ac County Cumberland, Lane Cove River	500 —		
	67 ac ditto, Worronora River Sutherland	1000 —		
	Portions 128, 129, 130 ditto ditto	3330 —		
	ditto 76 and 78 ditto ditto	9000 —		
	94 ac Parish St George, George's River	6000 —		
	[illegible number] Crown St (Cardigan Hotel)	8000 —		
	5 ac. 0r. 7p Parish Alexandria, South Head Rd	500 —		
	230 ac Curry's Hill, Kiama	1300 —		
	1/4 interest Leasehold Property, corner George and Bathurst streets	1000 —		
	1/3 share of 67 ac Woonona Estate near Bulli	4000 —		
Shares	1/10 share in Great Wollongong Pty Coal Co. Ltd	875 —		
	2000 shares United Land Building and Investment Co	200 —		
	3022 ditto Sydney Freehold Building Society	3173 —		
	250 shares Central Broken Hill Silver Mining Co paid up	900 —		
	1013 Big Oakey Gold Mining Co ditto	50 —		

	Particulars	Value		
Real Estate	*New South Wales Properties*	*£.*	*s.*	*d.*
Shares cont'd	250 Central Blocks Silver Mining Co contributing	6 —	6 —	0
	2300 Pinnacle Group Mining Co	1150 —		
	7754 New England Gold Mining Co	3892 —		
	36 Mount Limerstone Silver Mining Co	30 —		
	260 Preferential Shares, Katoomba Coal and Shale Co	22 —	18 —	0
	750 Patent Asphaltum Co Ltd	187 —		
		£66874 —	4 —	0
Personalty	Plate	250 —		
	1/2 share 360 cattle Tweed River	495 —		
	1/2 share 52 horses ditto	182 —		
Debts	The Hornsby Lands Co-principal and interest	11423 —	3 —	0
	Intercolonial Investment L. and B. Co—principal and interest	6202 —	8 —	8
	Thos Watters, St Leonards, grocer-principal	7500 —		
	Will. Wiley, Pitt St, Sydney—principal and interest	3756 —	13 —	4
	Will. Jenkins, "The Cardigan", Oxford St—rent	17 —		
	McCoy, Richard—promissory note due 16 May 1889	500 —		
	McFarland, Alfred & Co, Jr,—Amount guarantee	647 —	11 —	10
	Sir J. Robertson and another, Mortgage debt, £1000 + interest	1025 —		
	Collins, purchase money of North Queensland Co.	800 —		
	New England Gold Mining Co, balance purchase money and interest	1163 —	10 —	10
	A. L. Bloomfield, Sydney, amount of 10 promissory notes now due, less rebate	4279 —	9 —	2
	Thos Prise, Balance of Purchase Money	522 —	10 —	0

3.8 The lower depths

From the late 1850s, reformers condemned the houses, schools and factories in those parts of the cities where lived the most oppressed part of the working class. The slum landlords included some of the most respectable and powerful men in the community, such as George Wigram Allen, who was knighted in 1877, only a year after the publication of this Report. Note that this document refers to a moment in what is commonly regarded as 'the long boom'.

Source: 'Report and Evidence of the Investigating Committees of the Sydney City and Suburban Sewerage Health Board', *Votes and Proceedings of the New South Wales Legislative Assembly*, 1875–76, vol. 5, pp. 545, 628–9.

[From the Report] 14. *Neglect of property by owners.*—A perusal of the accompanying evidence will show that disinclination on the part of landlords to go to any expense in keeping their property in repair, even to the extent of an occasional coat of whitewash or paint, is the rule rather than the exception in Sydney. This argues a certainty of finding tenants to occupy the houses, whatever may be their condition, which would not be the case if dwellings for the working classes were not so scarce. This scarcity is proved by the fact that the rent of such houses has of late considerably increased. The evil referred to under this heading is intensified by the absence of any authority to compel the owners of properties to keep their tenements in habitable condition. Full powers should be given to the local sanitary authority to serve notice on owners so offending, and in default of remedy by them to make the necessary improvements at their expense.

The accompanying extracts will show how general is the complaint on the part of tenants that "the landlord will do nothing."

"What struck us most forcibly during our visit to these crowded localities was the total absence of any attempt on the part of the owners or landlords to do anything in the shape of repairs, or to improve the sanitary condition of the dwellings. We noticed no signs of lime, or white-washing, paint, or any attention paid to the drainage of the allotments. These essentials to the preservation of health do not appear to have engaged their attention at all, and there can be no doubt that the water used for domestic purposes in such abodes of filth and wretchedness must in many cases be polluted. The want of some sanitary authority, whose special business it should be to interfere in these cases, and to compel, where necessary, landlords to provide such accommodation as will render health and cleanliness at least possible, seems to us very urgent." p. 6.

The Dean of Sydney states in his evidence, in answer to question 4:—

"But I attribute a great deal of the bad condition of the dwellings to which I have alluded, to the landlords, who appear to leave them without any repairs or any purification whatever from year's end to year's end. I have known houses which have never been whitewashed or painted or improved in any way for many years. Not long ago I visited one family, and I learned from the mother, a respectable woman, who had lived there for thirteen years, that not the slightest repair had been done to the house since they came into it; the plaster had fallen off the walls and the floor was ripped up in several places. I asked why she lived in such a place, and she said she was applying continually to the landlord, but he would not so much as put a single nail into the floor. I believe that it has since been in some measure repaired; but that is only a sample of hundreds of houses which I have visited in this city." p. 1.

Referring to certain tenements in Clarence-street, the Committee say:—

"The tenants all state that the landlord positively declines to improve them; these people occupy them while in this condition solely because if they were to leave they would not know where to find other houses to live in, decent houses at a moderate rent being very scarce in the neighbourhood." p. 20.

"We examined another old brick house in Union-street, also owned by Walsh, containing two rooms, 10 x 10 ft. and 8 ft. high, occupied by a mangle-woman. This was also in a filthy state and badly ventilated. The tenant stated that she had lived there six years, and that during that time the house had never been cleaned out or whitewashed. The landlord positively refused to do anything." p. 32.

"The tenant of this house (Wexford-street), who has six children, told us that although she had lived there for five years the landlady had done nothing towards cleaning or repairing it." p. 54.

"In Paradise Row, off Abercrombie and Myrtle streets: This property consists of twenty-four weatherboard houses with slate roofs, owned by Thomas Broughton, Esq.—Carter, agent. The houses are chiefly two-roomed tenements, rented at 4s. per week. The neighbourhood in which they are situate bears about as bad a reputation as any we have yet visited; the houses are in a very dilapidated state, many of them being empty on account probably of their uninhabitable condition. The agent, a well-known character, with one arm, would persist in following us about during our examinations, and inciting the tenants to resist our entrance into their houses. I am sorry to say that in many cases he succeeded; his language was not of the choicest description and his conduct was very obstructive. He told us he had been fined on account of these places a short time ago, and 'he'd take (strong adjective) good care that he would not be sucked in again'."

[From the Evidence] G. F. Dansey, Esq., reported: We went next to Mount-street, where the houses are of a somewhat better class, but all of them fitted with the old-fashioned sash windows, and therefore badly ventilated; the closets are over common cesspits, but that cannot be avoided as there is no sewerage here.

We inspected a Public School in this street, which is in bad repair, the windows broken, and the weatherboards also in places. In the front room, which is 42 ft. x 26 ft., there is an average attendance of 110 children; and in the back room, 22 ft. x 16 ft., used for infants, there are between eighty and ninety. The floor is in such a broken state that a child might easily put his foot through the boards and get hurt; the building in fact is not in a proper state of repair to be used as a school.

Near this school are two houses, one built of brick and shingle, and the other of stone, with galvanised tile roof, containing each two rooms and a kitchen. In the stone house the solitary window in front has a fixed upper sash. In the brick house there is a family of seven; the closet is out of repair, and very offensive. This property belongs to Mrs. Brothwell.

In the front of these houses, at the corner of the street, is a building which has evidently been a butcher's shop, in a dilapidated state and falling to pieces; close by is a stone house which attracted our attention, but the tenants were out, and we could not enter it.

At the top of John-street, to which we returned, there is a cow-shed, the drainage from which was lying in pools in the yard, stinking, and creating a nuisance.

On the north side of this street we looked at a number of tenements, which are chiefly noticeable on account of the dirty and dilapidated condition of the back premises; they are mostly owned by Mr. Robinson. Here we found a two-roomed house, tenanted by a man and his wife and two children, and rented at 5s. a week, which must be a damp and unhealthy abode from the fact that the floors rest on the ground. The house is in bad repair, the roof being patched up with a variety of materials, and is a place which poverty alone would compel a man to live in. The children we were told are "middling healthy"; they go to St. Bede's School.

At the rear of John-street is a stone and shingle tenement in a shocking state of dilapidation, in the yard of which is a closet of the most wretched description, without any door, and almost tumbling down.

Close by is a house above which is painted—"Agent, Sydney Empire". No. 6 is on the door, but this does not tally with the street numbers. The tenant was not at home, and we could not make a closer inspection.

In Bowman-street we came to four houses built of rubble, with corrugated iron roofs, belonging to the Hon. G. Wigram Allen, rented at 7s. 6d. a week each. Attracted by the dirty appearance of the second house we entered it to make a closer inspection. The tenants informed us that it was a stinking hole, and that vermin abounded in it. We saw no reason to doubt either statement but everything to confirm it. The closet at the back is in a broken down dilapidated condition and in a filthy state, as was also the closet in the adjoining yard; we were obliged to leave hastily—we could not stand the smell. The drainage from these houses runs down along the surface gutters to a vacant piece of land close by, the stench from which is something frightful. The closet belonging to the house at the end of this row is in a shocking state of repair; the door is broken down, and a log of wood is placed over the seat to prevent the children from falling into the pit. The tenants of these houses all complained of ill health, and no doubt their dwellings are very unwholesome. The floors rest on solid earth, there being no excavation under them.

Thence we proceeded to Chowne-street, which is a street of recent construction, and the houses are in a good state of repair but badly ventilated; the back premises especially show the necessity of some law to compel owners of property to build in accordance with hygienic rules.

We next visited in rotation Point-street, Hill-street, the ascent to which is very steep; and Church-street, where we found the houses generally to be good and in clean order, being for the most part occupied by engineers and other employees of the A.S.N. [Australasian Steam Navigation] Co., and presenting a very respectable appearance internally as well as externally.

Dr. Read gave the following evidence on behalf of Mr. Chapman and himself:—

Met Mr. Chapman at the City Club at 11 o'clock on Thursday, 17th instant, and proceeded, accompanied by Sergeant Larkins, to a clothing factory in Clarence-street, connected with the firm of Macarthur and Co., and at the back of their premises in York-street. Ascending the stairs to the first floor, we entered a room 65 x 30 ft. and about 12 ft. high, which is used as a cutting room, and contained, at the time of our visit, only about twelve or fifteen male occupants, two or three being boys apparently at least 14 years of age. This room has eight windows, four on one side and four at one end, leaving two blank walls, and is, notwithstanding its size and the eight windows aforesaid, but imperfectly ventilated, considering the number of employees who are at times assembled in it. In the room above this, against the blank wall, is a stove used for heating the pressing irons, which does not tend to improve the atmosphere. A profuse perspiration came over me while I was in this part of the room, there being here no current of air to ventilate it. At the end of the room where there are no windows, at each corner, is a narrow staircase which leads to a closet, one for the women, the other for the men, the closets being some feet above the level of the work-room, an arrangement which is so far objectionable that it obliges the men engaged in the lower part of the building to pass through the women's department whenever they have occasion to make use of their closet. In the large room just described we found about eighty women and girls, besides three or four men occupied in pressing the clothes, and we observed that they took great pains to get as near the windows as they could. None of the girls, as far as we could judge, were under 13 or 14 years of age. This place seems to be very well constructed, and good order seemed to prevail. We were informed that not very long ago as many as 400 persons were employed in these two rooms, but the numbers are considerably reduced under the present management, encouragement being given to employees to take home work, a practice which should be encouraged, as the young girls who are engaged in the work are thus more under the care of their parents. The building is an old store of Macarthur and Co's converted into a workroom.

We next inspected Pascoe and Co.'s factory, in Wynyard-lane, owned by J. Marks. Here we found two rooms each 50 x 25 ft. and 8½ ft. high. The upper room only was occupied at the time of our visit, when there were about eighty workpeople in it, chiefly women and children, none of the latter being of tender age, certainly not under 12 years. This room has a dead wall at the back, and is imperfectly ventilated; the roof is composed of slate, and the heat was sickening. We were told that sometimes not less than 200 persons were employed in these two rooms.

We went downstairs, and passing through a passage came to a solitary closet, which is all the privy accommodation for the employees; there were three women in it, two of them *waiting their turn*; the closet is about 4 ft. square. We pointed out this deficiency to Mr. Pascoe, who expressed himself glad to receive any suggestions and to do anything he could to promote the comfort of his workpeople.

We returned at 1 o'clock.

Started from the "City Club" at 10 o'clock on the morning of Friday, the 18th instant, in company with Mr. Chapman and Sergeant Larkins, and proceeded to inspect a building in Macquarie-street North, formerly a Presbyterian Church, and a well ventilated, lofty, and commodious building. ... There are two galleries upstairs, one on either side, which are used for cutting rooms and for the storage of clothing. At either end of these galleries there is a shoot by which cloths ready for manufacture into clothing are shot down to the floor of the building. Here were between seventy and eighty girls sewing, some with machines and others by hand. Upon examining the back premises we found one very objectionable feature. Attention has been paid to the comfort of the girls by providing a nice little copper in the yard to boil water for tea. The closet for their use is in too close proximity to the store, and there is no separate entrance to it. There are two closets, side by side, marked respectively "Boys" and "Girls" erected no doubt for the accommodation of Sunday scholars when the main building was used for more reverent purposes, and now used by the girls employed in the lower room, and the men engaged in the cutting department up stairs, who have to pass through the lower workroom to go to their closet. We do not consider this decent, and we think a separate closet should be erected for the men on the other side of the yard.

We next went to Moore, Henderson and Boucher's factory in Bank Court off King-street, which is at the back of their premises in Pitt-street. This building has been an old store and is in a very tumble-down condition; it has already been shored up and strengthened with additional tie-beams to keep it from falling. It contains one large room 40 x 20 ft. and 9 ft. high, and one smaller room. The ventilation is very imperfect and the heat which comes from a stove in the room adjoining the large workroom and about 3 feet below its level, makes the place very close and unhealthy for the employees.

From this workroom we proceeded to Messrs. David Jones & Co's. establishment in George-street, which we inspected under the guidance of Mr. E. Jones, who said he was very glad to find that some steps were being taken to promote the comfort of the workpeople of Sydney. The rooms in this establishment are small but the ventilation is exceedingly good, ...

3.9 The skilled worker's budget

The bourgeoisie made many comforting assumptions about the economic position of the skilled worker in the colonies, and argued without embarrassment both for encouraging him to save and for reducing his wages. From the late 1840s, workers challenged these assumptions (see *People's Advocate*, 30 December 1848, p. 6).

Source: Melbourne *Argus*, 8 October 1863 and 17 October 1863.

The Condition of Labour

... That the workmen, with the prospect of regular employment, could manage well at present on lower rates will be obvious enough from the following comparative tables, showing the cost of living and the wages paid at different periods of the history of the colony:—

Estimate of the weekly expenditure of an artizan's family, consisting of a man, his wife, and three children, in 1850, 1854, and the present year, based upon the following rates of consumption.

	1850			1854			1863		
Bread, 28 lb.	£0	3	6	£0	12	6	£0	4	1
Meat, 21 lb.	0	3	6	0	16	0	0	7	0
Potatoes, 21 lb.	0	5	3	0	6	0	0	2	0
Flour, 5 lb.	0	0	8	0	2	2	0	0	10
Tea, 1 lb.	0	1	0	0	2	0	0	2	9
Sugar, 6 lb.	0	1	6	0	3	0	0	2	3
Soap, 3 lb.	0	1	3	0	1	0	0	1	0
Candles, 2 lb.	0	0	10	0	1	6	0	1	2
Milk, 7 pints	0	2	0	0	7	0	0	2	0
Butter, 2 lb.	0	2	6	0	9	0	0	2	0
Firewood, ¼ ton	0	2	0	0	10	0	0	2	6
Water, 1 load	0	1	6	0	7	6			
Rent o'cottage	0	6	0	1	15	0	0	6	0
Clothing	0	5	0	0	15	0	0	5	0
	£1	16	6	£6	7	8	£1	18	7

To test the present condition of the artizan with his past it is necessary to show how far his expenditure at the different periods given corresponds with his earnings. In 1850, when the colony was purely a pastoral settlement masons obtained from 6s. to 7s. per day; in 1854, the year which it may be said witnessed the termination of the great rush occasioned by the auriferous discoveries, their wages were £1 8s. per day; and at the present time the current rates are from 8s. to 10s. per day, the latter sum being more generally paid than the former. The following table will show the weekly wages of an artizan at the period given, together with the expenditure of himself and family:—

	1850			1854			1863		
Wages	£1	19	0	£7	10	0	£2	14	0
Expenditure, as shown above	1	16	6	6	7	8	1	18	7
Surplus	0	2	6	1	2	4		15	5

In 1850 single men could obtain board and lodging for 12s. per week, in 1854 the rate was 30s., and at the present time it is £1. The statements given above must be regarded, to a great extent, as merely comparative, inasmuch as families can be, and are, maintained with a less consumption than is there assumed. Taking that consumption as a basis, however, it will be seen that the artizans can at the present day—assuming full employment in both instances—put by a sum far beyond anything they could save in the pastoral era, when they worked longer hours, and consequently did more for their money. The surplus for the present year is somewhat smaller than that for 1854, but its purchasing power is greater, and under present circumstances more of the conveniences of life are placed within the man's reach than he could possibly enjoy in the former period.

LABOUR FOR FAMILY

TO THE EDITOR OF THE ARGUS.

Sir.—In your issue of the 8th inst. I find the first of an intended series of articles upon labour, remuneration, &c. Taking as granted you are sincere in your profession of good will, and wish only fair statements to be made, I beg to offer a few remarks, and respectfully request space for them. You say in 1863 a workman obtains about £2 14s. in wages weekly, and that himself, wife, and three children can live upon £1 18s. 7d. the same time. Now, allowing some of the items of food to be charged full and others under, I think it a fair statement upon the whole, as far as it goes (except rent); but you have not made any reference to several expenses not altogether unworthy of your kind remembrance. No provision is made for the education of his children, or for their attendance at any public place of worship or instruction. No sum set apart for the sundries which a good mother can so justifiably fill up; no provision for increase of family or for sickness, for loss of work, or subscription to benefit or building society—not even for green vegetables or fruits, which they say are necessary for health here. I do not mention beer or wine, though "a little wine for stomach's sake and often infirmity" is not an infidel recommendation. Then, again, I question whether the decorum of a well-regulated family can be carried out in nine cases out of ten in dwellings at 6s. per week, so that a larger sum would have to be put down to rent. I have merely stated a few facts, feeling personally their importance, and leave to abler hands the bearing it has upon the character and conduct of the rising generation, who are to take the place sometime their parents now occupy; and believing injustice or ungenerousness will never raise or maintain anything like a desirable state of things, I hope, for the working-man, as well as for the man of capital, you will raise your voice against the selfishness of mammon.

Yours,
M.

N.B. The foregoing remarks are against the presumption he can save 15s. 6d. per week.

(It will readily be seen that our correspondent's remarks do not affect the validity of our comparison between the working man's receipts and expenditure of the two periods in question.)

3.10 A worker makes it—with the help of his wife

There were hazards and costs involved in achieving economic independence—and good luck also played a part.

Source: Lucy Hart (Melbourne) to her Family, 3 May 1852, State Library of South Australia, D5063 (L).

... My Dear Mother I have had many trials and troubles since I saw you and a great deal of sickness but I have never wanted for anything amongst it all and for the first twelve months we was geting what I call on step forine and to back [one step forward and two back?]. I think I told you when I was home that Hart was very saveing and very fond of money which made me very uncomfortable has I could not save anything out of his wages has we had so much sickness and of course I had many little things to buy for such a time I could not save much you might think but Mother I have never been without a *pound* in my pocket since I have been *John Harts wife* and I think that is a great thing to say.

Should I have been so well off in England NO work hard and be half starved Australia is the place to live I would not come back to England again unless I had enough to keep me without work on no account neither would my husband I am speaking now the very sentiments of our hearts but people must be *saving industrious* and *persevering* we have deprived ourselves of many things we might have had but what was it for all to try to do something for ourselves so that my husband should not allways work under a *Master* and happy am I to inform you that we have gained that point he is now his own Master, My Dear Mother after I had quite recovered from my confinement and quite strong I was determined to work to help get a living I began to take in washing and ironing at 3 shillings per Dozen so I used to earn about 15 shillings per week which was as much as I could do with a young *Baby* then we could save a pound per week and live comfortable was then paying seven shillings per week for a house *garden* we was then geting on in the world very well for working people and just got things comfortable about us when my poor *husband* was taken ill with a violent *fever* fevers are very prevalent here and so they are in most hot climates when he was taken ill we had about 20 pounds in the house it was twelve weeks before he went to work again the very day he went to work we had but one shilling but thank God we did not owe any person a penny piece he went Back to his old place to work and you see My Dear Mother that through our own industry it kept us from the cold hand of *Charity* I still kept on my work all through his sickness so you might think my hands was full enough then I never expected him to recover the Doctor gave me very slight hopes of him after he got well and went to work again we was obliged to begin afresh and try to save a little more that is two years ago this month since then we neither of us has not had a days illness and everything have prospered then in a month or two we bought a *cow* and she used to turn me in about 12 shillings per week and a lot of poultry of my own rearing we was then doing well I had by that time a great deal of washing as my little girl could run about I did many weeks earn 30^{s} myself by my washing so I have not spent much idle time I was exactly like that when Mr. *White Brought* the letter to me that Stephen wrote and we had got 50 pounds in the Bank and all got by real hard work I must tell you Mother that Hart is a very steady sober man and would not spend a shilling in waste on no account neither would I myself... the diggins Broke out soon after Mr. White called on me well I beged of my husband to come here and try his luck has so many *Adelaide* people had been here and done well at last he made up his mind to come and leave me in *Adelaide* has I could get my living without touching the little money we had saved... in about 5 weeks after he left I received a letter from him containing the joyfull news that he had got his own share *200 pounds worth of gold* and also to tell me to sell my things and come to *Melbourne* as quick as possible so My Dear Mother gladly did I comply with that request I sold my things and took the first vessel Bound for Melbourne... where I found my husband anxiously waiting my arrival he was then determined that I should not work so hard any more of course I have no need to now for with the money that I Brought with me we could *raise 300 pounds* and now I consider myself well off in the world so I do nothing but my own work now... now Hart bought 2 *Horses* and a *Dray* he gave 100 and 50 pounds for them he is now taking stores to the diggins for shopkeepers and he is making 30 pounds per week and making money fast but he will be off to the *diggins* again as soon as the rain comes as they are obliged to wash all the earth after they dig it to get the *precious metal* I hope he will do something handsome this time...

3.11 Prodigal tradesmen

A teetotal compositor discovers that not all colonial workers were thrifty and not all mobility was upward.

Source: W. Calder's Journal: Jottings of a Trip to Adelaide and a Few Weeks' Stay There... 1858, State Library of South Australia, D4826 (L).

There are two daily papers in the Town, and Uncle had secured me a frame in either of them. I decided upon going to the *Register* and have had no reason to repent my choice. The work is very heavy. We go in during the day to distribute—generally between 12 and 2—and commence to set at 4 o'clock, tea between 6 and 7, and finish between 1 and 3 o'clock. The rate per 1000 [words of setting] is 1/4. My first week's bill was £5-2-8; the second, £5-4. I was scarcely begun work when I was told that the men were anxious to drink my health. I asked the sum and was told 7/6. I at once paid it and was done with it. I was horrified at the quantity of drink consumed in the office. The least excuse is made for drinking, and they drink Port Wine, Sherry, Brandy, and all sorts of Ale. They nearly all smoke at their work, but as the office has a very high roof and well ventilated the annoyance is not very great. The overseer—George Watson—served his apprenticeship in the *North British Advertiser*, and there are one or two Edinburgh men in the office beside myself. I was astonished at the freeness with which the men spend their money. One of them will think nothing of sending out for 5/- worth of drink, and some of them often take a dog cart to the Bay on a Saturday afternoon which costs £1. I was also astonished to hear of the freshness of their intelligence as to home matters. Not a man nor a movement could be mentioned but the minutest particular connected with it was known. ...It is curious to observe the difference in dress of the men in the office. While some of them are both very dirty and poorly dressed others are at the opposite extreme, wearing white hats and rings and very few wear aprons, and it is not the sober ones who are the best dressed. The best dressed man in the office being very unsteady being both a gambler as well as a drinker. But we are all very agreeable with one another and things go on very smoothly and pleasantly although we have occasionally a smart discussion about temperance v. drinking in which it is contended on the one side that moderation is the greater virtue and that they are all moderates. Mr. Hulls, the only other teetotaller in the office, shut them up the other day by saying that in looking round the room he saw several men who would have been independent today if it had not been for drink. This was too sharp firing, and irritated them not a little. ...

The greater proportion of the men in the office have been at the diggings, and little wonder may be felt at their loose morality. Most of them have been successful but alas it is now gone. One of them was at one time so far up the social scale that he kept a riding horse, but he is far enough down now. He has been a partner in all sorts of speculations — newspaper proprietor, baker, shoemaker, and cab-hirer. Another of the men got £800 as his share in the first hole he dug and on the first day. Drink, drink, what evil and misery thou hast caused...

3.12 Employer equals master

Immigrant workers often had to be taught that their position in the colonial labour market was subordinate. In this case, in which John Kerr, a shoemaker, was charged with absconding from hired service, the Immigration department as well as the judiciary was upholding the position of the employer.

Source: Melbourne *Argus*, 15 and 22 October 1863.

The defendant is one of two men who were engaged by Mr. Carter from the Immigration Depot, Melbourne. The following is a copy of the agreement. ... "Memorandum of Agreement made 7th. September, 1863 between G. L. Carter, of Fryerstown, of the first part: and John Kerr, free immigrant per ship——, of the second part. The conditions are that John Kerr engages to serve the said G. L. Carter, as maker of women's boots and shoes, by piecework (being a thoroughly competent and good workman) for the term of twelve months, in consideration of which services the said G. L. Carter agrees to pay the said John Kerr wages at the rate of 100 per cent in advance upon English prices".

G. L. Carter stated: The defendant entered my service from the 7th. September to 2nd. October. He did not give me any notice of his leaving. The agreement was written at Fryerstown, and finished by the Immigration Office, Melbourne. ... The first week he earned 14/-; the last three days he earned 16/-. The defendant could have earned 35/- to £2 per week. There are three kinds of work — order work, shop work and manufacturers' work; mine is manufacturers' work: the lowest price of all is paid for the latter class. ... I have received some encouragement to proceed with this case. The Immigration Department sent me a reply to a letter on the subject. I have not got that letter. I commenced the proceedings voluntarily, though I got some encouragement. I had an interview with Mr. Panton, sub-treasurer of Castlemaine, on the subject.

Edward Cleary stated, in answer to Mr. Makinson — I came out to this colony with defendant. I was employed in Manchester doing work. I have done all kinds of manufacturing work. I was not engaged in manufacturing work for Mr. Carter. The articles put in the boots are superior to what I put in manufacture. I told Mr. Carter he was not giving me 100 per cent on home prices. I got food from Mr. Carter. I could not go away. 2/6d. is the lowest price in Manchester; Carter gave us 3/- first; he then advanced us 4d. I get 2/6d. in Manchester for the same work. Carter and myself have cancelled our agreement. Burnett [another employer] gave me 6/- [per pair] in Fryerstown. Kerr could not make more than eight pairs per week. I swear that Carter has not given us 100 per cent advance on English prices.

Mr. Leech [for the complainant]—Mr. Carter has embarked in a new industry in this colony, and it would be a serious thing were he to be placed in a position in which not only would his character be damaged, but obstacles would be placed in the way of his developing the important industry in question. After some remarks on the character of Mr. Cleary's evidence, and the amount of reliance to be placed on it, the learned counsel proceeded to detail the kind of rebutting evidence which he would call. It was perfectly absurd to suppose that the prices stated by the witnesses for the defence were current in England: if so, the sooner the better the immigration commissioners wrote to the working classes of England and informed them that they were receiving far higher prices than were obtainable in this colony. ... A great deal of public money had been spent by the colony in bringing out workmen, but if on their arrival they were to be encouraged in breaking their agreements and acting as Kerr and Cleary had done, the sooner the importation of such men at the public expense was put a stop to the better.

The following witness, among others, was then called:— Matthew Peart, a boot and shoe maker, deposed—I have been eleven years in the trade. I came out as a Government immigrant, and arrived in this colony on the 6th. of June last. I am now living at the Junction. I never knew much difference in prices in England. There are three classes of work here. The boots produced (made by Kerr) could not be called "order" work; they would be called "manufacturers' work". When I left England, 1s. 9d. per pair was paid for this class of work.... This being the case for the prosecution.

Mr. Makinson [for the defence] proceeded to address the Bench. He criticised what he called the "gross vagueness" of the agreement. He could prove by numerous witnesses that the complainant had not paid an advance of 100 per cent on English prices. ... He concluded by characterising the conduct of the immigration agent, and all those who had promoted the prosecution, as cruel in the last degree. [He called a number of shoemakers, who supported Cleary's account of the state of English wages and who spoke of unemployment in the trade there.]

His Worship remarked that a good deal of evidence had been imported into the case which did not properly belong to the specified charge. On the previous occasion [i.e. the first day of the hearing] it had been clearly proved that the defendant had absconded from his hired service, and today it had been proved to his satisfaction that one complainant had kept his part of the contract. ... The defendant was not worthy of so-called "sympathy". He and his family had been brought out at the public expense and brought up from Melbourne to Fryerstown at the joint expense of the Government and Mr. Carter. His conduct was therefore inexcusable. He would inform the defendant that there was a Master and Servants Act in force in this colony; and in accordance with the provisions of that act he should sentence the defendant to one month's imprisonment in Castlemaine Gaol.

Defendant—May I make a few remarks?

His Worship—Your solicitor will inform you that if you wish to appeal, notice of appeal must be given. . . .

Mr. Makinson—I beg to give notice of appeal.

3.13 Strikers guilty of conspiracy

Seventeen striking compositors on the *Empire*, owned by the liberal politician Henry Parkes, were found guilty of conspiracy in 1854. They were gaoled for periods from one day to six weeks.

Source: *Sydney Morning Herald*, 11 and 15 February 1854.

The Attorney-General in opening the case pointed out to the jury that this was the first case of the kind which had occurred, and it was their duty to decide with strict impartiality between the employer and the employed. Mr. Parkes, he said, deserved great credit for the promptitude with which he had resisted this attempt at coercion. Nothing could be more injurious than that the practice of striking for wages should be suffered to grow into strength in this colony. It must be nipped in the bud. Combinations either of employers or of the employed to oppress the other class were equally illegal. . . . Either class could meet and discuss the rate of remuneration with a view to future operations, but they could not interrupt or affect existing engagements. The defendants might have terminated their agreements by giving the term of notice (a fortnight) required by the custom of the trade, and they might have lawfully arranged not to reengage unless their demands for increased wages were complied with. But it could never be tolerated that any set of men, believing their employer to be in their power, should determine upon leaving their employment at once unless he at once succumbed to them. . . . It was for the benefit of workmen themselves as well as of the masters that this system of striking should be nipped in the bud. It was quite impossible that the colony could continue to progress in industrial prosperity unless there was harmony and confidence between employers and employed. . . .

Henry Parkes, proprietor and publisher of the *Empire* newspaper . . . said he received on the 7th. January the following document from Cunninghame [the father of the chapel] "Resolved that it is the unanimous opinion of this chapel that according to the recognised principles of the business, and according to the unanimous opinion of the members of the profession in this colony, we are justified in the demand [for more money for specialised work] now made, and that the refusal of payment is tantamount to instant dismissal. We therefore agree to accept it as such, and to discontinue working in this office until such time as our just demand is complied with." Witness caused the hands to be summoned by his overseer to meet him (witness) in his room. He there explained to them his willingness to withdraw the objectionable matter—the tabular form of setting up the land sales. He also pointed out that the amount involved was one of small importance, not more than 35s in upwards of one hundred pounds, and that he trusted wholly to the decision of his overseer. But he offered according to the principle laid down in Savage on printing [probably James Savage, *An Account of the London Daily Newspapers and the manner in which they are conducted* . . ., London, 1811] to call a meeting of the employers and employed to settle the matter. He insisted, however, upon the resolution, so objectionable in its tone, should be first withdrawn. One of the defendants proposed accordingly to take this course, and Purcell seconded the proposition, but Bone exclaimed that this was not the way to settle—they were contending for a principle and must have another meeting... They all left... A number of them were found in a public-house near the office, and they sent word back that they would return if witness would pay the money and apologise for an expression which he had used characterising the movement and the resolution as an attempt to override his authority and to coerce him into compliance with their demands—equal to highway robbery....

Mr. Bone stated that whatever of prominence he had assumed in this matter had been forced upon him by circumstances. When he came to the *Empire* office, he found it in a state of turmoil, in consequence of the men not being prepared to assent to a code of laws which Mr. Parkes was desirous of having put in force. Before he had been in the *Empire* office one hour he found that it was a hotbed of discontent. He was not long allowed to remain neutral, for the next day after his employment Mr. Parkes withdrew his code of rules and named six men of whom he (Bone) was one to assist in drawing up a code according to the London rules and practice. At this time Mr. McKelly [the overseer] was absent in Melbourne, and finding on his return some changes, he expressed his dislike of these changes in strong terms, telling the defendant that "He would have none of his d—— London notions." All attempts at arrangements were met with abuse and threats of dismissal. As to the... circumstances... which were conceived to militate most strongly against himself, this defendant explained them thus:— He had resisted the proposition before Mr. Parkes to withdraw the resolution, not because he wished in the slightest degree to perpetuate the misunderstanding, but because he thought that if the resolution was to be withdrawn it should be withdrawn in the regular way, and this proposition was decidedly irregular. ....

[The jury found a verdict of guilty against all the defendants.]

The Chief Justice said... he felt called upon to make... reference to an advertisement which he had seen in the newspapers purporting to come from the "Operatives of Sydney". According to this advertisement these parties made common cause with these defendants, calling for the payment of subscriptions to indemnify them for the proceedings which had been instigated against them for this "alleged conspiracy". ... This, in fact, was a proceeding calling imperatively for the strongest reprehension from the Bench. The authors of this advertisement, calling themselves the "operatives of Sydney", who had dared to make common cause with parties duly convicted, and to set themselves against the law, who had presumed to designate that as alleged which, after a solemn investigation before a Court and jury, had been found to be proved, would if they could be brought to justice, be well deserving of punishment, for they had been guilty of a gross contempt not only of the authority of the court, but of the very laws under the protection of which they live. No man would be safe if combinations of this kind could be permitted. And the very interests of these classes themselves required a maintenance of the law in its integrity, for the labourer of today might be an employer of labour tomorrow. ...

3.14 Railway strike: Police versus labourers

These unskilled workers were not unionised. Despite the police attack, the strike continued for another week.

Source: Melbourne *Argus*, 7 November 1863.

STRIKE ON THE RAILWAY.—A disturbance took place on the railway line yesterday, which, but for the prompt manner in which it was met by the authorities, might have resulted in serious consequences. From time to time, since the commencement of the line to Echuca, attempts have been made by the workmen engaged on the line to obtain a rise of wages from 7s. per diem, the rate now paid by the contractors, to 8s. per diem, which the workmen think a more reasonable payment for their labour. Hitherto the efforts of the workmen have been unsuccessful, the demand for labour in the district having been of late comparatively slack. The opening up of a new field at the Raywood rush has been the cause of renewed dissatisfaction among the workmen, and seems to have induced a belief amongst them that an attempt to obtain a rise would at the present time prove successful. Under these circumstances, but little was required at any moment to cause a strike on the line. Nothing, however, appears to have been formally done for the purpose, and the present strike seems to have been more the result of accident than design. Yesterday morning, about half past nine o'clock, a labourer, named John Dynan, said to have been just discharged from the Sandhurst lockup, applied at the works, near Back Creek, to be taken on again, but at 8s. per diem. Being refused, he went to the men at the cutting and said to them, "Come out of that; I'll knock off your—— heads if you work for 7s. a day." He was at once given into custody for interfering with the men. The result was much disturbance; several men got out of the cutting, and refused to go on working under 8s. per diem; and finally the whole of the men at work, about 100 in number, knocked off, and went down the line calling upon others to join them. At the Back Creek-bridge, in M'Ivor-street, one of the men engaged at the crane refused to turn out, and offered to fight any man that would stand up to him. A rush was made at him from the bank by one of the mob, he was knocked down before he could put himself on his guard, and, either before or after he fell, struck between the eyes without, however, receiving any serious injury. Information of the proceedings was brought to the Town hall. The mayor adjourned the Police Court to twelve noon, and, accompanied by Mr. Cholmley, the inspector of police, and as many foot and mounted constables (eighteen of the foot-police . . .) as could be got together started for the Back Creek bridge. Meantime, the men continued their progress along the line. At the Crooked Billet, near Bridge-street, they found a body of masons at work; but, seeing a strong body of police coming, they passed on, and the masons continued their work. At the back of the White Hills, a gang of labourers at work there laid down their tools, as they saw the mob approaching, notwithstanding the presence of the police, who had orders to arrest any man who should interfere to prevent others working. Reinforced to about double their first number, the men on strike continued their progress as far as the commencement of Collier and Barry's sub contract, about the middle of the White Hills Hamlet, a distance of nearly three miles from the beginning of the line where the strike commenced. On the police reaching this point, inquiries were made of the contractors whether their men were being interfered with by the men on strike, and a reply being given that their presence interfered with the proper execution of the work, orders were given to clear the line. Several of the men were taken into custody for abusive and threatening language to the ganger, and with some little difficulty the others were compelled to leave the neighbourhood of the works. The men engaged on them continued their labour, and the police remained on the spot to protect them from further interference. At this spot Mr. Higgins, the contractor, pointed out to the police a man who had been active in inducing others to commence the strike, who had threatened "to knock the legs from under him," and had said that he had "buried many a —— better man than him in Bruce's contract." He was at once taken into custody, and secured in the White Hills lock-up close by. The man who committed the assault at the Back Creek-bridge was not to be found. He is said to have slipped out of the mob immediately after committing the assault. The names of the men already arrested are John Dynan, Charles Crosby, Martin Macmahon, and John Nash.

3.15 Violence on the picket-line

Tradesmen vigorously defended the Eight-hour Day. This strike, against an employer trying to introduce a longer working day, lasted six months, and was successful.

Source: Melbourne *Argus*, 16 December 1863.

At the District Court yesterday, a workman at present employed by Mr. Williams, coach-builder, at his factory at Batman's-hill, summoned a man who had been lately employed at the same shop, but who was now out "on strike", charging him with having assaulted the complainant and used threatening language towards him, with a view of inducing him to quit his employment. It seems that the men on strike keep watch on all of the approaches to Mr. Williams's factory, for the purpose of accosting the men who are at present at work there, on their way to and fro, and attempting to prevail on them to join the strike. In pursuance of this object, the complainant was stopped by a party of these men, and in the course of the conversation that ensued, threatening language and actual violence were used by the defendant, who gave the complainant a blow in the face, which was the assault complained of. The object in bringing the case into court being merely to prevent a recurrence of such actions, the Bench required the defendant to provide two responsible sureties, in £50 each, that he would keep the peace towards the complainant for the next twelve months. As many of the other workmen now on strike were pointed out by the complainant as being in court, Mr. Hackett took occasion to give them a few words of admonition, assuring them that any attempt at intimidation or violence would be severely dealt with if brought before the Court.

3.16 Management

In return for a percentage of the products, this manager took responsibility for the property of the owners and the control of labour.

Source: Memorandum of Agreement between the Whaling Company at Encounter Bay, South Australia, and Alexander Ewen, 1 June 1871, South Australian Archives, BRG 39 (xerographic copy of a contemporary manuscript in the possession of Mr George Ewen, Newland Town, Victor Harbour).

MEMORANDUM OF AGREEMENT made and entered into this first day of June in the year of our Lord one thousand eight hundred and seventy one—Between, Henry Banford, Henry Simpson and others, of the one part forming the Whaling Company at Encounter Bay in the Province of South Australia, And Alexander Ewen of Port Victor in the said province of the other party—That is to say—

The said Alexander Ewen doth hereby agree to take the management of the said Whaling Company of Encounter Bay and to use all means in his power to secure Whales on behalf of the above named Company, and doth hereby agree to take charge of, and securely keep all and sundry the property of the said Whaling Company. Viz: all Boats, Oars, Storegear, at present on the station and also any other property the said Company may from time to time add to the said Whaling Station at Encounter Bay.

And the said Alexander Ewen doth further agree and bind himself to send all Whale-Oil, and Whale-Bone (if any obtained) to Port Adelaide and to consign the same to the said Henry Banford, Henry Simpson and others of the said Whaling Company and that he the said A Ewen will not sell or allow to be sold or disposed of in any way whatever any portion of the Oil or Bone obtained from any Whales caught and secured by the said Alexander Ewen or the crews under his charge and controul, at any other place or in any other way except by the sanction of the said Henry Banford, Henery [*sic*] Simpson and others,—And further the said Alexander Ewen doth hereby agree and hold himself accountable to the said Henry Banford and others for all Boats, Oars, Stores, gear, and all other property now in the possession or to come into the possession of the said Whaling company and to be kept at Encounter Bay in the said province, and shall deliver them to the said H Banford and others in the same good order as he receives them (ordinary wear and tear excepted) at the end of the Whaling Season on or about the last day in August in this present year 1871.

In compliance with the above conditions the said Henry Banford, Henry Simpson and others on their part do agree to pay, or cause to be paid to the said A Ewen or his order the sum of Five pounds sterling money for every tun of Marketable Whale-oil and Five pounds per centum upon all monies realized by the sale of Whale bone as witness our hands this first day of June 1871

Witness to Signatures } Henry Banford on behalf of the said Company
Alexander Ewen

3.17 The formation of a Mechanics' Institute

The businessmen who set up the Mechanics' Institutes in Australia were not usually as proprietorial as Arthur Hardy, of Glen Osmond, a suburb in

Adelaide, for the structure of class power was expressed adequately enough through the ideology of these organisations.

Source: Minutes of First Meeting of the Glen Osmond Institute, 12th August 1854, State Library of South Australia, SRG57.

At a meeting held at Glen Osmond in the room intended to be used as a reading room and Mechanics' Institute on Saturday the 12th. August 1854:

Mr. Arthur Hardy in the Chair. Present also Mr. Justice Boothby, Mr. S. W. Bull . . . and several others.

Mr. Hardy opened the business of the meeting by stating that he had designated the building for the use of persons in his employment or living on his property. Neighbours and others having intimated their wish to participate in the benefits of the reading room, he had much pleasure in acceding to their request. It was his wish that the subscribers should themselves take over the whole management of the Institution upon themselves. He only required one restriction which he thought requisite at first at all events for the well being of the Institution viz: that no person should have a right to join or remain as a member of the Institute without his (Mr. Hardy's) consent. Mr. Hardy stated at the same time his wish to make the Institution as generally useful as possible and expressed his belief that he would not have occasion to exercise the power he retained. With this reservation he placed the room at the disposal of the Institute on every week day evening for such hours as should be found most generally convenient.

It was resolved that the Institute should be called "The Glen Osmond Mechanics' Institute".

It was resolved that the entrance money should be five shillings and the subscription sixpence per week payment in advance and that where the head of a family paid the entrance money any other members of the same family under sixteen years of age should be allowed to subscribe without paying any entrance fee.

It was resolved that children under 12 years of age should not be admitted.

It was also resolved that youths under 16 years of age whose parents did not subscribe should be allowed to subscribe without payment of entrance fee.

It was also resolved that the Institute should be managed by a Committee of twelve and that three should form a quorum. . . .

It was also resolved that the Committee should prepare a set of rules for the management of the Institution and submit them to a general meeting of the members to be held on Saturday evening next if possible and that the following should be included among the rules:

That no drinking, cards or gambling be allowed on the premises; that chess, draughts and dominoes be allowed but not for money; that no smoking be allowed. That the meetings on Saturday evenings be considered general meetings. . . .

It was resolved that the thanks of the Institution be given to Messrs. Dutton, Tomkinson . . . and Hardy for their donation of books.

(signed) Arthur Hardy
Chairman.

3.18 A children's temperance organisation

The small capitalists and working-men in the Rechabite movement, who embraced temperance as the highest bourgeois value, passed it on to their children via a ritual of fellowship, orderliness and obedience.

Source: South Australian District No. 81, Independent Order of Rechabites, . . . *Juvenile Tent Ritual*, Adelaide, 1888; State Library of South Australia, Pamphlets: Co-operation, vol. 2.

OPENING CEREMONY

C. R.—We are now about to open this Juvenile Tent. Those not members of our Order will please retire. The officers and members will take their places, and clothe themselves with their regalia.

The Deputy Ruler will see that the Guardian is at the door and report.

D.R.—Chief Ruler, the Guardian is at his post.

C.R.—Let no one be admitted while our Tent is being opened. The Levite will report if all have a right to remain.

LEVITE—Chief Ruler, all present are entitled to remain, and we are now ready to open the Tent.

C.R.—We will now stand and sing our opening ode, No. 1.

Tune—"Old Hundred."

1. As we're again assembled here,
May we all henceforth preserve,
And strive to spread the temperance cause,
In strict accordance with our laws.
In wisdom may we all increase
And, as true brethren live in peace;
And still from strength to strength go on,
Until the Temperance victory's won.

C.R.—I declare this Juvenile Tent duly opened.

MEMBERS—So it is.

INITIATION CEREMONY

C.R.—The Levite will see if there are any candidates for membership, and if so, collect their entrance fees, and report their names and ages to the Tent.

C.R.—The Levite will now introduce the candidates. Let us all stand and sing our ode of welcome, No. 2.

Tune—"Onward Christian Soldiers."

Welcome, kindly welcome
To our Tent to-day,
All whose hearts are with us,
Sons of Rechab say.
Sisters all we greet you
for our cause who feel
Brothers here we meet you
For the common weal.

Heartily we bid you
  Welcome to our band,
In our noble Order
  Firmly take your stand.

L.—Chief Ruler, Officers and Members, I have pleasure in introducing these friends for admission into this Juvenile Tent of the Independent Order of Rechabites.

C.R.—My friends, this Juvenile Tent has been formed to promote the principles of total abstinence, and to train the youth of our country therein. We are glad that you have resolved to join us, and to adhere to our time-honoured pledge. We are a branch of the oldest Temperance Order in existence, an Order which has, in the past, done much to promote the well-being of mankind, so you should therefore consider it an honour conferred upon you to be admitted into our fraternal band.

The Levite will now conduct you to our Deputy Ruler to assent to our Pledge.

L.—Deputy Ruler, I here present the candidates to receive the pledge.

D.R.—The members will now stand, and with the candidates repeat after me our pledge or

COVENANT

D.R. — I promise to abstain
ALL. — I promise to abstain
D.R. — From all intoxicating liquors;
ALL. — From all intoxicating liquors;
D.R. — And to do all I can
ALL. — And to do all I can
D.R. — To promote total abstinence;
ALL. — To promote total abstinence;
D.R. — To abide by all the Rules,
ALL. — To abide by all the Rules,
D.R. — To obey the officers.
ALL. — To obey the officers.
D.R. — And to strive to be at all times
ALL. — And to strive to be at all times
D.R. — A Faithful Rechabite.
ALL. — A Faithful Rechabite.

C.R.—The Levite will now invest the candidates with the badge of our Order, while we sing ode No. 4.

Tune—"National Anthem."

4. God bless our youthful band!
  O may we firmly stand
    True to our pledge!
May we to liberty,
Truth, love, and charity,
Evermore faithful be,
  From youth to age.

May Rechab's children stand,

A noble Temperance band,
  A joy to see;
And may our cause extend,
Until all people blend,
And one great shout ascend,
  "The world is free."

INSTALLATION CEREMONY

LEVITE—Worthy Superintendent, I now present the Juvenile Officers for Installation.

SUPERINTENDENT—Worthy Members, you have been chosen as the Officers of this Juvenile Tent for the ensuing quarter. I trust you will show by your carefulness and attention, that you fully appreciate the honour and responsibility thus conferred upon you. Remember that the success and future well-being of the Tent will depend very much upon you, and that other Members will look to you as their Officers to set them a good example. Be punctual and regular in your attendance, diligent in the discharge of your duties, and always endeavour to raise yourselves in the esteem and confidence of your fellow Members.

I will now repeat to you our Juvenile Officers'

COVENANT

I hereby pledge myself to perform the duties of my office to the best of my ability. I will attend every meeting, unless prevented by sickness or other important duty. I will be obedient to the Superintendents, and will do all I can to promote friendship and love amongst the Members.

Do you thus promise? If so, answer individually, I do.

OFFICERS—I do.

3.19 The formation of a church school

This Church of England project, which justified education in terms of self-help and Christian duty, was aimed at the children of the 'industrial classes' in a suburb of Adelaide.

Source: The Papers and Minute Book of the St Andrews Day School, Walkerville, State Library of South Australia, SRG54.

A SHORT ADDRESS TO THE INHABITANTS OF WALKERVILLE
[Extract from a printed circular]

Christian Friends—

It is proposed, if God permit, to begin a great work in your village—that work is the building of a school-house for a week-day school, and providing teachers capable of giving sound and useful instruction to such children as may become scholars. This is, in truth, a great work for education; a sound education, based on Christian principles, puts the young in possession of means which will enable them to turn to the best account the powers of body and mind which God has given them.

As the Minister of the Church at Walkerville I am most anxious that this work should go forward for your sakes—yes, for *your* sakes—it is the good of *all* of you that is sought. . . .

Now, you cannot expect this school to be built unless every resident in the place comes forward and does what he is able towards the carrying out of this object. Let no one of you deceive himself that *his* assistance will be but *little*, and that he is therefore justified in doing *nothing*. . . .

. . . Many, not in any way connected with the place, have promised their aid, but you cannot suppose that others will help you if you shew no disposition to help yourselves. Remember, as Christians, you are accountable to God for advancing or neglecting the best interests of your brethren. How then will you be held guiltless if you refuse to assist in the education of those about you?

Give us then, I would beg of you, your sincere prayers now, and your hearty assistance at the night of the meeting.

Your affectionate Minister,
T. P. WILSON.

Adelaide, November 28, 1848.

[Extracts from Minute Book]

Walkerville, Church of England Day School, a Public Meeting was held at the "Sussex Arms" Walkerville, on Thursday the 7th December 1848.

Present

C. I. Penny Esq. in the Chair—

Revd. T. P. Wilson	Revd. E. K. Miller
Messrs. I. W. McDonald	Messrs. C. T. Wilson
John Aubin	William B. Orde
John Chamberlain	O. K. Richardson
William Wright	Edward Rowlands
Richard Lambeth	Turner
I. Baddileys	Jarvis

Mr. Hawkes [Secretary] moved that in the absence of His Honor the Judge, Mr. C. I. Penny, to take the Chair—

Mr. McDonald Seconded the Motion

The Chairman, called upon the Revd. Mr. Wilson, to open the Meeting with Prayer.

The following resolutions were unanimously carried——

1st Resolution

Moved by Mr. O. K. Richardson,

Seconded by Mr. Richard Lambeth,

That in the opinion of this meeting it is most desirable to afford to the industrial classes of this favoured Province, the means of obtaining the advantages of a useful education, based upon sound principles of religion, and on such terms as need not exclude, even the poorest from its benefits.

2nd Resolution

Moved by Revd. T. P. Wilson

Seconded by Mr. William Orde

That in order to supply the urgent wants of the village of Walkerville, and

its vicinity immediate steps be taken for erecting a School House, in connection with the Church of England.
3rd Resolution
Moved by Revd. E. K. Miller
Seconded by Mr. Edward Rowlands

That the proposed School although to be established on the principles of the Church of England, shall be open to all such denominations as receive in common the authorized version of the Canonical Scriptures, and that its rules, and system of instruction shall approximate as nearly as possible to those of the Putteney street School.
4th Resolution
Moved by Mr. John Chamberlain
Seconded by Mr. John Aubin

That with a view of effecting the object named in the foregoing resolutions, a subscription list be now opened, and a Committee of Management formed to collect donations either in money or kind for such purpose, and to superintend the erection of a suitable building.

A Meeting of the Committee of Management of the Church of England Day School at Walkerville, was held at the "Sussex Arms" Inn on Tuesday the 6th February 1849.

Present

Revd. T. P. Wilson, in the Chair

Revd. E. K. Miller	Mr. I. W. McDonald
Mr. Richard Lambeth	Mr. John Aubin

and Secretary

Minutes The Minutes of the last meeting were read and confirmed.
Villagers The Committee, are of opinion that the feeling of apathy and indifference evinced by the villagers of Walkerville, will justify them in delaying the erection of a School Room, till such time as the Committee, shall be assured that an earnest desire, is felt, and a proper disposition is manifested by the villagers to assist in carrying out this object. In the mean time this Committee pledge themselves to use every exertion to collect the funds required to complete the projected School, and to prepare plans, and estimates of cost in the erection of any design which may be selected as suitable for a School Room.

A Meeting of the Subscribers to the fund, for the erection of a Church of England Day School at Walkerville convened by advertisement was held in the School House at Walkerville on Thursday the 5th day of September 1850

Present

The Revd. John Watson	The Revd. E. K. Miller
Mr. John Aubin	Mr. I. W. McDonald

Mr. G. W. Hawkes Secretary

The Revd. John Watson, was requested to take the Chair.

Minutes The Minutes of the last Committee Meeting were read by the Secretary, and confirmed.

The Chairman after some remarks recommended the adoption of the Rules and regulations for the Government of St. Andrews School Walkerville, which had received the approval of the Committee of Management, who desired to see them embodied in the Constitution of the School.

The following Rules were then carried unanimously—

Rules for the Government of
St. Andrews School
Walkerville

1. St. Andrews School, Walkerville, is established for the purpose of educating children of the industrial classes in the principles of the Church of England, but excludes none who shall conform to the rules hereinafter specified.
2. In the said School the authorized version of the Holy Scriptures, shall be read and explained daily; and such branches of Knowledge taught as from time to time shall be determined by the Trustees to constitute a sound Commercial education.
3. One or more lessons shall be given every week on the Liturgy and Catechism of the Church of England, but attendance at such lessons shall not be required of pupils whose parents being members of other communions wish them to be exempt.
4. The entire management of the School, and all properties connected therewith shall be vested in the following Trustees viz. the Incumbent and Wardens for the time being of St. Andrews Church, Walkerville.

3.20 Securing order in a voluntary organisation

The Green Ponds Tradesmen's Club was a sickness and funeral welfare association, the rules of which stressed order and duty.

Source: *Rules and Regulations of the Green Ponds Tradesmen's Club*, Hobart, 1861; Tasmanian Collection, State Library of Tasmania.

XIII. That any Member presenting himself in a state of intoxication at any meeting of this Society shall be fined One Shilling. Any Member interrupting another Member while addressing the chair shall be fined Three-pence for every offence. Any Member guilty of cursing, or any misconduct, during the hours of Meeting shall be fined Three-pence for each offence. Any Member leaving the room without permisson of the Chairman shall be fined Six-pence, and one of the Stewards shall represent all such fines to the Chairman who shall see them strictly enforced. No business connected with the Society to be transacted after 9 o'clock. If any Member disobey the Chairman or any other officer of the Society, when called to order, he shall be fined Six-pence for each offence; and any member dictating to the Chairman shall be fined One Shilling. Every Member when addressing the Chair shall do so standing or in default to be fined Three-pence.

XIV. That a Quarterly General Meeting of the Society shall take place every first Monday evening in the months of January, April, July, and October in each year for the election of Officers (as hereinafter mentioned).

At such Meetings, a Roll, containing the Members of the Society, shall be called over by the Secretary, immediately after the opening of the Meeting, and a second time, after the other business of the Meeting is over. Any Member not being in attendance at the first call (if not prevented by sickness or absence out of town, in any case to be proved to the satisfaction of those assembled) shall be fined One Shilling.

XV. That the Chairman of this Society be vested with the power to suppress disorder at Meetings, and shall, to the best of his ability, impartially administer and enforce the Laws of the Society, and shall not suffer any debate, or put any motion to the vote, which is contrary to the Laws, or can be determined by the Articles; or in default, to be fined Two Shillings each neglect.

XVII. That the Stewards of this Society shall hold office Three Months, and shall be elected at each Quarterly Meeting, from such Members as are eligible to hold office, to be chosen in rotation, as they stand on the books; and any Member refusing to serve (except he is sick or out of the District) shall be fined Two Shillings and Sixpence; and one of the Stewards shall attend alternately on the Meeting nights, or be fined One Shilling each neglect.

3.21 Development

On the second anniversary of the discovery of gold, the urban bourgeoisie celebrated the new social order. Thomas Sutcliffe Mort was a leading businessman.

Source: *Sydney Morning Herald*, 14 February 1853.

Gold Anniversary Dinner

Mr. T. S. Mort in rising to propose the toast to "The Commercial, Pastoral and Agricultural Interests of the Colony" said that although the discovery of our gold was of the very highest importance, these interests were no less important to New South Wales. ... The Commercial Banking Company's recent dividend, amounting to no less a sum than £100,000, must convince everyone connected with mercantile affairs that the gold discovery promised to make the merchants of Sydney like those of the once magnificent cities of the Mediterranean—"Merchant Princes" (Loud cheers). ... Who could afix a limit to the resources of Australia? (Hear, hear). Who that had sons before the gold discovery had any other resources than to send them to tend sheep in the interior, or to send them to Europe? Now a new state of things had arisen, and the colonists of New South Wales were about to build a new world. They would encourage, nay would raise, manufacturers, engineers and other skilled persons and what was done in the mother country would soon be done here. Consider the genial climate, the rich arable soil, the plains of pasturage, the wonderful mineral treasures of New South Wales, and then ask whether this indeed is not "the promised land". (Hear, hear). ... To another, and to a most important point, he would next solicit attention. He had adverted to the good effects of the gold discoveries upon the colonists in their capacities as citizens and fathers. He would now emphatically refer to the value of their discovery in making good Christians. (Hear). All the missionaries from all parts of the world who had so zealously laboured in the Islands of the South Seas for many years have done less than must inevitably be done in a very short time by the gold discoveries upon the great continent. Gold is the mainspring of commerce; commerce is the forerunner of civilization; and civilization is the handmaid of Christianity. (Loud cheers). Air—"Railway Galop".

3.22 Education for citizenship

George Kenyon Holden was a leading lawyer and businessman in New South Wales, from the 1840s to the 1860s. A liberal in politics, he was chairman of the National Schools Board and President of the Mechanics' School of Arts.

Source: G. K. Holden, *The Moral and Intellectual Culture of the People, Essential to Secure the Advantages of High Wages and Political Privileges, a Lecture delivered ... to the Sydney Mechanics' School of Arts, Tuesday, June 7, 1853*, The Empire Office, Sydney, 1853, pp. 9, 12.

It is no doubt a growing conviction of the necessity of qualifying the mass of the people to exercise wisely a power it is manifestly impossible to withhold from them, which has stimulated so many of those occupying the high places of society to exert themselves in the advancement of popular education. The most serious and far-seeing thinkers of our day clearly perceive that the only wise means of averting anarchy is to teach the people their own interests—to co-operate with them in the attainment of them—and to qualify both them and the classes above them to perceive in how many ways their interests may, instead of conflicting, be made to coincide. The people may thus be rendered not only a harmless, but a highly beneficial, conducting channel of political power—just as the same instrumentality by which a powder magazine may be exploded, may, under the guidance of a wiser art, be made to work an electric telegraph.

While the whole world, and especially that portion of it which speaks our own language, is pressing forward in this glorious career, it is surely not for Australia, with her golden resources, and her highly paid labourers, to lag behind in the race. Shall mechanics with incomes equal to those of the middle classes of other countries, remain content with their former pittance of education and intellectual advantage? No latitude of popular privileges, whether equalling or exceeding those of the mother country, can ever afford any real dignity or advantage, unless accompanied by the knowledge which qualifies for its intelligent exercise—which will enable you to appreciate the exertions of the honest public servant—to penetrate the disguises of the artful demagogue, who would flatter you for his own sinister ends—to check the rashness of the merely speculative politician—to take enlightened views of the great questions affecting our social welfare—to submit cheerfully to regulations entailing personal inconvenience, where their ultimate social results can be shewn to compensate the sacrifice—to exercise self-control—and resist the temptation to expend augmented wages in mere bodily indulgence—to cultivate habits of courtesy and mutual forbearance—to reconcile the difficult, but not contradictory, duties of following with conscientious decision your own religious convictions, and at the same time cherishing the most unalloyed charity towards all who differ from you—to take an intelligent part when your assistance appears requisite, in the management of useful public institutions, or furtherance of beneficial social movements—these and numberless other features in the character of good citizens must be established and generally prevalent among you before you can hope for any lasting social improvement. And these are the qualities which such an association as this School of Arts (or as I may again call it, the People's University) is calculated to promote....

Of political institutions this is not the place to speak, unless it be to repeat that such Institutions as this are equally entitled to the support of those who dread, and of those who rejoice in the advance of popular influence. Our mission is to quell the fears of the one by rendering the popular element innocuous—and to realise the hopes of the other, by ensuring its efficiency and durability. A popular form of Government without an educated people, is a dead shell, cast on a beach with no living inhabitant—while a people truly educated, will spontaneously form its own institutions as the nautilus forms its beautiful habitation, from its own vital secretions adapted to its own shape, growing with its own growth, repaired and renewed by its own inherent powers, whenever mutilated by accident or violence, and floating its fragile inhabitant safe through all the storms of that same ocean, which spurns the dead shell from its bosom to rot on the shore of oblivion.

3.23 Co-operation between labour and capital

Liberal democrats such as G. K. Holden were adept at mystifying class relationships and the power of large over small capital, especially when the goal of economic independence was receding.

Source: G. K. Holden, *An Enquiry into the New Relations between Labour and Capital induced by Co-operative Societies, Labour Partnerships and other Forms of Productive Industry in which Labour is Employed on a Footing more Independent than Common Hire* ..., William Maddock, Sydney, 1867, pp. 5, 6–7, 10–11, 13, 29–31, 33.

At a time when the growing political power of the working classes is exciting apprehensions among many thoughtful men ... it is scarcely possible to exaggerate the importance of any improvement in the relations between Labour and Capital which will tend to mitigate their antagonism, and open up to the labourer a perfectly just career of advancement, sufficiently encouraging in itself to remove all temptation to enter upon one of injustice.

The following enquiry will be directed to the indications of this improvement presented in the gradual development of Co-operative Societies, Labour-partnerships, and other forms of productive industry. ...

We have all heard more or less of Socialism, Communism, St. Simonianism, Fourierism, Owenism, and other schemes for reaping the advantages of co-operation without recognising those rights of property which are essential to maintain the natural stimulus of industry in each individual.

Their history is a uniform tale of deplorable failure. Nor could it possibly be otherwise, seeing that they have been in conflict with fundamental laws, established in the constitution of man by God himself,—laws as fixed and inexorable in the moral world as are those of gravitation in the physical. ...

So long as the false principles of Trades Unions preponderate, legitimate co-operation will not be appreciated as it deserves. There is a disposition on the part of the capitalist class to confound both together, as if they proceeded on a common ground of unjust aggression. But it is the grand advantage of co-operation, that it very soon outgrows the conditions of its own origin, as an exclusive association of working men,—and by the moral education it presupposes and cultivates in its managers and members, as the necessary elements of its success, it acquires a commercial credit, through which it is naturally and imperceptibly restored to an alliance with the capital of which it originally sought to be independent, and this under far more favourable conditions than before.

... Under the co-operative system a portion of the working class who were before wholly shut out from the position of capitalist through individual poverty,—have contrived, by prudent organization and management, to make the aggregate of their small contributions available to supply capital enough for many commercial undertakings hitherto beyond their reach. But so far as they thereby compete with existing establishments, it is in their newly assumed character of capitalists, and not of artisans. ...

The social movement we have been contemplating would still be very incomplete if we could not point out, simultaneously with the formation of these workmen's co-operative societies, a movement on the part of Master capitalists, impelling them to confer a voluntary boon upon their work people by admitting them to some share of profits, in lieu of, or addition to mere wages. ...

There is an aspect of the subject under consideration bearing on the political destinies of these colonies, of which it is impossible to exaggerate the importance. The danger of popular government is intensified exactly in proportion to the antagonism between the minority of capitalists, and the majority of manual labourers. Every social arrangement which tends to identify their interests, and bridge over the chasm which separates them, adds to the stability of such a government as ours. Those who would support democratic institutions have been quite consistent in endeavouring to encourage a population of small freeholders, cultivating their own land, in preference to that of either tenants or farm labourers. ... It remains yet to be seen whether the artificial encouragement of this class, by free selection, will succed in this object, in this colony. Hence the great importance of such a modification of the relations between capital and labour as will destroy their antagonism in all matters likely to come under the consideration of a legislature elected by their joint suffrages. This will be equally done whether the labourer becomes the member of a co-operative society, in which case he and all his associates become virtually capitalists; or whether he be admitted by his master to participate in profits, in which the smallness of his share, as compared with that of his master will no more prevent his acquiring the feelings resulting from a community of interest, than the small share of £50, held by one co-partner in a joint stock company will prevent his having a fellow feeling in commercial matters with the millionaire who holds £10,000 stock in the same company. As this movement proceeds, even though large numbers of both classes may not be reached by it personally, the line of distinction between them will become less marked, and as those who are embraced by it will partake equally of the feelings of both, they will gradually leaven with their moderate and equitable opinions, the whole mass of electors. ... The rock ahead in the extension of popular government has hitherto been a danger of the conflict of classes,—an apprehension of unjust legislation by a numerical majority, in the interest, real or imaginary, of one class only. This danger is, however, as we have already said, mainly consequent upon the line of demarcation between the two classes being sharp and definite. ... If the classes, on the other hand, pass into each other by imperceptible graduations, as is the case with the peerage and gentry of England—the prejudices which would otherwise naturally dominate in each, are so modified by social intercourse with members of the other, as to be rendered innocuous, and to preclude all danger of political collision. Great stress has been laid on this peculiarity of the upper strata of English society, by eminent historians and constitutional lawyers, and all their remarks upon this subject equally apply to the necessity of a like fusion between the labouring masses and their employers of the middle class, if they are to participate equally and safely in the exercise of political power.

... First came the era of master and slave, then that of capitalist and hired servant, and now we are approaching that of partnership or co-operation,—or rather we are consummating it, for it has long since embraced the whole of the capitalist class without reference to their relative wealth as individuals,—and all that remains is for it to comprehend also the labourer in a more perfect brotherhood of industry.

3.24 Qualifications for public office

How a successful businessman became a 'practical citizen', through marriage, and entered 'public' life.

Source: Sydney *Bulletin*, 21 August 1880.

The Right Worshipful Alderman Fowler, J.P., Mayor of Sydney

... in Mr. Robert Fowler we find a combination of rare qualities—an exquisite modesty combined with an energetic will, and a self-control that must have become habitual to him from the exercise of an enlightened discretion. It is not every man, however intellectually gifted, who, at forty years of age, reaches the social elevation which Mr. Fowler has attained, and still fewer who so unequivocally deserves it. The facts of his life are interesting because they teach a lesson of the best kind to young men—they point to a moral that needs only to be mentioned to be appreciated—they show how industry, regulated by common sense, leads to fortune, position, and (better than both) the conscientious discharge of duty. Without further comment or commendation, we give the particulars we have gathered of Mr. Fowler's career. He was born in George-street, South, Sydney, on the 13th of July, 1840, and received the rudiments of his education at Christ Church School in Pitt-street. His father, the late Mr. Enoch Fowler, belonged to that sturdy class of immigrant artisans many of whose sons have become so prosperous and distinguished in Australia. He was a native (as was his wife also) of the county Tyrone, Ireland, and soon after his arrival in Sydney established a pottery-business in Parramatta-street, near St. Benedict's Church. His son, the subject of our memoir, was at an early age apprenticed to the trade, and soon became an enlightened expert. He did not, like many of his youthful contemporaries, waste his evenings strolling about the streets, or "enjoying" themselves at the old Victoria Theatre. He devoted his spare time to study under private tutors, and has acquired a knowledge of history, natural philosophy, and the *science* of Political Economy far more extensive than most of his contemporaries imagine. While still quite a young man, he had charge of the extensive potteries erected at Camperdown. In 1867 he began life as a practical citizen by getting married (to Miss Seale of Burwood), and two years later, he was called to his first municipal honours, being elected alderman for the municipality of Cook. The year following he became its Mayor, and succeeded in uniting the boroughs of Cook and Camperdown into one corporate district, over which he presided as first Mayor, in 1870. On retiring from that position in 1871, he was entertained at a banquet in Camperdown, a flattering address presented to him, and an enthusiastic commendation of his impartiality and clearheadedness expressed by several speakers. In 1872 he was elected alderman for Denison Ward, by large majorities, and was soon after put in the Commission of the Peace. He has since been re-elected three times for that Ward in succession, without opposition, and was nominated for the mayoral chair last year, but was defeated by Mr. Roberts, or rather by the casting vote of the chairman (Mr. Ald. Merriman). In December last, Mr. Fowler turned the tables on his worthy predecessor, and became Mayor of his native city by a majority of three—the first to hold that office under the new Act. He has been appointed one of the local Commissioners for the Melbourne International Exhibition, and is likely to have a higher ambition satisfied—that is if he has any strong inflation for further honours—at the forthcoming general elections, as he has been asked to "run" for Newtown, with reliable assurances of his triumphant return. He is chairman of the Public School Board, No. 4, which embraces Petersham, Marrickville, Camperdown, and Darlington in its district. When to his numerous public duties are added the responsibilities of a large, and—we are happy to state—largely increasing business, it must be evident to all who read these remarks, that Mr. Fowler must possess indomitable energy, shrewd intelligence, and an innate love of fair play, or he would not be the popular man he is. The combination of such qualities—the main-springs of administrative success in a statesman—gives one an intimation that in the near future, he may be called upon to accept the port folio of Minister of the Crown. We wish him well in all his worthy life-pursuits.

4 The Working-class Challenge, 1890–1930

Patterns of Working-class Mobilisation

Working-class politics had its roots in the labour market organising of the 1860s and 1870s, but as a mass phenomenon it dates from the late 1880s, when regional patterns of mobilisation developed. The major pattern occurred in the cities, where the greater part of the working class began its political life in an alien urban setting, one whose functions in commerce and government it could not identify with its own origins in production. A generation later, as V. Gordon Childe commented in the 1920s, there were still practically no manufacturing towns in Australia. In other words, the characteristic form of urbanism during the period of working-class mobilisation was the commercial city or town. Of course, in some suburbs, factories grew in size and number, but the working-class communities that formed around them never became strong enough to impose on the city a new urbanism, the main function of which would be to organise the forces of production.

The working class primarily experienced this urban setting as a place where, because it was inhabited, work was available—as a structure of homes rather than a structure of workplaces. The development of trade unionism reflected this experience in two ways. Inter-union bodies, particularly the New South Wales Trades and Labour Council, were preoccupied with a certain form of political representation: with individuals, sometimes workers, who would represent the working class as another productive interest, one whose demands could be accommodated in the commercial ruling class's 'balance of interests' strategy. It was reflected, too, in the pattern of union growth. City unions with some institutionalised strength, such as the Amalgamated Society of Engineers, were those whose members had the opportunity to become, through job security and shorter hours, respectable home-owners and citizens. Accordingly, when working-class politics developed in this setting, it was primarily a form of local mobilisation to control the environment of the home.[1]

Not all workers were concentrated in cities. The primary production emphasis of the economy, with its large amounts of capital in the pastoral, mining, sugar, meat and shipping industries, meant that many wage workers were geographically dispersed and occupationally mobile. In mining regions and the smaller ports, workers came together for longer or shorter periods before moving on to another area and perhaps another occupation. In these areas, the pattern of mobilisation began in the workplace, and the regional concentration of workplaces made possible intra- and inter-industry alliances between workers. Charters Towers had a Trades and Labour Council in the late 1880s and a political organisation in 1890. In Port Pirie, the Working Men's Association from 1886 combined organising in the workplace and the electorate. There were similar developments in Townsville, Ipswich, Broken Hill and the West Australian goldfields. When workers mobilised in this pattern, they saw the locality as structured by work as well as the home.[2]

Evidence for the importance of the regional basis of working-class mobilisation can be found in the labour press. Between 1870 and 1899, 107 labour newspapers commenced publication in Australia, and of these 27 were published in towns or sought a suburban audience. These figures tend to underestimate the importance of the locally based labour newspaper, for if we look at how many labour papers were published year by year, we find that the graph for *all* kinds of labour newspapers reaches high points in 1891 (29) and 1896 (30), but then levels out between 1897 and 1899 (28); in contrast, the graph for labour newspapers published *locally* rises steadily, from 7 in 1891 to 13 in 1899. So in 1899, almost half of the labour newspapers appearing were published locally, six in Queensland towns and the others in such places as Balmain, Moonta (South Australia), Beechworth (Victoria) and Broken Hill (New South Wales). Country towns figure prominently in this list because in most of the cities, working-class suburbs also had access to labour newspapers of a more general kind. In Sydney, non-local labour papers such as the *Worker*, *Patriot*, *Co-operator*, *Transmitter* and *Dawn* all appeared in 1899.[3]

Working-class suburban communities at this time were closely knit, but they nestled in a bourgeois city, the functions of which encouraged cultural dependence. The intimacy of work and life bred a sense of place that normally overshadowed the workers' sense of exploitation. The pubs, the working-class sports (dogs, trotting, football and even the 18-foot skiffs on Sydney Harbour) and the local press built up the supportive local networks on which class action was based, but they were also easily diverted into suburban rivalry, culminating in professional sporting competitions. Then there were the voluntary welfare and uplift organisations—the co-operative stores, friendly and building societies—in which the working-class impulse to co-operation was contained within a bourgeois social form, the joint-stock company. They were the community-based analogues of the co-operative printing-works, mines and factories to which workers turned in strikes or periods of unemployment, and they were just as limited in their contribution to a class-based politics. Moreover, working-class traits of co-operation and solidarity in this setting ultimately became a source of what bourgeois observers called the 'Australian' culture of the First A.I.F., whose largest occupational group by state was industrial workers from New South Wales. Militarism became another form of containment of working-class culture.[4]

Some working-class communities developed in declining genteel suburbs such as Fitzroy or middle-class Balmain, which in 1910 had the second largest friendly society dispensary, one of the top ten building societies in Sydney, and whose co-operative society was the third largest in the state. Although home-ownership was limited in the cities—perhaps 30 to 40 per cent of homes were owner-occupied in Melbourne and Sydney between the 1880s and the First World War—it was a more prominent feature of working-class communities in suburbs of this sort and in the new subdivisions on the periphery of the city. On the other hand, in Redfern the Scottish and Australian Land Company, and other absentee landlords, owned great swathes of working-class terrace housing. Here, as in Collingwood or Port Adelaide, business and government power laid down the contours of development, blighting their working-class communities from the start. Health measures, for example, were resisted by businessmen with property in these localities, unless they were profitable. As Port Adelaide's Health Officer reported in 1889:

> one source of disease and death arises from overcrowding in dwellings and lodging-houses, from insufficient ventilation . . . household hygiene is extremely unsatisfactory in various parts of the Municipality . . . bedrooms ill ventilated, the floors not infrequently damp and uneven and well calculated to cause an accumulation of filth, thus affording a haven for disease germs; and the cellars gave off various unhealthy emanations. In many of the cellars, stagnant water is lying there in a putrescent state, a fruitful source of sickness.

Already by this date, serious epidemics had occurred in the most congested and depressed working-class areas, and state enforcement of public health regulations to check subsequent outbreaks was slow to improve the position. When the plague attacked Australia annually for six years from 1900, working-class suburbs provided its victims; amongst the 303 victims in Sydney in 1900, all whose occupations were specified (247) were workers.[5]

In the depressed, inner-city industrial suburbs, a distinctive working-class youth culture emerged in the larrikin push. It frightened the respectable by its indifference to the sanctity of property, but was channelled into serious

Horrors of childhood — II. A working-class child in the plague region of Sydney, 1900.
Source: N.S.W. State Archives, *Views taken during cleansing operations*: *Quarantine Areas, Sydney*, 1900, vol. III, no. 153.

crime mainly by police harassment. In fact, the larrikins diverted working-class energy from a frontal attack on property and class relationships into skirmishes with the police and soldiers. No wonder the most percipient bourgeois commentators counselled tolerance and advocated trade unions and dance-halls to turn the members of the push into useful citizens. From 1900, bourgeois writers began to romanticise the larrikin in novels, stories and ballads. The target of this larrikin literary tradition was not the unskilled and scarcely literate working-class deliquent; indeed, the problem for this literature was not larrikinism *per se*, whose roots went back to before the gold-rushes, but larrikinism in communities newly affected by working-class mobilisation. Diversionary the pushes might be, but they were still culturally the least tractable section of the working class. To prevent working-class politics assuming the cultural resistance of larrikinism, it was more effective to replace state persecution of the pushes with an attempt to persuade the 'respectable' section of the working class that 'we are all larrikins'. Literary 'larrikinism' promoted nostalgia for the values of a pre-industrial stage of class formation. It was a form of Australianism analogous to the *Bulletin*'s bush nationalism, and it served the same function. The fact that the literary 'larrikins' ended up as good husbands and soldiers, thus accurately reflecting the importance of the family and militarism to bourgeois cultural containment, hardly encouraged the transformation of the pushes into a street army of the proletariat.[6]

The suburban setting of working-class mobilisation was reflected in the surge of attempts from the late 1880s to enter municipal politics and to wrest control of the environment from local businessmen. As working-class votes were already electing businessmen to municipal honours, business resisted. One non-labour suburban newspaper told a newly formed Labor Electoral League in Sydney to stick to 'education' and 'propaganda'. Another response was for businessmen to become members of the new political organisations of the workers; indeed, businessmen helped to form the Labor Leagues in Ashfield and Leichhardt. But the most serious barrier to the emergence of municipal socialism in Australia was the leadership of the central Labor organisations. While some local organisations saw the advantage of controlling councils in order to secure relief works during periods of unemployment, to enforce minimum rates of pay and maximum hours and 'to supply local requirements, as food, clothing and other public necessaries by municipal enterprise', the official Labor programme for local government quickly settled down to being democracy, home-ownership and local progress.[7]

Working-class interest in local government as a field for class action ebbed just as the town-planning movement of technocrats and middle-class reformers appeared in about 1910. Where Labor aldermen controlled local councils, they now reacted with territorial defensiveness. Unable to prevent the zoning of working-class suburbs as industrial, they set out to woo new investment and consolidate their alliance with local small businessmen, in order to protect the community from major state intervention in the guise of 'slum clearance'. It was an alliance already strong in suburbs that had become retreats for the more highly paid workers. Here the most significant political division was between labour and local business on the one side and city or corporate capital on the other. In this pattern of mobilisation, the organisational expressions of the merger of interests between workers and local capital were the co-operative stores, dairies and butter-factories, and the Lib–Lab electoral alliance in local and state politics. Whatever the situation, as seats were tied-up and campaigns routinised, the Labor parties spawned formidable municipal machines, compensating local party workers for the loss of reforming zeal with the perks of office and the benefits of corrupt deals with business, both legitimate and criminal.[8]

A miner's hut, Lithgow Valley, N.S.W., 1900.
Source: Public Library of New South Wales, Sydney, T22.

The regional pattern of mobilisation in the pastoral districts, the non-metropolitan ports and the mining areas was produced by the interrelation of labour market organising and community control. This interrelationship was the material basis for the class awareness and militancy that characterised the 'new unionism' among bush workers, miners and transport workers, and that was so symbolically important for the development of parliamentary politics in this period. At the same time, the organisations that spearheaded developments in this pattern, the 'new unions', became in many cases instruments of containment of working-class politics.

The new unionism was not, as one of its leaders, W. G. Spence, later claimed, a natural product of bush work. Indeed, the shearers' union was put together in the late 1880s, in spite of an absence of solidarity between sheds and regions, by organisers who were paid according to results, that is, the number of members signed up. Gradually, however, the regional dimension of mobilisation stimulated union growth. Workers usually difficult to reach because they were migratory or thinly represented in a region, could more easily be organised where there was a strong regional class movement, as happened with the Bogan River carriers, the Newcastle shop assistants or the Charters Towers domestic servants.

Further, it was not a 'propensity to strike' among the leaders that was important in the industries covered by the new unions. There were, of course, important strikes associated with the development of these unions, which were fought on an industry-wide basis in order to bring particular employers into line. But it is important to recognise that the success of these strikes often depended a great deal on traditions of local militancy as well as on strong central leadership. Then, again, in Hindmarsh in the 1890s, a period of large-scale working-class action elsewhere, strikes were confined to single plants. Strike action in both of these situations tended to limit working-class consciousness to an instrumental and economist politics. But the critical strikes were those that spilt over into the community, and the critical periods those when the scale and variety of working-class action approached the level of a mass strike, as in 1890 and 1917.[9]

In these strikes, the crucial development was that workers, in such places as Broken Hill, Townsville and Wonthaggi, took the opportunity to lead their defensive organisations of the workplace into the cultural sphere. Often it began as a matter of sustaining a strike, but afterwards those who had been on strike, their families, other workers and eventually the businessmen of the town began to feel the presence of the union in their everyday lives. The union's brass band, the workmen's club, the union hall and the co-operative store were the most common signs of a union town. Later, unionists were found on the key town committees and in local politics.

To the extent that the unions gave leadership to the working class, they drew on its resources of co-operation and solidarity. These could be mobilised not just to defend the economic position of the workers but also the economic position and the social fabric of the town itself. Hence the support of local business people for the unions, even during strikes. Further, the unions, because of their leadership role in the working class, were often in a better position than business to understand and to organise solutions for the general problems of the town — for example, the scarcity of dental services or even the inadequacy of marketing arrangements for fuel and food. Thus there were occasions when unions performed functions for the town as a whole, in a way analogous to the role of the state in the wider society. Analogous, but not equivalent, for the unions' administrative and co-ordinating functions enlarged a sphere of co-operation, not of enforcement. In such a situation even the co-operative store could enhance class consciousness, as

Working-class mobilisation. A meeting of strikers during the Broken Hill strike of 1909.
Source: Mitchell Library, Sydney, Small Picture File.

when the Wonthaggi co-operative in 1934 loaned £1500 to the miners' union for strike pay.[10]

In view of the 'smooth' account of Australian history often given by historians of both the Left and the Right, it is worth emphasising the role of collective violence and mass demonstrations in the period of working-class mobilisation. In a union town such as Broken Hill, workers took mass action to combat the power of the state and of property: they commandeered transport, reconnected services to houses whose occupants were behind in their rates, and prevented the repossession of furniture. In several cities and towns, mass demonstrations enforced the laws on early closing of shops. Women in mining towns not only organised community support for the coal-miners on strike, but were the most effective members of demonstrations against scabs and the state employees who transported and defended them.

Private and state property was attacked (pubs and court-houses were favourite targets), as were scabs and policemen. In 1911, a nine months' strike and lock-out in Lithgow saw strikers break into the ironworks, take control of a mine and attack the property of the scabs. In this case, there was a very direct connection between regional mobilisation, working-class culture and collective violence, for the 'Lithgow riots' were precipitated when the scabs (who came from out of town) had the effrontery to stop work and dance to the music played by the town's brass band on the picket-line.[11]

Collective violence was so prevalent by the 1891 shearers' strike that Spence and other union leaders made secret contingency plans to *prevent* the workers taking possession of the country:

> The fight was bitter. It could not be otherwise. The marvel was that it did not result in civil war. The efforts of the leaders to try to effect settlement on reasonable lines, and the fixed idea of the men that they were engaged in an industrial strike, alone saved the country from civil war. At one time it was feared that it would come to that, and to prepare for such a contingency one of the leaders of the A.L.F. and myself held a private conference at three o'clock in the morning whilst travelling on the Adelaide express to Melbourne, and came to an understanding as to certain action to be taken by myself in the southern colonies. The men were becoming very exasperated at that time, and had they gone to extremes they would have taken possession of the country.

The leaders' fears, although exaggerated, cast a different light on the formation and structure of the new unions. They appear in this light as devices to contain working-class insurgency. Whereas workers were organising on a local basis, their leaders were obsessed with centralising control and top-level negotiations with business and the state. The same tension was apparent in the labour parties. In New South Wales, the cautious bureaucrats of head office really came into their own when Spence's union, the Australian Workers' Union, established its ascendancy over the party between the mid-1890s and the mid-1920s. By 1901, it was considered unremarkable for politicians, led by W. M. Hughes, to reconstitute the Waterside Workers' Federation. As Spence said, 'We need big unions, and big men at the head of them, and be prepared to pay big salaries to obtain them.' Of course, the other side of this argument was that the average unionists were *not* potential leaders — they were, in Spence's words, 'uncommonly like sheep' — although it was impossible to deny then, as it is possible today, that the success of the working-class's mobilisation rested on local groups of workers demonstrating their initiative, resourcefulness and class consciousness.[12]

Leadership: Intellectuals and Workers

Where do labour parties come from and how are the strategy and ideology of labourism explained in class terms? We start with the proposition that in capitalist society, the mobilisation of the working class is never simply a rearrangement of existing political resources. A mobilising working class creates a form of power that is collectively based and experienced in the capitalist mode of production. It reflects the emerging collective forces of production and as such is a form of power which challenges capitalist relationships based on private ownership. Secondly, this means that where the capitalist state has developed a parliamentary form, and access to decision-making positions in part of the state exists for representatives of the working class, there will be a tension in the politics of the class, flowing from its contradictory experience of two types of power, the extra-capitalist power of collective labour and the integrative power of decision-making within the capitalist state. Thirdly, the working class does not have a choice in this situation. Its leaders cannot choose to operate permanently outside the organisations of the State, because the class structure itself is constituted by the State. Moreover, as soon as the collective power of labour appears, the policies of the state are adjusted and new state forms created to integrate a subordinate class. (In other words, our second and third propositions are linked by the fact that changes in the form of the state and the class structure are related processes.) Together, these propositions point us away from one-sided interpretations of labourism that overgeneralise about the role of liberal ideology, of bourgeois intellectuals and of an over-hegemonised, 'corporate' working class.[13]

They also suggest that to focus on the formation of labour parties can mislead us about the scope and development of working-class politics. There was no 'turn to politics', not even to the politics of access to the state. This was not just because the liberal parliamentary form of the state preceded working-class mobilisation and thus lured workers away from their 'true' course. Rather, workers had to mobilise in relation to the state because the state, through both central and local government activity, was the largest employer, and the central government always played a major part in regulating the supply of labour. Thus workers participated in the political system as workers long before they formed labour parties. They lobbied politicians through separate unions, central councils of unions and organisations formed specially for the purpose, usually at elections. Some unionists were elected to parliament and then financially supported by fellow unionists (before payment of members of parliament). Of course, liberal ideology and the practice of parliamentary politics affected workers; there was a trend in the unions towards liberal, interest-group politics. On the other hand, the main campaigns of the period from 1860—for shorter hours, a minimum wage and a halt to assisted immigration, all of which involved state action—pushed the workers towards a sense of class interest and distinctiveness. The intensity of the demand for working-class representation in the state, a demand that arose during these campaigns, was more than a reflection of corporate, interest-group sentiment among the workers; in fact, the stronger the corporate sentiment, the more likely unionists were to be content with representation from sympathetic bourgeois liberals, as the history of labour politics in the 1890s in Victoria demonstrates.[14]

Class ideology and organisation required intellectual leadership, and from the 1860s the working class developed its own intellectuals, the men and women, usually remaining in working-class jobs, who organised and articulated its ideas and aspirations. By 1890, spokesmen for the churches and the bourgeois voluntary organisations were complaining not just of failure, but of failure to reach the working class, which had established its own intellectual life. There were socialist Sunday schools. There were debates and lectures in trades halls, Labor Leagues and union branches. Socialists, anarchists, single-taxers and co-operators founded networks of clubs and reading-rooms to educate the workers. And of course there were the labour newspapers, pamphlets and meetings. The 'public meeting' of the type common in the mid-century still took place, but for the working class, union meetings, strike meetings and workers' demonstrations were now more characteristic.[15]

Obviously, there were overseas influences on this new intellectual arena, and the transmission-belt was made mainly by non-working-class intellectuals. But the experience of mobilisation was evident in the way the main ideas were discussed in working-class papers and pamphlets. The local setting of working-class mobilisation was expressed in attacks on inequality, as working-class intellectuals realised the difference between 'Macleay Street and Red Rock Lane'. The scale and complexity of the labour market was then connected to depressed conditions in working-class communities. Unemployment was discussed in structural terms, as a product of machinery and the factory system. There were denials of ruling-class ideology on the causes of poverty (individual sloth or misfortune) and on its remedies (coercion or philanthropy). While in this way general propositions were made specific to the experience of mobilisation, working-class propaganda also focused on the process of mobilisation and its effects on the class structure.[16]

In fact, a class analysis was implicit in this treatment of mobilisation in working-class ideology. Four themes stood out. Firstly, the reason for mobilisation was tied to the notion of class structure in discussions that linked private property to the ills of society. This theme corresponded to the concentration of capital in key industries and the industrial pattern of mobilisation. Secondly, there was the ethic of solidarity, expressed in references to brotherhood, co-operation and unity. It was associated with the organising efforts of the class, especially rank-and-file initiatives. Thirdly, there were discussions of the methods of mobilisation: the forms of organisation, the need for discipline (for example, of politicians by the movement) and the Chartist theme of the relative strengths of moral persuasion and the use of force. Fourthly, there was the final goal, involving a radical break with existing society, in order to embark on social reconstruction, and variously referred to as 'the co-operative commonwealth' or 'socialism'. It coincided with the spread of co-operative experiments, most significantly involving unskilled workers such as laundresses and road-workers.

The fact that socialism failed as an electoral strategy when the socialists were excluded from, or moved outside of, the labour parties and formed their own parties, should not mislead us about the key role of socialism as an ideology in working-class mobilisation. After employers began to organise against the unions in the 1880s and after the state repression of the early 1890s, socialism corresponded not only to the sense of separate class identity but also to the mood of opposition and apocalyptic change that swept over workers, especially those in the transport and primary production sector. It made possible a new form of mass activity in the working class — the formation of a party, with constituency branches, a central organisation, a pledge for parliamentarians and provision of affiliation for the existing organisations of workers, mainly trade unions, but also clubs of socialists, single-taxers and other reformers. The rapid spread of this form of mass activity seems to have been connected to the strength of socialist ideology. In the suburban pattern of mobilisation, party formation and demands for municipal socialism went together. In isolated centres of industrial mobilisation, socialism remained a vital force even as an independent electoral programme; the only independent socialist elected to the New South Wales parliament, Percy Brookfield, came from Broken Hill in 1917. In Victoria, where the Labor Party was weakest, Tom Mann's socialism was the catalyst for the formation of Labor Party branches between 1902 and 1904. Although there were few members of socialist organisations, the pervasiveness of socialist ideas was critical for working-class mobilisation.[17]

Yet, the Labor Party was not a socialist party, a fact also with roots in working-class mobilisation. In the workers' suburbs, mobilisation meant an accommodation to local capital, especially as the central party organisations were dominated by union leaders who, having already made their accommodation with the capitalist state, made sure that municipal socialism was removed from the party's local government programme. However, the operation of integrative mechanisms, which ensured that the labour parties would settle for a reformist strategy of working through the capitalist state organisations, can best be seen in the class relations of working-class intellectuals. Not just articulators of the ideas of a mobilising class, they had also to make or influence decisions within the capitalist state. Inevitably, the tension between these two forms of power blunted and confused the class character of their ideas. Some were, in addition, influenced by their ownership of property; others by the processes of immigration and resettlement, which formed one aspect of Britain's late-nineteenth-century imperialist drive.

The general acceptance by the ruling class of trade unionism was a fact that the rhetoric of Spence and other union leaders has tended to obscure. During the strikes of the 1890s, employers' unions repeatedly asserted that they did not want to smash unionism. Leaders who could represent their members directly to the employer could be encouraged to represent them indirectly in parliament, for no matter how true to their ideals they remained, their membership of a state organisation separated them from the collective power of their class. But what of those union leaders who remained outside of parliaments and who continued to be exposed to the possibility of rank-and-file pressure for militancy and anti-capitalist programmes? For them, the new branch of state organisation for arbitration and wage regulation was developed, as the Victorian Chief Inspector of Factories recognised in 1915. Members of wages boards, he said, should be allowed a longer incumbency, so that the 'red ragger . . . freshly come from his working-bench full of main strength and zeal' could have enough time to learn 'gentler' methods: 'One of the most valuable influences of Wages Boards is the educative effect they exert on both employer and employee. Each side gets to know the difficulties of the other . . .'[18]

The involvement of working-class intellectuals in the organisations of the state, the logical outcome of the strategy of reformism, had important consequences for class analysis in the labour movement. Of course, it also meant the embourgeoisement of labour leaders by the perks and rituals of parliamentary culture. Further, it meant the creation of positions in new state organisations, those in the arbitration area, to which unionists could aspire. But actual physical involvement did not happen overnight, and before 1910,

Right: The Labor victory, 1910. Labor newspapers like the *Daily Post* in Tasmania played a key part in electoral organising.
Source: State Library of Tasmania, Hobart, NS 139/2/4.

THE DAILY POST
WILL YOU HELP
NOW FRIENDS
Sth AUSTRALIA
tried a
LABOR PREMI
for 4 Year
LAST SATURDAY
SHE RETURNED A
LABOR MAJORITY
AS A RESULT.
WILL YOU DO LIKEWISE?
AND WE DID
SENATE.
Campbell. 1989 Mulcahy 23736
Dobson. 23834 O'Keefe. 30798
Long. 30638 Ready. 29361
Macfarlane. 23452
REPRESENTATIVES
BASS.
Jensen 6548
Storrer 4937
DARWIN.
Fisher 3738
O.Malley 6545
DENISON.
Simmons 6097
Smith. 7079
FRANKLIN
McWilliams. 6211
Shoobridge. 5433
WILMOT.
Atkinson. 5312
Wilson. 4171
Final
3172
7170

the reformist strategy was implemented chiefly by non-labour governments. In fact, working-class intellectuals learnt to accept bourgeois-defined limits to the sphere of the state because, in this period, state action to integrate the working class was premissed on the mobilisation of workers by unions and labour parties. Just before he began a 35-year term as a workers' representative in the West Australian arbitration system, W. Somerville wrote in 1904 to the state's Liberal premier:

> Can you point to a party in the history of party politics the world o'er which has gone further on the way to abolish the prejudices of class and of calling than the Labour party? We have the Protestant and the Catholic, the superior civil servant (poor spiritless being) and the navvy, the doctor and the miner, the lawyer and the farmer. I know of course that within our party class prejudice is still strong and no one hates the evil thing more than I do . . .[19]

This perspective on class—as a prejudice to be overcome rather than a ruling power to be destroyed—reflected the impact of the integrative role of the state in the class structure at this time. Integration meant the institutionalisation, particularly through compulsory arbitration, of a certain level of working-class mobilisation. Labour reformists could therefore resist the dynamic, conflict-based logic of class analysis without dropping all reference to working-class interests. Reformism was not a demobilising strategy; it simply asserted that when organised workers were represented in parliaments and other sections of the state, it would be possible to supersede the clash of classes with a balance of interests and with a policy for the common good.

When a pamphlet history of the New South Wales Labor Party appeared in 1915, a large advertisement by a retail firm proclaimed: 'The History of Bon Marche is almost identical with the History of the Labor Movement.' Supplying goods and credit to the emerging working class had become a recognised business activity, one that often drew entrepreneurs from the working class itself. In Melbourne, John Percy Jones began a pay-as-you-wear clothing business in 1893, based on his experience of the 'clothing clubs' organised by working-men to give some of their number the chance (literally, for the clubs were sweeps) to escape the cycle of poverty. By the end of the 1890s he was a wealthy man and a leader of the labour movement whose extensive property interests were not seen as incompatible with his membership of the Victorian Socialist Party. Many other businessmen were active in the labour movement at this time, and not all of them were expelled, as Jones was in 1931 for supporting the Premiers' Plan. Another case was the coach-builder Alderman John R. Dacey, after whom a New South Wales labour government named a suburb that was meant to be a model for rehousing workers away from their traditional suburbs and the temptation of class militancy. With men like these in leading positions, the anti-property aspect of working-class ideology was necessarily stunted at birth.[20]

The beliefs of another category of working-class intellectuals can be understood in terms of their participation in the processes of late-nineteenth-century imperial expansion. The spread of European and American capital and the accompanying resettlement of 'white' population, following a presumed world-historical westward path, was justified at the time as a law of civilisation. It was further urged that the hopes of mankind lay in the 'new countries' of European investment and settlement, such as Australia. The racism, romanticism and environmental determinism of this rationale for imperialism were perfectly reproduced in the thought and action of William Lane. Lane came to Australia from England via Canada and the United States, and when he left eight years later it was to lead five hundred socialists to a 'New Australia', where they would be safe from the race war they imagined as threatening the end of civilisation. While in Australia, Lane was preoccupied with the bush — not just with bush unionism. His utopian socialism was of the same order as the mid-nineteenth-century radical idealism, and like that tradition it represented a surrender to the developmental mission of British imperialism and Australian capitalism. In the earlier period, the hegemonised pay-off was bourgeois freedom: the idea of economic independence; in the later period, it was nationalism and racial purity. Lane's novel, *The Workingman's Paradise* (published in 1892) eulogised the conditions of frontier work, which, he thought, made freedom and democracy 'natural' in new countries such as Australia. Socialism would follow if only men would be guided by their feelings and by the exemplary actions of their socialist mates. Lane spoke not only for those working-class intellectuals who supported socialist colonies along the River Murray or in Paraguay, but for all who connected social change with the natural environment of new countries. In the absence of a socialist analysis of the class relationships of frontier work, the development of natural resources proceeded along capitalist lines, even, after a few years, in the 'socialist' colonies. Gradually, the bush myth of the working-class intellectuals contracted to a racist and sexist nationalism, the assertion of the national distinctiveness of the white, male bush-worker.[21]

Working-class mobilisation also had an impact on traditional intellectuals, those in the professions and the bureaucracy, whose sympathies had in many cases already been aroused by the working and living conditions of the workers. They came in contact with working-class intellectuals in the anti-sweating and other reform movements of the time, where they were able to accomodate working-class concepts and demands to a liberal framework. Amongst liberal intellectuals in parliaments, the bureaucracy, and reform movements there were two influential groups. First, there were the clergymen, including Christian Socialists, who were seeking a way to make religion more relevant to their dwindling working-class congregations. Their earliest efforts can be seen in the sermons and tracts that appeared during the strikes of the 1890s. Secondly, there were the businessmen–journalists who initiated the 'new journalism' in Australia, in search of profit through a mass working-class circulation. Their greatest achievement was the Sydney *Bulletin*.[22]

So working-class intellectuals were separated from their class and cozened by traditional intellectuals. Some of them became property-owners, others became missionaries of frontier civilisation. In their intellectual development we see the effects of a partial class mobilisation, which challenged capitalism but was institutionalised by state power. By the end of the 1890s, there was a single intellectual milieu, where liberal and labour intellectuals met to produce the discourse of labourism.

Among the main themes of labourism was the stress on wealth as the main characteristic of the class structure, a stress that justified the strategy of redistribution through state intervention. This still left the problem of the manifestation of class differences in industrial conflict. The solution, a partnership between classes, was seen to rest on the introduction of such integrative devices as co-operatives, profit-sharing and workers' participation in management through consultative committees in industry. The term 'socialism' was applied equally to efforts of this kind as well as to enlarged state activity. If, during the transition to 'socialism' class conflict proved troublesome to order and property, it could be handled through the systems of compulsory arbitration, 'a new province for law and order'. The mobilisation of the working class would not be checked through head-on resistance, but by institutionalisation, legitimation by the state, and, in the industrial sphere, by a narrowing of its demands to the improvement of wages and conditions. Ruling-class power disappeared entirely from this analysis, and revolution or at least radical change could be defined as 'evolution', a gradual and peaceful process of mass education and enlightened legislation.

Reconstructing Bourgeois Culture

The growth of working-class politics with a regional basis was a more serious threat to capitalist institutions and values than the rapid electoral advances of the labour parties. While the political leadership of the working class embraced the idea that the state was neutral, the local political practice of workers was based on a collective form of power that posed a challenge to the idea of a neutral decision-making state. Yet, as we have seen, the community was also a source of weakness for the working class. It was here that the cultural defences of the working class were most vulnerable, and it was, therefore, the community that became a site of cultural intervention by the state in this period.

As cultural control enlarged as a sphere of state action, members of the emerging intelligentsia were increasingly involved with the state. Some of them were members of state organisations—for example, Peter Board, Director of Education in New South Wales from 1905 to 1922, but also an important public figure as an advocate of combining state and voluntary efforts to integrate young, unskilled industrial workers. Others remained outside of state organisations, but responded to the call to co-operate with the state. For example, there were the intellectuals in the universities and professions who dominated the Workers' Educational Association and whose activities were patronised by a string of high state officials. Church leaders were still important in the cultural area, despite their declining influence among the working class and their persistence with the strategy of private philanthropy, rather than state intervention. Indirectly, the Protestant churches contributed to the state's expansion in the cultural sphere by mobilising, through 'citizens' leagues', bourgeois morality as a force in electoral politics. And there were many church people who played a more direct role, as liberal individuals, in movements for women's rights, pensions, labour settlements for the unemployed, early closing, local option, and so on. Each of these movements sought state action in some form. Ironically, at the end of this period, it was customary for bourgeois intellectuals to lament the loss of the voluntary spirit and to blame it on the working-class strategy of seeking reforms through state action. This attack by intellectuals on the working class occurred in the context of a crisis of labour reformism in the 1910s, and was directed at the syndicalist and socialist alternatives, not at state action *per se*. Indeed, the intellectual programme developed at this time by Meredith Atkinson, Clarence Northcott and others aimed to justify the partnership of intellectuals ('social scientists') and the state in a project to replace class struggle with 'social efficiency'.[23]

State intervention rested on the argument that the working-class community was the seat of a dangerous moral contagion, which arose, so the scientists said, from the poor physical conditions of working-class life. But the argument was not always developed with scientific rigour. Bourgeois intellectuals attacked the working-class girl, who was just breaking away from the stereotype of sexual passivity, for not doing her 'personal duty' to 'her family, her country and her race'. They described working-class leisure activity as feckless and the larrikin youth culture as automatically criminal. And after the syndicalist and socialist challenges to reformism developed, the morality of a separate working-class culture was openly attacked as weakening the legitimacy of 'our social institutions'.[24]

When the state intervened in working-class life it tried to avoid paternalistic overtones. It aimed to break not only with the traditions of private charity but those also of the English state, whose poor law system the working class in these colonies of settlement remembered with horror. Further, it had to deal with the welfare demands of the labour movement, demands that in part reflected the growing cultural separateness of the working class. Pensions, for example, were demanded as a right of the aged members of the working class, not as a charitable response to individual misfortune and need. Thus the liberal-reformist governments of Victoria, New South Wales and South Australia eventually came round to justifying state intervention as a response to an inequitable situation caused by machinery and the economic system. This, of course, did not demobilise the working class, as private charity hoped to do, indeed it reinforced its level of mobilisation; but it did disguise the integrative functions of state intervention.[25]

If meliorism, the first strategy of cultural readjustment, operated at the level of the institutions and processes of working-class life, the second aimed to incorporate some individual members of the working class directly. The mobilisation of the working class had to be strategically accepted in this period, but the mobilisers, the working-class intellectuals, were so placed as to respond more quickly than their followers to the integrative thrust of the state's activities. To the extent that it succeeded, they were the more likely to endorse the point of view of the ruling class. On the other hand, the more they were personally incorporated, the more likely they would be to persuade their followers that state intervention was a victory for the workers as a class. Hence the importance of the cross-class alliances that the bourgeois reformers made with the trade-union leaders, politicians and publicists in the course of agitating for reform. For example, W. M. Hughes met the conservative politician T. R. Bavin, who later coached him for admission to the Bar, in the Early Closing League of New South Wales in the late 1890s.[26]

Middle-class women were particularly active in the various efforts to strengthen the family; indeed, one aspect of the first women's movement was the attempt to ensure that working-class women did not weaken the case for equal rights by escaping the restrictions of the family and bourgeois sexual morality. Maybanke Anderson, for example, the wife of a university professor, espoused women's suffrage and higher education for women on the one hand, but compulsory domestic science for schoolgirls, state aid for the family and sexual repression on the other. The university settlements and the kindergartens that were founded in the 1890s took working-class children off the streets, but their main object was to teach the mothers about authority and how to exercise it over the children. Similarly, the bourgeois men in Rotary who took up the cause of promoting the youth movement after the First World War were concerned with the wider ramifications of the breakdown of the working-class family. Although the ideology of 'service' inculcated in the various youth organisations and special activities—such as the 1924 Boys' Week, in Sydney—was supposedly classless, Rotary paid particular attention to the Church of England Boys' Brigade, which catered for working-class children. 'Service', in fact, meant learning to obey, as well as to exercise, authority: 'your boys of today are the foremen, managers and directors of tomorrow. What are *you* doing to teach them your high ideas of service?'[27]

Before the renovation of the family could be completed, housework had to be redefined in a way compatible with the emphasis in the bourgeois women's movement on the role of the mother and housewife in the reconstruction of society. To the working-class woman, motherhood and husband-nurturing could still be presented as natural or God-given roles, but for the middle-class women who promoted the 'education for motherhood' movement, a more sophisticated explanation was needed. Mobilised politically by the women's and other bourgeois reform movements, educated to an increasingly higher level and with greater experience of the organisation of work, these women in the early decades of the century were susceptible to the technocratic and nation-building ideologies of the time. Science and planning joined moral purity in the women's movement's recipe for national progress, and 'domestic science' and 'home economics' not only rationalised the confining of the working-class woman to the house, but in the form of labour-saving devices in the kitchen and the consumer market in household goods, it placated the 'new' bourgeois woman, who was trying to combine home duties and a restricted career.

State provision for the teaching of domestic science began in New South Wales in 1912. By this time, the state pension schemes (administered by the Commonwealth government after 1909) had already taken over certain functions usually performed by the family: the care of the aged and the sick. As the birthrate declined, the Commonwealth government intervened more directly into the family in 1912, by offering maternity allowances, to ensure the reproduction of labour power. Regulations to control the sale of contraceptives and abortifacients appeared early in the century and were strengthened on several occasions. Children outside the care and control of the family had been recognised as a state responsibility since the first years of the century, with Mrs King's orphan asylum, but there were stringent laws passed after 1900, to take children away from supposedly unsuitable families. Finally, the significance of the 1907 Harvester award for the working-class family was that it enshrined the concept of the family wage, thus confirming that the working-class woman's place was in the home, where she was expected to produce at least three children.[28]

Housing policy in this period functioned to defuse working-class campaigns against recalcitrant landlords, rent profiteering and 'rack renting' (payments to estate-agents in addition to rent to owners). These campaigns were particularly important in suburbs where great tracts of working-class housing were owned by one landlord. As the housing shortage in the cities grew, forcing up rents, trade unions and local organisations demanded rent control. Significantly, the periods when rent control was taken up as an issue by Labor politicians coincided with the periods of greatest working-class militancy: the period 1910–20 and the depression of the 1930s. Another housing venture by the state resulted in a particular section of the working class, Sydney's militant watersiders, becoming tenants of the state in 1900, when the government purchased thirty acres of private housing at The Rocks. Capital was poured into renovations of these houses, and when public housing became a class issue, Labor governments pointed to The Rocks. It was a long time before they could point to anything else; in its first eight years to 1920, the New South Wales Housing Board built only 453 homes, and most of these were in Daceyville, or as the working class called it, 'Canvass City', where the homeless squatted on the land the Crown had bought to demonstrate the social and moral advantages of garden suburbs for workers.[29]

However, the main thrust of state activity in the housing field was to encourage home-ownership among the working class. In New South Wales, the State Savings Bank was authorised in 1914 to make advances for home purchases to persons not already home-owners; by 1919, it had made 4400 loans. For those with a yearly income below £400, there was a special state home purchase loan scheme. This was not the end of state encouragement for home-ownership, for even the few homes built on Crown land by the state were offered for purchase to their tenants, a practice followed by the Commonwealth government when its War Service Homes Scheme began operating in 1919. These developments, apart from the symbolic state housing schemes, were welcomed by the residential real-estate and building interests, which about 1910 began developing new industrial suburbs based on home-ownership in such places as Altona (in Victoria) and Auburn, Clyde and Granville (in New South Wales). At the same time, traditional intellectuals responded to the cultural and political activities of the working class by developing an environmentalist ideology to justify the destruction of the slums and the separate zoning of factory and residential areas. Their town-planning movement spoke of 'social integration' as its aim and of the political instability that enclaves of workers portended. But the meliorist strategy of reformist governments was not to demobilise the working class but to integrate it; slum clearance did not become a major activity of the state until a later period. In the meantime, the town-planners successfully co-opted a number of Labor Party leaders into their movement.[30]

The introduction of cheap, compulsory elementary education in the 1870s and 1880s was one of the signs of the quickening process of class formation. The development of secondary industry coincided with a rise in the birthrate after 1865. Ten years later, child labour in the factories and loitering on the streets crystallised as issues for middle-class reformers. Both posed problems of social control more acutely than at any time since the 1850s. Accordingly, there was a close connection between the Factory Acts prohibiting child labour and the establishment of compulsory elementary education. Working-class youths, previously only intermittently exposed to training in bourgeois values, were drafted out of the factories and alleys and subjected to the discipline of the school.

The integrative function of public education after the reforms of the 1880s soon ran into trouble. In the first place, the regimen of the schools became accentuated under the pressure of numbers. The liberal idea of training working-men for citizenship was translated into rote-learning and physical drill, methods that imagined 'citizenship' for the working class as a form of vocational serfdom. Secondly, after the working-class youths left school at fourteen, they entered the factories where they were in fact little better than serfs, performing unskilled work that was poorly regulated by the state and managed in authoritarian fashion by the owners. Within a few years, the police were complaining that juvenile crime in the cities was not decreasing, that the juvenile offenders were becoming more literate, and that the factory system was clearly to blame. Educators too began to blame the factory system for the breakdown of 'social responsibility' and embarked upon an unrealistic campaign to provide educational solutions for problems arising out of the exploitative relationship of production (a tendency that has continued in educational circles until the present day). Four strategies were developed. Two of them involved the schools: a raising of the school leaving age (not achieved before the 1940s) and the 'new education', which recognised that the old methods of instruction were 'too vocational' and that more imaginative education meant better training for citizenship. A third involved state support for the 'youth movement', a cause vigorously championed by Peter Board, who saw Boys Clubs forming a link between the life of the school and that of industry, and extending the schools' work of inculcating a sense of social responsibility.[31]

The fourth strategy was to develop a special, and to some extent separate, system of technical education for the working class. As early as the 1870s, the newly formed Trades and Labour Councils and the professional bodies of engineers and others associated with manufacturing called for technical education. At first, the response of the state was cautious; it saw the problem as mainly organisational, setting up technical classes in elementary schools and networks of technical colleges under the control of the existing state body for education. By so doing, it merely continued the liberal principles of the old Schools of Arts, where the 'diffusion of useful knowledge' was chiefly valued for its 'moral utility'. This was not what the labour movement required from technical education, which it saw as a way to ensure the availability of skilled workers and hence a way to prevent dilution of the trades by unskilled workers and the reduction of wages. More importantly, it did not satisfy the manufacturing bourgeoisie. The working-class demand for a practical education was too corporate to withstand the ideology of technical education, which men like Norman Selfe, professional engineer and manufacturer, began to develop in New South Wales. Working-class youths in technical colleges came to be taught by men who proclaimed that technical education should be an autonomous part of the state education system, for the 'liberal arts' basis of the existing state system was seen as elitist and irrelevant to an industrial society. Technical education, when taught by practical men in a practical way, was said to be democratic, in tune with progress, and absolutely essential if the Empire wanted to keep up with Germany. Around

1910, the state at last began to recognise the force of these principles, at the same time as the labour movement began to adopt them. The conscious promotion by the state of technical education as a special branch of the system from this time (the first 'technical' man was appointed Superintendent of Technical Education in New South Wales in 1912) reinforced the ideologies of imperialism and of development through industrialisation — and strengthened their hold among the working class.[32]

When efforts were made to reinvest the family with moral authority, and when housing and educational policies were developed to manipulate the culture of the working-class community, appeals to propriety, thrift, home-ownership and progress were always wrapped up in the flags of empire and nation. Their full ideological ambit was the entire class structure; there were variations on the Anglo–Australianist theme to suit businessmen and the suburban or small town *petit bourgeoisie*. For the working class, there were the 'individualist notions of a nomad race', based on assumptions that were invented a long time before the 1890s. The romantic myth of individual opportunity in a 'new country' was present in the writings of Harpur and Kendall in the middle of the century, and of course the 'new country' theme was a key ideological support for the political settlement, based on access to opportunity, imposed by the liberal bourgeoisie in that period. In the 1890s this romantic position was refurbished, not least in the *Bulletin*. When J. F. Archibald characterised his ideal reader, 'The Lone Hand — very salt of the Australian people, the educated independent mining prospector', he was reasserting economic independence as a basic value, as well as indicating his preoccupation with the bush: which was the second key nationalist assumption. The idealisation of a bush ethos, stressing egalitarianism, resourcefulness, contempt for authority, sardonic humour, and so on, also had a long history before 1890 in English accounts of the bush, both literary and documentary. It was to be a long time before an urban/industrial myth was successfully substituted for it by the literary representatives of a new age of Australian capitalism. Thirdly, in an age of increasing imperialist rivalry it was assumed that Australia could not be fully independent, and that it needed protection from the 'races' to the north. Working-class nationalism therefore was also racist and militarist.[33]

Nationalism was an ideology, produced in a certain way, with certain key assumptions; it was not a vast, inexplicable change in mass consciousness. The method of its production required state and voluntary effort in campaigns that cut across class lines, such as those we have examined, as well as media of communication that could link an emerging working-class readership with bourgeois intellectuals. The printing-presses, in the main, were owned by businessmen who ran their papers and journals in order to make a profit and to counter the formation of opinions that threatened the system of property. The *Bulletin* was not a *tabula rasa* on which nationalist themes were inscribed by a collective thumb nail dipped in tar. Before the *Bulletin* could become the 'bushmen's Bible', it had to be a successful piece of property. The businessmen who ran the *Bulletin* and other popular journals were unlikely to feed an emerging working class ideas that challenged the rule of property. Instead, they devised an ideological package appropriate to the task of integrating a social order threatened by industrial militancy and political organisation.

Limits to Mobilisation: Ruling-class Reorganisation

It was not the spread of unionism but its militancy that worried businessmen in the 1880s, and the first organised response of the ruling class to working-class mobilisation, the formation of united fronts of businessmen in the labour market, made this plain. The most class-conscious businessmen regarded working-class mobilisation as a problem created by a legitimate economic interest group, the trade unions, forced into illegitimate interference with the rights of property by mistaken leadership. They believed that the closer organisation of businessmen would quickly defeat strikes, thus eliciting greater responsibility from trade-union leaders, facilitating wage agreements between organised labour and organised capital, and bringing pressure on the state for a more effective defence of private property.

Before 1885, co-operation among businessmen was slight. Although there were a few specialised industry-based bodies of employers, especially in building, they were more concerned to regulate competition than to oppose trade unions. Indeed, the trade unions encouraged this concern, hoping to prevent wage-cuts and unemployment by eliminating or reducing competition among employers. The formation of the coal vend in New South Wales was even assisted by the miners' union. Further, because many skilled workers in manufacturing retained a fair degree of control over production in small and technologically primitive shops, their employers, often still members of a trade union themselves, looked sympathetically on unionism. Even the New South Wales Employers' Union in 1890 shared this pro-union stance, although it feared that there were some union leaders who did not understand the obligations of labour to capital. Hence, when businessmen needed to organise against union militancy, they encountered a good deal of indifference in their own ranks, and in the long run it was the political leadership of the ruling class that offered the most effective resistance to working-class militancy.[34]

The first Employers' Union was in Victoria, formed in 1885 after a long and bitter fight in the boot trade; by 1889, an intercolonial conference could be held of Employers' Unions from Victoria, South Australia, New South Wales and Queensland. A second intercolonial conference was held during the 1890 strike, but the collapse of working-class organisation during the depressed 1890s removed the need for further employers' conferences. Their activities, the co-ordination of resistance to strikes and boycotts and the administration of funds to employers affected by them, could as easily be carried on by industry associations, whose spread the Employers' Unions had always assiduously promoted.[35]

In the meantime, the Labor parties were establishing an electoral base and the liberal-reformist governments adopting policies that strengthened the strategy of parliamentary reform among the working class. Since any form of mobilisation of workers on class lines was potentially dangerous for capitalism, business leaders turned their attention to this new front. Its importance was symbolised by the presence in 1899 of the pastoralist and non-Labor premier of New South Wales, W.J. Lyne, at the public meeting to announce the re-formation of the waterside workers' trade union, organised principally by W.M. Hughes, who was then a Labor member of the colonial parliament.

On the one hand, reformism was a sign that the working class was mobilising within the limits of bourgeois hegemony; on the other hand, every advance towards the welfare state, every new regulation of the labour market and every redistributive reform was a setback for free enterprise. Until the shift to industrial capitalism during the First World War posed the need for a new level of state intervention in the economy, many business representatives in the political sphere were opposed to any extension of the state and constantly were on the defensive.[36]

Businessman in politics. The merchant Sir George Dibbs (1834–1904), who was three times premier of New South Wales in the 1880s and 1890s.
Source: Portrait in oils by Percy Spence in the Public Library of New South Wales, Sydney.

Because Melbourne was the financial centre, the Victorian Employers' Federation, formed in 1901, was the first and most important of a new series of business organisations. By 1904 there was a Central Council of Employers of Australia, which grew to include Employers' Federations from every state in 1915. Although explicitly focused on parliaments, the Federations were slow to realise the need for a mass-based conservative party to meet the challenge of Labor. Their activities were modelled on the faction politics of an earlier age. They supported the entry of more businessmen into parliament and sought access to decisions as a series of pressure-groups. The continuing electoral successes of Labor parties and the formation of liberal-reformist governments, climaxed by Deakin's administration of the Commonwealth in 1905, produced a sense of reactionary desperation amongst the more ideological businessmen, who declared that they could already detect the advent of socialism in Australia. Increasingly, business representatives in upper houses blocked progressive legislation for as long as possible, and the courts saw a number of business-inspired challenges to the legislation that was passed. Employers' Federations took credit for these acts of resistance.[37]

Just as businessmen at this time were not embarrassed to give a naked ideological defence of employers' interests, for example against compulsory wage-fixing and arbitration, they did not hesitate to use directly the power of private ownership if at all possible. In Tasmania in 1912, the Employers' Federation organised a boycott of advertisers in the Labor newspaper, the *Daily Post*. When Labor parties gained office, of course, they were more vulnerable to the direct use of the power of ownership. In New South Wales, the Holman Labor government in 1912 was forced to drop its plans for a state-owned steel-works when B.H.P. threatened to move its proposed plant at Newcastle to South Australia. Perhaps the most notorious example of this kind of ruling-class resistance was the successful organisation by pastoral and commercial interests in Queensland of a boycott by the London money market of a loan for the Labor government of E. G. Theodore in 1920.[38]

While the businessmen were organising in the labour market, the conservative politicians were forced to recognise that the political sphere was no longer manageable in the old way. The faction systems operating in the colonial parliaments worked for as long as the mercantile bourgeoisie retained its cultural hegemony, electoral politics focussed mainly on local 'roads and bridges' issues and there were no organised interests representing different sections of property. However, in the 1880s, these conditions began to change. The leading businessmen–politicians who ran the faction systems were discredited as business, particularly in finance and property, began to show a want of the bourgeois virtues of probity and prudence. When the Queensland Bank collapsed and a series of bankruptcies ended the Victorian land boom, politicians were involved in business scandals; by the mid-1890s, a leading New South Wales conservative politician, John See, could face electoral challenge because of his business connections. Yet it was speculative enterprise rather than property as an institution that came under fire, and even the Melbourne land-boomers escaped with little damage to reputation, on the whole.[39]

At the same time, property-owners with grievances against the mercantile dominance began to organise politically, taking care, however, to speak on behalf of 'productive' property. In the 1880s, the Victorian manufacturers set up a legislative committee, while in New South Wales a recognisable protectionist group in the parliament appeared, with close links with the Chamber of Manufactures. Protectionist political parties followed. As Federation approached, the manufacturers stepped up their organisation, holding intercolonial conferences and establishing an Australia-wide body in 1903. In the meantime, the farmers on the agricultural frontier had also organised, at first in local improvement associations and then in regional and sectional bodies, which became increasingly more sophisticated in pressure-group tactics and electoral activity. Farmers' groupings appeared in parliaments in the 1880s and 1890s, and soon developed common policies of free trade, cheap labour and cheap money. With Chambers of Commerce continuing, as they had since the 1850s, to lobby for free trade and to encourage commercial men to enter politics, there was a three-way split, and the possibility of a conservative political coalition to meet the appearance of working-class interests and ideology in parliament was hampered by deep economic conflicts. The fusion of the non-labour parties between 1908 and 1910 was a temporary victory. It was followed by a split along new lines, with the formation of the first of the country parties in 1914, followed by others around the country into the 1920s. Within the urban non-labour parties, conflicts between sections of business were endemic until Menzies and the industrial capitalists reorganised conservative politics in the 1940s.[40]

Achieving conservative political unity was further complicated by conflicts of parliamentary strategy. In the decade or so after the depression of the 1890s, liberal-reformist governments in New South Wales, Victoria and South Australia sought to meet the challenge of working-class political mobilisation with a broad programme of reform. The beginnings of the welfare state, further reform of parliamentary democracy, regulation of the labour market and redistributive taxation were under way before the first Labor majority governments (in New South Wales and South Australia in 1910). Occasionally, the liberal-reformist governments depended on Labor Party support, but mostly they did not. Liberal reform, when seen in the context of working-class mobilisation, was not a series of measures to extract benefit from a worked-out Labor policy of support in return for concessions, but a strategy of containment. It was not even precipitated by the parliamentary debut of the Labor parties, as the Victorian factory legislation of the 1880s reveals. What the ruling class feared was the power of mobilisation; what the liberal-reformist strategy conceded was a guided mobilisation, by way of increasing state intervention.[41]

The alternative strategy was to oppose the extension of state power. There were two movements here, the first in the 1890s. The Young South Australian Patriotic Association, the South Australian National Defence League, the National Association of New South Wales, the Victorian National Association and the Queensland Political Association were organised by bankers, pastoralists, merchants and lawyers to combat liberal-reformism, which they interpreted as a spineless submission to Labor pressure. Because they were attempting to resurrect the political and cultural leadership of mercantile–pastoral capital, these conservatives concentrated on criticising the emergence of the party system, in the name of rule by the people and the need for 'sound men' in parliaments. There was also a heavy ideological content to their activities, with considerable emphasis on a populist rejection of class-based politics and a competitive individualism disguised as a law of nature: 'Property is simply an expression of human will and energy.'[42]

The second movement, which flourished in the first years of the new century, has been called a 'syndicalism of the right'. Embracing small property owners, especially in the countryside, it extended the anti-party feeling of the 1890s into an attack on parliament itself and engaged in a much more electorally sophisticated criticism of state intervention. The extension of state activities and the interest burden on state loans were seen as precursors to heavier taxation, and the environment of parliament and the public service were blamed for the perfidy of politicians, in much the same terms as the syndicalist left. The Kyabram movement in Victoria in 1901–2 and the People's Reform League in New South Wales after 1902, showed that electors could be mobilised for conservative ends by a programme calling for government retrenchment, particularly by reducing the salaries of politicians and top public servants, and for halving the number of politicians.[43]

By the late 1890s, the mercantile–financial section of the ruling class was lamenting the difficulties faced by 'practical' men in securing election to parliament. The *de facto* alliance between liberal-reformism, with its supporters in the protectionist movement, and the Labor parties forced the commercial men into an early recognition of the need for a mass-based conservative political party. But the early organising efforts were fitful, the branch structure collapsing after each election campaign. Greater success was achieved in the organisation of women as a separate conservative interest group. The technique here was to equate the family with the interests of property, through home-ownership. Until 1945, always the largest non-labour political organisation in Australia was the Australian Women's National League (which operated in Victoria only), with a nominal membership in 1906 of 10 000 and in 1914 of 52 000. Similar women's organisations were formed in 1902–3 in New South Wales and Queensland.[44]

The press played an important role in conservative politics, particularly when conservative party organisation was so intermittent and patchy. While the ability of the press to alter opinion, whether of the political leaders or of their followers, was the objective of those who owned, managed and wrote for the press, its more important function was to link leaders and followers, providing the information about issues and action without which a mobilisation of conservative voters could not be successful. Just as the labour press increasingly reflected the regional basis of working-class mobilisation, so the conservative press came into its own when the war and its aftermath provided the ruling class with the opportunity to effectively raise issues in the larger frameworks of empire and nation. There were 21 capital city dailies in 1903, 24 in 1919 and 26 in 1923.[45]

The war created for the first time a mass base for conservative politics. Despite the narrow victories for the Left in the conscription referenda of 1916 and 1917, it was business that gained in prestige during the war and the ruling class that began to solve one of its main problems: the creation of a separate political leadership. Businessmen, making large donations to the war loans and the patriotic funds, and putting voluntary effort into thousands of patriotic organisations, were thrust into positions of eminence and responsibility. As the State recognised their generosity and embraced their energies in advisory and regulatory bodies, their authority increased. At the same time, their participation in the conscription and loyalist campaigns gave them a taste of a mass, conservative mobilisation and an awareness of the need for experts to run it. The pattern of ruling-class leadership began to change.[46]

There were still some ruling-class leaders who were businessmen–politicians in this transitional period, for example Herbert Brookes, who was a director of Austral Otis, chairman of Australian Paper Mills and Deakin's son-in-law. He was already involved in conservative organisation in 1914, as president of the People's Liberal Party, whose importance lay not in its membership, which was small, but in its link with the Victorian Chamber of Manufactures, of which Brookes was also president. During the war, Brookes was prominent in the Lord Mayor's Patriotic Fund, the State War Council (which looked after repatriation), the State Munitions Committee, the Electricity Supply Board, the Federal Coal Board and the Federal Bureau of Commerce and Industry. All this made him an important member of the state apparatus, at the same time as he consolidated his position as a spokesman for business, through his presidency in 1918 of the Associated Chambers of Manufactures of Australia. Moreover, his political skills also took a quantum leap. He was a member of the Universal Service League, which campaigned for conscription, the Australian Defensive League (which assisted the Special Intelligence Bureau by spying on 'disloyal' elements) and was president of the Citizens' Loyalist Committee, which organised mass demonstrations against the Irish, the Catholic Church and Labor. Naturally he entered the new conservative political organisation, the Nationalist Party, as a back-room adviser. Meanwhile, in the Universal Service League were other men whose single forte was mass campaigning, such men as the New South Wales secretary, T. R. Bavin, who was later premier of New South Wales, and John Latham, the Victorian secretary, who later almost became prime minister. The Nationalist Party, with its extensive and semi-permanent organisation in the electorate, including women's branches of considerable size and influence on party councils, was the largest crop in the conservative field. But the ideological lesson of the war, that patriotism and development could be made themes in a conservative populism, was widely appreciated. It was expressed pre-eminently in *Smith's Weekly*, whose proprietor, the ex-Lord Mayor of Sydney, Sir Joynton Smith, discovered the thrill of conservative mobilisation in the war loan campaign of 1918, and set out consciously to use his paper to mobilise a 'League of Citizens'.[47]

Limits to Mobilisation: The State and the System of Property

State power protected the system of property, notwithstanding the strategic differences within the ruling class over how to deal with the mobilisation of the workers. We have seen how the bourgeois programme of cultural persuasion developed into a welfare system of state intervention into working-class family and community life. As well, the repressive organisations of the state were increasingly active in this period. Of course, using the police, the military and the legal system to contain popular discontent and to put down popular disturbances was not new in Australia. What was new was the explicitly integrative function of this activity, a response to the greater articulation of the class structure in this period. Now it was not just a matter of defending particular sections of property, nor of preserving individual interests during a breakdown of public order, but of ensuring the continuation of the system of property.

Extending the state's integrative function greatly enlarged the state. New departments appeared as part of the programme of concession and cultural persuasion. There were new relationships to enforce also, and these at first had to be imprinted on working-class consciousness through the real or threatened use of force. The police, for example, after the introduction of compulsory primary education, had to chase up parents who ignored the new enforceable aspects of their children's education. At the same time, traditional methods of working-class control, the laws against the sale of liquor and gambling, were more closely policed. But even when directly enforceable relationships were not involved, the police were key state personnel in this period, mediating between the state and its clients. Thus as well as being the state's repressive arm, the police rapidly became agents in the community for the state's bureaucratic power. By 1902, the Inspector-General of the New South Wales Police, who had been complaining in his annual report since 1894 about police work on behalf of government departments and charitable institutions, was so exasperated by the demands made on the police as the state increased its integrative function, that he was moved to quote:

> It is difficult to fix the precise limits within which it is proper that [the police] should act, but it is certain that by indefinitely multiplying their duties we run a [risk] of undermining the popularity of the force by exhibiting its members before the eyes of the people as universally interfering and censorious.[48]

The bureaucratic strengthening of the state turned one of its two fronts towards its own personnel. New South Wales in the 1890s gave its central personnel agency, the Public Service Board, wide powers. Victoria and Queensland also had central agencies to control their public servants by 1900, but they still had to overcome the vestiges of patronage and departmental autonomy that had been characteristic of the state services up to this time. The second front was turned against the clients of the state. In the police departments of the colonies, this meant centralisation of control, which had begun earlier in Victoria and New South Wales to cope with the breakdown of state authority on the goldfields. By 1900, after the working class had posed its threat to public order, all the colonies had reorganised their police forces on centralised lines. Special organisational steps to deal with working-class militancy were not usual, although the New South Wales Police Department decided to maintain a body of mounted police for duty in the metropolitan district in 1890, a year of bitter industrial conflict.[49]

The remarkable developments in the colonial military forces during the period of working-class mobilisation await proper historical treatment. There were certainly problems of imperial defence and renewed fears of invasion, but even a superficial look at military records suggests that the military were also valued as a guarantee of internal law and order. Like the police, they were reorganised between the 1880s and 1900. Moreover, their numbers tripled to about 29 000 in the same period. Much of this amazing expansion, at least in New South Wales, was in 'rifle companies', that is, volunteer units under the control of both reserve officers, who were often political notables, and permanent officers. When they were abolished in 1892, because from the military point of view they were difficult to train and mobilise, the Commanding Officer of the Military Forces of New South Wales recognised the need for the military to assume a repressive role inside the colony. He proposed a 'movable column', centred on Sydney, but equipped to move at short notice 'in case of war or national emergency'. In the next thirty years, there were several such 'emergencies' in the class struggle.[50]

Repression. Mounted police lead a demonstration of the forces of 'law and order' during the 1912 general strike in Brisbane.
Source: Oxley Library, Brisbane, VPQ71–21.

Although the state sided with the employers in the most militant strikes, its repressive activity should not be thought of as all savagery and naked support for business. The police, as we have seen, were also part of the cultural programme of persuasion and concession. However, cultural conflict in the class structure found one expression in the antagonism of the police and the working-class youth culture of the 'pushes' in the new industrial suburbs. So when the police found themselves on the front line in the battle between labour and capital, ordered perhaps to break up a gathering of strikers, there were strong cultural reasons why the orders were obeyed. But if the agents of the state were anti-working-class, and if the state necessarily defended the system of property, the object of the use of repressive tactics by the state was to integrate, not to smash, the working class. So long as the working class did not organise in such a way as to threaten the continued existence of property, the state directed its blows against those members of the working class who stepped out of line, while promoting in every such case, and in the many strikes where it did not have to intervene, the view that the state was impartial in the conflict between labour and capital.

The image of state neutrality was more easily promoted before the mounting of the challenge to business as a whole by revolutionary syndicalists and socialists between 1910 and the 1920s. In that earlier period, moreover, the political arm of the ruling class was divided and sometimes governments were cautious in dealing with disputes, like that at Broken Hill in 1892, for fear of losing office. But the First World War provided a more favourable ideological climate for conservative politics, as well as blowing away some of the cultural fog that prevented the acceptance by the workers of an anti-capitalist critique. Although none of the I.W.W., socialist or Communist groupings were large, or very influential in the labour movement, they were repressed and harassed with great severity, particularly by the Hughes and Bruce–Page governments.[51]

At this time, most of the machinery of the capitalist state in Australia was organised on a decentralised basis. The federal compact had explicitly relegated the Commonwealth government to a subsidiary role, looking after certain matters of interstate concern and leaving the remainder to the states. Meanwhile, the business structure of the ruling class, although affected by the colonial pattern of settlement, with relatively autonomous groups of capitalists in the major cities and towns, was in the operation of key sectors—for example, shipping, finance, mining and pastoralism—increasingly national, as was the labour market. But while these processes were occurring, the new federal political system retarded the development of unified state policies, even in such a crucial functional area as integrating the class structure. Social policy in this period was still mainly a state-level matter, although the development of Commonwealth welfare and arbitration policies could not be resisted by reluctant politicians. On the whole, however, the state apparatus was out of line with the class structure, a fact producing notable confusion in the history of state functions in the 1920s, when there was increased activity in the area of servicing sectors of business, but attempts by Prime Minister Bruce to dismantle the Commonwealth arbitration machinery. And the incredibly sustained repression of the revolutionary left during the 1920s, which seems so out of proportion to the scale of the challenge, is partly to be explained in terms of a conservative government being able to indulge its prejudices without the restraints imposed by the responsibility of managing the full complement of state functions.[52]

When the state assists one section of business, tension within the ruling class results. But in a period of working-class challenge, the service rôle of the state occurs within the overall context of the need to strengthen the system of property. In Australia, after 1910, the state embarked on a programme of assistance to the industrial section of capital, which was closely connected to the state's integrative activities, and which underpinned the growth of the corporate form of business organisation, and thus decisively strengthened capital's power to mobilise.

In the decade before the First World War, it became obvious that the export economy, which represented the dominance of mercantile capitalism, could not solve the problem of unemployment in urban areas, even though there was a big increase in the production of export items after 1904. When the outbreak of war cut off markets and reduced the import of manufactured goods, mercantile capitalism became a distinct embarrassment to the prosecution of the imperial war effort. Indeed, minerals producers were suspected of aiding the enemy because of their prewar refining contracts with German companies. In this situation, manufacturers saw their chance, for imperial interests could now be reconciled with economic nationalism. The Grimwade companies, for example, embarked on mechanisation and monopoly control of markets in glass and chemicals, and Russell Grimwade, like many other businessmen, entered the state apparatus, through consultative committees and statutory bodies. When the war ended, the state's assistance to business continued. The state had begun to orchestrate a shift in the balance of power within the ruling class.[53]

To get businessmen to accept state intervention was not easy. The War Precautions Act had to be invoked before one businessman, John Higgins, could be persuaded to assist the process. (He was later knighted.) But the fact that an ex-secretary of the Waterside Workers' Federation was the Prime Minister was a marked impediment, as a member of the Collins House group of companies recorded at the time. He, however, eventually overcame his antagonism to Hughes and arrived 'at the understanding that the individual was something less than the State'. Sometimes businessmen and farmers, invoking state rights to protect their specific interests, used the federal system to resist Commonwealth government schemes. And in the 1920s, there was a faltering in state support for industrialisation as mercantile and rural interests with British encouragement resisted on the political front. But the trend was never reversed.[54]

The critical events in the genesis of industrial capitalism, the establishment of B.H.P.'s steelworks at Newcastle and the reorganisation of the base metals industry, involved massive state assistance. B.H.P.'s decision to build at Newcastle was taken in 1912, after the New South Wales government had promised 'encouragement and consideration' (which meant land, wharves and harbour facilities), the newly formed Commonwealth Bank had guaranteed £1 million, and government contracts for rails were assured. The metals industry was reorganised by the Hughes government, which brought the producers together, encouraged the carrying out of smelting and refining in Australia, and assisted in securing overseas markets. Hughes' most spectacular coup in this area was a long-term contract between the zinc companies (dominated by the Collins House companies) and the British government.[55]

It is important to remember that these developments occurred when militant industrial battles, syndicalist ideas and the internal divisions of the ruling class were posing the problem of co-ordination to that class in a very sharp way. Finance committees emerged at this time to link the business leadership with the Nationalist political leadership, but within particular sections of business, organisation was either nominal or non-existent. However, by the end of the war it was apparent that state intervention might overcome the reluctance of business to organise both sectionally and as a class. Herbert Brookes, in his presidential address to the Associated Chambers of Manufacturers of Australia in 1918 foresaw a network of 'self-governing industries', co-ordinated by the new Bureau of Commerce and Industry, with the whole system encouraging 'a new corporate spirit'. During the war, businessmen had in fact been incorporated into the state in various industry-regulating boards.[56]

The intimate connection between the state-supported shift to manufacturing and the integrative function of the state can be seen in the way Brookes recommended that representatives of the workers should also be included in the government of industry, from the organisations of the state down to the factories. There was much talk at this time of 'industrial democracy' and 'co-operation'. A corporate liberalism was emerging among some businessmen and state personnel, who believed that in the future the state would regulate labour and capital, capital would admit labour to the government of industry, and labour would give up strikes and bolshevism. Such a programme was premissed on an integrated class structure and a ruling class organised, dominated by the corporate form of business, and committed to the pursuit of national economic interests.[57]

This programme for the advance of industrial capitalism had to contend with a small domestic market and the competition of British manufacturers, difficulties that were only partly overcome by the first avowedly protective tariff in 1920. It meant also an attack on labour costs via mechanisation and, more importantly, the new 'scientific' style of management to control the entire labour process in the interests of capital. When B.H.P. set up its Newcastle works, it began not only with modern machinery but also with a draconian system of labour discipline, a workforce artificially divided by a hierarchical job structure, in which promotion from one minutely differentiated grade to another depended on loyalty, not seniority, and with a workforce in the production area recruited especially for its non-union character. By the end of the First World War, other industrial capitalists were showing considerable interest in 'scientific management' and the state was encouraging intellectuals to propound the thesis that 'industrial efficiency' meant lowering the cost of labour.[58]

In the early stages of industrialisation, the working class had been able to hold certain defensive positions. At Lithgow, the iron-works operated on a contract basis in which the work-group played a key role in the organisation of production. The unions in the engineering trades were able to resist the introduction of piece-work fairly successfully until after the First World War. Many struggles were won to prevent dilution of the workforce in the wake of mechanisation. Indeed, the introduction of machinery was closely scrutinised by workers. In 1906, Edward Dyson was able to write about the sabotage by female workers of a paper-bag-making machine, with the story's humour directed against incompetent foremen and ignorant managers:

> Anything the Beauties could do to complicate matters and delay Luke in arriving at a complete understanding of the machine, they did with inimical good will, and bolts got into the cogs, and nails under the rollers in mysterious ways; nuts were loosened if Luke merely turned his back, and parts that worked in harmony one moment ceased to revolve the next, and when they were urged something always broke.

Ultimately, the machine 'insurrects' and the female workers keep their jobs.[59]

Yet gradually, the position of the unions in engineering, manufacturing and heavy industry was weakened. Increased productivity was not reflected in wages. Industrial accidents became more prevalent. Strikes were lost and lock-outs won, including a nine months' lock-out by B.H.P. in 1922–23, which ended only after the workers had taken a 10 per cent wage cut and B.H.P. had introduced even more efficient machinery. Company unions were set up in iron and steel, paper-milling, stevedoring, railways and tramways. The famous strike defeats in wharf-labouring, coal and timber at the onset of the depression during 1928–30 were not as significant as those that occurred in the First World War and immediately after, for these were the first victories for industrial capitalism. Moreover, they clearly underlined the importance of the state's integrative role, for the working class retreated without as much collective violence as marked the transition to industrial capitalism in the United States.[60]

Arbitration was used to legitimate the process of reducing the workers' control over production; awards incorporated piece-work, and dilutions of the ratios of apprentices to journeymen and workers per machine. State enterprises took the lead in introducing speed-up techniques, from about 1912. These were accompanied by 'Taylorism' or 'scientific management' of the sort that finally provoked the 1917 general strike in Sydney, which began in the government rail and tram workshops. In fact, throughout the war there was a rash of strikes in state enterprises, many of them caused by deliberate government policies to break down conditions and undermine the position of the craft unions. When the creation of new industries was discussed, the federal governments stressed the importance of the question of control of the labour process through piece-work, dilution, and so on. Where governments led, private businessmen saw no reason not to follow. Indeed, they pressed for stronger state regulation of the labour market. On one occasion, Hughes was forced to plead that he was not the 'Supreme Being', in the presence of businessmen demanding a guaranteed immunity from strikes in return for British investment in the Australian chemical industry.[61]

The contribution of the war to checking working-class advance offset the rapid shift to the left inside the labour movement. The war provided favourable conditions for governments to increase their offensive against the unions in state enterprises, and to step up the regulation of the labour market. The war gave a measure of natural protection to manufacturers and encouraged links between government and manufacturers, links that enabled the better organisation of the employers. From this strengthened position, the employers could proceed with their policy of securing greater control over production through mechanisation and new management techniques. Further, the war provided the favourable ideological climate in which the state could attack those unions that resisted speed-up and deteriorating conditions, as in the 1917 general strike. Finally, the war provided the experiences and ideas that could be fashioned by ruling-class spokesmen, like Brookes, into a new ideology of labour relations after the war: corporate responsibility, co-operation, industrial peace.

Notes

1. A quantitative approach to urbanisation, and the role of manufacturing growth in it between 1861 and 1891, can be found in N. G. Butlin, *Investment*

in Australian Economic Development, 1861–1900, A.N.U.P., Canberra, 1972, ch. 3. For a Marxist theoretical account of urbanism, as a way of mobilising, extracting and concentrating the social surplus, see David Harvey, *Social Justice and the City*, Arnold, Melbourne, 1975, chs 6–7. Childe's comment is in *How Labour Governs*, M.U.P., Melbourne, 2nd edn, 1964, p. 6. The social integration of trade unionism is the theme of N. B. Nairn, *Civilising Capitalism: The Labor Movement in New South Wales, 1870–1900*, A.N.U.P., Canberra, 1973, ch. 1. The conservative, home-owning city worker, supporting his union solidly, sometimes in spite of its radical leadership, is a familiar theme of union histories, although it is isolated from an analysis of the place of the union in the working-class community. See K. Buckley, *The Amalgamated Engineers in Australia, 1852–1920*, A.N.U.P., Canberra, 1970, pp. 95–100; R. T. Fitzgerald, *The Printers of Melbourne: The History of a Union*, Pitman, Melbourne, 1967; and J. C. Docherty, 'The Rise of Railway Unionism: A Study of New South Wales and Victoria, *c.* 1880–1905', M.A. (History) thesis, School of General Studies, Australian National University, 1973, introduction.

2. The history of the working class at the local level has not been written. There are some local labour histories, but their methodology focuses on the growth of organisation, not mobilisation. See, for example, H. J. Gibbney, 'The Goldfields and the Labour Movement in Western Australia', in *Labour and the Goldfields*, Australian Society for the Study of Labour History, Canberra, 1968, pp. 1–10; and G. C. Bolton, 'Labour Comes to Charters Towers', *Bulletin* of the Australian Society for the Study of Labour History, no. 1, 1962, pp. 25–34. See also G. Dale, *The Industrial History of Broken Hill*, Fraser & Jenkinson, Melbourne, 1918; and R. J. R. Donley, 'From Wheatport to Industrial Town: A History of Port Pirie, 1873–96', B.A. (Hons) thesis, Department of History, Adelaide University, 1965.

3. These figures on the labour press have been extrapolated from H. J. Gibbney (comp.), *Labor in Print: A Guide to the People who Created a Labor Press in Australia between 1850 and 1939*, Research School of Social Sciences, Australian National University, Canberra, 1975.

4. Working-class culture has attracted few scholars. J. M. Freeland, *The Australian Pub*, M.U.P., Melbourne, 1966, pp. 152–3, has figures showing the rapid increase in beer consumption and in licences during the period of working-class mobilisation. Sporting histories in Australia scarcely rise above the antiquarian level; for example, John Dunn and Jim Main, *Australian Rules Football: An Illustrated History*, Lansdowne, Melbourne, 1974. On social class and the eighteen-footers, see Bruce Stannard, 'Blood, Guts and Sails on Sydney Harbour', *National Times*, 1–6 March 1976. For examples of co-operative production, see J. Hagan, *Printers and Politics*, A.N.U.P., Canberra, 1966, p. 28; and E. Ross, *A History of the Miners' Federation of Australia*, Australasian Coal and Shale Employees' Federation, Sydney, 1970, pp. 23, 85. L. L. Robson, 'The Origin and Character of the First A.I.F., 1914–18: Some Statistical Evidence', *Historical Studies*, vol. 15, 1973, pp. 737–49, discusses C. E. W. Bean's Australianising of the A.I.F. and provides the figures on urban working-class recruitment.

5. Robert Irving, 'An Outline of History of Balmain', in John Wong, *The Houses of Balmain*, Horwitz, Sydney, 1969, stresses its mixed-class residential

character, as well as the unplanned nature of industrial development. The best study of the effects of business power on suburban origins and growth is B. Barrett, *The Inner Suburbs: The Evolution of an Industrial Area*, M.U.P., Melbourne, 1971, which deals with Collingwood and Fitzroy. See also G. Mitchell, 'Origins of Environmental Chaos: Wollongong, 1890–1910', B.A. (Hons) thesis, School of History, University of New South Wales, 1973. Kerry Wimshurst, 'Nineteenth Century Hindmarsh', B.A. (Hons) thesis, Department of History, University of Adelaide, 1971, is an excellent account of the hegemony of local small business over working-class residents. Recent contributions by economic historians to nineteenth-century studies have questioned the view that most Australians were home-owners; see A. E. Dingle and D. T. Merrett, 'Home-owners and Tenants in Melbourne, 1891–1911', *A.E.H.R.*, vol. 12, 1972, pp. 21–9; and by the same authors, 'Landlords in Suburban Melbourne, 1891–1911', ibid., vol. 17, 1977, pp. 1–24; and R. V. Jackson, 'Owner-occupation of Houses in Sydney, 1871–1891', ibid., vol. 10, 1970, pp. 138–54. The big increase in owner-occupation in Sydney and Melbourne occurred between 1947 (40 per cent) and 1971 (70 per cent); see M. Neutze, *Urban Development in Australia: A Descriptive Analysis*, Allen & Unwin, Sydney, 1977, p. 33. For corporate landlords in working-class suburbs, see *S.M.H.*, 23 July 1955, '99 Year Leases now Expiring in Sydney cause Legal Tangle'. The Port Adelaide health report is from E. Lumbers, *Centenary History of the Municipal Corporation of the City of Port Adelaide, 1856–1956*, Adelaide, 1956, p. 47. The effect of business control of local government on working-class health and living conditions is described in M. Cannon, *Australia in the Victorian Age, Volume 3: Life in the Cities*, Nelson, Melbourne, 1975, chs 2, 17. The figures for plague victims, of whom forty-five were females in 'domestic duties', come from N.S.W. Legislative Assembly, *Report of the Chief Medical Officer on Outbreak of Plague at Sydney, 1900*, Government Printer, Sydney, 1901, p. 31.

6. N. D. McLachlan, 'Larrikinism: An Interpretation', M.A. thesis, University of Melbourne, 1950; J. Murray, *Larrikins: 19th Century Outrage*, Lansdowne, Melbourne, 1973, is scrappy but reproduces verses on larrikinism from scandal and sex sheets like *The Dead Bird* (Sydney, 1889–91). Edgar Waters, 'Ballads and Popular verse', in G. Dutton (ed.), *The Literature of Australia*, Penguin, Ringwood, Vic., 1964, p. 271, has figures on sales of C. J. Dennis among the First A.I.F. There is no good published study of the larrikin literary tradition. Some examples: Louis Stone, *Jonah* (Methuen, London, 1911; repr. Angus & Robertson, Sydney, 3rd edn, 1965), in which the hero becomes a big businessman and his mate a small businessman—both redeemed by the family; Louis Esson, *The Woman Tamar* (a play), in *Three Short Plays*, Fraser & Jenkinson, Melbourne, 1911; Ambrose Pratt, *The Great Push Experiment*, Grant Richards, London, 1902; Rolf Boldrewood, *In Bad Company*, Macmillan, London, 1901.

7. *Leichhardt and Petersham Guardian*, 8 August 1891, criticising the Newtown Labor Electoral League's municipal platform (q.v. Document 4.1). The municipal socialism quotation is from *Australian Workman*, 30 January 1897, reporting the contribution of St Peters Labor Electoral League at the 1897 conference of the New South Wales Political Labor League. For Victoria, see H. McQueen's chapter in D. J. Murphy (ed.), *Labor in Politics: The State Labor Parties in Australia, 1880–1920*, U.Q.P., St Lucia, 1975, p. 321.

8. Leonie Sandercock, *Cities for Sale: Property, Politics and Urban Planning in Australia*, M.U.P., Melbourne, 1975, ch. 1; Peter Spearritt, 'Sydney's Slums: Middle Class Reformers and the Labor Response', *Labour History*, no. 26, 1974, pp. 65–81. On the Lib–Lab aspect of local mobilisation, see Wimshurst, 'Nineteenth Century Hindmarsh'; and, in relation to agricultural co-operation, D. N. Jeans, *An Historical Geography of New South Wales to 1901*, Reed Education, Sydney, 1972, pp. 257–9. The link between Labor municipal machines and crime is treated in Frank Hardy's novel, *Power Without Glory*, the author, Melbourne, 1950.

9. The best accounts of the 'new unionism' relate it to the structural principle of workforce concentration in key industries, but not to the patterns of class mobilisation; see R. Gollan, *Radical and Working Class Politics: A Study of Eastern Australia, 1850–1910*, M.U.P., Melbourne, 1960, ch. 6; L. Churchward, 'Introduction', in R. N. Ebbels, *The Australian Labor Movement, 1850–1907*, Australasian Book Society, Sydney, 1960, pp. 14–15; and W. J. Harris, *First Steps: Queensland Workers' Moves Towards Political Expression, 1857–1893*, Australian Society for the Study of Labour History, Canberra, 1966, pt 5. On Spence, see Coral Lansbury, 'William Guthrie Spence', *Labour History*, no.13, 1967, pp. 3–10. Despite Spence's ambivalence to the militancy of the struggles associated with the 'new unionism', his own books are still a good source for it; see *History of the A.W.U.*, Worker Trustees, Sydney, 1911, pp. 61, 73–5; and *Australia's Awakening: Thirty Years in the Life of an Australian Agitator*, Worker Trustees, Sydney, 1909. For Hindmarsh, see Wimshurst, 'Nineteenth Century Hindmarsh'. For the affiliations of unions and their estimated membership in New South Wales and Victoria in 1890, see Appendix 2 in Docherty, 'Rise of Railway Unionism'. Brian Fitzpatrick, *A Short History of the Australian Labor Movement*, Rawson's Bookshop, Melbourne, 1940, chs 6–8 and 12, comes closest to offering a 'mass strike' interpretation of the 1890s and 1917. The concept comes from Rosa Luxemburg, *The Mass Strike, the Political Party and the Trade Unions*, Harper & Row, New York, 1971 (first publ. 1906). See also J. Brecher, *Strike!*, Straight Arrow Books, San Francisco, 1972, p. 22 and ch. 7.

10. On 'union towns', see Dale, *Industrial History of Broken Hill*; Bolton, 'Labour Comes to Charters Towers', pp. 25–34; Peter Cochrane, 'The Wonthaggi Coal Strike, 1934', *Labour History*, no. 27, 1974, pp. 12–30; and Spence, *History of the A.W.U.*, p. 37 (re Narrabri).

11. Don Rawson's 'Political Violence in Australia', *Dissent*, nos. 22–23, 1968, deals with the formal political system. The Broken Hill incidents are in Dale, *Industrial History of Broken Hill*. The mobilisation of women in mining towns is discussed in Winifred Mitchell, 'Wives of the Radical Labour Movement', *Labour History*, no. 29, 1975, pp. 1–14. For mass demonstrations and direct action in early-closing campaigns, see G. Serle, *The Rush to be Rich: A History of the Colony of Victoria, 1883–1889*, M.U.P., Melbourne, 1971, p. 106; and B. Davies, *The Meat Workers Unite*, Australasian Meat Industry Employees' Union (Vic. branch), Melbourne, 1974, p. 18. E.F. Squires, 'Judas: A Strike Incident', in *Bulletin Story Book*, Bulletin Co., Sydney, 1901, is about community hostility to a scab, who eventually hangs himself. For the Lithgow riots, see Ross, *History of the Miners' Federation*, p. 215; and Helen Hughes, *The Australian Iron and Steel Industry*, M.U.P., Melbourne, 1964, p. 53.

12. Spence, *History of the A.W.U.*, p. 49, on secret meeting of union leaders, and p. 27, on workers as 'sheep'. His belief in big money for big leaders was put in a speech to a Workers' Educational Association Conference, reprinted in M. Atkinson (ed.), *Trade Unionism in Australia*, W.E.A., Sydney, 1916, p. 43. Ray Markey, 'The Return of Frankenstein's Monster: The Political Demobilization of the Australian Working Class in the Late Nineteenth Century', a paper delivered to the Class Analysis Conference, Sydney, 1976, notes the role of the A.W.U. in the institutionalisation of N.S.W. labour, but spoils his case by making a misleading distinction between 'working-class' urban unionists and the 'non-working-class' A.W.U. For politicians dominating the W.W.F., see L. F. Fitzhardinge, *William Morris Hughes: A Political Biography*, Angus & Robertson, Sydney, 1964, pp. 108–9.

13. We have in mind three recent influential studies: D. W. Rawson, 'The Life Span of Labour Parties', *Political Studies*, vol. 17, 1969, p. 316, argued that labourism occurs when intellectuals persuade the trade unions that power is a resource that can be transferred from the industrial to the parliamentary arena. This view has the merit of focussing on power relationships, although not on those of the class structure. John Saville, 'The Ideology of Labourism', in R. Benewick, R. N. Berkhi and B. Parekh (eds), *Knowledge and Belief in Politics*, Allen & Unwin, London, 1973, pp. 213–26, pointed to a material basis for labourism in the British working class, by suggesting that the mobilisation of a pre-industrial working class will result in workers accepting liberal ideology. But his notion of pre-industrial is without content, and in fact the argument proceeds at the level of ideology and organisation, leading to the tautological proposition that labourism is the working class's response to the intellectual and political supremacy of capitalism. George Lichtheim, *A Short History of Socialism*, Fontana, London, 1975, p. 220, believed that the British working class was 'instinctively labourist'. Like Rawson, he attributed a vital role in working-class politics to intellectuals, but in Lichtheim's case, they liberate the workers from the prison of corporate separateness. Our main objection to these three approaches is that they conceive of the working class as a stratum within a given structure, rather than as producing, and being produced by, that structure.

14. The growth in the working class of the politics of access to the state before the advent of labour parties can be traced in D. J. Murphy (ed.), *Labor in Politics: The State Labor Parties in Australia, 1880–1920*, Q.U.P., St Lucia, 1975; and Nairn, *Civilising Capitalism*. P. G. Macarthy, 'The Living Wage in Australia: The Role of Government', *Labour History*, no. 18, 1970, pp. 3–18, points to the way access politics developed because of the separate public sector in the economy. On the connection between corporate consciousness in the working class and representation by liberals, see H. McQueen's chapter, 'Victoria', in Murphy, *Labor in Politics*, pp. 296–302.

15. Our treatment of intellectuals derives from A. Gramsci, 'The Intellectuals', in Q. Hoare and G. Nowell-Smith (eds), *Selections from the Prison Notebooks of Antonio Gramsci*, Lawrence & Wishart, London, 1971, pp. 5–23. The defection of the working class from bourgeois intellectual activity in one city is discussed in R. Lawson, *Brisbane in the 1890's: A Study of an Australian Urban Society*, Q.U.P., St Lucia, 1973, pp. 175–80.

16. For overseas influences, see L. G. Churchward, 'The American Influence on the Australian Labor Movement', *Historical Studies*, vol. 5, 1952, pp. 258–77; and R. A. Gollan, 'American Populism and Australian Utopianism', *Labour History*, no. 9, 1965, pp. 15–21. B. E. Mansfield, 'The Socialism of William Morris: England and Australia', *Historical Studies*, vol. 7, 1956, pp. 271–90. Theo Gum, *The Only Solution of the Labour Problem*, Thomas & Co., Adelaide, n.d. (?1895), provides a structural account of unemployment. Christine Chinner, '"Earthly Paradise": A Social History of Adelaide in the Early 1890's', B.A. (Hons) thesis, Department of History, University of Adelaide, 1960; and D. P. Crook, 'Occupations of the People of Brisbane: An Aspect of Urban Society in the 1880's', *Historical Studies*, no. 37, 1961, pp. 50–64, both discuss poverty of unskilled workers and the growth of the belief that major social reconstruction was needed. The forces producing poverty are concisely surveyed in P. G. Macarthy, 'Labor and the Living Wage, 1890–1910', *A.J.P.H.* vol. 13, 1967, pp. 67–89. M. Pizer (ed.), *The Men Who Made Australia: Stories and Poems by Henry Lawson*, Australasian Book Society, Melbourne, 1957, pp. 227–8, reprints 'Macleay Street and Red Rock Lane'.

17. On socialism, see Spence, *History of the A.W.U.* (for co-operative experiments among the unskilled workers); P. J. O'Farrell, 'The Australian Socialist League and the Labour Movement, 1887–1891', *Historical Studies*, vol. 8, 1958, pp. 152–65; and *Harry Holland, Militant Socialist*, A.N.U.P., Canberra, 1964, chs 1–2; Bertha Walker, *Solidarity Forever!*, National Press, Melbourne, 1972, which covers the early life of Percy Laidler; and Tom Mann, *Memoirs*, MacGibbon & Kee, London, 1967 (first publ. 1923). Socialist agitation in the trade unions is obscure; a hint of how it occurred in the Amalgamated Society of Engineers after 1910 is found in Buckley, *Amalgamated Engineers in Australia*, pp. 189–90. For Brookfield, see Joe Harris, *The Bitter Fight: A Pictorial History of the Australian Labor Movement*, U.Q.P., St Lucia, 1970, p. 284.

18. The classic study of the embourgeoisement of Labor politicians is V. G. Childe, *How Labour Governs: A Study of Workers' Representation in Australia*, M.U.P., Melbourne, 1964 (first publ. 1923). See also H. V. Evatt, *Australian Labour Leader: The Story of W. A. Holman and the Labour Movement*, Angus & Robertson, Sydney, 1940, p. 568; and 'Report of the Chief Inspector of Factories, Melbourne, on Anti-Strike Legislation in Operation Throughout the Australian States, and Recommendations regarding such Legislation for Victoria', in H. M. Murphy, *Wages and Prices in Australia: Our Labour Laws and Their Effects*, Melbourne, 1915.

19. W. Somerville to W. James, 10 July 1904 (draft), Somerville Papers, General Correspondence, 1903–9, Battye Library, Perth (460A, item 11).

20. The advertisement appeared in George Black, *The Origin and Growth of the Labour Movement in New South Wales*, Worker Trustees, Sydney, 1915, p. 6. See also Graeme Osborne, 'John Percy Jones, 1872–1955: A Biographical Note', *Labour History*, no. 28, 1975, pp. 33–41. In the absence of a Dictionary of Labour Biography for Australia, the career of Dacey, and of others like him, can only be glimpsed, as in the biographical appendices to Murphy, *Labor in Politics*.

21. Grant Hannan's 'William Lane—Mateship and Utopia', in D. J. Mur-

phy, R. B. Joyce and Colin A. Hughes (eds), *Prelude to Power: The Rise of the Labour Party in Queensland, 1885–1915*, Jacaranda, Brisbane, 1970, provided the basis for this interpretation. On utopian colonies, see Gavin Souter, *A Peculiar People: The Australians in Paraguay*, Angus & Robertson, Sydney, 1968; Michael Davitt, M.P., *Life and Progress in Australia*, Methuen, London, 1898; and R. B. Walker, 'The Ambiguous Experiment: Agricultural Co-operatives in New South Wales, 1893–1896', *Labour History*, no. 18, 1970, pp. 19–31.

22. Protestant radicalism in this period is stressed in J. D. Bollen, *Protestantism and Social Reform in New South Wales, 1890–1910*, M.U.P., Melbourne, 1972. On the 'new journalism', see Ailsa Zainu'ddin, 'The Early History of the *Bulletin*', in M. Beever and F. B. Smith (eds), *Historical Studies: Selected Articles*, 2nd series, M.U.P., Melbourne, 1967, pp. 199–216. B. Andrews, 'Dynamite, Barricades, Brimstone: Price Warung's Political Themes', *Labour History*, no. 22, 1972, pp. 1–12, notes the ambivalence of traditional intellectuals who sided with the working class.

23. For Peter Board's views, see his paper in *Report of a Conference promoted by the Workers' Educational Association of New South Wales in October 1919 on Adolescent Education*, W.H.B. Printing Co., Sydney, 1919. The ideology of the W.E.A. is treated by Tim Rowse, *Australian Liberalism and National Character*, Kibble Books, Malmsbury, Vic., 1978, ch. 2. Also on the hegemonic role of intellectuals, see E. Williams, 'The Beginnings of the Australian University Extension Movement', in R.J.W. Selleck (ed.), *Melbourne Studies in Education, 1972*, M.U.P., Melbourne, 1972, pp. 185–210. The political activities of Protestants between 1890 and 1910 can be followed in Bollen, *Protestantism and Social Reform*; Lawson, *Brisbane in the 1890's*, ch. 8; and J. Rydon and R. N. Spann, *New South Wales Politics, 1901–1910*, Cheshire, Melbourne, 1962. Two characteristic examples of the attempt to substitute 'social efficiency' for 'class struggle' in the labour movement are M. Atkinson (ed.), *Trade Unionism in Australia*, W.E.A., Sydney, 1915; and C. H. Northcott, *Australian Social Development*, Studies in History, vol. 81, no. 2, Columbia University, New York, 1918.

24. *Report of a Conference ... on Adolescent Education*. See papers by Mrs Francis Anderson (for the comments about girls) and F. A. Bland and P. Board.

25. T. H. Kewley, *Social Security in Australia*, S.U.P., Sydney, 1965, ch. 2. Social welfare measures as part of a meliorist strategy by liberal-reformist governments are discussed by R. G. Boughton, 'Poverty and the Welfare State', B.A. (Hons) thesis, Department of Government, University of Sydney, 1975, ch. 4; and W. Higgins, 'A Working Paper on the Welfare State', *Arena*, no. 40, 1975, pp. 42–66.

26. L. F. Fitzhardinge, *William Morris Hughes: A Political Biography. Volume 1—That Fiery Particle, 1862–1914*, Angus & Robertson, Sydney, 1964, p. 99.

27. Maybanke (Mrs Francis) Anderson, *The Root of the Matter: Social and Economic Aspects of the Sex Problem*, Workers' Educational Association, Sydney, n.d. (*c.* 1916–17); 'The Education of Girls', in *Report of a Conference ... on Adolescent Education*; and *Woman Suffrage: A Refutation and an Appeal, by 'A Citizen' who has No Vote*, Australian Christian World, Sydney, n.d. (1895); and Peter Spearritt, 'The Kindergarten Movement: Tradition and Change', in D. Edgar (ed.), *Social Change in Australia*, Cheshire, Melbourne, 1974, pp. 583–

96. Anne Summers, *Damned Whores and God's Police: The Colonization of Women in Australia*, Penguin, Ringwood, Vic., 1975, ch. 10, is an excellent survey of the involvement of bourgeois women in the cultural reconstruction of this period, but because she does not discuss the changing pattern of family–state relationships in terms of the class structure, her stress on the 'middle class' or 'petty-bourgeoisie' is incomplete and slides off into idealist references to nationalism and puritanism; see pp. 317, 339. For the ideology of the 'youth movement' of the 1920s, see *Proceedings of the First Australasian Rotary Conference, Sydney, September 1924*; [*Programme of the*] *Boys' Week Exhibition, September 1924*, Sydney; and *Report of the First Official Rotary Conference*, Melbourne, March 1926 (catalogued under the heading 'Rotary' in M.L.).

28. Boughton, *Poverty and the Welfare State*, pp. 9–13. Edna Ryan and Anne Conlon, *Gentle Invaders: Australian Women at Work, 1788–1974*, Nelson, Melbourne, 1975, chs 3–4, document the sexist implications of the 'living wage' concept. On the teaching of 'Domestic Science', see our Document 4.11.

29. The housing issue in this period needs a full class analysis. Some sources: H. V. Evatt, 'A Fair Rent Experiment in New South Wales', *Journal of Comparative Legislation and International Law*, vol. 2, 1920, pp. 10–21; Evatt, *Australian Labour Leader*, pp. 321, 376; Spearritt, 'Sydney's Slums', p. 67; and Sandercock, *Cities for Sale*, ch. 1. On Daceyville, see *S.M.H.*, 1 October 1914.

30. *Official Year Book of New South Wales, 1919*, Government Printer, Sydney, 1920, pp. 646–50; T. A. Metherell, 'The Conscription Referenda: October 1916 and December 1917. An Inward Turned Nation at War', Ph.D. thesis, University of Sydney, 1971, pp. 56–76; and G. A. Taylor, 'City Design and Town Planning: What Australia is Doing', *Building*, 12 February 1920 (on real-estate profits through town planning).

31. A. Barcan, *A Short History of Education in New South Wales*, Reed, Sydney, 1965, p. 149; S. G. Firth, 'Social Values in the New South Wales Primary School, 1880–1914: An Analysis of School Texts', in R.J.W. Selleck (ed.), *Melbourne Studies in Education, 1970*, M.U.P., Melbourne, 1970, pp. 123–59; A. R. Crane and W. A. Walker, *Peter Board: His Contribution to the Development of Education in New South Wales*, A.C.E.R., Melbourne, 1957, ch. 6, on the place of training for 'citizenship' and 'national efficiency' in the 'new education', *c.* 1914. The Annual Report of the New South Wales Police Commissioner for 1883, in *Police Department: Annual Reports, 1883–1902*, M.L. (bound together in Q352.2N); and *Report of a Conference . . . on Adolescent Education*, for Board's views.

32. This interpretation developed from the work of S. Murray-Smith; see his 'Technical Education in Australia, 1788–1914: A Select Bibliography', in R.J.W. Selleck (ed.), *Melbourne Studies in Education, 1967*, M.U.P., Melbourne, 1968, pp. 210–45. See also: N. B. Nairn, 'The Role of the Trades and Labour Council in New South Wales, 1871–1891', *Historical Studies*, vol. 7, 1957, pp. 421–40; L. A. Mandelson, 'Norman Selfe and the Beginnings of Technical Education', in C. Turney (ed.), *Pioneers of Australian Education*, S.U.P., Sydney, 1972, vol. 2, pp. 106–7; J. M. Ritchie, 'The Development and Significance of Technical Education in New South Wales, 1880–1900', *J.R.A.H.S.*, vol. 55, 1969, pp. 245–61; and a newspaper report dated 22 February 1912 of a speech by the manager of Mort's Dock and Engineering Co.

to the Balmain Workingmen's Institute in J.P. Franki Papers, M.L. (MSS 69, item 4, p. 93).

33. Two other variants of nationalist ideology are discussed in C. S. Blackton, 'Australian Nationality and Nationalism, 1850–1900', *Historical Studies*, vol. 9, 1961, pp. 351–67; and in G. Lewis, 'Nationalism and Capitalism in Australia: The Queensland Economy, 1890–1930', *Arena*, no. 38, 1975, pp. 81–92. The view that a national self-image grew from 'the collectivist notions of a nomad tribe' was given a basis in historical argument by R. Ward, *The Australian Legend*, O.U.P., Melbourne, 1958, but it was held by literary nationalists in the 1940s, and its origins lie in the attempt by social-democratic intellectuals to appropriate nationalist ideology in that decade of war and Labor government. The individualist theme in the production of a nationalism for a mobilising working class is not treated elsewhere, although there are hints of its importance in the work of recent literary critics. See G. A. Wilkes, 'Going Over the Terrain in a Different Way', *Southerly*, vol. 35, 1975, pp. 141–55; and M. Wilding, 'A New Colonialism?', ibid., pp. 95–102. Coral Lansbury's *Arcady in Australia: The Evocation of Australia in Nineteenth-Century English Literature*, M.U.P., Melbourne, 1970, shows the pre-1890 and English origins of the 'new country' myth, and how the bourgeoisie (English and colonial) constructed the view that Australia was a workingman's (singular) country. Further work has established the ideological milieux in which literary nationalism was created; see John Docker, *Australian Cultural Elites: Intellectual Traditions in Sydney and Melbourne*, Angus & Robertson, Sydney, 1974, pp. 89–101; and David Walker, *Dream and Disillusion: A Search for Australian Cultural Identity*, A.N.U.P., Canberra, 1976. For militarism and racism in nationalist ideology, see McQueen, *A New Britannia*.

34. Studies of business peak organisations are not numerous. T. V. Matthews, 'Business Associations and Politics: Chambers of Manufacturers and Employers' Federations in New South Wales, Victorian and Australian National Politics to 1939', Ph.D. thesis, University of Sydney, 1971, operates within a pluralist framework. C. R. Hall, *The Manufacturers: Australian Manufacturing Achievements to 1960*, Angus & Robertson, Sydney, 1971, is a sketchy chronicle. On the formation of the coal vend, see Ross, *History of the Miners' Federation*, pp. 32–3. On the Employers' Union, see our Document 4.17.

35. Matthews, 'Business Associations and Politics', pp. 24–8. For industry associations in manufacturing, see T. G. Parsons, 'An Outline of Employer Organization in the Victorian Manufacturing Industries, 1879–1890', *Journal of Industrial Relations*, vol. 14, 1972, pp. 23–8.

36. Fitzhardinge, *William Morris Hughes*, p. 103.

37. Matthews, 'Business Associations and Politics', pp. 29–37. In New South Wales, over 25 per cent of the 1910–16 Labor government's bills failed to become law because of Legislative Council opposition; see G. N. Hawker, *The Parliament of New South Wales, 1856–1965*, Government Printer, Sydney, 1971, pp. 242–3.

38. *The Liberty of the Press: Boycott of the 'Daily Post' . . .*, Daily Post, Hobart, 1912. On the establishment of the Newcastle steel-works, see H. Hughes, *The Australian Iron and Steel Industry, 1848–1962*, M.U.P., Melbourne, 1964, pp. 53–66. On the Theodore government's problems, see B. Schedvin, 'E. G. Theodore and the London Pastoral Lobby', *Politics*, vol. 6, 1971, pp. 26–41;

and our Document 4.4. There were British investors in the Queensland pastoral industry.

39. G. P. Taylor, 'Business and Politics in Queensland, 1859–1895', *New Zealand Journal of History*, vol. 1, 1967, pp. 75–92; M. Cannon, *Land, Boom and Bust*, Heritage, Melbourne, 1972; and Papers of Sir John See, vol. 24 (Papers on Official Business), M.L. (A3672).

40. Matthews, 'Business Associations and Politics', pp. 38–43; B. Mansfield, *Australian Democrat: The Career of E.W. O'Sullivan, 1846–1910*, S.U.P., Sydney, 1965, p. 66; and B. D. Graham, *The Formation of the Australian Country Parties*, A.N.U.P., Canberra, 1966, pp. 47–53.

41. P. Loveday, 'Support in Return for Concessions', *Historical Studies*, vol. 14, 1970, pp. 376–405, argues the case against this labourist myth. B. de Garis, '1890–1900', in F. K. Crowley (ed.), *A New History of Australia*, Heinemann, Melbourne, 1974, pp. 237–42, provides a good survey of liberal-reformism. See also T. G. Parsons, 'Alfred Deakin and the Victorian Factory Act of 1885: A Note', *Journal of Industrial Relations*, vol. 14, 1972, pp. 206–8. J. Rickard, *Class and Politics: New South Wales, Victoria and the Early Commonwealth, 1890–1910*, A.N.U.P., Canberra, 1976, chs 4–5, has excellent detail, highlighting 'class' as a theme in political debate.

42. B. Dickey, 'The National Association of New South Wales, 1891–1898: A Conservative Response', *Teaching History*, vol. 8, no. 2, 1974, pp. 15–30; see *Australasian*, 17 October 1891, editorial, for the quotation.

43. Spann and Rydon, *New South Wales Politics*, p. 4; Rickard, *Class and Politics*, ch. 6; and H. L. Nielsen, *The Voice of the People, or the History of the Kyabram Reform Movement*, Arbuckle, Waddel and Fawckner, Melbourne, 1902.

44. I. Campbell, 'Groups, Parties and Federation', in P. Loveday and I. Campbell (eds), *Groups in Theory and Practice*, Cheshire, Melbourne, 1962, p. 67; and B. Irving, 'Women in Australian Politics: A Look at the Past', *Refractory Girl*, no. 7, 1975, p. 27.

45. H. Mayer, *The Press in Australia*, Lansdowne, Melbourne, 1964, p. 31; W. S. Holden, *Australia Goes to Press*, Detroit, Wayne State U.P., 1961; and R. W. Connell, *Ruling Class, Ruling Culture: Studies of Conflict, Power and Hegemony in Australian Life*, C.U.P., London, 1977, p. 194.

46. E. Scott, *Australia During the War. Volume XI of the Official History of Australia in the War of 1914–18*, Angus & Robertson, Sydney, 1936, pp. 333, 441, ch. 21; and M. Lake, *A Divided Society: Tasmania During World War I*, M.U.P., Melbourne, 1975, esp. chs 6–8. The fortnightly (and then weekly) pro-conscription journal, *Universal Service* reported on the activities of sixty branches of the Universal Service League in New South Wales in 1916. The honorary secretaries were T. R. Bavin, later conservative state premier, and Meredith Atkinson, a W.E.A. intellectual.

47. Rohan Rivett, *Australian Citizen: Herbert Brookes, 1867–1963*, M.U.P., Melbourne, 1965, pp. 52–63; J. Eyers, 'Herbert Brookes: A Political Biography', B.A. (Hons) thesis, Department of Government, University of Sydney, 1971; Sir Joynton Smith, M.L.C., *My Life Story*, Cornstalk Publ. Co., Sydney, 1927, pp. 261–9: and Claude McKay, *This is the Life: The Autobiography of a Newspaperman*, Angus & Robertson, Sydney, 1961, pp. 131–2.

48. Kewley, *Social Security in Australia*, pp. 50–3, 76–7, 104 and *passim*; and Hawker, *Parliament of New South Wales*, p. 226; *Reports of the Police Commissioners of New South Wales*, for 1894 and 1902. K. L. Milte and T. A. Weber, *Police in Australia: Development, Functions and Procedures*, Butterworths, Sydney, 1977, p. 31, suggest that the hostility to the police in Australia flows partly from their role as administrators of health and welfare regulations. The Police Commissioner's Report of 1902 quoted from W. L. Melville Lee, *A History of Police in England*, Methuen, London, 1901, p. 407.

49. K. W. Knight, 'The Development of the Public Service in New South Wales from Responsible Government (1856) to the Establishment of the Public Service Board (1895)', M.Ec. thesis, University of Sydney, 1956, sect. 6; R. S. Parker, 'Public Administration as the Study of Bureaucracy', in R. N. Spann and G. R. Curnow (eds), *Public Policy and Administration in Australia: A Reader*, Wiley, Sydney, pp. 224–31; G. E. Caiden, 'The Study of Australian Administrative History', paper delivered to Australasian Political Studies Association Conference, Melbourne, 1963, appendix. 'The Colonial Public Services, 1850–1900', pp. 1–27 (copy in M.L.); D. Chappell and P. R. Wilson, *The Police and the Public*, U.Q.P., St Lucia, 1969, ch. 1; and *Reports of the Police Commissions of New South Wales*, for 1890.

50. D. H. Johnson, *Volunteers at Heart: The Queensland Defence Forces, 1860–1901*, U.Q.P., St Lucia, 1975, ch. 14; 'Report of the Royal Commission into the Military Service', *Votes and Proceedings of the New South Wales Legislative Assembly*, vol. 7, 1892, pp. 559–883; and Annual Report of the Commanding Officer of the Military Forces of New South Wales, *Journal of the Legislative Council*, 1890–93, and later years.

51. B. Dickey, 'The Broken Hill Strike, 1892', *Labour History*, no.11, 1966, pp. 40–53; and I. Turner, *Industrial Labour and Politics: The Dynamics of the Labour Movement in Eastern Australia, 1900–1921*, A.N.U.P., Canberra, 1965. Anti-capitalism amongst the I.W.W. is given a psychological explanation by P. J. Rushton, 'Revolutionary Ideology of the I.W.W. in Australia', *Historical Studies*, no. 59, 1972, pp. 424–46. For a working-class perspective on the political counter attack of the ruling class in the 1920s, see Labor Council of New South Wales, *Industrial Peace and the Working Class*, Sydney, 1928, p. 32 (copy in the La Trobe Library).

52. R. Norris, *The Emergent Commonwealth: Australian Federalism: Expectations and Fulfilment, 1889–1910*, M.U.P., Melbourne, 1975, ch. 6, on social policy in the first decade of the Commonwealth.

53. J. R. Poynter, *Russell Grimwade*, M.U.P. Melbourne, 1967, ch. 7; W. S. Robinson, *If I Remember Rightly*, Cheshire, Melbourne, 1967, pp. 95–9; and Scott, *Australia During the War*, chs 14–15.

54. Robinson, *If I Remember Rightly*, p. 95; and Scott, *Australia During the War*, pp. 562, 597–601.

55. A. Trengove, *What's Good for Australia*, Cassell, Melbourne, 1975, pp. 89–101; Hughes, *Australian Iron and Steel Industry*, pp. 63–70; Scott, *Australia During the War*, pp. 567–9; and P. Mawson, *A Vision of Steel: The Life of G.D. Delprat, General Manager of B.H.P., 1898–1921*, Cheshire, Melbourne, 1958, ch. 12.

56. The involvement of industrial capitalists in state activity at this time can be seen in G. Currie and J. Graham, *The Origins of CSIRO: Science and the Commonwealth Government, 1901–1926*, C.S.I.R.O., Melbourne, 1966, esp. chs 3–4. See our Documents 4.18 and 4.19 (for Brookes' *Address*).

57. Robinson, *If I Remember Rightly*, pp. 158 ff., J. B. Holme, *The British Scheme for Self-Government of Industry, and Its Counterpart in New South Wales*, Government Printer, Sydney, 1918; and Littleton Groom, *A Vision for Australia*, lecture six in a series arranged by the Diocese of Melbourne, 1922 (copy in La Trobe Library).

58. Hughes, *Australian Iron and Steel Industry*, p. 96. The 'efficiency' theme is discussed by Rowse, *Australian Liberalism and National Character*, pp. 61–72.

59. Hughes, *Australian Iron and Steel Industry*, pp. 23–4; and Buckley, *Amalgamated Engineers in Australia*, pp. 238–42, 276–8. A strike in the glass industry over piece-work rates in 1917 is described in Poynter, *Russell Grimwade*, p. 118. E. Dyson, *Fact'ry 'Ands*, George Robertson, Melbourne, 1906, for the story, 'Introducing Machinery', pp. 221–35.

60. Hughes, *Australian Iron and Steel Industry*, pp. 93–5. On the violence of industrial conflict in the United States in the era of mechanisation and monopolisation of industry, see Brecher, *Strike!*, chs 3–4.

61. D. Coward, 'Crime and Punishment: The Great Strike in New South Wales, August to October, 1917', in J. Iremonger *et al.*, *Strikes: Studies in Twentieth Century Australian Social History*, Angus & Robertson, Sydney, 1973, pp. 51–80; Buckley, *Amalgamated Engineers in Australia*, pp. 236–56; and Poynter, *Russell Grimwade*, pp. 125–6.

Documents

Working-class Mobilisation

Labour Market

State and Working Class

Effects of Hegemony

Ruling-class Reorganisation

4.1 Control of the local environment

The municipal platform adopted by the Newtown Labor Electoral League in 1891. The only distinctively trade-union demand appears in the last line.

Source: *Leichhardt and Petersham Guardian*, 24 October 1891.

The abolition of property qualifications, the abolition of plural voting, the extension of the municipal franchise to all householders, irrespective of sex—only householders to be entitled to vote in respect of the premises they occupy. All elections to be held on Saturdays, and polling to be from 10 a.m. to 6 p.m.; the Mayor and returning officer to be elected by the people; upon a requisition signed by 10% of the electors, a plebiscite to be taken by the council on any matter of extraordinary or urgent nature arising during the period between the general elections; all assessments for rating purposes to be based on the capital value of the land irrespective of improvements; all buildings and other improvements affected by human exertion to be exempt from rates or taxes; one-half the cost of assessment to be defrayed by the Department of Water and Sewerage; compulsory registration with the local council of all private land, improved or unimproved, situated within the municipality; the council clerk's receipts for the rates due to date to be a necessary condition of transfer or conveyance in respect of any lands sold within the municipality; all plans of new subdivisions of estates within the municipality to be submitted to the council for approval before sales under such sub-division; no streets to be less width than 90 feet and lanes 22 feet; no lots to be less than 20 feet frontage by a depth of 100 feet; every lot to have a lane at rear, and not more than one dwelling to be erected on any one lot; all streets and lanes to be kerbed and guttered before sale by the vendor; every vendor to give guarantee to council's solicitor of certificate of Title to conditional purchases; every owner of land to prove to Council's solicitor his ability to give undoubted title. Cost of kerbing, guttering, paving and lighting to be defrayed out of the general rates, the council to have full control of the means of lighting within the municipality, and own their own lighting plant; all licence fees imposed by the municipality to be paid into the funds of the council; all parks, recreation grounds and public reserves within the municipality to be vested in the local council in trust for the people for all time, no encroachment to be permitted under any pretence whatever, and no impediments to the fullest and freest enjoyment of the people to be permitted except such as may be of absolutely necessary character; a free public library and reading room to be provided; the town hall to be let free upon the requisition of 50 householders for certain purposes; all municipal works to be carried out by day labor.

4.2 Working-class community: Class conflict and culture

A song written during the 1911 strike near Lithgow, involving coal-miners and iron-workers employed by Charles Hoskins. For ten months, with organised local and national support, the workers held out against scabs, 150 prosecutions, armed police and an 'impartial' Labor government. The strike was won.

Source: Recorded by Warren Fahey and Tony Suttor on *Man of the Earth*:

Songs and Ballads of the Australian Mining Industry, Larrikin Records no. 001, Paddington, 1975.

When We Get Our Twopence Back

It is strike time in the dear old Lithgow valley
The men on strike intend to do their best
A few scabs round the tyrant seem to rally
But there's not a spark of manhood in their breast
When the tyrant said he'd take them down for tuppence
Like a spirit each man seemed to disappear
As they said 'farewell' they added 'we'll return again
When you give that tuppence back Charlie dear.'

chorus: When you give that tuppence back Charlie dear
We can then return to work with conscience clear
But as heaven's sky is blue, we will never work for you
Till you give that tuppence back Charlie dear

As we wander up and down old Lithgow valley
The scenes of strife and want must give us pain
Standing for their rights like men of honour
Let us hope the struggle will not be in vain
Then we wander down the roadway to the furnace
And it makes us sad to see scabs working there
They'd be better off in the churchyard safely sleeping
Instead of being scabs for Charlie dear.

chorus:

4.3 Intellectuals and the working class

Two letters and a leaflet illustrating the range of propaganda and organising efforts of labour intellectuals, and their belief in the populist alliance and parliamentary reform. Significantly, Walter Alan Woods, before coming to Tasmania in 1895, and under his given name of Walter Head, had a career in New South Wales typical of the working-class intellectual: shearer, union organiser, journalist and secretary of William Lane's New Australia Co-operative Settlement Association. Woods became a Tasmanian parliamentarian in 1906.

Source: W. A. Woods Papers, Archives Office of Tasmania, NP 139/8/1, NP 139/9/4, NP 139/8/8.

(i) *Letter from ... Turnbull to W. A. Woods*

427 Rathdown St
Carlton. Melbourne

Jan 11th 1899

My dear Comrade Woods,

By this time I suppose Barker will have launched his first torrent out upon Hobartonians, and I trust he keeps up my statement that he would come on like an avalanche to sweep away all undemocratic debris, and make a clear way for the Social Democratic Party which is to come on to win the seat now being contested for. Tell him Turnbull is praying for him, for the candidate and for the party.... So that I may know how things are going kindly post on the "Clipper". I have only got two since leaving Hobart.

I note the reference to myself in last issue *re* organising work. I do hope something will come of the effort. The feeling I have is that a good push during the months previous to the next general elections, for Social Democracy, would help a long way to put up a good score for the Workers friends, at the time when the profession of Democracy comes to the point, as it assuredly must when candidates are looking for the honor of "M.H.A."

I received a letter from Mrs Smallhorn making an offer of the Victoria Hall for Sunday all day 15/- and over night during the week for social meetings 5/. For such a hall the terms to me seem fair. With the opportunity of a Labor Church work on Sundays, and each week a social lecture from somebody capable of interesting an audience, and discussing the question by the audience a centre could be formed of active workers, and also help to develop latent talent in propaganda work. Also once a month a popular Social to bring all Social Democratic workers in touch with each other would give tone to united brotherly efforts.

I shall be glad to hear from you as to whether, without my presence in Hobart to work up, something can be done to give some encouragement to my coming over within a few months.

Mrs T according to her last word to me will start for Melbourne tomorrow (Thursday) I need her help while I stay here. Of course everybody knows I cannot work successfully without her aid. As my dearest Chum she is indispensible. I had a splendid meeting last Sunday night. Good singing—seven numbers, and good speaking Dr Maloney was with me. Look out for the Doctor. I believe he will come over and see you. Now Adieu, but let me hear from you soon,

Yours fraternally,
Turnbull

(ii) *Draft of a letter from W. A. Woods to Mr Heyer*

10 High Street, Hobart,
Aug. 23/13

Dear Mr. Heyer—

Practically *all* the local clergymen have agreed to attend the preliminary mtg. Looking over the pile of letters on this subject, I find one or two that need a line of reply. Yours is one.

First let me say that I am very sorry if the circular seemed to hint a doubt as to all the religious, friendly, and Labor organisations professing working class sympathies. Apparently that sentence was clumsily worded. By an oversight I have not kept a copy—by the way, you might send yours, if you have not destroyed it—but I think the idea was that there might be a friendly society or two that would want to be free to claim that they represented or comprised or sympathised with *all* classes—the exploited class and the exploiting class—even as some churches, of more modern date than that of Laodicea, used to claim....

I do not think we should have on our Committee, (if it eventuates) any man who is a professed and prominent upholder of the glaringly unChristian state of Capitalism which renders complaints of unfair prices necessary. Such an one would die in his tracks before he would admit that prices were unfair, no matter what evidence was shown him. His notion and religious creed is that any prices one can possible get are fair prices. 'Buy in the cheapest, sell in the dearest market;' that is the motto of nearly 50 per cent of this and every other community. Twenty-five years ago it was the motto or the creed of 75 per cent; 85 years hence it will not be believed in by more than five per cent, and that little lot will not be at large. Of course this prophecy is made conditional upon nothing happening to radically deflect the path of peaceful reform. A universal revolution of blood, arising out of a general strike, say, would upset the prophecy. A great war between the nations would also upset it. But barring these horrors, Capitalism, which already challenges the hostility of all decent mankind, ('a pyramid trembling on its apex' as Hilaire Belloc describes it in his latest book) will be toppled over by the unanimous shove on one side of forces which have hitherto shoved on both sides; and there is no reason why the arrival of the united push should be delayed more than a decade or so. What the new order will be like no man knoweth; but much of its character may depend upon the part organised religion takes in its foundation-stoning—whether the churches join manfully in the pyramid pushing, or merely stand afar off and 'decline to take sides'. I believe that all the modern men in the churches now realise the position, and will push rather than perish. And even the ancients mean well, though their knowledge of economics is pretty shocking. Handel Jones, at King's X Hall, the other Sunday afternoon, to wit. Profit-sharing and sugar plums! The dear, good soul would usher in the millenium by compelling the Beef Trust to share its huge ill-gotten gains with its employees; and would shatter the Cinchona Bark Ring (which has just put up the price of quinine 33 per cent) with a powerful lecture on the beauties of co-operation and the evil of unrestrained competition! I suppose the estimable Jones would be genuinely surprised to learn that the Beef Trust's few employees all share fatly in the grab, and that the Quinine Monopoly, like Standard Oil and the Australian Shipping Ring, regards itself as a shining example of co-operation and as the most successful slayer of competition in all the world. But that doesn't save Handel's pocket when he buys beef or kerosene, or quinine or a trip on the ocean wave. Ditto Handel's congregation's pockets, and the offertory suffers. But wait until they understand, and Brother Jones understands. Then there will be a shindy!

Best wishes, yours fraternally,

(iii) *Leaflet*

Tasmanian Social Science Union

CONSTITUTION ADOPTED

Reprinted from *The Daily Post*, Saturday, October 25th, 1913.

A meeting of delegates from religious bodies, friendly societies, and labor organisations, was held at the Mechanics' Hall last night, to consider the draft constitution drawn up by a sub-committee for the proposed Tasmanian Social Science Union. Mr. W. A. Woods, M.H.A., presided over a fair attendance. Apologies for non-attendance were received from Bishop Mercer, Revs. Heyer and Bennett; Messrs. Williams, Gibbs, Giblin, and Barker.

After lengthy discussion the following constitution was adopted:—

Name.—Tasmanian Social Science Union.

Membership.—All persons who pay at least one shilling per half-year into the funds, and are admitted on a ballot by a majority of members present at a properly constituted meeting, and who agree to loyally conform to the rules, and uphold the objects of the union.

Objects.—To improve the conditions of living for the useful members of the community; to take such united action as the majority may decide in regard to unfair prices, methods of production and distribution, housing and recreations of the people, public health, industrial conditions, and any other branch of social science....

4.4 Limits of reformism

A socialist intellectual's class analysis of the failure of the Queensland Labor government, the one most sympathetic to, and strongly influenced by, the working class.

Source: *Labour Monthly* (London), vol. 6, 1924, pp. 282–5.

A LABOUR PREMIER MEETS HIS MASTERS

By V. G. CHILDE

The refusal of a loan to the Labour Government of Queensland by the City moneylenders created a sensation in 1920. But then the financiers won only a Pyrrhic victory. The Labour Premier declined to modify at their behest legislation passed by the elected Parliament of Queensland. He went back to the people of the State and, with "No dictation by foreign capitalists" as a battle-cry, managed once more to secure a victory for Labour at the polls. He even managed to secure a modest but costly loan in the U.S.A. At a time of universal depression, when the capitalist class has been making a mass attack on the standards of the workers, real wages in Queensland have remained higher than in any other State in Australia. The masters themselves have paid a striking tribute to the Labour Ministry by offering a bribe of £5,000 to a Labour member to desert his colleagues at a critical division.

Nevertheless these intervening years have been a period of disillusionment both to the proletariat of Queensland and to Mr. Theodore. The lack of loan moneys at once ruled out any "extension of the industrial and economic functions of the State" on lines which should on Australian theory pave the way to "Socialism". The financial embarrassments of the Government involved a partial cessation of public works which had been utilised to absorb the unemployed. The ranks of the latter were swelled by the inevitable retrenchment in the public service. In the absence of loans to cover the deficits, railwaymen and other State employees were sacked wholesale. No wonder the reiterated demands of the Party Conference, repeated with emphasis just the other day by the Brisbane Industrial Conference, for double pay for night work on the railways evoked a blank *non possumus*. And in the face of the general capitalist assault on hours and wages backed with the threat of a universal lockout, another plank of the Labour platform — the statutory 44 hour week — has had to be jettisoned.

The biting criticism of industrialists has only served to underline the Premier's lesson. And so he stands in Lombard Street in the garb of penitence. As the price of a short-term loan the Labour stalwart has reversed the position he adopted four years ago and acknowledged the superiority of economic to political power. In an apologetic letter to the interested companies he has promised that the weapon forged by Parliament in pursuance of a long established plank of the Labour platform shall rust in its scabbard.

This signal capitulation crowning four years of starved impotence is doubly instructive. The "silken cords" which bind the self-governing Dominions to the motherland are now revealed in their true nature. The imposition of conditions in return for a loan is only the obverse of that much trumpeted demonstration of complete Dominion autonomy in politics — the unhestitating Royal Assent to the obnoxious Bill for the abolition of the Queensland Legislative Council. The effective control over Dominion policy resides not in Westminster but in the City. And it is left to a Labour Colonial Secretary to give his blessing publicly to its exercise.

Secondly, the paralysis of legislation and the abrogation of parliamentary sovereignty exposes the fatuity of theories which promise the transformation of capitalism by evolutionary means; for it was precisely in Queensland that evidence for the feasibility of such politics might have been sought. The Labour Ministries which have ruled there since 1915 have some claim to be regarded as genuine workers' Governments. They made on their accession honest, if modest, attempts to give effect to the Labour policy for Socialism by the establishment of a number of State enterprises. Some of these, notably the State Butchers' Shops and the State Insurance Office, attained considerable dimensions, very substantially reduced prices and rates to the consumers, and earned an appreciable revenue for the State. The Insurance Acts giving the State Office a monopoly of workmen's compensation business and establishing a strict supervision over private insurers in other risks is particularly obnoxious to high finance and especially valuable to the workers. Similarly much admirable industrial legislation was passed in the interests of the toilers. The Industrial Arbitration Act went as far as it is possible to go within the limits of the compulsory system to give the Unions at once legal status and freedom of action. In administration again the Labour Ministers' policy contrasted favourably with that habitually pursued by "Labour" Governments in Australia — and elsewhere. Where the naked issue of the class war was raised, the Cabinet was distinctly, if perhaps reluctantly, on the side of the proletariat. While the Tory Government of New South Wales was crushing unionism on the railways there in 1917, the Queensland Minister concerned informed his colleague in the south that goods carried on non-union trains could not be accepted at the frontier for transmission over the Queensland lines. In the same year Premier Ryan ended the shipping lock-out by a threat to commandeer all ships in Queensland and man them on union terms. During the sanitary carters' strike at Townsville the Premier "cleansed" the town under the Public Health Act by paying the men the wages demanded and charging the cost to the Tory local authority.

The first reaction of capitalism against this regime was the adoption of fascist violence in 1919. To this end returned soldiers organised by Tory officers and encouraged by the Federal Government under the renegade W. M. Hughes were employed. The workers were unprepared and the State police insufficient to repel their attacks. Diplomacy was necessary, and Labour Ministers had to pose as upholders of law and order even at the cost of arresting militants for exhibiting the Red Flag contrary to Federal Law. So when the police at Townsville used firearms to repel an assault by armed strikers upon a non-union meat works, the Home Secretary condoned their conduct and despatched reinforcements to the town. The Minister for Railways suspended some unionists who refused to work the train conveying their extra constables, and only fully reinstated the victims under the cloak of the "Peace" celebrations when the crisis was passed. But the conspiracy to wreck the Labour Government by brute force was circumvented. The veterans' organisations were corrupted and their energy diverted to other channels.

It was after this partial defeat that the capitalists turned to their proper weapons. The post-war depression and the unemployment it entailed were utilised to undermine the position of the more militant unions. At the same time the financial boycott has robbed the Labour Government of its power to provide effective shelter to the victims of the attack. Mr. Theodore's capitulation is only the formal acknowledgement of defeat. The capitalist class have proved the efficacy against mere constitutionalism of that direct action which Mr. Theodore himself had once long ago preached to the workers when organising the unskilled navvies and lumberers of the north. The "responsibilities of Office" turned him against that doctrine, but its application has reduced his Cabinet and himself to the position of a subservient managing committee for the bourgeoisie.

4.5 Women in the factories

In 1923, the Printing Industry Employees' Union sponsored an investigation by a prominent doctor of women printing workers, including a medical examination of a sample of sixty. The following are the doctor's conclusions and her notes on some of the workers.

Source: Ethel E. Osborne, M.B., B.S. (Melb.), M.Sc. (Victoria and Leeds), *Report of an Inquiry into the Conditions of Employment as Regards the Health of Female Workers in the Printing and Allied Trades*, The Worker Print, Sydney, n.d. (*c*. 1924), pp. 17–19.

CONCLUSIONS.

1. In view of the facts which have been brought forward I consider that, under present conditions of work, the Printing and Allied Trades entail on the majority of women workers a heavy industrial burden.

2. From the employees I have medically examined I consider there is a high percentage of female workers who are fatigued definitely beyond the reasonable demands of the industrial day.

3. Factory environment varies between very wide limits, from excellent conditions to those requiring immediate remedial measures.

4. Owing to the fact that the working week is 48 hours, and is sometimes

concentrated into five days, the length of the uninterrupted spell of work is too great. It is desirable that no unbroken spell of work should exceed four hours for women workers.

5. As many workers have to expend a large period each day in travel it would seem desirable in city factories, where no outdoor change is possible, that the lunch break should be of an half hour's duration, but not less.

6. In view of the high percentage of immature females in the industry it is of the highest importance that the conditions of work should not be prejudicial to their health.

ETHEL E. OSBORNE.

APPENDIX I.
EXTRACTS FROM PERSONAL RECORDS OF EXAMINEES....

33. Very-nervy; tremor; frail, undersized; heavy financial responsibility; not fit.
34. Heavy responsibility; very nervy, frail, fagged out; not fit to work.
35. Nervy; irritable; thinks output could be maintained on shorter hours; boxmaking.
36. Very tired; feet ache; frail; suspicious tuberculosis.
37. Thinks work could be got into the shorter hours, and last half hour of day is very unprofitable.
38. Fine healthy girl; contented in work; has had experience on stapling and eyeletting machines; finds the use of one foot very trying, and has to knock off because of the pain; thinks two days is the limit to work constantly on these machines.
39. Working in gaslight; thinks that Saturday morning off is better for women workers, and does not think output is up to standard on Saturday mornings....
41. Thinks stapling very trying at periods; often girls have had to break the work for this reason; thinks punching machines very trying, especially using one foot all the time; nervy and knocked out with work; suspicious tuberculosis; 17 years [in the trade?].
42. Fit; likes work; thinks day is a bit long; hardly ever goes out at night, only at the week ends; 5-1/2 years.
43. Now forewoman; thinks all day stapling too much for any girl; has experienced both systems, and considers Saturday off a great boon to women workers; considers the work is "that monotonous that the girls must have a little pleasure"; 22 years.
44. Nervous breakdown; finds stapling all day very trying, especially at periods; 6 years....
46. Nervy and irritable.
47. Finds treadle stapling very tiring on the one side; had marked dysmenorrhoea [difficult or painful menstruation] while on stapling; is not nervous, but is tired and irritable; thinks the day too long and does not think output be diminished by small reduction in hours; 13 years.
48. Was on a folding machine for three years; had a lot of broken time; was advised to give up the work by a private doctor; complained of offensive smells in factory if windows were open; suspicious tuberculosis; 7 years....

51. Nervous; very tired and irritable; worn out; afraid of chest trouble; 5 years.
52. Very tired with work; thin, nervy, irritable; 6 years.
53. Very tiring on the one foot; has had nervous breakdown and "neuritis"; found dust worrying; very short of breath after exertion; suggestive tuberculosis; 7 years wire stitching.
54. Fit girl, but gets very tired at the end of the day.
55. Finds piece rates very hard; fagged out at the end of the day; fit girl; thinks output would not be materially affected on 44 hours.
56. Nervy; tired with work; irritable; feels burden of machine and looks it; fit, but thin; underweight; hollow chested; 14 years envelope machine.
57. Thinks hours are much too long for any girl; thinks Saturday morning off is a real boon, and considers output would not be materially affected by reduction of hours; 38 years.
58. Piece rates; thinks she would be much fresher if she worked shorter hours; works in gaslight; vibration is very worrying, and is tired out at end of day; envelope machine since 15.
59. Thinks girls are over-tired, and output would not be much affected by reduction of hours; working in gaslight; has always been interested in machinery, and wonders what girls find in their work who are not interested in machines; 15 years.
60. Envelope machine on piece rates; would prefer shorter hours at sacrifice of pay; is very interested in work, but finds it nerve racking; gets terribly irritable and could sometimes scream; she is not allowed to go out at night; feels dead beat when she gets home; she prefers the five-day week and shorter lunch break in order to get home earlier.

ETHEL E. OSBORNE.

4.6 Mechanisation and managerial control of the labour process

A manager explains the methods and advantages to capital of scientific management.

Source: *Australian Manufacturer*, 28 October 1916, pp. 21–3.

THE MAKING OF A COLLAR

By Mr. J. L. G. Law (Pearson, Law, Ltd.), Melbourne.

... To give you some idea of our growth, in 1907 we did a turnover of a little over £3,000 for the year; in 1914 we published our balance sheet, showing a profit of £7,800. Thus, you will see that in 1914 we made as much net profit as we did in turnover in 1907.

Six years ago in the shirt and collar trade, the minimum wages for a week of 48 hours was 16/- for females and £2/2/- for males; to-day the minimum wage is 22/6 for females and £3/5/- for males. It will, therefore, be noticed that the rates paid to females have increased from 16/- to 22/6, and the rates paid to males from 42/- to 65/-. Notwithstanding this fact, our labour cost per article shows a reduction of from 30 per cent. to 50 per cent., according to the article manufactured. Thus, you will see we have achieved what many people still believe to be impossible, namely, a high rate of wages with a low labour cost. Six years ago our cutting-room was on the ground floor. Collar cutters, who are males, were working piece work...; they used to cut about 250 to 300 dozen weekly, and on the average earned about £2/10/- to £2/12/6. They appealed to the Wages Board for an increase in wages and for the abolition of piece work. Their appeal met with success, and their wages were raised to £3/5/- per week of 48 hours, while piece work was abolished. The next thing that we knew was, they dropped their output to 200 dozen per week, and when asked the reason, stated that they had agreed among themselves that 200 dozen per week was a fair thing for £3/5/-. Just how they reconciled this argument with the fact that they cut 250 to 300 dozen for £2/10/- we cannot state. After a lot of discussion we decided that we had to get our costs, if possible, back to the old rate, and with this end in view we instituted a series of experiments. We lifted our cutting-room from the ground to the top floor, and took a lot of timings to get at the actual time required for each motion, and found it was possible for a cutter to cut a great many more than 250 to 300 dozen per week with a great deal less effort....

We then put every man on the minimum wage, namely, £3/5/- per week of 48 hours, and set a task with a bonus for every dozen of collars cut in excess of the task set. We met with opposition at first, as our cutters said we were asking them to do impossibilities, but as we had all out timings and records to put before them they accepted the position, and settled down to their work. The result is that our cutters are now earning from £3/5/- up to £3/12/6 per week of 48 hours—in fact, one of them the other week earned £4/1-, but I am only quoting average workers.... The quantity cut varies from 550–750 dozen per week, as against 250 to 300 previously, an increase of about 150 per cent. Thus, it will be seen that although our wages are 40 per cent. higher, our labour cost is from 33 per cent. to 50 per cent. lower....

The next operation, after cutting, is the stamping of the name and size on each collar, and this was a matter that also claimed our attention once we had our eyes opened to the possibilities of the savings that could be effected by handling the cutting-room correctly. ... The timings we got showed that one girl working efficiently could do all the stamping, so we picked out the smartest girl, who was getting 20/- a week, put her on piece work, and guaranteed that she would receive not less than 25/- per week—no matter what quantity she stamped—whilst we were instructing her in our methods. Our collar stamping was costing us a fraction over $\frac{1}{2}$ d. a dozen. When we told the girl the piece rate was to be $\frac{1}{4}$d. a dozen, and wanted her to do the lot, she said, "I can't possibly turn out the quantity, and what is more I could not earn enough to keep myself at $\frac{1}{4}$ d. a dozen." We had quite a difficulty in getting her to accept the position, but instead of her earning 25/-, in less than three weeks' time she had earned as high as £2/15/- a week, which was an increase of 175 per cent. in her wages, whilst our costs showed a decrease of 50 per cent. The result was we got all the collars stamped, our machinists were kept busy, and ultimately the stamping got ahead. This made it necessary to carry on the good work in our machine rooms, and after a little investigation we found it was necessary to standardise even more than we had done. ...

When we had got all these improvements working, we took a lot of timings, paying the same attention to detail as we had done in the cutting-room, and then set the piece work rates. We found that some machinists worked better on single collars, whilst others excelled on double collars; ... we gradually sorted out all our staff, until to-day we have specialists on every operation. After we had got the machining to our liking, we re-arranged the room, ... We got various devices in the shape of guides for our sewing machines, that enabled the girls to work a little quicker, and made the operations much more simple, following out what is now accepted as the correct thing to do, namely, wherever possible replace tedious operations requiring a lot of skill with machinery. ... The man in charge of our wash-house was a good, honest, hard-working man, and he used to be very much worried when things went wrong. ...

I spent three months in the wash-house, and found rule of thumb methods were being followed.... This, I could see, was the cause of the trouble, so experimented, and got at the exact quantity that had to be put into the machine at one time, the exact amount of water they had to be washed in, and the exact space of time each operation was to take, with the result that to-day, compared with three years ago, our costs for soap, starch, etc., show a decrease of 25 per cent. This saving was effected solely by supplanting old rule of thumb methods with more efficient standardised methods. We did not get this result without a lot of trouble. Our old employee felt that he was badly treated, when we took one of our smart young men and put him in charge of the wash-house and laundry, so he left our employ, taking his son, who was working in the wash-house with him. His resignation proved a blessing in disguise, for we found that ... we could do without this man and his son altogether, after increasing the wages of the employees that remained. After going thoroughly into our methods, wages, etc., we found that we had reduced our labour costs by a little over 50 per cent.

4.7 Scaled wages in industry

The move to heavy industry was accompanied by the introduction of a new job structure to eliminate the power of the craftsman. At B.H.P.'s steelworks, the hierarchical system of jobs, with minute differences in wage rates, was sanctioned by industrial law in 1915.

Source: *The Industrial Arbitration Reports of New South Wales*, vol. 15, 1916, pp. 473, 480–3.

[EDMUNDS, J.]

In re IRON AND SHIPBUILDING, NO. 19 AWARD

Award—Amendment—Broken Hill Proprietary Company's Steel Works—Industry carried on at a loss—Reduction of living wage.

Amendment by the Court of the award of the Iron and Shipbuilding Trades No. 19 Board, of 13th October, 1915.

... 17. Rates of Pay for Shift-work

The minimum rates of pay for the work usually done by the employees hereunder named shall be as follows:—

		Per hour. s.	d.
(a)	Blast Furnaces		
	Labourer (not on cast house floor), including labourers working or assisting pourers	1	3-1/8
	Labourers on cast house floor	1	3-5/8
	Pourers	1	3-3/4
	Ladleman	1	4-1/8
	Cinder potmen	1	3-3/4
	Stove tender	1	8-3/8
	Second helpers	1	3-7/8
	First helpers	1	6-1/8
	Keepers	1	9-1/8
	Pipe fitters	1	7-3/4
(b)	Steel Furnaces		
	First helpers	1	6-7/8
	Second helpers	1	5-3/8
	Third helpers	1	3-7/8
	First ladlemen	1	4-1/8
	Second ladlemen	1	3-5/8
	Assistant ladlemen	1	3-1/8
	Gasmen	1	5
	Ashmen	1	3-1/4
	Labourer	1	3
	Door boys, 1-1/2d. per hour over junior rates for day-workers.		
(c)	Rail and Bloom Mill—		
In Rail Mill—			
	First year on rolling	1	7-3/8
	Second year on rolling	1	10-3/8
	Third year on rolling	2	1-3/8
	Fourth year on rolling	2	4-3/8
	Fifth year on rolling	2	7-3/8
	Sixth year on rolling	2	10-3/8
	Thereafter	3	2
	Guide setter	2	2
In Bloom Mill—			
	First year	1	6
	Second year	1	10
	Third year	2	2
	Thereafter	2	6
	Manipulator men	1	6-7/8
	Roughers and finishers	1	6-7/8
	Shearsmen's helpers	1	3-1/8
	Wrenchmen	1	3-3/4
	Cropmen	1	3-1/8
	Bottom-makers	1	4-5/8
	Reheating furnacemen	1	4-5/8
	Reheating furnace helpers	1	3-1/8
	Soaking-pit heaters	1	6
	Soaking-pit helpers	1	3-1/8

	Per hour. s.	d.
Gasmen	1	5-3/8
Ashmen	1	3-1/4
Labourers	1	3-1/8
Door boys, 1-1/2d. per hour over junior rates for day workers.		

4.8 Resistance to 'scientific management'

The New South Wales government's introduction of the 'card system' into the railway and tramway workshops precipitated the Great Strike of 1917. The issue of control over production arose out of the experience of workers as Australian capitalism entered its industrial phase, but the issue was soon lost sight of by Labor leaders.

Source: *The Striker*, 13 August 1917; issued by the Unions' Defence Committee, Sydney. Copy in Mitchell Library, F331.8706/S.

THE CASE FOR THE MEN.

Official Statement by the Defence Committee

What, then, is the real trouble? What is meant by the card system? It means to the worker, not what the Commissioners would have us believe, but a system of speeding up the workman to his utmost capacity; of pitting him against his fellows and against himself—a system which aims to crush the last semblance of manhood out of him, and make him a machine in the crudest sense of the word. It means to him something that is not new, for he knows it well. He has had it tried on him in America and in England, and the thought of its introduction into Australia, where he has won for himself a measure of liberty, is unthinkable—for it means slavery!

The card system was first introduced about 1905, at the Midvale Steel Works, in Pennsylvania, a part of the American Steel Trust. The 'inventor' was the superintendent of the works, a man named [Frederick Winslow] Taylor. His first experiment was with men employed shovelling coal at the plant. A condition of employment was that men should be robust and of good physical strength, and must not be over 35 years of age. Experiments were made with laborers of extraordinary physique. Their motions while shovelling were scientifically analysed, timed, and tabulated. The men were then formed into gangs, with one of the 'super-men' to lead the pace, for which he received a cent or two extra, and a gang-boss or 'speeder', to watch the operations, speed the gang up to the pace set by the leader, and record the times for each portion of the operation. The quantity of coal moved and the height it was lifted was reduced to footpounds, similar to the method adopted in calculating the power of a steam engine. The hour's work was the unit on which the output for a ten-hour day was based. The gang became a machine, and worked as such, the human cogs being replaced when necessitated by death or desertion. This was the 'Taylor' system known in England as the 'card' system. The inventor proceeded to adapt it to all classes of work, and throughout America, the home of high speed, it was heralded as the greatest profit-producer of the times. Its suitability for machine shops and engineering works was specially stressed, and many of the big shops introduced the system. Each machine operator was 'carded' and a set schedule was laid out for his operations. He had to take so many cuts of such and such a depth over the material operated on. Each operation was timed by the 'speeder' and marked on his card, such time to be in accordance with the set schedule time for that particular operation. His individuality was completely smothered. He became part of the machine. He was worked till he could work no faster, and discharged when he failed any longer to keep up the pace required by the system and the 'speeder-up'.

The inevitable result was industrial strife. Labor troubles became the order of the day. More strikes were caused by the introduction of the Taylor system than had ever been known. To-day the system is used only in those centres where super-abundance of labor makes it possible to inflict it; and even in high-speed America, where, as everyone knows, the workers work hardest and die youngest, there is to-day no Union shop and no Government shop operating on the Taylor system. . . .

The system was introduced into England, as many of our men know to their sorrow. Your readers will surely remember the very recent report issued by the Commission appointed by the Imperial Government to inquire into the question of industrial unrest. The report stated that the chief cause of labor troubles was the operation of the card system!

This, then, is the system calmly referred to as a harmless time-keeping scheme. It is well known to us. We want none of it. The mechanics and artisans of the Railway Department are not shirkers; they can, and do, earn their pay. If they do not, the remedy is simple. Incompetent men should be discharged, and the department has surely foremen who are capable of picking out the incompetent ones without resorting to a system that involves the payment of a horde of non-producing sub-foremen as speeders-up, and which, in the land of its birth, has forced a man to dye his hair and massage his face weekly in order to save him from being discarded as 'too old at forty'.

4.9 Job control and industrial unionism

An extract from a speech by G. Pomfret, advocating union reorganisation on the basis of shop committees, at the Sixth Annual State Conference of the Victorian branch of the Australasian Meat Industry Employees' Union in 1913. Job control through shop committees, an expression of the impulse to create industrial unionism from below, had been spreading in the meat industry since before 1910.

Source: A. E. Davies, *The Meat Workers Unite*, Australasian Meat Industry Employees' Union (Victorian branch), Melbourne, 1974, pp. 46–8.

. . . Under the existing scheme of organisation, the whole responsibility for the control and success of Union activities is thrown upon the few officials. It is impossible at any time, for those officials to have that understanding with the rank and file, and to have that amount of control to enable them to keep the rank and file up to the mark. If progress is going to be made at all, that progress must be made by the rank and file, and by them alone, and that progress can only be according to their understanding; and the degree of understanding of the workers is just in relation to their responsibility under certain circumstances. They never appreciate those circumstances unless they, themselves, have to deal with them. If they, themselves, have not that responsibility to deal with, and the responsibility is thrown upon others, it means not progress but retrogression.

In reference to the first clause for the proposed scheme of re-organisation:

> "That wherever possible, Shop Committees be organised, such Shop Committees to form the basis of the Organisation."

I suppose that so far as our Organisation is concerned, we have, more than any other Organisation in the Commonwealth, experimented with Shop Committees; and in each case they were a success while they lasted, but ultimately they failed because wrong tactics were adopted while they were in existence. Such a thing as that we will have to be careful of in future. We will have to be careful that the members of the Shop Committees do not take action to secure something today that will bring upon them the ferocity of the master-class, when the conditions of the trade are not so favourable to the workers. In South Australia they really took control of the works in-so-far as it is possible to do so under Capitalism, but that drew forth the ferocity of the bosses, and later the Organisation on the works was smashed. At Angliss' it was the same, and also in Northern Queensland.

One of the main reasons that induced me to draw up this scheme was that for a considerable time there has been much criticism of our Management Committee indulged in, and also of the officials of this Organisation. ... There are sixteen or seventeen members on that Committee, including the officials, but it is not sufficiently representative of the rank and file. ... How can the Management Committee as a whole judge of the requirements, and also of the effectiveness of their work, unless each executive member is a true reflex of the needs of the members who elect him. I suggest that in this scheme before Conference, that will be overcome.

There is no more effective way of settling disputes than through the shop committees. The shop committee is a small union in itself. At a place such as the City Abattoir, the shop committee would be composed of delegates from each section of workers, beef, mutton and pig butchers, municipal workers, and so on and it would be fully representative of the whole of the men on the job. Each delegate would be continually in touch with the members who elected him. We talk a good deal about the One Big Union. Here is a more effective way of bringing about the O.B.U. along industrial lines than any other way put forward. We can meet and pass a resolution for the Federal Council to meet and adopt the O.B.U., but without having the basis for it, it is practically useless. We will never make any progress, nor meet the needs of the future unless we have the members taking a greater interest in their own affairs than they do at the present time. If the shop committee meets on a particular job, I say that the responsibility rests upon the members on that particular job for the correct control of their own affairs.

In dealing with the sectional Committees, the metropolitan delegates will agree with me that in many of the abattoirs, meat works, and several other places, there are no uniform working conditions, and they will agree with me that it is desirable that there should be uniform working conditions. Here with our sectional Committees, that should be overcome. First we have the

Shop Committees on the various works. Those Committees meet and discuss the needs and endeavour to settle any disputes on that particular job, and in turn each of those Shop Committees elects one delegate to a sectional Committee. On the export works every department should have a delegate on the Shop Committee.

Del. Fryer: Would you take in another section working on the job not in the A.M.I.E.U.?

Del. Pomfret: Most decidedly. In Adelaide the Board of Control was representative of every man on the job, butchers, engineers, firemen, cold storage men, everyone; and I understand that at Angliss' the girls had representation on the Board.

The President: They were represented by a delegate from the preservers.

Del. Pomfret: And that is the best way to bring about Industrial Unionism.

Del. Harris: Would you force the coopers into the Meat Industry Union?

Del. Pomfret: I would not force them in at all. I am not concerned from a cash point of view whether they join this Union or not. Whether a man is a member of the Coopers' Union or the Wool and Basil Workers' Union does not matter, so long as the Shop Committees are formed on these lines; and the Board of Control there controls the interests of the men on the job, I say, irrespective of what Union they belong to, that is Industrial Unionism in practice.

4.10 Repression

During the 1894 shearers' strike, the Queensland government prepared this manual for law officers. Its firm tone and positive identification of picketing and other forms of collective action as illegal were accompanied by an assertion of the state's neutrality.

Source: Manuscript in W. J. Gall Collection, Fryer Memorial Library, University of Queensland.

MANUAL: SHEARERS' DISTURBANCES 1894

Workmen whether unionist or non-unionist should in all cases be protected by officers of the law from anything approaching violence or forcible destruction.

The present strike is connected with a state of things not necessarily unlawful in itself and not necessarily tending to breaches of the peace or specific offences against persons or property but *in fact* it has this tendency and is accompanied by incidents of this kind.

To secure to every man the liberty which is dear to him, to provide against the consequences of the present strike before more serious crimes take place and to bring to justice all those who have already offended against the criminal law this manual is prepared for general instruction. Justices of the Peace, Police, special constables and other officers of the law should carefully study the information given them with a view to repressing crime with firmness and discretion. . . .

The primary offences embrace:

(1) Sureties of the Peace

(2) Sureties for good behaviour
(3) Intimidation
(4) Unlawful assembly
(5) Going armed so as to cause fear. ...

(1) *Sureties of the Peace*

If any person complains in writing that he is in fear of some present or future danger to himself or to his property and that the public peace is likely to be endangered, any Justice has a discretion and duty to require sureties and may issue a Warrant in the first instance and unless satisfactory sureties are forthcoming may commit to gaol for any period not exceeding six months. ...

(3) *Intimidation*

This is at present the most common offence for which the measure of punishment is imprisonment with hard labour not exceeding three months. The law justifies a reasonable degree of moral persuasion or pressure and therefore would not punish a man who did not exceed the bounds of information and peaceable conversation but in its desire to protect persons and property of, and to secure liberty to, those who dissent even from a majority of their fellow workers it does not permit any person to use or threaten to use violence to another or to injure his property. It is the practice for numbers of persons to specially attend at roll calls having in some instances recently ridden from other sheds and either to beset the place of operations in a threatening manner or to use such language as coupled with the number of the picketing party is calculated to deter persons desirous of working from commencing operations. In such cases all concerned are guilty of intimidation and it would be right to then and there arrest the ringleaders in this collective and organized intimidation and convey them to the nearest lockup. ...

(4) *Unlawful assembly*

The definition of this offence is:

If 3 or more persons assemble together (1) with intent to commit a crime by open force or (2) with intent to carry out any common purpose *lawful or unlawful* in such a manner as to give firm and courageous persons in the neighbourhood reasonable ground to apprehend a breach of the peace in consequence of it, this constitutes an unlawful assembly. Instead of the shearers and others on strike going into camp and remaining peacefully there it is the practice on this occasion for men to congregate together in a number of camps with the object of sallying forth, some to intimidate at the various roll calls, others to picket the roads and avenues to employment and more to commit felonies of a more or less serious character....

These assemblies sometimes develop into Riots. ... If any Justice finds 12 or more persons assembled together and acting in a riotous or tumultuous manner he should read the [riot] proclamation. ... and if further tumult continues should at once direct the Police to arrest the ringleaders. In case the circumstances call for it the Police will then act as an armed body and if called upon by the Justice it is their duty to obey. ... If rioters remain for one hour after the proclamation has been read they then become felons and should be dealt with as such. ...

In all the above offences constables should in endeavouring to arrest avoid as much as possible the use of firearms or other weapons but if in using the proper means for arresting or imprisoning they are resisted they may repel force by force and if death ensues in the struggle will be held harmless.

So far these observations have only dealt with what may be considered primary offences or misdemeanours. It is a matter of common knowledge that felonies have followed on the above offences such as

(1) Assault and battery
(2) Malicious injuries to property
(3) Sheep and cattle stealing
(4) Unlawfully wounding
(5) Shooting with intent
(6) Arson of buildings or grass
(7) Murder

In these cases the Police have greater powers and may arrest without warrant. ... In these cases they are armed to enable them successfully to overcome opposition to lawful arrests and to protect themselves against armed interference. It is their duty to arrest the felon as soon as they see him and if they cannot otherwise or secure him they must perform this duty even though they kill him and the law will protect them.

4.11 Persuasion: Ideology of family and citizenship in the schools

Extracts from the syllabus for girls in Domestic Science Schools, 1912.

Source: New South Wales Department of Public Instruction, *Course of Instruction for Domestic Science*, Government Printer, Sydney, 1912.

Superior Public (Day Continuation) Schools
Course of Instruction for Domestic Science Schools

TIME PERIODS

English	6	periods	5	periods
Household Accounts	5	”	5	”
Geography	2	”	2	”
Cookery and Laundry	4	”	—	”
Dressmaking and Millinery	3	”	3	”
Home Management	1	”	—	”
Hygiene, care of Infants and of the Sick	—	”	2	”
Botany and Gardening	3	”	2	”
Business Lessons	—	”	5	”
Moral and Civics (including History and Scripture)	4	”	4	”
Art and Home Decoration	2	”	2	”
Music and Social Exercises	2	”	2	”
Physical Training and Organised Games	3	”	3	”
	35	”	35	”

... HOUSEHOLD ACCOUNTS

The aim of this course is (1) to afford the girls practice in applying processes already learned to the solution of household problems; (2) to impart a knowledge of the method of keeping household accounts and of transacting such minor business operations as fall within the practice of the ordinary housekeeper; (3) fostering habits of accuracy in calculating and neatness in setting out; (4) giving such motive to the study as shall secure interest and sustained effort of the pupils. . . .

During the course the girls will learn something of the economic aspect of housekeeping, of the various factors which may be considered as income (e.g., productive labour within the household), of the regulation of family expenditure, and much incidental information upon the cost of food and clothing, of thrift and the reasons for saving, and of the necessity for efficient living (shelter, food, clothing, personal needs).

All of this instruction should help to produce a right attitude of mind towards domestic life, and the management of the finances of the household. . . .

BUSINESS LESSONS

Many girls at the end of their two years' course in the Superior School, will take up work in Commercial houses in the city. A limited course of instruction in business practice is provided for the purpose of affording them some insight into the modern methods of business houses. Even for girls who are to remain in their own homes the instruction given in this subject cannot but be enlightening and helpful, as tending to aid them in acquiring knowledge which is assumed by business people with whom the housekeeper necessarily comes into contact.

The thing to be aimed at is executive ability. Exercises in business practice may be so designed as not only to enforce accuracy and methodical habits, but to strengthen the judgment and initiative of the pupil. . . .

MORAL AND CIVIC OBLIGATIONS

FIRST YEAR

Good Manners.—"'Tis worth that makes the man, and want of it the fellow." Politeness means kindness in little things—social intercourse—rubbing off sharp corners by contact with each other—hence original meaning of "polite", "polished", etc. Source of good manners: regard for the feelings of others—importance of self-restraint—courtesy and respect towards all—bad manners an indication of selfishness—value of good manners to the individual and society.

Manners in the home (table conventions, morning salutations, entering rooms, etc.)—helpfulness to parents in the home—reverence and obedience of children to parents—care of younger brothers and sisters—manners towards brothers and sisters.

Courage.—What is a hero—examples of heroism and devotion to duty; heroic deeds done in the service of man. Self-sacrifice; chivalry; devotion of strong to weak; physical and moral courage. Importance of right decision; "He is a slave who dare not be in the right with two or three." Moral warfare against vice and wrong.

Patriotism.—Love of one's own land; national emblems; how each may serve his country; public spirit; military service; fighting for freedom; how to be a patriot; justice and charity towards all men; examples of patriotism.

Peace and War.—Value of peace; victories of peace; results of peace; "Blessed are the peacemakers." Self defence, when justified. International relations; how nations can help each other. Evils of war.

Justice.—In all social relations; fair treatment in trade; the spirit of fairness needed on both sides; "live and let live".

Capital and Labour.—Their mutual duties—justice on both sides; duty of employer to worker; worker's reciprocal duties—faithfulness in discharge of duty, promptitude, pride in thorough work. Honesty in dealing, a business asset. A fair day's pay for a fair day's work and *vice versa*.

Work, a Sacred Calling.—Personal qualities which make for success; choice of a vocation; value of special knowledge and skill; skilled and unskilled employment.

Self Knowledge.—"To thine own self be true, and it must follow as the night the day, thou can'st not then be false to any man." Self control; control of temper; use of leisure; temptations of a city—to waste time and money. Temperance; alcohol; cigarette smoking. Personal hygiene (nutrition, care of skin, etc.); thrift; simplicity of living; evils of betting and gambling; service as making for personal dignity; personal pride and dignity in conduct; ambition; the inner voice; having ideals.

SECOND YEAR

The Citizen's Duty to the State

How we depend upon one another and act together for a common purpose; how men's lives are bound up in institutions of many kinds; instances of such institutions, the school, the municipality, the State; their effect upon personal character in developing unselfishness, public spirit, mutual trust, social service.

The municipality and the shire—what they do for the citizen; the citizen's duty in response.

The State; the benefit the citizen gets from the State; the preservation of order, the protection of life and property, the provision of educational opportunities; help for those who suffer from such natural disabilities as weakness of physical frame or defective surroundings.

Reciprocal duties of the citizen towards the State: loyalty and obedience to the law; respect for the public property of the State; responsibility for taking fullest advantage of educational opportunities; public spirit towards benevolent institutions, public hospitals, libraries, art galleries, recreation grounds, etc.

Duty of the citizen to render public service—injury done to the State by man's neglect of public duty; duty of living and working harmoniously with others; value and benefit of co-operation.

Justice, the chief virtue of the citizen; the meaning of justice—fair play, honest dealing, respect for the rights and toleration of the opinions of others.

Public justice in the sense of the State's power to protect the rights of each.

The machinery of legal justice; police; courts of law; magistrates, judges, juries; the citizen's obligations as juror or witness; the relation of courts to one another.

The aims of laws; how laws are made; Parliament—how constituted; elections; the citizen's duty at elections.

The executive—its functions; how it is constituted.

The Commonwealth Government as distinct from the State; its powers; its constitution.

Defence a duty of the citizen; the army and navy; universal training; the training of military and naval officers.

4.12 Co-option

A state official justifies the existence of arbitration because of its embourgeoisement of class-conscious workers, and advocates strengthening trade-union and employer organisation to prevent strikes.

Source: 'Report of the Chief Inspector of Factories, Melbourne, on Anti-Strike Legislation in Operation throughout the Australian States and Recommendations regarding such Legislation for Victoria, 1915', in H. M. Murphy, *Wages and Prices in Australia: Our Labor Laws and Their Effects*, Melbourne, 1915, pp. 95–100, 132–6.

... During the current year I visited in turn South Australia, Western Australia, Tasmania, New Zealand, New South Wales and Queensland, and interviewed officials, representative employers and employees, and others, to obtain their views on the strike prevention laws in each case, and to ascertain the merits and faults of these laws. In making my recommendations, I have taken into consideration the knowledge thus gained, and supplemented it by the experience I have had as head of the sub-Department of Labour at Melbourne.

Apart from strike prevention, the practice of our neighbour States in such matters as transferring the workless from city to country districts by means of country employment agencies and free passes, the building of cottages, and the uplifting of the workers by transferring families from the low morality of the slums to the more healthful and moral surroundings of such places as Daceyville, near Sydney, has been of very great interest. ...

The comparative immunity from strikes in Victoria ... can hardly be ascribed to the fact that Victoria is the only State in Australasia where lock-outs and strikes may be undertaken at will without penalization. It would surely be fallacious to say that because we have no anti-strike laws we have few strikes. A better explanation is that the Wages Board system of regulating wages and conditions secures a greater measure of industrial justice for the workers than is afforded by systems in other States, and so takes away the necessity and desire for strikes. ...

The belief that industrial justice is a more powerful counter-strike factor than strike penalties is borne out by the fact that strikes—at least in Australia—are more frequent in high-wages trades than among the lower-paid workers. ...

I beg to suggest alterations in the Victorian Wages Board Laws in the direction of:— ...

Qualification of Members of Boards

Section 136 of the Factories Act requires that, as a qualification for membership, a person must be actually engaged in the trade concerned, or have been at least six months out of the past three years actively so engaged. This excludes managers of companies from representing employers, and Union secretaries from representing the workers. The object of the restriction appears to have been the desire to exclude the "red-ragger" from Boards. That it has not done, for the real red-ragger is more often the man freshly come from his working-bench full of main-strength and zeal, burning to achieve, but entirely lacking in knowledge of methods or of the rights and difficulties of the other side. His zeal is liable to be misdirected, his methods are of the sledge-hammer type, and much time is required before he learns gentler and more successful methods. The Act as it stands admits such a man to membership, but if the same man ceases to work at his trade for three years while he acts as a member of a Board he loses his qualification, yet his experience on the Board has made him a far more desirable and effective member than when he began. One of the most valuable influences of Wages Boards is the educative effect they exert on both employer and employee. Each side gets to know the difficulties of the other, and it is safe to say that, with very few exceptions, the "red-ragger" who has had three years on a Board is, under the present law, just coming to his best when he must make way for some one else, perhaps another "red-ragger". The section designed to exclude an undesirable class of representative has not been a success. For that reason, and because it is only fair that each side should have its claims put forward by the advocates they regard as the best, and in order to increase the confidence in the justness and efficiency of Wages Boards, and so heighten their usefulness in the direction of industrial peace, the area of selection should be widened. Any person who has at any time been engaged at the trade either as employer, manager, or worker for a period of at least three years continuously should be eligible for appointment. . . .

OTHER WAYS OF DISCOURAGING INDUSTRIAL UPHEAVALS.

THE INDUSTRIAL DISPUTES COMMITTEE OF THE TRADES HALL.

Notwithstanding the belief that is held in some quarters that Union secretaries and other office-holders of Unions are the real fomenters of industrial disputes, as a general rule these men are the force that holds the workers back. The Union secretary has a peculiarly difficult post. He is blamed by both sides. Of course he is most in evidence whenever disputes occur. It is he who must pull the strings for the man he represents, and so it is perhaps not surprising that he should be blamed. He is as a matter of fact frequently forced by a vote of the most ignorant, turbulent, and irresponsible section of his Union to take up a position which he knows to be wrong. It is inevitable that among Unions a section will be found that think reforms should be accomplished with a sledge hammer. These people are enemies of the legitimate objects of unionism, though they are unaware of it, and they are the thorns in the side of the Union officials, the majority of whom are honestly working for the upraising of the workers by equitable means. The lessening of strikes, provided fair demands can be satisfied by other means, is the aim of most Unions. . . .

Action was taken about three years ago to secure the proper consideration of all disputes before a strike could be declared. In order to safeguard Union interests and prevent the embroilment of unionism in a hasty or ill-considered strike, a committee was set up by the Trades Hall Council. This committee claims to have prevented sixty out of sixty-nine threatened strikes. . . .

EMPLOYERS' DEFENCE ASSOCIATION

In trades where such a combination is possible the banding together of employers with a pooling of interests, properly held together by money bonds and penalties, so that united action in case of a strike would be assured, would constitute (in my opinion) a stronger preventive of strikes than any penal law that can be enacted. It must be at once admitted that such an organization is impracticable in trades, crafts, or industries that are divided up between a large number of small employers, but in such occupations strikes less often occur. It is among largely held concerns that the greatest need of a strike-preventer exists, and it is here that their comparatively small number brings within reach of employers an over-powering weapon that, strange to say, has hardly been brought into use. It is scarcely within the scope of this report to go into details in such a matter, but I have in mind a trade which covers important interests, and in which there are probably less than 50 employers throughout Australia. If they combined, and under properly underwritten bonds agreed to close down all works for three months in case of a strike in any State, I venture to say the remedy would never be put to the test, because no strikers would knowingly enter upon three months' self-enforced idleness, but would prefer to submit their claims to the existing tribunals, and abide by the result.

4.13 Working-class youth culture

A defence of 'the push' by a reformer who understood its class basis, and its susceptibility to cultural manipulation.

Source: 'The Australian Pushes' by 'X.O.' (?Ambrose Pratt), unpublished manuscript, Hayes Collection, Fryer Memorial Library, University of Queensland.

... Writer remembers a Wharf Labourers or Coal Labourers Picnic at Chowder at which the "Rocks" and "Liver" and "Gipps" and other pushes met and will never forget it. The picnic committee knew certain pushes had arranged for a day out and had somewhere between a hundred and two hundred of their union sworn in as special constables. The pushes got to work and fought each other and the committee. No sooner would the committee eject one set of disputants from the pavilion than another dispute would start. In and outside the pavilion it raged till a boat load of police from Sydney arrived and found the pushes practically exhausted. One trick they tried during the day was to run down the pavilion with a stretched rope upsetting the dancers. Writer who has been there knows that a lot of the pushism originates in the school and is afterwards irritated into criminality by over officious policemen and busybody citizens. It was quite a usual thing in the early eighties for various schools especially of a denominational kind to jibe and jeer one another, to pelt each other with road metal and otherwise meet in combat. ...

... This feeling of school rivalry ... spread to localities and Writer remembers the boys of his neighbourhood, none over 15 years of age, at the time of the Egyptian war chasing the boys of another neighbour[hood] with sticks and stones. They were Egyptians; we were the conquering British. ...

... When said boys went to office or prenticeship, which came under the heading of "going to graft", the gregarious instinct survived. They would gather at night on a vacant allotment, or in the entry way of a warehouse, or on a street corner to yarn. Sometimes they were boisterous or a trifle coarse in their talk and drew upon themselves the wrath of some prim adjacent dweller. Retaliation in the shape of badinage or practical jokes inevitably fell to the interfering person or persons. Result a complaint to the police. If the police officer was a man of tact and understood boys, matters would be smoothe[d] over and the boys would select a quieter place and behave circumspectly—for boys. If the officer was a bully without tact he would succeed—has done so in many instances—in laying the foundations of several first class violent criminals. ... The hobble-de-hoys were reported as first class ruffians forming a bloodthirsty gang frequenting such and such a neighbourhood and police and push were in opposition. Youths of from 17 to 18 have been known to surround and beat into insensibility an obnoxious "trap". Every other little party of youths on that beat fell in for a share of the odium and were constantly hustled and harried by the police—truly an excellent guerilla way of training criminals. The regular result was arrests fines and imprisonment. ...

... From these isolated hard cases the big pushes were recruited. The Rocks push proper was recruited from many minor pushes or boys' kerbstone clubs in West Sydney. The Gipps Street push from the same sources all over Surry Hills, ditto other pushes. ...

... The law to the majority of these men was only a lop-sided tyrant. In many cases they had a genuine grievance against the law and their first acquaintance with it found the quality of mercy absent. Fresh introductions to gaol and fines followed. Special policemen were put on to suppress the push, sometimes the push suppressed the policemen. With avenues of employment closed, blackmail, robbery, and bludgery became the resources of the push and violence their only court of appeal. ...

... The "Black Reds" a Sydney suburban push was composed mainly of brick carters and brick makers or burners. They were a rough, excusably in a measure brutal, but industrious class. No great crimes lay at their door. They were willing to meet another push down the "Harbour" and have a go or to match their champion and generally held themselves pledged to prove their manhood against all comers.

The St Peters push was somewhat similar but the pristine glory of these pushes has faded. Their old component parts have married and settled down. Their neighbourhoods have been closely settled and their sway and liberty swamped by policemen and population. Wooloomooloo and Waterloo from the pushes of which participants in the Wooloomooloo and Mt. Rennie outrages were drawn are also practically extinct. The Liver Push, the "Liver" is a recognition of the Glebe Abbatoirs at which many of the push worked, the Abercrombie St push and Sussex Street pushes are not what they were. Police and the march of the warehouse obliterating the slum tenement cleared Sussex St and Wooloomooloo. The Rocks push will disappear with the perfection of the Resumption Scheme [land acquisition for the approach to the Sydney Harbour Bridge]....

... Always a kind of Freemasonry existed between pushes. A youth changed his residence and found an acquaintance resident in the new neighbourhood and associated himself with him and his clique. ...

... The promotion of a dance to raise the amount of "Bluey's" or "Knocker's" fine was and is still a common occurrence, the London coster's "Friendly Lead" is a parallel. Sometimes the fine was raised by subscription and ... the hotels, tobacconists or other shops or places in the neighbourhood were asked to buy tickets or subscribe; [that] is the usual procedure with every church or Charity Committee in the Commonwealth.

... Even up the conditions and pushism will disappear. Provide some national places for the hobble-de-hoy to meet and fraternise in a decent and orderly manner. His home is to[o] small to permit of social gatherings and as a rule is also required for more serious uses. You don't want to preach or prose to him and must needs let his feminine counterpart share in the benefits. Keep him off the streets and away from the low pubs. Give him a place and a status and run the country so that he is sure of a regular job. Under such circumstances a better state of affairs will come about. ...

... Dancing, reading, yarning, smoking and telling lies or playing games in which his girls can take a respectable part will keep him and his girl out of mischief such as leads to worse. Saving him from being run in will practically save him from further criminal bravado and malice towards the law, its makers and administrators. The spread of club rooms, trades unions, good dance and social halls, reading rooms, gymnasiums etc etc has done more to obliterate the push of the "eighties" than all the policemens feet and batons and magistrates and gaolors in Australia.

4.14 A working-class festival

The Rockhampton Labour Day celebration of 1921.

Source: Rockhampton Labor Papers, collected by Denis Murphy, Department of History, University of Queensland.

Rockhampton Labour Day Celebration Union

EUCHRE PARTY, SOCIAL & DANCE

School of Arts, Monday, May 2nd, 1921.

PROGRAMME

1. Labour Day Waltz ... ...
2. Waterside Workers Schottische ... .
3. Aust. Meat Employees Maxina ... .
   Song ... ... Mr. Bob. McLeod
4. Carters and Drivers Alberts ... ...
5. Painters and Decorators Two-Step ... .
6. Q.R Union Canadian Barn Dance ... .
   Song ... ... Mr. Con. Breen
7. Aust. Workers Union Mazurka ... ...
8. Boilermakers Fox Trot ... ...

9. Carp. and Joiners Waltz Cotillons ... .
   Song ... ... Mr. O'Leary
10. Coopers One-Step ... ...
11. Enginedrivers and Firemen Schottische ....
12. Engineers Valeta ... ...
    Song ... ... Mr. Jim Laffan
13. Storemen and Packers Two-Step ... .
14. Coachbuilders Flirtation Canadian
    Barn Dance .. ..
15. Moulders Fitzroys ... ...
16. Printers Employees Finale ... ...

M.C.'s Messrs. F. Conlon and M. Crowe.
Pianiste—Miss M. Dempsey. Secretary—I.H. Shackleton.

4.15 The Vice-regal connection

An illuminated address, from Catholic school children, to the Queensland governor in 1903, stressing loyalty to the Empire and respect for authority.

Source: Sir Herbert Chernside Addresses, John Oxley Library, Brisbane, OM 69–26.

The Children of the Convent School to
His Excellency Major-General Sir Herbert Chernside G.C.M.G., C.B.
Governor of the State of Queensland.

May it please your Excellency,

We desire to thank you for the kindliness of spirit and amiable condescension that have induced you to lay aside for a while the cares of your high office to meet us the little ones of the community. We shall ever treasure up in our hearts the memory of your visit to us, as an incentive to renewed endeavours to benefit of the able tuition given to us by our beloved teachers, so as to fit us for the duties of life which by the decrees of a wise Providence befall to all in this world.

The public voice has told us how readily your congenial nature has fallen in with the aspirations of our people and heartily seconded their own best wishes and endeavours for the success and prosperity of this our Austral land. The dear Sisters, our beloved teachers, have always told us that it is a paramount duty on the part of a child to pray for those in high places, to respect, love, and obey those whom God has placed over us. We shall ever pray that your Excellency who so nobly represents the Majesty of the throne and the August lady who bears your name, shares your exalted position, and so graciously adorns the high sphere in which she moves, may meet with length of days, and the highest rewards of merit. It were ungenerous on our part to express the wish that your Excellency may be long left to us. We shall only ask that when this new-born land of ours has taken its place in the orbit where gravitate around the high throne of the Motherland nationhoods representing the whole world, your name may be enshrined on the glorious roll of those mighty Empire-builders who have in the past and shall in future, shed such a glorious lustre upon our country.

We are your Excellency's humble servants,
The pupils of the Sisters of Mercy
Convent School, Mackay.

4.16 Learning the sexual division of labour in itinerant working-class families

Recollection of childhood in a railway labourers' camp, *circa* 1911–12.

Source: *Caddie*: *The Autobiography of a Sydney Barmaid*, Sun Books, Melbourne, 1975 (first publ. 1953), pp. 16–23.

... The camp site was called The Two Mile. It was fenced in with barbed wire to keep out straying cattle and had a large wire gate at the entrance. Most families had moved in when we arrived. Some had erected bark huts, others had merely pitched their tents. Much hammering was going on and dozens of kiddies played around while their mothers were seated on piles of bedding and belongings busily sewing corn bags which were to be used to line the inside of their dwellings.

... As we walked along, Mum was trying to pick out which place belonged to us, when she saw an old towel, which she recognized as one she had given Dad. It was hanging over the door of one of the bark huts. She seemed a little uncertain as to whether we should go in or not, when a big jolly-looking man came over and asked: 'Were you looking for someone, Missus?' Mum said she was looking for our place, and told him our name. He said that she was right there at our place. He said he knew father very well and that we'd be neighbours. It turned out that it was his dray that father had borrowed to fetch our things. He hoped we'd get better acquainted, and invited us to visit his family as soon as we were settled in.

Mum thanked him nicely, but although we lived there for about two years she never became over-friendly with anyone, and certainly never visited anyone. But for all that everyone seemed to like and respect her.

She was seldom seen around and was never known to do any shopping—Timothy and I did that.

Our place consisted of two tents (our sleeping quarters) and a stringy-bark hut which served as a kitchen and living room. The chimney was wide, built of stones and clay. In the yard near the chimney was a crude bench made out of saplings. On it stood a new tin dish, and beside it a cake of soap. It was obvious this was where Dad washed himself.

I followed Mum inside. The place was almost bare except for a box which Dad had been using for a table, and where he stored his food. In one of the tents where he'd been sleeping was a temporary bunk made of bags with sapling legs dug well into the earthen floor. Beside the bunk was another box; on it stood a candle in a pickle bottle. The candle was leaning to one side, where the grease had congealed around the bottle and on the box. A few old working togs, and heavy blucher boots lay in one corner.

... Later Dad and Timothy arrived with the furniture and belongings.

Mum got busy and straightened things up, then cooked the dinner in a camp oven which was suspended from a piece of wire fastened to an iron bar fixed in the chimney.

Because father was getting better wages in his new job, we had better food. We were allowed to have butter and mother used to make gingerbread. Sometimes she would make an apple-pie. Yet we were by no means well fed. We rarely saw fruit as it was considered a luxury.

There were no recreation rooms in the camp, so everyone had to make their own pleasures. There wasn't an hotel for miles, but that didn't worry anyone, as someone had already started a sly-grog shop.

We saw little of Dad, for which we were thankful, as he would hurry over his evening meal, then take himself off to the sly-grog, or down the scrub at the back of the single men's quarters for a game of cards or two-up. The men would sit around a big log fire in the open, telling blue jokes, and swearing like the devil.

... Timothy and I soon chummed up with the Medley family. Joshua the father we had met the first day. His wife's name was Emmy. His son Chris was about Timothy's age. He was boisterous and happy-go-lucky like his father. The daughter Esther was a nice girl with blue-black hair which she wore in pigtails. She had lovely brown eyes and a creamy skin. She was easy to get along with as she was quiet and reserved.

...Joshua went to great pains to make their camp home nice. He papered the walls, and even put boarded floors down and Mrs Medley bought cheap rugs and spread them out and made pretty curtains for the tiny windows. They were the only people in the camp to own a piano. That was the closest I had been to a real piano and believe me I thought it was the most wonderful thing in the world.

...The two Medley kids and Timothy and I became good mates. We even made a pact to stick together for ever. We had a sort of ceremony to make it binding. This was carried out under the Knapsack bridge one Saturday afternoon. Timothy seemed a bit sweet on Esther right from the beginning. He would always stay close to her and would carry her books to and from school. As far as I can remember sex matters, the mysteries of babies etc., were never discussed amongst us kids. However, someone in the camp owned a bright pink flannelette nightgown and it was the custom for it to be loaned to anyone expecting a baby; so when we happened to see it hanging on a line, we would whisper to each other about Mrs So-and-so must be getting a little baby soon. Sure enough we were right.

Timothy and I had to do all the chores, like carting water and keeping up the wood supply. We carried the water in two pails suspended from a yoke, in the fashion of the Chinese market-gardener with his baskets. Besides this, I used to mind Nellie's baby at mealtimes for an hour or so, until Nellie had got through waiting on table. They had a cow bell which Nellie would bring outside and ring to warn the men their meals were ready. But Dad didn't consider this was enough for me and when I was twelve he told mother it was time I got out and did a bit of work! He had come home fighting drunk—Albert's grog was not only hard on the purse but on the head and the stomach. Dad chucked things round, and roared that he was tired of sweating his guts out for us and reminded us how lucky we were. That he'd had to work all his life, and that the first pair of boots he ever wore he'd bought from the money he earned selling papers on the Quay.

He'd already got Timothy a job on the railroad as a nipper. A nipper was the name given to a young boy whose job it was to boil the billies and carry the various tools, such as picks and shovels, to the men when required. The first day some of the men got hold of Timothy and forcibly removed his pants to make sure (as they said) he was not a girl. This was a sort of initiation to the job.

Before long Dad had me installed at Mrs Hussler's boarding-house. I had to go there for an hour in the morning and after school. For this I was paid two and sixpence a week. Mrs Hussler was a tyrant to say the least. I had to work like a slave. I worked week-ends too.

... When I reached a certain stage in my life, mother told me one or two things concerning the facts of life; but not very much. Then Dad built a bark hut for Timothy, leaving me with the tent to myself.

It seemed now that I was growing up. I no longer wanted to go bird's-nesting with Timothy, or ride horses bare-back.

I made a patchwork rug for my bedside and trimmed my dressing-table, which was only a deal wood case, with some old curtains which I'd salvaged from someone's rubbish heap. I bought a small mirror from Paddy's shop and propped it up on the table. I got to looking at myself in the mirror and would put my hair up on top just to see what I looked like.

... I used to dream of the time when I would be able to get away from this sort of life. I began to turn my thoughts to Sydney. I'd get there somehow. I wanted to live in a proper house, wear nice clothes, get a nice job and some day I'd get married and have children of my own. I'd see they had a better life than I had. It was a dreary kind of existence. If there had been no trees to climb or horses around, I don't know what I would have done for amusement.

4.17 Reorganisation on the industrial front: Employers' meeting, September 1890

The merchants and bankers of Sydney organise a defensive alliance of employers.

Source: *The Labor Crisis*: *Issued by the New South Wales Exployers' Union. Meeting of Employers and Commercial Men . . . 2nd September, 1890, with A List of Those Present*, Sydney, 1890.

The Chairman, in opening the meeting, said:—Gentlemen, —You have been invited here this afternoon by the Employers' Union and Steamship Owners' Association to consider the very serious labor difficulties that have occurred, not only in this colony, but all over Australia.

Mr. HENRY HUDSON (President of the New South Wales Employers' Union) was called on to move the first resolution, and was received with loud cheers. He said:— Mr. Chairman and Gentlemen,—The resolution I am asked to propose is as follows:—

> That the time has arrived when it is absolutely necessary for all employers of labour, capitalists, and others directly and indirectly interested, to form themselves into an association for mutual defence and protection.

(Loud cheers.) In moving this resolution I thoroughly endorse everything said by the Chairman in introducing the object of this meeting. I am not one to make rash assertions, or to rush into what may be called a stand-up fight, but I think the time has arrived when it is absolutely necessary for us to do something to define the respective positions of employers and men. (Cheers). I am sure I am justified in saying that as far as the employers are concerned the present trouble is none of their seeking. (Hear, hear.) The present crisis is most unjustifiable, and has been brought about entirely by the action of the labour bodies—there can be no question about that. (Hear, hear.) . . . We should put ourselves in order that we may devise some means of meeting this trouble, and hence I ask you to pass the motion now before the meeting. . . .

Mr. THOMAS BUCKLAND (President of the Bank of New South Wales), who was called upon to second the resolution was greeted with loud cheers. He said:—Mr. Chairman and Gentlemen,—I must crave your indulgence, for I am but a poor speaker, but, having been resident in Sydney for close on sixty years, I may be able to give you some good reminiscences of what was the position of employer and labourer half a century ago, and up to within a very few years of the present time, as compared with the existing state of affairs. In days gone by, if a man was conducting a profitable business and went to the capitalist to borrow money, the first thing he did was to display his assets and then describe the nature of his business. The capitalist would say, well, your assets are worth, say, £10,000, but you have a good going business, and we will advance you money to the full extent of your assets, and also something on the prospects of your business. (Cheers.) What is the position now? If a manufacturer has £10,000 worth of solid assets in the shape of land, and, say, £50,000 invested in machinery, and goes to the capitalist to borrow money, what sort of a reception does he get? Why, he finds that he can get an advance to the full value of his land, perhaps, but the capitalist will not give him a shilling on his machinery or trade assets. (Cheers.) The capitalist knows well enough that any day a strike may occur, and render the whole of the manufacturer's property, with the exception of the land, utterly valueless. (Cheers.) . . . I employ a considerable number of people in the country in connection with the growth of stock. I pay rent to the Government for land and assist to grow wool, which I send to Sydney to ship or sell, and I say the Government are bound to see me unharmed. (Loud cheers.)

Mr. JAMES BURNS (Messrs. Burns, Philp & Co.), who was asked to support the resolution, rose amidst cheers and said:—In supporting the resolution, which has been so ably put before you, I must emphatically deny that the Steamship Owners' Association have in any way sought the present trouble. (Cheers.) . . . We hear a great deal about "Capital and Labor", but this does not properly describe the parties who are at present in conflict. (Cheers.) There is as much capital on one side as the other. (Hear, hear.) The present conflict is really one between dictation on the part of the employees and reason on the part of the employers. (Cheers.) We have been dictated to by the labor bodies on every point, until our business has been taken entirely out of our control. (Hear, hear.) In talking about "Capital and Labor" the labor bodies seem to think that they have a great majority on their side, but that is not correct. I have gone into this matter with care, and I find from the returns of the shareholders of the various shipping companies that nine companies out of thirty-four have nearly 4,000 shareholders, the exact figures being 3,759. Now, if the other companies have similar numbers of shareholders, there must be between 10,000 and 12,000 shareholders, with capital invested in shipping and represented in the Steamship Owners' Association. If we take in addition our employees (our clerical staffs) we have fully 12,000 people who are interested with the members of the Steamship Owners' Association. (Cheers.) I need not take up your time by going into further matters of detail, but I simply wished to remove the false impression existing as to the relative positions of so-called "Capital and Labor." There is no such thing as "Capital" in the sense in which the term has been used by the labor leaders. (Cheers.) A large number of the shareholders in the coastal steam shipping companies are working men, settlers, and others, who have invested their money in the shares of the steamship companies. (Cheers.) In the Tasmanian S.N. [Steam Navigation] Company there are not less than 800 shareholders, a large number of these being ladies in Tasmania, who are dependent upon their dividends for their bread. (Hear, hear.) These are the "Capitalists" who are supposed to be crushing out labor at this moment. (Cheers.) ... Unionism in a moderate degree is a good thing, but when it becomes aggressive, I might almost say pestilential, it is the duty of all men, even the workers themselves, to stop it. (Cheers.)

Mr. A.W. MEEKS (Gibbs, Bright & Co.), Vice-President of the New South Wales Employers' Union, was entrusted with the third resolution, and was greeted with loud cheers. He said:—Mr. Chairman and Gentlemen—The resolution I have to submit to you is as follows:—

> That it is desirable that all employers not members of the Employers' Union should at once join that Union to ensure united action. This meeting calls on all persons directly and indirectly interested to express their sympathy in a practical manner by recognising that the shipowners and others connected with maritime labour are fighting the battles of the community against aggressive unionism, and agrees to subscribe to a fund to assist them.

Some two years ago a meeting was called in Sydney to inaugurate an Employers' Union. I had the pleasure then, although not long in this Colony, of supporting a resolution recommending that an Employers' Union should be formed in this city. That Employers' Union was formed, and has been in existence since, but, without some crisis such as the present to force them to the front, employers are often inclined to hold back, as they do not see the necessity for action which others who have been in the conflict have had fully brought home to them. Therefore the Employers' Union has not been such a generally recognised institution in this land as it ought to have been. (Cheers.) Nevertheless, it has done an immense amount of good. (Hear, hear.) The Employers' Union was not started as a fighting institution, but a large number of people here saw, as had been previously recognised in Adelaide and Melbourne, the necessity for combination. ... The Employers' Union has been of some assistance in the past, because, whereas in years gone by the Unions would have thrown their rules down and insisted upon the employers adopting them literally, they now come to ask us if we are prepared to adopt them. Conferences have been held which show that the labour organisations recognise the Employers' Union as a certain power, and what we seek now is to make that power something more than it is to-day. (Cheers.) We want every person who is engaged in business, everyone who has a stake in this country, to come forward and join our ranks, and so this resolution affirms that every employer not at present a member of the Employers' Union should join it at once. (Hear, hear.) I am glad to say that during the past few days we have had very valuable accessions to our ranks. Some of the largest houses in the city have joined us and are working heartily with us. (Cheers.) When we have got a flourishing institution round which we can rally, the Trades and Labour Council will find itself confronted by a thousand or more men engaged in business, who are prepared to stand up and protect that which belongs to them. (Cheers.) We have expressed sympathy with those who are engaged as employers in the present conflict, and this sympathy must take the form of something more than a formal resolution. We must have funds to carry on the work. (Cheers.) The action taken by the labour bodies recently has been aggressive in the extreme, because the strike has not been confined to those who have real or supposed grievances, but has been extended to those who have no possible grounds for complaint. The wharf labourers, for instance, have decided on a certain course, and have stopped work all round, broken their agreement, and, joining those who have come out on strike, have brought the whole trade of the port to a standstill. Now is the proper time for claiming that freedom of contract to which every man is entitled, but which has been denied us by the labour bodies. (Cheers.)

4.18 Reorganisation on the political front: Finance committees

After 1910, when Labor won control of both houses of federal parliament and proposed to alter the Constitution to extend the Commonwealth's powers over monopolies, the dominant fraction of capital set up 'finance committees' to co-ordinate the political fight against Labor. The committee in Victoria was known at first as the Constitutional Union; its trustees represented pastoral, shipping and financial interests.

Source: *Australian Worker*, 4 May 1911; and reprinted in C. Joyner, *The Commonwealth and Monopolies*, Cheshire, Melbourne, 1963, pp. 25–6.

Constitutional Union Committee
Nos. 10 and 11, Third Floor
Equitable Buildings,
Collins St.
Melbourne, 1st February

Dear Sir,—To ensure united action on the part of all opposed to Labor-Socialism in Federal, State and Municipal Elections, the Constitutional Union Committee, consisting of representative businessmen has been formed. Its main objects are:

1. To collect donations for a Central Fund for the support of all organizations opposed to Labor-Socialism, namely, the Australian Women's National League, the Commonwealth Liberal Party (with which is shortly to be merged the Farmers' League), and the Victorian Employers' Federation.
2. To make this committee the only body for collecting Special Donations (other than the subscriptions and small contributions to these organiza-

tions), so that subscribers to this Central Fund will not be asked for donations by any of these other bodies.

3. To promote united action of the political organizations in opposing Labor-Socialism, and to exercise supervision over the expenditure of money donated to them from the Central Fund. The Central Fund is vested in the following trustees: Mr. E.E. Smith, Mr. Wm Riggall, Mr. George Fairbairn.

Much more money than we have received is needed for opposing the referendum next April, as well as for perfecting the organization of the Political Leagues, so that they may prove an effective fighting force against Labor-Socialists at the next State and Federal elections.

The Political Leagues have resolved to work together in opposing the referendum. A Council of the Leagues has been formed, consisting of three delegates from the Australian Women's National League, the Commonwealth Liberal Party, and the People's Party respectively, one delegate from the Constitutional Union, and a Chairman. This body will deal with questions relating to overlapping, etc., in the working of League branches, supervise the preparation and distribution of League literature, and promote an active campaign against the referendum.

Donations from the Central Fund, collected by the Constitutional Union Committee, will be given to the Leagues from time to time, as long as they can show that they are actively carrying out the objects for which they were formed. To successfully oppose the referendum next April and win we have only to get our people to vote "No". This needs money for organization.

We urge on you the necessity of contributing to the Central Fund, as no doubt you are opposed to the referendum and to the aims of Labor-Socialists. You must see the absolute necessity of fighting the Socialists, who spend thousands in political work, and who had the money to assist all candidates advocating Socialist views at the recent Federal elections.

Please give this letter your early consideration, and send your contribution to the hon. treasurer, Mr. Wm. Riggall, 120 William St., Melbourne.

We are, dear Sir,
Yours faithfully,
Wm. Riggall
Hon. Treas.
George Fairbairn
} Trustees
John West, Secretary

4.19 Corporate liberalism: The state and business in 1918

Herbert Brookes, President of the Associated Chambers of Manufactures of Australia, reports on the efforts of the State to organise the shift of capital into manufacturing during the First World War, and propounds an appropriate ideology of corporate responsibility to the community, class collaboration and state planning.

Source: Associated Chambers of Manufactures of Australia, *President's Address, 1918*, Melbourne, 1918.

... Thrown almost completely as we have been and are on our own resources, and cut off by the circumstances and needs of the great war from the general flow of basic commodities, Australia has an opportunity now such as may not come her way again for many generations—we trust may never come again from the same terrible causes. We all realise this fact to a greater or less degree, and most of us have been talking about it and letting our efforts expend themselves with the breath that has uttered them. But there does indeed now appear to be a very serious endeavour being made to translate these thoughts and these industrial ideals into realities. I happen to know, placed as I have been as your chief Executive Officer of the past year in a very responsible position, that the Federal Government has made considerable progress and is continuing to make further progress in the direction of assisting in various ways in the establishment of basic industries.

NEW INDUSTRIES

In the great staple industry of Wool, many developments are being projected, and some accomplished, among others a very great increase in our modest Spinning capacity in Australia.

In the Metal Trade, in zinc and tin and copper and iron and steel, many new additions are being realised. I need not stress this point, since all of you are more or less familiar with the fine work of the various committees controlling these sections of industries.

In the White Lead and accompanying manufactures, definite and practical steps have been taken.

In the Alkali Industry, for the manufacture of Caustic Soda and Soda Ash, a big move has already been made.

In the Paper, the straw-board, and pulp board industries, great expansion within the next year or two is already assured.

The Federal Government is sparing no effort in all these directions, and deserves our heartiest commendation. It fully realises that one of the weak spots in our Industrial armour is the almost total absence of well-developed oil-fields. Accordingly, it is endeavouring to encourage by a broad general policy the development of the Shale Oil Industry. . . .

Associated with, and subsidiary to, the great Iron and Steel Industries at Newcastle and Lithgow, several key industries are being encouraged; and it seems to me before the term of my successor has elapsed he will be able to record the founding of such highly significant industries as the manufacture of black sheet iron, of corrugated iron, of tinplates, of solid drawn tubes, of wire drawing plants all of sufficient magnitude to cope with a large portion of the consumption of these commodities throughout the Commonwealth. With these in active operation, so many other collateral industries become practicable and desirable. For instance, along with negotiations for those basic industries I have mentioned, are others which are being carried on by the Government for the establishment of factories for the manufacture of Water Tube Boilers, Marine Boilers, Super Heaters and Economisers. The Government are really determined that the Commonwealth shall never be caught again as industrially unprepared as it was when war broke out. I am authorised by the Acting Prime Minister to make these general statements, as a member of the Board of Trade. The details are naturally matters of private negotiation at present.

SELF-GOVERNING INDUSTRIES

The Federal Government is to be congratulated, and in particular the Prime Minister and the Acting Prime Minister, upon their successful establishment of a number of very necessary and useful bodies.

Am I right in mentioning first that Board to which I have the honor as your nominee to be appointed—The Federal Board of Trade. To this body the Cabinet when it sees fit can commit any question of a commercial or industrial character for report and advice. It is anticipated that in the ordinary course of events we shall have something to say about possible amendments of the tariff.

Then there is the Bureau of Commerce and Industry, which may yet with our co-operation as manufacturers develop into an organization of organizations and link them all together under one Director who will be in a position to make representations to the Minister who has been appointed as head of that department. . . .

The opportunity has been afforded us by the Prime Minister of adopting and developing this organization under the Bureau of Commerce and Industry. If we do not take full advantage of all it offers we shall be blind to our own interests and to the Industrial expansion of the Commonwealth. By means of this Bureau a new corporate spirit can be introduced into all our industries, "a larger appreciation of the rights and duties of the industry as a whole, a new sense of the danger of uncontrolled economic forces, and a new consciousness of the place and share to which the workpeople are entitled in the government of the Industrial world." . . . Goods, commodities, are good, but men and women, real capable men and women who are interested in, and have joy in their work and as far as possible have a personal interest in the business are better. For we are further convinced that the democratising of the whole world, which shall be the result of this war, must be the extension of the principles of democracy to industry, and this must spell the application to a greater or less degree where practicable of the method and principles of co-operation.

We realise, too, that Government regulation, which after all can be called a form of socialism, has come to stay and play a more permanent part in the industrial order of the British Empire.

WE WOULD HAVE THE WORKER, THE REAL LOYAL WORKER, UNDERSTAND US BETTER. We can make no appeal nor do we desire to appeal to the sham-worker, the red-rag unionist, the I.W.W., the shirker, and the disloyalist. All these are the curse of the Labour Movement, and all alike live by sowing dissension between class and class, and preaching disloyalty to Empire and State. With all these and their bitter press and vicious sectarian rags we can do nothing. We know that with such it is war to the death as with the Hun. But with the real Labour man, the true and rational and loyal unionist, we would say—"Come, let us reason together let us co-operate and create goodwill, and make this rich young country flourish, and let us share the produce according to the respective services we have rendered in evoking it." . . .

We of the employing class at present are prepared to admit that we have learned much from this world-struggle, and that great changes are likely to be made and to become permanent before the final settlement takes place. We realise that the fight is for democracy and that we are going to be carried further than we anticipated when we set out to defend the freedom of the world. But whithersoever it leads us we are willing to follow. We realise for instance that we who live in that world of romance known as the Modern Industrial World can no longer regard PROFIT as the end and aim of our endeavour. SERVICE to the community henceforth must be our prime endeavour. If we inscribe SERVICE upon our banner we know that we can trust the intelligent majority of our countrymen to see that justice is done to us as by us. And they on their part will recognise as true co-operators to the same end that it is their duty, as it is our duty, to the community to produce as much as it is possible to produce, working together with a will, and sharing the products of our united efforts according to the respective measure of the contribution each of us has made. We shall then have ONE GREAT NATIONAL PARTY IN AUSTRALIA, and we shall know then how to deal out their desserts to the disloyalist and sectarian traitor and Bolshevik in our midst. No longer shall a treacherous alien institution be permitted to sow the seeds of discord within our midst and preach disloyalty to the State in peace as in war. Then and not till then we shall have free industries, free men, and a free Australia. To this end let us dedicate our lives, and by so doing make Australia a fit country for the returned men who have risked their lives for us, for our Empire and for Civilisation.

4.20 The Workers' Educational Association

In the W.E.A., liberal intellectuals tried to 'educate' the working-class leaders to accept responsibility for increasing the 'efficiency' of capitalist production. Note how the working *class* is blamed for the apparent dead-end of the reformist strategy, as well as for its proletarian resistance to that dead-end.

Source: Meredith Atkinson (ed.), *Trade Unionism in Australia*: *Report of a Conference held in June 1915 under the auspices of the Workers' Educational Association of New South Wales*, Burrows & Co., Newtown, N.S.W., pp. 11–17.

The group of papers embodied in this report does not claim to present a complete account of Trade Unionism in Australia. They were written by men of great experience in the world of economics and industry, but differing widely in training, and writing without any attempt at collusion or conference prior to the actual reading of the papers. It is remarkable, therefore, how clearly can be traced, through most of the papers, certain leading ideas which give them some claim to incorporation in one book under a comprehensive title. To bring this fact into high relief we place below a series of extracts exhibiting this central idea.

"... The Wages Board system has already produced a race of union secretaries who are little more than expert advocates of the case for their members before boards or courts. It seems not unfair to say that these men have been driven to become officials instead of leaders. Their life of specialised routine unfits them for the spacious vision and keen study absolutely essential to right leadership. Nor is there much consolation to be found in turning for leaders to the sphere of politics. The very success and high concentration that has brought decisive victories to Labour at the polls has created a form and spirit of government alien to the production of the best type of leader.

"... In the last ten years especially the workers have learned to lean upon the State to a degree altogether subversive of the finer spirit of positive effort and social idealism which characterised the earlier history of the Labour Movement. The Australian worker has become more or less content to shout orders to his Parliamentary employees, and to sit and wait for pleasing results. ...

"The main difficulty to be emphasised, as already suggested, is the increasing impatience of the Australian worker with anything like discipline from above, a characteristic which does him credit in his struggle to better his condition, but one which, if carried forward into the sphere of co-operation, would result in certain failure." (M. Atkinson) ...

"So it is claimed higher wages and standards of living and shorter hours of work have resulted in social progress, and this ultimately reacts upon efficiency. There is much truth in this contention, but the results claimed have been indirect and unintended ... and the fact still remains that Unionism has not seriously considered the question of efficiency. ...

"Working men have shown that they are capable of a high degree of organisation for special purposes. Their weakness to-day it seems to me is that their ideals and purposes have not developed with the times. My conviction is that their traditional aims must be enlarged so as to include the hundred and one social problems on the solution of which further progress and Welfare depend. This enlargement means much more than putting planks, often unseasoned, into a platform. It means a resolute determination to study and learn and discuss, and a willingness to co-operate with every other group of thinking and sincere men. Only by so doing, it appears to me, can the movement retain the creative force and idealism it once possessed." (Prof. R. F. Irvine) ...

"Apathy and easy-going carelessness has been the curse of the workers. It would seem as if their economic dependency on some other man for the right to work had sapped and dried their initiative. ... Wage slavery will continue, unemployment will increase, cost of living keep on rising, and a host of other self-evident evils associated therewith, multiply themselves, if the trades unions fail to get out of the old rut and tackle the admittedly tremendous problem. ...

"We must not expect too much from even a Labor Parliament. Much has been accomplished and there will be advance, and inevitably some mistakes but that, after all, is what a sane mind expects of all human actions." (W. G. Spence) ...

"The workers are tame, fat, scant of breath, and scant of moral and intellectual ideals. I am not a candidate for Parliament, so I can afford to speak the truth, and there is no one who needs the truth from one who believes in them more than the Australian workers. I have frequently been shocked at the backbiting and recrimination the disloyalty and lack of solidarity displayed. ...

"... The industrial legislation in Australia involves no revolutionary change in the relation of employer and employee. It recognises the wage system, and perpetuates it. It checks any attempt to upset it. ... This summary of this phase of Australian development presents a characteristic incident in social evolution. First, a rapid advance, overcoming the obvious barriers to progress, and then a deadlock, in which further progress seems difficult, if not impossible, and we are inclined to question the advance that has been made. The real truth is, that further advance demands qualities in the human beings involved of an altogether higher order, and until these are forthcoming advance is impossible. This seems to be just the position in Australia. We have gone as far as legislation and mechanical means can take us. We have our higher wages, our increased comfort and the like; but we have not inaugurated a new order. We still have the crude antithesis between capitalist and proletariat. We have not seen the appearance of a higher order of being but still the mass, with its narrow outlook, its somewhat low aims, and its disorganisation. The complete lack of any intellectual grasp of the difficulties of the problem, and of any alternative methods to meet the situation, is conspicuous. Hope for the future depends upon new ideas and more refined methods. We may get Labour Governments in power, but without a revolution in the spirit of the worker, and a higher quality of his mentality there will not be real progress." (Mr. F. W. Eggleston) ...

The leading points in these extracts stand out with telling clearness, and are worthy of enumeration and some little discussion.

(1) It is generally agreed that Trade Unionism in Australia, and its political expression, the Labour Party, has reached the end of a great phase in its programme of development. It is suffering chiefly from a lack of ideas. ...

(2) The workers have learnt to rely far too much upon Parliamentary effort alone. This has produced two main effects:— (a) A belief that things economic are easy to understand, and easy to change; (b) inevitable disappointment in the failure of Labour Governments to make a new heaven and a new earth. The workers have not yet learnt that something more than abuse and criticism of their elected representatives is necessary to solve the problem of Labour.

(3) The questions of Labour and Capital are still being treated in the old-fashioned, traditional ways. The worker is still content to fight the capitalist with all his might without ever seeking to analyse the complexities of commerce, or ever thinking that they have any vital relation to him. There is a most pressing need of study by the worker of economic problems that seem at first sight to carry in them nothing of interest to him. Labour leaders themselves have learned, by a short experience of the responsibilities of government, how entirely necessary is such close study.

(4) Very few workers realise that their own movement is teeming with facts and processes not yet analysed, the study of which is of incalculable value to themselves and the race. ...

(5) The self-complacency of the Australian workers greatly retards their intellectual progress. Though the achievements of their movement are very remarkable, the present barrenness of ideas threatens it with a stagnation worse than defeat. They must learn to assess alike the realities and the illusions of progress, and to reinterpret progress constantly in the light of ever-changing situations.

... We must avoid the peril of mistaking advanced social legislation for advanced social efficiency. The latter can only be attained by the intensive cultivation of the citizen-mind, a slow and discouraging process but the only one that will ensure the continuous ferment of thought and life, without which real progress is impossible.

5 The Industrial Ruling Class, 1930–1975

By the 1920s the social dynamic of colonial capitalism had been played out, a profound political and economic deadlock had been reached. Of those who understood this at the time, probably most expected it to be broken by a crisis leading to socialism. What occurred instead was a crisis, more exactly a succession of crises, which catalysed sweeping changes in the ruling class and enabled it to establish hegemony on a new economic and political basis. This change operated at many levels: the construction of a welfare state, the massive expansion of suburban housing, the advent of the motor car and mass retailing; but above all, it centred on a restructuring of the economy around manufacturing. Blast-furnaces rather than flocks became economically and politically decisive; engineers and technocrats such as Essington Lewis moved into the leadership of the ruling class; ironworkers and metalworkers became the storm-centres of organised labour.

The reasons for the industrialisation of what had once been a reasonably successful primary exporting and mercantile economy are of course complex. Some are matters of changes in technology (electrification most notably), the social roots of which are remote; but the principal structural reasons are in the class deadlock itself. The possibilities of capital accumulation in the fringe-imperial economy were becoming exhausted; from the 1890s to the 1930s there was no substantial rise in living standards to persuade the working class that capitalism actually delivered prosperity. The political labour movement was blocked but still menacing, the parliamentary deadlock driving militants even farther to the left; and the convulsions of international capitalism, notably the 1914–18 war and the 1929–33 depression, ripped through the frail defences of a dependent economy. Other options were blocked; the Australian ruling class had to industrialise. It did so in several spasms, gradually gaining in strength and co-ordination (with increasingly conscious direction of the business by the state), until in the late 1930s it took off in a sustained industrial boom that lasted for the next generation and created the context of contemporary life.

The Rise of Industrial Capital, 1900–1950

'Industrialisation' meant a great deal more than putting some serrated roofs in suburban skylines. It involves changes in the corporate system and the organisation of capital; changes in the labour process and the structure of power in business; and changes in the general organisation of the economy, including circulation and the economic role of the state. Of course, it did not start from nothing. Small-scale manufacturing had long been needed to feed the cities' appetite for bricks, clothes and processed foods; in the decade 1910–20, an average of 18 per cent of the paid workforce was employed in manufacturing. Some of the companies involved were already large, such as C.S.R. with a capital of £2 million at the turn of the century; others were created by merger in the palmy days of the trust movement, such as British Tobacco (1903–4) and Carlton and United Breweries (1907); while manufacturers were already showing signs of organisation in their Chambers of Manufactures and in trade journals such as the *Australasian Manufacturer* (1916). But the decisive steps that were to transform the Australian economy were not simple extensions of these beginnings. In some respects, they involved sharp discontinuities; and here the role of the state and the political balance of class forces becomes particularly clear.

Launching heavy industry in the context of twentieth-century technology, especially under competition from imports, required heavy capital outlays. B.H.P.'s Newcastle blast-furnaces *began* with a workforce of 1450 men, and even with government assistance and the financial strength of 'The Proprietary', they struggled for a decade before becoming profitable. B.H.P.'s main rival, Hoskins of Lithgow, had to bring in British capital to form Australian Iron and Steel and start new steelworks at Port Kembla in 1928, and then were promptly ruined by the depression. For a time, the labour movement toyed with a strategy of growth made possible by the political success of reformism, using its control of the state to form capital and establish state-owned heavy industry. The New South Wales Labor government got as far as introducing a State Iron Works Bill in 1912. But the backing for such ventures was slight; the N.S.W. government withdrew under pressure from B.H.P., and when the federal Labor government became involved in metal projects as the war cut off international trade, it was as an ally of the Baillieu group, not a rival. With only a little difficulty, then, private capital shook off the only immediate alternative to capitalist industrialisation. The new industries were launched by the existing corporate rich and took the traditional corporate form.

At the start, it was Melbourne mining capital that was decisive, launching the two major empires in heavy industry that emerged between the wars. B.H.P. shifted from silver-lead mining to steelmaking as its Broken Hill mine became exhausted. It already held iron-ore leases; it now moved into shipping to transport the ore, coal-mining to supply its blast-furnaces, and set up various subsidiaries and joint ventures with British firms, such as wire-rope works, to process the steel. By wage-cuts and lock-outs, it drove its own wage costs down; by well-timed price-cutting, it drove its Port Kembla rival to the wall and in 1935 absorbed it. In twenty years, the company built a vertically integrated monopoly in the most basic of modern industries. The strategy was carried through by Essington Lewis, its general manager from 1921, and Harold Darling, its chairman from 1922, both sons of South Australian merchants. Lewis, a tough and taciturn man who had trained as an engineer, became the most powerful businessman in the country and arguably the most important figure in twentieth-century Australian history. He personified a new drive for technology and precision in combination with reactionary social attitudes, hostility to unions and a determination to promote accumulation and growth regardless of social cost. In that, he was impressively successful.[1]

The manufacturing enterprises of Collins House were also based on mining profits. Around 1905, a group of brokers and financiers operating in Melbourne, Adelaide and London bought into the mines at the ends of the

Broken Hill lode and began to finance a new process for the recovery of zinc. The mines proved to be richer than B.H.P.'s own, and the flotation process, in the modest words of one of the Baillieu group, 'earned a wonderful stream of dividends'. From this, the group moved into base-metal refining, taking over the Port Pirie smelters from B.H.P., setting up Electrolytic Zinc (1916) in Tasmania to use state-supplied hydro-electric power in a new American technique, and in alliance with Mount Morgan interests setting up Metal Manufactures (1916) in Port Kembla to refine and make copper products. In due course the group moved into other industries, the most notable being its establishment of Associated Pulp and Paper Mills (1936) with a local monopoly of the production of fine paper. This was an empire of a different kind from the tightly integrated structure of B.H.P. Its central figure was the durable financier and politician W.L. Baillieu; it employed technologists but was not dependent on them, and was integrated mainly by common ownership rather than interlocking management. The earlier companies were in effect used as holding companies for the later ones. To some extent, Collins House followed B.H.P.'s drive towards vertical integration; but the more significant feature of the group's organisation was that it became an international operation, with several of its leading members living in London and operating on the international metal and capital markets. This achieved an integration of Australian and world capitalism of a different kind from the traditional one institutionalised in the Anglo–Australian banks and British-owned pastoral companies and mines.[2]

Though it did not immediately create new fortunes, the emergence of Australian-based heavy industry irreversibly changed the conditions in which fortunes could be made by other entrepreneurs. Firms supplying specialised materials and services were now able to grow on a completely new scale; and through the cut-throat conditions of the 1920s and 1930s, a number scrambled up to a size that enabled them to boom and diversify after the depression. The motor industry illustrates the process well. American manufacturers moved inside the Hughes tariff barrier in the 1920s: Ford set up Victorian plants in 1925 to assemble chassis and build bodies, and within a year employed 1000 workers; General Motors set up its first chassis assembly plants in 1926, and in 1931 took over its local supplier of bodies, Holden's. With heavy political encouragement, both became involved after the war in local manufacture of complete (or nearly complete, to be precise) cars. Around them, other things began to move. Beaurepaire's, a family tyre-retreading business, gave birth in 1933 to the Olympic Tyre and Rubber Co., in order to manufacture its own tyres; during the war, the group began producing insulated electric cables; and after the war expanded into a diverse manufacturing empire. The Auto Grinding Co., a two-man reconditioning business in the early 1920s, had 500 employees when floated as a public company called Repco in 1937; with a huge growth in the 1950s and 1960s, it is now an employer of more than 10 000 workers. While these grew to be giants, a mass of smaller enterprises proliferated: specialised parts manufacturers, retailers, repairers. By the 1950s this complex of companies,

Right: The new ruling-class leadership in the context of the old. Two pastoralists, a solicitor, a merchant, a mining engineer and a manufacturer—the board of B.H.P. on the eve of achieving monopoly in the steel industry.
Source: *The B.H.P. Review*, Jubilee Number, June 1935, p. 152.

closely interlocked by function, contract and licensing, though not by common ownership, had become the most important industrial grouping in the country.[3]

Because of this pattern of growth industrialisation did not lead to a markedly more centralised corporate structure. The major industries characteristically were dominated by oligopolistic companies, or monopolies created after the healthy example of the beer and cigarette makers. Glass and chemical firms in the different states merged into national combines (Australian Glass Manufacturers, later A.C.I., 1922; Drug Houses of Australia, 1929), as did paper men (Australian Paper Manufacturers, 1926). In the 1920s, about 6 per cent of establishments accounted for 50 per cent of the workers in secondary industry. But the spawning of new companies and plants nearly kept pace with the mergers and growth of the heavies, so the level of concentration rose only slightly over the years of industrialisation. There was no marked shift, that is, to monopoly as the form of corporate organisation, which might be taken to mark the advent of 'monopoly capitalism'; though there were certainly new kinds of dependence on the major corporations, illustrated by the motor trade.

There was also a clear shift of economic activity into the new sectors. Not so much the workforce: manufacturing absorbed 18 per cent of the paid workforce in the decade from 1910, 20 per cent in the 1920s, and a little over 25 per cent in the later 1930s and thereafter—there was spectacular expansion, of course, in such places as Newcastle and Wollongong, but the manufacturing workforce as a whole did not grow very much faster than the rest of the economy. Manufacturing output did. It accounted for about 16 per cent of gross national product in the 1920s, 18 per cent in the 1930s, and 30 per cent by the 1960s (a figure comparable to countries such as the United States). Obviously, the capital intensiveness and labour productivity of manufacturing was rising over this period; it can be estimated to have doubled since the period before the First World War.[4]

What this meant, among other things, was changes in the labour process. Though the actual details have been very little studied, the general outlines are evident. The plants of the new industries were factories, properly so called, with hundreds of men and women labouring together under the dominance of the machine. The close co-ordination of masses of workers was required by the rhythm of production from blast-furnaces and rolling-mills in the metal industries, and by the production-line techniques that were introduced in the 1920s by motor-body manufacturers. This demanded a new routine and regularity in the actual conduct of work; industrialisation in Australia, as everywhere else, demanded an offensive against the freer pre-industrial work habits. One notes, for instance, six o'clock closing of hotels being introduced in the interest of national efficiency during the First World War. Within the enterprise, it required greater managerial control of the work process. This was almost caricatured by Essington Lewis, prowling round his plants with pockets crammed with technical notes, firing men on the spot for 'slacking', finally retiring from the office with a text on the wall reading: 'I Am Work.' But the matter was much more serious than personal idiosyncrasy. Management control of the new labour processes meant breaking the power of craftsmen and their unions: so it was not by accident, and not purely for immediate profit considerations, that B.H.P. set out to break the Ironworkers' union in 1917, that un-unionised women were welcomed into the new electrical manufacturing industries; nor was it from pure sexism that the unions often opposed the classification of work as capable of being done by women, for in a sexist society that meant basically unskilled, a confession of the degradation of formerly skilled work.

The labour process in manufacturing industry. Workers assembling Wirraway parts during the Second World War.
Source: C. Meeking (ed.), *Pictorial History of Australia at War, 1939–45*, Canberra, 1958, vol. 2, p. 133.

Changes in the environment of work accompanied changes in the labour process. The sheer size of plants multiplied, the larger ones sprawling across tens of acres in hump-backed sheds, filled with the din of packed tyre-moulding, wire-twisting, tin-pressing or glass-moulding machines. Even the medical profession began to wonder about the physical effects of constant, repetitious labour in such circumstances (though characteristically, the fears were mostly for its effects on the child-bearing capacity of female workers). The psychological effects also go deep. Under conditions of mass production, the worker was patently, overwhelmingly, someone else's tool. Craftsmen might cling to their separate unions and their pay margins, but even they were absorbed in the authority structure of the factory. It is profoundly interesting to see how the heroic figure of the idealised labourer, so common in the turn-of-the-century union and radical press, disappeared as manufacturing advanced. The novelist Kylie Tennant caught the symbolic significance of this, opening her novel about social change in inner Sydney with a description of the traditional procession in which groups of unionists marched in working gear with floats illustrating their trades:

> The change in Foveaux, that momentous slow change that was to creep over it, had just begun in 1912. Perhaps the last time Foveaux came out in all its old glory was the day of the Eight-Hour Day Procession.

After that came war, development and loss of confidence. Fifty years later, it was the idealised manager and technologist who dominated the image of industry.

Another change in imagery showed the social distance within enterprises that opened up with advanced technology and large scale under capitalist relations. The managers separated themselves socially, and often physically, from these work-places. B.H.P. had its head office in Melbourne, despite the fact that none of its steelmaking was carried on within four hundred miles; Collins House, a square, brown office building in Collins Street, was the centre of the whole Baillieu mining and industrial complex. In photographs of nineteenth-century manufactories, we typically see the workforce drawn up, staring at the camera, with the proprietors in the centre of the group, distinguished by coats, collars and top hats. Symbolically, the separation has become complete. Big businesses' photographs of their factories now show the workers working, or the managers on inspection, but never the two as a group.[5]

Industrial technology and the new needs for planning, co-ordination and control meant a reorganisation of power in business at the top as well as on the shop floor. Again this has been little studied, but one can see the outlines of a new group of technocrats who had risen into the top leadership of the ruling class: men like Lewis of B.H.P., 'Gunboat' Smith of Australian Glass Manufacturers and Herbert Gepp of Electrolytic Zinc, whose position was based on technical knowledge and skill in organisational politics rather than personal or family capital. Keith Murdoch, a journalist who between the wars built a new corporate empire in the media (the Herald and Weekly Times), is another man of this style, who thrived on the mass publicity needs of a mass-production economy. As these men rose, some of the older business families began to be displaced. The process is well illustrated by the very wealthy Grimwade family in Melbourne, whose fortune grew out of a wholesale drug and bottle manufacturing business of the late colonial period. As their enterprise grew in scale and technical complexity in the early twentieth century, they reorganised the family partnerships as family-owned companies. Between the wars, under pressures of technical change and foreign competition, these companies were merged into national monopoly combines—Australian Glass Manufacturers, Drug Houses of Australia, and the oxygen business into Commonwealth Industrial Gases. As professional managers became more dominant in these combines, the Grimwades became increasingly rentiers, a leisured upper-class group living off the profits of share ownership.

Paradoxically, this process was accompanied by a new wave of family capitalism, working through the new corporate structure. Many of the new companies were based on family firms; and as they were incorporated and grew, such families as the Beaurepaires, Coles, and Myers in Melbourne, and the engineering Perrys in Adelaide, retained a good deal of operating control and a large slice of the ownership. Continuities were also maintained in the process of capital-raising, where the dependence of many of the new men on the old became apparent. Capital was raised for the expansion of a small business through the existing capital market, typically through a stockbroker, who thus became an important member of the entrepreneurial group. Stockbrokers placing shares naturally turned to their existing customers, thus diffusing ownership of the rising industries among the existing class of owners, while this class was expanded by the new entrepreneurs. (Olympic's twenty-seven shareholders at its flotation in 1933 included one R. G Menzies.) When Frank Beaurepaire went into politics, it was in the conservative framework; similarly with Frank Perry in South Australia, who became a prominent figure in the Liberal and Country League inside and outside parliament.[6]

Nevertheless, political change was implicit. It is nicely symbolised by Arthur Coles of the Melbourne chain-store family. After being Lord Mayor of Melbourne, he was elected to federal parliament; and in 1941 was one of the independents who tipped Fadden out and brought Curtin in, an action that helped catalyse a drastic political reorganisation of the ruling class. When this reorganisation occurred, it was partly on the basis of the extent to which the state had been drawn into the new industries. Manufacturing investment found a great deal of sympathy from governments regardless of party: federal Labor governments saw it as a strategic resource and a necessary part of 'development', state Labor governments saw it as a way of creating or guaranteeing jobs, however much they might resent the same companies' industrial relations policies. State governments provided land and power, federal governments provided tariff protection and at times negotiated export markets. The state also became a vital market for the new industries, as public investment rose even above the high levels of the nineteenth century. The Collins House companies sold their zinc to the British government under very profitable long-term contracts, and sold their copper products to the expanding electricity grids and telecommunications systems of Australian governments. During the Second World War, most of the manufacturing complex that went over to war production worked on a 'cost-plus' (that is, guaranteed profit) basis for the federal government, and that government reciprocally stepped in to organise war production and regulate profits—appointing as director of the national industrial effort one Essington Lewis.

But it was the South Australian government that went furthest in designing a whole system of state support for manufacturing. Urbanised but dependent on primary industries, South Australia had been ravaged by the depression. In 1935 a group of businessmen and civil servants led by the Auditor-General J. W. Wainwright, devised a policy of regional industrialisation, which they sold to the conservative state government. It was in clear contrast with the earlier tentative moves towards state-based industrialisation in New South Wales, using state power not to form capital directly, but to create local conditions that would attract manufacturing investment from outside companies by—in effect—guaranteeing profitability. Company tax and freight charges were lowered, cheap land, electricity and water were provided; and most strikingly of all, labour costs were directly lowered by government provision of cheap housing for the workers, price control, and the avoidance of strikes by a co-operative union movement. With this package, some adroit blackmail (B.H.P.'s ore leases were renewed in exchange for a promise to build South Australian steelworks), and vigorous salesmanship to eastern and overseas capitalists by successive premiers, Butler and Playford, a diversified manufacturing sector was built up in Adelaide and Whyalla.[7]

The Working Class and Industrialisation, 1920–1950

Though we tend to think of 'industrialisation' as something that happened to the whole economy, it was always something that happened in a specific place, and often had a strong and immediate impact on its environment. Newcastle had been a coal port, threatened with decline as the Maitland coalfield developed; B.H.P. started there with nearly 1500 workers and poured in capital to get economies of scale, its workforce rising to about 5000 in 1935. The population of Newcastle more than doubled in the same twenty years. Metal Manufactures and another copper company began the transformation of Port Kembla at the time of the First World War; the Hoskins' iron-works in the 1920s continued it, and when B.H.P. directed its main capital flow there from the late 1930s, Wollongong–Port Kembla became an industrial city. Whyalla's population trebled in three years as a blast-furnace and shipyards were established around 1940; massive paper mills at Burnie in Tasmania followed the foundation of A.P.P.M. Under the hands of B.H.P. and Collins House, industrial towns sprang up in the Australian countryside, which before (apart from Lithgow and Port Pirie) had known only mining and railway towns as working-class settlements. The local elites that had run towns such as Wollongong were brushed aside; they often reacted with considerable hostility, but did not carry the weight, in the new configuration of Australian capitalism, to be more than a small nuisance to industrial capital.

Most of the industrial expansion, however, was near the main markets and labour pools, that is, in the existing cities. Room was found for it by two methods. The first was an assault on the inner suburbs, particularly working-class suburbs where land was fairly cheap and wooden houses easy to demolish. Factories and workshops in increasing numbers were squeezed into the arcs of suburbs around the south and west of Sydney and the north and west of Melbourne, into the north-west of Adelaide and the river-flats of Brisbane. Big industry still depended on rail and sea transport, but the truck traffic it generated, and the demolitions and rebuilding, began a process of carving up the inner suburbs that reached critical levels in the 1950s.

Other industries clustered along lines of transport just outside the suburbs, where land could be bought at semi-rural prices and plants could spread themselves. Some gleams of new-town planning ideas seem to have been involved. Though some city-fringe plants, like the Electrolytic Zinc works at Risdon near Hobart, were blots on settings of great natural beauty, others, such as British Tobacco's 'Raleigh Park' development at Kensington in Sydney, achieved a modest grace. In some fringe areas, notably Bankstown, a whole complex of new plants grew up, and after the Second World War the main thrust of industrial development was into areas like this. The workforce followed, and the fringe sites were steadily swallowed by suburban expansion, driving up land prices again. New leaps were made to cheap land at such places as Liverpool, Dandenong and Elizabeth, with governments generously supplying much of the housing. Private building filled in the gaps, and the car-based conurbations of the 1950s and 1960s were produced.[8]

Kylie Tennant's 'momentous slow change' was not just a loss of community in the inner suburbs. Though no one seems to have realised it until it was half completed, what was happening was a remaking of the working class as a whole. A colony of settlement, prosperous on primary exports though highly urbanised, Australia had developed a clearly defined capitalist class structure before being industrialised. If our argument is correct, industrialisation occurred partly because of the class struggle so produced, which forced capitalist development along a new path. The working class increasingly became an industrial proletariat; but within a situation where it already had considerable defensive strength; and at a stage in history where technology and (post-war) the massive inflow of capital could sustain industrial growth without a sustained pressure on working-class incomes. The transformation of work habits, neighbourhoods, and conditions of everyday life thus occurred in a very different context from the industrialisation of England (with which comparisons were usually made) or even the United States. This altered sequence is crucial in explaining the relative peacefulness of the process in Australia, and the marked economism of the working-class responses that did occur.

The workforce of the industrial plants between the wars was probably mostly native-born, certainly mostly male. Some of the British immigrants of the 1900s and 1920s no doubt went into factories, but the heavy migrant concentrations in industry came much later. Port Kembla drew surplus labour—unemployed men—down from Sydney; in fact, until the 1940s there was always a substantial reserve of unemployed in the country. Heavy industry was male. Most machinery still demanded strength and toughness, universally supposed to be male properties; the skills of machine making and repairing were taught in apprenticeships and trade courses that were closed to women. About 80 per cent of all factory workers were men. But the 20 per cent was significant, and the figure was far higher in a few industries: the clothing trades, traditionally a women's field; electrical manufacturing, relatively clean and physically light. Women were also increasingly used in clerical work as that became more of a routine mass occupation, with the growing scale of companies and government departments and the multiplication of administration and record-keeping. Despite the low wages compared to men's, young women (older women being mostly married and out of the paid workforce) preferred the freedom these jobs gave them to the long hours and close supervision characteristic of domestic service. Women's jobs thus reflected the rationalisation of the economy and the trend away from preindustrial labour patterns, without for the most part being directly implicated in heavy industry.[9]

Standards of living as the economists measure them—that is, average incomes in real terms—rose slowly and inconsistently between the wars: in

1935 the figure was about what it had been in 1920. The physical conditions of life in the inner suburbs deteriorated, with the impact of factories and the decay of houses let by landlords who would not or could not pay for repairs. Around some of the new industrial plants there was little housing at all; at Port Kembla, for instance, in the 1930s single men and families lived in humpies and tents, A.I. & S. declining to interest itself in such matters, as long as the workers still clamoured for jobs. Life in such settings was for most people a battle with the system, a matter of scrapes and lurks, cutting corners and making shift. Trots, dogs, football and boxing gave an outlet to the men, with a vigorous growth of gambling and small-time crime around them. It was mostly the women who kept up the informal networks of co-operation and friendship on which working-class families relied heavily at times of unemployment, separation or death. The unions themselves came to rely on this strength, as a series of lock-outs and strikes in coal-mining demonstrated: the women of the mining settlements organised food, household necessities and other services during the disputes, turned out for demonstrations against blacklegs, and from the late 1930s ran a highly successful women's auxiliary to the Miners' Federation. Attempts to expand such formal organisation beyond the close-knit mining settlements were unsuccessful; but it is clear from retrospective interviews, and much of the social-realist literature of the 1930s and 1940s, that the domestic skills and informal networks of women were crucial components of working-class strength.[10]

Two main forms of working-class mobilisation already existed: the unions and the Labor Party. Union membership had grown rapidly in the first two decades of the century, levelling off at about one-third of the workforce in the 1920s. It was hard hit by the depression, the union movement practically disintegrating in some industrial centres in the trough; but recovered with the tightening labour market in the late 1930s and an extension of unionism among white-collar employees, reaching a new peak of about half the workforce in the 1950s. The curve of Labor Party support had risen much earlier, outstripping its union base: in 1910, when Fisher won a federal election with 660 000 votes (50 per cent of the total) there were only 300 000 unionists in the country (17 per cent of the workforce). The climacteric of the party's mass appeal had already been reached; since then, the Labor vote has normally oscillated between 40 per cent and 50 per cent in both state and federal elections. The federal party has never won more than 53 per cent of the vote in general elections (the level it reached in 1943), and in only one state election has the total Labor vote gone over 60 per cent (Tasmania in 1941).

The divergence of these two curves says a lot. The early Labor Party was predominantly working-class (never exclusively so), but not the party of an industrial working class. The main form that the conscious mobilisation of industrial workers took, as their numbers and power grew, was economic: the expansion and consolidation of their unions. This was more than economism, for unions became vehicles of political consciousness to a large extent; conversely, the main waves of socialist activity, around 1920 and again in the 1940s, had a strongly syndicalist character. The Labor Party, which picked up a broader popular radicalism, was in a strategic deadlock with the conservative parties in parliament from the time of the First World War. It was unable to expand; but equally it was irreducible, strongly entrenched in working-class communities and closely interlocked with major

Figure 5.1 Unionisation and the Labor vote, 1901–72

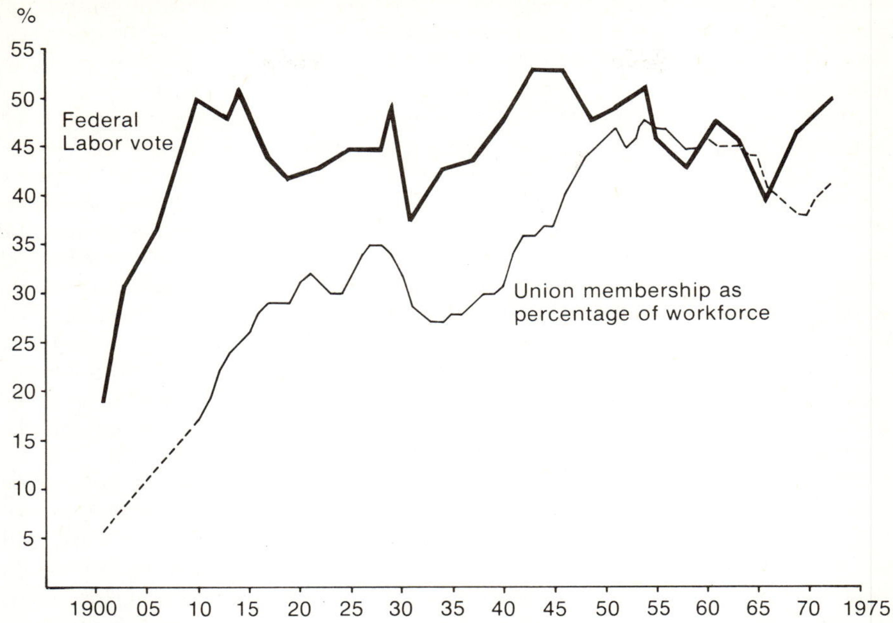

Note: The unionisation figures for the final decade are estimates, adjusted for comparability from statistics calculated on a different base. Voting figures are national percentages in House of Representatives elections.

unions. As the working class changed beneath it, the politics of the change revolved around the fact of this party-in-being: whether it could be changed in decisive ways, or smashed by a new force based in the industrial unions—or neither.

There is in fact no clear break that marks a shift of the focus of industrial class conflict into the manufacturing sphere. B.H.P. was heavily embroiled with its workers almost as soon as the Newcastle plant opened, trying to create a company union to replace the Ironworkers and locking the men out in 1922; but the company already had a reputation for militancy from its silver-mining days, and these struggles followed closely the massive transport and mining strikes of the war decade in Brisbane, Sydney and Broken Hill. The Hoskins works at Lithgow was equally turbulent. It was established industries—mining, transport and timber-getting—that were the scenes of the most bitter, and sometimes bloody, clashes before the depression: on the Fremantle wharves in 1919, and on the northern New South Wales coalfield in 1929, working men were killed in clashes with the police. Perhaps the best marker is the most famous strike of the 1930s, the demonstration at Port Kembla against the export of iron to Japan that earned Menzies (who tried to settle it on behalf of B.H.P.) the title of 'Pig-Iron Bob'—a strike over industrial exports, though it was waterfront rather than industrial workers who took the action. By the 1940s, manufacturing had clearly become the key to industrial class conflict. The hard-fought metal trades dispute of 1946–47 in Victoria was the crucial post-war test of strength with employers.

When won by the Engineers and Ironworkers, it established rates and conditions that soon flowed on to other industries. In the following years, the metal trades became accepted as the major test cases in the arbitration system; and the focus of strike action shifted from mining and the waterfront to manufacturing.[11]

In the most basic form of working-class mobilisation, then, the period of industralisation saw, after initial disaster, a growth both relative and absolute, the involvement of new groups of employees and a shift of initiative towards the unions in heavy industry. This hardly amounted to a new form of class mobilisation. The craft unions, and some mass unions of manual workers, were by now established institutions, and their unbalanced structure—giants such as the A.W.U. jostling tiny craft unions and feuding with their Trades and Labour Councils—proved very difficult to change. To make unions into organs of industrial government, which was the strategy of the leading socialists in the period around 1920, required drastic reorganisation. In fact only modest changes, like the formation of a national union council (the A.C.T.U.) with little authority, were forthcoming; and the expanding white-collar unions mostly remained aloof even from that.

The big unions as they stood were significant power resources, especially when interlocked with the Labor Party. The A.W.U. leadership in Queensland under Theodore, McCormack and Fallon in the 1920s and 1930s, and in New South Wales under Bailey, practically constituted a labour establishment, almost independent of rank-and-file control, and with great power in the party machine. For union organisation to become the vehicle of a radical response to industrial capitalism required in the first instance a struggle against the controllers of this structure; and then, when a militant leadership was established in one union (as it was, for instance, in the Miners' Federation), to extend its influence in the umbrella organisations of the labour movement. Thus the history of grass-roots socialism in this period becomes the history of 'factional' conflict within labour organisations. Much of this revolved around the unions' relationship to the state. Arbitration and other forms of wage regulation had never been completely accepted, and a number of unions, or radical groups within unions, more and more explicitly rejected them as tools of ruling-class control. As the miners' paper *Common Cause* remarked, it is 'the legal machinery of the Capitalist Class and it holds the working class sheep tight while he is being shorn by the boss'. As the Labor Party was committed to arbitration and the defence of its awards, the system became the subject of clashes between militant unions and Labor governments, and among unions themselves. Conflicts over attitudes to the state and responses to industrialisation were gradually deepened by the failure of the movement as a whole to achieve a major redistribution of income.[12]

Neither changing nor outflanking the Labor Party proved easy. The reasons for its conservatism are usually sought in sell-outs by parliamentary leadership or the development of bureaucratic power-groups in the party machine. Both of these arguments have force; but both depend on something more. The more profound reason is in the way the party had become embedded in working-class communities. Its early involvement in municipal politics has been mentioned; between the wars, a firm control was established over the municipal government of many inner-city areas and industrial and mining towns. Union activists were prominent in this—at the time of the depression, for instance, there were four union officials who were mayors of Melbourne suburbs and two others who had recently been—and municipal politics was often a stepping-stone to parliament, so it integrated rather than divided the organised labour movement. Control of local councils in fact was the nearest the labour movement in most states came to sustained state power—and it was power of very restricted scope, except in a few isolated cases such as Broken Hill. With some ability to introduce schemes such as preference to unionists, relief measures in the depression, etc., Labor councillors could do little about the major influences on the local environment of working-class life: property values, rents and incomes, industrial development, the growth of motor traffic. Labor councils became notorious more for corruption than for class consciousness—scandals such as that in the Sydney City Council in 1927–28 gave splendid propaganda to conservative politicians, and petty graft made the labour movement stink to many whose only direct contact this was. Graft in turn was a key element in the construction of regional factions within the party machine (the most celebrated being that built by John Wren, a millionaire S.P. bookie and sporting promoter, in and around Collingwood) through which the power of property reached into the heart of the labour movement. It was almost unopposed except as 'corruption', for the movement generated no theory of working-class mobilisation for control of the local environment. Labor councillors were ideologically naked, and soon came to adopt ruling-class mores. Labor mayors at first often refused to wear robes and chains of office; but soon they were back, clinking and sweating, welcoming Royal tours with the best of them. The Labor mayor of Sydney went back to his robes in 1949, explaining that the dignity of the city overrode Labor practice: 'My decision is not a mere gesture', said Ald. O'Dea. 'It is a tribute to tradition, and to the high status of Sydney, the second city of the British Empire.'[13]

The parliamentary leadership of the Labor Party was hardly more able to articulate a class response to industrialisation. There were few industrial workers among them, for a start; they were often embroiled with the union militants for control over party platforms, it being conventional wisdom that moderate policies gave them better electoral chances; and in some ways, the ideological framework of parliamentary Labor aligned them with the industrial capitalists rather than against. Having taken over the colonial liberal rhetoric of progress and prosperity for all, Labor came to claim, in effect, that it was better at development than the conservatives. Where Labor held office, this could make it a party of local boosters, very strikingly so in the case of the Collier government in Western Australia in the 1920s and 1930s; where it was not directly responsible, developmentalism could still lead it to support rather than oppose such things as Playford's programme of subsidised capitalist development in South Australia, and the disembowelling of Australia's oldest working-class community to build a bridge for North Shore commuters in Sydney.

Though developmentalism constantly compromised responses to industrialisation, the pressures on the working class were still too severe to allow this to be the only response. One of the mainstreams in the Labor parties was a radical populism, and this was constantly recruited by the rise of union militants or radical activists from the crowded inner suburbs or working-class towns. One such was Eddie Ward from East Sydney, who rose in the machine as a protégé of radical unionists (notably Beasley and Garden) and became the Lang group's first standard-bearer in Canberra in the party crisis of

1931. Lang himself, a successful faction leader in the 1920s, is the classic example of Labor populism, with huge (but temporary) popularity, militant rhetoric, mild action and sharp anti-communism. As premier in the depression, he defined bankers and financiers as the enemies of the people. By postponing some interest payments he struck them with little more than a feather-duster, but immediately came up against the ruling class *en bloc*. He also came up against the federal Labor government, which called this 'repudiation' and overrode him — thus in effect defining the full rights of pri-

The working-class inner-urban environment in the 1940s.
Source: 'Tenements', in O. L. Ziegler (ed.), *Australian Photography 1947*, Sydney, n.d.

vate property as the boundaries within which the labour movement could act. But there were monetary radicals in the federal party too, notably Theodore and then Chifley, who led a drive to control the banks in the 1940s.[14]

This radicalism, however, was addressed to a business power structure that was already passing; it was incapable of handling the strategic problems of the integration of business and the state, and working-class militancy directed against the state. Its last important revival, 'post-war reconstruction' movement of the 1940s, was essentially defensive, intended to prevent a repetition of the recession, boom and depression that had followed the First World War. Its main ideas were captured, as will be seen, by a new conservative leadership. The Labor Party, throughout this period, remained without a plan for moving out to seize control of production as a whole, without a coherent response to the configuration of industrial and social life being produced by the Lewises, the Baillieus, and the Gepps, the Myers and the Murdochs. And a significant part of the working class, while continuing to vote for the Labor Party through this period, was clearly dissatisfied with the achievements of reformism. State employees were involved in some of the greatest industrial upheavals from the Victorian railway strike of 1903 to the Queensland one of 1948, and often enough it was Labor governments, and moderate union establishments, that they were directed against. Attempts by militants to use machinery such as party conferences to push the Labor leadership to the left became almost routine. And, most significantly, new attempts were made to organise outside the official Labor framework.

Socialism in this period had acquired a gritty industrial flavour from the militant unions that provided its chief strength, which distinguished it from the utopian and theoretical socialism of the generation before the First World War. On several occasions socialist ideas achieved considerable grass-roots support: in the I.W.W.'s campaign of 1914–16; the 'One Big Union' movement only a few years later, at the same time that a socialisation objective was forced by unions and radicals on the Labor Party; and the 'Socialisation units' in the N.S.W. Labor Party in 1930–33, first supported, and then smashed, by Garden and Lang. In the 1940s socialism appears to have had its widest support ever (at the same time, be it noted, as the peak of Labor Party electoral strength), gaining considerable influence outside the organised labour movement. Intellectuals such as the Melbourne Anglican priest Father Maynard declared their support; socialist alignments among artists and writers were common; and a local literature of socialist theory began to appear.[15] Above all, much of this activity was organised by, or around, a second working-class party, which now mounted a serious challenge to the Labor Party.

The Communist Party of Australia was launched in 1920 on a wave of enthusiasm for the Russian Revolution by a fractious group of unionists and socialists, who had considerable influence for some years in stiffening the militancy of unions and the Labor Party in New South Wales. Eventually excluded from the Labor Party, it struggled along as a small propaganda group until after being reorganised along Stalinist lines. Its members were distinguished for militancy in the depression, especially as organisers of the unemployed, and won support as the official labour movement fumbled and split. As the union movement revived in the late 1930s, many came to be leading officials with a reputation as tough negotiators. C.P.A. membership boomed in the middle 1940s, to a peak of 23 000. For a few years there was a significant second working-class party, which had swept up most of the industrial opposition to reformism into a disciplined organisation. It did not last long. After the war, a series of clashes with the Labor Party leadership, culminating in the Queensland railway strike of 1948 and the New South Wales miners' strike of 1949, split the movement. Both sides blundered, the Hanlon and Chifley governments overreacting with force, the Communists pushing their hard-left line beyond the capacity of unionists to sustain it; and both sides lost. Their struggles helped let in the Menzies government in 1949 and prepared the Labor Party split of 1954, while the Communist Party rapidly lost strength in the unions and went into a permanent decline.

The theory of the Communist Party was part home-grown and part imported, in a spirit of solidarity with the international working-class movement and subservience to Stalin. The significant threads in it were a rhetoric of class conflict, which it shared with the Labor Party Left; a stress on unions as the practical agent of working-class activity provided they had Communist leadership; and periodic attempts to organise, when the line of the international Communist movement allowed it, a coalition of 'the people' against 'the monopolists'. The chief monopolists identified were B.H.P. and the Baillieu group, which at least shows that the party was focusing on the process of industrialisation; but it groped for an analysis of it, and lacked any effective theory of class relations in a dependent and quasi-colonial environment. The thinking was still to a considerable extent populist, as these diagnostic words show; the differences from Labor Party militancy were not as great as the Communists themselves often wanted to believe.[16]

The Communist Party was broken partly by its own errors, these partly forced upon it by the Russian connection which represented socialist internationalism at the time; but also by counter-mobilisation from the Right, which mounted in intensity in the later 1940s—the catholic-based 'Movement' in the trade unions and the linked 'Industrial Groups' formed by the Labor Party; attacks from the press, mounting in its level of hysteria as the Cold War got under way; and intimidation by the state. The socialist summer of the 1940s in some ways had been a chancy combination of the onset of sustained industrialisation, a tight labour market, a military alliance with the Soviet Union, a period of disarray in conservative politics, and a wide-spread if vague desire for thorough social reconstruction after the experience of depression and war: all of which gave power or prestige to the Left.

This moment was, perhaps, the lowest ebb of hegemony since the convict era. In fact, throughout the period of industrialisation the ruling class was culturally on the defensive. Its power rested less on consent and more on force than it had done before, or was to do later. Strikes and lock-outs in this generation repeatedly turned into riots, police violence against unionists was widespread, and several times paramilitary organisations were formed against the Left, of which the best-known but by no means the only example was the New Guard mobilised against Lang in New South Wales. This having been said, it is necessary to recognise that cultural controls did still operate, and often powerfully. The miners' wives may have formed union auxiliaries and backed strikes; but many other women were influenced by an ideology of the family that defined anarchism, bolshevism and socialism as deadly threats to family life and womanhood. Enid Lyons, the wife of the leader of the Labor Party in Tasmania, got him to cancel his subscription to the *Australian Worker* so that their children would not absorb class hatred as they learned to read. Lyons had already dropped his socialism and republicanism before he went to Canberra, headed for a Labor cabinet post, the prime ministership in a conservative coalition, and a visit to the King's Silver Jubilee. He was only one of a whole series who split away to the right from the Labor parliamentary parties in political crises: the anti-pledge group of the 1890s, the conscriptionists of the First World War, the sound finance supporters of the depression, the anti-Communists of the 1950s, not to mention individuals who were absorbed into business (including Watson and Theodore). The movement called them 'rats' and blamed their defections on weakness of character, but the process is so pervasive that it must be more than that. All of these splits, in fact, occurred over issues where bourgeois ideology had some grip within the movement, though not a complete one: parliamentary custom, nationalism, and the sanctity of property. The long series of splits is not mysterious; it is one of the signs of a working-class struggle to free itself from an only partly understood and only partly opposed bourgeois hegemony. Industrialisation changed some of the terms of that struggle, but it was neither sudden enough, nor oppressive enough, to spark the widespread changes in working-class consciousness on which militant socialists depended for any part of their programme to work. When the conservative reaction came, it met some resistance, and made some strategic concessions to working-class economic power, but also had a swift and thorough political and cultural victory.[17]

The Political Crisis of the Ruling Class

The ruling-class political leadership came out of the 1910s shaken, but with definite cause for relief — the big expansion of Labor votes stopped, the Labor Party split, a mass conservative party created. Yet the position was not stable. Farmers were sufficiently restive to have formed separate parties; and political Labor came back — by 1926 it governed in five states, and in 1927 even carried Victoria, the citadel of Australian capitalism. The depression, though it did not immediately produce a revolutionary response, plunged the ruling class into a lengthy political crisis.

The mainstream conservatism of the inter-war years was socially extremely conventional, and markedly defensive. It stood for loyalty to the Empire and British traditions; strict law and order, including the absolute right of property-owners to control those they hired, and to fire them if they couldn't; it assumed that property and respectability conveyed a moral right to rule. It saw the Labor movement as a grasping, sectional, and sometimes subversive force: with union bosses regimenting the politicians and bribing the voters with promises of wealth they had not produced; with agitators and foreign influences causing unrest among otherwise decent workers. Within this rhetorical framework, of course, the conservative parties did more pragmatic things: selling some state enterprises set up by Labor, but equally establishing some of their own (notably in electricity supply); launching services such as the Council for Scientific and Industrial Research and a national broadcasting network; pouring money into urban development in the 1920s; and continuing the traditional policy of state-financed immigration. But the body of conservatives systematically resisted those kinds of reforms that might imply a reduction of their class income or of their class power: tax-financed welfare schemes, central control of the economy, and the extension of union authority or worker control in industry. In the depression crisis, they were largely able to impose these constraints on Labor governments, by control of upper houses, the power of banks, and in the final analysis, in New South Wales, by a constitutional coup against Lang.[18]

In important respects, this politics was simply an extension of the social morality of the urban bourgeoisie—maintenance of decorum, respect for property and rank, sexual and social repression. It was supported by household tradition, so far as one can judge the character of social relations inside bourgeois households in this period; and this survived such experiences as the depression, which was very unequal in its impact (contrary to the 'all in the same boat' rhetoric), if anything tending to heighten in bourgeois families a sense of their social distance from the unwashed and feckless. Orthodoxy was further supported by the weight of organised religion. There were a few lingering currents of Protestant radicalism, which surfaced in the 1940s and later again in the peace campaigns of the 1950s and 1960s; but the official stance of the churches was massively conservative on such issues as 'repudiation' in the depression. The alliance of the Catholic hierarchy with Labor over conscription never extended to socialism, militant unionism, or even fiscal radicalism; and in the later 1930s, a militant anti-communism emerged in Catholic circles in response to the Spanish Civil War. More mundane backing for conservatism was found in the peak organisations of business. 'Recent investigations show that the spirit of association is no less manifest in the case of employers than in the case of workers,' remarked the Commonwealth Statistician in 1922, as he began counting them: he found a stable membership of 50 000 to 60 000 in employer organisations (excluding farmers') for most of the next two decades.[19]

From such sources a class antagonism to Labor might be expected among property-owners and their dependents; and an ideological antagonism produced by the forces of nationalism and respectability could be expected from much wider groups. These responses still had to be articulated and organised, to form an effective political defence. From the middle of the first war to the middle of the second, a series of improvisations were tried, which temporarily held the line but successively collapsed. The details, like those of the factional politics of the labour movement, are too intricate to follow here; but as in that case, we can identify the underlying problems which were faced.

Basically, the political techniques of the colonial bourgeoisie were proving increasingly inadequate in the face of organised labour and an economy that was fluctuating out of control. The first important response was to create mass organisations on the model of the Labor Party. This was first successfully done in the Nationalist movement; but after the enthusiastic mobilisation of the war years the new party struggled, and remained dependent on money provided by big-business finance committees. This remained a standing point of conflict in the Nationalist and its successor parties, sometimes breaking out into open conflict: as in 1941 when Hollway, leader of the United Australia Party in Victoria, publicly denounced 'the financial moguls', 'this non-elected group of kingmakers', who controlled the finances of his party and sought to use it as a lever on the parliamentarians. With a fragile organisation, the leadership relied heavily on the reliably conservative press as an organising device. As we have noted, this was a period when the major newspaper groups were moving towards mass-marketing techniques, and their increasing importance as a channel of communication between the conservative leaders and their mass base gave the newspaper proprietors an unusual role. At a time when other big businessmen were withdrawing from direct involvement in politics, they were becoming structurally more important. Hence they were enabled to play at times a decisive role in the factional politics of conservatism, as when Murdoch promoted Lyons as a coalition leader in 1931, and when the Fairfaxes helped break Menzies' leadership ten years later.[20]

The problem of a mass base remained; and the strains of depression and war eventually tore this ramshackle structure apart. A business leadership, or a business-based leadership, was no longer widely trusted: for more than a generation the level of welfare had increased very little, and though capitalism survived the depression of the 1930s, it was widely believed that it would not survive another. The stand-pat conservatism of the conventional was increasingly under strain with the socialist attack on property, structural changes in the economy, and the evident retreat of British imperial power; and it was incapable of producing a theory of the role of the state that was adequate to the new situation. In the 1940s a general fragmentation of conservative organisations occurred, more drastic than ever before. Labor came to office federally and swept the 1943 election; the upsurge of socialism promised even worse to come.

The revival that occurred in the space of a few years was dependent on the structural changes that have already been outlined, but is also a tribute to the organising abilities of a small group of politicians and businessmen, and the depth of the fear inspired in property-owners by working-class strength in the 1940s. In effect a major ruling-class political mobilisation occurred, consciously planned and directed by a revived leadership and supplied with a new ideology.

This mobilisation marked the arrival of a new cadre of political leaders; more than that, a new type of political leadership. A turnabout on the role of the state required a political leadership sufficiently independent to carry through a strategy at odds with the conventional wisdom of business. The groundwork for this had been laid by the growth of mass conservative parties, however unstable, and by the expansion of the state organisations that had been quickened by war and Labor. It was a long and slow transition from the colonial parliaments, where leading businessmen and leading politicians were often the same men; the inter-war 'finance committees' and the careers of such men as Bruce and Massy Greene (who were leading figures in both spheres, but at different stages of their careers) were transtitional forms. Top political management was now moved decisively into the hands of specialists who ceased to have any significant personal connection with business — men like Playford and Menzies, later Bolte and Askin, and increasingly the senior civil servants through whom they governed. This progressive bifurcation of political and business leadership in the ruling class created problems of co-ordination that at times became open conflict — Playford for instance had to fight a sharp battle with the Adelaide establishment to force through his plans for electrification — but it was essential in establishing the flexibility that allowed ruling-class control of the process of industrialisation.[21]

Of course, connections with business remained, and the politicians on their own could have done little; but they were aided by the changes within the business leadership that flowed from industrialisation and the shock of the depression. Some large welfare schemes had been mooted by conservative politicians before the war, and some businessmen, big enough to be able to play with options, had begun to look on investment in a contented workforce as money well spent—most notably W. S. Robinson of the Collins House group. About the middle of the Second World War, this crystallised into a coherent form. In 1942 a group of manufacturers in Melbourne launched the 'Institute of Public Affairs' as a propaganda centre for business. For a time it behaved (as did the group of the same name in New South Wales) as a finance committee for conservative politics, but soon concentrated on the reconstruction of business ideology. It formulated a growth-and-welfare social programme, which it sold to the Victorian business establishment; and after a considerable amount of resistance had been overcome, its main views were adopted as the programme of the Liberal Party in 1945. At the same time, partly through the persuasion of intellectuals such as Keynesian economists, but also because of practical experience of industrialisation in South Australia and the meshing of government and big business in the war economy, the notion of government 'management' of the economy was becoming increasingly respectable. The business establishment vigorously resisted the Labor government's proposals for central control of the economy, in the 'powers' referendum of 1944 and in the clashes over banking in 1945–49, but it accepted regulation through macroeconomic policy without much more demur. The new conservatism understood the state theoretically as a part of capitalism, better than much of the labour movement did.[22]

These changes in theory fed into a political reorganisation. This too had its forerunner, also in South Australia. Here the disparate forces that had combined to defeat Labor in the depression election were welded into a single organisation, the Liberal and Country League, in 1932. The League had internal finance committees tapping urban business, and a mass membership, largely in the country; and it enjoyed a remarkable success in controlling state politics. It formed proportionately the largest state branch in a new national party when the electoral triumphs of the Labor Party had put the final pressure on the disintegrating U.A.P.

Some fourteen separate organisations, by Menzies' count, came together in a unity conference at Canberra in 1944 to form the Liberal Party. He persuaded them to merge their machinery, while leaving the parliamentary groups intact. The pressure for reorganisation is shown by the fact that even the Australian Women's National League, which had outlasted three federal conservative parties, agreed to immolate itself. The party's officers, rather than 'outside' committees, were responsible for raising finance. The money still came ultimately from the same sources, and business influence in the party continued, symbolised by the part played by the I.P.A. in the actual drafting of the Liberal programme; but the relationship was no longer an immediate source of disruption in the party machine. Finally, the party adopted a mass-membership organisational model; indeed, the first Federal Council in 1945 adopted the fantastic aim of a membership of one million. A very impressive growth did occur: by 1950, the national membership was probably over 150 000. One can exaggerate the centralisation of the Liberal Party, which remained an alliance of largely independent state branches. But it did effectively co-ordinate campaigns and provided, in the welfare conservatism and developmentalism brilliantly expounded by Menzies, a common platform for the conservative revival.[23]

The offensive broke over the Chifley government's attempt after the war to control and then nationalise the private banks. Though the banks were no longer central to the economy, the conservatives chose to regard the issue as a crucial threat. They launched a pre-emptive attack on the labour movement, throwing out the Victorian Labor government and starting a massive campaign, not merely to block bank nationalisation, but to destroy the Chifley government. The mobilisation extended far beyond the Liberal Party, with business publicity and financial resources being co-ordinated by the banks—the chief manager of the National Bank, L.J. McConnan, working practically full-time on the campaign. The Liberal president R. G. Casey, a scion of Mt Morgan money, raised large campaign funds from English capitalists; Menzies built the issue into a general campaign against rationing and government controls as a foretaste of socialist dictatorship; and the Labor cabinet went down to defeat in 1949, hardly knowing what had hit it.[24]

From an attack on the parliamentary Labor Party, the conservatives moved immediately to an attack on the radical wing of the labour movement. The new government attempted to ban the Communist Party, and when its legislation was blocked in the courts, took the issue to a referendum. This was narrowly defeated in a dramatic campaign by the new Labor Party leader, H. V. Evatt. But the power of the Communists had already been shaken by opponents who had begun ejecting them from control of a series of unions in the late 1940s. It was indeed convenient for Menzies to have some Communists still in power in unions, as he hammered the theme of Communist influence in the Labor Party, and successfully engineered a spy scare just before the 1954 election. In this strategy he struck at a vulnerable point, an issue where religious hegemony was still strong: the Catholic right, schooled to hatred of 'godless Communism', could be split from the rest. The Labor Party cracked under the stress, expelled its right wing, and went into the wilderness; its state governments fell one by one, and the federal party— level pegging with the Liberals in the early 1950s—became a permanent opposition. After nearly ten years' continuous struggle, a new conservative regime had been built.[25]

The political contours of this sequence of events are well known; their significance in terms of class relations less well understood. We have called the conservative reaction of the late 1940s a ruling-class mobilisation, and it was clearly that, in terms of its leading participants, the scale of the involvement of companies and other property owners, the issues on which battle was joined. But it was also, crucially, a mobilisation that went beyond the ruling class as such. In the defence of the private banks, the owners and managers were joined by many white-collar workers, most notably their own employees including the bank officers' union (which had been resisted bitterly by the companies when first formed). Menzies began to campaign on an appeal to 'the forgotten people', by which he basically meant ununionised middle-income earners and the declining group of the self-employed, in the war years; and though the response was delayed, it does seem likely that these groups shifted to the right in the late 1940s. In the attack on militant socialism in the unions, the conservatives were joined, in some measure forestalled, by 'the Movement' and the A.L.P. Industrial Groups, i.e. groups within the working class who were for a variety of reasons hostile to the Communists. (Among the Communists' most effective opponents were men like Laurie Short of the Ironworkers, who had come from a Trotskyite background, that is, marxists opposed to stalinist control.) The Communists themselves split the labour movement and delivered support to the conservatives by taking a hard-left line at a moment that fatally coincided with the ruling-class offensive. Contradictions within the working class, in short, were destroying the apparent unity of the mid-1940s and helped make possible the shift to a new period of capitalist dominance. Out of the smash came, not just the personal ascendancy of Menzies in federal politics, but a reconstructed capitalism: an industrial welfare capitalism, pacifying the workforce with rising material standards, providing profits out of growth, managing economic incoherencies and social tensions by expanded state intervention, and cementing the classes with an ideology of anti-communism and development. There were new contradictions in this, but it took another couple of decades for them to mature.

Capitalist Expansion: The 'Second Long Boom', 1950–1970

The pattern of welfare capitalism, though reached by a peculiar local route, was reasonably similar to what developed in other parts of the capitalist world after the period of revolutionary upheaval in the 1940s. In the re-establishment of world capitalism, American military and financial power were crucial; the financial pre-eminence of the British had been destroyed in the war and the United States emerged as the main source of international investment, as well as the defender of the boundaries. It remained the base of most of the growing multinational companies that controlled the capital flow, and that rapidly increased their stake in Australia. There was thus a hard material basis, as well as the military motives provided by the Japanese assault in 1942 and the fantasied Communist attacks of the 1950s and 1960s, for a shift by Australian governments into the American orbit. Curtin and Evatt began it, albeit under pressure; Menzies swallowed his Britishry and followed suit.[26]

This was not the only way that Australia became integrated into the new world order. The reconstruction of capitalist economies in Europe and North America on a high-technology basis absorbing most of the local workforce, created new demands for pools of unskilled labour which should be highly mobile and subject to political control. In these regions, and in Australia, the need was increasingly met by immigration — a form of development aid, as it has been remarked, from the poor countries to the rich. With women, who had provided a large part of the labour force for wartime production, being pushed back into the home and child-rearing, and with Aborigines disregarded in the outback, the labour had to come from overseas. The federal Labor government, spurred on by racist fears reawakened by the Pacific war, launched a European immigration programme, which was taken over by the Liberals. A steady, heavy inflow totalled nearly two million in two decades. The migrants fed the industrial workforce, providing, for instance, three-quarters of the 1945–55 increase at B.H.P.'s Newcastle and Port Kembla steelworks, and much of the labour with which Playford got his power system supplied from the remote Leigh Creek coalfield and the eastern states got hooked to the Snowy Mountains. They also supplied an increasing proportion of labour for unskilled jobs in the major cities; with migrant women, drawn into jobs in much higher proportion than Australian-born women, the most heavily exploited of all.

Sponsored immigration had been a traditional resort of capitalists wishing to drive wages and conditions down. Though the new workers were vulnerable, as migrants always are, and some more so because of language barriers and social isolation, they did not generally (at least in the short run) depress standards. Money wages rose and continued to rise in the 1950s and 1960s, real income following more slowly because of inflation. With increasing inequality in wage rates after about 1950, native-born workers did better out of the boom than the migrants, since the latter were more concentrated in unskilled jobs. What happened, rather, was an increased segmentation of the working class. As in other capitalist powers—though less markedly than in Germany or the United States—the migrants formed a relatively exploited and isolated lower stratum of the working class, with little representation in unions or political organisations, lower than average wages, and often the worst housing and provision for education. Concentrations of migrant workers and their families began to form in the old inner-city working-class suburbs such as Redfern, Leichhardt, and Carlton. In some ways, this reproduced in an ethnic framework the dense social networks of the generations before the boom, but for the most part lacked the old connection with labour politics and working-class consciousness.[27]

The capital for expansion came from both internal and external sources. Some companies were able to finance the growth of their plant out of their own profits: B.H.P., for instance, was notorious among capitalists for passing on only a modest dividend to shareholders and financing expansion from the retained earnings. Others raised new capital on the Australian share markets, or by loans. Some important new sources were becoming available. Insurance companies changed their rules and began investing in shares and supplying inter-company loans; by the late 1950s it was reckoned that they were supplying about one-fifth of all new money in the share market, and they rapidly became the biggest shareholders in the major public companies. The banks also shifted from their previous heavy concentration on the pastoral industry, becoming more closely interlocked with manufacturing.

It appears, further, that direct share ownership became more widespread; certainly the numbers of shareholders in individual companies rose markedly. Olympic rose from 50 in 1933 to about 13 000 at its founder's death in 1956. C.S.R., a big company with nearly 5000 shareholders in 1934, rose to over 12 000 in 1954. Through the 1960s the numbers rose again, and a dozen or more companies had more than 30 000 shareholders in the early 1970s, with B.H.P. reaching 180 000. Such figures were acclaimed by business ideologists as evidence of 'people's capitalism'; the interpretation is a little soured by the fact that the biggest 5 per cent of shareholdings controlled more than 50 per cent of the shares, and the sketchy evidence available about the actual social composition of shareholders shows most of the men to come from the upper levels of the occupational structure. Effective power in companies was not diffused. But in these ways the fund-raising network of corporate capitalism was spread more widely. As with savings, employment was increasingly absorbed into the corporate structure and the state. The proportion of the workforce who were 'self-employed' had been gradually declining from the 1920s—from 16 per cent in 1921 to 8 per cent in 1966.[28]

The growth in the scale of companies that these figures suggest was related to changes in the process of production, the beginnings of which have already been sketched: an advance of mechanisation; the routinisation of many labour processes, both manual and clerical; and changes in the demand for different categories of workers. By the 1960s, conferences were being held and learned opinions given on the impact of 'automation', and a small computing industry began to develop (though the computers themselves were always imported). Ideas of a technological revolution were exaggerated, but there certainly was a general mechanisation of farming, earth-moving and materials handling, which reduced the demand for old-fashioned brawn—most spectacularly with containerisation on the wharves in the 1960s and 1970s. At the same time, clerical and administrative work was reorganised along factory lines, with large offices in the city centres organised for the mass processing of people and information by a division of labour among relatively unskilled workers. Seeking the cheapest labour, the managers of these offices created a segregated labour market for women; especially young women, for whom routine clerical work became the standard occupation in the way domestic service had been two generations before. These processes were of course going on in other industrial countries at the same time. The shifts in the structure of labour were masked in Australia by the fact that the move to secondary industry was occurring simultaneously with the growth in tertiary industry (administration, services); but even so, the relative numbers of 'white-collar' workers grew from about 30 per cent of the workforce in the decades before the Second World War to about 40 per cent in the decades after. The percentage rose more steeply among women than among men.[29]

These changes were spurred by the import of capital, in increasing volume, from overseas, often bringing new technology with it. The arrival of foreign-based manufacturing companies behind the import control and tariff barriers has already been noted—a process vigorously encouraged by federal and state governments in pursuit of development. American firms in particular made very high profits in the 1950s, but even when the rate fell in the 1960s, their profits remained higher than those of Australian firms. The total of foreign capitalists' investment in Australia rose from about £500 million in the late 1940s to about \$10 000 million in the early 1970s, the American share having risen to near par with the British. By then, a quarter of the fifty largest companies in the country were subsidiaries of multinational corporations; official inquiries, when finally made, reckoned that foreign capital held between a quarter and a third of the entire corporate business of the country. Japanese investment followed American in the 1960s. From being an appendage of one, Australia had graduated economically to a field for the play of forces from several of the international centres of capitalism.[30]

The most spectacular example of this was provided by the British-based mining company Rio Tinto-Zinc. Under the leadership of Sir Val Duncan, one of the most vigorous entrepreneurs in post-war history, this firm moved into mining operations in Australia as part of a world-wide programme. It set up huge projects in aluminium in Queensland, iron in Western Australia and copper in New Guinea, took over uranium and zinc interests and aluminium refining facilities. Its operations were characterised by international loan finance, long-term international sales contracts, and mass production techniques at the sites on a scale far beyond the tentative beginnings of mechanised mining in Australia between the wars. By the 1970s its local holding company, Conzinc Riotinto of Australia, formed in 1962, was the second largest concentration of capital in Australia; and the copper-mining operation alone was so profitable that it became politically embarrassing.

C.R.A. was only the most conspicuous example of a large-scale move into mining by foreign-owned and local companies. Stimulated by an upsurge in world base-metal demand, mining became in the 1960s the major growth point of the economy, considerably outstripping the rate of investment in manufacturing; and a series of new mining towns grew in the outback, most notably in the Pilbara iron-ore region of Western Australia. With high-technology, mass-production methods, these were in many ways closer to manufacturing industries than to traditional underground mining, and the companies paid very high rates to attract skilled workers. But it remained an enclave industrialisation—'decentralisation and development', as the companies preferred to call it—with plants widely separated, and much of the produce shipped off in raw or semi-processed state overseas.[31]

The industry that made the deepest impact after steelmaking was the motor trade. We have sketched the origins of this as an industrial complex between the wars. Its significance changed qualitatively in the late 1940s: in twenty more years, it had become the biggest in the country, with ten of the top fifty companies, car and truck manufacturers (Chrysler, Ford, G.M.H.), part and tyre manufacturers (Repco, Dunlop, Olympic), and petrol refiners and distributors (Ampol, B.P., Mobil, Shell). The car became a central feature of working-class life and culture, a basis of the economics of everyday life.

The growth of this complex represented a massive change in the way a basic social service, transport, was provided. The change was not expected or planned; in the 1920s for instance N.S.W. authorities were planning the expansion of the city of Sydney on the assumption that the mass transport of the future would be trains, and built its Bridge and Underground on that assumption. The motor car was first a toy of the ruling class (there is a fine photograph of S. M. Bruce standing proudly beside his Rolls-Royce) or of technical enthusiasts. Manufacturers began building them as a modest market opened up among the affluent. Federal governments gave the manufacturers protective tariffs in line with the general policy of protection, and encouraged them to build locally because of the military advantages of a motor industry. Demand surged post-war because of the suburban expansion, already discussed, into areas where there were no good alternative means of transport; and the spread of cars in turn permitted the spread of suburbs farther from railways, so the two spiralled together. Mass production cheapened the relative price of cars and brought them in range of rising working-class incomes; the growth of hire-purchase solemnised the marriage, while binding workers in new forms of economic dependence. The phenomenal growth of car, home and appliance ownership in turn boosted the business of the finance companies, formerly poor relations of banking, to the point where they rivalled and in some cases dominated the business of the banks themselves. While this massive change in the basis of transport was going on, conservative and Labor governments alike contented themselves with supplying roads to service the new traffic. They provided inadequate bus services, hardly increased rail networks at all, and in Sydney actually dismantled the tram system because it interfered too much with cars. No group who commanded the state authority or the private capital to act effectively, took any serious steps to deal with the immediate material effects of the new transport system, the rising numbers of deaths and injuries from motor accidents and the rising pollution of the cities by exhaust and noise. It is a remarkable illustration of the process of social change under capitalism.[32]

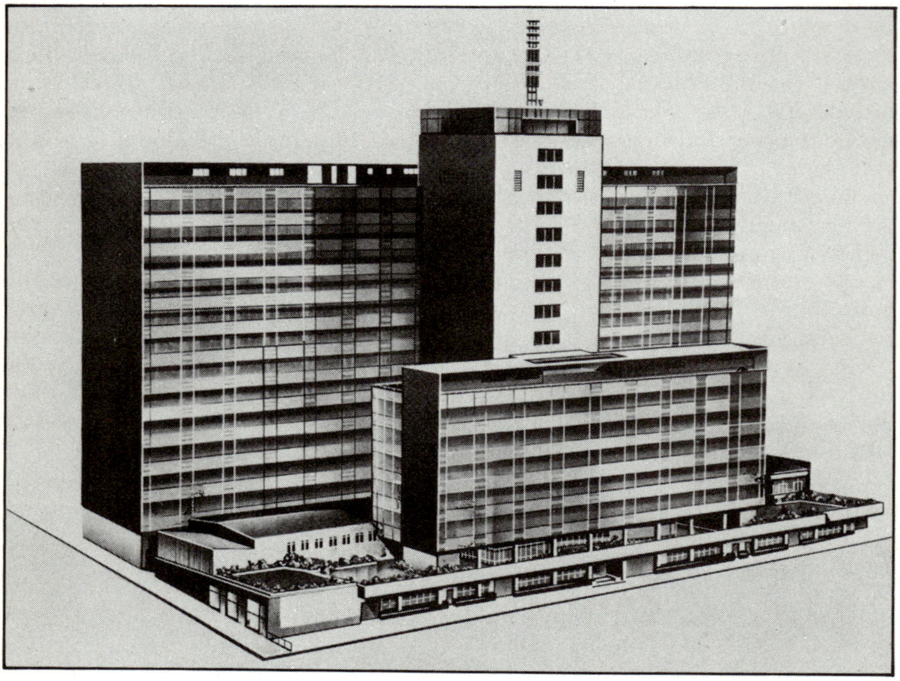

The new temples of Mammon: one of the first of the post-war office blocks.
Source: *The MLC Head Office Building, North Sydney*, Sydney, 1957, a booklet published by the MLC to mark its opening by R. G. Menzies.

In something of the same fashion the cities were rebuilt. In the late 1940s suburban building revived, and from 1950 produced a steady 80 000 houses a year: almost all being suburban bungalows designed for (but not by) housebound wives. Part of this growth was provided by government housing authorities, most by private builders. The construction firms which did best were concentrating on another target, the central business districts of the cities. Symbolically, a petrol firm began this: H. C. Sleigh opened a nine-storey headquarters in 1955, the first new office building in Melbourne since the war. In the next few years a massive demolition and rebuilding of the city centres began, on a scale that had not been seen since the 1880s. It was largely financed by the insurance companies, notably the A.M.P. in Sydney, which had heavy surpluses of funds to invest; and by the big mining and industrial companies which wanted new head offices. Sydney, now coming to rival Melbourne as the centre of Australian capitalism and point of entry for international capital, set the pace with the M.L.C. building and then a forest of office blocks near the harbour. The big Melbourne companies soon followed: B.H.P., whose headquarters had lived in dingy rented offices throughout its rise, built itself an Essington Lewis House; the pace of growth soon outstripped it and in 1972 it moved into B.H.P. House, a dark tower dominating the city skyline. Simultaneously, attempts were made to introduce freeway systems to service this expanded commuter centre and build outer-suburban nodes for corporate retailing (Roselands, Chadstone). To prevent interference with this from over-zealous planners and Labor organisations, the corporate leadership mobilised its political resources in the very complex system of councils and state authorities that governed the cities; but it must be admitted that until the end of the 1960s there was little articulate resistance of any kind, the whole thing being justified by the ideology of development and governments pacified by the prospect of increased rates and taxes.

The office blocks of the central cities are more than the functional centres of companies. Like the classical temples of the nineteenth-century bankers, and indeed the Georgian mansions of the pastoralists, these buildings are the visible expression of class power, the symbols of a new ascendancy. Each one built because companies wanted prestigious and modern (terms that were practically equated) head offices, they are collectively the statement of an industrial ruling class. The functional, abstract, metallic style is of course international—B.H.P. House was largely designed in Chicago—but perhaps that makes it even more appropriate to the contemporary Australian ruling class.[33]

Hegemony and the Working Class

The changes in business ideology catalysed by the I.P.A., and the changes in architecture just noted, were not isolated. Both shared the theme of modernisation, which can be understood as the cultural form taken by traditional developmentalism in the period of industrial capitalism. Parallel developments can be found in many art forms, such as the marked growth of abstract painting and sculpture. The economic links here are obvious: businessmen bought paintings and art objects to decorate the new office blocks, affluent professionals bought them for their homes and waiting-rooms. They wanted prestige, modernism, and no awkward social content; abstract art, or art that mythologised the Australian past, supplied them. In literature, less marketable, the links were less direct; but here too a change occurred towards subjectivity and elitism in a revulsion from the radical enthusiasms of the 1930s and 1940s. At the simplest level, poetry became more unintelligible (except to litterateurs) as its practitioners pursued technique and subtleties of consciousness. At a rather more complex level, the preoccupations of novelists shifted from social critique, of which the last landmark was Frank Hardy's *Power Without Glory*, a massive indictment of Wren and the corruption of labour politics, to the exploration of psychological and ontological issues epitomised by Patrick White. Commenting on some related changes in academic writing, one conservative journalist wrote in 1962 of 'the counter-revolution in Australian historiography'. This was exaggerated; but it is undoubtedly true that there was a broad shift towards conservatism among Australian intellectuals, or where not explicitly conservative, at least towards concerns and techniques that served to cut them off from the politics and everyday life of the working class.

The high culture of the period, for all the occasional dissidence of particular artists, was essentially affirmative; it crowned the world of industrial capitalism with prestige and unsubversive elegance. The Opera House, Cultural Centre and Festival Theatre of Sydney, Melbourne and Adelaide were perfect epitomes. In the much broader sphere of popular arts, industrial design, home decoration, and so on, the same styles spread. Home ownership in the suburbs as a desirable form of life, as well as the equipment necessary for it, was actively sold to the working class and provided a context for this. Popular magazines after the war spread the gospel of 'modern' styling, along with the message of high consumption; the electrical equipment increasingly invading the household spread the same tastes. The rising popularity of motor sport, massively publicised by the motor and oil industry from the Redex reliability trials of the early 1950s to Jack Brabham's international racing triumphs of the 1960s, spread the gospel of technique among working-class youth.[34]

From the point of view of the working class, re-establishment of bourgeois hegemony is a process of demobilisation, of some withdrawal from a state of class distinctiveness, class consciousness, and organisation for struggle. A defeat is not necessarily equivalent to a demobilisation, as is shown by many industrial and electoral losses after which the labour movement has sprung back. But the political defeats around 1950 were followed by a demobilisation, and the reasons plainly extend far beyond politics into changes in domestic life, new patterns of division in the working class, and changes in the role of the state as well as the cultural ascendancy of the industrial bourgeoisie.

In the new outer suburbs, working-class families found more physical freedom, but a new economic dependence. Most of the housing had been built for sale, rather than rent, and finance companies supplied a large volume of credit to allow home-buying on terms. The loans were long-term, usually twenty or twenty-five years, and represented a big commitment to stability and continuity of work, quite apart from the upkeep of what were commonly ill-designed and indifferently-built houses. As the suburbs, developed at minimal cost by private builders or housing commissions, lacked collective services and equipment, the cost of cars, washing-machines and vacuum-cleaners, television sets and refrigerators went into household budgets and on to hire-purchase bills. Unions found their members increasingly reluctant to enter long disputes, and many shifted tactics towards short demonstration strikes.[35]

The social life of these suburbs was very much home-centred. Most leisure time was spent working around the home, in the garden, on the car; and if survey evidence is to be believed, any extra leisure on the part of housewives would have been spent on more housework. With the spread of television, in

Selling the suburbs. The cover of a magazine devoted to suburban expansion and selling household commodities, using the figure of the modern classless housewife to tie it all together.
Source: *Australian Home Beautiful*, April 1946.

half the houses in the late 1950s and in practically all by the late 1960s, entertainment became mainly home-centred as well. Kinship networks were kept up, by telephone, visiting, and mutual help in family crises. But the neighbourhood networks of the older working-class suburbs were mostly lost, and with it much of the municipal strength of Labor politics. In the new suburbs, it was typically professionals and local businessmen who provided the 'civic leaders' and tried to whip the inhabitants into participation in 'community affairs', as they defined them. Periodically working-class neighbourhoods might mobilise around a class issue, such as rent or repayments; but even this was very difficult to organise, for except in housing-commission areas, it was rare for neighbours to share the same landlord or financier and hence be able to act jointly.[36] Such forms of collective action as union womens' auxiliaries died away, even in the old mining towns; in the new mining towns of the far north, domestic life was markedly privatised and kept at arms' length by the unions.

'Suburbia' and 'affluence' (the two hardly distinguished) were often regarded by intellectuals at the time as direct reasons for the decline of political Labor. This is too simple: as a new generation of Labor leaders (notably Whitlam, Dunstan and Wran) showed, the electoral decline of Labor could be reversed, and that partly by campaigns on suburban issues. But it is undoubtedly true that the sense of class distinctiveness was eroded in the new environment, along with the municipal base of traditional Labor politics. The low-density suburb was a living environment created by business, initially unplanned, full of problems for its inhabitants, lacking public land, buildings and services. It had to be made to work, and a great deal of effort went into making it habitable; but it was so structured that most of this effort had to be organised on a household-by-household basis. It was very difficult to make or sustain a collective response to diffuse pressures and isolating geography; and that was compounded by the fact that the adults who spent most time in this setting, the married women, had the bulk of their energy absorbed by child-rearing and solitary domestic labour. The post-war suburbs did not abolish the working class, or class consciousness, but they certainly helped fragment it.

Other events tending to divide the working class have been mentioned. One is the inflow of migrants and their concentration, initially at least, in the worst-paid jobs. It is difficult to estimate the cultural and political effects of this. There was certainly widespread prejudice, against Southern European migrants especially, on the part of Australian-born workers, though direct economic competition was slight; and this is one reason for their slow entry into union posts, party politics, and so on. But the encounter of a pre-industrial population with industrial capitalism is notoriously turbulent, and the migrant workers were not entirely passive. At the Mount Isa lead-zinc and copper mine in Queensland, a fierce struggle with the American owners and the Queensland government broke out in 1964; migrants were among the most militant. A big strike against General Motors in Victoria in the same year began in a workshop almost entirely composed of Greeks. In the nine-week strike against Ford in 1973 at Broadmeadows, one of the most bitter confrontations since the 1940s, it was largely migrant workers who insisted on holding out when even Communist union officials were willing to compromise.[37]

Similarly, the expansion of 'white-collar' occupations— clerical, administrative and technical workers—increased the stratification of the working class; but as these became mass occupations and their work routinised, they organised. White-collar unions expanded—against some resistance by employers, but nothing as fierce as the opposition encountered by the clerks and bank officers around the time of the First World War—and became industrially more active. Startled by the employers' application in the federal wage case in 1952 to reduce the basic wage and increase standard hours of work, and a 1954 declaration by the court that margin increases would not be automatic but would have to be fought for, the white-collar unions decided on central organisation. The New South Wales and Victorian peak organisations federated to form the Australian Council of Salaried and Professional Associations (A.C.S.P.A.) in 1956. Notably, they did not join the A.C.T.U.: and a fair number of white-collar unions, especially public service unions which had their own federal organisations, stayed out. The event was hardly a triumph of working-class solidarity. But even semi-professional groups began entering the industrial arena: in 1961–62 the engineers used the arbitration system very effectively to establish their claims for professional pay and conditions, and during the 1960s, air pilots' and teachers' strikes scandalised the orthodox.[38]

In some ways, what was happening here was a reversion to a very old pattern—the use of techniques of industrial action by privileged groups in the workforce to maintain their distance and extend their privileges over other employees. The 'labour aristocracy' of the nineteenth century was reincarnated, on a basis not of traditional manual skill, but of professional knowledge certified by specialised higher education. The expansion of higher and technical education, which the labour movement in a vague way supported, developed in a socially divisive way. To the extent that working-class youth entered the new mass universities and colleges (which remained, nevertheless, mainly the preserve of the affluent), they were cut off from their age-mates and inducted into a new form of hegemonised class consciousness, the ideology of professionalism, which was assiduously spread among new mass occupations such as engineering and teaching. Some of this filtered into other parts of the workforce—there were some comic attempts to 'professionalise' company management, more serious attempts to restructure some of the new labour processes by professionalising a fraction of workers such as technicians (for example, computer programmers) and reducing the rest to the status and pay of routine operatives. Most important of all, the doctrine of higher knowledge validating higher privilege was reinforced in the schools, where it was spread to the mass of working-class children, who under no circumstances could become professionals; and this helped confirm them in a new sense of their inferiority in the technological age and undercut the sense of dignity and equality that was one of the most important legacies of traditional radicalism.[39]

With the growing demand for administrative and welfare services, and in despite of the nominal policy of conservative governments, the numbers of public employees grew, the Commonwealth government at a brisker rate than others. By 1970, government employees totalled more than a million. With the scale of foreign intervention in Australian business, this created a striking situation: less than two-thirds of the Australian working class was actually directly employed by Australian capitalists. When this is taken together with the pervasive influence of wage regulation and welfare services,

When you call our Telephone Freeway reservations room, we'll answer your call, on average, in less than two seconds.
Two seconds.
And you're on a direct line into our reservations computer system, Ansamatic.
That means we'll reserve and confirm your flight, hotel room, Avis Rent-a-car and any other special request you might have, in seconds.
We'll arrange your holiday, and if 15 or more of you belong to a Common Interest Group we'll give you a 10% Group Travel discount.
Which all goes to make our Telephone Freeway the fastest way to fly.
At Ansett Airlines we give you Air Service. It's the kind of helpfulness that starts on the ground.
ANSETT
AIRLINES OF AUSTRALIA
Air Service
The fastest way to fly.
Ansett Airlines' Telephone Freeway.
For reservations call
Sydney 20 631, Canberra 47 7522, Melbourne 345 2222.
Brisbane 24 0222, Adelaide 212 1111, Perth 250 251.
Hobart 34 7466, Launceston 31 7711 Darwin 80 3333.

it can be seen that class relations, to a very marked degree, had become indirect — mediated through the state and through international structures of ownership. With the elaboration of grades in administrative hierarchies, both public and private, the revival of margins in arbitration awards, the development of selective higher education as a means of controlled access to well-paid jobs, even the creation of status grades in suburban developments built by public authorities, the working class was coming increasingly to live in an environment of planned inequalities rather than inequalities produced directly by the labour market.[40]

The benevolence of these arrangements, by the late 1960s, was increasingly subject to doubt. Welfare conservatism, during the period when political opposition had wilted, had been able to get away with some schemes that amounted to welfare frauds — notably a medical insurance scheme that subsidised the incomes of doctors and insurance companies, but was too costly for the groups who needed it most. If the administered labour market meant administered inequality, a number of groups were hardly able to use it at all: Aborigines, age pensioners, deserted wives and single mothers, and 'the unemployed'. The continued existence of such groups began to penetrate through the mists of the propaganda of affluence, as intellectuals began to talk again about 'the poor': estimates of their numbers ranged upwards to half a million. The invention of this social category is a telling sign of the extent of hegemony. In a series of political debates and official inquiries, it was accepted on all sides that there was a category of 'the poor' that was somehow *outside* the social structure, and that the appropriate response was an overhaul of state welfare measures; the debate was over the necessary adjustments to pensions and social services rather than over the social structure that generated such a situation. By defining a 'poverty line' — essentially basic wage plus child endowment — the existing equilibrium in class relations was reproduced by the state welfare apparatus.

Militant Aborigines were the first to shift the argument to a more general ground, stressing the inbuilt racism of white Australian society. In the early 1970s the systematic reasons for poverty among women, institutional sexism and the dominance of the traditional family, were similarly pointed out by the new women's movement. Not until the rising unemployment of the mid-1970s, and the evident breakdown of the now traditional techniques of macroeconomic regulation, did the specifically capitalist character of a society that distributed income through the labour market come into focus.[41]

A period opening with a series of electoral defeats, and continuing with an increasing economic and domestic fragmentation of the working class and an increasing cultural strength of conservatism, was hardly propitious for labour politics. Its municipal base weakened and its parliamentary leadership unpopular, the Labor Party was unable either to close or override the split of the mid-1950s. At one point in the late 1960s, it was not in office in any parliament in Australia, for the first time since before the First World War. The Communist Party staged some revival in the unions as the A.L.P. Industrial Groups were weakened and then disbanded. But within a few

Left: The industrialisation of office work: from a newspaper advertisement intended to convey the office's efficiency.
Source: *Australian*, 29 October 1974.

years, it entered a period of internal disintegration with factional disputes among its leaders exacerbated by the shock-waves of the breakup of international communism. By the 1970s, nothing much remained but some left-wing ginger groups, perhaps one-tenth of the size of the party at its 1944 peak. But the Labor Party machine stayed in being; the D.L.P. was not followed out by other groups willing to form a new centre party. The defensive strength of working-class organisation established in the previous generations was impressively demonstrated, as it also was by the unions. Their growth, in terms of coverage of the workforce, stopped and retreated slightly from the peak of the early 1950s; but they were aided by the high level of employment and the heavy imports of capital to keep a strong bargaining position. Even approximate stability in class shares of national production meant a rise in working-class incomes on average, though they were more unequally distributed between categories of workers.

When the Whitlam government eventually came to office, one socialist intellectual, who had himself suffered from the anti-communist hysteria of the 1950s, called it 'the end of the Ice Age'. Certainly, these two decades were a chill time for the Left. The attempts by Fabian socialists to work out a theory of parliamentary socialism petered out about the time of the split. Attempts in the following decade to reconstitute socialist ideas by Labor Party figures, notably J. F. Cairns, and marxist intellectuals set adrift by the break-up of the Communist Party, had little influence. A radical mobilisation broke out after the federal government sent troops to Vietnam in 1965, but suffered a stunning defeat in 1966. Nevertheless this episode stored up trouble for the Liberals. Resistance to the war, based on a coalition of radical unionists and young professionals, notably students, stiffened after the 1966 election even though the Labor Party officially became more cautious, culminating in a campaign of illegal resistance to conscription that won wide underground support, and mass demonstrations, the Moratorium movement, on a new scale in 1970. The universities unexpectedly became a focus of disaffection; and even some businessmen began to doubt the wisdom and morality of the war in Vietnam, though their attempts to split the Liberal Party failed. The 1966 election had also let in a new federal leadership which was a more formidable parliamentary opposition.[42]

The Whitlam leadership represented much more than a change in federal parliament, as is suggested by the emergence of similar leaderships in South Australia and eventually New South Wales and Victoria. It was the expression of a number of changes in the social bases of the party, which have already been indicated, and responded to the new situation in cautious but intelligent ways. From the 1940s there had been a definite decline in the occupational-status polarisation of the vote, that is, the tendency for Liberal and Labor votes to split along white-collar/blue-collar lines. Labor was electorally depending far more on people who did not automatically think of themselves as working class, but who still had class interests that could be spoken to through the hegemonic language of modernism—as Whitlam did in expounding his urban policies. Not many white-collar unions had affiliated with the party, but their membership could be reached. The attempt was made easier by the increasing numbers of professionals and semi-professionals in the Labor leadership. There had of course been white-collar workers in the party before (including the two previous federal leaders); they now became the preponderant part, particularly after the 1969 election. And as the upper levels of the party changed, industrial workers were further cut off from organised political expression. In the early 1970s a dozen militant sects of marxist inspiration competed for their attention, but only the unions remained to them as an effective form of organisation.

The new leadership of the Labor Party accepted the constitutional bar against anything like socialism—a point Whitlam had made in a famous lecture in the 1950s—but devised ways to use the executive and planning powers of central government to rationalise capitalist development. Like the welfare capitalism of Menzies and the I.P.A. in the 1940s, it was a strategy that was being widely canvassed in other countries, and it struck gold, electorally, in Australia. Industrialisation and urban expansion by this stage had left a series of dislocations. It had eroded and polluted the inner suburbs, and created wide tracts of outer suburbs without elementary public services. It had expanded education and health services, but unequally, and as already noted had revealed 'pockets of poverty', as they were called, inadequately served by existing welfare measures. The policy of the Whitlam leadership essentially amounted to cleaning up the mess left by the long boom, financing the operation out of the profits of further growth. When a period of conflict in the ruling class undermined the Liberals, a coalition of the old unions, the new intelligentsia, and the outer-suburban working class was just strong enough to put Whitlam in office. It was not strong enough to keep him there for long.[43]

State and Ruling Class after Industrialisation

The techniques of conservative government in the boom are familiar. The states competed to attract and subsidise corporate investment. Playford won the development stakes in the 1950s with an integrated 'new town' north of Adelaide called Elizabeth, floated on weapons research but supplied with a diverse manufacturing base in the 1960s. Bolte followed with a huge industrial complex for the quiet semi-rural area around Westernport. Queensland and Western Australian weighed in with the mining boom—though in the Pilbara at least the potential profits were so huge that some companies were prepared to build the necessary towns and railways themselves.

At the federal level, the government provided such direct services to capital as research, marketing aid, bounties and grants (mainly to rural capitalists); but more importantly, it provided guarantees of growth and stability. For the first, it held open the gates for immigrant capital as well as immigrant labour, with the effect of constantly increasing the scale of markets and total investment. For the second, it adopted policies intended to pacify and integrate the working class, providing a bed of consent for the flower of capital accumulation. The most important point here was employment. The Labor government in a celebrated White Paper of 1945 formulated an objective of full employment, which the Liberals, after the ideological reconstruction of the 1940s, accepted. Full employment, from a business point of view, had the happy effect of guaranteeing demand for consumer goods and the safety of the loan finance system. Unemployment was discovered to be unnecessary as a method of labour discipline when most of the workforce accepted wage regulation through arbitration; wage rises were constantly conceded, but also largely recouped through inflation of prices. The techniques of juggling credit and controls so as to produce full employment with modest inflation became a routinely accepted part of conservative government, to the point where McMahon could rise to be Prime Minister with his skill at this business as his main claim to the leadership. It was only when he had won it that the techniques broke down.[44]

Once the course had been set, the ship sailed on for a couple of decades with little more than administrative attention. It was as much top civil servants as ministers through whom Menzies and Playford governed; and this is the period when the upper levels of the Commonwealth bureaucracy became a *corps d'élite* who in many respects themselves were the holders of state power. As managers of the techniques of integration of the capitalist order, they developed channels of consultation with the business leadership—and often retired to a directorship or two when the days of labouring in the public interest were over. This is familiar in the modern capitalist state. Unlike the pattern in the United States, however, the Australian state bureaucracy remained insignificant in forming and promoting a socially integrative ideology, a task that remained with the parliamentarians until the spate of inquiries and commissions that followed the dislocations of the early 1970s.[45]

With the growth of companies of really massive size, the business leadership of the ruling class itself came more and more to resemble a bureaucracy. We have already noted the importance of salaried career managers in high-technology industries, and this pattern was also true of large retail and finance companies. (In some respects it was pioneered, in Australia, by the nineteenth-century banks.) Like shareholders, these men were dependent on the extraction of profits for their income; but here the profits were appropriated in the form of high salaries, and a fascinating and increasingly complex system of non-cash benefits—share options, company cars and houses, and many more ingenious schemes designed for tax avoidance. Combined with the increase in indirect ownership of companies via insurance firms, investment trusts, etc., which in effect gave prerogatives of ownership to the managers of these mediating firms, this reshaped much of the leadership of big business as a salaried elite, with gradations of income and power apparently continuous with those of technical and clerical workers. Echoes of the 'managerial revolution' thesis began to be heard.[46]

The reality beneath this was a highly centralised capitalism based on the undamaged rights of property. The actual numbers of companies grew to a remarkable extent: in 1969 there were nearly 150 000 companies registered in Australia, a few years later nearly 200 000. Most were small, often being private companies set up to conduct a modest business or to hold personal property for tax avoidance or concealment. In 1969, 50 000 recorded no profit. Major industries continued to be dominated by small numbers of large companies. Some, such as steelmaking, were outright monopolies; others, like oil-refining and banking, were controlled by tightly organised oligopolies.

The major companies had become very large, by pre-war standards, though they did not approach the scale of the biggest American and European firms. B.H.P. had a workforce of 55 000 in 1972, and a working capital of $1800 million. Other manufacturing companies had smaller, though still formidable, numbers: G.M.H. employed 26 000, Dunlop 24 000, A.C.I.

22 000, C.S.R. 16 000. A number of retailers and banks were in the same range: Woolworths with 34 000, Myer 29 000, Coles 28 000, A.N.Z. Bank 19 000, Bank of New South Wales 18 000. Some of these leviathans, such as Dunlop and Woolworths, had been created by a string of takeovers; others, such as B.H.P. and C.S.R., had spawned a series of enterprises by diversification from a base in a single industry. Serious problems of co-ordination and complexities of ownership resulted. In a number of cases, there was a reorganisation of ownership into a holding company structure, with the actual business being done by subsidiaries, and the listed public company having no other function than that of ownership — adding a further step to the series of mediations through which property relations now passed.[47]

Worker militancy in heavy industry. An incident during the long strike at Ford's Broadmeadows car assembly plant.
Source: *Australian Financial Review*, 31 July 1973.

The problems of co-ordination of enterprises on this scale, of controlling such numbers of workers, managing suppliers, markets, and governments, forced changes in the pattern of control in business. At earlier stages, companies were often effectively controlled by one or two men, often a general manager plus board chairman combination like the Lewis–Darling tandem in B.H.P.'s drive towards steel monopoly. It was still possible for individuals to hold considerable personal power, as did W. O. Bourke, who drove Ford towards market equality with G.M.H. in the late 1960s, or E. Dunshea, who moulded Dunlop into a large conglomerate by a remarkable series of takeovers in the same period. Personal entrepreneurship is still characteristic of the small (albeit rich) firms that operated in the stock-market booms; and where small companies grew rapidly, as for instance Ansett Transport Industries and Thomas Nationwide Transport, their managers could often retain personal power. Thus another wave of new men such as Ansett and Abeles climbed into the top leadership of the ruling class, as the Myers, Perrys and Coles had done before. But in the largest companies, personal entrepreneurship is no longer a feasible way of doing business; and here the appearance of a bureaucratic leadership has substance, with a division of functions — control of production, personnel, marketing, finance, etc. — among a corps of career managers with relatively clear-cut lines of command. In some companies the devolution of power and formalisation of policy has become very marked, as in the American-owned car manufacturers which developed an elaborate committee structure within management, Chrysler going so far as to set formal goals for achievement by each executive.[48] In such firms, of course, the bureaucracy is an international structure, and the term of office of any Australian manager is likely to be merely a segment of a career line that may reach over several continents.

The attempts to guarantee profit by rationalisation and long-term planning that are characteristic of this stage of capitalism go well beyond the individual firm. They amount practically to a system of inter-company planning. Price rings and agreements on restrictive practices are familiar and long-established features of Australian capitalism as devices to control competition and soak the consumer. In 1967–68, when a federal Trade Practices Act demanded registration, more than 10 000 restrictive agreements were registered within the year. There was now something more than that: a new tendency towards inter-company integration in making large investment decisions and operating the production facilities set up. The mining boom was the most conspicuous case. It would be tedious to list examples, but most of the big mining ventures of the 1960s and 1970s were established by consortia, often linking big local companies with the multinationals; and a number of big processing and manufacturing plants likewise. Such marriages have often used long-term loans from international capital markets, rather than share capital, as the main means of finance. Partly for this reason, partly because of the scale of investment itself, this has meant a close involvement with government in the planning of investment, a search for guarantees by the state. This generally has payoffs for development-minded cabinets, and it has been common for large investment decisions to be announced, not by the companies, but by the local premier. With this mutual involvement in investment planning, and the extension of central economic control, added to traditional activities like wage regulation and lobbying, the care and maintenance of diplomatic relations between big firms and governments has become one of the major activities of management — on both sides.[49]

It would be misleading — very badly misleading — to leave the impression of corporate capitalism having become one happy family at the top. On the contrary: this system of co-ordination, both through the state and outside it, is necessary precisely because of incoherencies and conflicts that are endemic in the system. Competition is not obliterated, though some of its effects are mitigated in these ways and it has tended to take new forms. One is the competition *within* companies for the control of their administrative machinery, in which poor profitability can be decisive; another is the possibility of takeover, which as T.N.T.'s attempt to swallow Ansett in 1972 showed can affect quite large companies. Competition may also take the form of rivalry for the favours of a government which, for instance, controls mining leases. Pressure from international capital is always possible, even for so well-loved a local monopoly as Carlton and United Breweries, which found itself faced by the British-based Courage. In much of Australian manufacturing, the preservation of tariff barriers against competition from imports is crucial to profitability: motor manufacturing is merely the best-known.[50]

For all its potency, direct foreign investment did not produce the kind of stratification in the ruling class that developed in those countries where local entrepreneurs became 'comprador' capitalists, essentially local agents of productive capital from overseas. Some local firms did fit into this role, including a good many brokers and merchant bankers, and some producers (such as Thiess) who supplied mining leases and local political connections to big multinationals (as in the Thiess Peabody Mitsui coal venture in Queensland). Foreign capital dominated the motor manufacturing and oil-refining complex. But local manufacturing and mining firms — B.H.P., C.S.R., Western Mining, A.C.I. — matched the scale of the largest foreign-owned manufacturers and miners. And finance, transport and retailing remained firmly in the hands of local capital, which was certainly not acting principally as agents of circulation for foreign-based producers.

The integration of international and local capital was more complex, in some ways more incestuous, than that. The joint ventures in mining have been mentioned. Two of the biggest venturers, B.H.P. and Western Mining, had at one time (between the wars) been majority owned in England, but the bulk of the capital had been repatriated — economic ownership could flow in and out of a given corporate structure. In 1976 the last of the British-based banks, which had been so important in Australian financial history, decided to shift its domicile to Melbourne. R.T.Z., no doubt largely for political reasons, sold shares in its mining companies and its local holding company (C.R.A.) on Australian stock exchanges — and on one occasion offered advance options on a share issue in a subsidiary company around a spectrum of Australian politicians, bureaucrats, journalists, and their wives. Specialised local industries as well as heavy industries might attract international buyers — this happened to most of the remaining Australian book publishers, not forgetting Cheshire, which has passed through several hands, including those of the Xerox Corporation of America and the British-based Longman. In short, international capital became enmeshed with the whole structure of Australian corporate business rather than forming a distinctive sector. Its managers, similarly, showed little tendency to form a socially distinct group in the Australian ruling class.[51]

It was this that made conflict over the inflow of foreign capital, when it did develop in a serious way at the end of the 1960s, very difficult for Menzies' successors to handle consistently. At the same time a number of other conflicts of interest within the ruling class deepened, coinciding with a period of factional conflict in the conservative political leadership. The result was a breakdown of business support for the Liberals and the advent of the Whitlam government. The turbulence of 1972–75 showed, among other things, how firm the structure of co-operation between central government and big business had become. Consultation on development went on, businessmen remained on the statutory corporations, and participated in a major inquiry on policy for manufacturing industry. Only in the mining field did an energetic minister make a serious attempt to control business operations, and that was partly directed to getting them higher prices overseas by means of 'resources diplomacy'. Connor certainly caused friction, as did Whitlam's adventures with the tariff; and there were some attempts to mobilise business more generally against Labor on the model of 1947–49. They failed. When the Labor Party in 1974 launched an appeal for \$750 000 to build a national headquarters, it was publicly backed by some of the most notable developers of the long boom: Sir Thomas Playford, Sir John McEwen, the chairman of Shell, the vice-chairman of C.R.A.—and the chairman of B.H.P. The government was destroyed with some co-operation from business, certainly, but not by a ruling-class mobilisation—simply an astute ruling-class coup.[52]

The Whitlam government was let in by a local episode in the world-wide turbulence of capitalism that began in the late 1960s. It promised reform of some of the more obvious dislocations produced by the long boom, and it offered to the ruling class the possibility of integrating the organised working class into the political order during a difficult economic passage. The coalition was fragile, and had begun to break up before the coup: capitalists breaking away because of a squeeze on profits that began to bite in 1975,[53] parts of the intelligentsia because the government proved unable to deliver on welfare reforms as its own financial and political difficulties deepened. Union support remained, though increasingly qualified; and at the moment of the coup, when there was a wave of anger in working-class organisations and proposals for a general strike in response, the Labor Party leadership sat on it. Fraser had judged the electoral climate better. His government represented a ruling-class retreat from the strategy of integration and hegemonic control. It began to take higher risks in rejecting the economic demands of the labour movement, though this was aided by a rising level of unemployment. It seems likely that this change will be carried through at the cost of a revived radicalism outside the major-party structure. What forms it might take are still unclear; but some developments in the union movement in the 1970s have foreshadowed new forms of opposition to corporate capitalism and its state: most notably the 'green ban' movement and its offspring, union opposition to the Newport power station and to the export of uranium; and the beginnings of a conscious movement for workers' control of production which, significantly, has emerged within advanced manufacturing industry.

The hegemony of the industrial ruling class in the last generation was bought at a price: on the one hand, a closer integration with the state and with the networks of international business; on the other, an abandonment of a moral for a pragmatic defence of capitalism, a justification by social prosperity rather than the old claim of the absolute rights of men of property. The combination worked with spectacular success for a generation; but it left the position of the ruling class more vulnerable to crisis, and Fraser is a child of that crisis.

Notes

1. H. Hughes, *The Australian Iron and Steel Industry, 1848–1962*, M.U.P., Melbourne, 1964, is an excellent survey of these developments. For the workforce, see *Seventy-five Years of B.H.P. Development in Industry*, B.H.P., Melbourne, 1960; for the politics of the move to Newcastle, H. V. Evatt, *Australian Labour Leader*, Angus & Robertson, Sydney, abridged edn, 1954, pp. 223–32; for Lewis, G. Blainey, *The Steel Master*, Macmillan, Melbourne, 1971—perhaps the most illuminating single book on Australia's recent history. There is now a general account of B.H.P.: A. Trengove, *'What's Good for Australia . . .'*, Cassell, Sydney, 1975.

2. For origins of the Collins House group, see M. Cannon, *The Land Boomers*,

M.U.P., Melbourne, 1966, pp. 131–8. For their move into mining and the operation of their international network, see G. Blainey, *The Rush that Never Ended*, M.U.P., Melbourne, 2nd edn, 1969, pp. 276–82; and W. S. Robinson, *If I Remember Rightly*, Cheshire, Melbourne, 1967 (see p. 41 for the comment on flotation quoted)—after *The Steel Master*, this is the most valuable inside account of the Australian ruling class in this period. For propagandist but useful illustrated narratives of the Collins House industrial projects, see M. H. Ellis, *Metal Manufactures Limited: A Golden Jubilee History*, Harbour Press, Sydney, 1966; and *E. Z. Review: 50 Years of Progress*, Electrolytic Zinc, Hobart, 1966. Their sprawling corporate structure fascinated pamphleteers, not only on the left; for a remarkable map of the interlocks, evidently meant as an investor's aid, see A. P. Warren, *The Kingdom of Collins House*, Sydney, 1939.

3. W. M. Corden, 'The Tariff', in A. Hunter (ed.), *The Economics of Australian Industry*, M.U.P., Melbourne, 1963, pp. 174–214; C. Forster, *Industrial Development in Australia, 1920–1930*, A.N.U.P., Canberra, 1964, an extremely useful survey of the whole field, which has details of motor manufacturing; P. Stubbs, *The Australian Motor Industry*, Cheshire, Melbourne, 1972; Department of Manufacturing Industry, 'The Motor Vehicle Industry', in R. G. Jackson *et al.*, *Policies for Development of Manufacturing Industry*, A.G.P.S., Canberra, 1976, vol. 4, pp. 395–487; G. Lomas, *The Will to Win*, Heinemann, Melbourne, 1960, on Beaurepaire; and 'It All Began in an Old Tin Shed ...', *Repco Record*, 50th birthday special issue, vol. 16, no. 62, 1972.

4. N. G. Butlin, 'Some Perspectives of Australian Economic Development, 1890–1965', in C. Forster (ed.), *Australian Economic Development in the Twentieth Century*, Allen & Unwin, London, 1970, pp. 266–327, summarises the aggregate statistics of industrialisation; C. B. Schedvin, *Australia and the Great Depression*, S.U.P., Sydney, 1970, pp. 301 ff., shows manufacturing's importance in the recovery. On the increase of capital intensiveness and productivity, see H. R. Edwards and N. T. Drane, 'The Australian Economy, July 1963', *Economic Record*, vol. 39, 1963, pp. 259–81. B. D. Haig, 'Manufacturing Output and Productivity, 1910 to 1948/9', *A.E.H.R.*, vol. 15, no. 2, 1975, pp. 136–61, suggests a lower figure for the growth of productivity. Concentration raises many problems of measurement, and no single measure is completely satisfactory. For evidence of the general maintenance of an initially high level, see C. P. Haddon-Cave, 'Trends in the Concentration of Operations of Australian Secondary Industries, 1923–1943', *Economic Record*, vol. 21, 1945, pp. 65–78; I. Gordijew and N. T. Drane, 'Concentration of Employment in Australian Factories, 1938–9 to 1956–7', *Economic Record*, vol. 37, 1961, pp. 214–16; P. Brown and H. Hughes, 'The Market Structure of Australian Manufacturing Industry, 1914/1963–64', in Forster, *Economic Development*, pp. 169–207. For sketches of the new monopolies, see J. R. Poynter, *Russell Grimwade*, M.U.P., Melbourne, 1967; and 'A.P.M.'s Part in History of Australia', *A.P.M. News*, June–November 1959; for post-war mergers, J. A. Bushnell, *Australian Company Mergers*, M.U.P., Melbourne, 1961.

5. There are no substantial studies of changes in labour process or social relations in the workplace in Australian industrialisation: it is one of the great gaps in the history of the period. These remarks are based on fragments in a number of company histories already cited, which have pictures

of plants and workshop interiors and occasional descriptions of production processes; and more general sources such as P. Spearritt, 'Women in Sydney Factories *c.* 1920–50', in A. Curthoys *et al.* (eds), *Women At Work*, Australian Society for the Study of Labour History, Canberra, 1975, pp. 31–46. By the 1940s, industrial production and machinery had begun to fascinate artists, as may be seen in publications such as *Australian Photography 1947*. Tennant's observation is in *Foveaux*, Sirius, Sydney, Australian edn, 1946, p. 17. The change in industrial iconography can be traced in the glossy picture-packed company reports that now shower forth at annual-general-meeting time from almost all the big companies (Woolworths, and the Collins House companies, are among the few to have maintained their earlier austerity). Contrast them, for instance, with the mid-Victorian image of the P. N. Russell engineering works shown in the illustration on page 133. For Lewis' habits, see Blainey, *Steel Master*, pp. 51–2, 71–6.

6. Sources on Lewis, Beaurepaire, Grimwades already cited; on Gepp, C. D. Kemp, *Big Businessmen*, Institute of Public Affairs, Melbourne, 1964; on the Myers, A. Marshall, *The Gay Provider*, Cheshire, Melbourne, 1961; the others mentioned do not seem to have attracted biographers as yet.

7. On Collins House's links with the state, see Robinson, *If I Remember Rightly*, pp. 94–100; there are close parallels with the negotiations for car manufacturing described by L. J. Hartnett, *Big Wheels and Little Wheels*, Lansdowne, Melbourne, 1964. On the process of integration in wartime, see S. J. Butlin, *War Economy, 1939–1942*, Australian War Memorial, Canberra, 1955 (pp. 308–11 on the 'cost-plus' system and profit). On the South Australian system of state-supported industrialisation, see the important article by T. J. Mitchell, 'J. W. Wainwright: The Industrialisation of South Australia, 1935–40', *A.J.P.H.*, vol. 8, 1962, pp. 27–40; D. Nicholas, *The Pacemaker*, Brolga, Adelaide, 1969 (a remarkably bad book—not even listing Wainwright in the index—but with useful details of Playford's tactics and style); and R. M. Gibbs, *A History of South Australia*, Brolga, Adelaide, 1969.

8. There has been little analysis of the social structure of the new industrial towns, though there are many clues in novels; see, for example, D. Cusack, *Southern Steel*, Constable, London, 1953, interesting especially for the account of status tensions produced by technological change in Newcastle. L. Richardson, 'The Labor Movement in Wollongong, 1928–1939', Ph.D. thesis, Australian National University, 1974, has an excellent account of the impact of steel-making on the N.S.W. South Coast. For pictures of the Risdon works, see *E. Z. Review*: *50 Years of Progress*; for Raleigh Park, 'History of British Tobacco Company (Australia) Limited', ms. held by Amatil Ltd, 1954. On the growth of Bankstown, see M. I. Logan, 'Suburban Manufacturing: A Case Study', *Australian Geographer*, vol. 9, 1964, pp. 223–34; and on the suburban spread of manufacturing in other cities, see T. McKnight, 'Industrial Location in South Australia', *Australian Geographical Studies*, vol. 5, 1967, pp. 50–72; R. J. Pryor, 'The Recent Growth of Melbourne', ibid., vol. 6, 1968, pp. 120–38; D. R. Scott, 'The Suburbanisation of Manufacturing in Perth, W.A.', *Australian Geographer*, vol. 9, 1963, pp. 125–6; and *Manufacturing Development in the Sydney Region*, Australian Institute of Urban Studies, Sydney, 1970.

9. M. Keating, 'Australian Workforce and Employment, 1910–11 to 1960–

61', *A.E.H.R.*, vol. 7, 1967, pp. 150–71; Curthoys *et al.*, *Women at Work*; S. Encel, N. MacKenzie and M. Tebbutt, *Women and Society*, Cheshire, Melbourne, 1974, pp. 151–69; and B. Kingston, *My Wife, My Daughter and Poor Mary Ann*, Nelson, Melbourne, 1975.

10. Literary accounts of working-class life in the period that illustrate these points are L. Esson's play 'The Bride of Gospel Place' (1926), in *The Southern Cross and other Plays*, Robertson & Mullens, Melbourne, 1946, and K. Tennant's novel *The Battlers*, Gollancz, London, 1941; perhaps the most vivid account is *Caddie: The Autobiography of a Sydney Barmaid*, Sun Books, Melbourne, 1975 (first publ. 1953). H. Brownlee, V. Gerrand and R. C. S. Trahair, 'Women Through the Depression: An Empirical Study', *La Trobe Sociology Papers*, no. 17, 1976, though suffering somewhat from abstracted empiricism, confirm some of these impressions from retrospective interviews. M. Dixson, 'Stubborn Resistance: The Northern New South Wales Miners' Lockout of 1929–30', in J. Iremonger *et al.* (eds), *Strikes*, Angus & Robertson, Sydney, 1973, pp. 128–42; and W. Mitchell, 'Wives of the Radical Labour Movement', in Curthoys *et al.*, *Women at Work*, pp. 1–14, treat the story of the women of N.S.W. mining towns.

11. Hughes, *Iron and Steel Industry*, pp. 78–9, 93–5; L. Richardson, 'Dole Queue Patriots: The Port Kembla Pig-iron Strike of 1938', in Iremonger *et al.*, *Strikes*, pp. 143–58; M. Dixson, 'Rothbury', in R. Cooksey (ed.), *The Great Depression in Australia*, Australian Society for the Study of Labour History, Canberra, 1970, pp. 14–26; B. K. De Garis, 'An Incident at Fremantle', *Labour History*, no. 10, 1966, pp. 32–7; T. Sheridan, 'Labour v. Labor: The Victorian Metal Trades Dispute of 1946–47', in Iremonger *et al.*, *Strikes*, pp. 176–224. For the 'test' role of the metal trades, cf. O. de R. Foenander, *Studies in Australian Labour Law and Relations*, M.U.P., Melbourne, 1952, ch. 6, 'The Basic Wage Inquiry Case of 1950'. The changed pattern of strike activity in the post-war period is traced in P. Bentley, 'Recent Strike Behaviour in Australia: Causes and Responses', *Australian Bulletin of Labour*, vol. 1, no. 1, 1974, pp. 27–56.

12. Substantial histories of two of the most important militant unions are now available: R. Gollan, *The Coalminers of New South Wales*, M.U.P. and A.N.U., Melbourne, 1963 (see p. 161 for the working-class sheep); and T. Sheridan, *Mindful Militants*, C.U.P., London, 1975, on the engineers; we badly lack something comparable on the A.W.U. The attempts to create a unified organisation can be followed in I. Bedford, 'The One Big Union, 1918–1923', in *Initiative and Organisation*, Sydney Studies in Politics, no. 3, Cheshire, Melbourne, 1963; and J. Hagan, *The A.C.T.U.: A Short History*, Reed, Sydney, 1977.

The calculation of trends in the distribution of income is as difficult as the calculation of industrial concentration. D. W. Oxnam, 'A Note on Wage Earners' Share of the Proceeds of Industry', *Economic Record*, vol. 27, 1951, pp. 70–4, studies manufacturing and shows wage shares fluctuating between 50 and 55 per cent over the period 1920–49. K. Hancock and K. Moore, 'The Occupational Wage Structure in Australia since 1914', *British Journal of Industrial Relations*, vol. 10, 1972, pp. 107–22, studies wage rates, the dispersion of which fluctuates but seems to return to fairly similar levels over the long run. H. Lydall, *The Structure of Earnings*, Clarendon Press, Oxford, 1968, pp. 190–1, using estimates based on taxation returns, finds the dispersion of incomes falling between 1938 and 1953–54, but increasing again at the end of the 1950s. So far as this uncertain data will take us, it seems that the distribution of income became more equal during the two peaks of class struggle, in the 1910s and 1940s, but then less equal after the ruling-class political victories.

13. *Daily Mirror*, 1 March 1949. Depressing examples of this ideological cringe are the municipal histories of working-class areas; to take only one example from a large field, in reading E. Lumbers, *Centenary History of the Municipal Corporation of the City of Port Adelaide, 1856–1956*, Adelaide, 1956, one would simply not know that this was a centre of working-class radicalism, or even that it had a Labor council! Labor's municipal history has been largely ignored by historians, political scientists and current critics of the party. For a little insight into the inter-war situation, see L. J. Louis, *Trade Unions and the Depression*, A.N.U.P., Canberra, 1968, p. 213; J. Fitzpatrick, *The Barrier Industrial Council*, B.I.C., Broken Hill, n.d. (*c.* 1965). Evidence of the importance of municipal involvement of Labor Party activists can be seen in the potted biographies in S. O'Flaherty, *The Labor Party in South Australia*, A.L.P., Adelaide, 1956. For a summary of the Sydney scandal, which helped to destroy the Lang government in 1927, see A. Birch and D. S. Macmillan (eds), *The Sydney Scene*, M.U.P., Melbourne, 1962, pp. 290–1. F. Hardy's novel *Power Without Glory*, the author, Melbourne, 1950, is a fictional account of Wren's career; for his experiences with the machine in researching it, see *The Hard Way*, Australasian Book Society, Sydney, 1961. For a Catholic counterblast in the form of a biography, see N. Brennan, *John Wren, Gambler*, Hill of Content, Melbourne, 1971, which misses the main point of Hardy's critique of the Labor Party; and for a Catholic critique of Wren, see the speech of S. M. Keon on 27 July 1948, in *Victorian Parliamentary Debates*, vol. 227, pp. 1867–74. R. F. I. Smith, 'Collingwood, Wren Left-overs and Political Change', *Labour History*, no. 30, 1976, pp. 42–57, rather ponderously gives an account of the machine's latter-day decline.

14. On the Collier government in the 1920s, F. K. Crowley, *Australia's Western Third*, Macmillan, London, 1960, pp. 227–31. The depressingly diagnostic tale of development and The Rocks is told by P. Spearritt, 'The Consensus Politics of Physical Planning in Sydney', B.A. thesis, Department of Government, University of Sydney, 1972. On radicalism, E. Spratt, *Eddie Ward*, Rigby, Adelaide, 1965; I. Young, *Theodore*, Alpha, Sydney, 1971; L. F. Crisp, *Ben Chifley*, Longman, Melbourne, 1961; J. T. Lang's story has been told in every book that touches on the depression; for his own account, see *The Great Bust*, Angus & Robertson, Sydney, 1962; and for a recent survey of his whole career, see H. Radi and P. Spearritt (eds), *Jack Lang*, Hale & Iremonger, Sydney, 1977.

15. On socialism in the 1910s, see I. A. H. Turner, *Industrial Labour and Politics: The Dynamics of the Labour Movement in Eastern Australia, 1900–1921*, A.N.U.P., Canberra, 1965; on the socialisation units, R. Cooksey, *Lang and Socialism*, A.N.U.P., Canberra, 1971; and on the revival of socialism in the 1940s, W. J. Waters, 'Labor, Socialism, and World War II', *Labour History*, no. 16, 1969, pp. 14–19. M. Dixson, 'Ideology, the Trades Hall Reds, and J. T. Lang', *Politics*, vol. 6, 1971, pp. 53–65, is an extremely interesting

account of militancy and factional manoeuvering in the 1920s. None of these studies has much evidence about the rank-and-file. Examples of the intellectual socialism of the 1940s are the N.S.W. Fabian Society pamphlets, especially *Towards a Socialist Australia*, Sydney, 1949; and K. Merz, R. Gibson and F. E. Maynard, *A Fair Hearing for Socialism*, Fabian Society, Melbourne, 1944; the latter is a reprint of lectures at St Paul's Cathedral in Melbourne arranged by Father Maynard, who had been a worker-priest in the Mt Morgan mine.

16. A. Davidson, *The Communist Party of Australia: A Short History*, Hoover Institute Press, Stanford, 1969, revolves around the idea of the party moving away from and returning to an Australian tradition of socialism; curiously, the party was strongest when it was dominated by stalinism. R. A. Gollan, *Revolutionaries and Reformists*, A.N.U.P., Canberra, 1975, fills out the character of life in the party in its heyday. F. Farrell, 'Explaining Communist History', *Labour History*, no. 32, 1977, pp. 1–10, reviews the debate over the reasons for the party's stalinisation; M. Dixson, 'Reformists and Revolutionaries in New South Wales, 1920–1922', *Politics*, vol. 1, 1966, pp. 135–51, describes the context of its formation and the union militants' influence in the Labor Party. An excellent account of the social bases of communist union strength in one town is Richardson, 'Dole Queue Patriots'; J. T. Lang, *Communism in Australia: A Complete Exposure*, Century Publications, Sydney, n.d. (1944), is a very hostile but perceptive and well-informed account of communism in the unions. For the clashes of 1948–49, see M. Cribb, 'State in Emergency: The Queensland Railway Strike of 1948', in Iremonger *et al.*, pp. 225–48; Gollan, *Coalminers*, pp. 230–5; Crisp, *Chifley*, pp. 350–67. For the major statement of Communist Party theory in this period, see L. L. Sharkey, *The Trade Unions*, Current Book Distributors, Sydney, 1942. L. H. Gould (ed.), *The Sharkey Writings*, Sydney, n.d. (*c.* 1972), is a useful collection of C.P.A. ideas.

17. H. McQueen, 'The Social Character of the New Guard', *Arena*, no. 40, 1975, pp. 67–86, has forcefully argued the ruling-class character of the New Guard and similar manifestations. For the newspaper episode, E. Lyons, *So We Take Comfort*, Heinemann, London, 1965, p. 145. H. McQueen, 'Who Were the Conscriptionists?', *Labour History*, no. 16, 1969, pp. 44–8; and J. Lonie, '"Good Labor Men": The Hill Government in South Australia, 1930–1933', *Labour History*, no. 31, 1976, pp. 14–29, are useful accounts of two of the splitting groups that point to their relative distance from the industrial working-class sections of the Labor coalition.

18. For typical samples of conservative thought in this period, not a notably theoretical one; see such pamphlets as: Constitutional Association of N.S.W., *A Recipe for Revolution*, Sydney, n.d. (1932?), an attack on Lang; business histories such as Elder, Smith and Co., *The First Hundred Years*, Adelaide, 1940; and autobiographies such as E. Page, *Truant Surgeon*, Angus & Robertson, Sydney, 1963. D. Carment, 'Sir Littleton Groom and the Deportation Crisis of 1925: A Study of Non-Labor Response to Trade Union Militancy', *Labour History*, no. 32, 1977, pp. 46–54, is a good account of the way these themes come together in a tactical crisis.

The Hancockian interpretation of Australian politics in terms of 'initiative and resistance' (see D. W. Rawson, 'Another Look at "Initiative and Resistance"', *Politics*, vol. 3, 1968, pp. 41–54; and M. Goot, 'Parties of Initiative and Resistance: A Reply', *Politics*, vol. 4, 1969, pp. 84–99) essentially mistakes a tactical situation, fairly common in the period 1910–30, for the basic structure. The strategic situation in this period was ruling-class resistance to working-class mobilisation; this sometimes involves resistance to Labor policy 'initiatives', certainly, but also involved 'initiatives' by the conservatives such as those listed in the text. And when the ruling-class reorganisation of the 1940s got under way, the tactical initiative in party conflict generally passed to the conservative parties.

19. Brownlee *et al.*, 'Women Through the Depression', provide useful evidence of its differential impact; Kingston, *My Wife...*, traces the steep decline of domestic service after the depression, which may have contributed to the changing social consciousness that found political expression in the 1940s. Figures on employer organisations are given in the annual *Labour Report* in this period; the quotation is from the 1922 *Report*, p. 15. For statements by prelates on repudiation, see L. J. Louis and I. Turner (eds), *The Depression of the 1930s*, Cassell, Melbourne, 1968, pp. 70–5; for a sketch of Catholic anti-communism in the 1930s, J. G. Murtagh, *Australia: The Catholic Chapter*, Angus & Robertson, Sydney, 1959, pp. 167–78; for its political context, D. Watson, 'Anti-communism in the Thirties', *Arena*, no. 30, 1975, pp. 40–51, who convincingly argues it was a product of genuine fear and confusion and not just red-scare electioneering.

20. B. Irving, 'The Nationalist Party, 1919–1930', unpub. thesis, University of Sydney, 1972, notes that nationalist ideology stressed the parliamentary party rather than the organisation; cf. J. R. Williams, 'The Organisation of the Australian National Party', *Australian Quarterly*, vol. 41, no. 2, 1969, pp. 41–51. For further details on financial organisation, see B. D. Graham, 'The Place of Finance Committees in Non-Labor Politics, 1910–1930', in C. A. Hughes (ed.), *Readings in Australian Government*, U.Q.P., St Lucia, 1968, pp. 367–79; and J. R. Williams, 'Financing Conservative Parties in Australia', *Australian Quarterly*, vol. 43, no. 1, 1971, pp. 7–19. For Hollway's statement, *Argus*, 14 November 1941, p. 3. H. Mayer, *The Press in Australia*, Lansdowne, Melbourne, 1964, is the fullest account of the politics of the press. For further argument on the view stated here, see R. W. Connell, *Ruling Class, Ruling Culture: Studies of Conflict, Power and Hegemony in Australian Life*, C.U.P., London, 1977, ch. 9.

21. Apart from Askin and the civil servants, these careers have been traced in biographies; see C. Edwards, *Bruce of Melbourne*, Heinemann, London, 1965; C. D. Kemp, 'Sir Walter Massy-Greene', in *Big Businessmen*, I.P.A., Melbourne, 1964, pp. 85–140; K. Perkins, *Menzies: Last of the Queen's Men*, Rigby, Adelaide, 1968; Nicholas, *Pacemaker*; and P. Blazey, *Bolte*, Jacaranda, Brisbane, 1972.

22. The story of the I.P.A. is told by D.A. Kemp, 'The Institute of Public Affairs—Victoria, 1942–1947', B.A. thesis, University of Melbourne, 1963; see also Kemp, *Big Businessmen*. J. L. Carrick, *The Liberal Way of Progress*, Sydney, 1948, is a very capable statement of welfare conservatism from New South Wales. For other welfarist stirrings in business, see Robinson, *If I Remember Rightly*, pp. 158 ff; cf. the softening in Lewis' views noted in Blainey, *Steel Master*, p. 177. There was certainly no sudden victory of a new ideology.

For continued rock-ribbed conservatism led by the Adelaide Establishment, see W. J. Waters, 'The Opposition and the "Powers" Referendum, 1944', *Politics*, vol. 4, 1969, pp. 42–56; and for a reaffirmation of free-enterprise fundamentalism by the Federal President of the Liberal Party, see W. H. Anderson, *Dynamic Liberalism*, Sydney, 1956. P. Tiver, 'The Ideology of the Liberal Party of Australia', *Politics*, vol. 11, 1976, pp. 156–64, shows the persistence of some of the old themes long after the war.

23. On the foundation, R. G. Menzies, *Afternoon Light*, Penguin, Ringwood, Vic., 1969, pp. 281–96; J. R. Williams, 'The Emergence of the Liberal Party of Australia', *Australian Quarterly*, vol. 39, 1967, pp. 7–27. For contemporary scepticism about the continued links with business, see 'Has the L.P.A. Dumped the I.P.A.?', *Smith's Weekly*, 6 January 1945; and 'Finance of the "New Liberal Party"', Voice of Labor broadcast by E. D. Gray, in 'Labor Party Broadcasts', T.S.A. (NS 113). The fundamental work on Liberal organisation is K. West, *Power in the Liberal Party*, Cheshire, Melbourne, 1965 (who makes a count of eighteen merged organisations in 1944: pp. 221–2). For membership objectives, see Liberal Party of Australia, 'Report of Proceedings and Minutes of the Inaugural Federal Council Meeting', 1945, Battye Library (1291 A/5); this Report claims a national membership of nearly 100 000, proportionately strongest in South Australia. Blazey, *Bolte*, p. 48, notes a party membership of 46 000 in Victoria at the start of the 1950s and a gradual decline thereafter. This is nearly double the 1945 figure for Victoria, but as business mobilisation there was particularly intense, it is unlikely that national membership had also doubled. West, *Power in the Liberal Party*, pp. 269–70, reports financial members of state divisions in 1961–62 that add to about 120 000, almost half of the total being provided by South Australia, where most of the membership was somnolent. A. Watson, 'The Party Machines', in H. Mayer and H. Nelson (eds), *Australian Politics: A Third Reader*, Cheshire, Melbourne, 1973, p. 364, reports a national membership of 100 000 in 1972. Very probably, the years around 1950 were a peak both in numbers and in the membership's active participation.

24. The organisation of this campaign, with fascinating detail of the political techniques of business, is described in A. L. May, *The Battle for the Banks*, S.U.P., Sydney, 1968; G. Blainey, *Gold and Paper: A History of the National Bank of Australasia Limited*, Georgian House, Melbourne, 1958; and C. D. Kemp, 'Sir Leslie McConnan', in *Big Businessmen*, pp. 141–64. Our interpretation of the campaign is spelt out in more detail in R. W. Connell and T. H. Irving, 'Yes, Virginia, There is a Ruling Class', in H. Mayer and H. Nelson (eds), *Australian Politics: A Fourth Reader*, Cheshire, Melbourne, 1976, pp. 81–92.

25. For detailed narratives of these events, see L. C. Webb, *Communism and Democracy in Australia*, Cheshire, Melbourne, 1954; and R. Murray, *The Split*, Cheshire, Melbourne, 1970. Murray gives an extraordinarily detailed account of the factional politics of the Labor Party, but is unable to grasp the whole matter theoretically—when it comes to the decisive event, Evatt's open attack on the Movement in October 1954, he has to fall back on mental instability as an explanation. I. Campbell, 'A.L.P. Industrial Groups—A Reassessment', *A.J.P.H.*, vol. 8, 1962, pp. 183–99, has balancing remarks on the tactical errors of the groupers, and interesting evidence of financial support of their activities by business.

26. The shift is traced by A. Watt, *The Evolution of Australian Foreign Policy, 1938–1965*, C.U.P., London, 1967; this book itself is an interesting document of cold-war ideology in the upper levels of the civil service. For the politicians' view, see P. C. Spender, *Exercises in Diplomacy*, S.U.P., Sydney, 1969. The major divergences from the American line were over Suez (see Menzies, *Afternoon Light*, pp. 149–85) and West Irian, both issues to do with rival Western imperialisms.

27. There is a very large literature on post-war immigration. For an excellent short review of the subject, see C. A. Price, 'Immigrants', in A. F. Davies and S. Encel, *Australian Society*, Cheshire, Melbourne, 2nd edn, 1970, pp. 180–99. Systematic evidence of their use as an industrial workforce is in J. Kmenta, 'Economic Mobility of Immigrants in Australia', *Economic Record*, vol. 37, 1961, pp. 456–69; for the steelworks, B.H.P., *Seventy-five Years*, pp. 27–8. The best study of migrant industrial life is J. Zubrzycki, *Settlers of the La Trobe Valley*, A.N.U., Canberra, 1964. R. Blandy *et al.*, 'Migrant Workers in Australia: Industrial Cannon-fodder?', *Australian Bulletin of Labour*, vol. 3, no. 2, 1977, pp. 20–31, deny this can be explained in terms of 'dual labour market' theory; mostly an exercise in bashing straw men, though it usefully points to upward mobility over migrants' working lives. For the basis of the view put in the text, see J. Collins, 'The Political Economy of Post-war Immigration', in E. L. Wheelwright and K. Buckley (eds), *Essays in the Political Economy of Australian Capitalism*, A.N.Z. Book Co., Sydney, 1975, pp. 105–29; and 'A Divided Working Class', *Intervention*, no. 8, 1977, pp. 64–78; Collins' concept of segmentation tends to be more statistical than structural, but there is no reason to doubt the main conclusions.

28. On the new support of the stock market, see A. R. Hall, 'Industrial Investment in Listed Company Securities', *Economic Record*, vol. 34, 1958, pp. 375–89; and the A.M.P. Society's *Annual Report 1972*, p. 5, which has a summary of the post-war shift of investment towards shares and real-estate. L. Rivers and J. Hyde, 'The Dominance of Finance Capital', *Arena*, no. 39, 1975, pp. 5–30, give a useful account of the insurance firms' business and political links, though they build rather too much on one episode of opposition to Labor in concluding that this sector now holds political leadership of the ruling class. P. J. B. Rose, *Australian Securities Markets*, Cheshire, Melbourne, 1969, is a useful general account of the exchanges. P. Cochrane, 'Australian Finance Capital in Transition', *Intervention*, no. 6, 1976, pp. 21–36, traces the reorientation of the banks towards industry. On the numbers of shareholders, Lomas, *Will to Win*; Turnbull, 'Diverse Ownership'; and recent *Annual Reports* of B.H.P. and other companies. For statistical evidence of the concentration of the ownership of shares, see R. K. Yorston, 'Some Accounting Implications arising from the Corporation viewed as a Social Unit', *Australian Accountant*, vol. 22, 1952, pp. 41–54, 77–87; E. L. Wheelwright, *Ownership and Control of Australian Companies*, Law Book Co., Sydney, 1957; E. L. Wheelwright and J. Miskelly, *Anatomy of Australian Manufacturing Industry*, Law Book Co., Sydney, 1967; T. Sykes, 'In a Few Hands', *A.F.R.*, 12–16 February 1973. On self-employment, see the figures in Census reports at the following places: 1933, vol. 2, p. 1654; 1954, vol. 8, p. 156; 1961, vol. 8, p. 217; and 1966, vol. 1, pt 8, p. 14. There are of course difficulties in comparing these figures; on the face of it, they suggest a rise in self-employment between 1911 and 1921, but then a regular though gradual decline.

29. A summary of changes in occupational distributions is in L. Broom and F. L. Jones, *Opportunity and Attainment in Australia*, A.N.U.P., Canberra, 1976, ch. 3. For an example of the concern with automation, see the conference recorded in G. W. Ford (ed.), *Automation: Threat or Promise?*, A.N.Z.A.A.S., Sydney, 1969.

30. Official statistics in *Overseas Investment in Australia*, Treasury Economic Paper no. 1, A.G.P.S., Canberra, 1972. For a general survey of foreign investment up to the mid-1960s, see B. Fitzpatrick and E. L. Wheelwright, *The Highest Bidder*, Lansdowne, Melbourne, 1965; and for the new sources, D. T. Brash, *American Investment in Australian Industry*, A.N.U.P., Canberra, 1966, which has useful survey data though its concept of effects is almost purely economic. For the greater profitability of foreign-owned companies, B. L. Johns, 'Private Overseas Investment in Australia: Profitability and Motivation', *Economic Record*, vol. 43, 1967, pp. 233–61.

31. C.R.A.'s story is told from its own point-of-view in *Submission to the Senate Select Committee on Foreign Ownership and Control*, Melbourne, July 1972; and from a critical point of view in R. West, *River of Tears*, Earth Island, London, 1972. There are some inaccuracies in West's book, but it is valuable in putting the local events in the context of the world-wide operations of R.T.Z. P. J. Rose, 'Aspects of Financing the Mineral Industry in Australia', *Australian Economic Review*, no. 4, 1969, pp. 7–18; and R. B. McKern, *Multinational Enterprise and Natural Resources*, McGraw-Hill, Sydney, 1976, give the general background. For detail on one Pilbara company's techniques, see *Operations of Hamersley Iron*, Hamersley, Melbourne, n.d. (1972?).

32. The basic work on cars, written from an economist's angle but with much useful political and organisational detail, is Stubbs, *Australian Motor Industry*. On oil, see J. McB. Grant, 'The Petroleum Industry', in A. Hunter (ed.), *The Economics of Australian Industry*, M.U.P., Melbourne, 1963, pp. 247–88; and R. Murray, *Fuels Rush In*, Macmillan, Melbourne, 1972. For the Sydney planners, see P. Spearritt, *Sydney Since the Twenties*, Hale & Iremonger, Sydney, 1978, ch. 7. For an early account of the decline of public transport, G. R. Webb, 'Urban Transport—The Emerging Problem', *Australian Economic Papers*, vol. 2, no. 1, 1963, pp. 76–84; D. Atkinson, 'The Transport Trap', *Arena*, no. 42, 1976, pp. 40–59, ties the issues more closely to the nature of corporate power.

33. Statistics of post-war housing completions are in the *Commonwealth Year Books*. For the pride taken in the first post-war skyscrapers, see H. C. Sleigh Ltd, *The First Sixty Years*, Melbourne, n.d. (1955); and Mutual Life and Citizens', *The M.L.C. Head Office Building, North Sydney*, Sydney, n.d. (1957). For a sketch of the emergence of this style, see J. M. Freeland, *Architecture in Australia*, Cheshire, Melbourne, 1968, pp. 298–305; on B.H.P. House, P. Corrigan, 'Bronze Medal and Brute Steel: Melbourne's B.H.P. Building', *Meanjin*, vol. 35, no. 1, 1976, pp. 34–41. For a very illuminating study of the finance and politics of central rebuilding, see R. T. M. Whipple, 'Redevelopment and the Real Estate Market in Sydney's Central Area', in P. N. Troy (ed.), *Urban Redevelopment in Australia*, A.N.U., Urban Research Unit, Canberra, 1968, pp. 250–303. There is now a considerable literature on Australian cities: M. Neutze, *Urban Development in Australia*, Allen & Unwin, Sydney, 1977, usefully collates the statistical evidence, though its theory is

derisory; H. Stretton, *Ideas for Australian Cities*, Georgian House, Melbourne, 2nd edn, 1975, fills in political background and cultural meaning with great verve. L. Sandercock, *Cities For Sale*, M.U.P., Melbourne, 1975, is by far the most important in exploring the class nature of urban politics and development processes.

34. On the art market, see J. M. Main, 'Painting: Taste and the Market', in A. F. Davies and S. Encel, *Australian Society*, Cheshire, Melbourne, 1965, pp. 176–89; and for an example of the use of modern paintings in business, see the report of the modern art collection of Consolidated Gold Fields Australia in Sydney, 'Executive with a Feel for the Masters', *Australian*, 5 June 1971. For suggestions about the contrast of Hardy and White, we are indebted to an unpublished paper by Bruce Russell, postgraduate student in the Department of Government, University of Sydney, 1972. For a denial of political intent in the new drama, see D. Williamson, 'The Removalists: A Conjunction of Limitations', *Meanjin Quarterly*, vol. 33, 1974, pp. 413–17. On the 'counter-revolution' in historiography, P. Coleman, 'Introduction: The New Australia', *Australian Civilization*, Cheshire, Melbourne, 1962, pp. 1–11; and on the 'new critics' of this period and their connection with industrial capitalism, T. Rowse, *Australian Liberalism and National Character*, Kibble Books, Melbourne, 1978. For a conscious attempt to spread modernism in design, see the post-war issues of the *Australian Home Beautiful*, and guides to interior decoration in popular handbooks, such as *Australian Women's Complete Household Guide Illustrated*, Colorgravure Publications, Melbourne, n.d. (*c.* 1950). For an example of the corporate promotion of motor sport, see *Repco Record*, vol. 16, no. 62, 1972, pp. 28–9. For examples of 'modernism' in political argument, see Liberal Party pamphlets such as *Back to Methuselah: The Faceless Men and the Power Structure of the Labor Party*, Sydney, n.d. (1965?). On the selling of home-ownership and suburban life, Connell, *Ruling Class, Ruling Culture*, pp. 215–17; J. Kemeny, 'The Ideology of Home Ownership', *Arena*, no. 46, 1977, pp. 81–9; and 'A Political Sociology of Home Ownership in Australia', *A.N.Z.J.S.*, vol. 13, 1977, pp. 47–52.

35. On the migration from the inner suburbs, see R. J. Pryor, 'Urban Fringe Residence', *Australian Geographer*, vol. 11, 1969, pp. 148–56; on its economics, M. R. Hill, *Housing Finance in Australia, 1945–1956*, M.U.P., Melbourne, 1959; and (a fine capitalist celebration of 'the meteoric rise' in hire-purchase debt), V. H. S. Low, *The Philosophy of Hire Purchase*, Australian Hire Purchase Conference, Melbourne, 1959.

36. Three important surveys in Melbourne and one in Adelaide give evidence of these processes: D. Scott and R. U'Ren, *Leisure*, Cheshire, Melbourne, 1962; A. F. Davies, 'Social Class in the New Suburb', *Westerly*, no. 3, 1961, pp. 15–18; 'Politics in the New Suburb', *A.J.P.H.*, vol. 8, 1962, pp. 214–23; and *Images of Class*, S.U.P., Sydney, 1967; L. Bryson and F. Thompson, *An Australian Newtown*, Penguin, Ringwood, Vic., 1972; and J. I. Martin, 'Suburbia: Community and Network', in Davies and Encel, *Australian Society*, 2nd edn, pp. 301–39. For evidence of home-centredness, see also R. Lansbury, 'The Suburban Community', *A.N.Z.J.S.*, vol. 6, 1970, pp. 131–8: and for evidence of its impact on women, the non-survey — i.e. accounts written by the women themselves — in G. Wesson (ed.), *Brian's Wife, Jenny's Mum*, Dove, Melbourne, 1975. For the new mining towns, see the excellent study

by C. Williams, 'Working Class Women in an Australian Mining Town', *Hecate*, vol. 2, no. 1, 1976, pp. 7–20.

37. For a case-study of migrant settlement in the cities in the 1950s, see F. L. Jones, 'Italians in the Carlton Area', *A.J.P.H.*, vol. 10, 1964, pp. 83–95; on their politics, J. Jupp, *Arrivals and Departures*, Cheshire–Lansdowne, Melbourne, 1966; and A. F. Davies, 'Migrants in Politics', in *Essays in Political Sociology*, Cheshire, Melbourne, 1972, pp. 67–81. On their involvement in industrial action, see Stubbs, *Motor Industry*, p. 206; G. H. Sorrell, 'The Dispute at Mount Isa', *Australian Quarterly*, vol. 37, no. 2, 1965, pp. 22–33; and reporting of the Broadmeadows strike: for example, *A.F.R.*, 24 July 1973. For a general discussion of this strike, see P. Bentley, 'Australian Trade Unionism 1972–73', *Journal of Industrial Relations*, vol. 15, 1973, pp. 419–30.

38. On this process of unionisation, see R. D. Williams, 'White-collar Unions', in P. W. D. Matthews and G. W. Ford, *Australian Trade Unions*, Sun, Melbourne, 1968, pp. 146–64. J. I. Martin, in 'Class Identification and Trade Union Behaviour', *Journal of Industrial Relations*, vol. 7, 1965, pp. 131–48, disputes the view that white-collar unions are less political than blue-collar unions, but it can hardly be denied that they are generally less class-conscious.

39. The most important attempt to grapple with these questions was undertaken by theorists connected with the Melbourne socialist magazine *Arena*; see the discussion of the '*Arena* thesis' in W. Osmond, 'Towards Self-awareness', in R. Gordon (ed.), *The Australian New Left*, Heinemann, Melbourne, 1970, pp. 166–216. The *Arena* thesis is right about the significance of change in the realm of production, but seems over-optimistic about the implicitly socialist content of intellectual culture. On professionalism, see P. Bishop, 'Values and Legitimation in Professionalism—The Primacy of Status', *A.N.Z.J.S.*, vol. 9, 1973, pp. 37–41; on knowledge and consciousness in the schools, Connell, *Ruling Class, Ruling Culture*, chs 7–8.

40. On the elaboration of hierarchy in administration, see S. Encel, *Equality and Authority*, Cheshire, Melbourne, 1970; on the revival of margins, Hancock and Moore, 'Occupational Wage Structure'; on selection in education, T. Roper, *The Myth of Equality*, N.U.A.U.S., Melbourne, 1970; on status grades in planned suburbs, Stretton, *Ideas for Australian Cities*.

41. For collations of data that stimulated the discussion of poverty in this framework, see R. G. Brown, 'Poverty in Australia', *Australian Quarterly*, vol. 35, no. 2, 1963, pp. 75–9; 'Poverty in Australia—The Evidence', *British Journal of Sociology*, vol. 15, 1964, pp. 150–65; and J. Stubbs, *The Hidden People*, Cheshire–Lansdowne, Melbourne, 1966; and for its development by economists, A. F. Henderson, A. Harcourt and R. J. A. Harper, *People in Poverty*, Cheshire, Melbourne, 1970. This defined the 'poverty-line' approach that was carried through in Henderson's official inquiry, Australian Government Commission of Enquiry into Poverty, *Poverty in Australia*, vol. 1, A.G.P.S., Canberra, 1975. For the critique of the assumptions of this approach and analyses of the role of the 'welfare state' as a means of the reproduction of capitalist social relations, see A. Pemberton, 'Towards a Radical Critique of Social Work and Welfare Ideology', *Australian Journal of Social Issues*, vol. 6, 1971, pp. 95–107; J. Roe, 'Social Policy and the Perma-

nent Poor', in Wheelwright and Buckley, *Political Economy*, pp. 130–52; W. Higgins, 'A Working Paper on the Welfare State', *Arena*, no. 40, 1975, pp. 42–66; J. Collins and R. Boughton, 'Capitalism and Poverty: A Critique of the Henderson Report', *Intervention*, no. 7, 1976, pp. 3–33.

42. On the trough in the fortunes of the Labor Party, see Murray, *The Split*; D. W. Rawson, *Labor in Vain?*, Longman, Melbourne, 1966; R. Ward, 'The End of the Ice Age', *Meanjin*, vol. 32, no. 1, 1973, pp. 5–13. There is now a general survey of the D.L.P.: P. L. Reynolds, *The Democratic Labor Party*, Jacaranda, Brisbane, 1974. On the vicissitudes of the Communists, see Davidson, *Communist Party*; R. Mortimer, 'Communists and the Australian Left', *New Left Review*, no. 46, 1967, pp. 45–54. The main product of Fabian socialist intellectuals was A. Davies and G. Serle, *Policies for Progress*, Cheshire, Melbourne, 1954. The 'socialism of magazines' centred on *Overland* (1954–), *Outlook* (1957–70) and *Arena* (1963–), with *Nation* (1958–71) and *Dissent* (1961–) representing the non-Marxist Left; for a survey of these developments, see A. Barcan, *The Socialist Left in Australia 1949–1959*, A.P.S.A. Monograph no. 2, Sydney, 1960. J. F. Cairns, *Socialism and the A.L.P.*, Victorian Fabian Society Pamphlet no. 8, Melbourne, 1963, was the most important theoretical statement of socialism in the Labor Party; for the later development of his thought, see G. Summy, 'The Revolutionary Democracy of J. F. Cairns', *Politics*, vol. 7, 1972, pp. 55–66. For a remarkable photographic record of the peak of the anti-war campaign, see J. F. Cairns, *Silence Kills*, Victorian Moratorium Committee, Melbourne, 1970.

43. On the change in the electoral base of the Labor Party, see R. R. Alford, *Party and Society*, Murray, London, 1964, p. 178; and 'Class Voting in the Anglo-American Political Systems', in S. M. Lipset and S. Rokkan (eds), *Party Systems and Voter Alignments*, Free Press, New York, 1967, pp. 67–93 (needless to say 'class' here means occupation); D. Kemp, 'Social Change and the Future of Political Parties: The Australian Case', in L. Maisel and P. M. Sacks (eds), *The Future of Political Parties*, Sage, Beverly Hills, Calif., 1975, pp. 124–64. S. Encel, 'Political Leadership in Australia', *Australian Journal of Social Issues*, vol. 1, no. 2, 1962, pp. 2–10, already noted the declining dominance of manual workers in the Labor Party leadership. For Whitlam's position in the 1950s, see 'The Constitution *versus* Labor', in *Labor and the Constitution*, Victorian Fabian Society Pamphlet no. 11, Melbourne, 1965. Note that his final argument in 1957 was to change the Constitution: as the difficulty of that became more apparent, he gave increasing stress to the use of executive power within the existing Constitution. For his accession to office, L. Oakes and D. Solomon, *The Making of an Australian Prime Minister*, Cheshire, Melbourne, 1973. For a comprehensive statement of the programme of the new reformism, see J. D. McLaren (ed.), *Towards a New Australia*, Cheshire, Melbourne, 1972. R. Catley and B. McFarlane, *From Tweedledum to Tweedledee*, A.N.Z. Book Co., Sydney, 1974, offer a detailed critique that overstates the integration of these policies, but correctly points to their rationalising function.

44. Information on Elizabeth supplied by the S.A. Housing Trust; on the Westernport development, see L. Sandercock, 'Politics, Planning and Participation', *Australian Quarterly*, vol. 46, no. 3, 1974, pp. 48–64; on the Pilbara, *The Pilbara Study*: *Report on the Industrial Development of the Pilbara, June 1974*,

A.G.P.S., Canberra, 1974. An excellent survey of these relationships at the national level is K. Rowley, 'The Political Economy of Australia Since the War', in J. Playford and D. Kirsner (eds), *Australian Capitalism*, Penguin, Ringwood, Vic., 1972, pp. 265–324.

45. The major study of the bureaucratic elite is Encel, *Equality and Authority*; see also J. Playford, *Neo-capitalism in Australia*, Arena, Melbourne, 1969, on relationships with business. G. Caiden, *The Commonwealth Bureaucracy*, M.U.P., Melbourne, 1967, is the orthodox survey of organisation; B. Juddery, *At the Centre*, Cheshire, Melbourne, 1974, has much more detail of internal politics and the readjustments of the early 1970s.

46. For the fullest account of the business leadership in this period, see Encel, *Equality and Authority*, esp. pp. 390–415; on the 'professionalisation' of company directors, M. Baume, 'The Grey Men of Business', *Quadrant*, vol. 8, no. 1, 1964, pp. 13–29; on salaries and fringe benefits, H. Gepp, 'Executive Salaries: Policies and Practices', *Personnel Practice Bulletin*, vol. 17, no. 3, 1961, pp. 22–7; and D. Gunzburg, 'Executive Salaries and Benefits in Non-manufacturing Firms', *Personnel Practice Bulletin*, vol. 27, no. 1, 1971, pp. 11–45.

47. For company numbers and profits, see *Commonwealth Taxation Assessments 1969–70*, Bulletin no. 9, pp. 37, 42. The figure for B.H.P.'s capital represents funds employed. On workforces, see *Annual Reports* for 1972 of the companies named; not all companies give this information, but it is becoming increasingly common. Examples of holding company structure in the Top 50 are Wormald (1949); Olympic (1953); C.R.A. (1962—the biggest); Johns Perry (1966); M.I.M. (1970). Carlton and United Breweries is an interesting inversion—until its corporate reorganisation in 1973, the merged breweries had in effect been holding companies in it.

48. On Ford, see 'Bill Bourke Keeps His Foot Flat', *Australian*, 15 May 1972; on the management structure of Chrysler, Stubbs, *Motor Industry*, p. 153. Personal power in a personally built business is classically illustrated by D. F. Packer; see R. S. Whitington, *Sir Frank*, Cassell, Melbourne, 1971; and the interview with him in R. Moore, *Profiles of Power*, Australian Broadcasting Commission, Sydney, 1970, pp. 91–104. Management by committees is more characteristic in the bigger companies; B.H.P. has even created a post of 'general manager corporate affairs' concerned purely with co-ordination (*Australian*, 17 September 1974).

49. On restrictive agreements, Commissioner of Trade Practices, *Fourth Annual Report*, Canberra, 1971, p. 15; for a general review of such rings in the 1950s, see A. Hunter, 'Restrictive Practices and Monopolies in Australia', *Economic Record*, vol. 37, 1961, pp. 25–52. As one example of the joint ventures, all the major companies in the aluminium industry except Alcan are owned by consortia; see *The Australian Aluminium Industry*, Aluminium Development Council, Sydney, n.d. (1969?), p. 4. The most massive consortium project of all, a proposed nine-company 'jumbo' steel plant in Western Australia, seems to have folded, though something new may now develop in the Pilbara.

50. For accounts of some of the takeover struggles, see 'The Takeover Specialist', *Australian*, 15 April 1972; 'The Deal of a Lifetime', *Daily Telegraph*,

17 October 1972; and 'A "Proud Capitalist" who Gives it a Go', *Australian*, 21 March 1972; and M. Indyk, 'Establishment and Nouveau Capitalists', *A.N.Z.J.S.*, vol. 10, 1974, pp. 128–34.

51. There is a somewhat diffuse literature that presents Australian capitalism in this period as essentially subordinate to foreign capital, from the socialist perspective of E. L. Wheelwright, *Radical Political Economy*, A.N.Z. Book Co., Sydney, 1974, to the national-bourgeois perspective of most commentary on foreign takeovers; for example, G. McCarthy, *The Great Big Australian Takeover Book*, Angus & Robertson, Sydney, 1973. Control of the publishing industry is sketched in T. Barr, 'Foreign Bound: Australian Publishing', *Arena*, no. 35, 1974, pp. 23–4, 60–3. Some reasons for shifting this emphasis are given in Connell, *Ruling Class, Ruling Culture*, but it really needs much more detailed argument. On the Comalco share offer in 1970, see West, *River of Tears*, pp. 101–8.

52. *Ruling Class, Ruling Culture*, ch. 6. On the appeal for John Curtin House, see *Australian*, 6 September 1974. A flood of articles and books on the Whitlam government and its demise is still coming, most at the level of Canberra in-fighting.

53. There is dispute over what actually happened to shares of national income, but it may be presumed that the view argued by R. A. Price, 'The Effect of the Government's Economic Policies on Industry, 1973–1975', *Australian Quarterly*, vol. 48, no. 2, 1976, pp. 81–94, that there was a redistribution of income that 'caused a severe profit slump and exacerbated the critical capital shortage' was at least widely *believed* by capitalists in 1975; Price works for the Victorian Chamber of Manufactures.

Documents

Ruling-class Organisation

Ideological Struggle and the State

The Labour Market

Family Life and Hegemony

5.1 Monopoly in heavy industry

From a socialist pamphlet, illustrating both the concentration of industrial capital and the radical critique current at the time.

Source: B. Fitzpatrick, *The Rich Get Richer*, Rawson's Book Shop, Melbourne, 1944.

MONOPOLY is the worm in the bud of the common man's future in Australia. There is no "century of the common man" before us unless the people of Australia, through their Governments, restrain the small group of irresponsible business organisations which dominate the national life. There is no prospect of social security in Australia, while our Governments continue to burk the issue of control of business monopolies. On the contrary, as things are shaping now, opportunities for the private enterprise of unprivileged citizens will be narrower and fewer after the war, than they were before it. At present, while Monopoly continues unrestrained, planning by the Ministry of Post-war Reconstruction is no more than mental exercise for the university graduates who form the departmental staff. The planners may have plans, but they have not the power to carry out those plans. . . .

B.H.P.'s £30,000,000 Monopoly.—Take first the Broken Hill Pty. Co. Ltd., registered in Melbourne in 1885. B.H.P. is the archetype, the supreme example, of monopolistic organisation in Australia. It has assets worth more than £30,000,000, the most valuable of all private holdings in Australian business apart from the banks' holdings. B.H.P. shareholders, who own this great wealth, are credited on the books with nearly £14,000,000 of share capital paid up, which is the largest paid up capital of any company engaged in Australian industry. B.H.P. shareholders' funds—paid-up capital plus reserves and undistributed profits—amount to more than £23,000,000, a holding only rivalled by the funds of the Colonial Sugar Refining Co. Ltd.

If the bulk of that £30,000,000 worth of assets were owned by a large number of Australian residents, as B.H.P. propaganda has implied—"we have 20,000 shareholders . . . 30,000 shareholders"— then the fact that the B.H.P. and its many satellite companies have a complete monopoly of steel making might not be wholly objectionable. *If* ownership of B.H.P. assets were spread widely among Australians, and if their votes as shareholders really counted in the control of this great organisation, then perhaps only irreconcilable opponents of the principle of private ownership of the means of production might cavil at the monopoly. But the facts are otherwise.

Not a single B.H.P. share has ever been offered for public subscription. The company started silver-lead mining 58 years ago, and steel production 29 years ago. In the beginning the "paid-up" capital was £320,000, of which only £18,000 was subscribed in cash, the rest being issued free to the promoters. When the steel enterprise was started in 1915, "paid-up" capital was still less than £500,000, of which less than £200,000 had been subscribed in cash, the balance being the "water" of bonus issues; shares given free to those who had got in on the ground floor. Nowadays, B.H.P.'s so-called paid-up capital is nearly £14,000,000, or about thirty times the 1915 capital. The whole of the enormous additional capital has been kept "in the family," except for about £1,300,000 issued to shareholders whose businesses, mostly overseas firms' branches, B.H.P. took over. All the rest went to companies or individuals already holding B.H.P. shares. They received some additional shares at par, that is, at £1 a share, the nominal value of shares worth perhaps double that amount on the market. They received other shares at a premium, that is, at a price above the face value but, nevertheless, less than the market value.

Well over £6,000,000 of the £14,000,000 capital of B.H.P. was issued *free* to shareholders, including a bonus issue of more than £4,000,000 made just before the outbreak of the present war.

That is how ownership of Australia's greatest monopoly was distributed. The general public enter the B.H.P. picture only when some B.H.P. shareholder disposes of shares on the stock exchange. B.H.P. shares being valuable possessions, with a prospect of being added to by bonuses, not much B.H.P. capital moves through the stock exchanges. Those who have B.H.P. scrip hold it if they can. *And those who hold B.H.P. scrip in quantity are a few rich Australians and Anglo-Australians, some other Australian and Anglo-Australian companies, and rich English interests which early saw the prospect of huge profits in the Broken Hill silver-lead lodes, and with their accumulated weight of capital, their call on technical skills, and their ownership of refining plants, were in a position to overwhelm the handful of sheep station employees whose searches uncovered the mineral wealth of the Barrier long ago.*

B.H.P. keeps share registers in London and in Melbourne, and by spending a good deal of money, it would be possible to trace the ownership of great blocks of the company's shares. But this fact will do as an indication: in 1912, not long before B.H.P. switched "from silver to steel", 760,000 of B.H.P.'s shares (nominal value then 5/- a share) were held in London. (R. L. Nash: "Australasian Joint Stock Companies' Year Book," 1913–14.) That is nearly 80 per cent. Nearly all shares issued in the 30 years since then have been issued to individuals and companies already holding shares. So it is reasonable to suppose that the great bulk of B.H.P. capital is still held by overseas capitalists. The complicated ramifications of the Australian steel monopoly, through Australian, British and American company organisations, are of a kind to support this view of B.H.P.

5.2 Defensive political organisation in the depression

Narrative of the organisation of an anti-Labor coalition in South Australia, by the academic who became chairman of the 'Emergency Committee', clearly illustrating ideology of the period. The Citizens' League was a middle-class anti-party organisation. Lyons had been Treasurer in the Labor federal government, and at this time was seen as future leader of a 'national' government, which he shortly became. This extraordinarily interesting document was softened by the author in preparation for publication; the original text is given here.

Source: A. Grenfell Price, 'The Emergency Committee of South Australia and the Origin of the Premiers' Plan 1931–2', typescript, State Library of South Australia.

By the end of 1930 Australia was becoming alarmed at the strange new doctrine of inflation which was emanating from Theodore, and when I took my family to Victor Harbour for our annual holiday I took down various books on the course of inflation in other lands. My wife and I discussed the question at great length, and I finally drafted a pamphlet of about 30 pages which compared the drift in Australia with that in Germany. The main authority I used was D'Abernon, on the German inflationary crisis, and the comparison seemed quite clear.

This pamphlet was published in March, as "The menace of inflation" and apparently made an impression, as it appeared in the middle of the Scullin–Lyons controversy. The Banks and Insurance Companies took it up and it ran into a large number of impressions and sales exceeded 30,000 copies. Professors Shann and Melville were very pleased with the little effort—indeed Shann was mainly instrumental in securing the large sale. ...

The business men also asked me to give the "Menace of Inflation" in the Town Hall as a public lecture. Winterbottom, the Secretary of the Chamber of Manufactures made the arrangements, but the attendance was poor. Bagot promised to cooperate with the Citizens' League, but could not have done anything much. Two days afterwards I had a letter from Arthur Champion, Manager of the Colonial Sugar Refining Company, saying that I must get in touch with more influential people if I was to do anything. Others expressed the same opinion, and emphasised the necessity of action in the national crisis.

The chance came a few days later. The Hon. W. G. Duncan and C. A. S. Hawker M.H.R. asked me to lunch at the Adelaide Club and invited me to take on the job of bringing the anti-socialist organisations together. These men were Liberals and they made no secret of their anxiety as to the immediate danger of the Citizens' League. If the League came in and formed a new Lyons party it would split the vote. If, on the other hand, the League could be kept under control until after the crisis it would collapse through lack of funds. The other organisations to be brought in were the Country Party, Political Reform League, and Business Men—no doubt the last two seemed to the Liberals to be simply Liberal pups. Charles Hawker (who was on the St. Mark's Council) was, as usual, delightfully frank. He stated that they had looked over the possible people and that I was the least offensive. The final choice was apparently Sir Joseph Verco (who was almost blind and very old) or myself. ...

My first duty was to try and get the parties and leagues together, but before I issued an invitation for a conference I saw all the leaders concerned. The time was most inauspicious as the Country Party and Liberals were at daggers drawn over the election of Senator Kneebone, but I went down to the House and saw A. G. Cameron and the Hon. A. P. Blesing, the two leaders of their party of four. I also saw Bagot, who was non-commital, but I worked the League through L. V. Pellew and C. W. Andersen, whom I knew well. Over the others there was no doubt—the Liberals, Political Reform League and Business Men were all ready to come in. ...

On my return to Adelaide [after consultation with conservatives in Melbourne] we faced three lines of work: First the committee had to raise funds; second we had to organise the State for the Federal election, and thirdly we had to choose a combined team of Federal candidates.

The first job was to raise funds. On May 14th I spoke to the Business Men of Adelaide in the Wool Exchange putting the need for funds as strongly as possible. My speech is fully reported in the "News" of that day.

The speech seemed to have a very good effect. We had already formed a Finance Committee consisting of Norman Taylor (Chairman), Copley (L.F.), Parsons (C.P.), Queale (C.L.), and Hogben (P.R.L.), and myself. We now formed a strong Advisory Committee in finance consisting of such men as Tom Barr Smith and Sir Wallace Bruce. Bruce and others were against an immediate appeal for funds, even though the Federal election seemed imminent. Fortunately I made a very strong appeal that funds should be raised immediately. Had I not done so the E.C. would have been absolutely up against things in regard to finance, for, as the chance of an immediate election faded away, there would have been no possibility of obtaining money. As it was I used the information obtained in Melbourne that the financial position of the country was desperate and that two or three more members of the Scullin party were wobbling and might come across. This decided the matter, and we entered the field before Scullin and Theodore saved themselves by submitting to the Premiers' Plan.

The financial appeal was a wonderful success resulting in subscriptions of £6,000–£7,000. Much of this we placed upon deposit. The balance we used for what we called organising and educational work. At first we paid the organisations on the following basis: Liberals £250 a month. C.L. £250 a month. C.P. £60. P.R.L. £50. Later we lowered this to two-thirds of these amounts, much to the fury of Bagot, who had wild ideas of needing enormous sums for the South Australian campaign.

The men who did the financial work were—N. H. Taylor (the Chairman), and D. C. Turner and C. B. Jennings, Financial secretaries, but behind the scenes men like Sir Walter Young and T. Barr Smith did wonders. D. C. Turner was splendid—quite the outstanding figure in finance. As chairman of the St. Mark's College Finance Committee he had proved himself a marvel at raising funds, and one of my first steps was to ask him to be Financial Secretary of the Committee. He had great energy, a well-deserved reputation for generosity, and, although not widely known in business circles, a great pull with the people that mattered most. ... Actually most of the money that came in was Liberal money, and a very large part went to the C.L. But the League deserved substantial assistance, for it was the League more than any other body which was educating the public and pulling the floating vote.

Our second job was that of organisation. We formed a Campaign Committee consisting of myself as Chairman, Page (L.F.) Bagot (C.L.), Cameron (C.P.), and Wilson (P.R.L.). In the city work Wilson took the lead. He strongly criticised the Liberal organising work, and took an immense amount of trouble in preparing a city organisation. Our final plan was to form an Emergency Committee for each electoral subdivision, which in turn formed Polling Booth Committees. The city work was done by the Liberal, C.L. and P.R.L. Had the election come on rapidly these Committees would have done good work, but as it was they varied in their efforts as the imminence of the election faded away. We began this organising with divisional meetings in the banqueting room of the Town Hall. Boothby for instance met on 19th May. ...

As time went on we built up our organisation of the country districts. The Campaign Committee recommended the expenditure of a substantial sum, and we appointed six country organisers from the various bodies to carry on the work. These were: H. Hudson (Citizens' League), R. J. Champion (Citizens' League), W. G. Alexander (Country Party), W. T. Strahan (Liberal),

J. Rundle (Liberal), G. King (Liberal). They were sent out to form an Emergency Committee in every important country centre—these numbered hundreds. By the opening of the final election campaign at the end of the year the organisers had just about finished their work. Their reports were most interesting. Everywhere there was a strong swing from Labour. Old Labour men made secret offers of assistance, provided that their names and connection with the committee were not published in the press. These reports more than any other factor convinced me that we were on a winning horse.

All through the year members of the committee supplemented the Country Organisers' work. Walter Duncan and I were all over the place, speaking at Mt. Gambier, Maitland Y. P., Riverton, Clare, and many other centres. Everywhere the reception we received was excellent, and there was practically no opposition at all. We also got out a tremendous lot of country publicity by means of the "Advertiser" and the Country Press. Hogben organised an excellent city press section which fed the "Advertiser" as the newspaper which circulated everywhere, and I boiled down the publicity articles sent out by Martin Threlfall from Canberra, and the Country Press published a great deal of this work. We were also helped by several important visitors. Lyons came over and spoke at Nuriootpa and other centres; Latham spoke in the country during his visit, and we had a most amusing visit from Earle Page, the Federal Country Party leader. . . .

The Scullin Ministry fell on November 20th., we had just four weeks for the election campaign. We at once took over half the Executor Trustee Building and had 70 typists and other workers installed after the week end of the 29th. Page and his most able staff moved in, and the huge job of getting out hundreds of thousands of circulars was done in a warehouse in Stephens Place. I immediately organised the following committees:

1. *Finance* under Taylor and Turner (who was well again). They called together the Advisory Body, and under Morphett (George and Ralph) they raised some £7,000 additional. Turner moved in as permanent Chairman, and he and Hogben did all the financial work.
2. *Page took the Campaign Directorate* and managed all the arrangements for the campaign. He did a wonderful job without a single hitch.
3. *I took the general supervision*, and the *Chairmanship of Publicity* with Langsford as paid organiser.

   We formed the following committees:

   Posters and Hoardings—Langsford.

   Press—Parish and Martindale from the Advertiser with a permanent salaried man—Sexton of the Advertiser.

   Letter Writing: Hogben and committee.

   Illustrated Leaflets: Lavington and Jack Bonython.

   Pamphlets, etc.: A. G. P. Wilson, Hogben, and A. M. Bills of St. Marks, who did some great work. He had just taken a literary degree.

In our building were all the City Divisional Committees. Adelaide (Harper), Hindmarsh (Simmons), Boothby (Mrs. Boundy) etc.

The six country organisers who had just finished the preliminary work got out again and finished the campaign.

I had a colossal amount of work. I got up at 5 a.m. at college and drafted advertisements, slogans and pamphlets, and worked in the office from 9 a.m.

to 11 p.m. getting home for a few hours sleep. Sir David Gordon and Walter Duncan kindly came in to censor all the work. There were a few troubles. The main difficulty was the attitude of the C.P. over Wakefield. Badman, however, stood firm against Collins, and behaved splendidly, and Blesing and Cameron went to the west coast and helped there in the campaign, thus avoiding Wakefield.

Everywhere enthusiasm was intense, and we won 9 out of the 10 seats. ...

In the broad issue the results of the election of 1931 were remarkable. The nation had been stirred to its foundations. For the extravagant Bruce Ministry it had substituted in 1929 a Government of wobblers, and financial extremists, who pleased few and frightened almost all. The mistakes of the Scullin Ministry had roused an indignant nation, which had developed a political interest such as Australia had not seen since the stirring times of the foundation of the Commonwealth. Above all, the crisis had found the nation sound on a number of fundamental principles. First, as in the Conscription issue, the individual proved finer than the machine. As usual with the Labour Party the good men refused to be bound. Second, the nation showed its willing determination to face hard facts, and to make such sacrifices as might be required. We spoke plainly on the platform in South Australia. Neither Lyons nor the local leaders made any of the usual glowing promises. We spoke of sufferings, of sacrifices, and of duties, and the nation, although it had been spoon-fed by arbitration, by pensions, and by a dozen socialistic policies, which had temporarily sapped the foundations of individualism, responded to the call. Thirdly and most of all, the people showed their British traditions and their Imperial affections. They rallied against communism throughout the length and breadth of the land. I was never certain of the real value of our currency policy: I disliked intensely our cooperation with the manufacturing interests, who were utterly selfish in their tariff attitude, but I was certain of this one point—that the future of our country depended upon her maintaining her membership as an honest partner in the British Commonwealth of Nations, despite all the machinations of Communist Langs and Irish Scullins. I am certain that it was primarily the appeal of British minded Australians to a British people that gave the victory to our hands.

5.3 Political revival: The Liberal Party

These reports of the party's inaugural Federal Council illustrate some of its organisational and policy measures. Note the stress on publicity and the welfare content of its policy.

Source: *Sydney Morning Herald*: (i) 29 August 1945, p. 45; (ii) 31 August 1945, p. 3; (iii) 1 September 1945, p. 3.

(i) *Liberals' policy and publicity*

The problem of dealing effectively with policy and publicity was of outstanding importance in the struggle ahead, said the Leader of the Federal Opposition, Mr. Menzies, at a meeting of the Liberal Party Council in Sydney yesterday...

The meeting of the Federal Council was the first since the inception of the party and was attended by delegates from all States.

Mr. T. Malcolm Ritchie, who was elected unaminously first Federal president of the Council, was in the chair.

FREMANTLE DEFEAT

Mr. Menzies, mentioning the party's defeat at the Fremantle by-election, revealed his disappointment that a candidate of outstanding qualifications and with a war background had failed to wrest the seat from the Government...

He had returned from that State strengthened in his belief that the Liberal Party must have a strong central office—a real Federal Secretariat—which could be responsible for the preparation of publicity material.

They must give extremely close attention to policy and publicity at the meeting of the Liberal Party's Federal council.

COUNTRY SUPPORT

Consideration must also be given to primary industries, and the party must show that it understood rural problems and was prepared to do something constructive.

"If we can present to the people six or eight considered statements on six or eight live issues," he said, "we will be able to satisfy the minds of hundreds of thousands of good people who are still sceptical about us, although they want to be with us."

"We are not in a position to say that we command the support of a majority of the people of Australia."

"It will be one of our tasks at this meeting to devise ways and means of making progress with the people of Australia by presenting to them extremely well-considered ideas with all the arts of publicity."

Liberal Party delegates from all States, including the Premier of South Australia, Mr. Playford, heard Mr. Menzies...

Mr. Ritchie said that the real problem before the Liberal Party was the development of all the resources of Australia quickly, and with a determination to make it fit for all free men and women to live in, each with a sensible share of all that modern life had to offer.

CONSTITUTION ADOPTED

The meeting adopted the constitution of the Liberal Party as framed by the Albury Conference...

(ii) *Policy planning by Liberal Party*

The Federal Council of the Liberal Party of Australia yesterday defined the authority of the Federal executive of the party.

The executive, which consists of the president and one member from each State division, shall subject to the party's constitution and to the control of the council, have power to manage all the affairs of the Federal council, except matters affecting the alteration of the constitution of the party or the raising of money.

The new Federal executive consists of Messrs. T. Malcolm Ritchie (president), W. H. Spooner (N.S.W.), W. H. Anderson (Vic.), P. A. McBride (S.A.), H. Bushby (Tas.), J. L. Paton (W.A.), and J. B. Chandler (Q.)...

The Leader of the Federal Opposition, Mr. Menzies, took an active part in discussions at the council meeting, and members said afterwards that he had played a leading part in its deliberations...

FEDERAL SECRETARIAT

The Council attaches much importance to the creation of a Federal Secretariat.

The resolution favouring its establishment said that the plan of organization of the Federal Secretariat should be the basis of a long range scheme of organisation for co-ordinating the development of the Liberal Party through the State divisions...

Members of the Council expect that when the Secretariat is in full operation, it will have a very constructive and far reaching effect on public opinion.

WOMEN'S PART

The women's activities sub-committee of the Council yesterday decided to co-opt women members from all State divisions to inaugurate an Australian-wide drive to interest women in the Liberal Party.

In presenting a progress report to the Council, Miss M. Battye of Western Australia, said that, in many Federal electorates there was already a preponderance of women voters, and that special efforts must be made to secure the interest and support of all women.

(iii) *Tax cuts and adequate housing are main Liberal planks*

An "all round reduction of the taxation burden" and an adequate housing programme were placed in the forefront of the Liberal Party's policy by the Leader of the Federal Parliamentary Liberal Party, Mr. Menzies, in a speech in Sydney last night.

Mr. Menzies, who was speaking at the official inauguration of the party to a crowded audience in the Assembly Hall, Margaret Street, made the following policy points:—

TAXATION

There was every reason why taxation should be reduced at once, for there could be little doubt that even substantially reduced taxation would hardly affect the total tax yield in the next few years, when civil production would be enormously increased.

Special consideration should be given to the family taxpayer, particularly with reference to allowances for children, medical and education expenses...

HOUSING

The present grave shortage of houses demanded the application of a policy envisaging the co-operation of the Commonwealth, State, and local authorities...

SOCIAL SECURITY

The Liberal Party would vigorously pursue a policy of generous provision for superannuation, incapacity, sick-pay, medical, unemployment, and widowhood expenses. There would be no means test.

EMPLOYMENT

The party stood for employment for all in a free society. It urged the co-ordination of Government activity and individual initiative to encourage the full development of long-term employment.

PRIMARY INDUSTRIES

There should be stabilisation schemes, based on guaranteed prices, to be ascertained each year by tribunals on the model of the Tariff Board.

EDUCATION

Reforms in education should include increased facilities for secondary, rural, technical and university training, and adult education. Further, the Commonwealth should accept responsibility for the provision of financial assistance to the States.

5.4 Welfare conservatism

From the I.P.A. policy document that formulated a new political position for business, extracts that illustrate the reasoning behind welfare proposals, and some examples of the means proposed to reduce class conflict.

Source: Institute of Public Affairs, Victoria, *Looking Forward: A Post-War Policy for Australian Industry*, Melbourne, 1944.

In Australia, industry requires a fresh spirit, a finer vision, a greater objective. To fall back into the attitude of the pre-war years, to fail to resolve the antagonisms plainly manifest during the war, would spell disaster, a certain loss of much for which the sacrifice of the war has been made, a betrayal of the fighting men. We should prepare now not for new and bitter sectional struggles, but to bridge the gulf of division in an intelligent reconciliation of conflicting claims. . . .

Sources of Industrial Discontent

4. It is necessary to note that the dissatisfaction of the employee section of industry may be due to either one or both of two causes. First, it may arise from discontent with the rewards, conditions and treatment which employees receive in the organisation in which they work. This is a common, but under today's conditions not the major, cause of ill-will between employer and employee. The major cause is the absence of confidence of great numbers of employees in the system under which industry has been conducted to provide them with security of employment and income, and with protection for themselves and their families against economic misfortune.

It is impossible to see how industrial relations can be constituted on a satisfactory basis unless the great body of workers has a reasonable assurance that the mass unemployment of the decades preceding the war will not recur. Over and above such an assurance it will be necessary for employees to know that, in return for honest service, they and their dependents will be provided under all contingencies with the means to sustain themselves in a decent minimum of physical well-being. It is probably true that the greatest demand which has grown out of the present world conflict is the demand for security. It is an entirely legitimate demand and it requires a concrete and practical answer. . . .

The Role of the State

8. The goods and services to be produced should, in the main, be decided by the people in their capacity as consumers, and not by the state acting

through its executive officials. The latter policy would necessitate a far-reaching system of government controls and of state regimentation of the life of the individual, and would usurp the individual's prerogative to choose the commodities on which to spend his income. This means that a return should be made, as soon as possible after the war, to a price and market mechanism sufficiently free to register the real demands of the people.

9. The functions of the state in the control of the economic system should be basically fourfold:—

(a) To assist in preventing the periodic recurrence of large-scale unemployment;
(b) to provide for all responsible citizens (through social legislation) protection from the fear and degradation of economic misfortune;
(c) to regulate private business so as to encourage the maximum enterprise and initiative of individuals and groups;
(d) to conserve, in the interests of the nation those natural resources fundamental to its future security and prosperity.

10. The state and private industry should regard themselves as partners in the task of improving the living standards and security of the community. The representatives of the state and of private business should work in the closest collaboration. . . .

Industrial Relations

32. The following steps to improve relationships between employers and employees are recommended:—

(a) The wide adoption of consultative councils consisting of an equal number of representatives of employees and of management.
(b) Employees to be fully informed of the activities and plans of their organisations through regular reports and house magazines.
(c) The introduction of profit-sharing schemes, wherever practicable.
(d) The institution of a minimum annual holiday of two weeks, with pay, for all employees engaged in industry.
(e) The regulation of hours of work, factory conditions, and the introduction, where necessary and when practicable, of medical, dental and canteen services, and encouragement and assistance in establishing sports facilities in the interests of the health, happiness, and general well-being of employees.
(f) The provision by larger industries of assistance in the proper housing of their employees.
(g) The supplementing of national social security benefits by company superannuation and welfare schemes, where financially possible both for employers and employees.
(h) Regulation of the conditions of employment to conform to the need for a vast expansion and improvement of the educational facilities of the nation after the war. Vocational training of employees should be adequately assisted and special training plans made to help service men and women to take up satisfactory occupation in civil life.
(i) The widening of opportunities to give every individual the chance to rise to positions of responsibility commensurate with their capacities.
(j) The education of the public in an understanding that greater production, and therefore higher wages and incomes, are seriously handicap-

ped through industrial strife, and that any action inducing industrial strife is anti-social and as damaging to the national effort in peace as it is in war.

5.5 Developmentalism: State intervention

Extracts from the remarkable series of reports in which J. W. Wainwright formulated the policy of state-backed industrialisation as the answer to unemployment and regional stagnation.

Source: Auditor-General of South Australia, *Annual Report*, *Parliamentary Papers*, no. 4, Adelaide, 1935 and 1938.

[1935]

South Australia does not get anything like a fair share of the secondary industries which have been established by tariffs, partly due to free trade between the States, but also to the fact that the objective of public policy in the past has been most concerned with the developing of the primary industries. These industries do not now offer much inducement for further extension, and South Australia must in future have as the objective of her policy a greater development of secondary industries and less dependence upon exported primary products. There is no economic reason why this State should not have a greater share of secondary industries than she has to-day, and with reasonable encouragement by the State, the public, traders, and the press, some thousands of persons now unemployed and a burden upon the State could become again independent people with money to spend, which would bring about still more employment and prosperity to all, and more revenue to the State, less expenditure on rations, and reductions in taxation.

[1938]

Permanent New Industries are Necessary.

...The primary industries of Australia have a prosperous future ahead of them, and are still capable of expansion in some products; but no such expansion as has been experienced in the past can reasonably be expected in the near future from agricultural and pastoral pursuits. As a means of employing increased numbers of breadwinners they offer no possibilities.....

Approximately 70 per cent. of the natural increase since 1901 of persons engaged in these industries have sought other than rural occupations. That future expansion must be in secondary and service industries is *not a matter of opinion*; *there is no alternative*!...

The Small Business.

Most new industries still grow from small beginnings, without a large capital outlay, and employing few persons. Many are for long periods struggling concerns, unable to develop fully their technique through lack of resources, unable to take full advantage of a potential market, unable often to gauge the extent and nature of their potential market. Many are inefficient because they are struggling, and struggling because they are inefficient. Some go out of business when a little advice, or extra capital would have made success and expansion possible. The very large proportion of small concerns operating in secondary industries in South Australia is shown by the following figures. . . .

Provision of Developmental Capital is Difficult.

One of the most serious disabilities experienced by promising new industries is the difficulty in obtaining sufficient capital to expand rapidly in order to cope with an expanding market. The provision of developmental capital is not looked upon by the existing financial institutions as within their province. The Industries Assistance Corporation which was recently formed in this State to assist in this way, has been able to facilitate re-organization of a number of established small industries upon a sound and promising basis, but much more could be done if funds were provided. . . .

A Practical Employment Policy is Impossible without Research.

If the thesis is sound that a practical employment policy must have its main effect in the extension and expansion of secondary and service industries, and it cannot be seriously contended otherwise, then a necessary prerequisite to the formulation of such a policy is much more complete knowledge of these industries, their problems, their possibilities and their trends. Study is needed of markets and market conditions. Technological improvements should be noted, studied, if possible forecast, and their effects analysed. New departures in industry and new types of industry should be followed up and scientific research conducted. Problems of financing, factory lay-out, accounting and of management should be studied at close quarters, and methods of dealing with specific problems formulated after close study of the practical problems. To know beforehand what are the difficulties confronting industry and the changes taking place, is to be forewarned of the approach of the causes of unemployment, and would render immeasurably the easier, the formulation of plans and policies to maintain employment, national income and general prosperity at as high as possible a level.

In all countries individual initiative must be relied upon for the production of both primary and secondary products. The part the State should take in supporting individual initiative in primary production has been developed in detail in most countries, but the State's part in secondary production has not, except in the totalitarian countries. It seems obvious that the State can combat unemployment only by the development of a sound secondary industry policy.

5.6 Developmentalism: Labor and business

From a series of speeches by the party's leader in 1973, patching up relations with the business leadership.

Source: Speech by E. G. Whitlam to Chamber of Commerce and Industry, South Australia, at the G.M.H. dining-hall, Woodville, 21 September 1973 (press release).

Once already this week I have had occasion to draw attention to the remarkable number of manufacturers' dinners I have been eating, or will eat in the space of a fortnight—five in all. Manufacturers well know the way to my heart.

These eating engagements are, of course, also speaking engagements. I am happy to speak to Australian manufacturers because, quite frankly, I think we have a good story to tell. I believe there is no section of the Australian business community which shares greater common interests, more common ground with the present Australian Government than Australia's manufacturing industries. It is an historical fact that the strength of Australian manufactures and the strength of the Australian Labor movement have grown together. This has been no accident. It is of the essence of the political and industrial development of this nation; and this community of interest between Labor and industry was never greater than at this time in our history when we have an Australian Labor Government.

First, the Australian Government has an unqualified commitment to genuine full employment. However acute our perception of the social and economic evils of inflation may be, we are not prepared to seek a solution through the weapon of massive unemployment. In Australia, massive unemployment means empty or half-used factories. It means, whenever that weapon has been tried in this nation, *your* loss, *your* bankruptcy, the retarding and sometimes even the end of your careers as businessmen. There is no matter on which the people we represent and the industries you represent should share so strong a common view and a common determination. And that means that whatever measures we take to deal with the day-to-day problems of economic management, even when those problems have a high international component, they will not be solved—by us at least—by creating significant unemployment or closing your factories.

Secondly, we are committed to a national economy running at the highest level of its capacity and real productivity. We are a Government of growth. That means that the manufacturer and the investor can plan with complete assurance on the maintenance of the highest level of growth. We cannot be content with the two or three per cent growth prevailing in the year before our election. We need to sustain and, if possible, surpass the seven per cent already achieved, not just through our efforts in the last nine months but through your efforts and the efforts of your employees.

Thirdly, you need, as we need, a high level of real wages and high level of real purchasing power. Your prosperity and our success depend alike on the ability of the consumers—overwhelmingly employees and their dependants—to buy your goods and pay into our revenues.

Fourthly, we have a vested interest in your achieving fair profits. We need the growth which the investment of your profits brings; and quite frankly we need healthy taxes from your healthy profits.

As to these last two matters—wages and profits—you may recall that in my policy speech last November, I acknowledged that our program of vast social reform could only work successfully within a framework of strong, uninterrupted growth. The expectation of reasonable profits is as much a factor in achieving that growth as is the reasonable anticipation on the part of employees that their real standards will rise.

Fifthly, there is the overwhelming importance to the well-being of all Australians of our social program itself, our social goals, our social priorities. ... When governments take initiatives where none existed before, it is private enterprise, private manufacturing which share in the first fruits of such initiatives.

5.7 Communism as union militancy

Extracts from a major theoretical work of the Communist Party, in the period when it was growing towards the peak of its influence in the unions.

Source: L. Sharkey, *The Trade Unions*, Current Book Distributors, Sydney, 1942.

Our Party to-day has a similar task, to raise the political understanding of the masses to the level of a Communist understanding of society and the consequent tasks of the labour movement. Marx and Engels, Lenin and Stalin, have given us an understanding of the historical tasks of the working class in regard to the revolutionary change-over from Capitalism to Socialism. The advance guard of the proletariat have been able to grasp these theories, to master Marxism-Leninism; it has to be taken to the masses who, unaided, are unable to raise themselves to the level of a theoretical understanding, are unable to advance beyond the immediate practical tasks of wages, conditions, strikes.

The Trade Unions are the most important mass organisations of the working class and therefore, have a special importance for the Revolutionaries. "Without the Trade Unions a revolution is impossible," Lenin has written.

What are our tasks in regard to the Trade Unions?

These tasks fall into two main sections: (1) The raising of the theoretical level, the winning of the workers for a revolutionary objective, and (2) the practical-organisational...

A GOOD UNION WORKER

In order to equip themselves as not only the best theoretical and political leaders of the Trade Unions, but also as the best practical Trade Unionists, militants must master the Awards, as they cover their industry or factory, they must know the Rule Book of the Union and its organisation, history, customs and practices. Only in this way can they become the best Trade Unionists. ...

Comrades in the Unions must study the conditions and problems of Union Members and draw up programmes of demands for the Union to be able to give a lead, in good time, on all matters affecting the Union and strive at all times to unite the Union Membership and foster good relations with other Unions.

Speaking in the Union is also an art. We do not want to bore the workers with long and windy speeches, or go over their heads by being too "theoretical." We must deal with the questions before the meeting in an attractive fashion. This does not mean that we confine ourselves solely to economic questions. "No politics in the Union" means bourgeois politics in the Union. We must skilfully seize appropriate moments and opportunities to discuss politics and Socialism with the workers at Union meetings and elsewhere. Our goal is to raise the consciousness of the Unionists to the level of a Socialist understanding. ...

"ARISTOCRACY", REFORMISM, ARBITRATION

The Australian Trade Union Movement has been permeated and for long dominated by the ideology of the reformists. Reformism, Lenin has explained, is the outlook of the higher paid, skilled craftsman, the "aristocrats of labour." This "aristocracy" is given concessions on the basis of Imperialist exploitation—super-profits—from the colonies. This induces the belief that workers' conditions can be continuously improved within the framework of the capitalist system, and that there is therefore no need to struggle for Socialism. The reformists substitute class co-operation, class peace, class collaboration for class-struggle.

Reformist class-collaboration expresses itself in the adherence of the unions, in Australia and New Zealand, to legalism—to the State-instituted Arbitration Courts, the Arbitration system. The function of Arbitrationist legalism is to prevent strike struggles and to enforce acceptance, by law, of a low standard of living. It will at once be seen that Arbitration is detrimental to the development of the class-struggle, and class-consciousness and of that genuine and fundamental solidarity and perfected organisation necessary to the revolutionary struggle for Socialism. Nor has the Arbitration Court given any real concessions without strikes and mass political campaigns. The basic wage to-day, the real wage, related to the cost of living, is no higher than that first basic wage awarded by the Courts, the Harvester judgement of 1907. . . .

Strikes, properly led and conducted and properly timed, are a revolutionary weapon. *Strikes develop the labour movement, organise and unite workers and win the intermediate social strata to the side of the revolution.*

The general run of strikes in Australia have been of an economic character, or confined to economic demands, by the reformists. Political strikes have been few in number (Port Kembla, against scrap iron for Japan, for the release of Ratliffe and Thomas, against the execution of Sacco and Vanzetti in the U.S.A. and possibly a few more.) Political strikes are a higher form of struggle than economic strikes. Such strikes challenge the Government, the State, the rule of the capitalist class. One of our chief Trade Union tasks is the politicalisation of strikes.

Strikes are also important in that they reveal the class line-up to the more backward workers. The bourgeoisie, its press and politicians, and most of the parsons all unite to fight the strikers with every possible weapon. The law, the police, even the army, are used to crush the workers. The reformists oppose the strikers and thus expose themselves. The hypocritical mask is off. In a flash, the real character of the capitalist State is revealed to the masses.

5.8 Anti-communism

A relatively restrained example of propaganda put out during the referendum campaign on banning the Communist Party; illustrated by a map of Australia with a giant red arrow descending on it from the north.

Source: N.S.W. Liberal Party leaflet, Sydney, 1951.

SMASH COMMUNISM'S FIFTH COLUMN WITH A YES VOTE ON SEPTEMBER 22

Ten Reasons Why you Should Vote "Yes" on Sept. 22

---

1 AN overwhelming majority of the Australian people on December 10,

1949, endorsed the Menzies Government's undertaking to introduce legislation to ban the Communist Party, to remove Communist leaders from office in certain key trade unions and from the Commonwealth Service.

2 The Communist Party Dissolution Bill carried out the promise. In its final stages it was supported by all parties in the Federal Parliament—AND IS STILL SUPPORTED BY A LARGE SECTION OF THE LABOR MOVEMENT.

3 THE legislation, however, was found by the High Court to be beyond the peace-time constitutional powers of the Commonwealth.

4 AT the general election of April 28, 1951, the people gave the Menzies Government a specific mandate in terms of the Prime Minister's policy speech. "We will" said Mr Menzies, "promptly decide whether to seek the power we need by asking the States to refer it to us under the Constitution, or by seeking a straight-out Constitutional amendment."

5 FOUR States agreed to refer the power—Victoria, South Australia, West Australia and Tasmania. Only New South Wales and Queensland declined to refer the power.

6 BECAUSE action to ban the Communist Party and to deny Communists the right to hold office in certain key unions must be taken on an Australia-wide basis, the refusal of New South Wales and Queensland makes a Referendum necessary.

7 IT is necessary because no existing law—including the Crimes Act—authorises the Federal Government to take the steps sanctioned by the people at two elections.

8 THE ACTION IS URGENTLY NECESSARY BECAUSE THE COMMUNIST PARTY IS AN ANTI-AUSTRALIAN ORGANISATION WORKING IN THE INTERESTS OF A FOREIGN POWER. ITS LEADERS ARE FIFTH COLUMNISTS AND THEY ARE IN THE STRONGEST POSITION TO SABOTAGE OUR ECONOMY WHILE THEY ARE ENTRENCHED IN KEY INDUSTRIAL UNIONS.

9 AT this very moment Communist Thornton, former general secretary of the Ironworkers' Federation, is in Peking as Australasian representative on the Australasian–Asian Bureau of the W.F.T.U., the Kremlin's instrument for Red sabotage in the Pacific; and Communist J.J. Brown who holds office in the Australian Railways Union, is in Russia for orders.

10 AS the ultimate objective of Communism is to destroy our liberties and overthrow our Constitution, we must protect both our liberties and our Constitution by giving the Government the power to destroy the Communist Fifth Column.

COMMUNISM IS A CONSPIRACY AGAINST AUSTRALIA.

5.9 A coal-miner's story

Narrative of work and struggle in the coal-mines on the south coast of New South Wales, before and after mechanisation in the 1950s.

Source: B. Collins, 'Work: The Coal Miner', *Outlook*, no. 3, 1970, pp. 5–6; no. 4, pp. 6–8.

To work on the pit top and understand what's going on underground is a bit difficult, so from there, having this position [as a union representative], I decided to go underground. It wasn't as easy as all that to go underground; for some reason or other the Manager wanted me to stay where I was, but he eventually allowed me to go to the pit bottom.

You generally go there first, you don't go straight to the coal face, you work at the pit bottom, you do clipping, shift work. Clipping is clipping empty or full skips on to a continuous wire rope that goes through the entire pit; it pulls the full ones out of the pit and takes the empties back. That's the first job underground. Then you go to shift work, you may jump to a wheeler, from a wheeler on to the coal face.

I went from clipping to wheeling, and from there on to the coal face, once I got a mate. I bypassed shift work, which is mainly putting up timber where it's needed to support the roof, or putting rails down, or you may have to do some other type of labouring work, whatever is needed.

I went on to the coal face, and found it one of the hardest jobs I'd ever tackled. I had tackled timber cutting and found that most difficult, cutting on contract, and I found this contract work of pick and shovel most difficult too, most tiring, and in some of the places we worked, very hot.

You'd finish up with sweat in your boots before you were finished, and you could wring the sweat from your pants and from your belt. My mate and myself were not what you call "hungry miners". A hungry miner is one on contract who will work practically the full shift. In coal mining you take approximately an hour for travelling, each way from the pit top to your work place. Doing a full shift on contract work you'd start in the vicinity of eight o'clock and knock off at two o'clock.

You got paid according to the number of skips you filled. My mate and I actually worked hard while we were there, getting around eighteen or nineteen tons of coal when we had our man wheeling the coal away from us. Some others would prefer to do their own wheeling. Some would get as many as thirty or forty tons of coal plus doing the wheeling, that is, they'd fill their skips, one of them would pull four or five skips away with the horse, and pull the empties in and get stuck into it. There was no easing up. You didn't do such a great deal of picking, you might get some of the coal face down with a pick, but the majority was shot down and you'd shovel it into your skips. When you'd cleaned your place up it was the end of the day, unless you got the shot firer in to drill some more holes and blew the place down and got stuck into it again.

An indication of the hardness of this work was the look of the men themselves who worked at this job. Their weight was down to a minimum, around about ten stone, ten stone five or six. My weight is around eleven and a half stone now, but we no longer do contract work, we work with mechanisation and some of our members have jumped up three stone or more. So it was pretty solid work, and hot work, you'd certainly lose a lot of weight.

Some of the men wouldn't bother to wear much; it was a necessity to wear safety boots, but some of the men never worried. My mate ploughed around better in sandshoes. It wasn't a good policy of course, because if you got an injury to the foot you'd be battling with the company to get compensation.

I can recall that some of them would just wear helmet, belt, boots. The belt was a necessity, to put the battery on for your light, and that was about all they wore.

There came a stage when we got a new manager in there, and he was going to clamp down on this. He maintained that men had to be decently dressed, and it developed into quite a donnybrook over it. We had a meeting, he said we had to wear shorts—some of the fellows used to wear a piece of skirt. Old Blue Ridley wore a skirt, and Dagger Wales—I can remember him getting his photo in the paper when this strike was on; we finished up having seven days over this particular blue—he had his wife's skirt around him in this photo in the paper. That was probably the most comfortable to wear. . . .

I'll just touch on the changing of the system, that is, the changing from contract mining to mechanisation, which is important. It is important to note that when the Company decided to change, their rotten tactics got the workers' back up.

We had all received a letter that the Company was going to spend some considerable money on changing from contract to mechanisation, and unfortunately they'd have to lay 120 men off, unless we were prepared to agree to the Company's proposals.

Well, I was a member at that particular stage of the Communist Party. We had quite a good branch at our pit, and rather than throw your arms up in the air and say, well, we've got to accept what they say, otherwise someone's going to get laid off, we decided to put in a counter blow. This had the support of the miners, mostly at this stage those involved were members of the Miners' Federation, and our Executive discussed with the Company a shorter working week, which would assist in the employment of labour, and also an increase of £5 per week because we wouldn't be making so much as some of the men were on contract work.

Eventually it worked out that everyone was found a job, no one was laid off; unfortunately (this is going back eleven years) we didn't receive the shorter working week, but they came up with the increased wage in the form of a bonus system. . . .

From what I see of it now, with the change of managers, I think they're beginning to make a study of how to handle workers. There has been a change with managers, they call it psychology, in how to handle the leaders of particular unions. I've found with our Union that the manager is always prepared to meet the executive, and yet a few years ago they weren't going to recognise the CMU, the Combined Mining Unions, in the pit.

But times have changed, the CMU is united, and they are always prepared to meet us. They use psychology with the executive and this has its good points. It has its bad points too. You can discuss around the table like a family, you may discuss fishing before you get on to the main things on hand. This can have a detrimental effect on the basis that you get too friendly with the opposite side.

On the good side, often you can come to an agreement. He may see your point of view, you've got to see his, and you run things fairly smoothly. I always feel they've got to be on the defensive, and this way sometimes they have you on the defensive, and instead of continually rolling up and fighting for better conditions, you can become friendly relations officers.

But if you can continually win small points, sometimes it's valuable and for the betterment of the members that a pit can be run pretty smoothly, without losing conditions.

5.10 Working-class immigration

From the narrative of a Dutch migrant housewife, whose husband came to work in Gippsland in the early 1950s.

Source J. Zubrzycki, *Settlers of the Latrobe Valley*, Australian National University, Canberra, 1964, pp. 196–9.

The train stopped; where were we now? It was already passed 9 o'clock and we could not see a thing anymore and that was Moe 8 years ago, small and primitive. We were given a cordial welcome to Australia by our Dutch friends who had been looking so well after my husband and son. My husband did office work in Holland but in Australia one has to take on any job at all when one wants to be a *good* migrant (and as 500 people had been sacked that moment at the paper factory amongst whom was my husband, he took a job with a contractor who was laying sidewalks. When you are not used to this sort of work, it is not easy and he had to give up. He was severely ill for 6 weeks). We were welcomed with a lovely Dutch cup of coffee and a beautiful Australian laid table. This was one of the first things that was very strange to us, especially pumpkin, one has to learn to eat that. All the lovely meat, pudding and when one thinks one is finished then you get a cup of tea with lovely homemade cake. Yes the Australians are excellent cooks. And now the great moment had come . . . we were going home . . . home . . . to our own home. I could cry with joy. The roads were very bad and the street lighting was even worse, with 2 torches we moved bit by bit to 62 Wirraways Street. . . .

But that was not a house, but a superb residence, compared to our house in Holland. 3 Bedrooms (mattresses on the floor), a lounge, that would most likely stay empty for the first 2 years, a beautiful dining-kitchen and there was an electric stove. I could not believe my eyes, this stove belonged to the house, what a luxury. But that was not all, we had a beautiful bathroom, yes a bathroom with a bath. This is in Holland only meant for rich people, they think that a labourer does not need such a thing, if *he* comes home tired and dirty from work, he can wash at the kitchen tap and if one can spare the money you might go to the public bath house once a week. . . .

We are almost 9 years in Moe and have seen the place grow, so many things have improved in that time and building is going on. Another 5 years and Moe will not be a country village any more but a nice country town. Our path was not always paved with roses during that time. We had lived in Australia for one year. My husband worked with the SEC. I was woken up one night by a lot of stumbling and noise. I got out of bed and what was wrong? My husband had been brought home, he had had an accident, had broken his leg badly. During that time we got to know the Australians. As long as my husband was home we hardly got any money (all this has improved since). But they did *not* leave us in the lurch. They had a collection for us at the SEC and a crate with potatoes and vegetables and a piece of meat was delivered home. *That is how the Australians are* when they know somebody is in trouble. I myself have been in hospital ten times which cost a lot of money. It was not only doctors' bills but also commitments on furniture and everything we had to buy. And yet I have *often* been told: 'I do not understand... you come here with nothing, and within 2 or 3 years you have a house full of furniture and some money in the bank, or a house of your own'. Yet, it is difficult to answer.

5.11 Formation of the CRA mining group

Extracts from the history of the CRA group, as presented by the company itself in two documents. Note the constant changes in corporate structure to accommodate new ventures, and the interaction of British and Australian capital.

Sources: Conzinc Riotinto of Australia Ltd, *Facts About CRA*, Melbourne, 1972, pp. 52–4; and *Submission to the Senate Select Committee on Foreign Ownership and Control*, 1972, p. 8.

1905 The Zinc Corporation, Limited (ZC) registered in Melbourne, September 1905, to treat zinc bearing tailings at Broken Hill, NSW.

1911 Decision made to acquire a producing mine because of limited life ahead in treating zinc tailings. Leases of Broken Hill South Blocks acquired, and ZC reconstituted with head office in London.

1915 ZC participated with other Broken Hill mining companies to acquire a controlling interest in the Port Pirie, SA, smelters of The Broken Hill Proprietary Co. Limited (BHP), resulting in formation of The Broken Hill Associated Smelters Proprietary Limited (BHAS). In 1925 BHP sold its remaining interest, and ZC increased its interest to 25%. ZC's interest was further increased to 50% in 1945. ...

1949 The merger in Britain of ZC and Imperial Smelting Corporation resulted in the creation of Consolidated Zinc Corporation (CZC), and the Australian subsidiary Consolidated Zinc Pty Ltd (CZP).

1951 Management of ZC and NBHC transferred from London and CZP appointed manager in Australia for ZC, NBHC, and other Australian interests. ...

1953 Territory Enterprises Pty Limited formed by CZP to manage uranium mining project at Rum Jungle, NT, on behalf of Commonwealth Government.

1954 Mary Kathleen Uranium Ltd (MKU) formed to develop the uranium deposit discovered by prospectors in July. Main shareholders at that time were the prospecting syndicate and Australasian Oil Exploration Ltd.

1955 Interstate Oil Limited (IOL) formed by CZP to take over its one-third interest in Frome-Broken Hill Co Pty Ltd. CZP discovered extensive bauxite deposits at Weipa on Cape York Peninsula, Qld.

1956 CZP formed Commonwealth Aluminium Corporation Pty Limited (Comalco). The Rio Tinto Mining Company of Australia Pty Ltd (RTMA) commenced operations as a wholly owned subsidiary of The Rio Tinto Company Limited of London, and development of the Mary Kathleen, Qld, uranium project began.

1957 British Aluminium Company Limited entered a three-year association in partnership with CZP through Comalco to develop the Weipa bauxite deposits.

1958 MKU commenced operations in June and up to November 1963 produced 9,000,000 lb of uranium oxide for the United Kingdom Atomic Energy Commission. . . .

1959 Construction of new smelter complex at Cockle Creek for Sulphide Corporation began. The smelter is centred around the Imperial Smelting Process, in which both lead and zinc are produced simultaneously and separately by the one furnace.

1960 Following a re-arrangement of interests, the partners in Comalco became CZP and Kaiser Aluminium & Chemical Corporation. These companies formed Comalco Industries Pty Limited and the Comalco group began its rapid development as an integrated aluminium producer.

1961 RTMA became a public company and began investigations into iron ore occurrences in the Pilbara region of Western Australia.

1962 Conzinc Riotinto of Australia Limited (CRA) formed in July through the merging of the Australian interests of CZP and RTMA. Pilbara iron ore exploration continued, culminating in the discovery of Mount Tom Price orebody, in September. Hamersley Holdings Pty Limited formed in October by CRA in association with Kaiser Steel Corporation of USA. The wholly owned subsidiary Hamersley Iron Pty Limited (HI) also established.

[The following section is taken from the Senate Committee submission.]

2.01 A. The merger in 1962 to form CRA

C.R.A. was formed in July 1962 through a merger of the Australian operations of The Consolidated Zinc Corporation Limited (Consolidated Zinc), registered in London, and of The Rio Tinto Mining Company of Australia Limited (Rio Tinto Mining) which was an Australian public company and an 88.2% owned subsidiary of The Rio Tinto Company Limited registered in London. At the time of the merger, there were approximately 1,000 shareholders in Rio Tinto Mining with Australian addresses holding approximately 10% of the equity. There were also a number of Australian shareholders in Consolidated Zinc.

2.02 At the time of the merger, the principal assets of these two Groups in Australia were:

Consolidated Zinc Group

Consolidated Zinc Proprietary Limited	100%
The Zinc Corporation, Limited	100%
New Broken Hill Consolidated Limited	32%
Sulphide Corporation Pty. Limited	75%
The Broken Hill Associated Smelters Proprietary Limited	50%
Comalco Industries Pty. Limited	50%
Interstate Oil Limited	52%

Other interests included mineral and oil exploration, power generation, beach sands, timber, and mining and chemical projects under development.

Rio Tinto Mining Group

Mary Kathleen Uranium Ltd.	51%
Rio Tinto Collieries Pty. Limited	100%
Fitzpatrick Industries Pty. Limited	75%
Rio Tinto Brick Pty. Limited	100%

Other interests included mineral exploration and the Pilbara iron ore investigations.

2.03 At the time of the merger, the public shareholding in C.R.A. became 9.9%. R.T.Z. owned the remaining 90.1%. The public shareholding steadily increased and is now 19.35%. The public shareholding is owned by some 34,000 shareholders.

2.04 At the time of the merger C.R.A. shareholders' funds consolidated on an equity accounting basis became $85,145,000 with 42,732,111 ordinary shares of 50 cents fully paid and 1,400,000 7% redeemable cumulative preference shares of 50 cents fully paid. At 31st December 1971, the shareholders' funds of C.R.A. on the same accounting basis totalled $338,675,000 with 144,252,712 issued shares of 50 cents fully paid.

5.12 Conflict in the motor industry

The outbreak, and consequences, of the big Holden's strike of 1964, as told by an official of the Vehicle Builders Employees' Federation. The strikers were roundly beaten by an intransigent management, which applied heavy pressure through the arbitration system.

Source: H. P. McCarney, 'The General Motors-Holden's Dispute', *Journal of Industrial Relations*, vol. 7, 1965, pp. 326–31.

In July a resolution was carried by members working in the foundry calling on the Union to examine their wage structure in comparison with other foundries and seeking to be paid an inducement wage of £3 per week. This was endorsed by the Victorian Branch and referred to the Federal Office. The Federal Executive requested further information from the Victorian Branch. In August a further report from the Victorian officials advised that there was grave discontent among all employees and that the claim for £3 had now been extended to all employees. On Thursday, 20th August, the Union claim was made on the Company for increased wages for foundry workers. On Tuesday, 25th August, meal break meetings were held at 12 noon, 1 pm, 7.30 pm and 8.30 pm.

On Friday, 28th August, the Company replied as follows:—

"As you will have seen, the Company has given careful and detailed consideration to all the matters you put forward in your 'Summary' of the claim for a further £3 p.w. and made on behalf of your members employed here at Fishermen's Bend. In the light of—(a) the present over-award payments being made; (b) the extensive improvements soon to be expected in regard to foundry conditions; and (c) the fact that the other grounds put forward in support of your claim should, in view of their application to industry in general, be properly dealt with by the Conciliation and Arbitration Commission, the Company can find no substantial or sound reason as to why this claim should be granted."

On Friday, 11th September, the Union again met the Company and pressed the claims on behalf of the men. On Thursday, 17th September, the Company met V.B.E.F. officials and again rejected the claim. On Friday, 18th September, a meeting of foundry workers took place commencing at 12.10 p.m. No member on day shift resumed work after the meeting. Only 41 members offered for work on the afternoon shift out of 291. At the meeting the following resolution was carried:—

> "(1) That a ban on overtime in the foundry be imposed; (2) That an attempt be made to arrange a meeting of all Unions on Friday, 25th September, at 2 p.m.; (3) That V.B.E.F. members employed on afternoon shift in the foundry hold a meeting before starting work."

On Monday, 21st September, foundry workers resumed normal duties.

On Friday, 25th September a meeting of all members of the V.B.E.F. employed at Fishermen's Bend was held to hear a report on the £3 claim. Also in attendance were members of the Amalgamated Engineering Union, the Electrical Trades Union and some Australasian Society of Engineers members. During the meeting a deputation of Union officials conferred with the Company's representative on the claim. Discussions proved unsuccessful and members of all Unions went home.

On Monday, 28th September, a meeting was held in Festival Hall. [This meeting recommended a return to work to allow further negotiations on the £3 claim.]... On 29th September Company representatives and Union officials again conferred on claims; once more, discussions proved unsuccessful. ...

On 2nd October, a mass meeting of Dandenong workers decided to join Fishermen's Bend employees in their claim. On 5th October, a mass meeting of all G.M.-H. employees held at the Festival Hall carried the following resolution:—

> "This meeting of G.M.-H. employees calls on the Trades Hall Council Disputes Committee to demand that the management of G.M.-H. negotiate immediately an unconditional increase in the wage rates of all G.M.-H. employees, and in view of the management's refusal to negotiate this demand with officers of the Melbourne Trades Hall Council, this meeting call upon the Disputes Committee to decide we remain on strike until our demands are met."...

[The return to work occurred nearly a month later.]

The number of members of V.B.E.F. involved were:— On strike: Victoria 5,870, South Australia 6,774; total 12,644. Stood down: New South Wales, 1,529, Queensland 276; total 1,805. Total involvement of the V.B.E.F. was 14,449. A stand-down took place in Western Australia.

The V.B.E.F. gave £25,000 to the strike fund, £10,000 was given by both South Australia and Victoria, £5,000 was given by New South Wales. Other unions paid their financial members in accordance with their respective policies and unfinancial members were paid out of the strike fund the same amount as paid by the V.B.E.F. Payments were made in all States whether on strike or stood down. Fines were imposed as follows:— V.B.E.F., A.S.E., A.E.U., and E.T.U., £2,000 each; Sheet Metal Workers' Union, £1,500. All plus costs. Up to 26th October when a recommendation was made to resume work, the unions were liable for a further £9,000 for the V.B.E.F., A.S.E., A.E.U., and E.T.U., and £4,500 for the S.M.W.U., a total of £40,500 plus costs.

An examination of this dispute taken after the return to work and settlement of some portions of the dispute leave me with the following impressions:—

(a) New Australians. Whilst the work force is made up of many nationalities, the two strongest national groups within the Company are Italians and Greeks. With both of these groups there is an inability of the trade union movement when an industrial dispute is pending, or in fact in operation, to communicate. Too much dependence is placed upon interpreters who do not necessarily understand some of the tactics involved in an industrial dispute. In this particular instance in the foundry, too high a percentage of Greeks were employed and in addition had language difficulties. Perhaps the strongest influence upon national groups are the clubs of which they are members. This again, because of their numbers only, is felt more strongly through the Greeks.

(b) The issue capable of being exploited affected the control of the dispute. General Motors-Holden's is an American company. It is the financial success story of the post-war period. It had bought out the Australian shareholders and failed to publish balance sheets in the early part of the complete control by Americans. It has made the biggest profits in the history of Australia. Hence the claim was for wage increases, notwithstanding the present over-award payment, the possibility as the dispute continued of the issues being diverted from a question of wages to one of the penal power of the Conciliation and Arbitration Act, or the fact that strike originated from within what is a so-called moderate union.

(c) In this dispute General Motors-Holden's were represented finally by Mr. D. Hegland, Managing Director, Mr. W. Gibb, Manufacturing Director, and Mr. S. McManamy, Industrial Department, and as the story was unfolded it must have been obvious that on the Company side they had no officers with practical experience in the settlement of industrial disputes. There had been only two previous disputes since the war, one in South Australia in the mid-forties and a morning tea dispute in New South Wales in November, 1962. Most of the statements issued by the Company and later by the Company and the A.C.T.U., and the printed statements, although written differently, did not depart from the original answer.

(d) Provocative statements issued by the leaders of the Federal Government in Parliament further aggravated the dispute.

5.13 A mass base for conservatism

A key speech by R. G. Menzies, in which he launched an appeal to the 'forgotten people' as the backbone of the nation—and the mass base of the conservative revival. Note his skilful identification of the social customs and prejudices of these groups with the strategic interests of capitalism, and the role of the family in making the connection.

Source: R. G. Menzies, *The Forgotten People*, Angus & Robertson, Sydney, 1943, pp. 1–10.

In a country like Australia the class war must always be a false war. But if we are to talk of classes, then the time has come to say something of the forgotten class — the middle class — those people who are constantly in danger of being ground between the upper and the nether millstones of the false class war; the middle class who, properly regarded, represent the backbone of this country.

We do not have classes here as in England, and therefore the terms do not mean the same; so I must define what I mean when I use the expression "middle class".

Let me first define it by exclusion. I exclude at one end of the scale the rich and powerful: those who control great funds and enterprises, and are as a rule able to protect themselves. . . .

I exclude at the other end of the scale the mass of unskilled people, almost invariably well-organized, and with their wages and conditions safeguarded by popular law. . . .

These exclusions being made, I include the intervening range — the kind of people I myself represent in Parliament — salary-earners, shop-keepers, skilled artisans, professional men and women, farmers, and so on. These are, in the political and economic sense, the middle class. They are for the most part unorganized and unself-conscious. They are envied by those whose social benefits are largely obtained by taxing them. They are not rich enough to have individual power. They are taken for granted by each political party in turn. They are not sufficiently lacking in individualism to be organized for what in these days we call "pressure politics". And yet, as I have said, they are the backbone of the nation. . . .

Now, what is the value of this middle class, so defined and described? First, it has "a stake in the country". It has responsibility for homes — homes material, homes human, homes spiritual. . . .

The material home represents the concrete expression of the habits of frugality and saving "for a home of our own". Your advanced socialist may rage against private property even while he acquires it; but one of the best instincts in us is that which induces us to have one little piece of earth with a house and a garden which is ours: to which we can withdraw, in which we can be among our friends, into which no stranger may come against our will. . . .

Then we have homes human. A great house, full of loneliness, is not a home. "Stone walls do not a prison make", nor do they make a house. They may equally make a stable or a piggery. Brick walls, dormer windows and central heating need not make more than a hotel. My home is where my wife and children are. The instinct to be with them is the great instinct of civilized man; the instinct to give them a chance in life — to make them not leaners but lifters — is a noble instinct. . . .

And finally, we have homes spiritual. This is a notion which finds its simplest and most moving expression in "The Cotter's Saturday Night" of Burns. Human nature is at its greatest when it combines dependence upon God with independence of man. . . .

The case for the middle class is the case for a dynamic democracy as against a stagnant one. Stagnant waters are level, and in them the scum rises. Active waters are never level: they toss and tumble and have crests and troughs; but the scientists tell us that they purify themselves in a few hundred yards.

That we are all, as human souls, of like value cannot be denied. That each of us should have his chance is and must be the great objective of political and social policy. But to say that the industrious and intelligent son of self-sacrificing and saving and forward-looking parents has the same social deserts and even material needs as the dull offspring of stupid and improvident parents is absurd. ...

If the new world is to be a world of men, we must be not pallid and bloodless ghosts, but a community of people whose motto shall be, "To strive, to seek, to find, and not to yield". Individual enterprise must drive us forward. That does not mean that we are to return to the old and selfish notions of laissez-faire. The functions of the State will be much more than merely keeping the ring within which the competitors will fight. Our social and industrial obligations will be increased. There will be more law, not less, more control, not less.

But what really happens to us will depend on how many people we have who are of the great and sober and dynamic middle-class — the strivers, the planners, the ambitious ones. We shall destroy them at our peril.

5.14 Urban families: The respectable

Findings from a survey of 1954–55, showing the stress on the closed family unit and the conservatism of relationships inside it.

Source: H. Fallding, 'Inside the Australian Family', in A. P. Elkin (ed.), *Marriage and the Family in Australia*, Angus & Robertson, Sydney, 1957, pp. 54–81.

During a period of fifteen months spanning those two years I made the intimate acquaintance of twenty professionals' and eighteen tradesmen's families in Sydney. These families were approached through a variety of sources to avoid bias as much as possible, and represented various political and religious positions, various residential areas and various occupations on the part of the father. Each family had two or more children, and only fairly long-established families were included, so that in most of them at least one child had entered adolescence. ...

Close solidarity with neighbourhood was also generally absent. Most people preferred to "keep to themselves" rather than have their neighbours "tell them what to do". For the parents of most families neighbourhood played an almost negligible part in supplying friendships. The prevailing relationship can be described as polite curtailment. Contact was restricted to friendly greeting and petty help, like borrowing a ladder or a back number of a magazine, helping to lift a load, or keeping an eye on the children. But accompanying sentiments like the following were always expressed: "I believe in having your friends away from where you live," "They're nice enough people but I don't believe in having too much to do with them," "We say 'good day' but would never go near one another's homes — except, perhaps, for a drink at Christmas." A high proportion had tales to tell of venturesome relations, followed by strain, drawing back, and subsequent caution.

However, there were eight families who frequently exchanged visits with neighbours, allowing themselves to become intimately involved and accepting the obligations and rule of opinion that entailed; although no case was entirely free from some kind of curtailment. These families were found at different social class levels, in localities ranging from closely settled industrial areas to spacious outer suburbs. The environmental factors common to them all were a strong prohibition on pretentiousness throughout the whole neighbourhood, a rough equivalence in the economic status of neighbours, and the existence of similar interests among them.

Moreover, none of the suburbs exhibiting neighbourliness was *very* new; they had all been settled slowly enough and for long enough to allow assimilation to a type to occur. The four cases in which neighbourhood relations were most sharply and deliberately curtailed were those where professionals, owing to some special circumstance, were living in residential areas of considerably lower class status.

The prevailing relationship of polite curtailment seems to be due, then, to lack of assurance that one is sufficiently like one's neighbours. Two things contribute to this anxiety. An open-class society can place a person in the position where he doubts whether his class qualifications are acceptable to his neighbours. Secondly, secular society allows a diversity of aims to develop amongst its members, and too much association between people having different aims can lead to their making a convenience of one another. Many complaints were forthcoming that neignbours, whose "business" was not of the kind one cared about, were too ready to presume, impose, or make a nuisance of themselves if they were given encouragement: using the telephone, making a habit of borrowing, wasting one's time in telling their troubles, and so on. Thus, where aims and attitudes are not assimilated to a type, doubt about acceptability and fear of over-familiarity have led to polite curtailment in the attempt to keep relations cordial.

Solidarity with kinsfolk, while it may not have been as wide or intense as in less urbanized communities, was by no means extinct. To the parents of all save one of the families of the sample relatives were far more close than the friends of choice. This was so although, verbally, relatives sometimes suffered devaluation in comparison with friends and some were regarded as diabolically difficult. They were cherished more, helped more, depended upon more, seen more, and spoken of more than friends—and usually much more. . . .

The third element to consider is the transmission from one generation to the next of a traditional conception of family roles and of one's place in society. In all families of the sample there was some departure from the traditional conception of the roles of parent and child, and in a number of them from the traditional conception of the roles of husband and wife also. These departures, however, were hedged around with cautions. There was a general tendency to conservatism: in all but the most unstable families parents strove to preserve (or to restore if it had been lost) the element of authority in their relations with their children, and husbands and wives divided authority for family control between them in the traditional way, accepting the customary responsibilities of bread-winner and homemaker respectively. There were some signs of a returning pendulum-swing after a wave of experimentation. . . .

Other productive activities were divided between the parents. Mothers made clothing, mainly for themselves and the children, made effects for the home, did nearly all the repetitive cleaning, washing and ironing, and the shopping to stock the home with provisions, prepared the meals and baked cakes and pastry, and perhaps engaged in some flower-gardening. Tradesmen's wives had no outside assistance in these tasks, but nearly one half of the professionals' wives had part-time helpers. All of the tradesmen, but only half of the professionals, made a deliberate point of giving their wives some token help in this work by washing or drying the dishes, making morning or evening cups of tea, and so on. It was essentially the mother's burden that was being lightened, however, for the men did not regard these tasks as belonging properly to them. More constructional and outdoor tasks were the man's work: building cupboards, laying paths, designing gadgets, repairing and painting the house, keeping the yard tidy, growing vegetables, chopping wood, cleaning and overhauling the car. But a third of the professionals had to excuse themselves from most of this work, either because of incompetence or over-busyness, and engaged tradesmen to do it. . . .

The families were fairly uniform in the way the productive tasks were divided. They were less uniform in matters of family management. In twelve of the eighteen tradesmen's families the fathers could be said to be in effective control; in three the mothers were in effective control; and in the remaining three something like a partnership in management was found. In nine of the twenty professionals' families the fathers were in effective control; in one the mother was in effective control, and in ten there was partnership. The over-all picture is one of patriarchy, being challenged by a pattern of partnership. But this surface classification masks the various forms that control and partnership took.

5.15 Urban families: The unwashed

A description of one of the situations covered by the 'poverty' research of the late 1960s.

Source: J. Paterson, 'Outsiders: Those Who Have Not', in J. Rigg (ed.), *In Her Own Right*, Nelson, Melbourne, 1969, pp. 111–23.

Lack of direct contact with the poor, ignorance of the total story, and a deeply engrained belief in such virtues as work, saving, planning and insurance inevitably gave rise to criticism. 'Why doesn't he take a second job; he's not even prepared to do an honest day's work.' 'She's a bad manager, probably dull.' 'Why do they have so many children?' 'No wonder they're in trouble with hire-purchase, they're not prepared to do without a thing—I caught a glimpse of her frig one day—it was bigger than ours!' Do these diagnoses fit the K's?

'*Why doesn't he take a second job*?' Mr K is thirty-four, an unskilled labourer who is currently employed as a truck driver. He has been in the job for five months and take-home pay (he's taxed as a single man as a form of saving) is $41.15. He likes the job and the boss seems to like him, and Mr K is crossing his fingers that it lasts, because he hasn't what you'd call a good job record. One of the reasons is that as well as being unskilled he can barely read or write and is so embarrassed about this that on occasions he's walked off the job without being paid rather than admit it. Another reason, which he's probably not conscious of, is that his bitter experiences with his father, who used to beat him up when he was drunk, made Mr K supersensitive to people who try to 'throw their weight around', behaviour which can be attributed to most 'bosses' at some time. It also made him fiercely determined that his own sons would get a decent education and be able to fight for a place in the world. He worries about the future because of his back trouble—he knows there's no light work for an unskilled labourer.

'She's a bad manager ...' Mrs K is thirty-one and when she and Mr K were married she was seventeen and pregnant. They lived in a series of rooms, and the first place they didn't have to share with another family was a Commission house they got shortly after the birth of their fourth child. She'd never before had a kitchen to herself and remembers being 'struck dumb by so many cupboards'. They had to buy furniture on hire-purchase because what they left behind was only fit to burn, and they had a sense of really getting going for the first time. Mrs K also wanted curtains so that the house would look nice from the street, and to further this aim she hung them inside out. She was aware that it would have been cheaper to make them up herself, but she didn't have a machine and had never even learned to sew.

With only primary education behind her, she was faced with the task of maintaining a household of nine people on $41.15 a week. Her general plan was to put aside the rent money of $10, pay whatever bills were really urgent, and make the rest go as far as possible on food. Mr K was the only one to eat butter (actually she often tricked him by wrapping margarine in butter paper), but she prided herself on the fact that her kids rarely went hungry. Her figure was testimony to a diet of toast and tea, but she was spared anxiety about the missing eggs, cheese and oranges because they didn't learn about proteins and vitamins in primary school. On pay night when there's nothing in the house she turns the setback into a treat by taking the children to meet her husband and then on to the fish and chips shop.

'Why do they have so many ...?' Mrs K always wanted a large family and didn't start thinking about birth control until after the fifth, and then when she asked the doctor he said she was 'only young and good for a few more yet'. She doesn't like talking about the whole thing because her mother always said you had to give men what they wanted and it wasn't natural to use anything, so they just tried to be 'careful'. She knows about the pill now but wonders how on earth she'd ever put aside $1.95 a month. The other problem is Mr K. 'He's funny about birth control; he's so proud of the kids, he says they're the only thing he's had anything to do with that's come out good.'

'They're not prepared to do without ...' Like most of the other families in the street their television is on hire-purchase and so are the furniture, the frig and the motor mower. The Welfare doesn't consider television essential but the K's do. They say it's not only the cheapest form of entertainment for the whole family but it keeps the kids off the street, and several of them are even called after television personalities. The lounge furniture could have been bought second-hand, but the second-hand firm didn't accept instalments and the K's had no hope of paying out almost a week's pay in one go. They admit the frig is larger than they need, but the salesman insisted that it had a better trade-in value and they hadn't realised at the time they'd end up paying nearly half as much again in interest. The motor mower is also a worry because it was supposed to be a way of Mr K making extra money on

the weekends, but he hasn't been able to do anything for several weeks because of his back.

If the K's were asked what they wanted, they'd probably say enough money in his wages so they could pay their way without having to take charity. Even though they've had to rely on other people's help for ages, they still hate it. For them it would be a luxury to go just one week without owing anybody anything.

5.16 Class consciousness of professionals

An editorial in the journal of a powerful and conservative association in an occupation that was strategic in the process of industrialisation. Its status problems were intensified by the conflict of 'professional' claims with the fact that most engineers were employees, producing a hegemonised consciousness that can be found in other growing white-collar employee groups, though this is a particularly acute case.

Source: 'To Raise the . . . Status . . . of the Profession of Engineering . . .', *Journal of the Institution of Engineers, Australia*, vol. 31, September 1959, pp. N 57–8.

The history of those professions which have achieved today a high status both for the professions themselves and the members of them, discloses that their position in the community and in society was not always as it is today. In some cases there was a long and hard struggle to achieve, in the first place, respectability, and later a degree of social eminence. Their present position was achieved ... by adopting high standards of education and training for the profession itself, and by the combined efforts of individuals in adopting a professional outlook and approach to clients and by exercising care in speech, dress and social habits. Enhanced status led to increased remuneration until today the members of these professions, shortly after they are established in their careers, have the financial resources to maintain the status won for them by their predecessors. ...

The Council has done much to raise the prestige of the Institution and the status of the profession. It has safeguarded the standards of qualifications for professional engineers, raising the requirements for admission to the various grades from time to time to meet world standards and advances in scientific and technological developments. It publishes technical material of originality and high quality, encouraging members to contribute to their own publications. This year it has increased the number of its publications, essentially to enhance the standing of The Institution and its members. By exchanging its publications it ensures that the standing of Australian engineers and their achievements are brought to the notice of appropriate bodies throughout the world. ...

If we want to restore that which seems to have been lost, it is not good enough to leave the matter of status entirely in the hands of the Council. It is a matter in which we all have a responsibility—to ourselves, our colleagues, our profession and the community.

As professional men we are often judged not only on our academic qualifications and technical competence, but on a host of small and often very minor details associated with our appearance, bearing, habits and family life. We are often so judged by employers as well as by the general public. We cannot afford to be either careless or flamboyant in our dress. In a democratic community those who wish to sponsor dress reform are at liberty to do so, but they cannot complain if they are not recognised as professional men.

The tendency to judge by appearance has changed little since Polonius advised Laertes:

"Costly thy habit as thy purse can buy,
But not express'd in fancy; rich, not gaudy:
For the apparel oft proclaims the man;"

On more than one occasion, members calling on business at The Institution have been mistaken by junior members of the staff for workmen. It is not unusual to see at a meeting of the Institution, one or two members in casual clothes suitable for a beach resort. There is always difficulty in selecting photographs for publication with the report of an Annual Conference, because in most of them there are members whose attire is hardly likely to enhance the status of the profession. Peculiarly, those who are most unprofessional in their dress are often loudest in their demands for corporate action to increase their status.

We may be judged when we least expect it on our appearance, our speech, or the stationery we use. When applying in writing for a position or writing to someone we have not met, it must be remembered that we will be judged first by the stationery we use and what we write on it. A large employer informed us some years ago that more than fifty per cent of the applications his firm received for important engineering positions were handwritten on cheap stationery, and that such applications went unread straight into the waste paper basket. We have no reason to doubt this statement, as many of the letters members write to criticise the Council's attitude to status give an impression of rough drafts on scrap paper rather than communications from professional men.

Afterword

At the start of this book, we emphasised the connection between class analysis and socialism; at the end, it seems right to reflect on this again. Our first plans envisaged a final section of the book, almost as long as the historical narrative itself, in which its implications for an understanding of the state, of Australia's position in imperialism, for the relationship between the social structure and its environment, and for labor movement strategies would be spelt out. The project has grown too massive for us to attempt all that in one book, and we will not even try to sketch a position on these issues now. Being out of breath, we leave it to the readers to carry on. But we would like to say a few words of encouragement, and at least gesture towards lines of thought that seem to us to have come out of the research.

First, an argument against schematism. There is no simple reading-off of political strategies from a view of history. Our account of class relations and their development matches none of the versions of the past that have so far been used to justify the position of one tendency against another in the socialist movement. Perhaps that is inevitable; history is science, not myth, and only myth can be used as polemic. History *informs* socialist thinking, it does not fix it; we studied the past, in part, in order to escape it. Yet that *informing* is crucial, because social reality, human experience, are historical. To ignore the coming-into-being of the present is to be forever trapped in its particularity, to take the immediately given as the real.

A good many contemporary ideologies in Australia seem to us to be based on that fundamental error, or the cognate one of reading the past in an 'essentialist' rather than a historical way. That Australia is 'the working-man's paradise', or in more contemporary idiom, that Australia is culturally a working-class country which only needs the workers to shrug their shoulders for the parasites to disappear, is a traditional one that appears simply incredible in the light of the narrative above. At best, it is serious over-generalisation from the situation at the height of the working-class challenge to colonial capitalism; but it was not true even of the decade 1910 to 1920. On the other hand, this history lends no credence to the view (now popular in some Labor circles as a justification for retreat) that Australians are 'innately conservative' and that this accounts for the trouble Labor has in winning or holding political power. Radical mobilisations have, on occasion, gained wide support; and, more importantly, the character of the working class is not a simple determinant of events. Ruling-class responses, with all the economic and cultural power that can be mobilised by them, are also vital in determining the course of political struggle. Ignoring the effects of ruling-class power leads, curiously, to a position of political passivity.

That the working class is essentially conservative, or naturally revolutionary, or invincibly racist—all are equally wrong. The working class are simply people, who improvise their lives in certain situations, which may or may not be changed by their responses. A historical understanding of these situations and responses rejects essentialist views of the working class, its ideas and its organisations—which for example would see the unions as 'essentially' reformist, or the Labor Party as 'essentially' *petit-bourgeois*. In fact the Australian working class and its organisations have produced an astonishing variety of responses, struggling against racism as well as reproducing it, mobilising against capital as well as helping it to organise, and so on. The mass unions themselves have sometimes represented a militant strategy for socialism, and sometimes a barrier to working-class mobilisation. The possibilities of an organisation, or for that matter of a class, must always be taken in the context of its situation. That implies, in some basic sense, a limit to what history can 'teach' us. (As already mentioned, we cannot *read off* present strategies from a historical analysis.) But it returns to politics its essential character of practice. Political judgement is practical judgement, not the application of scientific laws.

It hardly needs stressing that a serious historical study shows the absurdity of the theme of the 'withering away of class', the obsolescence of class categories, that is currently popular among some journalists and political scientists. That there has been a demobilisation of the working class since the 1940s is evident. But one must be a very determined Liberal indeed to think that the political and cultural victory of capitalism means an end to class society. That, in turn, points to the fallacy in the reciprocal view on the left—the idea that hegemony is so absolute, so effective, that we might as well give up the game. The short answer to that is that there have been periods of hegemony before—and they have been broken, not by accident, but by forces that emerged out of the bowels of class society. Admittedly, television and suburban dispersal are in some ways a tougher proposition for the working class to challenge than the daily newspapers and self-help organisations of the first long boom. But the technological and organisational advantages of the ruling class in that period were met by a political response in the emerging working class. Superior technology was not a trump-card then, nor should it be now.

The historical analysis, more positively, gives us some perspective on what an adequate socialist strategy must be and do. Unlike those socialists who have given up on history, and whose theory explicitly rejects 'historicism', we find that socialist strategy must centre on the process of the remobilisation of the working class, rather than the organisation of militant minorities capable of exemplary actions. There is no reason to think exemplary action by a latter-day Ned Kelly should be any more effective today in altering the balance of class forces than it was in the 1870s. The working class is not an undifferentiated mass requiring detonation before it enters the historical process. It is a highly complex structure whose points of articulation must be laid bare by theoretically informed activity. More than that, it is part of an historically determined class structure, with a range of interconnected processes: industrial, urban, cultural, political. The strategy for remobilisation, then, must understand the historical connections between these processes. As we write, a conservative federal government is reversing a generation of integrative state activity directed towards the working class. It is this historically situated aspect of the relationship between state and class structure that socialists must grapple with, rather than abstractions about the state in general.

Research reports traditionally begin with a statement of grandiose purposes, and end with an apology for not having achieved them — together with suggestions for 'further research'. We can hardly ignore so fine a precedent, even at the risk of producing what seems like a shopping-list. Perhaps the most urgent work to be done to fill out — and perhaps substantially revise — the picture we have drawn, is a detailed historical analysis of state functions and organisations in the Australian context, and in the context of the imperial connection (which continued to be of profound importance to the state structure well into the twentieth century) and the evolution of the world capitalist system. Among other things, this would require an evaluation of the place of state employees in working-class politics. (In the light of current theoretical debates about whether state employees are really part of the working class or not, it is notable that in Australia, state employees' unions such as the A.R.U. in Queensland have often been in the vanguard of militancy, even against Labor governments.)

Scarcely less important is research on strategy and structure in the ruling class. The history of the integrative strategies businessmen have used in the workplace, from co-partnerships and profit-sharing schemes to workers' participation, is obscure but important. There is a gaping hole where there should be a body of research on the power, strategies and impact of the largest firms, both in politics and the economy. Some work is currently being undertaken on these lines, but it is only a beginning; a library of company-by-company analyses is required to build up a solid picture of the structure and operation of the class.

On working-class organisations there is, comparatively speaking, research in abundance; much less on the working class beyond. The relationship between alienation and mobilisation, which appears in a shadowy form in our account, requires detailed research, tracing processes across the range from popular rejection of hegemonic values to class organisation. The changing form of the working class in response to changes in the organisation of production, and the reciprocal effect of working-class struggle on the production process, have yet to be studied in depth. And while historians have given a number of useful accounts of episodes in the interaction of intellectuals with labour organisations, a systematic evaluation of the intellectual intervention of socialists and their role in the process of working-class mobilisation would be of immense value. So much for a research shopping-list. Whatever course future study takes, it is bound to affect the picture offered in this book; we claim no more than provisional validity for it. Yet in ten years, if the study were to be done again, it could still be no more than provisionally valid, in its turn. If we wait for the final word on history before setting course, we will be a very long time in port.

And that *is* the goal of the enterprise, not the multiplication of research (though that will go on automatically in the context of an active socialist movement). A final word about that. Some historians (not all) look back on the period discussed in Chapter 4 as the heroic age of Australian radicalism, now dead and gone, leaving only embers and ashes behind. Of course that mobilisation is long past; but its *significance* is not. In that period the Australian working class earned the reputation of being one of the most politically advanced and effective in the world. The reputation was not always deserved, but it had some substance, within the peculiar limits of colonial capitalism. The Australian working class once again has the opportunity of playing an important, perhaps decisive, role in world socialism. Australia is one of the places where the issue of hegemony, perhaps the key strategic issue in this stage of the transformation of capitalism, presents itself in a particularly naked way, where it can be directly challenged and overcome. And it may be, precisely through the evident insanity of a system based on profit and prepared to risk the future of the world for the sake of development. The issue of uranium export sums up a great deal. Forty years ago, the workers of Port Kembla struck to prevent the export of war materials to the fascist regime in Japan. Australian capitalists now have a greater opportunity: just possibly, they may help to blow up the whole planet. The achievement of workers' power in Australia has very plainly ceased to be of merely local interest.

Index

Name Index

Subject Index

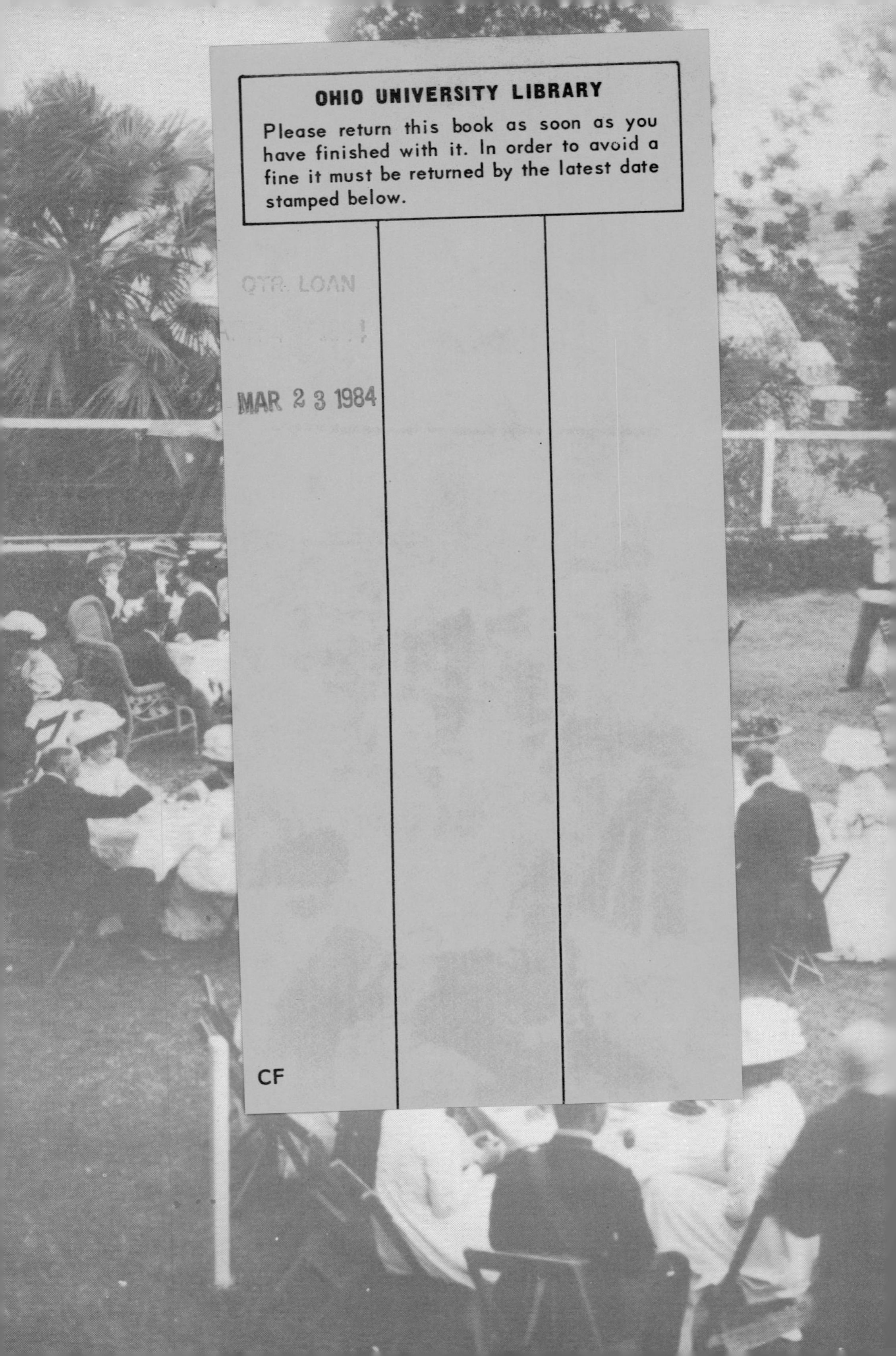